Stone Artifacts of Texas Indians

STONE ARTIFACTS OF TEXAS INDIANS

Completely Revised Third Edition

Ellen Sue Turner
Thomas R. Hester
Richard L. McReynolds

Illustrations by Richard L. McReynolds
Foreword by Harry J. Shafer

TAYLOR TRADE PUBLISHING
Lanham · New York · Boulder · Toronto · Plymouth, UK

Published by Taylor Trade Publishing
An imprint of The Rowman & Littlefield Publishing Group, Inc.
4501 Forbes Boulevard, Suite 200, Lanham, Maryland 20706
http://www.rlpgtrade.com

Estover Road, Plymouth PL6 7PY, United Kingdom

Distributed by National Book Network

Copyright © 2011 by Ellen Sue Turner, Thomas R. Hester, and Richard L. McReynolds

All rights reserved. No part of this book may be reproduced in any form or by any electronic or mechanical means, including information storage and retrieval systems, without written permission from the publisher, except by a reviewer who may quote passages in a review.

British Library Cataloguing in Publication Information Available

Library of Congress Cataloging-in-Publication Data
Turner, Ellen Sue, 1924–
Stone artifacts of Texas Indians / Ellen Sue Turner, Thomas R. Hester, and Richard L. McReynolds ; illustrations by Richard L. McReynolds ; foreword by Harry J. Shafer. — Rev. 3rd ed.
p. cm.
Rev. ed. of: A field guide to stone artifacts of Texas Indians / by Ellen Sue Turner and Thomas R. Hester.
Includes bibliographical references.
ISBN 978-1-58979-464-1 (pbk. : alk. paper) — ISBN 978-1-58979-465-8 (electronic)
1. Indians of North America—Texas—Antiquities. 2. Indians of North America—Implements—Texas. 3. Projectile points—Texas. 4. Stone implements—Texas. 5. Texas—Antiquities. I. Hester, Thomas R. II. McReynolds, Richard L., 1935– III. Turner, Ellen Sue, 1924– Field guide to stone artifacts of Texas Indians. IV. Title.
E78.T4T87 2011
976.4'01—dc22 2011018073

Printed in the United States of America

We honor the past and dedicate this book to the future of our grandchildren.

As for man, his days are as grass: as a flower
of the field, so he flourisheth.
For the wind passeth over it, and it is gone;
and the place thereof shall know it no more.

PSALM 103:15–16

Contents

Foreword ix

Acknowledgments xiii

1. INTRODUCTION 1

Projectile Point Typology 3

2. THE MANUFACTURE AND USE OF STONE TOOLS 9

Making Chipped Stone Tools 9

Determining the Function of Stone Tools 28

3. CONTEXT AND CHRONOLOGY 41

Context 41

Chronology 43

Archaeological Sequences in Prehistoric Texas 44

4. PROJECTILE POINTS: TYPE DESCRIPTIONS 53

Dart Points 56

Arrow Points 176

5. CHIPPED STONE TOOLS 219

6. GROUND, PECKED, AND POLISHED STONE ARTIFACTS 251

Appendix 1. Archaeological Societies in Texas 287

Appendix 2. Sources of Illustrations 289

Appendix 3. County Symbols for Archaeological Site Designation: Texas (41) 301

Appendix 4. Texas Archeology Awareness Month 305

Appendix 5. Groups to Contact Around the State 307

References 311

About the Authors 351

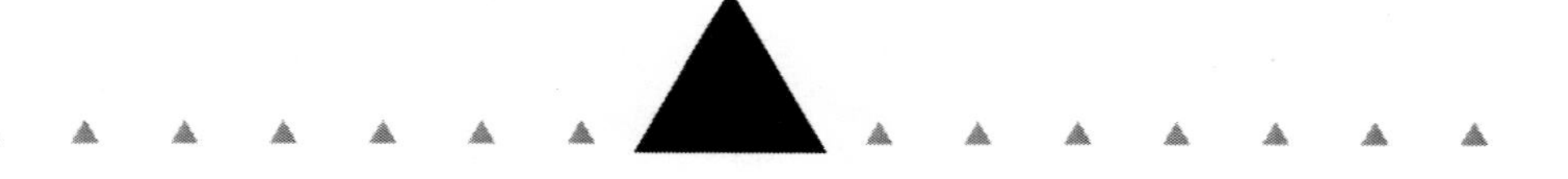

Foreword

THE FIRST procedure of scientific study of any subject is to establish order among the objects in question. Carl Linnaeus established this precedent in the 18th century with his classification of living organisms, and the biological sciences have continued to use his basic system of nomenclature to this day. A classification, or taxonomy, reveals relationships that could not be perceived in chaos and hence lead toward a further inquiry. A classification system then is the foundation for scientific study.

In the early years of Texas archaeology, from about 1915 to the mid-1930s, prehistoric cultures were classified according to some notable characteristic of the regional archaeology (e.g., Big Ben Basketmaker, Upper Mound culture, and Small Scraper culture). Since the late 1940s and early 1950s though, archaeologists working in Texas have relied on the pioneering efforts of J. Charles Kelley and Alex D. Krieger. These two were the first to establish order among the material collections from archaeological sites across Texas. The magnitude of the task they undertook can be appreciated by those who have viewed the massive collections at the Texas Archeological Research Laboratory; their work was the direct result of hands-on analysis, done at a time when computers were nonexistent. With the publication of *An Introductory Handbook of Texas Archeology* in 1954, the labors of Krieger and Kelley, with the added contributions of Dee Ann Suhm and Edward B. Jelks, led to an awakening in Texas archaeology. The typologies followed Krieger's rule, published in his 1944 article in *American Antiquity*, that types must have meaning in time and space. That is, a type must occur at a specific interval of time within a given geographic space to be credible.

Professional archaeologists (and there were surprisingly few employed in Texas at that time) and a growing corpus of avocational enthusiasts now had access to an amply illustrated, easily comprehended guidebook of typologies. No single publication has stimulated more interest or contributed more to Texas archaeological literature and research. The immediate response was to use the "*54 Handbook*" as a means of classifying a collection of projectile points or pottery. In doing so, the suggested typology was being rigorously tested; new types were proposed when workers recognized that not all projectile points or pottery types were known or described. With the advent of radiocarbon dating, attention was focused on documenting change through time. As initial chronologies were proposed, refinement in taxonomies ensured more refined chronologies.

The *Handbook* encouraged students of Texas archaeology to adopt a hands-on approach to the study of artifact collections necessary for the analyst to gain a "feel" of the specimens in question, which Krieger considered so essential in typological analysis. The *Handbook* provided a solid foundation of facts for student archaeologists in Texas during the fifties through the seventies, this writer included.

I do not wish to overlook the importance of quantification in science, an essential ingredient in archaeology given today's computer-assisted technologies. There is no substitute, however, for the kinds of experience gained through hands-on analysis and seeing the forms, material, and patterns in the artifacts themselves. Attributes can be coded, measured, and counted. But each projectile point has a history of its own, including material, style, technology, and context; the point's history may also include even impact, repair and reworking, impact again, breakage, and discard. The type, which includes form and technology, cannot always be quantified to the extent that all of the observed nuances are captured. This is where quantification combined with experienced qualification is good science.

Imperfect and incomplete as the *Handbook* classifications seem to us today, they are the real foundation on which much of our understanding of the state's prehistory rests. The present chronologies of central and southwest Texas, which are perhaps the best defined in North America, were the direct result of putting Kelley's and Krieger's taxonomies to the test. Once the temporal controls were established, spatial or geographic relations became more comprehensive and valid. And once the archaeologist had good control on the time frame of a certain layer or deposit under investigation, more specific questions or working hypotheses about his activities and behaviors of the ancient people under study could be addressed.

The original *Handbook* soon went out of print. It was replaced in 1962 with *Handbook of Texas Archeology: Type Descriptions* by Dee Ann Suhm and Edward Jelks, a reprinted version of the pots and points descriptions from the original *Handbook* with only minor additions. This volume was reprinted twice, the last time in 1968, evidence of its popularity and demand. Both the 1954 *Handbook* and 1962 *Type Descriptions* have been reprinted once again by Gustavs Library Publishing. Neither volume was updated.

Cultural resource management (CRM) brought forth a need for a revised typological guide for lithics, stimulated largely by the explosion of new information and research in Texas in the 1970s and 1980s. The publication of the first issue of E. Sue Turner and Thomas R. Hester's *A Field Guide to Stone Artifacts of Texas* in 1985 with updated information on the types and, more importantly, radiocarbon-dated chronological ages of points—something that was not available in any of the previous typological guides or in the reprinted versions—proved to fill in this important need.

Our understanding of the archaeology of Texas is undoubtedly more complete today than it was fifty-five years ago. We have access to a much richer body of both site data and theory for our research and our interpretations. Advances in general archeological theory, lithic technology, site formation processes, understanding the relationships between human populations and their environs, paleoenvironmental studies, zooarchaeolgy, and ethnoarchaeology have all contributed to a better awareness of how the archaeological record came to be, along with new tools for interpretation. The new advances and new goals of archaeology have not changed the fact that the basic sources of comparative data are the site or survey report. It is in these reports that material remains are described, and central to this description is a common language of understanding, or a standard taxonomy. Classification is an analytical tool, and not an end unto itself; but it is an essential step to establish order. This revised edition of *Stone Artifacts*, like its predecessors, is intended to provide just that: a standard taxonomy for stone artifacts in Texas.

This new edition of the *Stone Artifacts* book is extensively updated with regard to known types, new information on chronological age for each type, and more illustrations of each type provided by Richard McReynolds's excellent drawings. New information on formal tools other than projectile points and a primer on lithic technology complete the book.

The authors of the book are certainly the most qualified archaeologists to put such a comprehensive study together. Sue Turner has accomplished a monumental task of compiling information on projectile point types across the state, contacting professional archaeologists and avocationals alike to gather information and examples of points and other stone artifacts. Since the first publication of *Stone Artifacts*, she has devoted much of her energy toward gathering new information on point types, dates, and distributions as they become available. To keep up with the growing body of information, especially that generated from CRM work, is not easy, and she has been assisted in this effort by her coauthor Thomas R. Hester.

Tom Hester has spent his entire career working in central and south Texas, and has the most intimate knowledge of the region's prehistory of anyone I know. One of his research interests is in developing and refining lithic chronologies. He has been instrumental in establishing the typological framework currently used for the Great Basin, Maya Lowlands, and in central and south Texas. Tom's publication list in Texas archaeology, lithic technology, and Maya archaeology together numbers in the hundreds, including books, peer review articles, book chapters, journal articles, and monographs.

The fine artifact illustrations by Richard McReynolds add to the book and enhance its usefulness. Richard is a noted artifact illustrator, and his artwork can be seen in many volumes of the regional journal *La Tierra*. He is an active avocational archaeologist and has worked with professional archaeologists on many occasions in Texas and Belize in addition to his own work. He has authored and coauthored numerous articles in *La Tierra* as well. What makes Richard's drawings so informative is not only the detail but also his knowledge of south Texas archaeology and lithic technology. He is familiar with the artifacts and understands the details of flaking attributes; he has the admirable skill of projecting what he sees to the drawings.

Together, these authors make a formidable team when it comes to typology and chronology, and artifact illustration, and have provided a new edition to *Stone Artifacts* that should be in the hands—and backpacks—of every practicing archaeologist and avocational in the state and surrounding areas.

—Harry J. Shafer

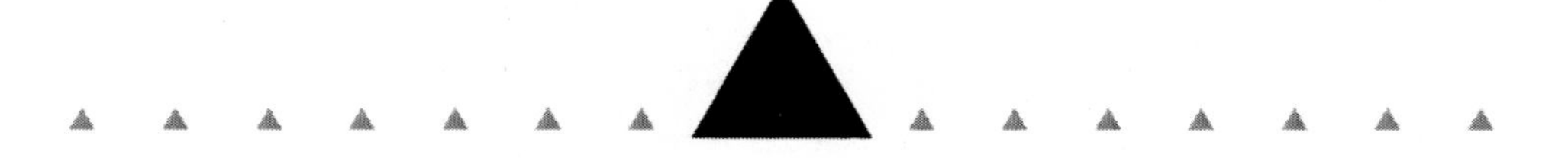

Acknowledgments

WE WISH to express our gratitude to the many persons and several institutions whose assistance in a variety of ways has made it possible to undertake and complete this book. A considerable number of the illustrated artifacts are in collections in the Witte Museum, San Antonio; the Center for Archaeological Research, the University of Texas at San Antonio; the Panhandle-Plains Historical Museum; the Texas Archeological Research Laboratory, the University of Texas at Austin; the Museum of the Coastal Bend, Victoria College at Victoria; and INVISTA. Laura H. Nightengale, head of collections at TARL; Jeff Indeck at the Panhandle Plains Museum; Marybeth Tomka at CAR/UTSA; Amy Fulkerson at Witte Museum; Sue Prudhomme at the Museum of the Coastal Bend; Amy Hodges, manager, Texas Public Affairs at INVISTA; and Robert Mallouf at the Center for Big Bend Studies gave their time tirelessly to searching collections for us. A special thank-you goes to Ben McReynolds who for thirty years constantly urged his brother, Richard, to do the illustrations for a book such as this. Richard finally acquiesced! The accuracy of the illustrations was made possible by having collections made available to us and by the gracious loan of specimens from friends and colleagues throughout Texas: Tom Atkinson; Byron Barber; David Beason; Laura Beavers; John R. Boland; Bill Birmingham; Don Black; Earl Bly; Jimmy Bluhm; Bob Bonneau; James Boyd; Richard Brady; Randy Holden Brandt; Bill Bredenridge; Keith Brown; Kenneth Brown; Doug Bryan; Kai Buckert; David J. Burrows; David Calame; Todd Chism; Dick Clardy; Kit Corbin; David Crain; Darrell Creel; Ruth and Walt Carruthers; Bucky Densford; Carl Dillard; E. D. Dorchester; Frank Dudley; Roy Ekstrum; Geffert-Barrett; Hue Fadol; Robert Flores; R. E. Forrester; Jon Gerber; Pat Gilstay; Phillip Lee Green; Lane Gregson; Frank Griffin; Keith Grunswald; Tom Gudergan; Joe Guillory; Claude Haby; John Haberer; Tony Hardon; Curt Harrell; Robert Haynes; John Neil Hernandez; Donald Higgins; Curtis Hodges; Barry Holleron; Keith Horton; Bob Huston; Howard and Marilyn Hunt; Timmy Johns; Shannon Jones; James Kasen; Terry Kelly; Erwin Kramer; Mike Krzywonski; Don Kumpe; Terry Kumpe; Marc Land; D. Lehard; Kirk Loftin; Tommy Long; Emmit Long; Al Lopez; Joseph Louvier; Calvin Mansell; Buck Maspero; Roberta McGregor; Jody and Floyd McKee; Wilson McKinney; Ben McReynolds; Michael McReynolds; Richard Mentzer; George Meyar; Connie and Keith Mohan; Pat Mercado-Allinger; Victor Milales;

Brian R. Miles; Tom Miller; Homer Mills; Allen Mitchell; Jimmy Mitchell; Ed Mokry; Ted Namic; Bo Nelson; Hugh O'Brien; M. F. Palmer; Tim Perttula; Eugene Pilarczyk; Mike Redwine; James Richmond; Scott Reilley; Jay Roach; Barth Robbins; Dwain Rogers; John Roland; Richard Rose; Jack St. John; Barney Sam; Jim Schroeder; Steve Schwarz; Cliff Scott; Harry J. Shafer; W. Slaughter; Lewis B. Smith; Ray Smith; Mike Redwine; Cindy and Roy Smyers; Randy Snider; Leslie "Skip" Stewart-Abernathy; Paul Tanner; Joel Z. Taylor, MD; Steve Tomka; Mary Beth Trubitt; Robert Turner; V. V. Turner; Tom Valley; Clayton Vandergriff, MD; Armando Vela; Rusty Vereen; Mark Walters; Carey Weber; Mrs. John West; Larry Wilhot; H. E. Womack; Billy Woods; Thomas Wooten; James Wright; and Bill Yoder.

We are grateful to production editor Alden Perkins, at Taylor Trade, for being so kind and patient with us.

Finally, a special word of appreciation to spouses Lynda Hester and Carolyn McReynolds who gave so much of their time, effort, and forbearance to make this project possible and to Ellen Turner Scott who shared her time and expertise to help us sort through computer challenges. We were all saddened by the untimely death of Carolyn before the book was published.

1

Introduction

As archaeologists, we are at the same time collectors and interpreters.

—Sir Mortimer Wheeler

THIS VOLUME provides a compilation of the types of projectile points and other stone tools made and used by the Indians of prehistoric Texas. It is designed to serve as an introduction to the study of stone tools for the interested public and, we hope, to function as an aid to research for student, avocational, and professional archaeologists. Thus, we have used a straightforward format that emphasizes illustrations and general descriptions for quick reference, followed by a list of pertinent sources that can be consulted for scholarly research. The purpose of the volume will be achieved if it both promotes an awareness of the scientific importance of stone tools and provides a baseline for further detailed studies of Texas lithic assemblages.

Many of the projectile point types described here were originally defined in the 1940s in the writings of J. Charles Kelley and Alex D. Krieger. In 1954, Krieger, along with Dee Ann Suhm, and with the aid of Edward B. Jelks, published their classic study, *An Introductory Handbook of Texas Archeology*. It contained a detailed review of the state of knowledge of Texas prehistory at that time and presented formal descriptions of numerous projectile and pottery types. This was followed in 1962 by the *Handbook of Texas Archeology: Type Descriptions*, authored by Suhm and Jelks and published by the Texas Archeological Society and the Texas Memorial Museum. Although that volume was issued in a format designed to permit the inclusion of subsequently published type descriptions, none were ever added. In 1958, Robert E. Bell of the University of Oklahoma issued the first in a series of spiral-bound volumes entitled *Guide to the Identification of Certain American Indian Projectile Points*. This, and following volumes, later authored by Gregory Perino, incorporated many of the Texas types and added others from Oklahoma, Arkansas, Louisiana, and adjacent areas. The Bell and Perino volumes were similar to the earlier efforts of Suhm, Krieger, and Jelks in that they emphasized projectile points (and did not include other types of stone tools) and featured detailed descriptions and illustrations. Another compendium of Texas lithics, with some attention to shell and bone artifacts, has been published by Davis (1991).

All of these volumes have long been out of print (the Texas Archeological Society has recently permitted new printings of the Suhm, Krieger, and Jelks [1954] classic and the 1962 work by Suhm and Jelks by Gustav's Library of Davenport, Iowa). Further, since 1962, there has been an incredible growth in the practice of Texas archaeology—by professionals, students, and avocationalists. As a result, many new projectile point types were defined, and descriptions were also set forth for certain distinctive chipped and ground stone tool forms. These were often defined and illustrated in widely scattered publications, ranging from papers in the *Bulletin of the Texas Archeological Society* to local or regional journals and newsletters. Additionally, the monographs and reports put out by the various state, academic, and private consulting archaeological programs throughout Texas often included new type descriptions. And many of the original Suhm, Krieger, and Jelks types were modified through new data—distributional studies, radiocarbon dating, and technological analysis—generated by excavation, survey, and laboratory analysis.

Our book serves to update projectile point typology since the publication of Suhm and Jelks's (1962) work, as well as our first edition of 1985 and our second edition of 1993. It provides current information on type revisions, along with several additional type definitions. We have further added a series of descriptions of various kinds of chipped and ground stone tools found at archaeological sites in the state. This book also includes chapters on stone tool technology and function, as well as the context and chronology of these artifacts. We hope these chapters provide a better perspective from which to evaluate the typological materials and their use in archaeological studies.

Projectile points are among the most distinctive and popular artifacts sought by amateurs and professionals alike. The hobby of random relic collecting, however, can cause havoc. In recent years, the untrained digging of sites has caused great damage to Texas archaeology. There has also been a tremendous increase in the "commercialization" of artifacts, at Indian relic, gun, and knife shows; in dozens of websites devoted to artifact sales; and in advertisements found in urban newspapers for the purchase or sale of artifacts. The days of a local "digger" spending several years at a specific site (and disturbing comparatively little of it) are being rapidly replaced by "pay digs" that feature the use of front-end loaders and backhoes to scoop up the intact site deposits, putting the materials on large screens manned by hobbyists paying as much as 200 dollars a day to "Easter egg hunt" through the debris. Such excavations usually eliminate or severely damage entire sites.

Collecting of sites on federal properties in Texas has attracted the attention of law enforcement agencies, and arrests have been made at Lake Amistad, Lake Georgetown, and several east Texas lakes. Collecting and excavation on private property is, of course, up to the landowner and the people who seek access to his land. Thus, an untrained excavator should never undertake an undisciplined excavation of a site, because irreplaceable information will certainly be lost. Even casual surface collecting can be damaging, unless the sites are properly recorded and the artifacts are cataloged or kept separated according to site.

Archaeological sites are exhaustible resources, and a constant effort is being made by avocational and professional archaeologists in Texas to preserve the archaeological heritage. While this book can assist the hobbyist in identifying and interpreting stone tool collections, we hope that the materials presented here will also demonstrate the scientific importance of these artifacts. We encourage the hobbyist to become involved in avocational archaeology and change a potentially destructive recreational pursuit into one that contributes information to the study of our prehistory. We urge the reader to consult the agencies and organizations listed in appendix 1 and become a part of the Texas archaeological community. The scientific contributions made by avocational archaeologists cannot be overemphasized; a synthesis of south Texas prehistory (Hester 1980), and the decades-long work of the Texas Archeological Society and the Southern Texas Archaeological Association, all clearly demonstrate the critical role that avocationalists have played in the study of the archaeology of much of Texas.

PROJECTILE POINT TYPOLOGY

The projectile point type can be a valuable research aid for archaeologists. Once it has been demonstrated that a particular type has meaning in terms of its geographic and temporal distribution, it becomes valuable as a "time marker," allowing the archaeologist to quickly date excavated archaeological deposits or surface sites found during surveys. Most types have regional distributions, as the index map found with each type description illustrates at a glance. Most have fairly limited time spans and are preceded or replaced by points of different shapes. Archaeologists still do not fully understand why ancient Indian groups changed the style of projectile points through time; such changes may have reflected different forms of hafting, shifts in the kinds of animals hunted, or even the movement of certain populations. It is fortunate that these changes in style were made, however, as they provide invaluable indicators of the chronology of culture change in different regions of Texas.

There are two major forms of projectile points in Texas and North America—dart points and arrow points. Dart points are generally large, thick (5 to 10 mm) specimens that were used to tip spears thrown with the *atlatl* or spear-thrower. They are commonly known to the public as "arrowheads," although they did not serve that specific function. Dart points, spears, and spear-throwers comprise the major weapon kit for prehistoric Texas Indians from earliest times, around 9200 BC, through the early centuries of the Christian era. Indeed, in some parts of the state, the spear-thrower was in use until a few centuries before the Spanish conquest.

The spear-thrower or atlatl (see Dickson 1985) makes use of the principle of centrifugal force, the force that tends to move an object outward from the center of rotation. When a spear is thrown with the hand, the amount of force that propels it depends largely on the length of the arm. In effect, an atlatl lengthens the arm, permitting the spear, or dart as it is called in the archaeological literature, to be thrown harder and farther. Atlatls found preserved in dry caves in the lower Pecos of Texas and western regions of Texas, the Southwest, and the Great Basin (Hester et al. 1974; see fig. 1-2) usually consist of a narrow, flattened stick of hardwood about two feet long. The end of the atlatl that is held in the hand is sometimes equipped with a pair of animal hide loops into which the fingers are inserted to permit a better grip (fig. 1-3). Near the opposite end is a short groove and a projecting spur on the upper surface of the atlatl. This spur engages a small depression in the base of a dart. The atlatl and dart are held over the shoulder (fig. 1-1). The arm is quickly brought forward, and the dart is released almost simultaneously to be propelled toward its target. The dart used with the atlatl is often a "compound dart" made of two main parts, the mainshaft and the foreshaft, which when assembled form the whole dart. The foreshaft (fig. 1-3; see also fig. 2-18, hafted Langtry) usually consists of a short piece of wood about six inches long and tapered at one end. The opposite end is notched to hold a chipped stone projectile point fastened in place with sinew and sometimes strengthened with pitch or asphaltum. The tapered end is often rather rough so that it will fit snugly into the hollow end of the mainshaft and not be accidentally jarred loose.

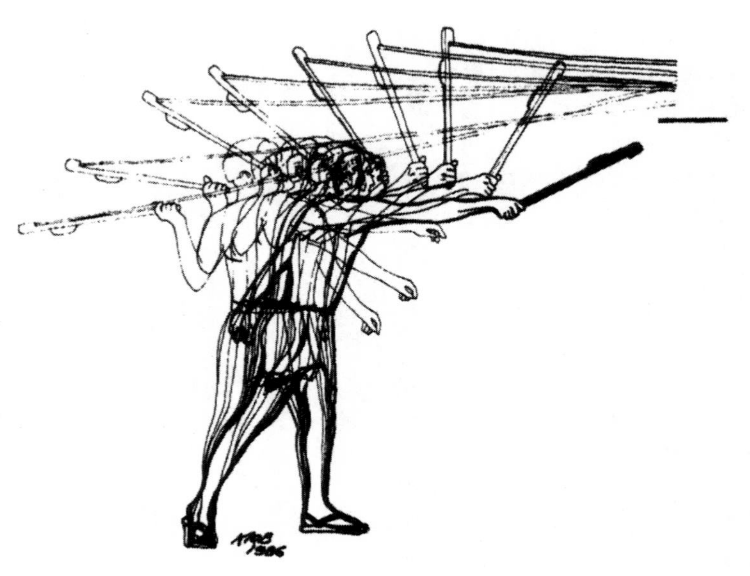

Figure 1-1. *Propelling the dart with an atlatl.* Illustration by Kenneth M. Brown. Originally published as the cover of *Bulletin of the Texas Archeological Society* 56 (1985). By permission of the Texas Archeological Society.

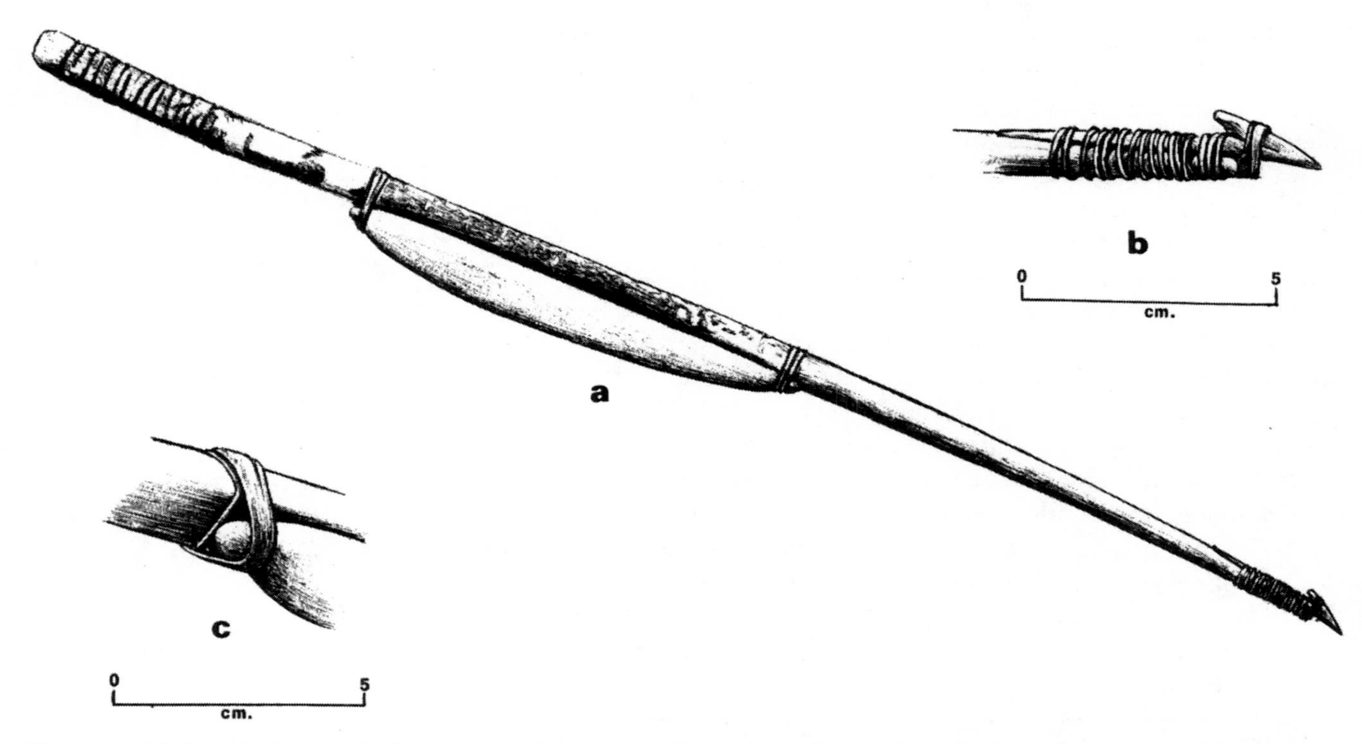

Figure 1-2. *Atlatl from the Great Basin.* The specimen is from a site near Winnemucca Lake, Nevada, and is radiocarbon dated to at least eight thousand years ago. It has a simple form (compared to fig. 1-1), with a large boatstone attached as a weight (a, b) and a spur carved of bone lashed to the end (c). From Hester (1974, fig. 4). a, atlatl or spear-thrower; b, use of atlatl; c, atlatl dart foreshaft; d, dart foreshaft inserted in mainshaft. Length of the atlatl is 58.1 cm.

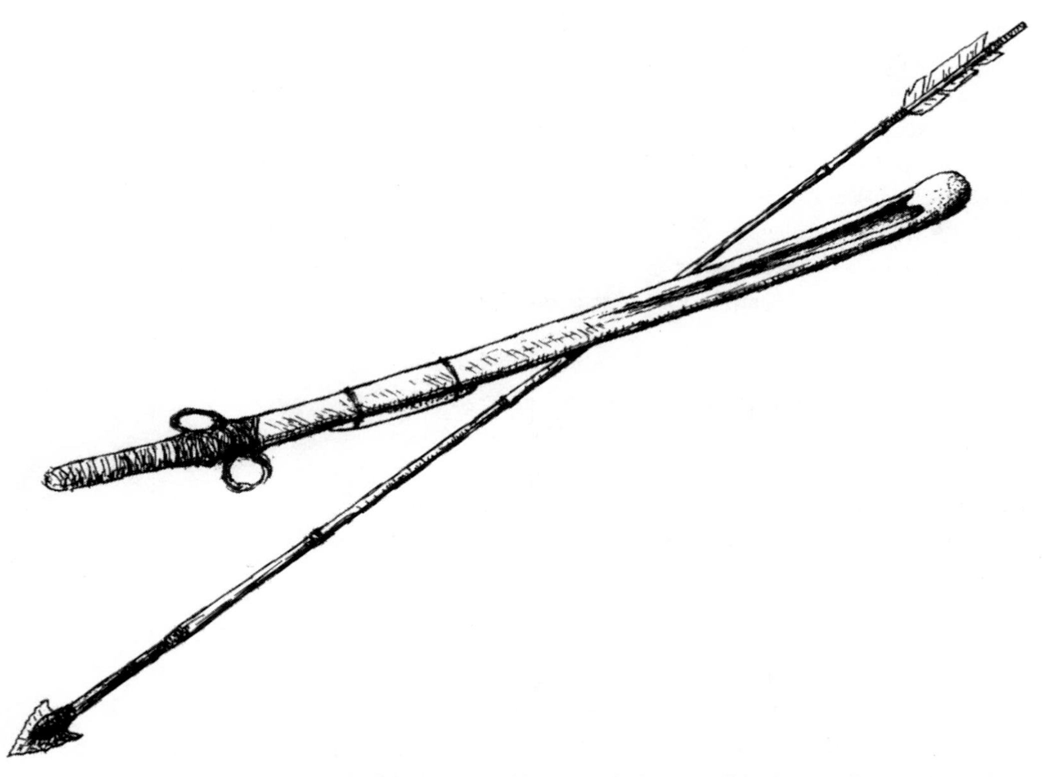

Figure 1-3. *Atlatl.* This is Richard McReynolds's conception of an atlatl and dart shaft, based on archaeological specimens. Note the loop handles, an attached weight, and the spur carved into the far end of the atlatl. Overall length would be about 55 cm.

Not all foreshafts are fitted with stone points. Examples have been found where the foreshaft was merely wood sharpened to a point and fire-hardened or where a sharpened bone point was used (Hester 1974). When completely assembled, the atlatl dart measured somewhere between fifty and seventy inches long.

Arrow points are tiny, delicately chipped, thin (1 to 4 mm) artifacts introduced along with the bow and arrow around AD 700–1000. While many collectors refer to them as "bird points," they served to tip arrows that could be used to kill anything from birds to buffalo and, given the testimony of burial sites of this era, other humans.

Most dart and arrow points found in Texas have distinctive shapes and can be sorted into a variety of groups, categories, or "types." Intensive archaeological research is needed to demonstrate whether these groupings are simply ones of convenience, which permit the archaeologist to describe a collection, or whether they have greater meaning in terms of defining a certain style with specific boundaries in time and space or even specific ethnic groups (Johnson 1989a). There has been, and continues to be, much controversy in North American archaeology as to the use of projectile point "types." We cannot resolve this, but we can make explicit how we conceive of these types and how we intend that they be used by other archaeologists. We follow the typological theory employed by Krieger (1944) and by Suhm, Krieger, and Jelks (1954) in their original studies of Texas typology. Krieger (1944, 272) set forth this objective of typology: "The purpose of a type in archeology must be to provide an organizational tool which will enable the investigator to group specimens into bodies which have *demonstrable historical meaning in terms of behavior patterns*." Suhm and Jelks (1962, viii) provide a further, and clear-cut, expression of how types in the Texas typological system are meant to be used:

> A type is not just a descriptive category, but must have cultural and historical meaning if it is to be employed successfully as a tool for archeological interpretation. . . . For example, arrow points that are quite similar to the *Perdiz* type in shape, size and chipping occur in California, Spain and Japan. These fit the physical description of *Perdiz* rather well, but they do not fit the geographical and temporal position of *Perdiz*; therefore, they should not be called *Perdiz* points. . . . *Continuity in distribution of a type is the principal criterion for demonstrating that it is a valid cultural entity.* In short, these are cultural types, not descriptive types, and they should not be used out of context because to do so would imply cultural relationships that may not have actually existed.

Thus, these are types whose definitions rest on evidence from the archaeological record of Texas and adjacent states and which reflect identifiable ancient cultural patterns in this region. They cannot be used, in a scientific fashion, for describing projectile points of similar shape in distant areas with wholly different cultural systems. Unfortunately, this has occurred quite often in Mesoamerica, where Texas typology has been applied to points of similar shapes but with totally different cultural contexts (for example, one does not have Marcos points in the Late Preclassic cultures of the Valley of Mexico [Hester 1986]; see also Perttula 2009).

We would further make note of typological approaches put forth by David Hurst Thomas (1979), as these generally follow the approach followed in this book. Thomas first describes "morphological types" (217), the grouping of projectile points into similar categories on the basis of shape alone. These are merely descriptive clusters, but they allow the archaeologist to record the characteristics or attributes of particular groups of points to begin the detailed studies necessary to establish more formal classifications. As Thomas notes, "Morphological types are of limited value as end products; their primary function is descriptive, to convey the overall appearance of a set of artifacts" (216).

Thomas also defines "temporal types" (222–25), a typological concept paralleling that employed in this guide. If, for example, an archaeologist finds that a grouping of similar artifacts—a "morphological type"—is found to occur in archaeological deposits of a certain time period within a certain region, it can be elevated to the level of a temporal type. Such types have "significance in time: they change" (222). As Thomas warns, however, and as we shall discuss in chapters 2 and 3, temporal types are but stepping-stones toward better understanding of ancient cultural patterns: we have to look at how these types reflect activities (such as changes in hunting patterns); what they reflect in terms of technology (are some types simply unfinished versions of another?); how they are altered or modified in shape through use; and, overall, their particular role in an ancient culture. It is all too easy to become fascinated with projectile points and to forget the essential mission of archaeology—disclosing the true nature of the people behind the artifacts.

Those uninitiated in projectile point typology will wonder where the names come from and, perhaps, why these types are named. The names are largely geographical in origin; an archaeologist defines a type and often chooses the name of a local town, creek, or landmark in the region to apply to it. Very rarely, a type is named in honor of a person, usually a landowner or an individual who has been instrumental in obtaining information on the new type. As to why the types are named, we can simply say that it is to foster communication. Once a new type has been defined and illustrated, the name attached to it carries communicative value when archaeologists are discussing certain projectile point forms in meetings or in print. In the Texas typological system, a single term is used, without a descriptive adjective. We talk, then, of Montell points, rather than using the original term, suggested by J. Charles Kelley, "Montell Split Stem"; and of Nolan points, rather than "Nolan Beveled Stem." However, this binomial system is sometimes still used in other parts of North America (e.g., the Great Basin: Heizer and Hester 1978; Thomas 1981).

Here are two final notes of explanation and caution: First, this volume does not include descriptions for *every* possible point type in Texas. Some remain to be defined; some we have undoubtedly missed; for some, we simply had insufficient information; and there were a few we felt no longer served a valid purpose. Additionally, in some areas of the state, especially in far west Texas and the Panhandle (and adjacent parts of eastern New Mexico), there is limited typological information available in comparison with the rest of Texas. Fortunately, with the help of colleagues in those areas, we have incorporated new data.

Finally, it is obvious that no ancient projectile point maker had a copy of any typological guide that permitted every point to be made in strict conformance with the descriptions and illustrations provided here. While the prehistoric flintknappers certainly must have had certain stylistic ideals in mind in many cases, the variability of skills and of raw materials resulted in a wide range of shapes within some of the types that we currently recognize. Furthermore, not every ancient projectile point fits within known types. Points were often reworked extensively during their use-life, and reshaping of the body (and sometimes the stem) can make typological placement impossible. This should be clearly recognized by the reader, circumventing, we hope, the frustration of trying to force every point into a specific typological niche.

This guide is by no means the final word on stone tool typology in Texas. Some types, such as Merrell (this volume), need much more work in terms of definition, distribution, and dating. Similarly, some suggested Paleo-Indian types, such as Berclair, Lubbock, and Thrall, need work (Bousman et al. 2004). Some may be based on only a few specimens, or others may actually be linked to previously established types. Mallouf (1990) has suggested that Hell Gap points sometimes occur in the southern Rolling Plains of west Texas. Some regional specialists disagree with that type label, noting that the name has been widely applied in recent years to a broad range of specimens.

Bill Young has loaned us examples of dart points from Dallas, Henderson, Navarro, and Ellis counties that he types as Jakie Stemmed and Rice Contracting Stem, known best from Arkansas and Missouri (impinging on northeast Texas; Justice 1987). He has shown these to other professional archaeologists who concur with his typology. A comparison with some of the local types in that region suggests that more research has to be done to verify their presence.

Frankly, we are skeptical about the validity of some of the types presented here; a few have been eliminated since the first edition, but others remain for lithic researchers to review, modify, or discard. Detailed attribute and multivariate analyses (Johnson 1989a; see also Peter 1982a, Mallouf 1987, and Bement 1991b) will doubtless serve to tighten up many of the typological groups. We note such research in progress by Elton R. Prewitt, working with Central Texas Archaic types, and the late Thomas C. Kelly's studies of Paleo-Indian projectile points in the state.

The Manufacture and Use of Stone Tools

CRUCIAL TO the study of projectile points and other stone tools is an awareness of the manufacturing techniques used to produce them. Similarly, we must ask questions about how certain stone tool forms functioned in the daily life of ancient Indian cultures. Both areas of inquiry play a major role in modern archaeology. Lithic technology is the study of stone tools, from the initial stages of manufacture through completion, use of the tool in various ways, and its eventual discard. A great deal of attention has been given to tool manufacture; archaeologists now analyze the thousands of waste flakes found at occupation sites, looking for clues to the manufacturing process; others have become experts at replication, the experimental production of stone tools using ancient techniques.

Stone tool function is another major concern within lithic technology. Archaeologists formerly labeled tools "knives" or "scrapers" based on a subjective appraisal of their shape or form. Now, sophisticated techniques of microscopic analysis have been developed that reveal minute traces of wear—and these wear patterns are often diagnostic of specific tool functions. Coupled with microwear studies are experiments in actual tool use—for example, the butchering of a deer with stone flakes or making a spear-thrower with a stone scraper—designed both to see how a specific tool form actually works under "primitive" conditions and to examine the microscopic traces of wear produced under controlled experimentation.

MAKING CHIPPED STONE TOOLS

The manufacture of stone tools is a subtractive process, a systematic reduction of a piece of stone designed to achieve a desired shape. The sequence of events that results in a finished stone tool leaves a great deal of waste debris in the archaeological record; however, even this material can be analyzed as a source of information on the ancient toolmaking process.

The raw material for stone toolmaking varies across the state, although the most common is chert or "flint." Technically, chert is a term broadly applied to "all sedimentary rocks composed primarily of microcrystalline quartz, including flint, chalcedony, agate, jasper, hornstone, novaculite, and several varieties of semiprecious gems"

(Luedtke 1992, 5). Luedtke (1992, 5–6) places any materials referred to as "flint" within the chert category, as has long been the American usage of these terms. British researchers usually distinguish "flint" by using the term to refer to the dark nodular materials found in the Cretaceous chalk formations in southern England. "Chert," on the other hand, is a "lesser-quality" material found in nodules in limestone outcrops or in shale beds.

Cherts and other cryptocrystalline materials occur in the form of seams, ledges, nodules, and cobbles at various outcrops in different parts of the state. The serious lithic researcher should try to obtain a copy of *From Mountain Peaks to Alligator Stomachs* (Banks 1990), the only comprehensive study of stone tool resources in Texas and adjacent states (see also Holliday and Welty 1981).

Obsidian, a volcanic glass, does not occur in artifact-quality form in Texas, and its presence on archaeological sites is indicative of ancient trade. Hester and colleagues (1985, 1991a) have documented obsidian from Mexico, New Mexico, Idaho, and Wyoming at Texas sites, utilizing techniques such as X-ray fluorescence and neutron activation analysis. Once the geologic source has been chemically characterized, the obsidian of which an artifact is made can be "fingerprinted" and linked back to its source. Hester and colleagues (1985) found that a Clovis-age biface from Kincaid Rockshelter (41UV2) was made of El Paraiso obsidian, from the Mexican state of Queretaro 600 miles to the southwest (see Hughes and Hester 2009). As Hester and colleagues (1991a) have noted, obsidian from the Malad source in southeastern Idaho is widespread in Texas, especially at Late Prehistoric sites along the Balcones Escarpment. This may be reflective of a north-south trade network out of the Plains. Sites along the Colorado River in San Saba and Llano counties have also yielded pieces of obsidian, many of these linked to the Obsidian Cliff source at Yellowstone Park, Wyoming. New Mexico obsidian is scattered across the state. Hester and colleagues (1991b) documented Late Archaic obsidian artifacts at Arenosa Shelter (41VV99) in the lower Pecos. The obsidian was from the Cerro de Toledo source in the Jemez Mountains of northern New Mexico. Another source in that same area, Cerro del Medio, is also widespread in Texas. Obsidian artifacts are particularly common in the Texas Panhandle, and most are attributable to interaction between Pueblo and Plains Native American groups in Late Prehistoric times.

Figure 2-4 shows the location of some of the major lithic resources in Texas, as described by Banks (1990). Some of these resources are widespread, such as the Catahoula Formation, with quartzites and petrified woods (from the overlying Fleming Formation). The Uvalde Gravels, usually small lag gravels of chert, quartz, quartzite, jasper, limestone, and silicified wood, occur widely in the state and are especially common in south Texas, where they cap the hills and high terraces (Hester 1975).

Along the Rio Grande, the "Rio Grande Gravels" contain cobbles of red, black, green, and other colorful cherts, quartzites, and basalts derived from the Big Bend area and deposited on the river's high terraces millions of years ago.

The Edwards Plateau is, according to Banks (1990, 59), "one of the largest sources of chert in the United States." The Edwards limestone formation contains seams, ledges, beds, and nodules of high-quality chert. For example, on the north side of San Antonio, there are extensive exposures of Edwards cherts, often a fine-grained grey to brown material, and there are many quarry locales where these were procured by the ancient peoples of that region (Katz 1987; McGraw and Valdez 1978). In the Georgetown area, there is a dark gray to blue chert of exceedingly good quality, used extensively in prehistoric times and sought today by flintknappers. In the Junction area, a "root-beer colored translucent chert" is often found in archaeological sites and ancient

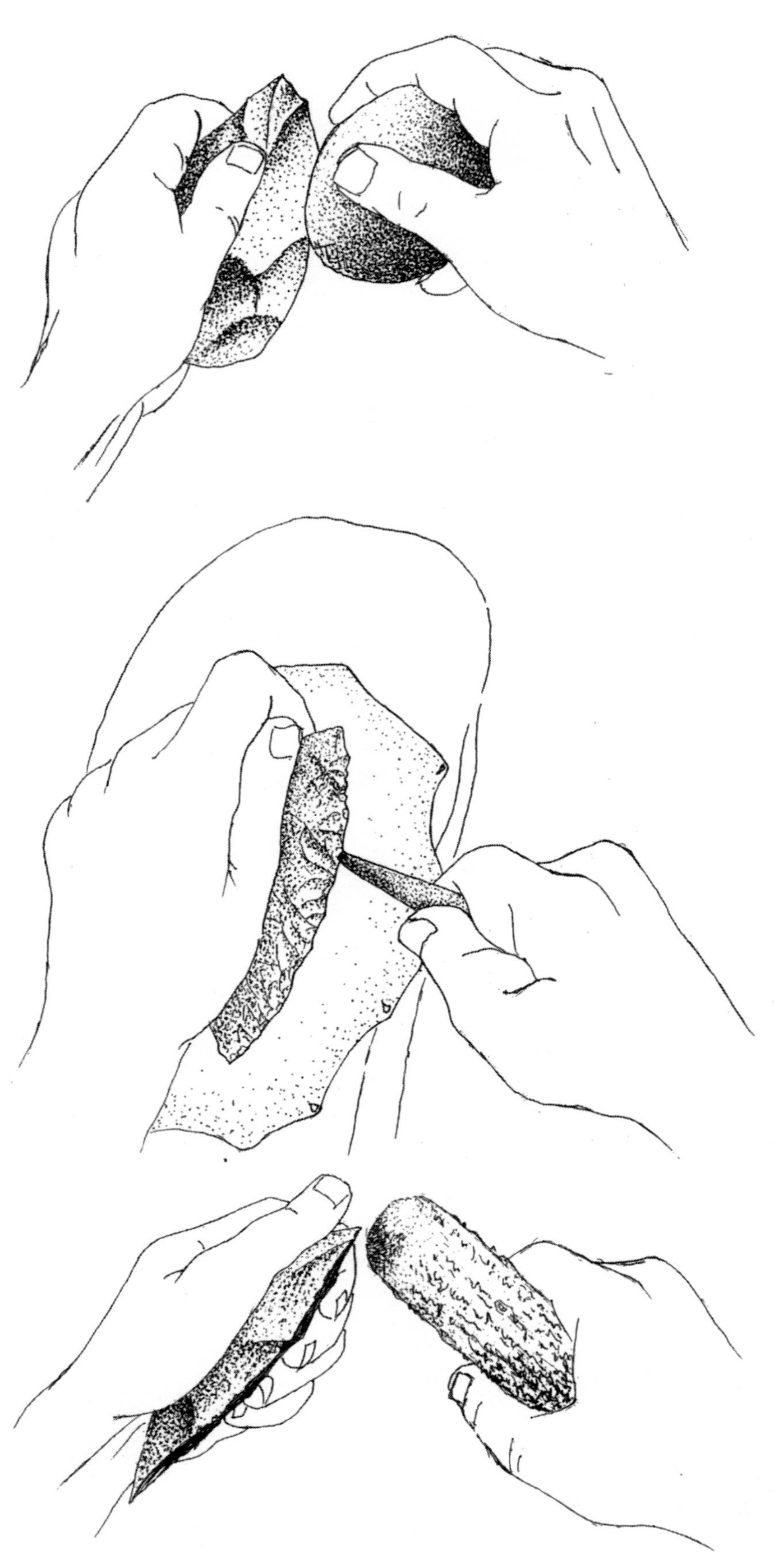

Figures 2-1 to 2-3. *Examples of flint-knapping techniques.* 1, hammerstone percussion; 2, pressure flaking, using a bone or antler flaking tool; 3, "soft-hammer" (billet) percussion, using an antler hammer.

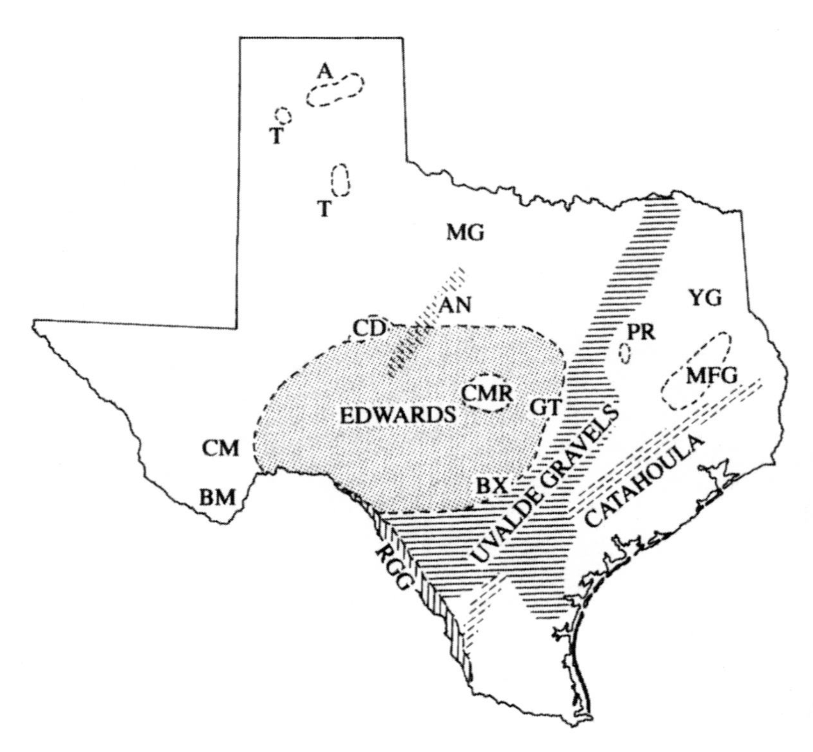

Figure 2-4. *Lithic resources in Texas.* Approximate locations of selected major lithic resources are shown. Detailed information can be found in Banks (1990). Key: A, Alibates; AN, Antlers Formation; BM, Burro Mesa; BX, Bexar County cherts; CD, Callahan Divide; CM, Caballos Mountain; CMR, Central Mineral Region; GT, Georgetown cherts; MFG, Manning fused glass (and sites with artifacts from this material); MG, Markley Conglomerates; PR, Pisgah Ridge; RGG, Rio Grande Gravels; T, Tecovas formation; YG, Yegua Gravels.

quarry exposures (Banks 1990, 60). The Llano Uplift, or Central Mineral Region, of central Texas contains some distinctive cherts but was also used in ancient times for the procurement of serpentine and soapstone and for granites used locally for milling implements.

In north central Texas, the Callahan Divide, just north of the Edwards Plateau, is the source of high-quality light gray to blue-gray cherts. These occur in lenses and nodules in that area (Banks 1990).

The Trans-Pecos, including the Big Bend, has several chert sources. One of the best known is the "Burro Mesa" material, a colorful chert with variegated red, brown, and white colors, often striped or mottled (Banks 1990, 84). The Caballos Novaculite of west Texas yields a chert, glassy in texture, and blue-gray to green in color (85). A white novaculite is also present, and Banks (1990, 86) reports that it encompasses the whole 1,200-foot-high north face of Caballos Mountain.

On the Llano Estacado, the most famous raw material source is Alibates, found along the Canadian River. Many of the major quarries are now part of a national monument (Wishoff 2010). This "chert" (agatized dolomite) ranges in color from white, yellow, red, or purple—often mottled or striped combinations. It is known to have been procured for stone tools beginning in Paleo-Indian times and widely traded in the Plains and in Texas (e.g., Mallouf and Wulfkuhle [1991] report a cache of Alibates cores and bifaces in southwestern Kansas). The Tecovas cherts or jaspers occur near Quitaque and into Oldham County, not far from Alibates, and are sometimes confused with it. They have color combinations or ranges of white, yellow, red, and brown—often characterized by white speckles (A. J. Taylor, personal communication).

A sampling of other Texas lithic resources, studied in detail by Banks (1990), include Manning Fused Glass (formed by the "fusion of volcanic ash as a result of burning lignite underlying the ash itself" [53]) found in east and southeast Texas (see Brown 1976; it is often a light grayish blue, used from San Patrice times up through

Caddo [Shafer 1973]); the Yegua Gravels—quartzites and petrified woods in east Texas; the Pisgah Ridge Cherts in the Corsicana-Richland Creek areas of north Texas; the "ironized sandstone" of the Woodbine Formation in the Eastern Cross Timbers, used for metates, axes, and choppers (Banks 1990); the Markley Conglomerates, in the Brazos River area near Graham, where workshops of chert and quartzite are found; and the Antlers Formation, exposures of chert and quartzite gravels in the San Angelo area (Banks 1990).

In some areas, where chert or quartzite was not of the best quality for flaking, the prehistoric Indians would subject the cobbles to heat treatment. This could consist of baking the materials under the coals of a campfire for twenty-four to forty-eight hours, based on ethnographic accounts (Hester 1972a). Experimentally, heat treating is known to alter chert in terms of its microcrystalline structure, making it easier to chip; heat treating is evident in some areas of the state: it produces a pink to purple discoloration of the chert, along with a vitreous "greasy" appearance (Hester and Collins 1974). Most cherts can be heat treated between 250 and 450 degrees Celsius, sometimes using a gradual elevation of temperatures during the process. But each chert is different—some may not respond to heat-treating efforts, and for those that do, the processes used and the level of heating are all imprecise.

Since heat treating of cherts was done by some Native American groups well into the early 20th century, early observations of the technology may have given rise to the old tale, still heard commonly today, that "arrowheads were flaked by drips of water placed on a heated piece of stone, or flint." In the September 5, 1908, issue of *Field and Stream* magazine, a lengthy letter to the editor involved an account from a "Dr. Bishop" who worked among Arizona tribes in the late 19th century (Kelpie 1908, 371). Dr. Bishop described a process in which a piece of flint of "straight grain" was placed in an informal wedge made on the end of a split twig. Then it was placed in a small fire where it was "gradually heated until it was hot enough to suit the arrow maker." The stone was then removed from the fire, the end of another small twig was dipped in water and then quickly applied to the flint, "and a part of the stone would scale off where the wetted stick had touched it." The stick continued to be wetted and applied, and the arrow maker even used a finger, dipped in water, as the process became more "exact." Dr. Bishop stated that "this is the only way that arrowheads can be made."

Thus, in order to initiate the making of a stone tool, the prehistoric knapper had to find the right type of stone, and sometimes had to alter it through heat treatment, before beginning to work it. The subsequent reduction process that resulted in the manufacture of a tool could take several different trajectories (Fox et al. 1974; Patterson 1977; Tunnell 1978). Most typically, in the manufacture of a biface (especially a dart point), a core (fig. 2-5) was formed by striking flakes off a cobble using a hammerstone percussion technique (fig. 2-1; fig. 2-6). The first flakes removed from the cobble were designed to create a platform, and by directing percussion blows at the edge of the platform, additional flakes were detached from the sides of the core. Ideally, the knapper was looking for a flake of appropriate size and thickness (fig. 2-8) for further reduction into a bifacial point. First, however, the exterior surface (cortex) of the core had to be flaked away, creating distinctive primary cortex flakes (fig. 2-9). Further chipping produced secondary flakes, showing both earlier flake removals and traces of remaining cortex (fig. 2-10). Finally, interior flakes (fig. 2-11) with no remaining surface cortex, could be struck off and one of appropriate size selected for further work. There are other types of flakes that represent specific events (for example, overshot flakes, fig. 2-12, discussed later; see also fig. 2-13 for terms used in describing flakes and blades). Bifacial chipping—removing small flakes on both sides by striking at the edges of the

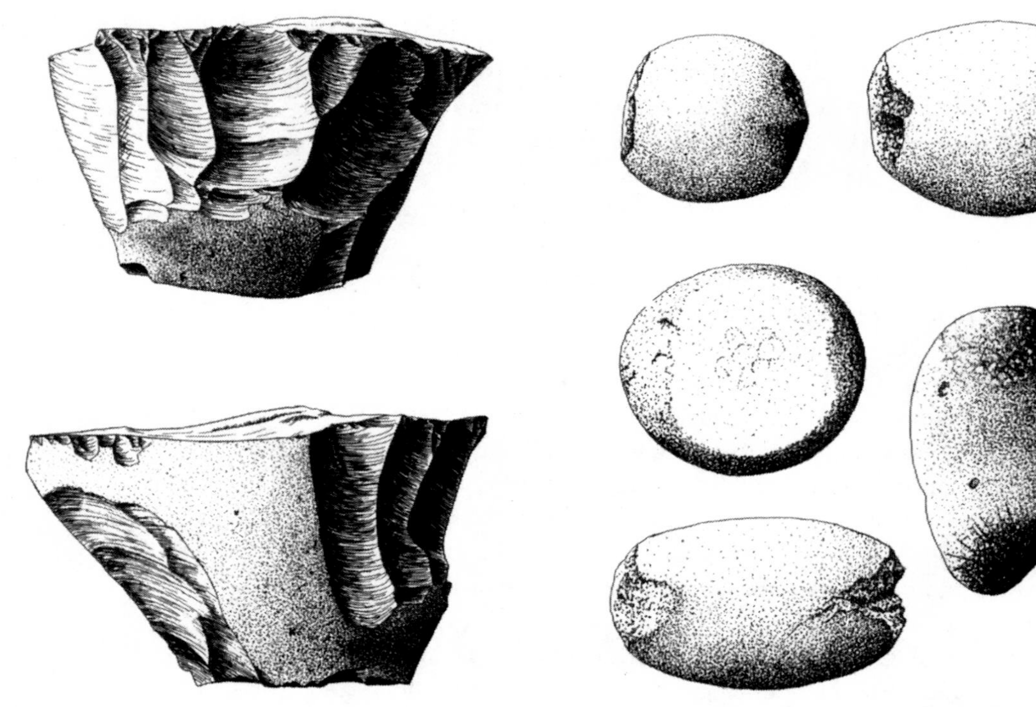

Figure 2-5. *Core*. A large flake core from northern Bexar County, Texas. A large chert cobble was split, and the broad surface (platform) used to strike off flakes. Top specimen is 13 cm across platform.

Figure 2-6. *Hammerstones*. These specimens are made on quartzite pebbles. Note the battering on the ends resulting from use in percussion flaking. Length of bottom specimen is 6.8 cm.

flake—proceeded using hammerstone or billet percussion. It was then a question of continued thinning and shaping of the flake, leading to final completion of a point. Very often, the knapper would make a mistake or would encounter a flaw in the chert. The partly completed specimen would be discarded. These abortive efforts at toolmaking are, of course, preserved in archaeological sites and represent "fossilized" stages in bifacial reduction. Archaeologists once simply described these as "knives" or put certain shapes into specific "point" types, not realizing that they were looking at part of a process. The larger, thick bifaces at the beginning of the process are often called blanks. They often have cortex on one or both surfaces, particularly if, instead of reducing a core and picking proper-sized flakes, the knapper chose to reduce a tabular cobble with the intention of chipping it into a finished product (fig. 2-7).

The "quarry blanks," which are often large and crudely flaked, are characteristic of quarry and lithic processing sites found at raw material outcrops. Sometimes, the thinner, better-made blanks were collected and buried in "caches"—items perhaps hidden away for future use or being transported as part of a trade network (Lintz and Saner 2002). These "cache bifaces" (fig. 2-16)—often in groups of thirty or more specimens—are intriguing, as their reasons for their deposition in caches reflects ancient behaviors that we know little about (Bement 1991b; Miller 2007; see also Fields et al. 1991).

Sometimes, the large, thinned blanks occur as single specimens found at a considerable distance from the raw material source. These can be described as "trade blanks" (fig. 2-17), having entered into other areas through prehistoric trade (Hester and Barber 1990). Such large bifaces also sometimes end up in mortuary offerings, as documented by Taylor and Highley (1995) at the Loma Sandia (41LK28) Archaic cemetery, and by Lovata (1997) at the Silo site.

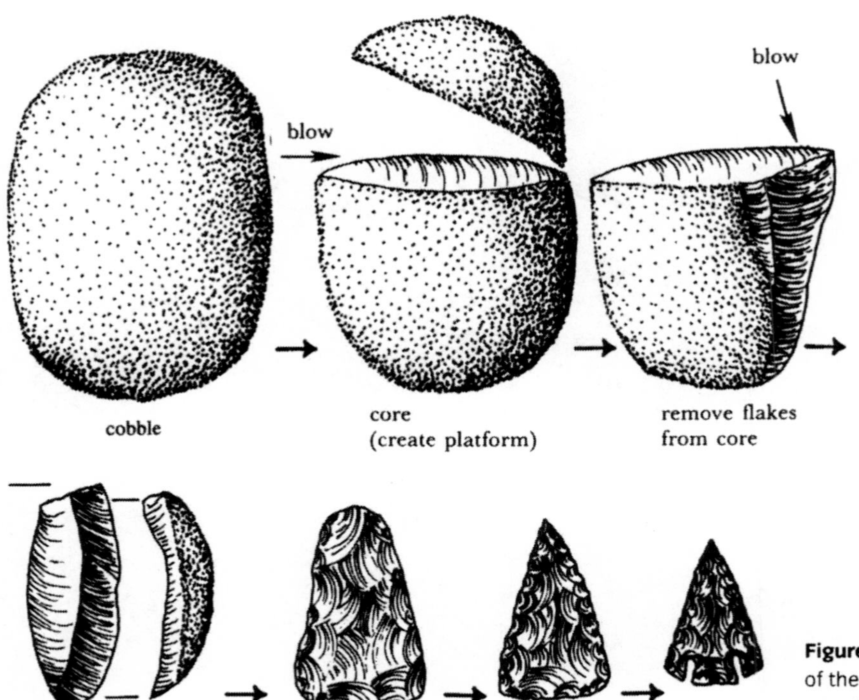

Figure 2-7. *Sequences of bifacial reduction.* Idealized view of the making of a stone tool starting with a nodule and core. Length 7.2 cm.

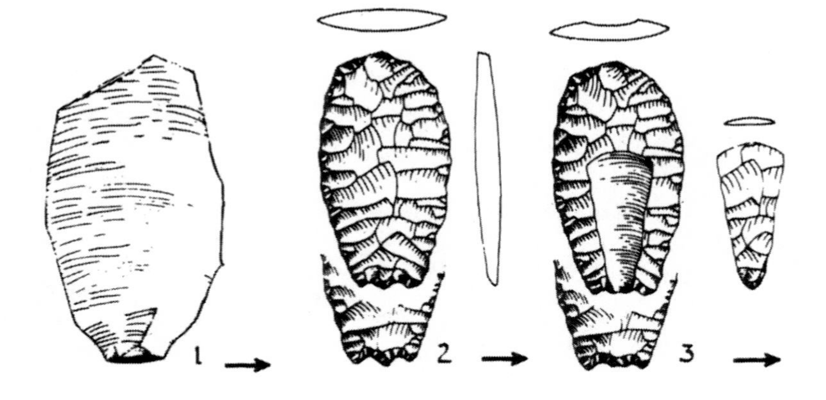

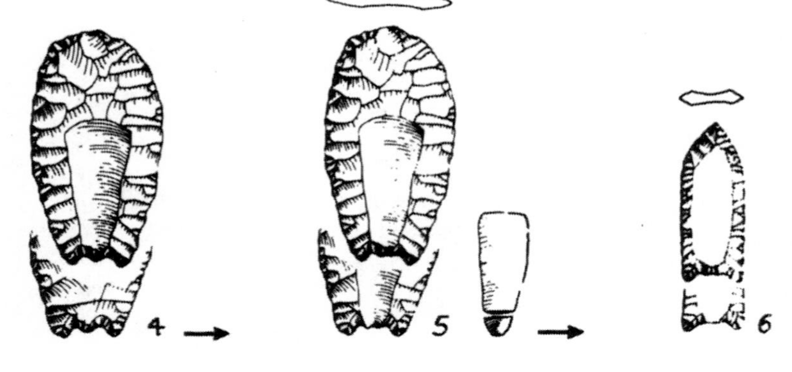

Figure 2-8. *Sequence of fluted point manufacture from the Adair-Steadman Folsom site, Fisher County, Texas.* 1, flake blank; 2, preform with flute removal platform in center of base; 3, removal of flute; 4 and 5, stages of trimming the basal edge; 6, trimming of point to final shape. From Tunnell (1975, fig. 2). Courtesy of the Texas Historical Commission.

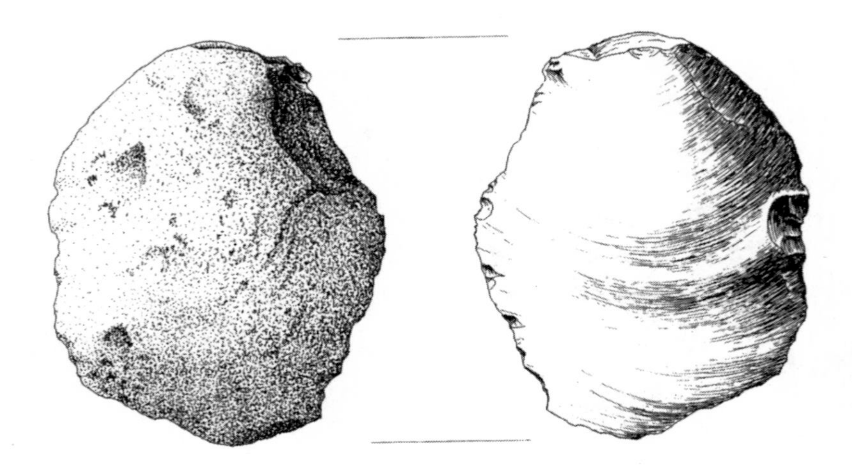

Figure 2-9. *Primary flake.* The initial flakes struck from a core usually have most of their outer surface covered with the cortex (weathered exterior of cobble).

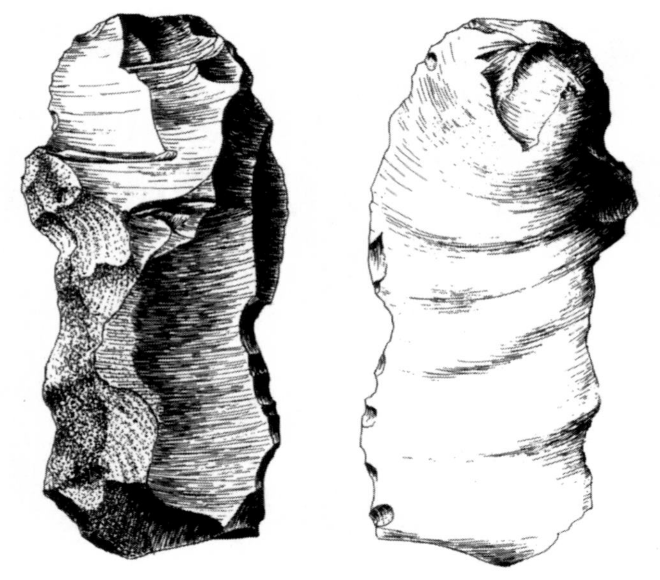

Figure 2-10. *Secondary flake.* Further removal of flakes from a core produces flakes whose outer (dorsal) surfaces show both previous flake removals and some cortex remnants.

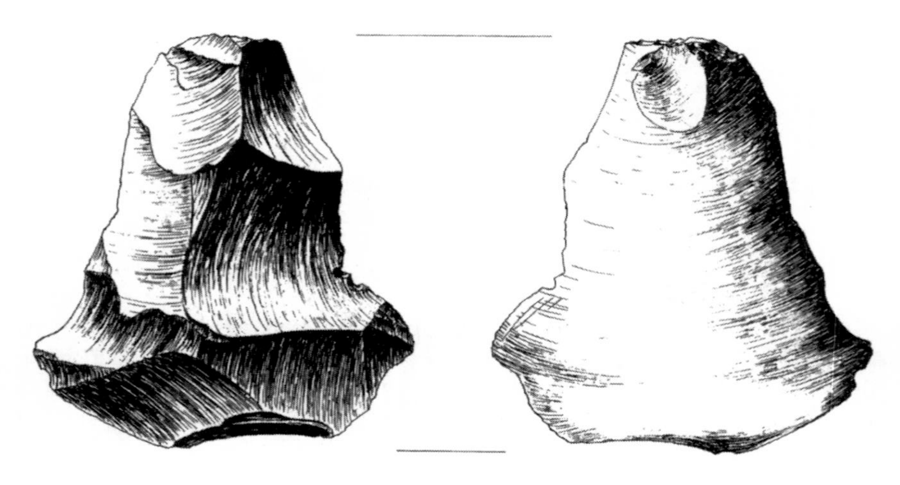

Figure 2-11. *Interior flake.* These flakes are removed from a core once it has been prepared and shaped. Such flakes were intended for use as blanks in making dart points, or for knifes, scrapers, or other functions.

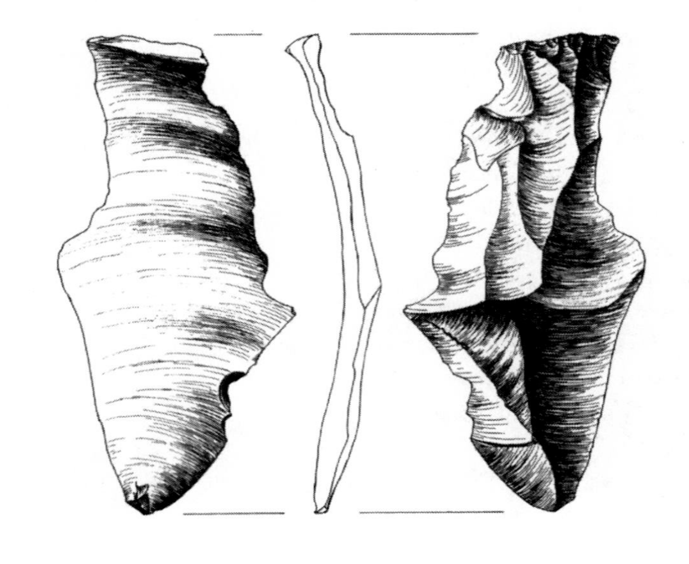

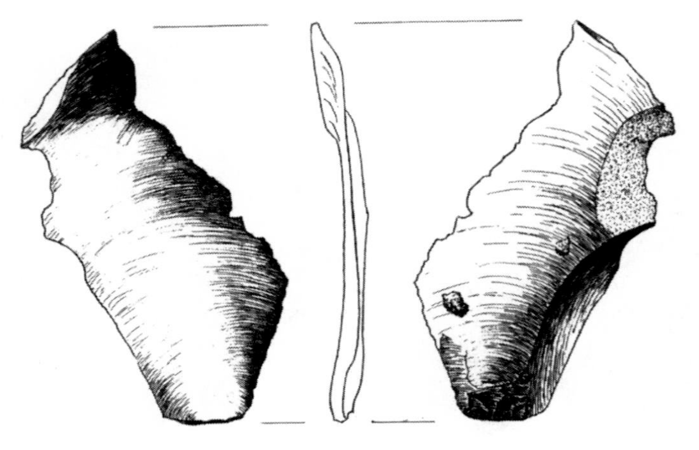

Figure 2-12. *Overshot flake*. An overshot flake represents a flake struck from one edge that carries across the biface and removes a section of the opposite edge. In Clovis technology, overshot flakes were intentionally removed in making Clovis points. However, many in other time periods represent mistakes by the flintknapper. Length of top flake, 11.3 cm.

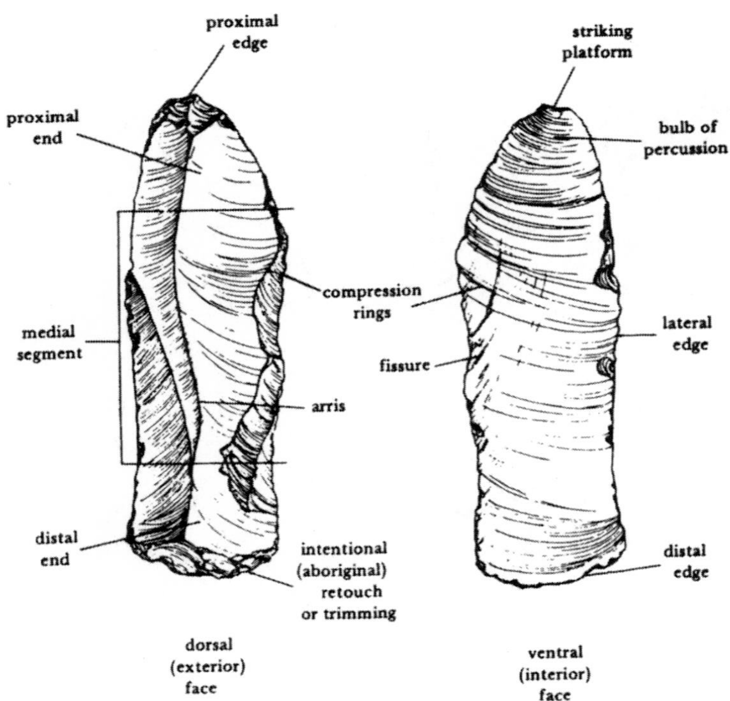

Figure 2-13. *Attributes of flakes and blades*. Terminology used by archaeologists to describe the various portions of a flake or a blade are shown. From Mallouf (1981a; specimen 6, Brookeen Creek cache). Courtesy of the Texas Historical Commission.

However, if the biface blank continued to be thinned and reduced in a lithic reduction sequence, it entered a stage that we call a preform (figs. 2-14, 2-15). While preforms may themselves go through several stages, they are generally fairly thin and approach the shape and size needed for the final artifact. Indeed, when the preform has been thinned as much as possible by hammerstone percussion (or, in some areas, by percussion with antler cylinder-hammers or billets), pressure flaking with a deer antler tine (fig. 2-2) is used to finish and straighten the edges and to form the notches and stem that serve to complete the projectile point. The classification of preforms presents a number of problems. Some of the projectile point types that we describe in a following section of the book are probably preforms (figs. 2-14, 2-15). Unfinished Langtry points are sometimes called "Almagre" (see fig. 2-14); Pandora and Refugio may not be valid types at all but rather preforms for several different point styles. Thus, in assigning types when sorting a large stone tool collection, the archaeologist has to view the whole range of chipped stone lithics with an eye to the toolmaking process. Specimens that may be preforms have to be examined for evidence as to why they were abandoned (e.g., flaws; short "hinge" flakes; stacks, lumps, or knots on the biface that could not be removed; or the detachment of "overshot flakes" that removed the opposite edge of the

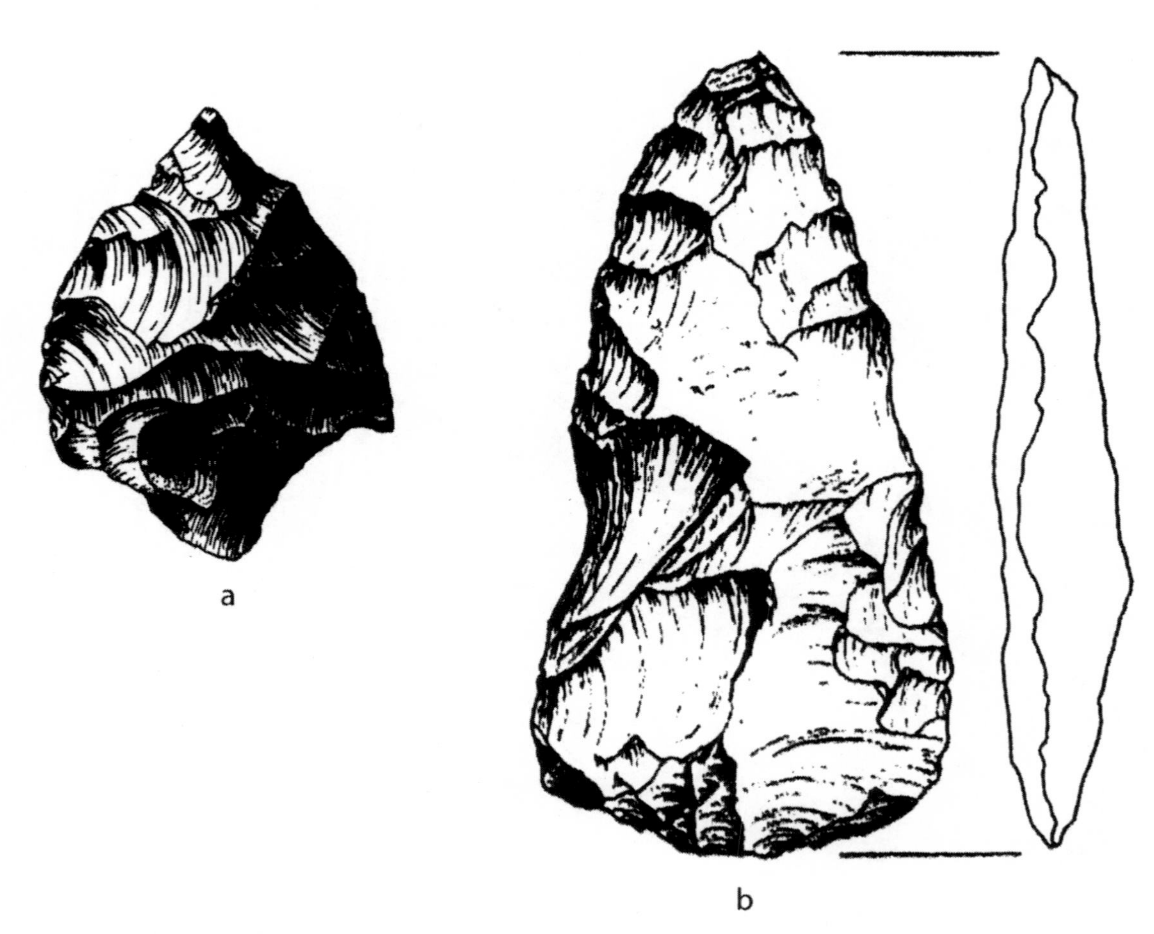

Figure 2-14. *Dart point preforms*. Left = a, right = b. Length of b is 125 mm. These are bifaces designed to be finished as dart points but were abandoned during the process. Left, Langtry preform (so-called Almagre points); right, bifacial preform, central Texas. Drawing by Dennis Knepper.

Figure 2-15. *Arrow point preforms*. These preforms are from a site in Uvalde County, Texas, and represent unfinished Sabinal points.

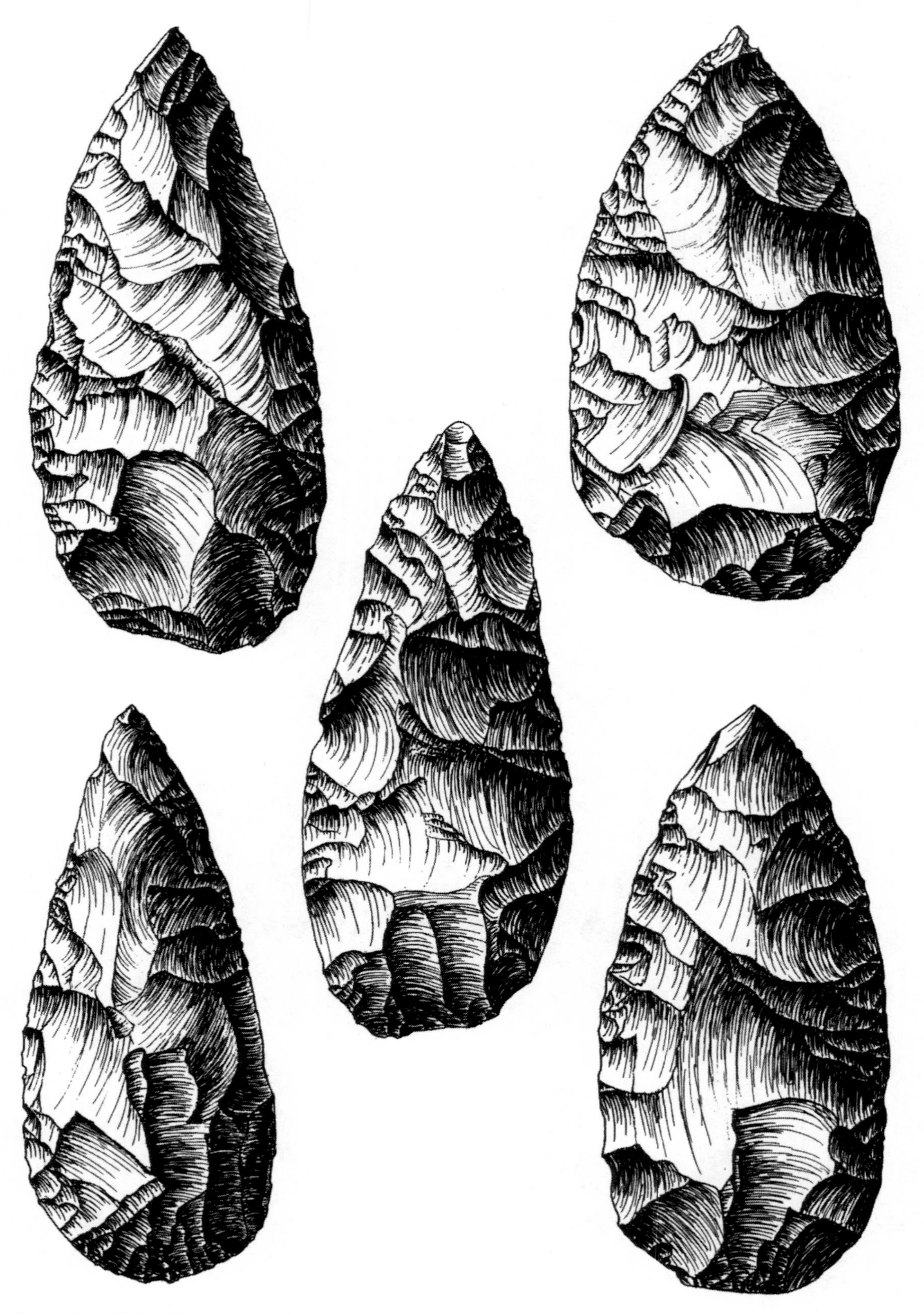

Figure 2-16. *Cache bifaces*. Caches often consist of a number of bifaces that were placed in a pit or otherwise hidden to be used at a later time. There are a number of reasons behind caching strategies. But it often seems they represent the transport of processed lithics from a flint-rich to a flint-poor area. From the John Haberer collection. Length of specimen in upper left is 11 cm.

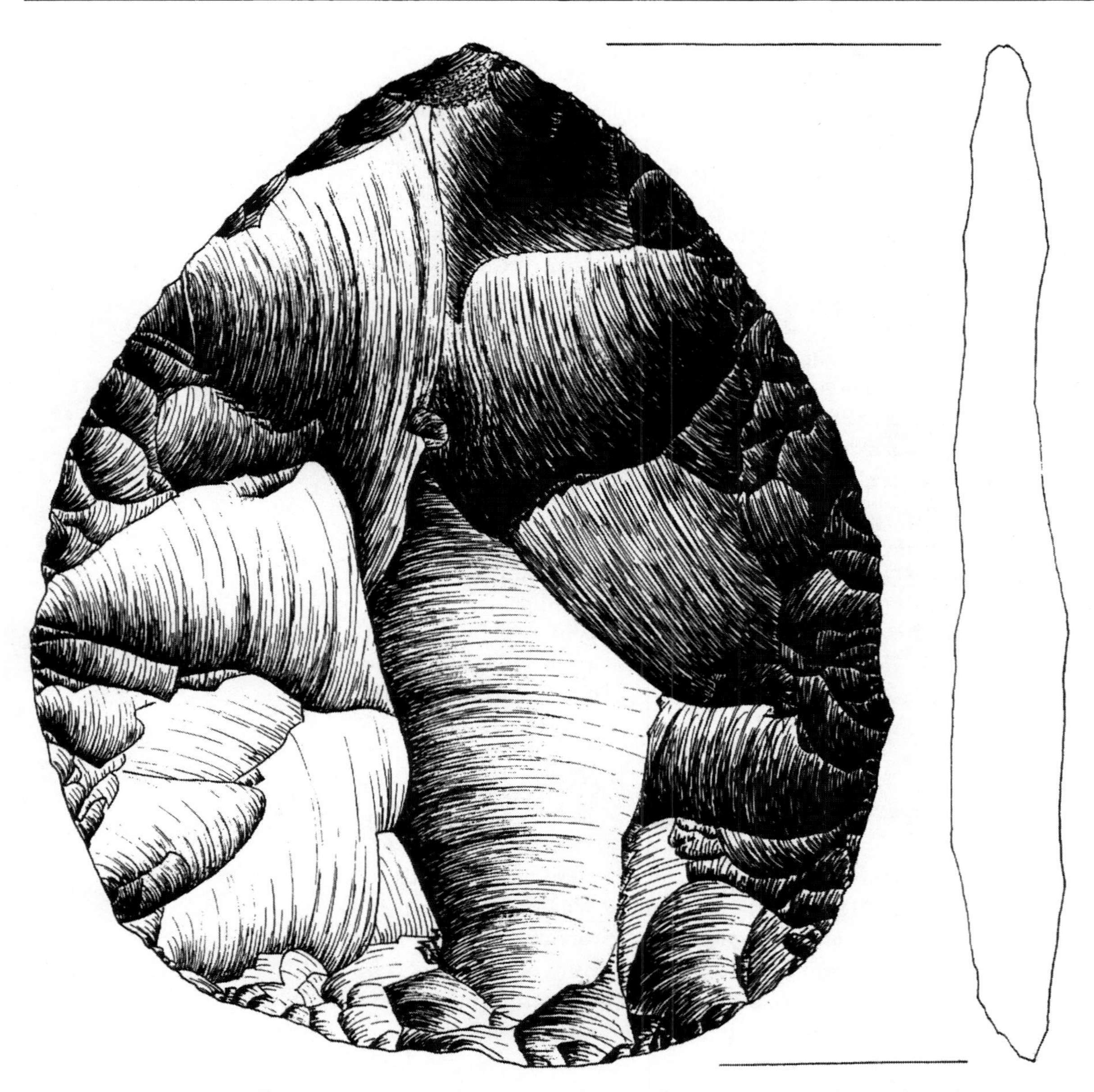

Figure 2-17. *Trade blank.* Large, thinned bifaces are sometimes found as caches or occasionally as individual specimens, again likely related to the trade of lithics. From the Medina Lake cache, south central Texas. Courtesy of the Texas Historical Commission and David L. Calame Sr. 15 cm. long.

biface. See fig. 2-12). Additionally, the archaeologist learns to recognize specific types of breakage patterns that are the result of fractures caused during the reduction process.

The manufacture of arrow points is generally less complicated. Most are made by pressure flaking on small flakes or elongated flakes known as blades (fig. 2-13), yet some go through a preform phase. And if the point is never completed, the archaeologist recovers tiny, arrow point–sized preforms at the prehistoric campsite (fig. 2-15). Again, if the reduction process is not kept in mind, some of these preforms may erroneously be classified as arrow point "types" (for example, the "Granbury" type defined in central Texas in the 1960s or perhaps the "Cliffton" [see Perdiz] and Young points described below).

Making a uniface, a stone tool chipped on one face (see chapter 5), is not as complex as biface reduction. A core is reduced and selected flakes used for uniface manufacture. Some unifaces, typically called scrapers, are fairly casually made, with an edge formed by chipping along one side of a flake. Others reflect much more care, both in the selection of a proper flake and in careful chipping to form the working edges and to achieve a desired shape. End scraper unifaces are particularly characteristic of this kind of careful treatment, often being made on long flakes or blades. On occasion, unifaces or blades destined for uniface manufacture have been found, like biface blanks, stored or hidden away as caches (for example, the Gibson cache in Coke County, reported by Tunnell [1978], and the Brookeen Creek cache in Hill County, described by Mallouf 1981a).

The finished artifact, be it point or scraper, has a "life span" or use-life during which it may undergo modifications that will significantly alter its shape. Some specimens that we classify as projectile points may have been used, at least at times, as knives. Use of the cutting edge causes dulling, and the edge then has to be rechipped or beveled, often giving the specimen a different shape. (A bevel is a steeply angled edge, usually on a biface edge, that usually results from resharpening of that edge; see also Patterson and Sollberger 1990).

Examples of reworking or resharpening of formal lithic tools are common in Texas. For example, the two-and-four beveled knives (see pp. 222–23) were extensively resharpened during use, often causing changes in overall outline. The so-called Meserve points are simply Plainview, Golondrina, or Dalton points that have been extensively reworked, either because of breakage or because they were used as knives and resharpened. Goodyear (1974, 29) has done a study of Dalton points and records the different shapes they take as they are resharpened and modified during use (see also Ballenger 2001).

Sometimes a projectile point was broken by impact when it hit a bone in an animal carcass or missed its target, striking the ground. Perhaps rather than removing the point from the shaft, the broken tip was rechipped, producing a distinctly different shape for the distal end. The projectile point stems were often fractured or broken and sometimes reworked. Flenniken and Raymond (1986) and Flenniken and Wilke (1989) have used experimental data on stem breakage and subsequent stem reworking as an argument against the utility of point types as time markers in the Great Basin. Bettinger and colleagues (1991) present a very different view, arguing that these experimental data do not change the archaeologically observable evidence that point forms do indeed change through time. Our experience in excavating and analyzing projectile point forms, especially in central Texas, indicates that stem shapes were important (for whatever reason) to the prehistoric peoples and that a great deal of attention was given to stem detail. When stems were broken and reworked, the ancient craftsman seemed intent on restoring their original shape (the "mental template" concept that we discussed earlier in terms of our typological approach). Of course, in the analysis of hundreds of points from a site, there are always a number whose stems or other attributes do not permit classification; these may be unrecognized types, unique specimens, or the reworking of a stem in a casual fashion. As is clear on preforms from central Texas, the careful shaping of the stem—on a biface or large flake blank—preceded the completion of the point (see Hester 1988b; Johnson 1995). This certainly suggests that standardized stem shape or form was important in prehistoric Texas point-making technologies.

The completed chipped stone artifact was often hafted for use. This is obvious with the projectile points; the shape of their stem often reflects how they were inserted and bound on a spear or arrow shaft. Archaeologically, we can see examples of hafting from preserved specimens found in lower Pecos and northeastern Mexico shelters and caves (figs. 2-18, 2-19). Figure 2-18 shows a hafted Langtry point and a hafted Toyah point.

Hafting the specimen on a shaft may require binding with cordage or application of a gummy resin (as with the Langtry point in fig. 2-19) or use of natural tar or asphaltum. The latter is seen on the bases of Morhiss dart points from Victoria and Goliad counties. Some large, thin, triangular bifaces were hafted as knives, as in the illustrated example from the Cueva de la Candelaria burial cave in southwest Coahuila, Mexico. The biface base was set into a shallow notch in the wooden handle and secured in place with pine resin. Of course, some bifaces were handheld during use; an example is the Kerrville biface, a butted knife chipped so that it would fit easily in the palm of the hand.

Unifaces, too, were usually hafted (fig. 2-19), although some large gouges and scrapers may have been handheld. We often see efforts at thinning the end of the uniface, such as an end scraper, opposite the thick working end, suggesting that it was to be inserted into a haft. Tiny end scrapers had to be hafted, especially those used in such tasks as working bison hide. Many of these may have been inserted in L-shaped handles of the kind used by Plains Indians in early historic times (Metcalf 1970; Wedel 1970). Casually chipped unifaces or edge-trimmed flakes were, somewhat surprisingly, also hafted at times. There are surviving examples from the dry caves of the lower Pecos region, including a tiny flake hafted in a split sotol stem and a pointed, trimmed uniface set into a socket in the middle of a short, wooden handle. Some hafting may have been informal, simply wrapping the end of a flake or uniface with a strip of leather or a plant leaf, to keep it from cutting one's hand during use. At the Witte Museum in San Antonio, the lower Pecos collections include a sharp-edged flake set in a "handle" or sheath made of woven basketry (Shafer 1986, 123). Thus, when we look at stone tools from most parts of Texas, where preservation is usually poor, we have to keep in mind that tools were probably hafted in a variety of ways (for further examples from the western United States, see Heizer 1970; Hester 1970b, 1974).

Some further comments are offered here regarding the occurrence of blades and blade cores in Texas archaeological sites. A blade is a long, parallel-edged flake resulting from intentional removal (by percussion) from a specially prepared blade core. Blade-like flakes sometimes occur in the flake technologies so common in Texas, but here we are describing a specialized core-blade technology. Such a technology can be seen in the Late Prehistoric in Texas, along the coast (Hester and Shafer 1975), and in the Toyah Phase of south and central Texas (see the small polyhedral core in fig. 2-20; see also Green and Hester 1973). On the coast, blade-making may have been an efficient way to use scarce chert resources. In the Toyah Phase, blades were used in making Perdiz points (Green and Hester 1973, fig. 2) and unifacial end scrapers (fig. 5).

However, since the early 1990s, studies have shown that core-blade technology was important in Clovis times, 11,200 years ago. Green (1963) initially reported a cache of Clovis blades from Blackwater Draw, the Clovis type site. In addition, Young and Collins (1989) describe a cache of Clovis blades found near the Trinity River in Navarro County (fig. 2-21). The specialized polyhedral blade cores from which these have been removed are noted by Collins (1990) from the Kincaid Rockshelter (41UV2), 41LL3 in Llano County, and 41GL175 in Gillespie County. Another Clovis blade core was excavated by Hester and Collins in 1991 at the Gault site (41BL323) in central Texas (fig. 2-22). A surface find of such a core from Victoria County, on the Texas coastal plain, is shown in figure 2-23. The distinctly curved Clovis blades (fig. 2-21) and the polyhedral, prepared-platform blade cores are traits of the Clovis cultural pattern that will surely be recognized at more and more sites across the state. Indeed, as Collins and his colleagues have continued the excavations at the Gault, more polyhedral blade cores have been found, as well as wedge-shaped cores from which blades were detached (fig. 2-24, from Kerr County).

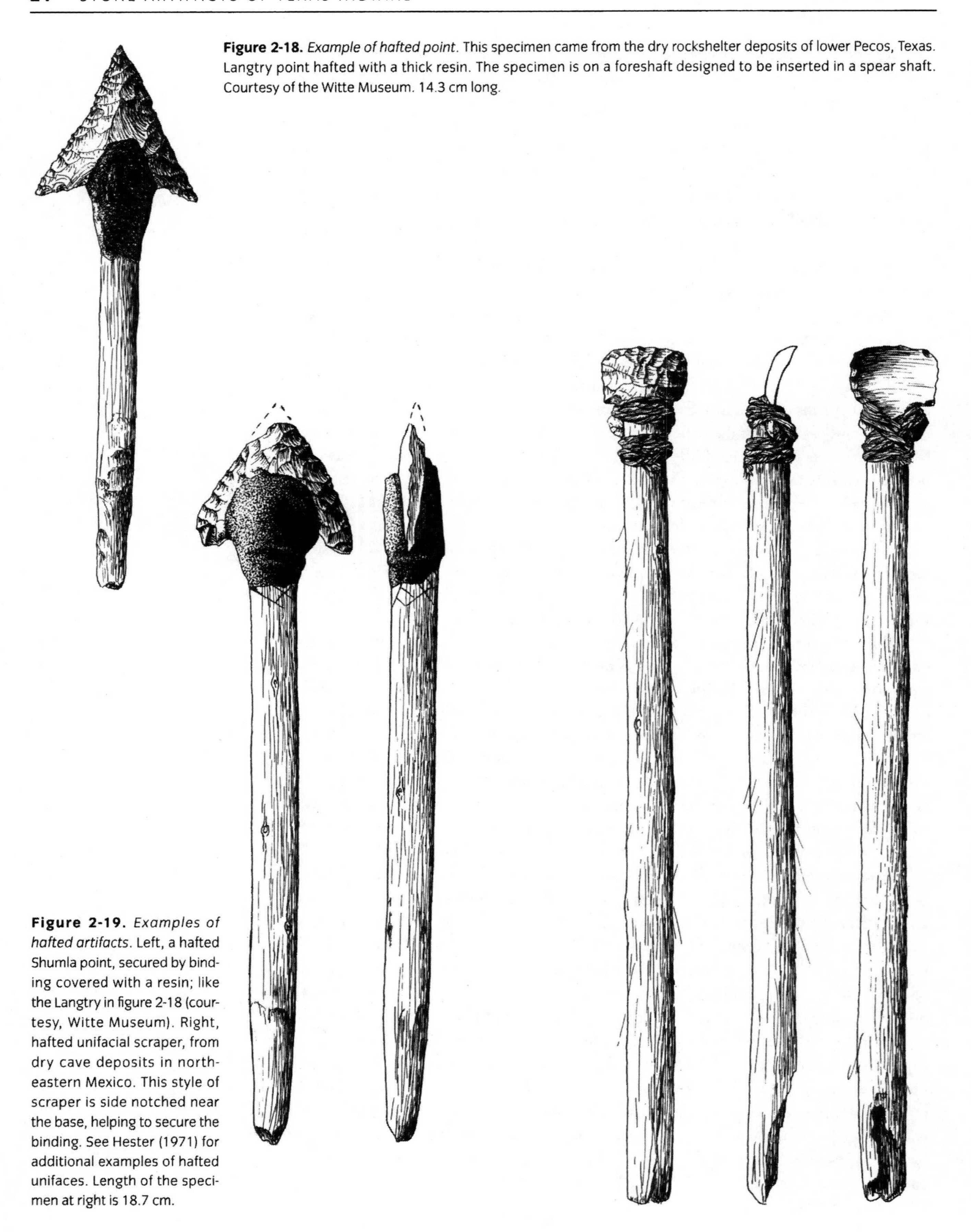

Figure 2-18. *Example of hafted point.* This specimen came from the dry rockshelter deposits of lower Pecos, Texas. Langtry point hafted with a thick resin. The specimen is on a foreshaft designed to be inserted in a spear shaft. Courtesy of the Witte Museum. 14.3 cm long.

Figure 2-19. *Examples of hafted artifacts.* Left, a hafted Shumla point, secured by binding covered with a resin; like the Langtry in figure 2-18 (courtesy, Witte Museum). Right, hafted unifacial scraper, from dry cave deposits in northeastern Mexico. This style of scraper is side notched near the base, helping to secure the binding. See Hester (1971) for additional examples of hafted unifaces. Length of the specimen at right is 18.7 cm.

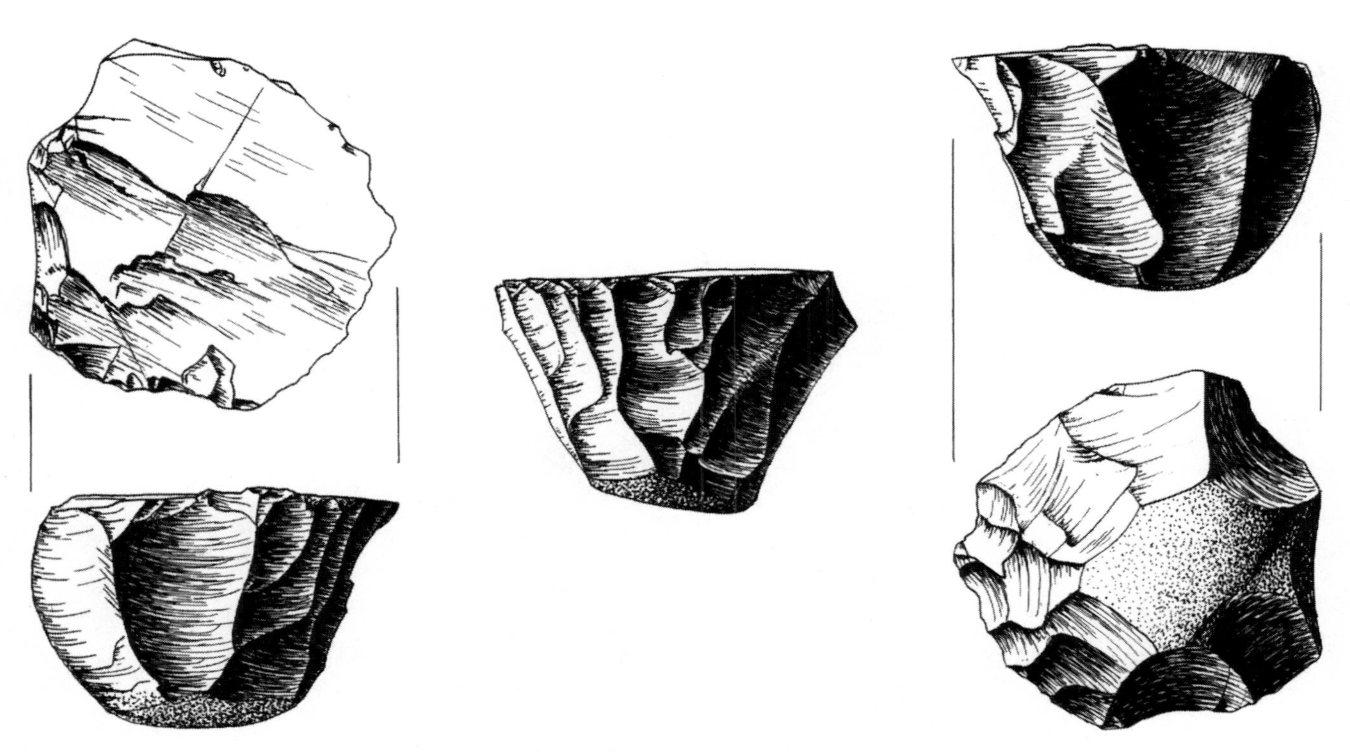

Figure 2-20. *Small polyhedral blade core*. Five views of the core are shown. Small polyhedral blade cores of this sort are typical of the Late Prehistoric II Toyah culture, where characteristic Perdiz arrow points were often made on blades. Width across platform is 6 cm.

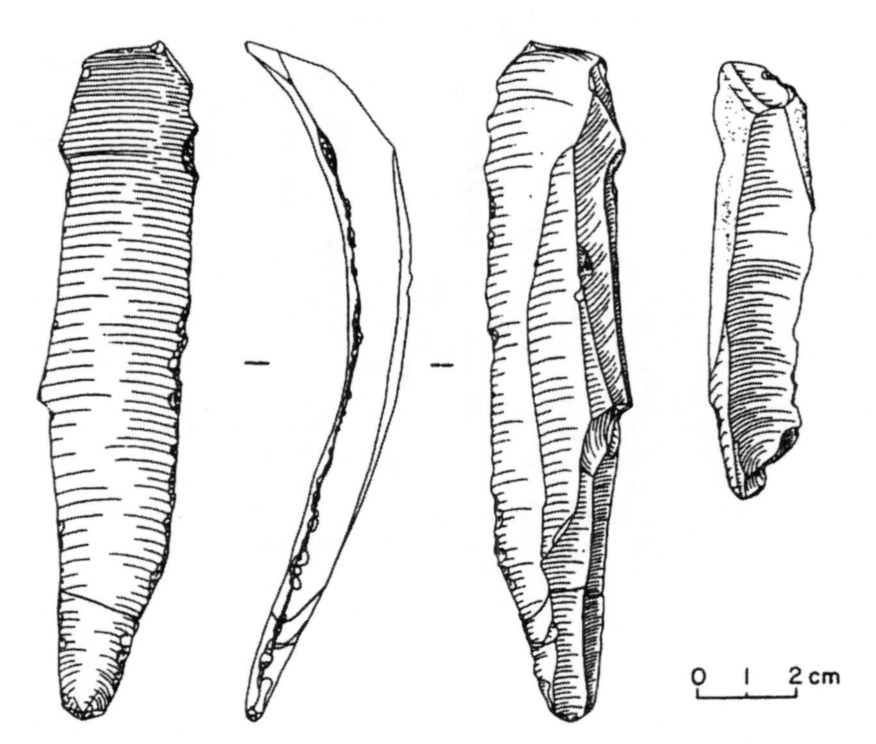

Figure 2-21. *Blades of Clovis age from Navarro County*. From a cache found at site 41NV659 (Young and Collins 1989). Courtesy of *Current Research in the Pleistocene*.

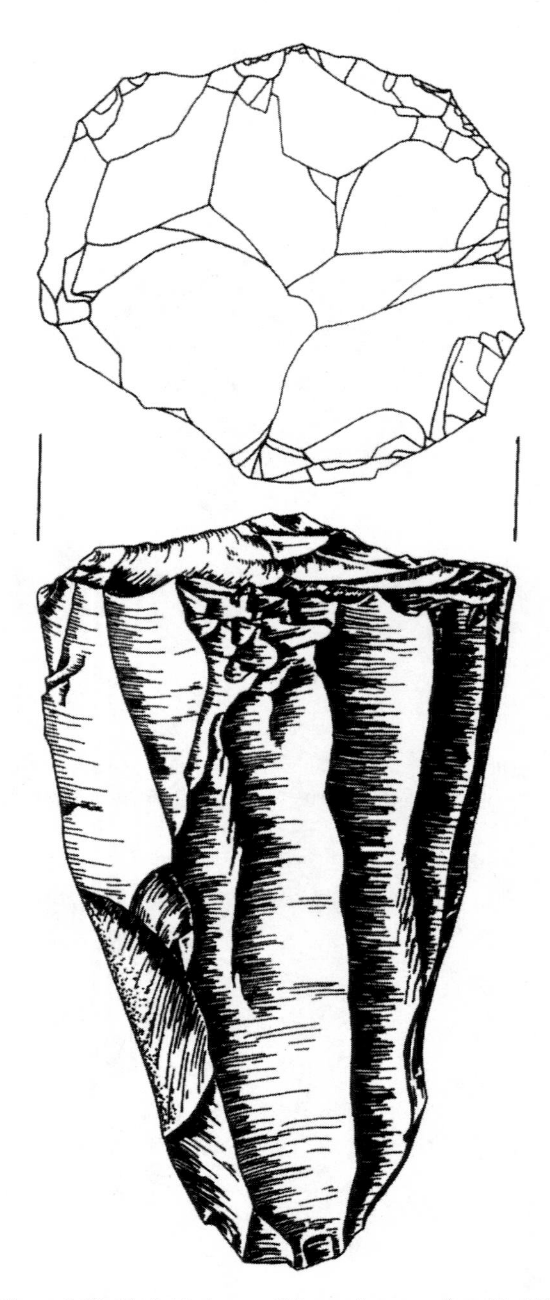

Figure 2-22. *Clovis blade core*. This specimen was found in 1991 excavations at 41BL323 by Hester and Collins. The side view indicates the nature of blades removed; also shown is a top view of the multifaceted core. Drawing by Pamela Headrick. Courtesy of the Texas Archeological Research Laboratory. (Length of specimen, 12.7 cm.)

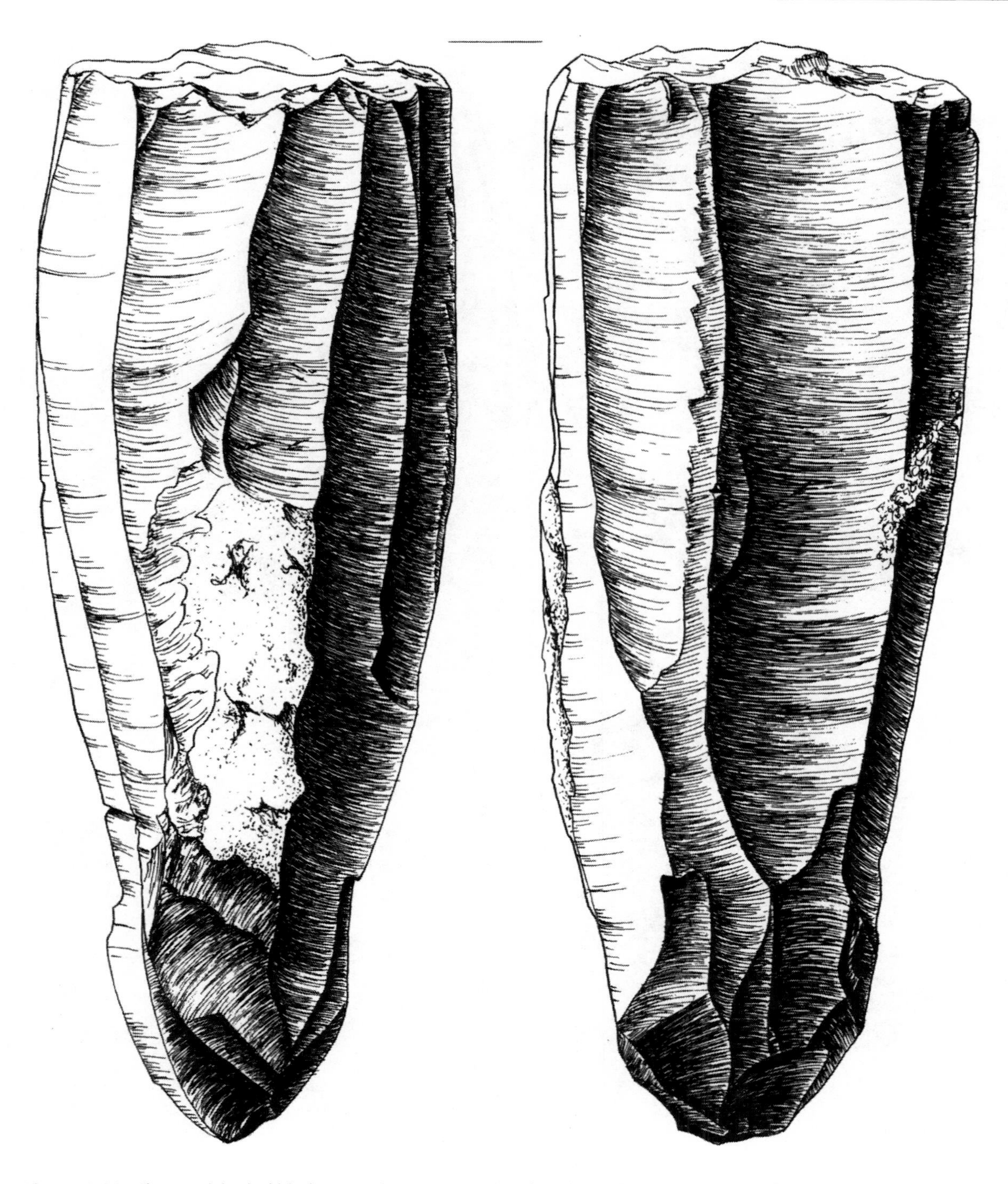

Figure 2-23. *Clovis polyhedral blade core*. This specimen was found in Victoria County, Texas, in a surface context. See Birmingham and Bluhm (2003).

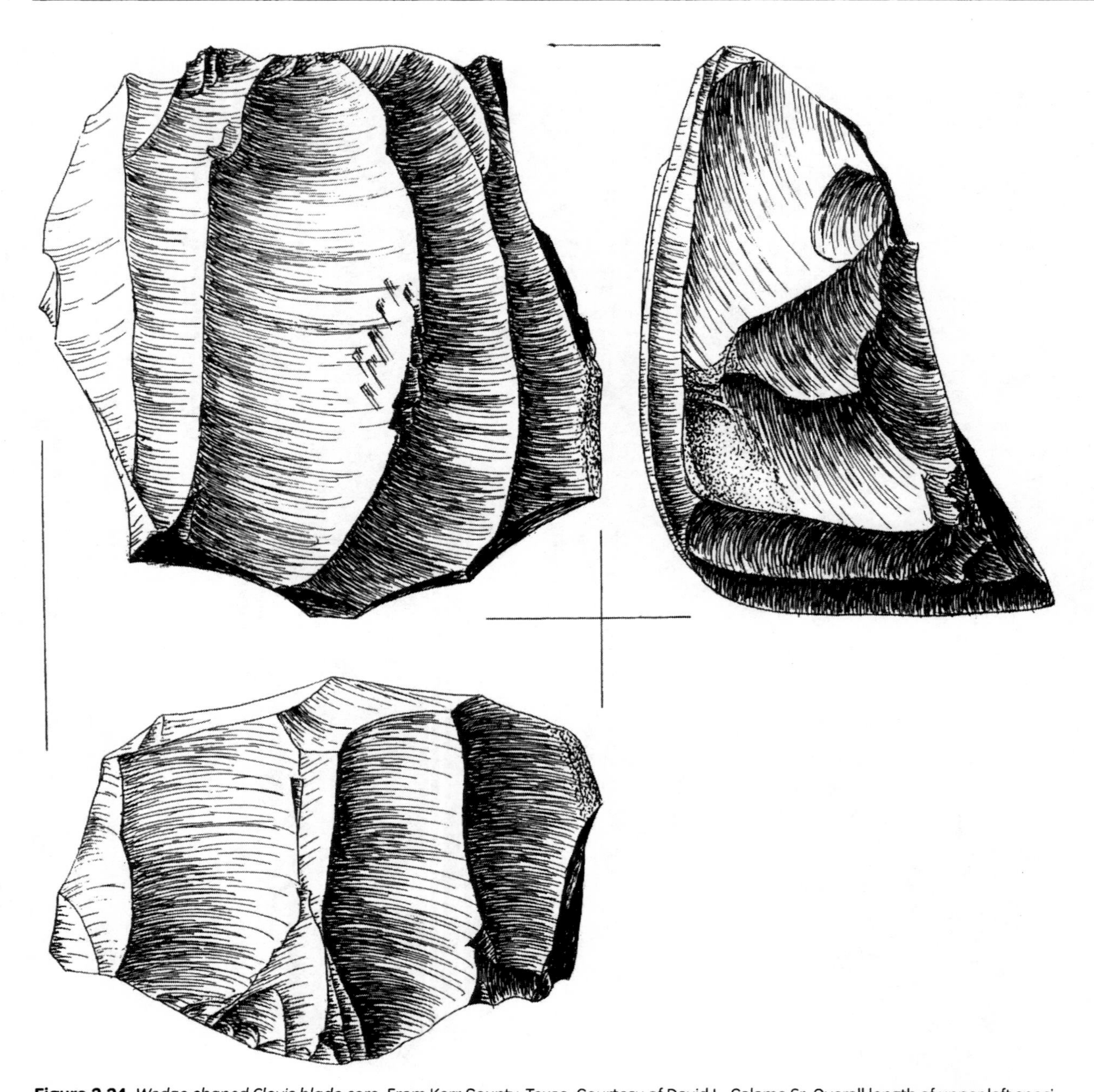

Figure 2-24. *Wedge-shaped Clovis blade core*. From Kerr County, Texas. Courtesy of David L. Calame Sr. Overall length of upper left specimen is 9 cm.

DETERMINING THE FUNCTION OF STONE TOOLS

Over the past thirty to forty years, there has been intensive archaeological research directed at scientific determination of tool function. Many early typologies of stone tools were based largely on tool shape and the function such shape suggested (e.g., knife, scraper, chopper, and gouge). Spurred largely by the pioneering efforts of Semenov (1964), archaeologists have developed ways of ascertaining the actual function of a prehistoric tool. Most investigations have combined microscopic examination of tool edges with experimental use of tools in various tasks required of prehistoric cultures.

Microscopic investigations, called wear pattern studies, have led to the recognition of specific traces of ancient tool use—polish resulting from cutting meat or soft plants, scratches or striations linked to scraping hides, and crushing of the edges from cutting bone or scraping wood. Some of this wear can be observed under low-power microscopes (up to 75X); some can only be seen or interpreted under high-power microscopes (1,000X). Some research has even been done with powerful scanning electron microscopes (10,000X). Wear pattern research indicates that some tools had specific tasks, while others were used for many activities, as a pocketknife would be used today.

Microwear patterns have led to the analysis of tool function—using a combination of microscopic data from ancient and experimentally used artifacts. We have learned that some artifacts thought to be projectile points were sometimes used as knives. Some "scraper" unifaces were used as cutting and slicing tools. "Gouge" bifaces sometimes functioned as adzes in woodworking (Hudler 1997). In many cases, we cannot immediately interpret the observed wear patterns; this requires controlled experiments with stone tools on wood, hide, and plants, with subsequent microscopic study of the experimental edge to see what kind of wear resulted. Although great progress has been made in this type of study in recent years (Hudler 2003; Shoberg 2010), it still requires many hours of intensive research. Still, it provides a way for archaeologists to understand better how tools were actually used and to sort them into meaningful functional categories.

Use-wear analysis still remains in the "art, not a science" stage, despite many advances in technology. It is very capable of recognizing distinct patterns of wear and to suggest, buttressed by experimental data, the function of stone tools. Unfortunately, some analysts use limited wear data from a single site to make authoritative, often erroneous, statements about tool function (Root et al. 2008). This is a dead-end strategy in that use-wear studies have to remain broadly comparative and the analyst (or his or her editor) cognizant of the regional wear pattern literature.

Detailed wear pattern research is desperately needed for Texas stone tools. Some good studies have been done, but more intensive work is necessary. For example, there are only a few wear pattern studies of corner-tang bifaces. These specimens elicit much interest, but eight decades after they were first published, we still do not know how they were used. Similarly, the "Kerrville bifaces" of Late Archaic central Texas exhibit visible polish on the tips, which might result from cutting meat or slicing up soft plants, but no detailed wear research has been published to shed light on this situation. It may well be that many of the preforms, bifaces, and some point types are "knives" as some have suggested. Only wear pattern research can offer a solution. The various beveled tools from south Texas and other regions (Clear Fork, Nueces, Olmos, etc.) might have been used as scrapers or adzes—we simply do not know in most cases. Hudler (1997) has done experimental research and systematic high-power microscopy to establish that Clear Fork tools were used in woodworking, primarily as adzes. Prior to his comprehensive study, there were several small studies of Clear Fork tools that are useful (see Chandler 1974; Hester et al. 1973; Howard 1973; Shiner 1975). Figure 2-25 illustrates a sequence of beveled bifaces from southern Texas, indicating that there is chronological variation; however, evidence of function is still not wholly resolved.

Another avenue of determining tool use is through residue analysis. Shafer and Holloway (1979) have applied this technique to flake tools from Hinds Cave in Val Verde County, Texas. Using analyses of organic residues still adhering to chert flakes from this dry cave, they were able to determine what the flakes were being used for (mostly cutting and processing plants) and what types of plants were being used. Studies like this indicate that many of the stone tools of aboriginal groups were the so-called waste flakes—the debris from toolmaking. If a casual knife or scraper was needed, it seems likely that a flake was picked up, used once or twice, and then discarded. Little visible evidence of use is left on the tools, although microscopic study of flake edges, and the rare and fortunate preservation of organic residues, can give us clues as to their actual function.

Residues identified as asphaltum are often seen on the stems of Morhiss points and on other lithics from the Texas coast. This reflects the use of this natural tar in hafting the artifact. In figure 2-26, traces of asphaltum are shown (in black) at the base of a large Clear Fork tool from the Texas coastal plain.

More recent studies have focused on fatty acids, or lipids, that have survived as residues on ancient artifacts. Marchbanks (1989) was able to recover and identify, as plant or animal, such residues from Caddoan ceramic vessels. Some residues on stone tools have been identified as human or animal blood (Loy 1983), although a recent review of some of these analytical procedures has raised serious question as to their validity (Manning 1991). Needless to say, archaeological lithics from dry caves are prime candidates for residue preservation and should not be handled or washed. It is even possible that certain kinds of residues are preserved on lithics from open sites, and some archaeologists are careful not to handle or to wash stone tools as they come into the laboratory. Obviously, if the reader encounters a stone artifact with residue, great care should be taken to preserve it.

Some prehistoric tool forms are perplexing from the standpoint of both technology and function. Perhaps most intriguing in this regard is the burin (fig. 2-27), a form first recognized in the Texas area by Epstein (1963). Burins had long been known in Europe (see Pitzer 1977). They are tools formed by the removal of long, narrow, sliverlike flakes (burin spalls), which create a chisel-like edge. The term "burin" also refers to the chipping technology that forms the burin edge—precise percussion blows often directed perpendicular to the long axis of the specimen. Burins can be formed on flakes, on broken bifaces, or on projectile points. Often, we do not understand why a burin was created; for example, why do some Paleo-Indian points have burins at the corners of the base (e.g., could these be related to impact fractures created by the haft or foreshaft?). In figure 2-27, burin spalls have been removed from the edges of Paleo-Indian point fragments, though the purpose of these is unknown. Another type of burin is seen on Olmos bifaces, apparently a technique to resharpen a dulled working edge. Burins probably designed to serve as engraving or incising tools have been made on flakes found in lower Pecos caves and in central Texas (Epstein 1963; Sorrow, Shafer, and Ross 1967). However, in many cases, microscopic examination of a burin indicates no evidence of use. Indeed, in many cases, the burin is actually a "core"; the spalls from the "cores" make excellent drills, especially for boring shell and other tough materials. We have not included burins in our formal descriptions, because they are found on such a wide variety of lithic artifacts, are of uncertain function, and may have been formed primarily for the production of the spalls and not the burin edge itself. This is another area of stone tool technology in Texas that needs much more research. In this regard, an excellent study of burins and burin spalls has been published for the Wilson-Leonard site (Dial and Collins 1998).

Certainly, the most common tool in an ancient tool kit was not the projectile point or the other kinds of tool forms shown in chapter 6. That distinction goes to the ordinary flake, perhaps one that was selected for its size, sharpness, and ease of handling. Or perhaps a discarded flake was picked up off the surface at the camp to serve an immediate need. These flakes often have nicks or small areas of retouch along the edges and are generally called utilized flakes (fig. 2-28). Flakes were much better cutting

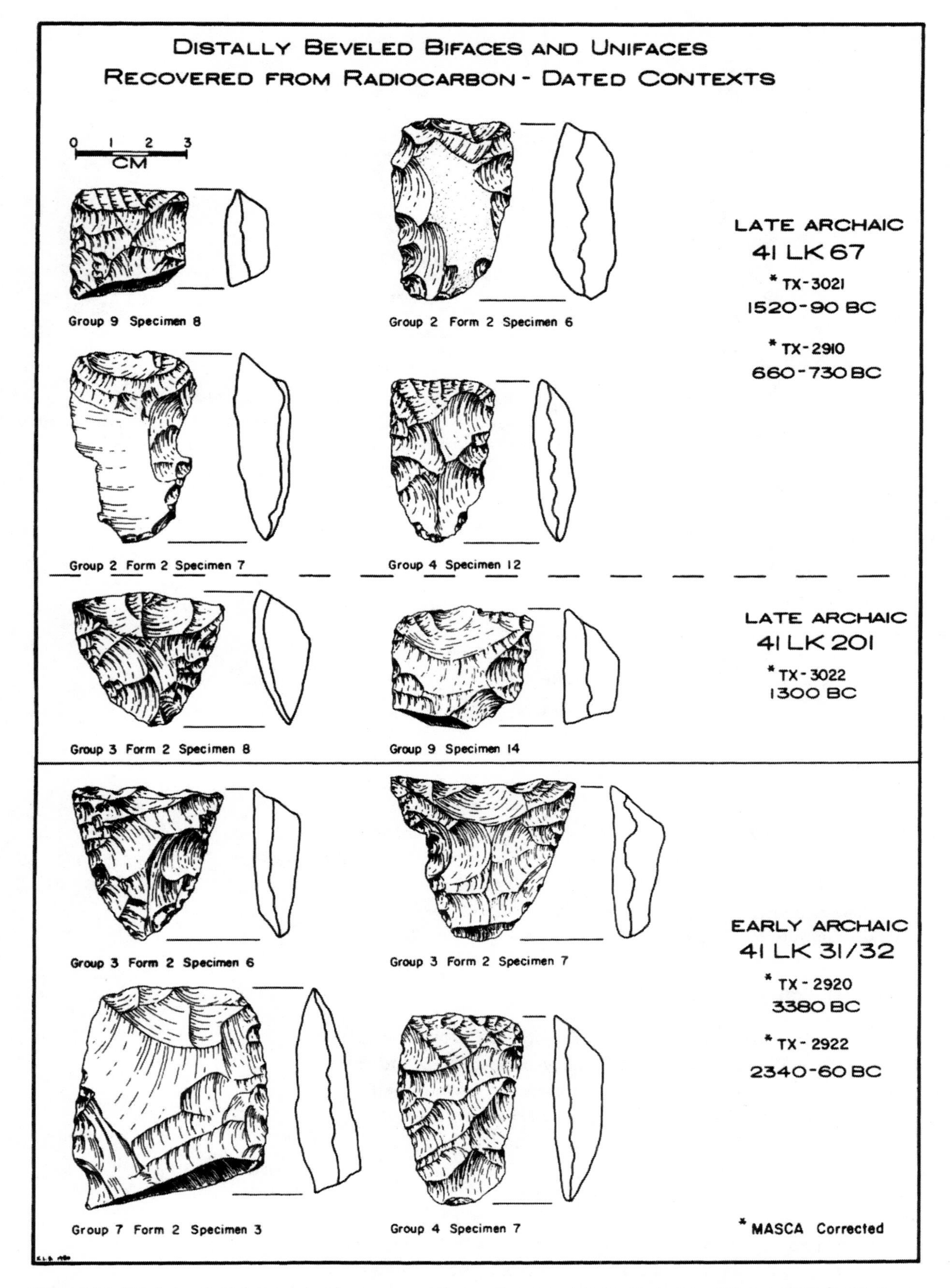

Figure 2-25. *Distally beveled bifaces and unifaces recovered from radiocarbon-dated contexts*. From Hall et al. (1982, fig. 79). By permission of the Center for Archaeological Research, University of Texas at San Antonio.

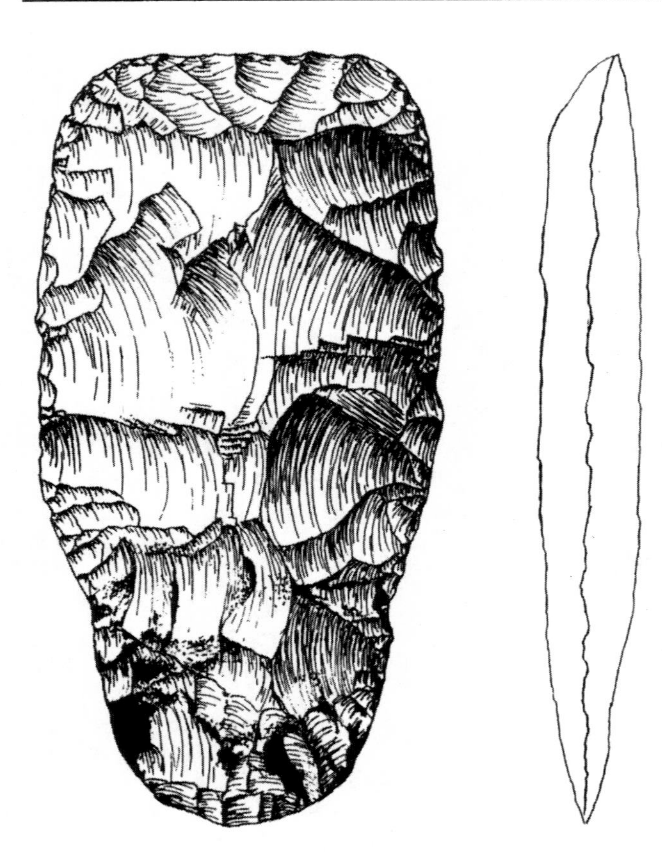

Figure 2-26. *Use of asphaltum for hafting stone tools.* Bifacial Clear Fork tool from site 41VT69, Victoria County, Texas. The black areas at the proximal edge indicate presence of asphaltum, a sticky substance used to haft the artifact. Asphaltum occurs as natural "tar balls" along the Texas coast. Length 10.3 cm.

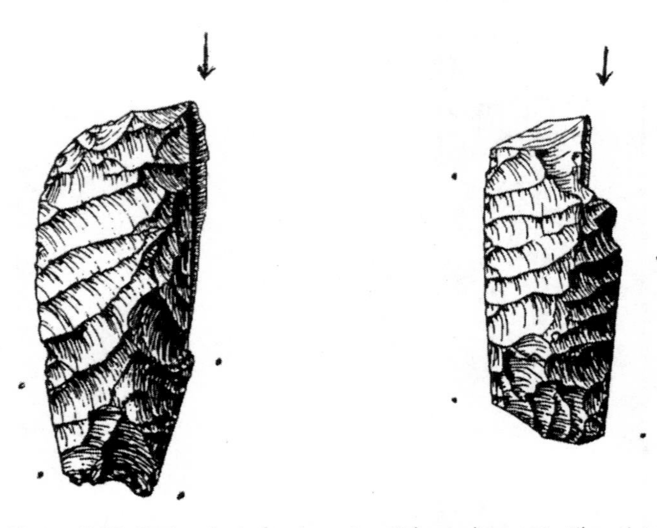

Figure 2-27. *Burins.* Burin facets on two Paleo-Indian projectile points. After the points were broken, burin blows (see arrows) removed spalls that were triangular in cross section. Length of left specimen is 4.3 cm.

tools than the bifacially flaked "knives." Archaeologists have conducted many experiments in which a deer was butchered using a small group of flakes; common bifacial "knives" were commonly of no value. Sometimes the flakes show very little wear after such use—much like the illustrated utilized flakes. When obsidian flakes are used in deer butchering, they seem to resharpen their edges as the work is being done.

Nature Tries to Make Stone Tools

The early days of archaeology were marked by many controversies about the stone tools of the first human cultures. Some believed that crudely chipped flakes and cobbles were the primary candidates, and these were called "eoliths" or "dawn stones." Other specialists believed the eoliths to have been shaped and formed by natural forces. Many experiments were conducted among British archaeologists, and the prevailing view was that eoliths were not fashioned by human hands.

Two similar situations developed in California in the mid-20th century. First, crudely chipped specimens were collected from high marine terraces near San Diego. George Carter claimed great antiquity for these materials and published a book on the "Texas Street site." Other archaeologists thought the specimens to be naturally made and labeled them "Carterfacts."

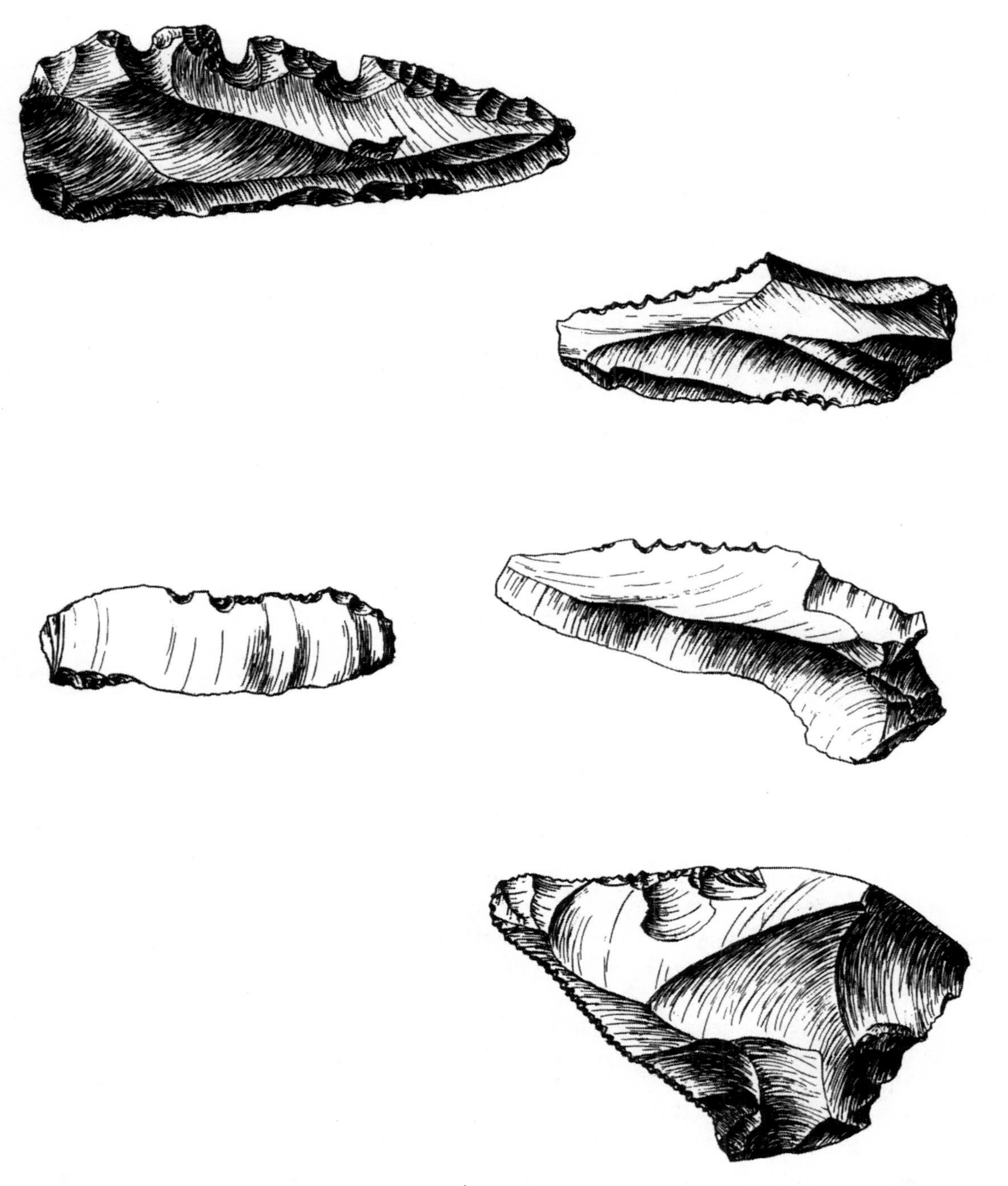

Figure 2-28. *Utilized flakes and blades*. Sharp edges were using for cutting or shredding, with visual evidence of use-flakes along the edges. Also shown is a deeply notched flake that resembles a "saw" but its actual function is unknown. Length 7.9 cm.

Greater controversy developed at Calico Hills in the Mojave Desert, where California archaeologist Ruth Simpson, with the blessings of Louis Leakey, claimed artifacts from deposits as much as two hundred thousand years old. There were many problems with the whole scenario, including the lack of patterned flaking on the specimens, but further study by geoarchaeologist Vance Haynes proved that the "artifacts" were cobbles within a thick deposit of cobble and boulder gravels, which were occasionally "flaked" while being pushed and churned in a high-energy alluvial fan (Dillehay and Meltzer 1991). Haynes used the term "geofact" to describe this kind of naturally chipped stone object. That term is used in archaeology today to refer to any object whose shape has been modified by nature; nature-fact is another label that is applied. Below, we will review a few situations that apply to Texas archaeology.

Incidental Percussion

The streambeds in many parts of Texas contain huge quantities of gravels, limestone, flint/chert, basalt, quartzite, and other rock. High-velocity floods can pick up a cobble and hurl it against a larger rock on the bottom of the stream, or it can tumble along the bottom, striking embedded cobbles. These, and their innumerable variations, can lead to the removal of percussion flakes. The British scholar Alfred S. Barnes (1939), who did critical research on distinguishing geofacts from artifacts, called this "fortuitous concussion." And there are well-documented examples of chert cobbles that erode and fall from a high bluff, and impact on chert cobbles and boulders below. Such "falling percussion" is also suspected for the creation of geofacts in some South American shelter caves for which some researchers have claimed great antiquity. Regardless of the type of "natural percussion," such geofacts can often be distinguished by having only a few flake removals, and these are in no particular pattern. The edge angles are much steeper than on humanly flaked tools (fig. 2-29).

These, and other contexts, such as soil creep or solifluxion (the slow downslope movement of soils containing gravels or other materials), can also "pressure flake" a cobble. Sometimes, both percussion and pressure flakes occur on the same geofact found in one of the contexts noted above.

Thermal Fracture

The fissures and cavities in cobbles or boulders of chert or other raw materials can be penetrated by water, and with freezing, the cobble can split into fragments that resemble stone tools (Sieveking and Clayton 1986). This fracture process is sometimes called "freeze-thaw" and leads to the formation of starch fractures, with fracture planes that mimic blade removals (fig. 2-30). Indeed, one experienced southeastern archaeologist found such items in an early site and initially interpreted them as "probable microblade cores from the pre-Clovis zone" (Goodyear 2000).

Heat fracture creates disc-shaped flakes, called "potlids," that pop from the surface as a result of moisture in the stone reacting to rapid heating—or temperatures that exceed 573 degrees Celsius. These plano-convex flakes, with no bulb of percussion, are often found in debitage from a site. Chert cobbles that have been extensively potlidded can resemble the flaking and form of a stone tool (see fig. 2-29, lower). Similar features, though more shallow, can also be caused by frost-pitting of chert.

One group of geofact illustrations (fig. 2-31) is of river pebbles found in a streambed in San Antonio, Texas. At first glance, the patterns seem to suggest the handiwork of humans. However, these were more likely formed in a streambed context where filled solution cavities were eroded away. Geofacts of naturally shaped stones are very common in Texas. In any riverbed, one can pick up rocks with natural holes worn through them. Sometimes, wind, sand, and water have combined to shape rocks into humanlike figures—and, in some cases, to wear a convenient hole through such an anthropomorphic specimen. Any archaeologist has seen hundreds of such rocks, brought to them (sometimes, in a pickup load) by a finder who is convinced they are ancient sculptures or other types of man-modified artifacts. The geoarchaeologist Paul V. Heinrich has an interesting study of these posted on the

Figure 2-29. *Geofacts: nature chips stone*. Upper, a chert pebble fractured by indirect percussion, other cobbles striking the edge as they rolled along a flooding stream; lower, two chert pebble fragments covered with potlids, deeply concave features that were formed by heat fracture.

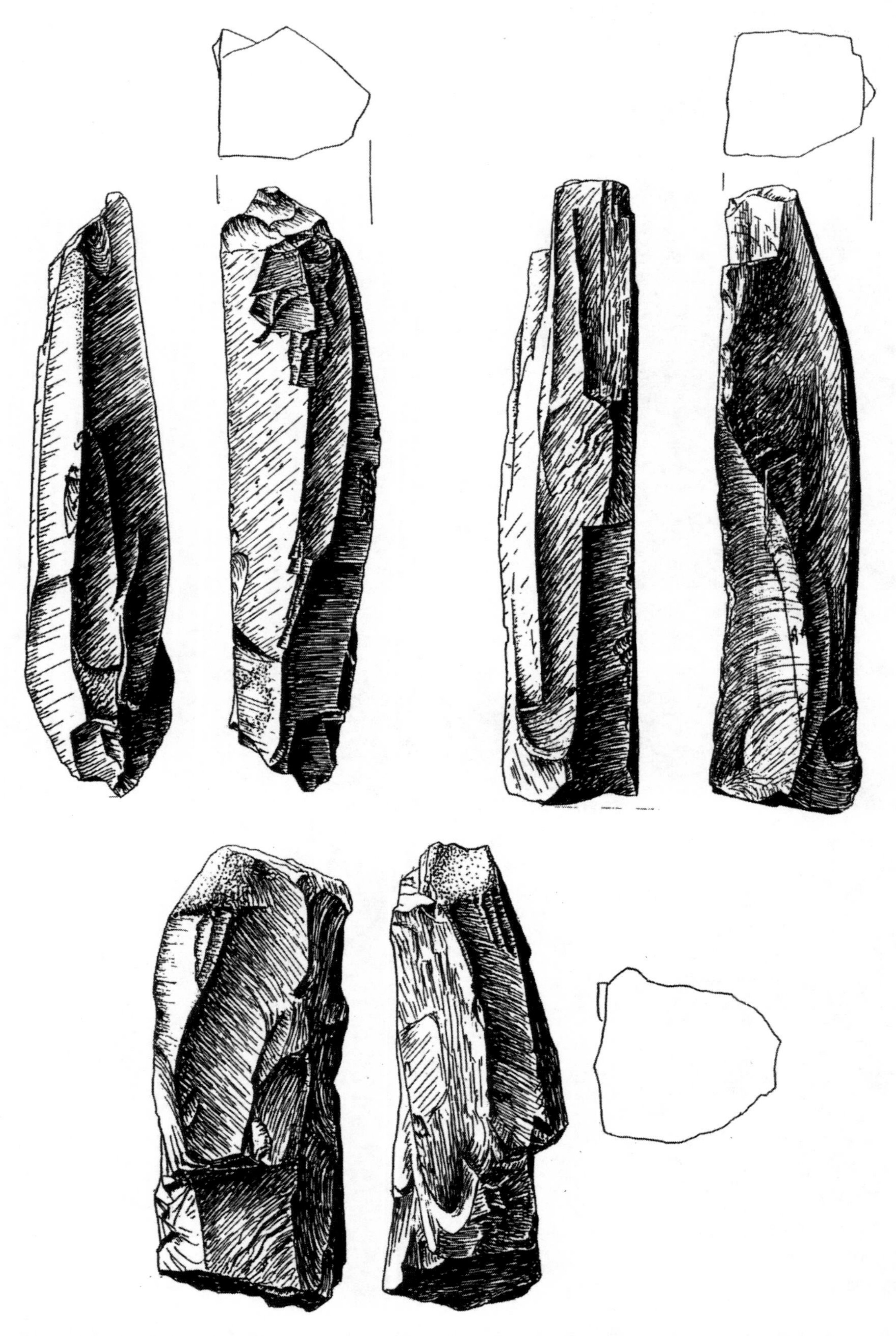

Figure 2-30. *Geofacts: nature chips stone*. Views of three starch fractures found in central Texas. These resemble, and have been mistaken for, specialized blade cores. Top left 11.5 cm.

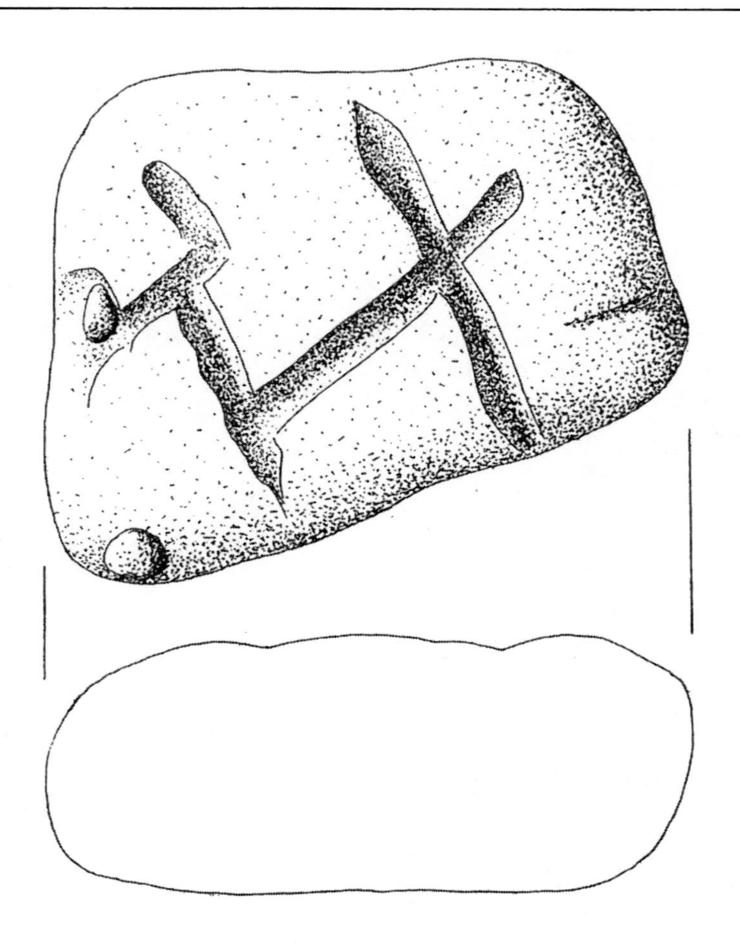

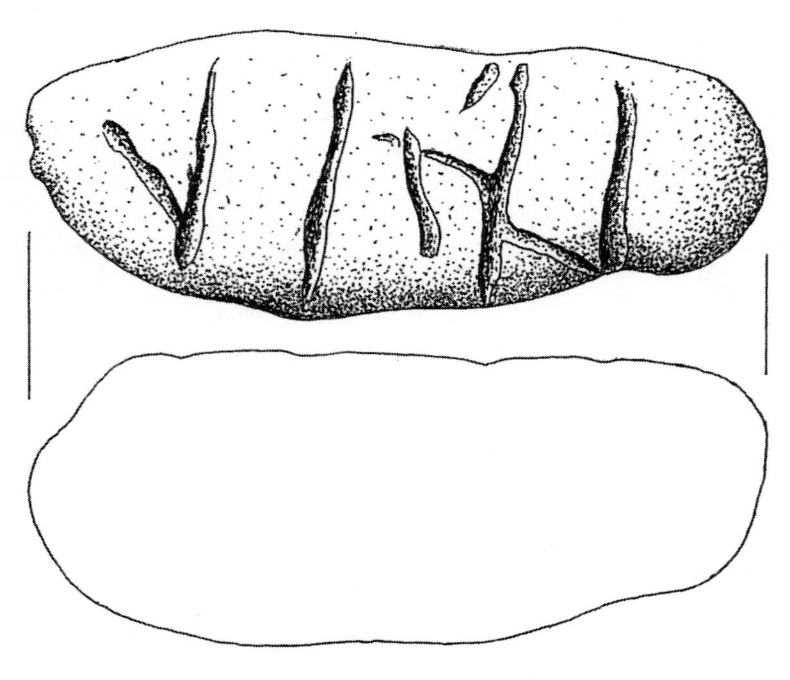

Figure 2-31. *Geofacts: nature shapes stone*. The deep channels seen on these two cobbles were formed by long-term erosion of inclusions or soft zones that formed naturally in chert. From San Antonio River Gravels at Goliad, Texas.

Internet (http://www.intersurf.com/~chalcedony/geofact.html). Here he illustrates a number of rock geofacts, such as those described above, collected around High Island, Texas. The intent of his study was to demonstrate that claims of stone sculptures and pseudo-effigies from the Gulf of Cambay in northwest India are nothing more than geofacts.

And Then There Are the Fakes

There is a long history in archaeology of the production of fakes—chipped stone items—often greatly embellished—designed to be sold as the real thing. This is different from the replications made by modern-day flintknappers, but with the tremendous growth of that hobby, even these replicas are sometimes passed off and sold as "real" by unscrupulous practitioners. The best-known commercial flintknapper was Mack Tussinger of Oklahoma, who in the early 1920s began making incredibly intricate, often large, "eccentrics."

One of the most common fakes is the chert fishhook (fig. 2-32); all experts agree—there is not, and never has been, a single authentic specimen of this form. Bone and shell hooks dominated the fishing technology of American Indians. In a similar vein, there are all kinds of chert "thunderbirds" (fig. 2-32), some small like the one illustrated and others very large with tremendous wingspans! Like the chert fishhook, every chert thunderbird is a fake.

The massive chert bifaces (fig. 2-32), often with fancy notching along the edges, are usually made from long, flat chert blanks sawed from a large block. If one looks at these things closely, they are flat from base to tip and there are no bends to be seen, nor any other natural traits of an ancient biface. The owner of such a fake will often argue that his grandfather found it out in a field; maybe that is true—but it was just after he acquired it from someone else! Fluted points, typical of the Paleo-Indian period, are among the most widely faked artifacts; usually, the flutes are removed in an inaccurate way, the specimens are too thick, or they are made of specific kinds of cherts.

Figure 2-32. *Examples of fake flint artifacts*. Shown here are three specimens often found in chert or flint fakes. The "wildly notched specimen" on the left was created on a blank sawed from a block of chert; the "fish-hook" and the "thunderbird" are common among small fakes that are widely sold. All examples of this sort are fraudulent. Length 20.3 cm.

3

Context and Chronology

STONE TOOLS occur at a variety of prehistoric archaeological sites. Just how they occur provides information on the function of the site and on the ancient activities that were carried out there. This is what we call *context*—the relationship of the artifacts to one another and to the site deposits within which they are found.

In addition to contextual information, stone tools can also provide data on the age or antiquity of a site. Although they cannot be directly dated, associated organic remains (such as wood charcoal from a hearth) can be assayed by the radiocarbon method, yielding a date for the points and tools at the same level of the hearth. Excavations can also provide relative dates, by determining which styles of artifacts are earlier or later than others. Once a chronology is established at several regional sites, types of known dates can then be related to the same type at other sites. Gradually, a framework of prehistoric cultural patterns can be built up in a sequential fashion. Many of the types described in this book are "time-sensitive"; excavation and subsequent analyses have shown they change through time, making them valuable chronological aids for archaeological research.

CONTEXT

An archaeological site is, technically, any spot on the landscape that has been modified by humans. Common among these are *campsites*, where daily life took place; *quarries* or the *processing areas*, the locales of stone-chipping; *temporary campsites*, representing brief hunting or gathering forays; *kill-sites*, where bison or other mammals were slaughtered and butchered; *rock art sites*, overhangs or shelters with pictographs (rock paintings) or petroglyphs (rock carvings); *caves and rockshelters*, protected overhangs in canyon walls, which some Indian groups, particularly in west Texas, used for daily occupation; *mound sites*, purposeful accumulations of earth, found in east Texas, used as platforms for dwellings or for burials; *burned rock middens*, incidental accumulations of fire-cracked rock from earth oven technology, often in a moundlike fashion and found associated with campsites in central and west Texas; *shell middens*, accumulations of shellfish collected as food, principally of oyster shell on the central coast and *Rangia* clam on the upper coast; *cemetery sites*, specific areas for the disposal of the dead, found in the Early Archaic, Late Archaic, and Late Prehistoric eras in central, coastal, and east Texas; and *sinkholes* in the Edwards Plateau, often used for disposal of the dead in ancient times (Bement 1994). This is by no means an exhaustive catalog of site types in Texas but serves to suggest the diverse ways in which the ancient populations utilized the terrain and took advantage of its plant and animal resources. At many of these sites, the only surviving cultural remains are stone tools. If we are to understand the prehistoric use of the site, and indeed specific activities within the site boundaries, it is important that we know the context of the stone tools.

For example, at *kill-sites*, proper excavation will usually discover projectile points and cutting or butchering tools in association with the animal bones. The most common type of kill-site in Texas is the bison-kill of Paleo-Indian times, from 9200 to 6000 BC. For example, at Bonfire Shelter near Langtry in Val Verde County, excavations revealed a mass of bison remains associated with Folsom and, possibly, Plainview points, accompanied by miscellaneously shaped flakes and bifaces used for processing the slaughtered animals (Dibble and Lorrain 1968). A number of Late Archaic bison-kill-sites have been documented in the Llano Estacado and Panhandle of Texas and into western Oklahoma.

At *quarries* or *lithic processing areas*, controlled surface collection will often yield great numbers of large, crudely chipped bifaces, the early stage of toolmaking known as the quarry blank (Assad 1978; Kelly and Hester 1975; Lukowski 1987; Wishoff 2010). Rarely are projectile points or other finished tools found, since this is a locality where the basic levels of stone-working took place—securing good chipping materials, removing cortex flakes from the cobbles, and roughing-out the blanks for further reduction elsewhere. These are important sites for archaeological study, though they have long been ignored, as they shed a great deal of light on a fundamental activity in prehistoric cultures.

Campsites are, throughout the state, found along streams or other water sources; most are "open occupation" sites, though caves and rockshelters were themselves often used for habitation. Many represent the villages of hunters and gatherers, the main way of life throughout ancient Texas, until late times, when farming was introduced in east Texas and in parts of the Panhandle and far west Texas. They were the locales of daily life and were perhaps occupied for a few weeks or months before the group moved on to exploit the plant and animal foods of another area. These are the most common sites and contain great quantities of stone tools, flakes, and other debris. Context is particularly important in these sites. Even the surface collecting of an eroded campsite can ruin fragile patterns of tool distribution that, under controlled conditions, might tell the archaeologist a great deal about site function and the ways in which different parts of the site were used. Excavation presents an even larger challenge. Test pits can plumb the depths of the site, sometimes giving us information on the sequence of occupations by recovering stone tool types from different levels. However, to understand the behavior of the ancient inhabitants and the activities they carried out, a fairly large block or open area excavation is usually required. In this fashion, we can plot in place the projectile points, scrapers, choppers, and flakes and study the patterns of their horizontal distribution. This often shows the archaeologist where toolmaking took place, where animals were being skinned and butchered, and where bone tools were being made or wooden spear shafts fashioned. Therefore, the relationships of the tools to the area of the site and to other stone tools provide contextual information vital to archaeological interpretation.

We hope these comments serve to demonstrate that not only are the artifacts important, but also their relationships within a site are even more crucial. Casual collecting and indiscriminate digging destroy these vital links. Thus, a cigar box of points dug out of a site by an untrained person may make an interesting collection to show friends, but it has little or no scientific value in the study of ancient Texas Indians. Only through proper recording and documentation in the field, and follow-up cataloging once back from the site, will the materials have any lasting meaning. It is beyond the scope of this book to detail the procedures of recording and cataloging. A number of books and manuals are available through local archaeological societies or through bookstores. A partial list of these includes *Field Methods in Archaeology* (Hester et al. 1997; 2009); *Excavation* (Roskams 2001); and *Excavation* (Carmichael et al. 2003). Proper field and laboratory methods cannot be fully learned from a book, and we encourage interested readers to join the Texas Archeological Society and their local or regional archaeological societies in order to take advantage of the training opportunities these organizations provide.

CHRONOLOGY

In this section, we have two objectives: first, briefly to describe some of the dating methods used to ascertain the age of stone tools; second, to review the general cultural sequence as it is known statewide.

There are basically two types of archaeological dating: absolute and relative. Absolute dating provides calendrical dates for archaeological remains. The most widely used technique in this regard is radiocarbon dating. It can only be used for organic remains (charcoal, wood, plant parts, etc.) that have been preserved in archaeological sites. A date obtained through this method has little significance unless the archaeologist is certain of its association with distinctive cultural remains. One date often means very little; we generally need a series of dates in order to ascertain the age of a particular cultural level that might contain diagnostic kinds of stone tools. Radiocarbon dating is also expensive, with most laboratories charging around $400 per sample. Samples of ideal size are around twenty grams or more of charcoal; even then, the resulting date is expressed with a possible range of error, perhaps fifty to one hundred years earlier or later than the central date.

Much smaller organic samples can be dated through accelerator mass spectrometery (AMS) dating, usually at about $600 per sample.

Still, this is the most widely applied and most useful of the absolute dating techniques in North America. Other methods of absolute dating can be used in some areas, but most are still experimental in their application; good general archaeology texts, such as *In the Beginning* (Fagan 1981), provide a review of such techniques as thermoluminescence, archaeomagnetic dating, dendrochronology, and obsidian hydration dating. Thermoluminescence, the measurement of alpha particles emitted from ceramics or other fired or burned materials, and archaeomagnetic dating, the study of remanent magnetism in heated clays (such as fire pits or hearths), have been used for some Texas sites and materials, but their application is still limited.

Optically stimulated luminescence (OSL) dating is a largely experimental dating technique that has been applied at several sites in Texas (see Collins et al. 2003) over the past twenty years. The approach involves the precise measurement of a "luminescence signal" found in a mineral's crystalline structure. The signal continues a "natural clock" that increases with time until it is released in the laboratory. Collecting samples for OSL is a very rigorous and complicated process; the results obtained through OSL are most often used in dating sediments.

Relative dating provides the archaeologist with not calendar dates but rather approximate dates based on the vertical context of archaeological specimens. In an excavation, a certain point type may be found at a level deeper than another style; thus, we can date it as older than this latter type on a relative basis. Stratigraphy plays the key role in relative dating. If excavations reveal a sequence of occupational deposits, we can assume that materials in the bottom zone are the earliest, those in the middle come later, and so on. Stratigraphic data from a series of sites allow cross-comparison of site sequences and permit the archaeologist to build a chronology of cultural patterns for a region. In some central Texas and lower Pecos sites, where there are deep middens representing repeated occupations over thousands of years, a detailed chronology can be developed, based on relative dating established through stratigraphy. In other areas, as in the campsites of south Texas, archaeological remains are more scattered, and constructing a sequence of artifact forms based on excavations can be a long, slow process (see Hall, Black, and Graves 1982; Hall, Hester, and Black 1986) (see fig. 2-5).

Cross-dating is an important technique for establishing the age of archaeological sites in some parts of the state. This involves comparison of artifacts of the same type among sites within a region or between regions. For example, as excavation of stratified sites continues in central Texas, and as some cultural patterns and their diagnostic artifacts are radiocarbon dated, it is then possible to cross-date artifacts of known date with sites in areas less well known or where stratigraphy and radiocarbon dating have not established a firm sequence. If Bell points are found in deposits stratified at the base of sites at Stillhouse Hollow, central Texas (Sorrow et al. 1967), and placed in an Early Archaic time frame, we can assume that similar points found in another part of central Texas (for example, in Bexar County) are of the same age. And carrying the cross-dating further, if Bell points that are typologically and technologically identical to those of central Texas are found in adjacent south or east Texas, we can speak of occupations of similar age at sites in those regions.

ARCHAEOLOGICAL SEQUENCES IN PREHISTORIC TEXAS

Archaeological work has continued in parts of Texas for eighty to ninety years. Some areas, such as central Texas, have been intensively studied, and detailed archaeological sequences have been established. In other regions, such as the southern part of the state, research has intensified only in the 1970s, and much remains to be learned about the history of prehistoric cultures. In this section, we provide a general chronological framework for the state, designed primarily to permit readers to understand better the temporal position of the projectile points and tool forms defined below. Obviously, cultural change proceeded at somewhat different rates over this vast area; in some regions, there were hunting and gathering cultures throughout prehistory, while in others, cultures with farming and settled village life appeared.

Four volumes published in the Arkansas Archeological Survey Research Series in 1989 and 1990 are the result of "regional overviews" done for the Southwestern Division of the Corps of Engineers. Hofman and colleagues (1989) synthesize north Texas, the Llano Estacado, and Panhandle; Simmons and colleagues (1989) examine the Trans-Pecos; Story and colleagues (1990) summarize east Texas; and Hester and colleagues (1989) provide overviews of the archaeology of south, central, and lower Pecos Texas.

However, the most current review of the chronology of the various parts of Texas can be found in the edited volume by Perttula (2004), which is highly recommended to the reader. These include summaries of central Texas, south Texas, central and lower coast, southeast Texas, the eastern Trans-Pecos, the lower Pecos, the southern High Plains, and east-central and northeast Texas.

A general summary of the major time periods, their approximate dates, and certain major characteristics appears below (see also fig. 3-6).

Paleo-Indian

While some claims have been made for greater antiquity, the earliest known inhabitants of the state, during the Late Pleistocene (Ice Age), can be linked to the Clovis Complex around 9200 BC. The distinctive Clovis fluted point is widespread and was, at least in some cases, used in mammoth hunting. A mammoth kill-site, Miami, is found in Roberts County in the Texas Panhandle. Ferring (1990) has excavated a deeply buried Clovis campsite at the Aubrey site in Denton County; a Clovis point, Clovis blades, and thousands of flakes were found. But clearly the most important Clovis site in Texas, and perhaps North America, is the Gault site (41BL323), excavated by Michael B. Collins over the past decade (for the most recent data, see Bradley et al. 2010). An amazing number of Clovis points, preforms, cores, blades, and all other facets of this early lithic tradition have been found at Gault. The Folsom Complex, around 8800–8200 BC, is distinguished by Folsom fluted points and is known from sites where now-extinct forms of bison were killed and butchered (Bonfire) or from campsites (Adair-Steadman) where the points are found along with other stone tools. The Clovis and Folsom materials might be considered to fall within the early part of this period. Although fluting ceases to be an important trait of Paleo-Indian points after Clovis and Folsom, later Paleo-Indian points maintain an overall lanceolate, parallel-sided form, often with careful parallel-flaking and with the basal edges dulled to facilitate hafting. There is a great diversification of point types, several of which we still cannot precisely date. Dalton and San Patrice points may date around 8000 BC in east Texas; Plainview points are found from the Panhandle into south Texas at around 8200–8000 BC and are associated with kills of Pleistocene bison at Plainview and Bonfire. However, a fair amount of concern is focused on Plainview typology and whether or not its traits have been applied too broadly. The definition of the St. Mary's Hall type helps to clarify some of this problem, but much more research needs to be done. By around 8000 BC, the end of the Pleistocene, remnants of the animals of that era—mammoth, bison, camel, horse, and sloth—have disappeared. Climates became more like those of modern times, yet in some regions, projectile point traditions continue to follow the patterns of earlier times. In east Texas, there are Scottsbluff points from around 6500 BC; in the lower Pecos and south Texas, hunters and gatherers used Golondrina points, radiocarbon dated at 7000 BC, and Angostura, dated a few hundred years later. While we are still learning more about the lifeways of these late Paleo-Indian cultures, we can trace their presence and distribution with these time-sensitive point styles.

Archaic

Much of Texas prehistory is subsumed within a long time span of hunting and gathering cultural patterns known collectively as the Archaic. It begins around 6000 BC and is notable for changes in the style of projectile points and tools, the distribution of site types, and the introduction of grinding implements and ground stone ornaments, all reflecting a gradually increasing population utilizing the abundant plant and animal resources of environments similar to that of modern times.

The details of the Archaic sequence vary from region to region within the state. In general, it can be divided into Early, Middle, Late, and Transitional eras. Each period is represented by specific point styles, and in some regions, each can be subdivided

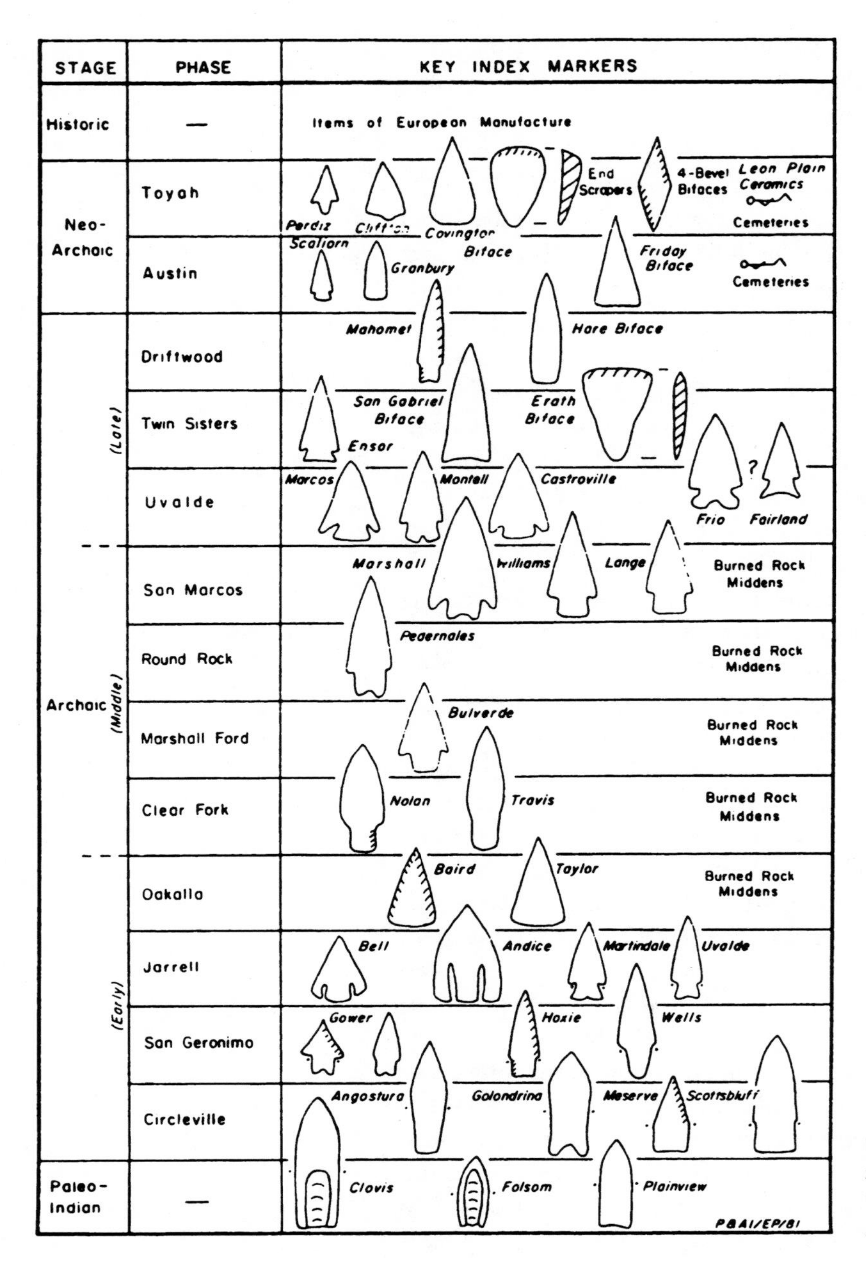

Figure 3-1. *Sequence of projectile point and chipped stone tool types in the central Texas region.* From Prewitt (1981a, fig. 4). By permission of the Texas Archeological Society.

into several segments, sometimes called phases. The Early Archaic (6000–2500 BC) is poorly known in its earliest phases, though a number of point and tool types can be linked to that era (fig. 3-6). In general, settlement appears more scattered, and there are broader relationships among several regions, as indicated by the widespread occurrence of distinctive points, such as Martindale, Uvalde, Early Triangular, and Bell (McKinney 1981). The Middle Archaic (2500 BC–1000 BC) marks a time, throughout the state, of significant population increase, large numbers of sites, and abundant lithic artifacts of various forms. It, too, can be divided into segments in some areas. Certain regions appeared to be typified in the Middle Archaic by one or two distinctive points; for example, Gary and Kent points in east Texas, Pedernales in central Texas, Langtry in the lower Pecos, and Tortugas in south Texas. In some regions, specific types of sites are recognized, especially the burned rock middens of central Texas and shell middens on the Texas coast. Additionally, cemeteries with large numbers of interments begin to

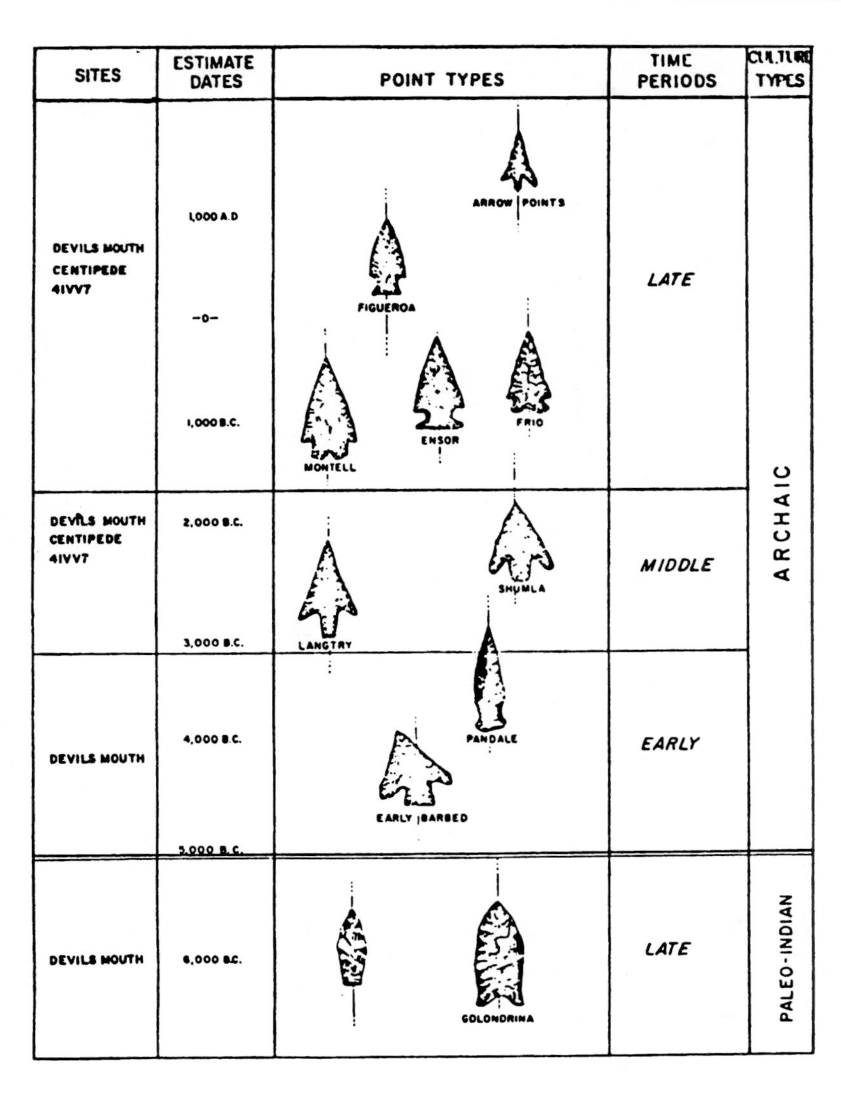

SITES
ESTIMATE DATES
POINT TYPES
TIME PERIODS
CULTURE TYPES
DEVILS MOUTH
CENTIPEDE
41VV7
1,000 A.D
-0-
1,000 B.C.
ARROW POINTS
FIGUEROA
MONTELL
ENSOR
FRIO
LATE
DEVILS MOUTH
CENTIPEDE
41VV7
2,000 B.C.
3,000 B.C.
SHUMLA
LANGTRY
MIDDLE
ARCHAIC
DEVILS MOUTH
4,000 B.C.
PANDALE
EARLY BARBED
EARLY
5,000 B.C.
DEVILS MOUTH
6,000 B.C.
GOLONDRINA
LATE
PALEO-INDIAN

Figure 3-2. *Projectile point sequence in the lower Pecos region, Texas.* Based on excavations at the Devil's Mouth site, Val Verde County. From Johnson (1964, fig. 25). Courtesy of the Department of Anthropology, University of Texas at Austin.

appear late in the period, perhaps reflecting territoriality on the part of some hunting and gathering societies. Similarly, trade connections are established, bringing in artifacts of stone and shell from distant areas.

The Late Archaic (1000 BC–300 BC) sees the continuation of hunting and gathering lifeways in most of Texas, again distinguished by certain types of projectile points and stone tools (fig. 3-6). In east Texas, pre-Caddo ceramic sites mark the beginning of settled village life shortly after 500 BC. Cemeteries are more notable in some regions, as in southeast Texas (Hall 1981). Bison appear to be an important game resource in central Texas and in the lower Pecos, where another bison-kill occurs at Bonfire Shelter (Dibble and Lorrain 1968). Other bison-kills are known in the Texas Panhandle and southern Plains at this time (Hughes 1976).

The Transitional Archaic (300 BC–AD 700) marks an interval that in some ways is little more than a continuation of the Late Archaic. Still, there are distinctive point styles. While this time period is an important one in the Archaic sequences of central and lower Pecos Texas, it is not part of the east Texas archaeological record, where village sites (such as the George C. Davis site of the Gibson Aspect) make their initial appearance. These often have large mounds, with flat-topped examples sometimes used to support structures and conical mounds for burials.

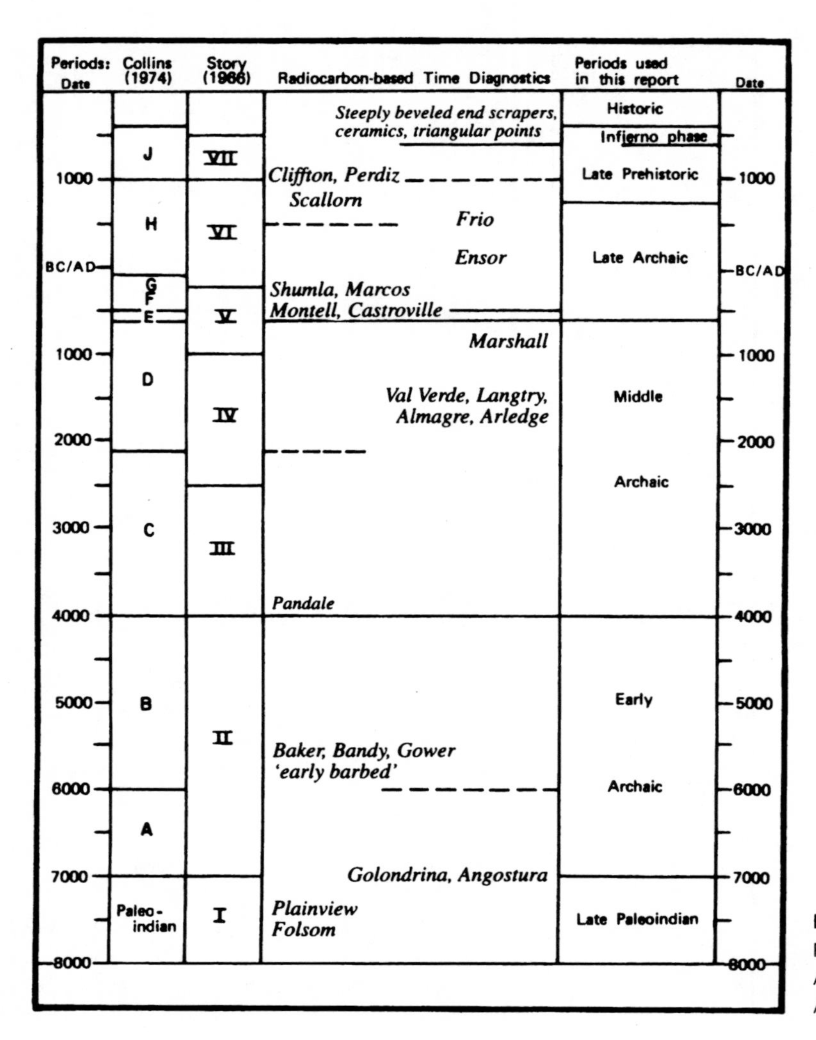

Figure 3-3. *Archaeological sequences for the lower Pecos.* From Turpin (1982, tab. 2). By permission of the Texas Archeological Research Laboratory, University of Texas, Austin.

The Late Prehistoric (AD 700 to historic times) is particularly noticeable in the archaeological record throughout the state. The bow and arrow is introduced, along with other distinctive types of stone tools. Pottery is also present, even among hunters and gatherers in central, south, and coastal Texas. Bison hunting appears to be very important in most regions. The occurrence of tiny arrow points, such as Scallorn, Perdiz, Cuney, Friley, and Catahoula, marks the spread of the bow and arrow throughout the state. Many local types develop: Livermore in the Trans-Pecos, Lott and Garza in the Llano Estacado, and McGloin and Bulbar Stemmed on the coast. In some areas, we can discern distinct shifts in arrow point styles through time, especially with Scallorn (Austin Phase) and, later, Perdiz (Toyah Phase) in central Texas.

Although a hunting and gathering lifeway continues, as in the Archaic, the material culture, hunting patterns, settlement types, and other facets of Late Prehistoric times mark a fairly distinctive break with the past. In east Texas, around AD 1200, the Gibson Aspect gives way to the Fulton Aspect, which continues into the Historic era and is linked with the Caddo. In the Panhandle and Llano Estacado, settled villages are found in the Antelope Creek Phase on the Canadian River around AD 1400, and in Andrews County, village sites with links to southeast New Mexico appear around the same time. In the far west Trans-Pecos area, a sequence of settled horticulturalists, with strong ties to the Southwest, commences in the early centuries AD, developing more

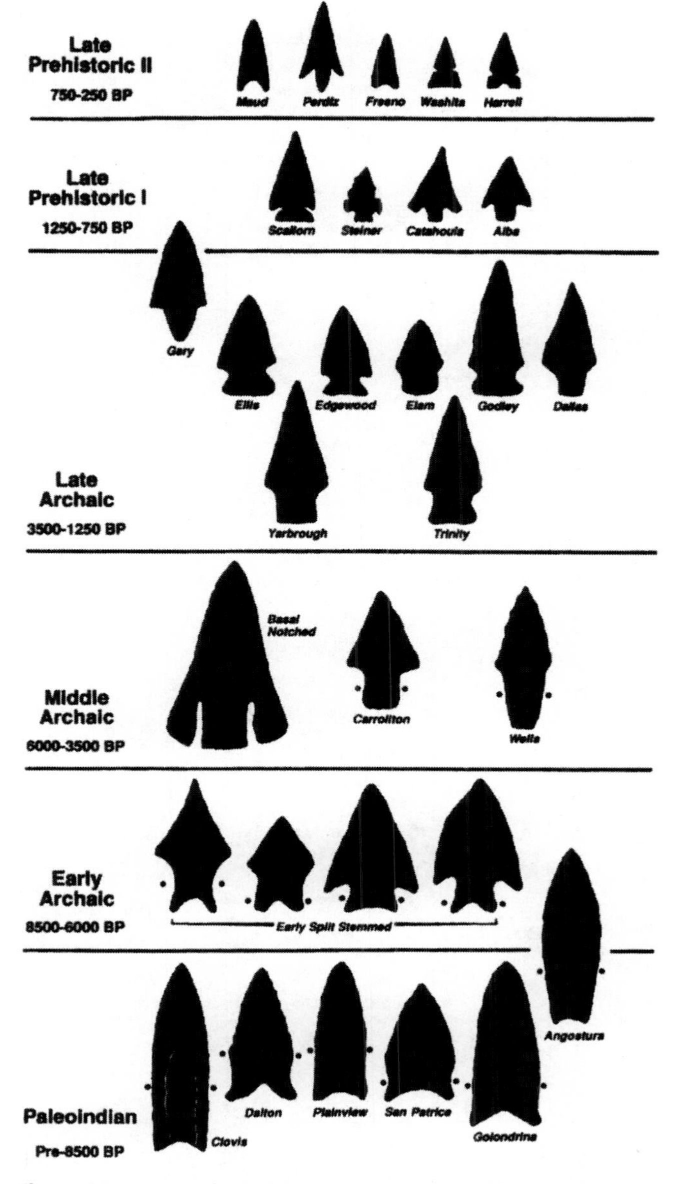

Figure 3-4. *Proposed projectile point sequence for north central Texas.* From Prikryl (1990, fig. 24). By permission of Texas Historical Commission, Austin.

fully around AD 600 (Whalen 1980), marked especially by pithouse dwellings. Down the Rio Grande, near Presidio, another center of agriculturally based villages, the Bravo Valley Aspect dates to around AD 1200–1400 (Kelley 1986; Suhm et al. 1954).

The Historic era (after ca. AD 1600) marks the beginning of the end for the native Indian cultures of the state. Some projectile points in east Texas continue into historic times (e.g., Turney and Cuney). Similarly, such types as Toyah and Fresno certainly date in part to historic times in parts of the state. With the advent of the Spanish mission system, the Indians who adopted mission life continued to make stone tools (Fox 1979b, 1983; Hester 1989c), and a distinctive point type, Guerrero, is often found in missions, ranchos, and Indian campsites of that era. However, by the late 18th century, stone tools give way to glass, and brass and iron points replace those chipped from stone, ending an 11,000-year tradition.

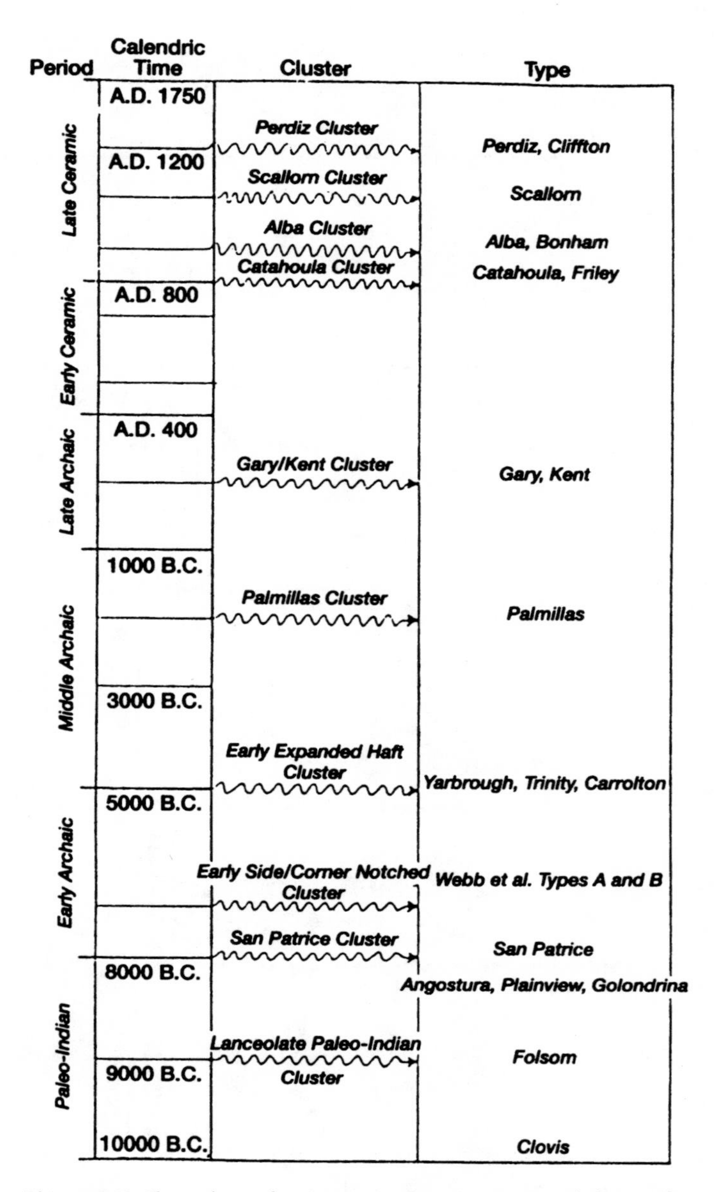

Figure 3-5. *Chronology of major projectile point types and clusters for inland southeast Texas*. From Ensor, Dockall, and Winchell (1991, fig. 2). By permission of the Archeological Research Laboratory at Texas A&M University.

Figure 3-6. *A quick guide to major time periods and stone tool forms in Texas prehistory.*

PERIOD	APPROXIMATE DATES	SELECTED POINT TYPES	SELECTED TOOL FORMS
HISTORIC	1700 1600	Guerrero, Turney	end scrapers, gunflints, drills, flake tools
LATE PREHISTORIC II	1200	Perdiz, Cuney, Bonham, Alba, McGloin, Fresno	end scrapers, small drills, beveled knives, Gahagan bifaces
LATE PREHISTORIC I	AD 700	Edwards, Scallorn, Sabinal, Zavala,	Pipe Creek bifaces
TRANSITIONAL ARCHAIC	300 BC	Ensor, Darl, Frio, Ellis, Edgewood, Fairland, Paisano	Olmos, Bristol bifaces
LATE ARCHAIC	600 1000	Montell, Shumla, Marcos, Castroville, Lange	Kerrville bifaces, corner-tang knives
MIDDLE ARCHAIC	1200 2500	Pedernales, Langtry, Gary, Kent, Morhiss, Marshall, Kinney, Tortugas, Motley, Pontchartrain	large perforators, Nueces tools, smaller Clear Fork tools
(early Middle)	3100	La Jita, Pandale, Nolan	
EARLY ARCHAIC	3500 6000	Bell, Andice, Early Triangular, Martindale, Uvalde, Baker, Bandy, Hoxie, Wells, Laguna, Gower	Guadalupe bifaces; Clear Fork unifaces, bannerstones; sequent flake tools
LATE PALEO-INDIAN	6500	Angostura, Scottsbluff, Firstview, Early Stemmed, Lanceolate	Clear Fork bifaces
MIDDLE PALEO-INDIAN	7000	Golondrina, St. Mary's Hall	Clear Fork bifaces
	8200	Plainview	
EARLY PALEO-INDIAN	8500 9200	San Patrice, Dalton, Folsom, Clovis	Albany tools; Dalton adzes, end scrapers, gravers; Clovis blades and blade cores; engraved stones

Projectile Points
Type Descriptions

PROJECTILE POINTS are the most familiar single artifact of the North American Indians and the principal tool utilized by ancient cultures for the last 11,000 years. As discussed earlier in this book, the shapes and sizes of projectile points change through time in most regions of the country. As such, those categories or times that have distinct attributes, and time-space contexts, can be used as time-diagnostic items in archaeological studies. The majority of these specimens possess the same general morphological traits when considered from the standpoint of the manufacturing process (see chapter 2). Both the large, thick dart point and the tiny, thin arrow point are bilaterally symmetrical, bifacially (or in some cases, unifacially) flaked artifacts that are thinned and pointed at the distal end. Usually, they possess a haft element (stem) distinguished from the body by means of edge-grinding, basal, and/or laterally opposed notches or other modifications for the apparent purpose of attachment to the haft.

Points have often morphological "styles" such as side- and corner-notching in common with types in widely scattered areas; yet, they may be thousands of years apart in time. Thus, it is essential to acquire a working knowledge of the technology, dating, and distribution of a type (see chapter 3). Site reports, guides (such as this one), and archaeological journals are a good way to gain access to this knowledge. Studying actual collections of points will always be the best way to familiarize oneself with the variability of forms.

In order for types to serve as a useful means of communication, it is important that readers and authors attach the same meaning to the terminology used in the type descriptions. Figure 4-1 graphically describes much of the nomenclature used in this guide. The dart and arrow points follow and are listed separately in alphabetical order with the descriptive data for each type.

The illustrations are usually at actual size unless a scale is indicated. We have minimized the description, choosing to let the drawings portray most of the features. For example, the extent of grinding and smoothing on Paleo-Indian points is indicated with dots.

For the distal, pointed part of projectile points, we use the term "body" (see fig. 4-1), instead of the much-abused label of "blade." A blade, technologically speaking, is a parallel-sided flake, at least twice as long as it is wide, intentionally removed from a core prepared for such blade production. But the term is often used by avocational and professional archaeologists to refer to the distal section of points or to describe large, thin bifaces.

Within the description, numerous references are usually listed, and additional detailed information can be obtained from these publications. We have made an effort to select sites that show the known distribution of the type and have been excavated under controlled conditions with associated tool assemblages carefully recorded (readers should be aware that these sites are on private property and not open to the public). Additional references that contain relevant studies or pertinent information useful to the type description are also included.

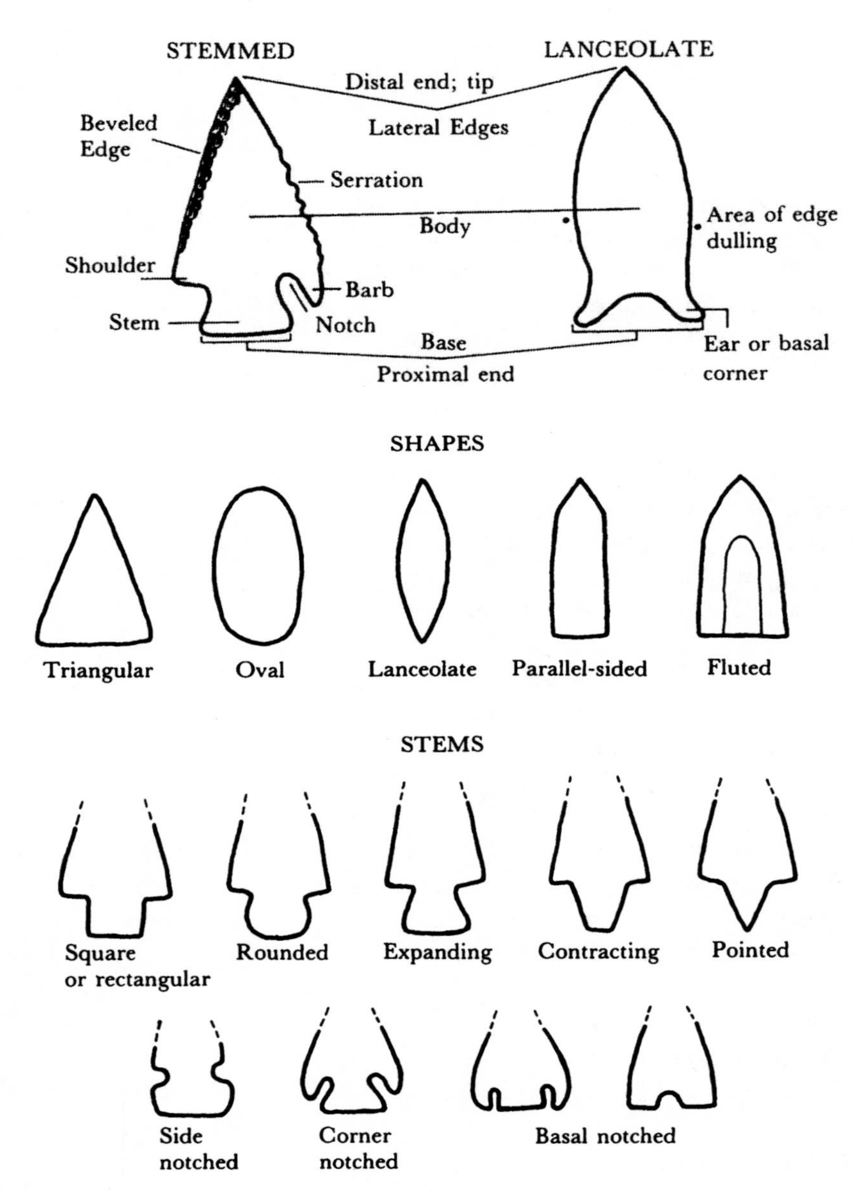

Figure 4-1. *Terminology used in artifact descriptions.* Based largely on Cambron and Hulse (1975).

The site designations used here are based on the Smithsonian trinomial system, adopted in the 1950s by the University of Texas at Austin, where it continues in use in the central archaeological data files of the Texas Archeological Research Laboratory. In this system, forty-one indicates Texas, the county is denoted by a two-letter abbreviation (see appendix 3), and the site is numbered in sequential fashion.

The estimated age, based on known radiocarbon dates and stratigraphic contexts, is included with the cultural affiliation (Paleo-Indian, Archaic, Late Prehistoric, or Historic), and a general distributional range of reported specimens is indicated on an index map of Texas.

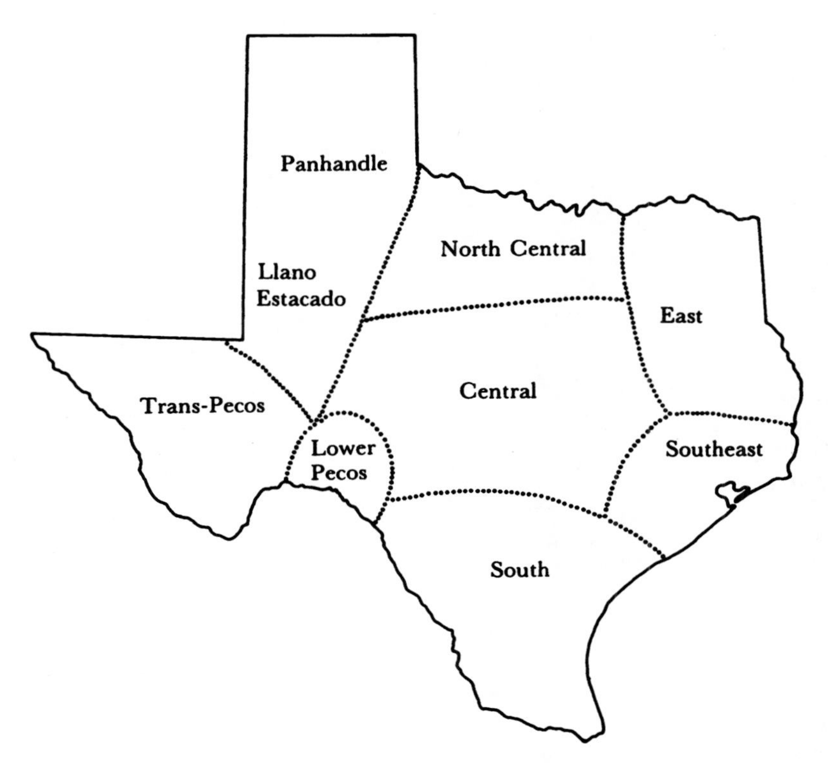

Map 4-1. *Major archaeological areas of Texas.* This map depicts the archaeological areas referred to in this book.

DART POINTS

ABASOLO

This large, unstemmed triangular point has a distinctive well-rounded base. The lateral edges may be beveled, and the base is sometimes thinned. It is similar to Catán but larger in size. Abasolo specimens often have impact fractures reflective of their use as dart points, although microscopic use-wear is sometimes observed on the lateral edges.

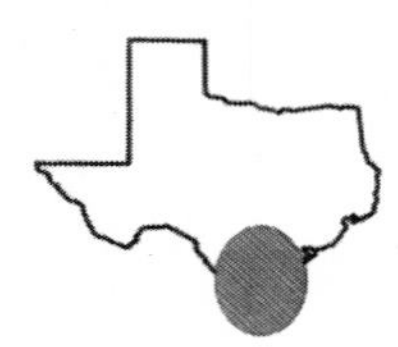

Distribution: Common throughout south Texas, especially in the Rio Grande drainage and continuing into northeastern Mexico. **Period:** Early to Middle Archaic. **Sites:** Choke Canyon; Oulline; La Perdida; Sierra de Tamaulipas, Mexico; Killam Ranch; Boiler.

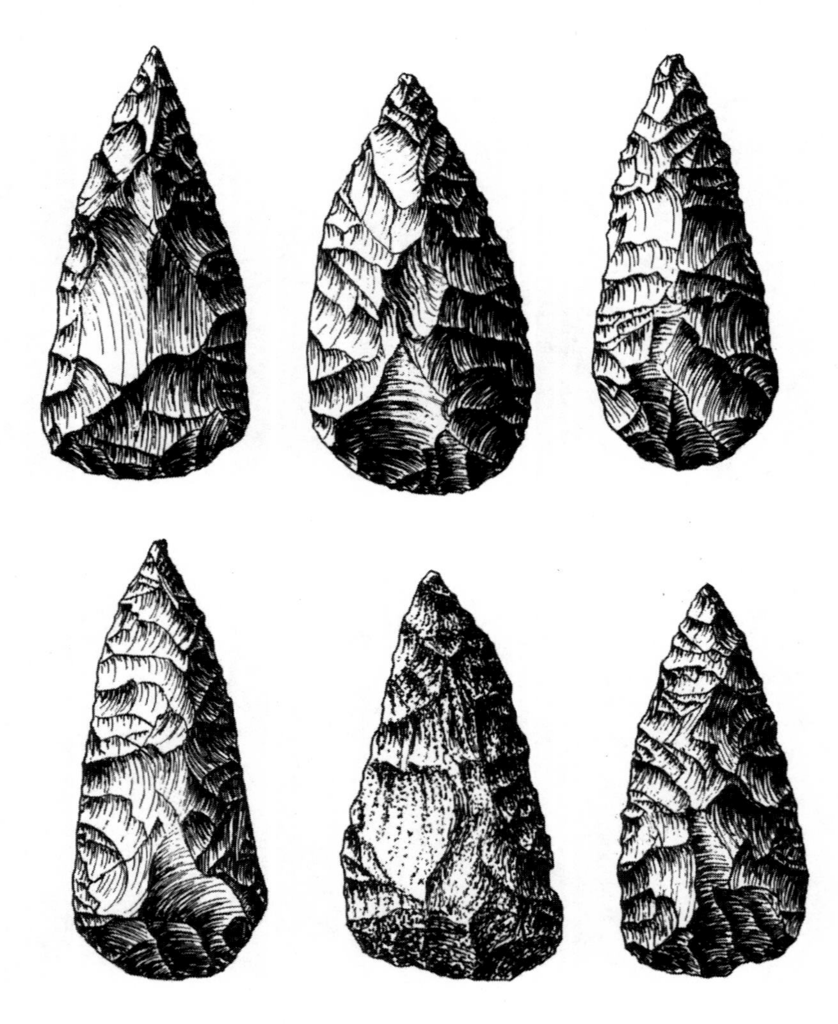

References: Bettis 1997; Hall, Black, and Graves 1982; Hester, White, and White 1969; MacNeish 1958; Quigg et al. 2002; Suhm and Jelks 1962; Weir 1956.

ANDICE

Andice points are large, broad, triangular points with straight to convex lateral edges and a long, essentially rectangular, stem. Prominent, massive barbs extend downward and are narrowest at the juncture with the body (resulting in high breakage frequency). The characteristic deep notches produced a distinctive "notching flake" that can identify the presence of Andice, even absent the finished point. Andice are closely related to Bell morphologically but are distinguishable by their greater size, stem length, and barb length (Bell stems are usually more expanding and rarely exceed 16 mm in length).

Andice and Bell are part of the Calf Creek Horizon, found in Missouri, Arkansas, Oklahoma, and most of Texas (Calame et al. 2002; Wyckoff 1994). Proposed hafting techniques are illustrated by McReynolds (2002). A remarkable find in Oklahoma revealed a shattered Andice point embedded in the forehead of a bison (Bement et al. 2004). Indeed, a number of southern Oklahoma sites have Calf Creek assemblages that add greatly to knowledge of this tradition. For example, at the Primose and Stillman sites, stockpiled (or "banked") triangular chert blanks and early stage preforms awaited manufacture as Andice points (see Bartlett 1994).

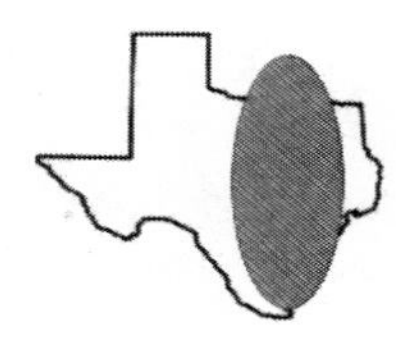

Distribution: East and south central Texas, across the Gulf coastal plain to Victoria–Corpus Christi area. **Period:** Early Archaic, ca. 4500–3500 BC. **Sites:** Gault; Collins; Coleto Creek; Cuero I Reservoir; 41UV351; Sutherland Springs Sand Pit, Wilson County; Barton; White's Point (41SP156).

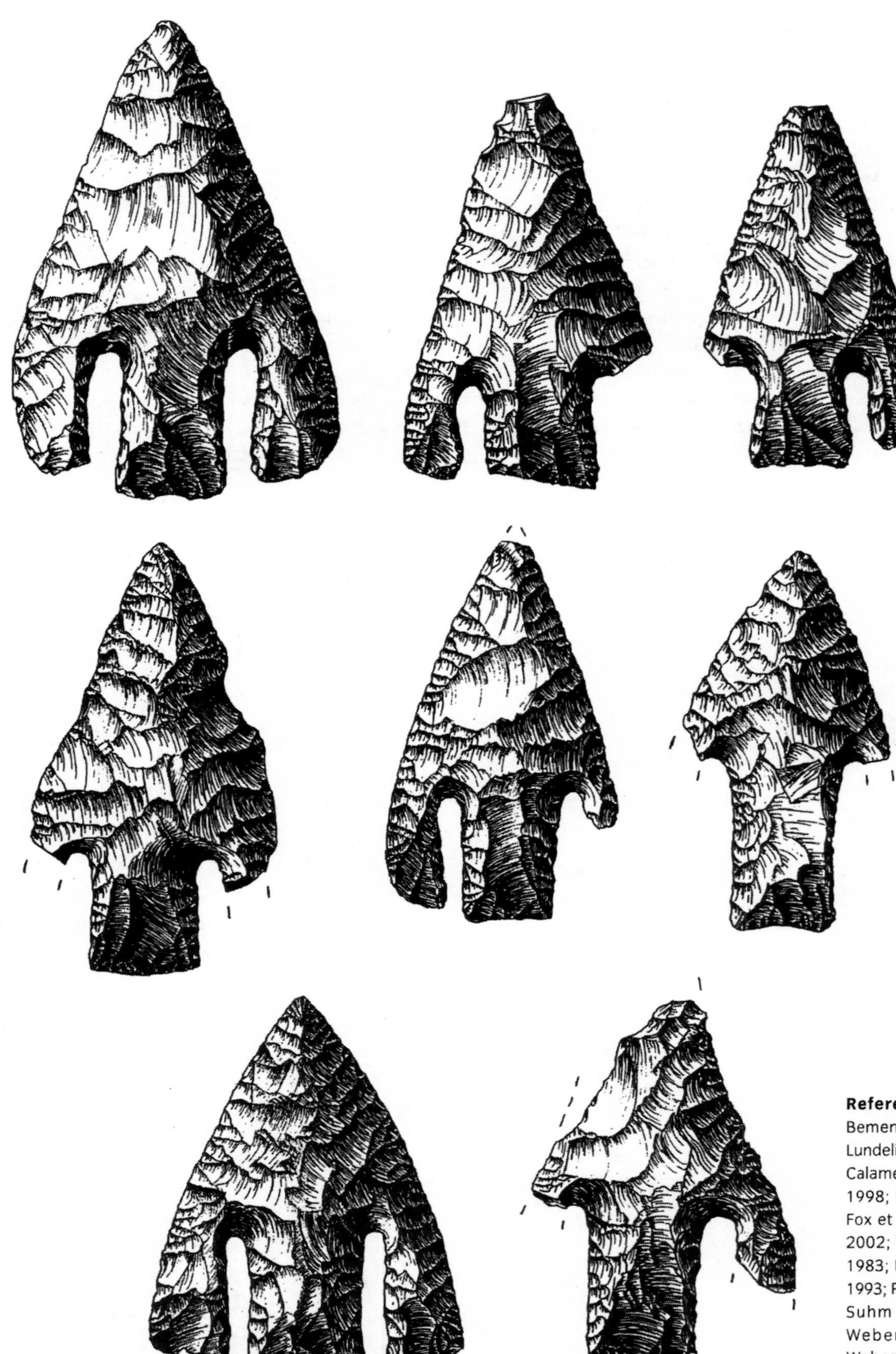

References: Bartlett 1994; Bement et al. 1989; Bement, Lundelius, and Ketchum 2004; Calame et al. 2002; Dial et al. 1998; Fox and Hester 1976; Fox et al. 1974; McReynolds 2002; Moore 1989; Prewitt 1983; Prilliman 1998; Ricklis 1993; Ricklis and Collins 1994; Suhm 1955; Weber 2000; Weber and Collins 1994; Weber and Patterson 1985, 1986; Wyckoff 1994.

ANGOSTURA

This long, slender, lanceolate point can have oblique parallel-flaking or can be more casually flaked. It has a narrow, concave, or irregularly straight base and ground basal edges. Angostura was originally defined for the Plains. Specimens attributed to the type in Texas are very common and widely distributed. They vary widely in shape and flaking, causing problems in definition. Kelly (1983b) suggests two other types of this point, which he labels "Texas Angostura" and "Zella." Additionally, the Thrall type as proposed at the Wilson-Leonard site in central Texas is, in our view, largely made up of Angostura points.

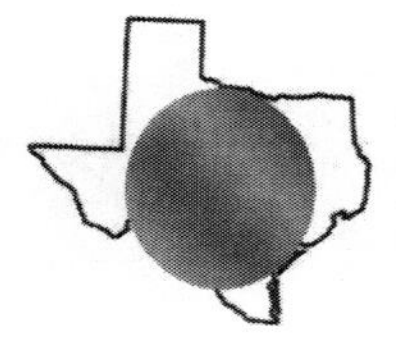

Distribution: Throughout much of Texas. **Period:** Late Paleo-Indian. An AMS C-14 date on wood charcoal of 8805±75 BP (6855±75 BC) came from a deposit associated with an Angostura point at 41BX831. At the Armstrong site (41ICW34), date ranges of 8490–8080 and 8080–7960 BP came from radiocarbon analysis. **Sites:** Strohacker; San Miguel Creek; Levi Rockshelter; La Perdida; 41BX831; 41BP19; Armstrong.

References: Alexander 1963; Bement et al. 1989; Bousman, Baker, and Kerr 2004; Dial et al. 1998; Hester 1968; Kelly 1983b; Nightengale et al. 1985; Sollberger and Hester 1972; Suhm and Jelks 1962; Thoms 1992; Weir 1956; Wormington 1957.

ARENOSA

This point is distinguished from a wide range of other Middle Archaic contracting stem styles on the basis of stem termination, which is pointed to slightly rounded. Short barbs are common. It is similar to and contemporary with both Langtry and Val Verde points.

Distribution: Lower Pecos, Big Bend, eastern Trans-Pecos, and south to southern reaches of Rio Grande and northern Mexico. **Period:** Middle Archaic. **Sites:** Arenosa Shelter (41VV99); Val Verde County; parts of the Trans-Pecos; and occasionally the southwestern Edwards Plateau.

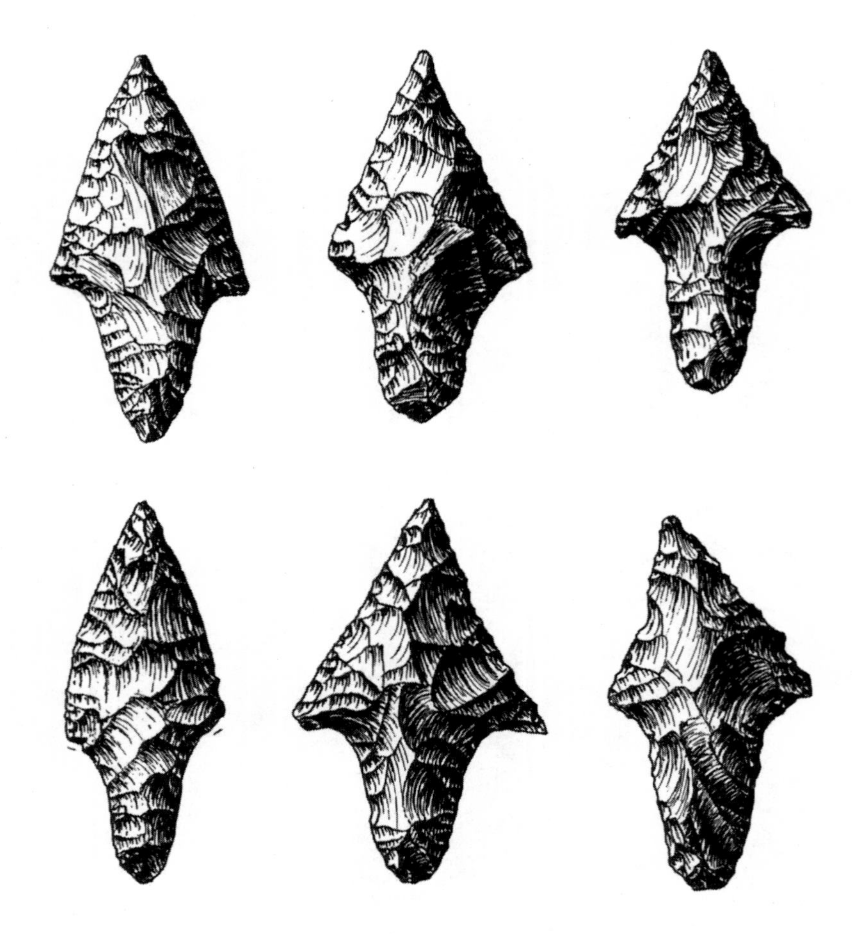

References: Bement 1991a; Mallouf et al. 2006.

AXTELL

This medium-sized stemmed point is thicker than most dart points (7–10 mm) and generally has a crude appearance. The straight to gently convex lateral edges are commonly lightly serrated, and many have light edge-beveling. The shoulders are slight to moderate in size and rarely barbed. They have been called "Penny Points" because of the distinctive, generally rounded stem, which is sometimes heavily ground. There is considerable variation in the outline of the stem. It is similar to Palmillas, but rounding of the Axtell stem begins closer to its shoulders.

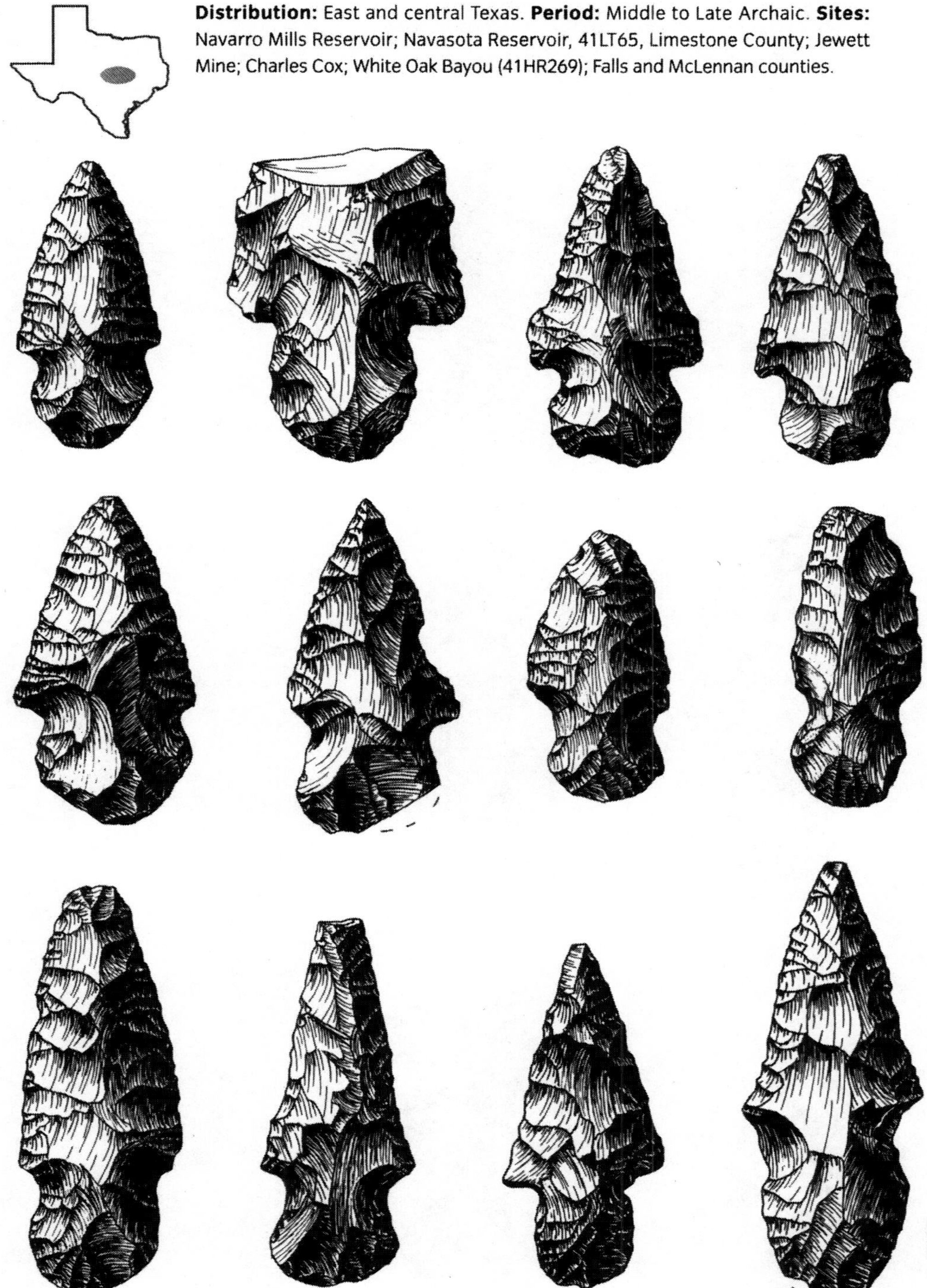

Distribution: East and central Texas. **Period:** Middle to Late Archaic. **Sites:** Navarro Mills Reservoir; Navasota Reservoir, 41LT65, Limestone County; Jewett Mine; Charles Cox; White Oak Bayou (41HR269); Falls and McLennan counties.

References: Bryan 1930, 1936; Fields 1988; Fields et al. 1990a, 1990b, 1991; Prewitt 1974b; Prewitt and Chandler 1992.

BAKER

The body of this point is thick in cross section, and it has straight to slightly convex lateral edges, and shoulders or strong barbs. The stem is expanding, and the base is bifurcated. A second variety is less commonly barbed, and the convex stems have a "bowlegged" appearance; the notches in the base are more open, and the base of the notch is rounded. It is similar to the Uvalde type in central Texas, and specimens are often classified as Baker or Uvalde.

Distribution: Lower Pecos into the southwest Edwards Plateau. **Period:** Early Archaic, ca. 6000 BC–4000 BC. **Sites:** Baker Cave; Hinds Cave; Varga; Gatlin.

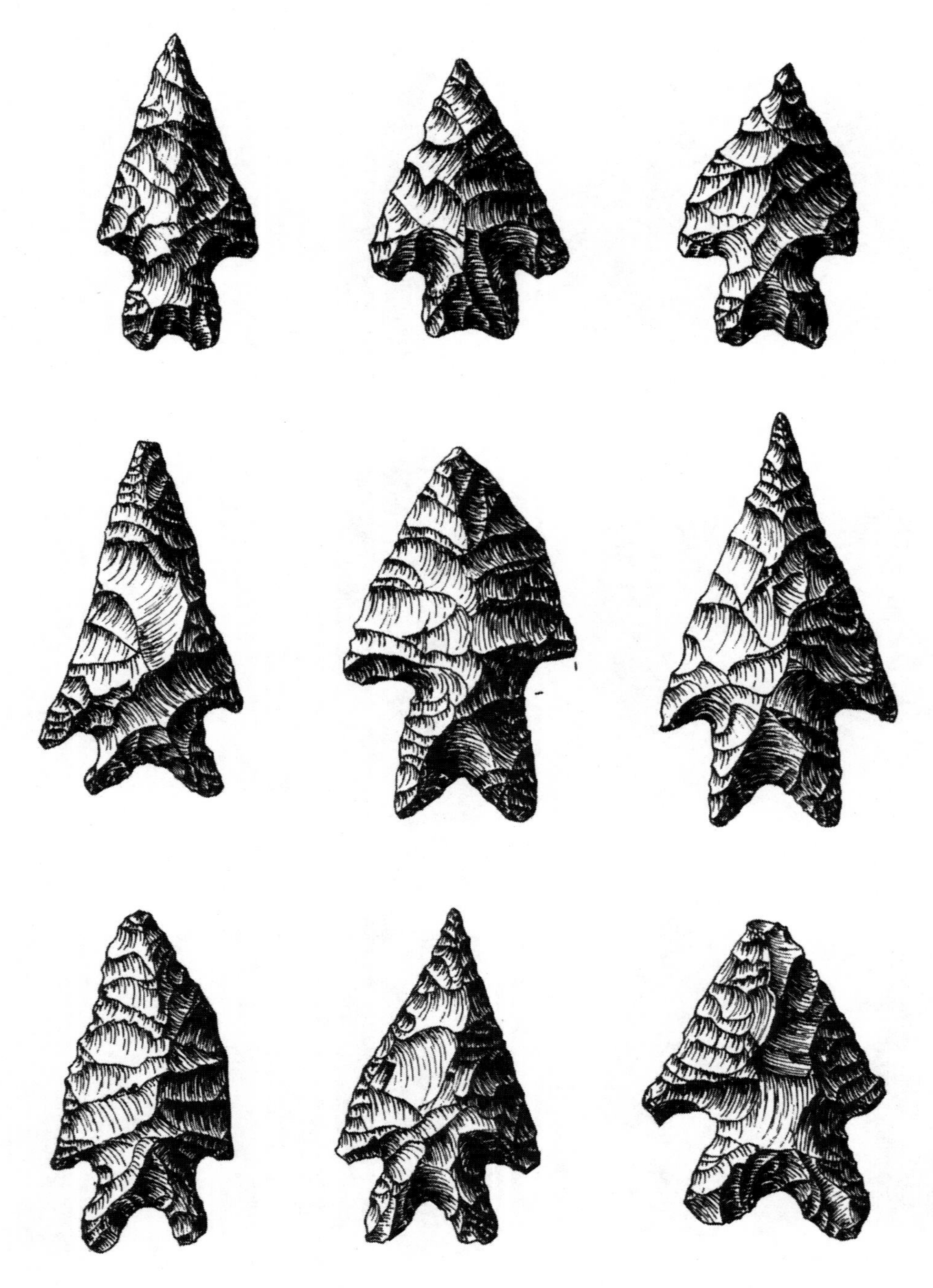

References: Chadderdon 1984; Hester 1978b; Houk et al. 2008; Quigg et al. 2008; Shafer 1984; Shafer and Bryant 1977; Word and Douglas 1970.

BANDY

The lateral edges on this point vary from gently convex to slightly recurved, and corner-notching produces strong barbs with narrow or V-shaped notches. The stem is slightly expanding, and the base often has a "fishtail" appearance. It is very thin in cross section, especially the base, and is very well made. It may be the lower Pecos equivalent of the Martindale type of central Texas. Indeed, Bandy points have been reported from key sites in the southern Edwards Plateau.

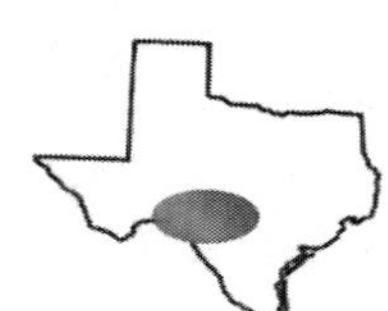

Distribution: Lower Pecos and lower central Texas. **Period:** Early Archaic, ca. 6000 BC–4000 BC. **Sites:** Baker Cave; Hinds Cave; Wilson-Leonard; 41WM235; Varga; Gatlin.

References: Chadderdon 1984; Dial et al. 1998; Hester 1978b; Houk et al. 2008; Quigg et al. 2008; Shafer and Bryant 1977; Weir 1984; Word and Douglas 1970.

BARBER

The Barber type is represented by long, thick, parallel-flaked, lanceolate points that expand near mid-body. It has a deep basal concavity and recurved basal edges that contract more than Plainview (Kelly 1983a). The basal concavity and edges are ground, and the deep, recurved, or bell-shaped concavity (up to 12 mm) is the deepest of any Texas Paleo-Indian point. We see many specimens that have been misclassified as Barber, and we continue to consider it to constitute a distinctive regional type, mainly in Gillespie and surrounding counties. At the Wilson-Leonard site, Barber was "combined" with Golondrina, constituting a "Barber-Golondrina" grouping that we feel is not useful. The late Tom Kelly (1983a) had identified a few distinctive Barber points in the Wilson-Leonard collection.

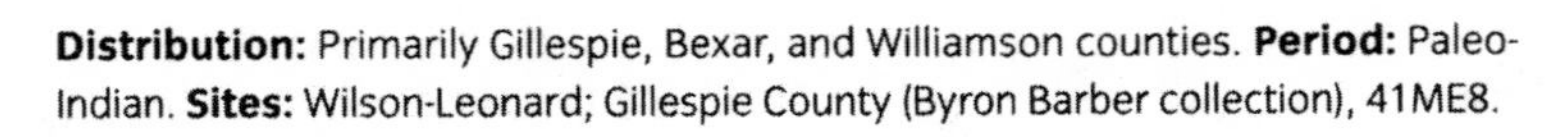

Distribution: Primarily Gillespie, Bexar, and Williamson counties. **Period:** Paleo-Indian. **Sites:** Wilson-Leonard; Gillespie County (Byron Barber collection), 41ME8.

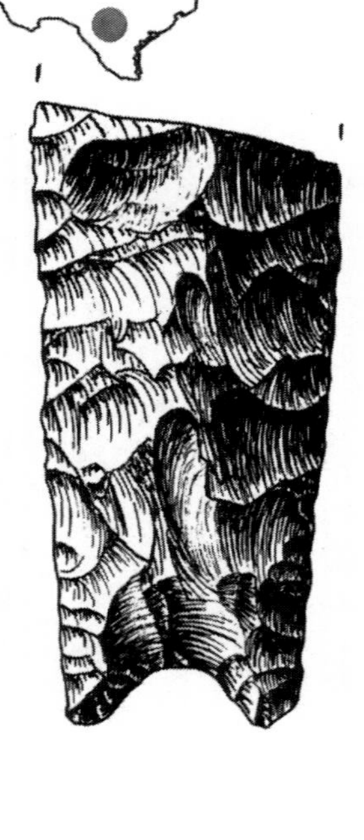

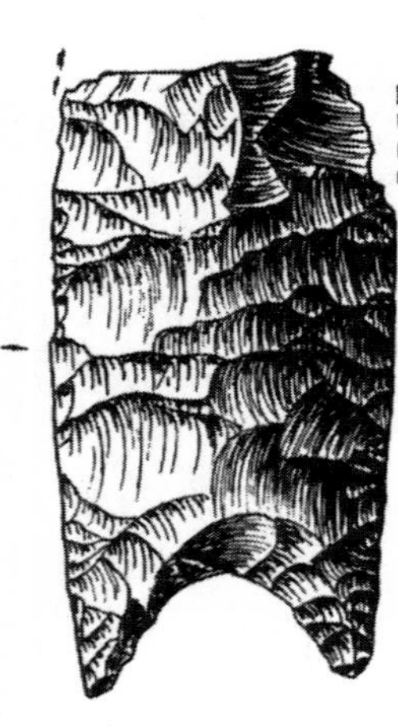

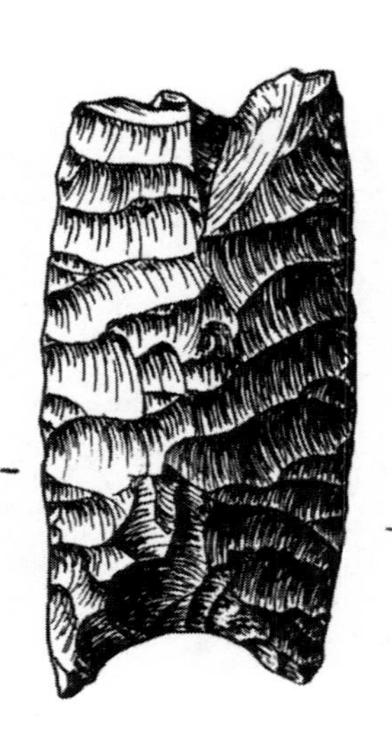

References: Dial et al. 1998; Guderjan et al. 1992; Kelly 1982, 1983a; Weir 1984.

BELL

The distinctive attributes of this point are its wide, thin, triangular body and long, narrow barbs formed by basal notching. It is similar to Andice but smaller in size and has expanding stems. Bell points are part of the Calf Creek Horizon.

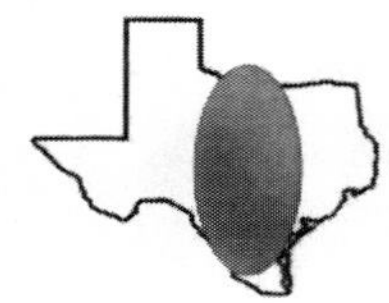

Distribution: Most common in central Texas but also found in south Texas, the eastern edge of the Llano Estacado, east Texas, and the central Texas coast. **Period:** Early Archaic, at 41MM340, 5660–5460 BP; at Cibolo Crossing, 5300–4800 BP. **Sites:** Landslide; Eagle Cave; Bonfire Shelter; Jetta Court; Cibolo Crossing; Gatlin; White's Point (41SP156).

References: Dibble and Lorrain 1968; Houk et al. 2009; Kibler and Scott 2000; Perino 1985; Ricklis 1993; Ross 1965; Sorrow, Shafer, and Ross 1967; Weber 2000; Weber and Collins 1994; Weber and Patterson 1985, 1986; Wesolowsky, Hester, and Brown 1976.

BIG SANDY

This type has been long known in the southeastern United States and has only been recognized fairly recently in Texas. Texas specimens are usually somewhat smaller than Big Sandy artifacts illustrated by Perino (1985). They are more compatible with those published by Justice (1987, fig. 13). The specimens are side notched with the corners of the stem often squared. Serrations are sometimes found along the lateral edges of the point. Much more research needs to be done on the Big Sandy type in Texas, and identification of these points should be done with caution.

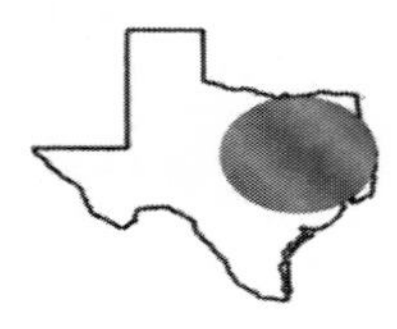

Distribution: In Texas, from east and southeast regions into the Edwards Plateau; Louisiana. **Period:** Late Paleo-Indian. Justice (1987, 62) dates them between 8000 and 6000 BC in the southeastern United States, and Mary Beth Trubitt (2009b, 4) recently excavated specimens in Arkansas from Sample 2008-328-121 that came back at 7070±40 BP, which has a calibrated intercept of 5980 BC. **Sites:** McFaddin Beach (41JF50); Gault (41BL323); Camp Bullis (near 41CM96); Lake Tacoma; Gatlin; Jones Mill, Ark.; 41MM376, Milam County; 41RF10, 11, Hopper's Landing, Refugio County; Fort Polk (La.).

References: Anderson and Smith 2003; Dial et al. 1998; Duffield 1963b; Gerstle, Kelly, and Assad 1978; Houk et al. 2008; Justice 1987; Long 1977; Perino 1985; Prewitt and Lawson 1972; Story et al. 1990; Trubitt 2009b.

BULVERDE

This strong-shouldered to barbed point has a long rectangular to slightly contracting stem thinned by a broad flake or two or three contiguous vertical flakes. Most distinctive, however, is a thin, finely chipped stem base that is wedge shaped in cross section.

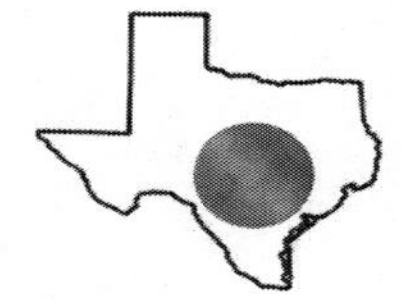

Distribution: Principally a central Texas point but occasionally found in south and east Texas. **Period:** 1500–2000 BC; Middle Archaic. **Sites:** Landslide; Greenhaw; Smith Rockshelter; Wunderlich; 41BN108; Eckols (41TV528), Panther Springs Creek; Gatlin.

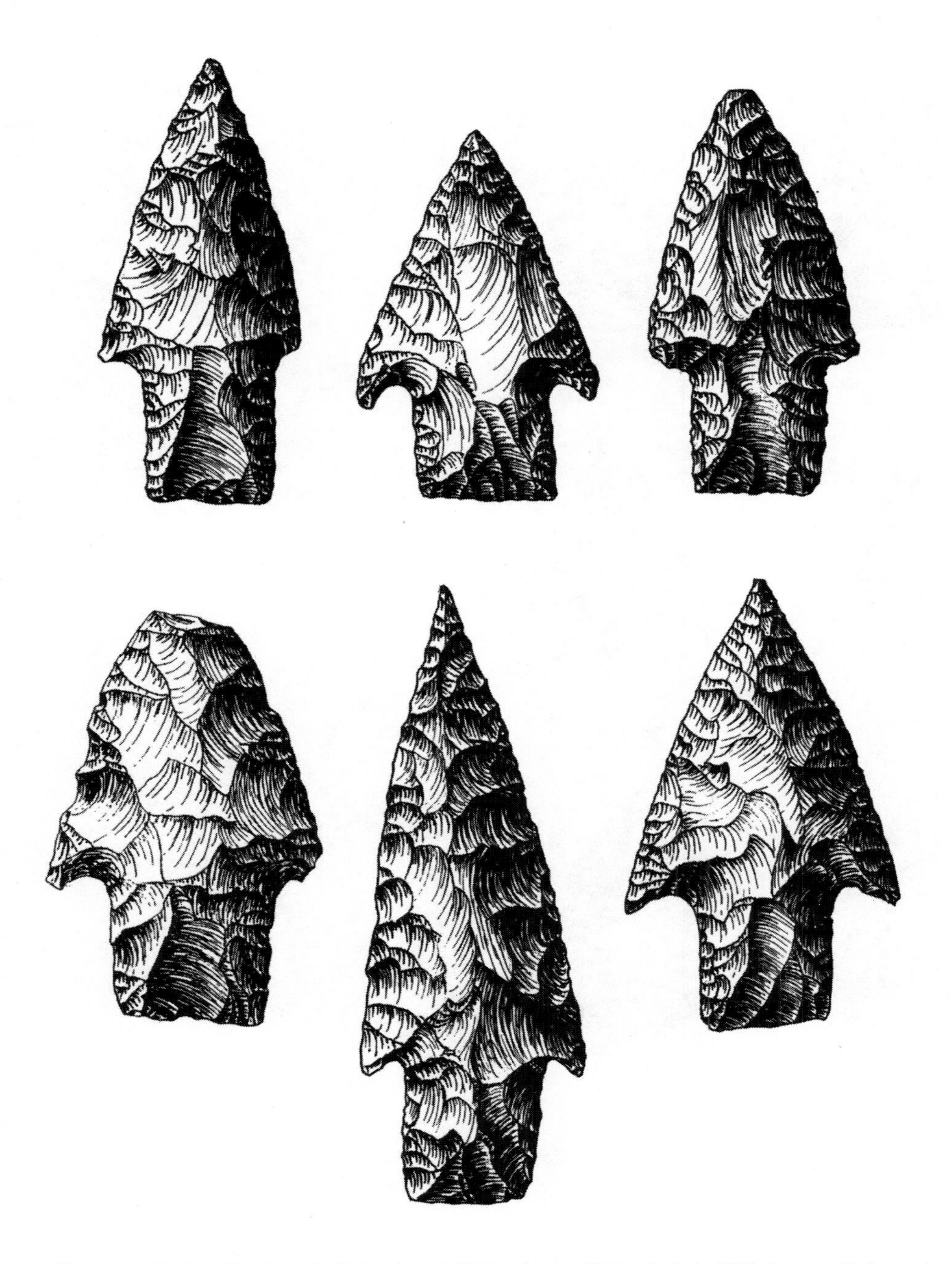

References: Black and McGraw 1985; Houk et al. 2008; Johnson 1962a; Karbula 2000; Sorrow, Shafer, and Ross 1967; Suhm 1957; Suhm and Jelks 1962; Weir 1979.

CARLSBAD

A basal-notched point that has a highly variable shape and convex base. These points often have bodies and shoulders that are reduced in size from resharpening. There is some overlap with the Hueco dart point type, particularly in regard to stem length.

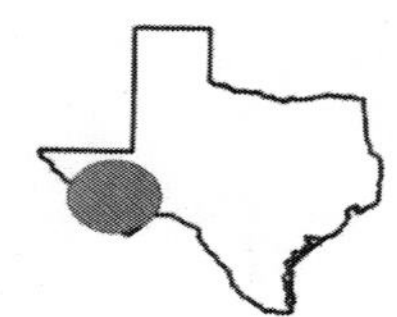

Distribution: Southeastern New Mexico extending south across the Trans-Pecos to the Big Bend. **Period:** Late to Transitional Archaic. **Sites:** Culberson County; Roberts Shelter; Hueco Tanks.

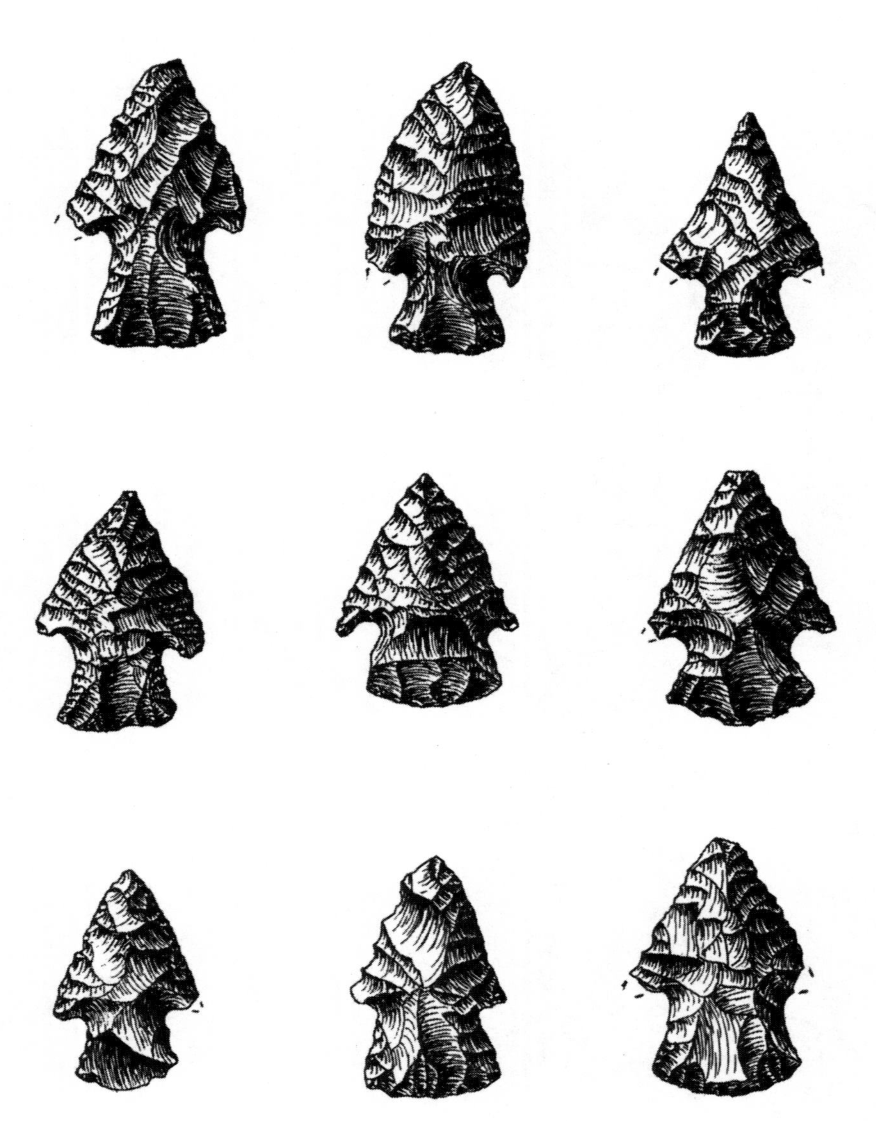

References: Howard et al. 2010; Leslie 1978; Roney 1995, C. Smyers, personal communication.

CARRIZO

This unstemmed, triangular point has slightly convex lateral edges and a single, deep notch carefully chipped in the center of the base. It is usually finely flaked and occasionally made of heat-treated chert. There have been a number of points with concave basal edges or unusual notches in the base that have been misclassified as Carrizo at some Edwards Plateau sites.

Distribution: Primarily south Texas, the Middle Rio Grande, and some central Texas sites. **Period:** Middle Archaic. **Sites:** San Miguel Creek; Panther Springs Creek; Greenhaw; Loma Sandia; Dimmit County; and Middle Rio Grande.

References: Black and McGraw 1985; Hester 1968; Hester and Whatley 1997; House and Hester 1963, 1967; Nickels et al. 2001; Nunley and Hester 1966; Perino 1968; Taylor and Highley 1995; Weir 1979.

CARROLLTON

This point has a triangular body with prominent shoulders, which are squared or barbed, and a long, rectangular stem. While some are rather crudely flaked, others are well made, but the stem and basal edges are sometimes smoothed. Carrollton points are commonly resharpened with the end result being a stem about as long as the distal end.

Distribution: Dallas area along the terraces of the Trinity River. **Period:** Middle Archaic, 3786 BP at 41FT226. **Sites:** Wheeler; Lake Dallas; Jake Martin; Culpepper; 41DL30; 41TR21; 41FT226; Trinity River drainage.

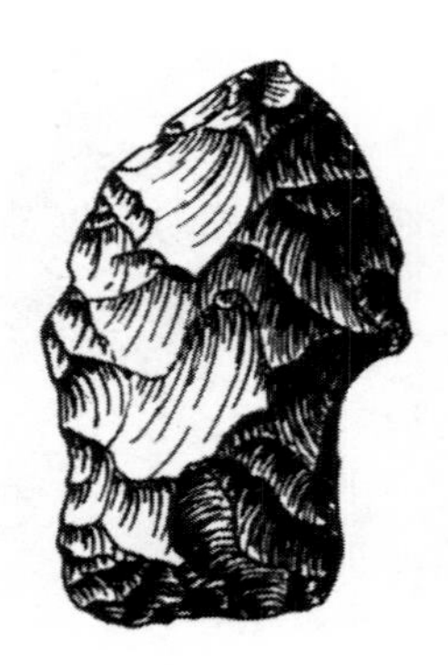

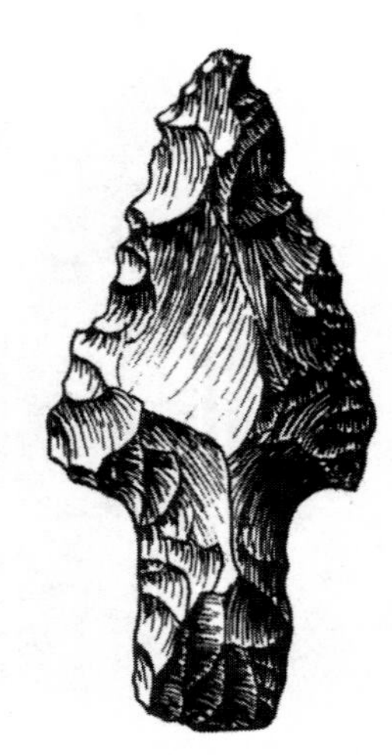

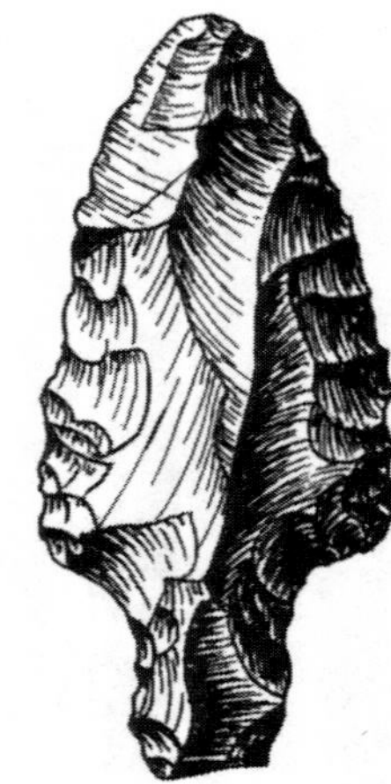

References: Crook and Harris 1952; Davis and Davis 1960; Prikryl 1990; Richner and Bagot 1978; Scurlock 1962; Suhm and Jelks 1962.

CASTROVILLE

Classic Castroville points have large, triangular bodies, with massive barbs formed by basal notching. Barb ends are pointed to squared. Stems are expanding, with the basal edges straight to slightly concave.

Specimens were found with the Late Archaic Bone Bed 3 bison-kill at Bonfire Shelter, with four radiocarbon dates that average 2645±75 BP (around 700 BC). Interestingly, points of similar shape have been found with bison-kills in the Texas Panhandle and western Oklahoma. The specimens from the bison-kills have not been assigned to any type by researchers, though they point out the similarities to Castroville and to Lange. Boyd (1997a, 268–70) assigns them to the Transitional Archaic.

Caches of Castroville points and preforms have been found in several sites, though the only scientifically recovered example is from Uvalde County (Mueggenborg 1994). A major cache found in central Texas was accompanied by finished points, preforms, antler billets, and a well-used hammerstone.

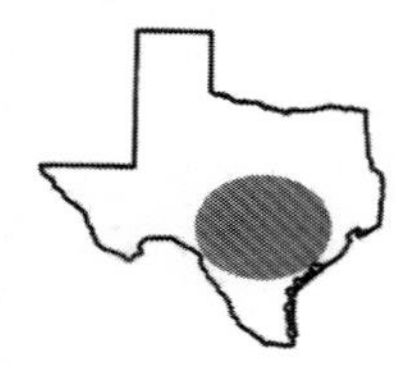

Distribution: Principally central Texas but also found in south Texas and the lower Pecos. **Period:** Late Archaic, ca. 800 BC–400 BC. **Sites:** Bonfire Shelter; Jetta Court; Scorpion Cave; Piedra del Diablo; 41BX195; 41UV159; Harrell.

References: Arnold 2003; Bement and Buehler 1994; Boyd 1997; Collins 1968; Dibble and Lorrain 1968; Highley et al. 1978; Johnson 1995; Mueggenborg 1994; Prewitt 1970; Quigg 1997, 1998; Story et al. 1990; Suhm and Jelks 1962; http://www.texasbeyondhistory.net/; Tunnell and Hughes 1955; Wesolowsky et al. 1976.

CATÁN

This triangular, unstemmed point has straight to slightly convex lateral edges that are sometimes beveled and a convex, well-rounded base that is sometimes thinned by the removal of one or two broad, arc-shaped flakes. The outline is similar to Abasolo, but Catán points are smaller. Detailed studies of Webb County lithics reflect a high percentage of impact fractures on Catán points.

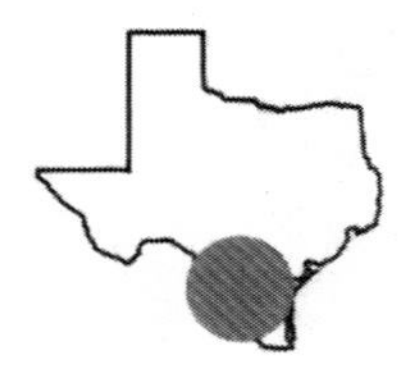

Distribution: Typical of south Texas and into northeast Mexico. **Period:** About AD 1000 at 41SP120. **Sites:** 41DV1, 41DV2, 41DV3; Sierra de Tamaulipas, Mexico; Cueva de la Zona de Derrumbes Rockshelter, Mexico; La Salle, McMullen, and Webb counties; 41SP120.

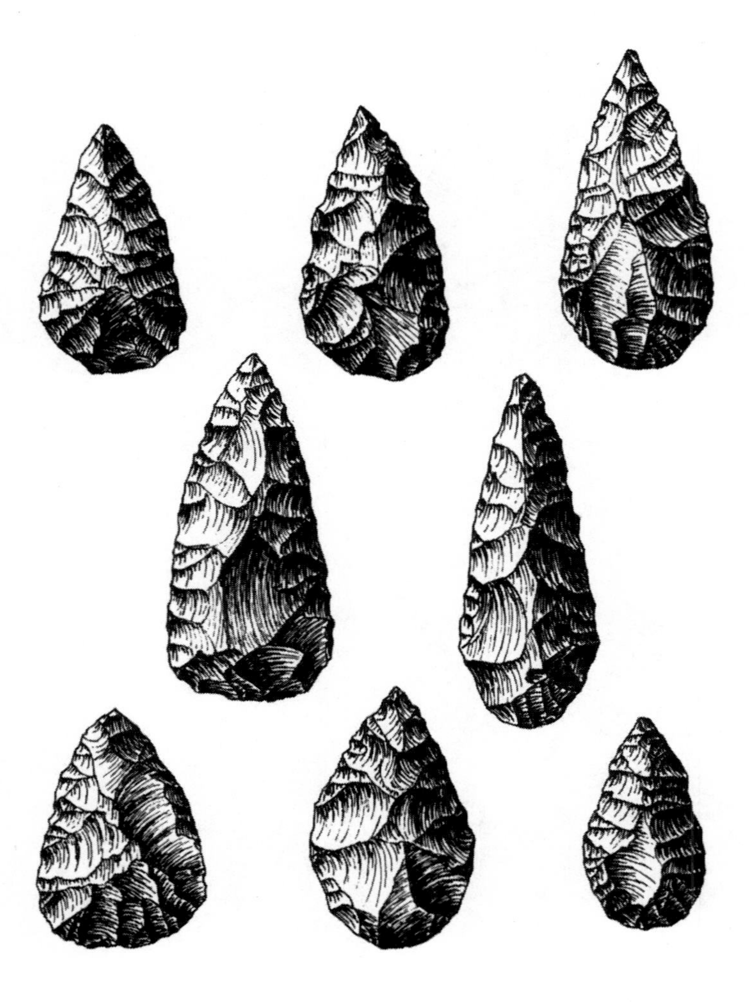

References: Bettis 1997; Hester 1972b; MacNeish 1958; McClurkan 1966; Suhm and Jelks 1962; Weir 1956.

CHARCOS

This point has a triangular body with straight or convex lateral edges. The shoulders are asymmetrical, with one barb longer than the other. On the side with the shorter (or absent) barb, there is a well-chipped notch in the lateral edge. This is a well-known form in southwestern Coahuila. In the second edition of this book, we mistakenly "extended" the range into "south Texas and the Big Bend." This was incorrect; they are confined to Coahuila, especially the areas around Torreon. While many Charcos points are found for sale on websites and listed as being from "Zapata" or "Starr" counties, all are smuggled in from Mexico.

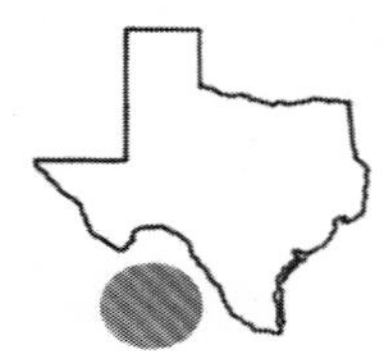

Distribution: Coahuila (northern Mexico). **Period:** Middle to Late Archaic. **Sites:** Comarca Lagunera; Desierto de Charcos de Risa; Cueva de la Candelaria; Poza Salada (all in Coahuila).

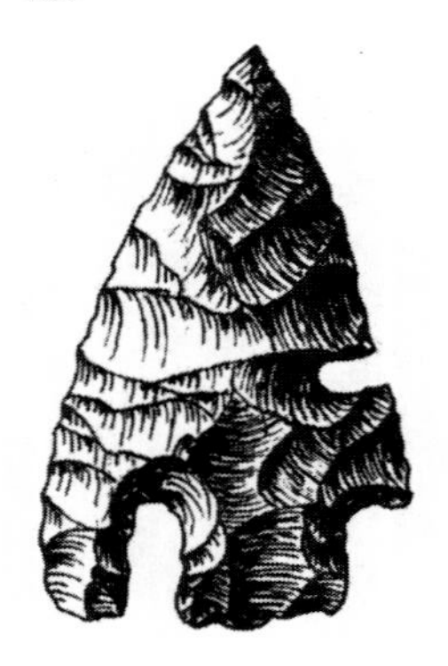

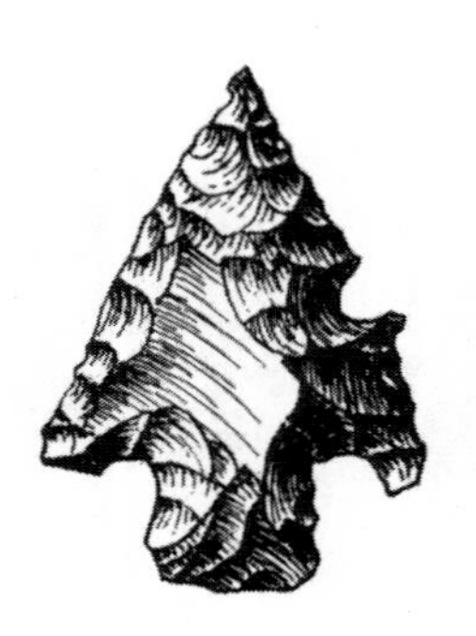

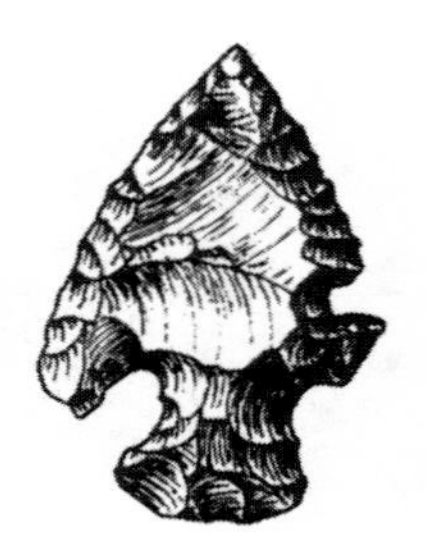

References: Aveleyra et al. 1956; Campbell 1967; T. N. Campbell, personal communication; Greene 1971; Heartfield 1975; Hester 2002a; Utberg 1969.

CLOVIS

Clovis points have a lanceolate outline with short flutes usually on both sides of the base. The basal edges are heavily ground, and after fluting, the base was often further thinned. A technological trait seen on most Clovis points is the presence of four or five broad flakes removed across the face of the body during preform flaking. Clovis points have biconvex cross sections and are thicker and heavier than the Folsom point. These points have been found with mammoth skeletons at the Miami kill-site in the Texas Panhandle. It is the earliest diagnostic point form known in North America. The Gault site in Williamson County, Texas, is perhaps the largest scientifically excavated Clovis occupation site in the New World.

Clovis point manufacture has been described for various regions of North America (e.g., Morrow 1995). Caches of Clovis age have been found in several states. Distinctive artifacts associated with Clovis include large polyhedral cores (this book), blades (Collins 1999), intricately engraved stones (this book), and a variety of bifaces, including many examples of points broken during the manufacturing process (Collins and Hemmings 2005).

Distribution: Widespread throughout Texas (see Bever and Meltzer 2007) and across North America. **Period:** Paleo-Indian, ca. 9200 BC. **Sites:** Miami (Roberts County); Lubbock Lake; Scharbauer; Clovis (N.Mex.); 41BL323; 41JF50; 41DN479; 41TV1364; McFaddin Beach (41JF50); Pavo Real.

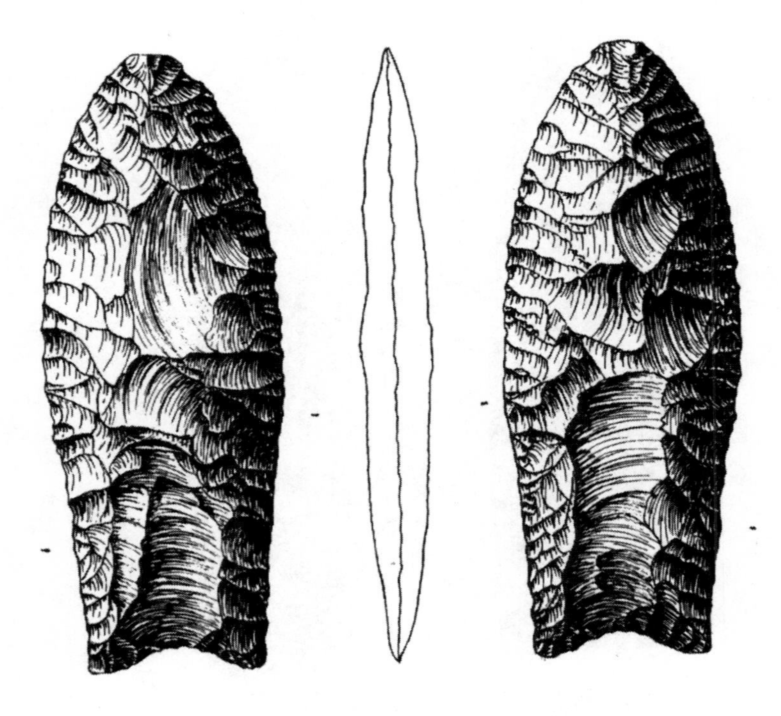

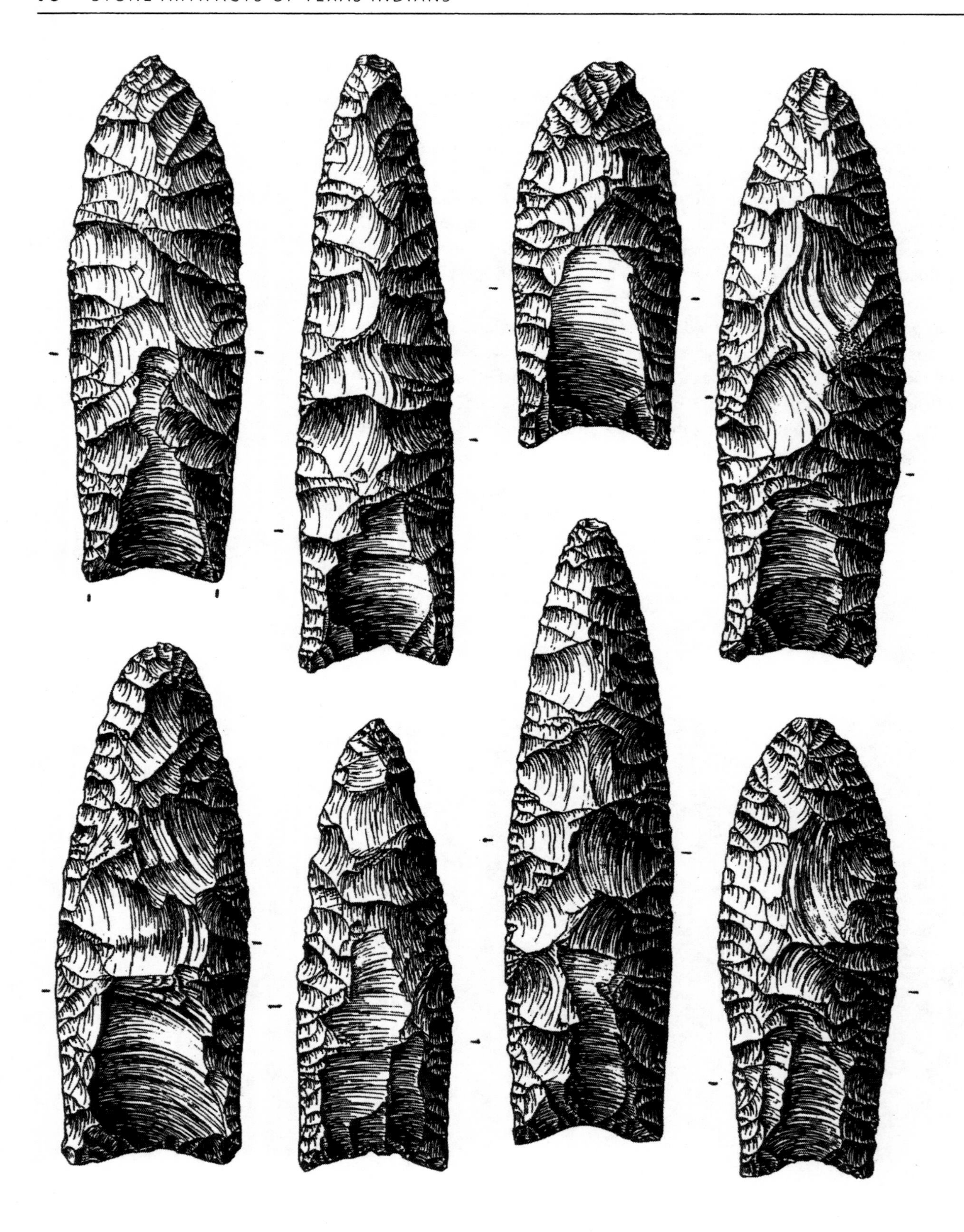

References: Bever and Meltzer 2007; Bousman et al. 2004; Bradley et al. 2010; Collins 1990, 2004; Collins and Hemmings 2005; Collins et al. 1990; Collins et al. 1991; Collins et al. 2003; Ferring 1990; Haynes 1966; Haynes and Agogino 1966; C. Howard 1990; E. Howard 1935a, 1935b; Johnson and Holliday 1980; Meltzer 1987; Morrow 1995; Sellards 1952; Suhm and Jelks 1962; Wendorf et al. 1955; Wormington 1957.

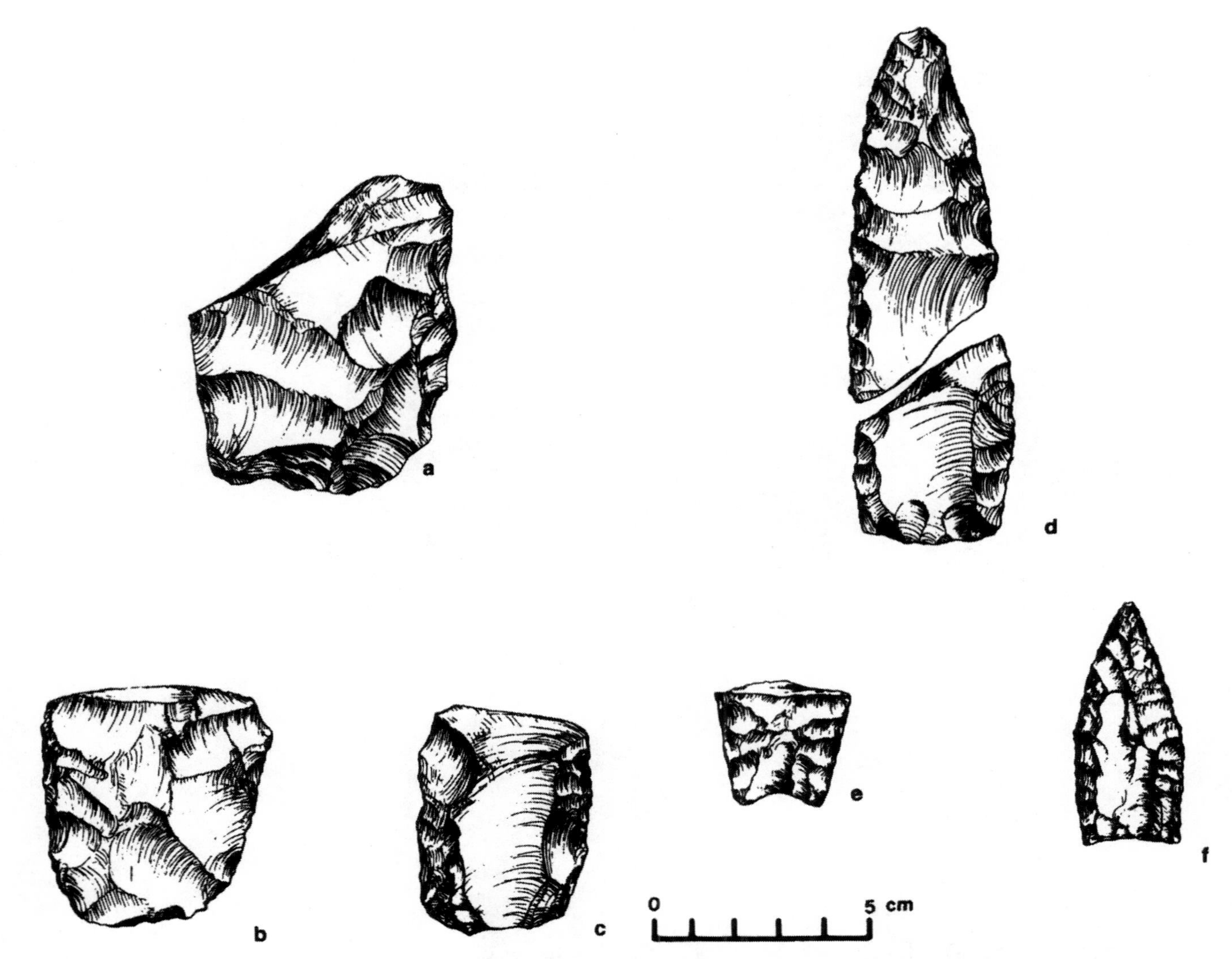

Clovis artifacts from Kincaid Rockshelter. a, b, early reduction stage failures; c, fluting failure; d, thinning failure after first fluting; e, obsidian base fragment; f, resharpened Clovis point. From Collins et al. 1989. Courtesy of *Current Research in the Pleistocene*.

CONEJO

This is a subtriangular point with shoulders that have pointed barbs that "turn" back toward the stem. The expanding stem is formed by corner notches, the base is often concave, and lateral edges are usually convex.

Distribution: Lower Pecos, upper south Texas, and occasionally the Big Bend area. **Period:** Late Archaic. **Sites:** Bear Creek; Devil's Mouth; Amistad Reservoir; Castle Canyon; 41DM59.

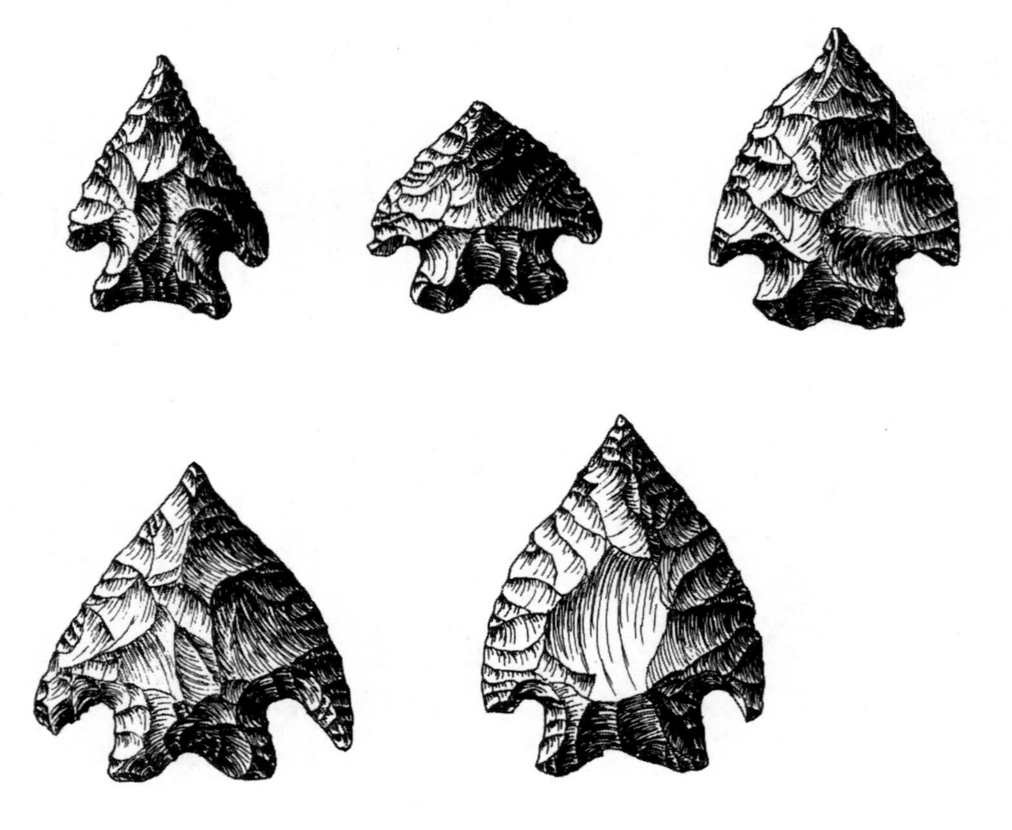

References: Graham and Davis 1958; Greer 1966; Hester and Whatley 1992b; Johnson 1964; Marmaduke 1978.

DALTON

Distinctive features of this point are beveled lateral edges, often serrated, and a roughly parallel-sided haft area that is distinguished from the body by edge-dulling or a change in outline. The base is concave and thinned by one or more relatively large vertical flake scars on both faces. Considerable variation in the point probably reflects morphological changes as well as use, resharpening, and probably temporal and/or regional variations (Johnson 1989b, 18).

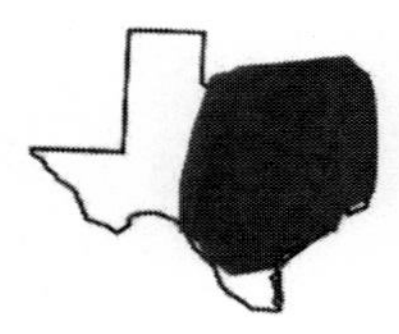

Distribution: Northeast Texas. Similar points found in the Southeast, including Arkansas, Missouri, and Oklahoma. **Period:** Paleo-Indian, ca. 8500 BC–7900 BC (according to Goodyear 1982, 382). **Sites:** McFaddin Beach; Sloan (Ark.); Chowning collection; Conway, Faulkner, and Perry counties; Big Eddy, (Mo.). Courtesy of Leslie C. "Skip" Stewart-Abernathy.

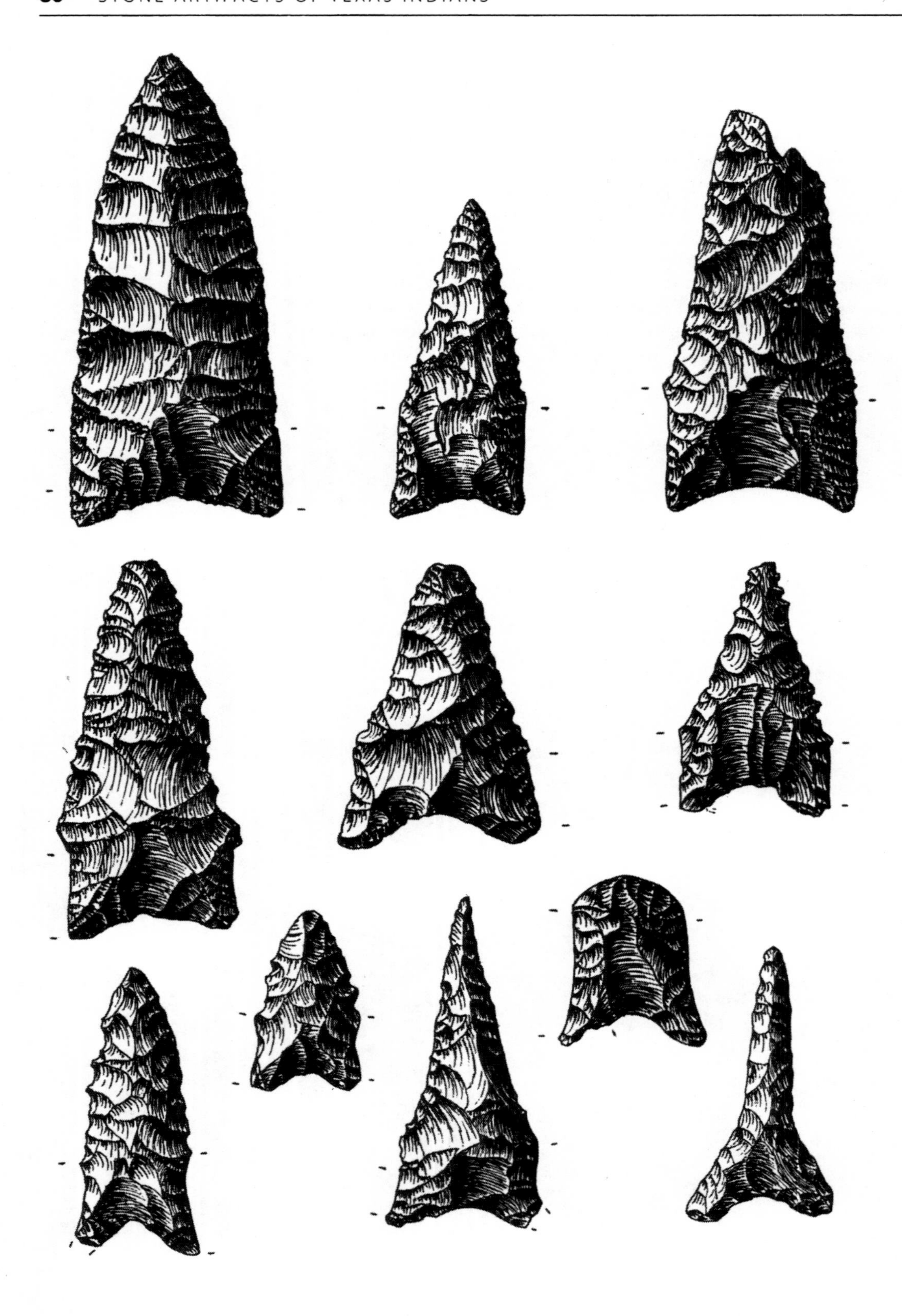

References: Ballenger 2001; Bousman, Baker, and Kerr 2004; Ensor 1987; Goodyear 1974, 1982; Johnson 1989b; Logan 1952; Luchterhand 1970; Morse 1997; Morse and Goodyear 1973a; Myers and Lambert 1983; Ray et al. 1998; Stright et al. 1999; Wood and McMillan 1967; Wormington 1957.

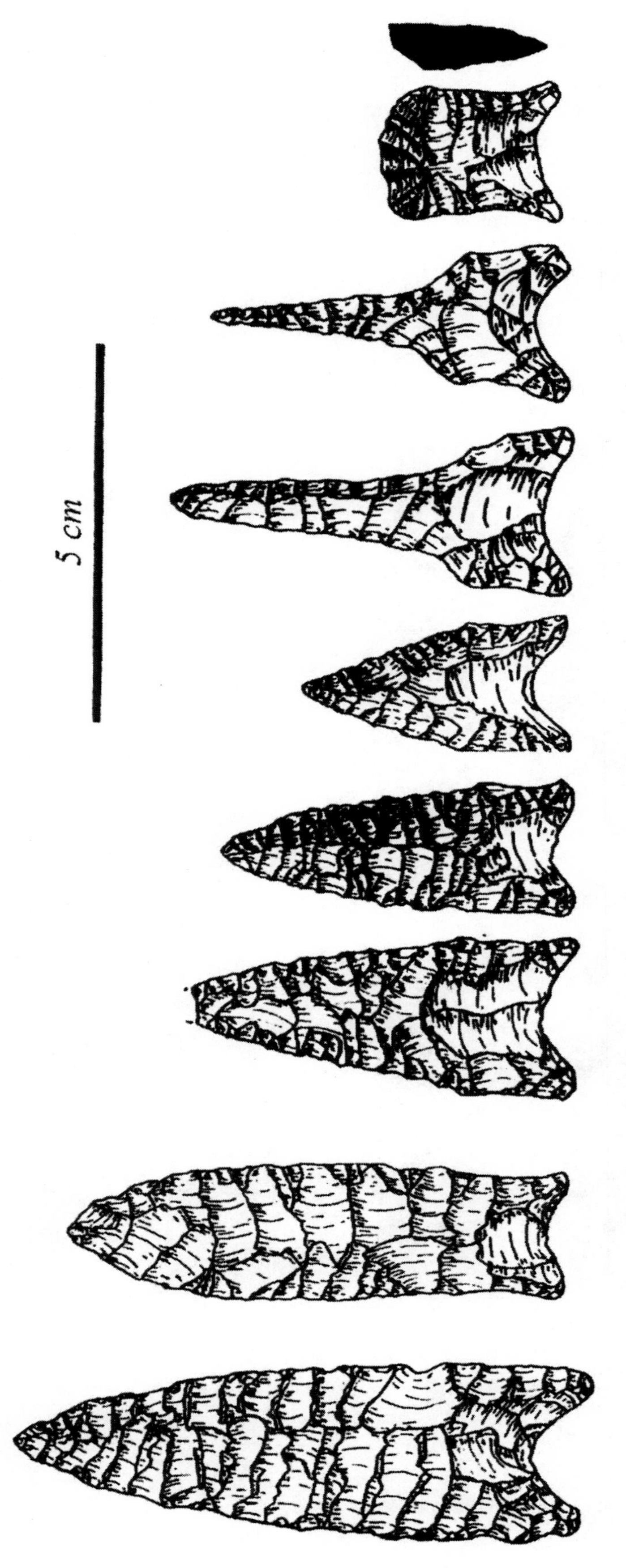

A sequence, left to right, of the resharpening/reworking patterns for Dalton points, showing how they change in shape and form. From Ballenger 2001; with permission of the Oklahoma Archeological Survey.

DARL

This is a small dart point with a long, slender body. Lateral edges are sometimes serrated. Specimens are carefully flaked (often parallel-flaked) with an expanding or rectangular stem. The lateral edges and stem are sometimes beveled. Basal edges vary from straight to concave.

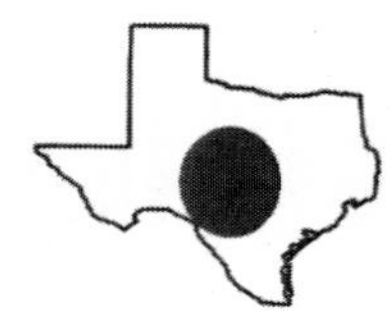

Distribution: Central Texas and eastward onto the coastal plain; north central Texas and northern parts of south Texas. **Period:** Transitional Archaic, ca. AD 200. **Sites:** Loeve-Fox; Tombstone Bluff; Jetta Court; Evoe Terrace; 41TV933; 41HY209M; Harrell; High Bluff.

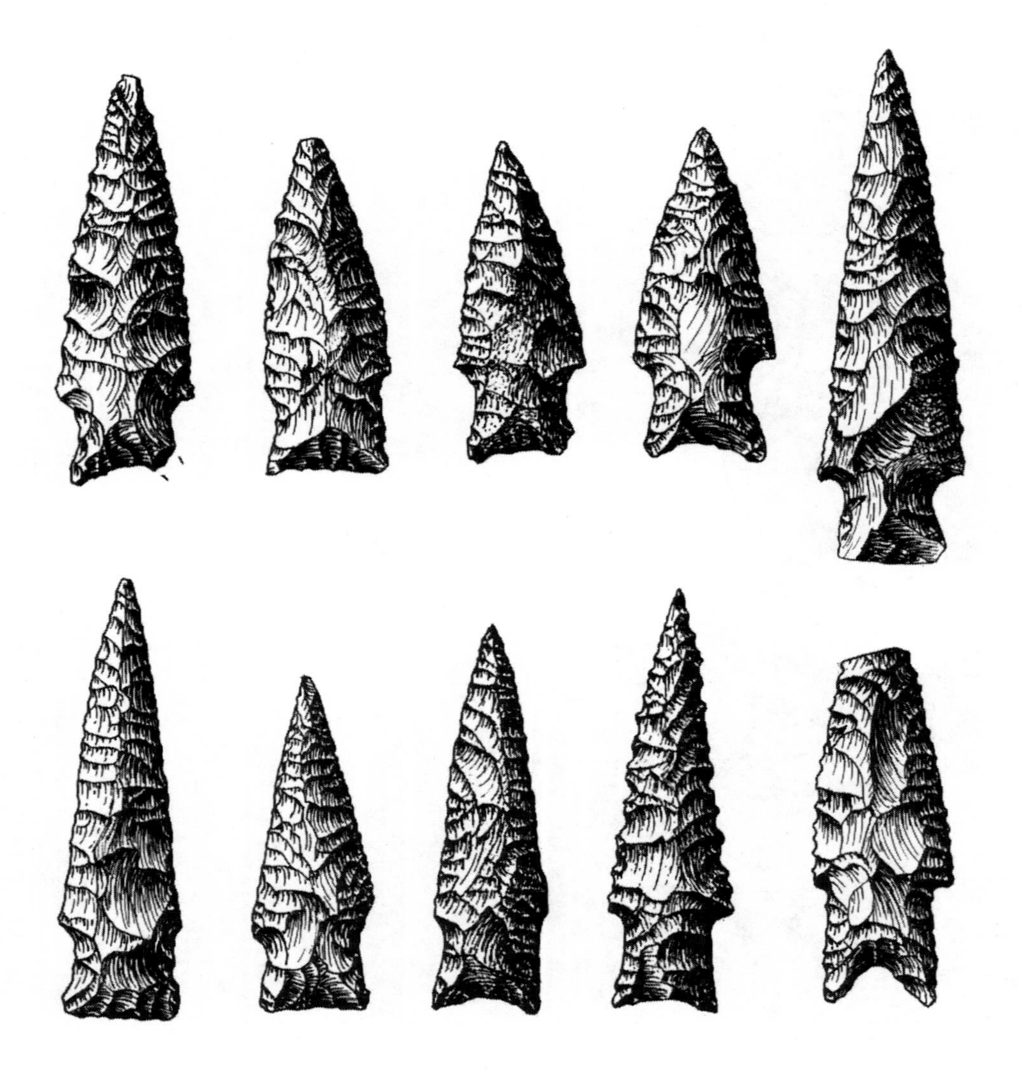

References: Flinn and Flinn 1968; Kotter et al. 1985; Prewitt 1981a; Ricklis and Collins 1994; Sorrow, Shafer, and Ross 1967; Suhm and Jelks 1962; http://www.texasbeyondhistory.net/; Wesolowsky et al. 1976.

DELHI

The Delhi point (Ford and Webb 1956) is a type that occurs within the Poverty Point Phase centered in Louisiana. Webb and colleagues (n.d.) separates it from the Motley type. Specimens are described as "pleasingly symmetrical . . . and well made," with rectangular stems that are often slightly concave. The distal portion is long, with straight to slightly concave lateral edges. Justice (1987, 179) further describes them as biconvex in cross section and, sometimes, barbed shoulders that project downward.

Distribution: Eastern Texas; Trinity River drainage; Polk and San Jacinto counties, Texas. **Period:** ca. 1300–200 BC, according to Justice (1987, 179). **Sites:** McFaddin Beach (41JF50); Resch (41HS16); Oak Hill (41RK214); Poverty Point and Archaic sites, La.

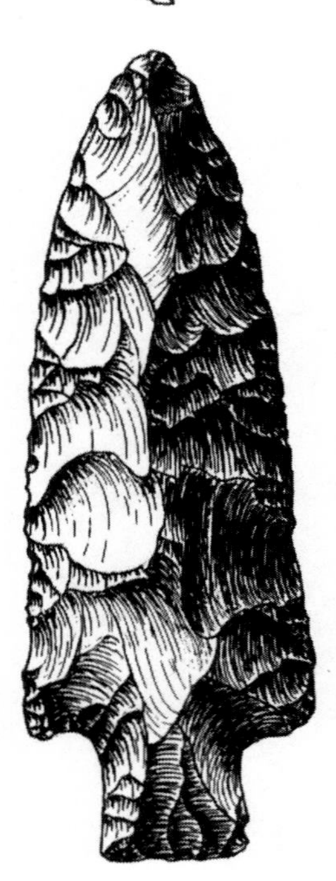

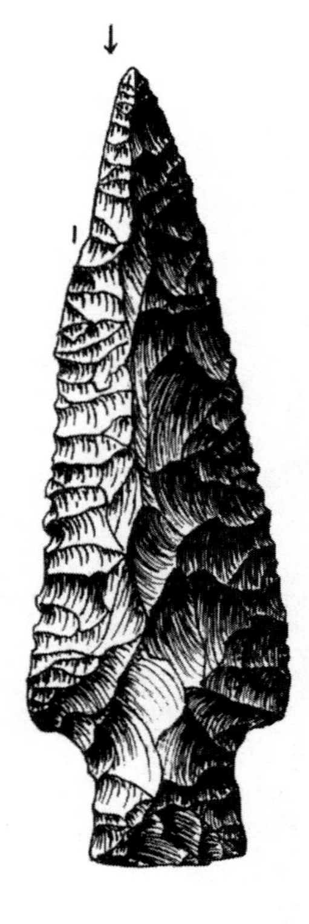

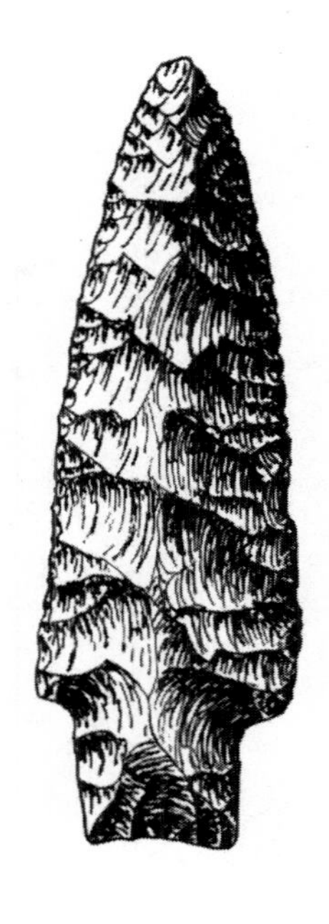

References: Ford and Webb 1956; Justice 1987; Rogers et al. 1997; Webb et al. (n.d.).

DESMUKE

This small, lozenge-shaped point has a characteristic contraction from the lower part of the body toward the base. The maximum width of Desmuke is in the basal one-third of the point. The lateral edges are often alternately beveled and may be slightly serrated. Impact fractures are common, as is the use of heat-treated cherts. Actual specimens from this type are very restricted geographically, and reports of "Desmuke" points from south central Texas are in error, especially when "dated" to much earlier time frames.

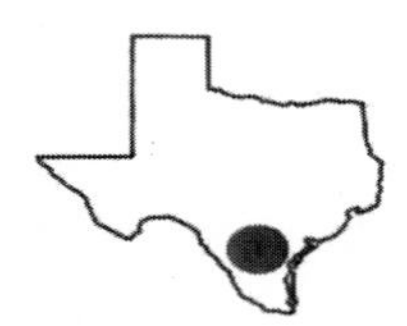

Distribution: Mainly in a small area of south Texas, between the middle Nueces River and the Rio Grande. **Period:** Late Archaic. **Sites:** Oulline; La Perdida; San Miguel Creek; Duval County (41DV1,2,3); La Salle and McMullen counties; Webb County; Killam Ranch.

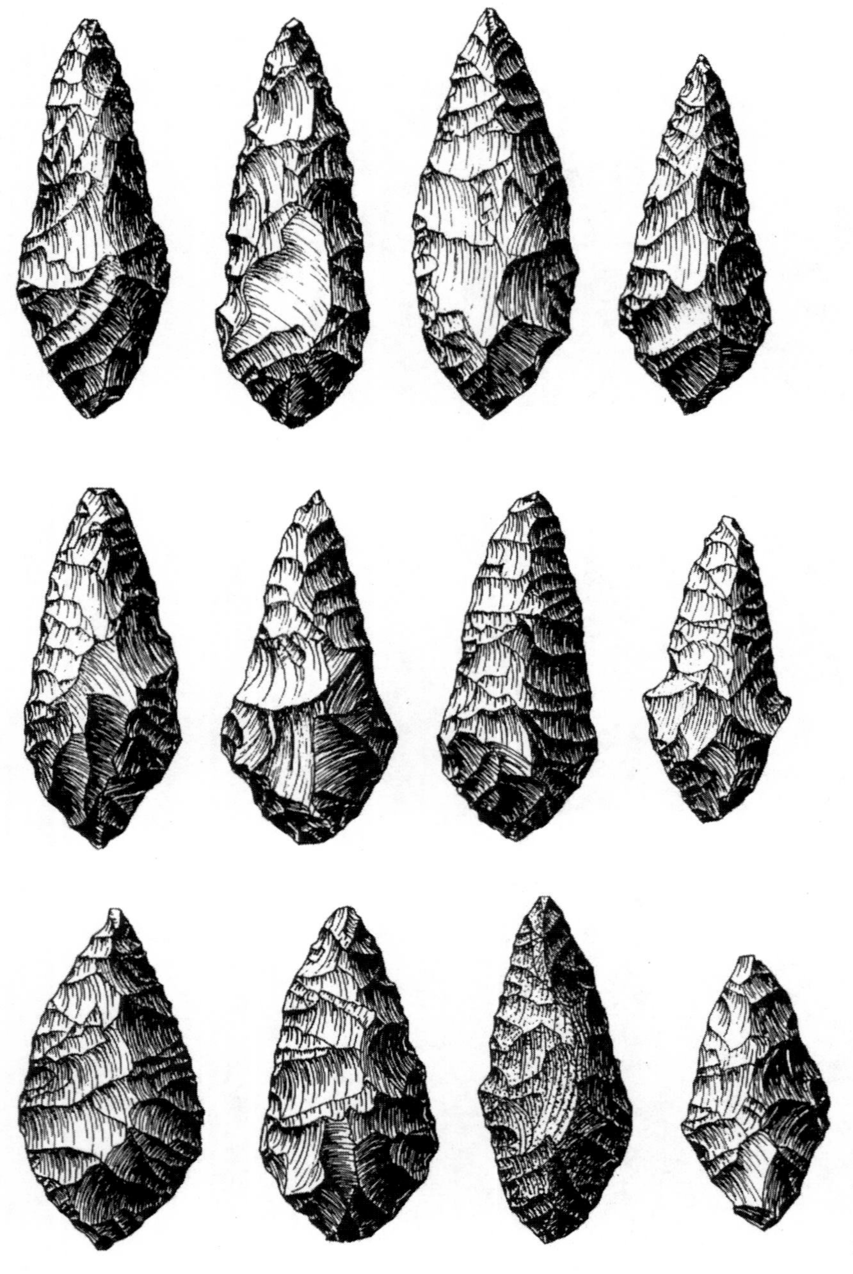

References: Bettis 1997; Hester 1968, 1972b; Hester, White, and White 1969; Kelly 1989; Suhm and Jelks 1962; Thoms and Mandel 2007; Versar and Parsons 2008; Weir 1956.

DURAN

These small dart points are characterized by rounded to expanding stems and by one or two notches in the lateral edges. The type was defined by Taylor (1966) for the Cuatro Cienegas region of Coahuila. These do not occur in Texas, despite claims on some artifact dealer websites. There are some notched specimens similar to Duran in parts of the Big Bend, but not enough is currently known about these artifacts. Complicating the Duran typology is the fact that, in Nuevo Leon, Coahuila, and into eastern Durango, there are a variety of points with multinotched lateral edges.

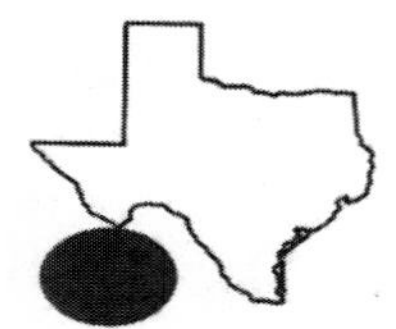

Distribution: Coahuila to eastern Durango. **Period:** Middle Archaic (Coahuila Complex of Taylor 1966). **Sites:** Cuatro Cienegas; Desierto de Charcos de Risa; eastern Durango.

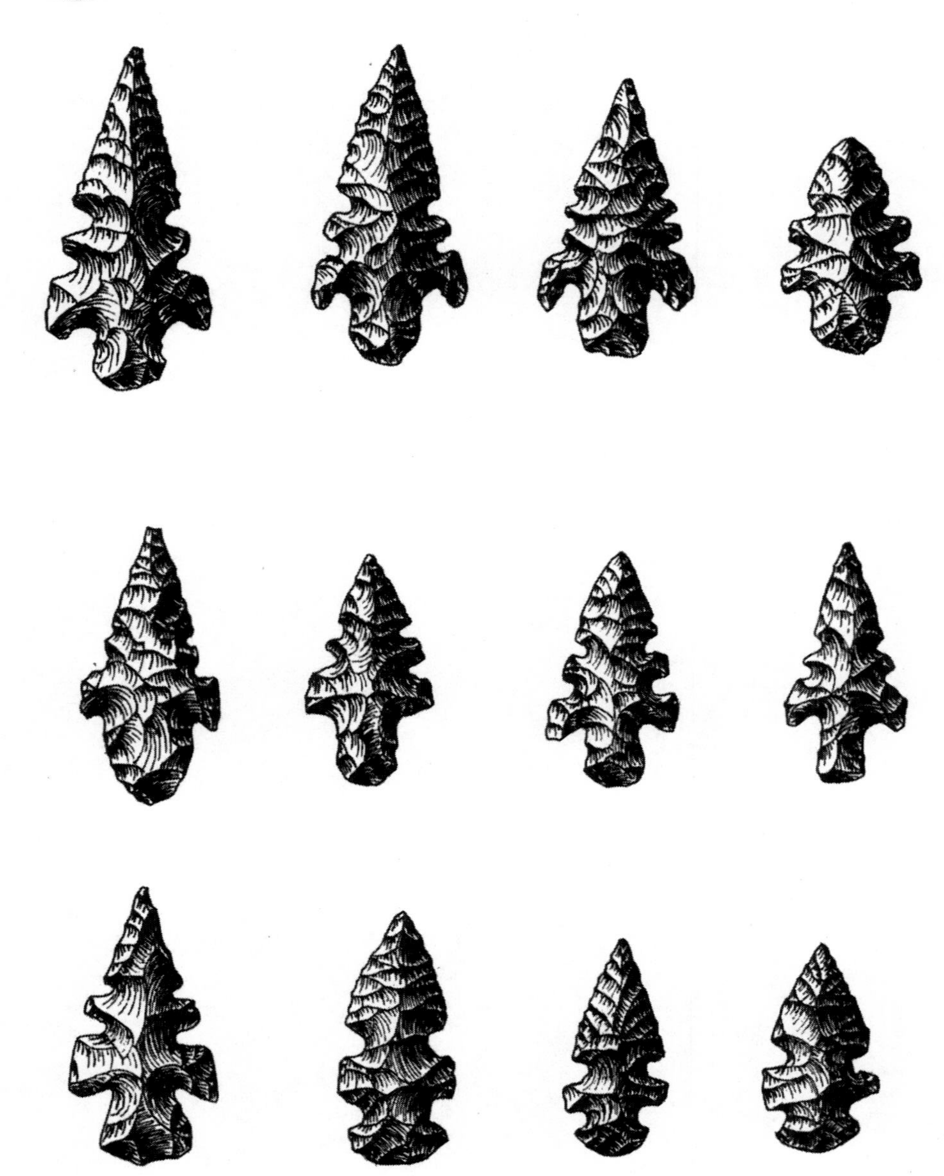

References: Heartfield 1975; Hester 2002a; Silva and Hester 1973; Taylor 1966.

EARLY STEMMED LANCEOLATE

Projectile points in this category have long, lanceolate outlines with weak shoulders forming ill-defined stems, the edges of which have been dulled. They have been found in loose association with other Paleo-Indian projectile points and are thought to date from that era. Much typological research is needed to define this group further; Kelly (1983b) tentatively included them in his Victoria type. A more definitive review of this type and the Victoria type has been done by K. M. Brown (2008). The top point on the right and the first on the second line look the most like Brown's Victoria point. Due to the ongoing confusion over what constitutes a "Victoria" point, we suggest that the Early Stemmed Lanceolate is the preferable label (see Flaigg 1995).

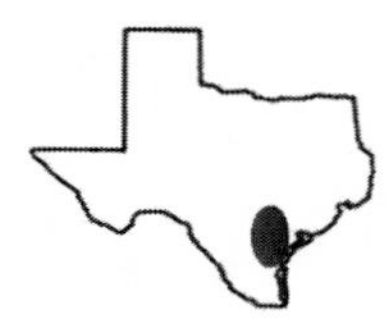

Distribution: Central portion of the coastal plain, especially in Victoria County, but similar forms extending into central Texas. **Period:** Late Paleo-Indian. **Sites:** Johnston-Heller; Gillespie County; Wilson-Leonard; Granite Beach; Berclair; 41BP19; Berger Bluff; Olmos Basin.

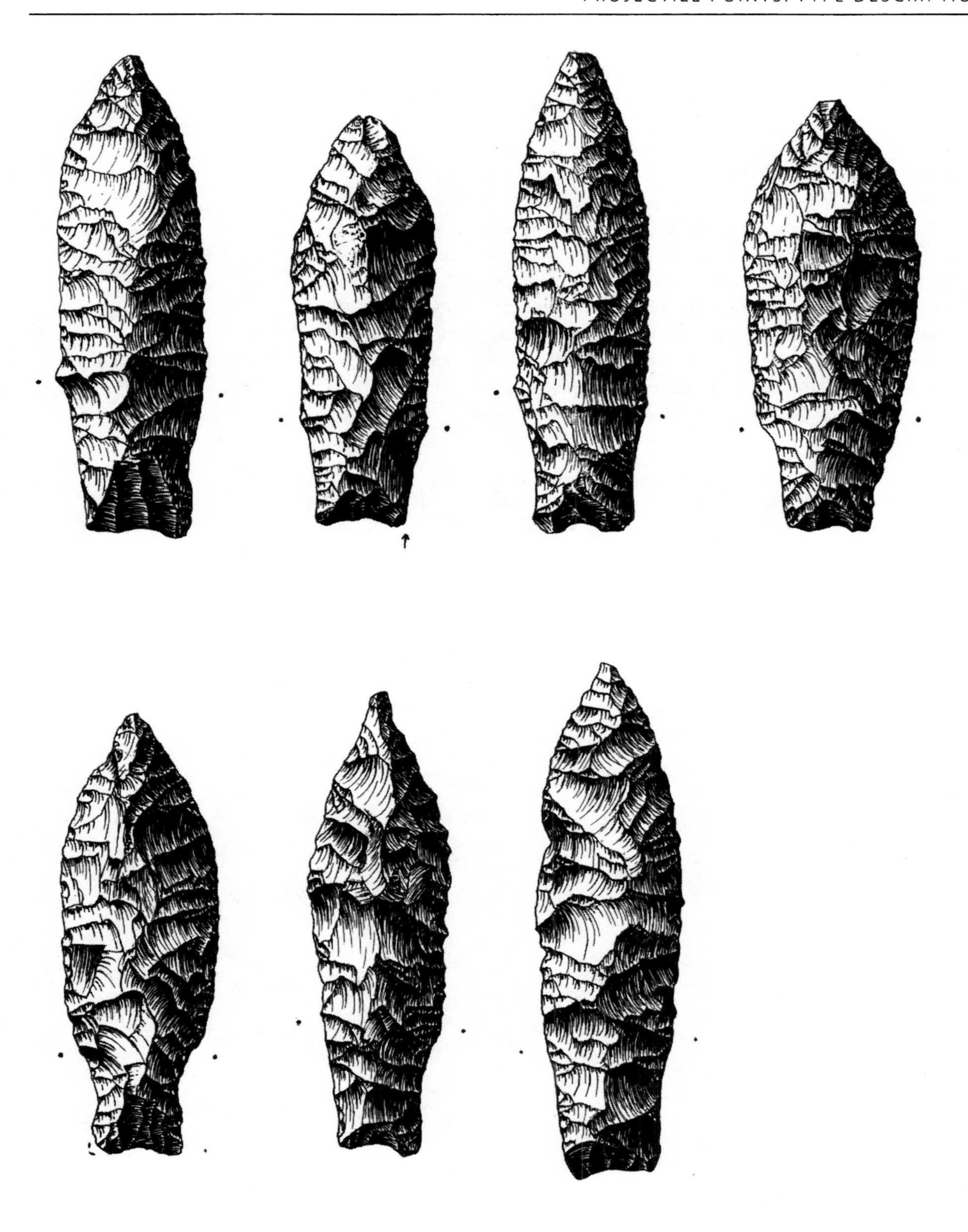

References: Bement et al. 1989; Birmingham and Hester 1976; Brown 2008; Kenneth M. Brown, personal communication; Chandler 1994a; Crawford 1965; Flaigg 1995; Kelly 1983a; Thomas C. Kelly, personal communication; Sellards 1940; Frank A. Weir, personal communication.

EARLY TRIANGULAR

These are triangular points usually characterized by careful parallel-oblique flaking, straight to slightly concave bases, and alternately beveled lateral edges (which may also be slightly serrated). Because there has been considerable confusion in the typology of triangular points, we have used this descriptive name (following Hester 1971) for those triangular forms that occur in the late part of the Early Archaic. They are chronologically earlier than Tortugas points in southern Texas. In central Texas, such specimens have been called (by Kelley [1947]) Baird Beveled Blade and Taylor Thinned Base (or Taylor and Baird; Sorrow 1969). However, no specific attributes for clearly separating these two groups have yet been published. Indeed, Black and McGraw (1985) postulated that these specimens are knives, with the shapes changing through use and subsequent beveling (resharpening) of the lateral edges. However, a microwear study by Harry Iceland demonstrated minimal use of the lateral edges and, combined with a high frequency of impact fractures, argued that these are mainly projectile points (Decker et al. 2000: 256–63).

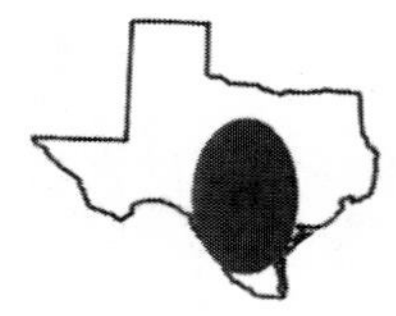

Distribution: North and south central, south, and southwest Texas; lower Pecos. **Period:** Overall, 5800–5700 BP; at Royal Coachman site, 4840–4779; [for Early Triangular and Bell: 41NU221, 5919–5336 BP; 41NU184, 5592–5326 BP; 41NU267, 4986–4862 BP]; at the Varga site, 3910–4820 BP. **Sites:** Panther Springs Creek; Landslide; La Jita; Dan Baker; Wounded Eye; 41BN107; Varga; Woodrow Heard; McKinzie; Royal Coachman; Montell Rockshelter.

References: Black and McGraw 1985; Coleman et al. 2001; Decker et al. 2000; Hester 1971; Kibler and Scott 2000; Luke 1980; Mahoney et al. 2003; Medlar 1991; Peter 1982b; Quigg et al. 2008; Ricklis 1995; Schmiedlin 2000a; Sorrow, Shafer, and Ross 1967; Suhm and Jelks 1962; S. Van der Veer, personal communication.

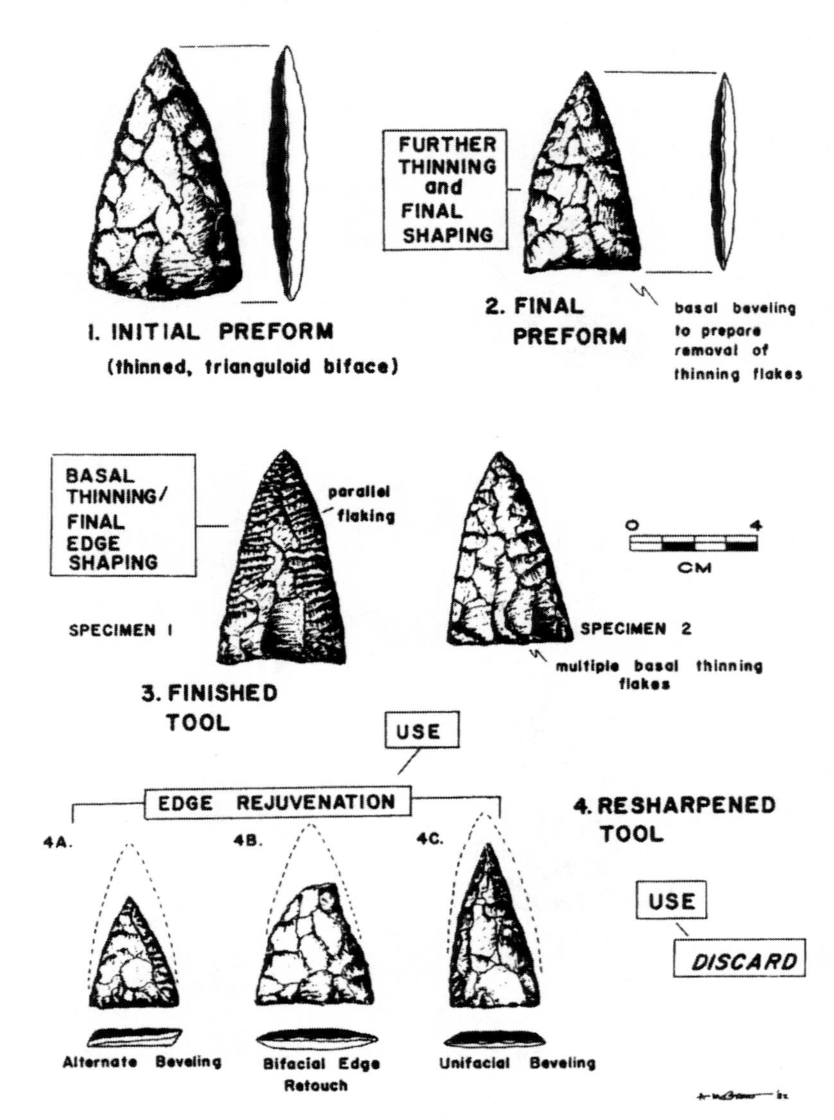

"Thinned-based Early Triangular" manufacturing and resharpening sequence model. From Black and McGraw (1985, fig. 24). By permission of the Center for Archaeological Research, University of Texas at San Antonio.

EDGEWOOD

This short, triangular corner-notched point has prominent to well-barbed shoulders and a widely expanding stem. The basal edge of the stem is concave to straight base, distinguishing it from Ellis points.

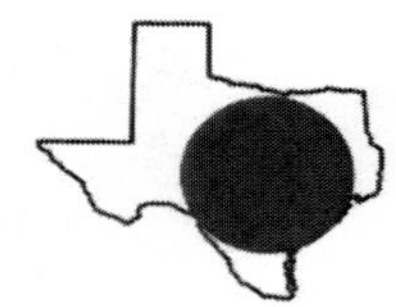

Distribution: Common in northeast Texas but also known in central and south Texas, including the coast. **Period:** Transitional Archaic. **Sites:** Mackin; Pecan Springs; Cooper Reservoir; Jake Martin.

References: Davis and Davis 1960; Duffield 1959; Mallouf 1976; Prikryl 1990; Sorrow 1966; Suhm and Jelks 1962.

ELAM

This small point has slight to prominent shoulders and a parallel-sided stem that is approximately one-third to one-half the length of the point. The stem edges are sometimes ground. This stubby form features heavily resharpened distal ends, and it may well be that many such points are actually other types, such as Ellis and Trinity.

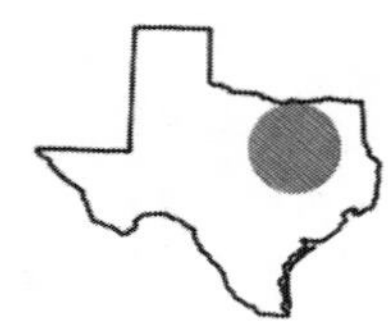

Distribution: North central Texas into east Texas. **Period:** Late Archaic. **Sites:** Yarbrough; Limerick; Milton; Jake Martin; 41DN6; Trinity River drainage.

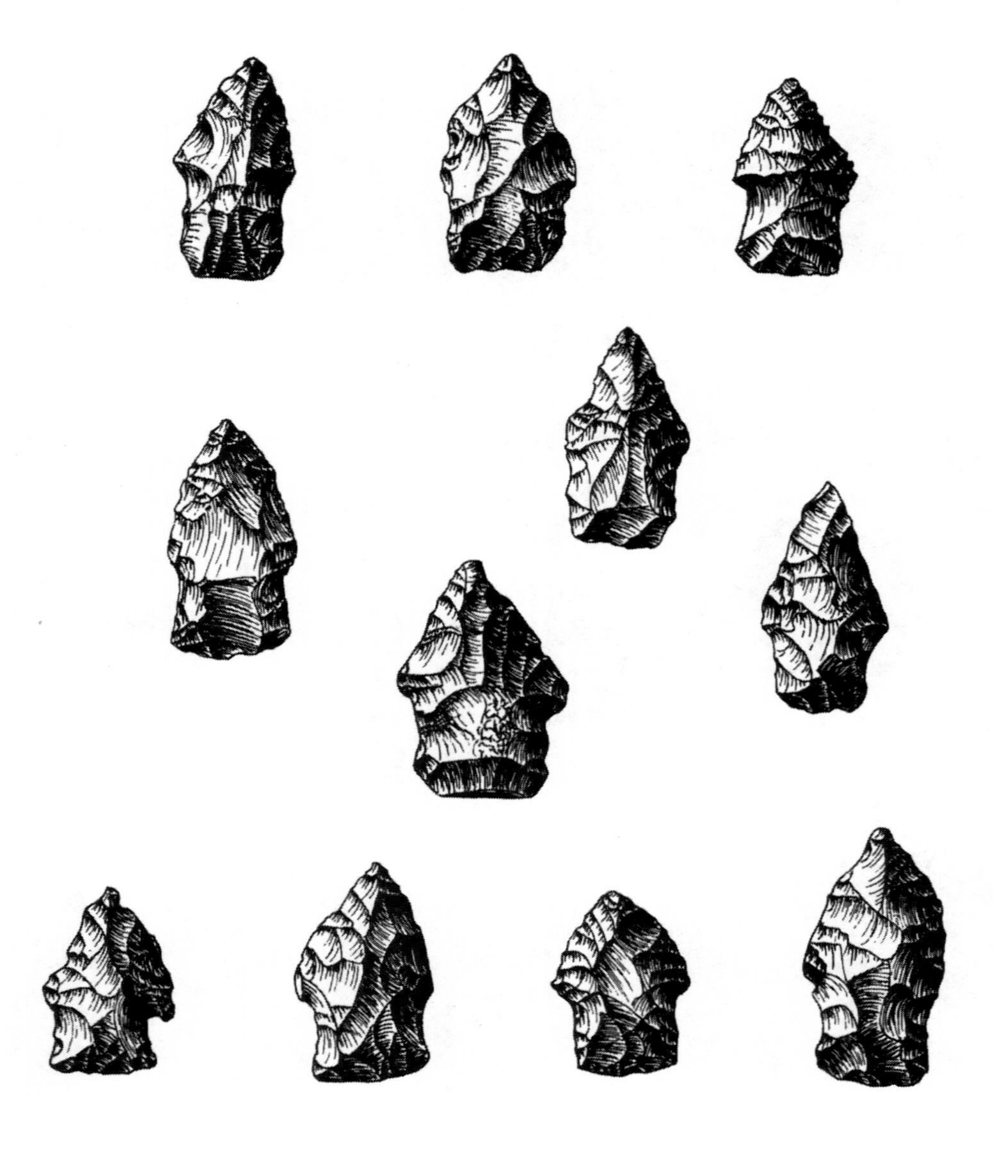

References: Crook and Harris 1954b; Davis and Davis 1960; Duffield 1961; Fields 1988; Johnson 1962b; Prikryl 1990.

ELLIS

These points have a short, thick body; shallow corner notches or side notches; barbs; and an expanding stem. It is often difficult to distinguish morphologically from Edgewood and Ensor, and Prikryl (1990) compares them to Marcos.

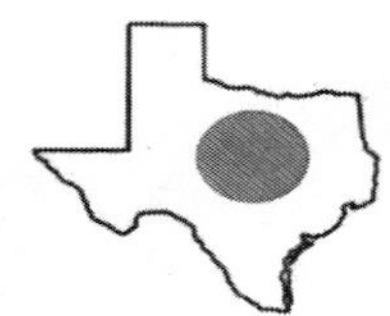

Distribution: Primarily north central to northeast Texas and into Oklahoma; points typed as Ellis are occasionally found in south and central Texas, Panhandle, west Texas, and also adjoining areas of Louisiana and Arkansas. **Period:** Late to Transitional Archaic, ca. 1000 BC. **Sites:** George C. Davis; Tankersley Creek; Yarbrough; Mackin; Ray Roberts Reservoir.

References: Anthony and Brown 1994; Johnson 1962b; Mallouf 1976; Newell and Krieger 1949; Prikryl 1990; Shafer 1973; Story et al. 1990; Suhm and Jelks 1962; C. Webb, personal communication; Young 1981.

ENSOR

This point varies considerably in all dimensions, but broad expanding stems, shallow side or corner notches, and generally straight bases tend to identify the type. Specimens with a V-shaped basal notch are sometimes called "Ensor-Frio." Typology is sometimes difficult, because there appears to be much gradation of basal forms from Frio to Ensor. Additionally, Harry Shafer (personal communication) suggests that there are two major variations in Ensor forms. The corner-notched version occurs mainly between the Colorado and Brazos rivers, along and on both sides of the escarpment. The markedly side-notched specimens are found in the lower Pecos and eastward to San Antonio with an admixture of both between San Antonio and the Colorado River.

Ensor is a key marker of the Transitional Archaic, mainly in campsites, but also in burials and cemeteries.

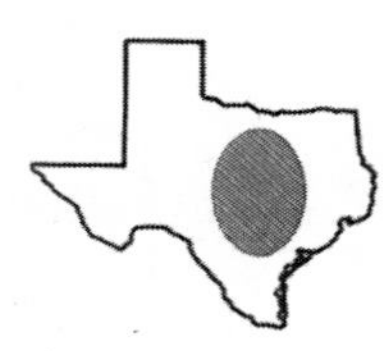

Distribution: Widespread in central and south Texas, coastal plain, the lower Pecos, and west Texas. **Period:** Transitional Archaic, ca. 200 BC–AD 600 (or later). **Sites:** Loeve-Fox; La Jita; Choke Canyon; Panther Springs Creek; Smith Creek Bridge, Silo, 41LK21.

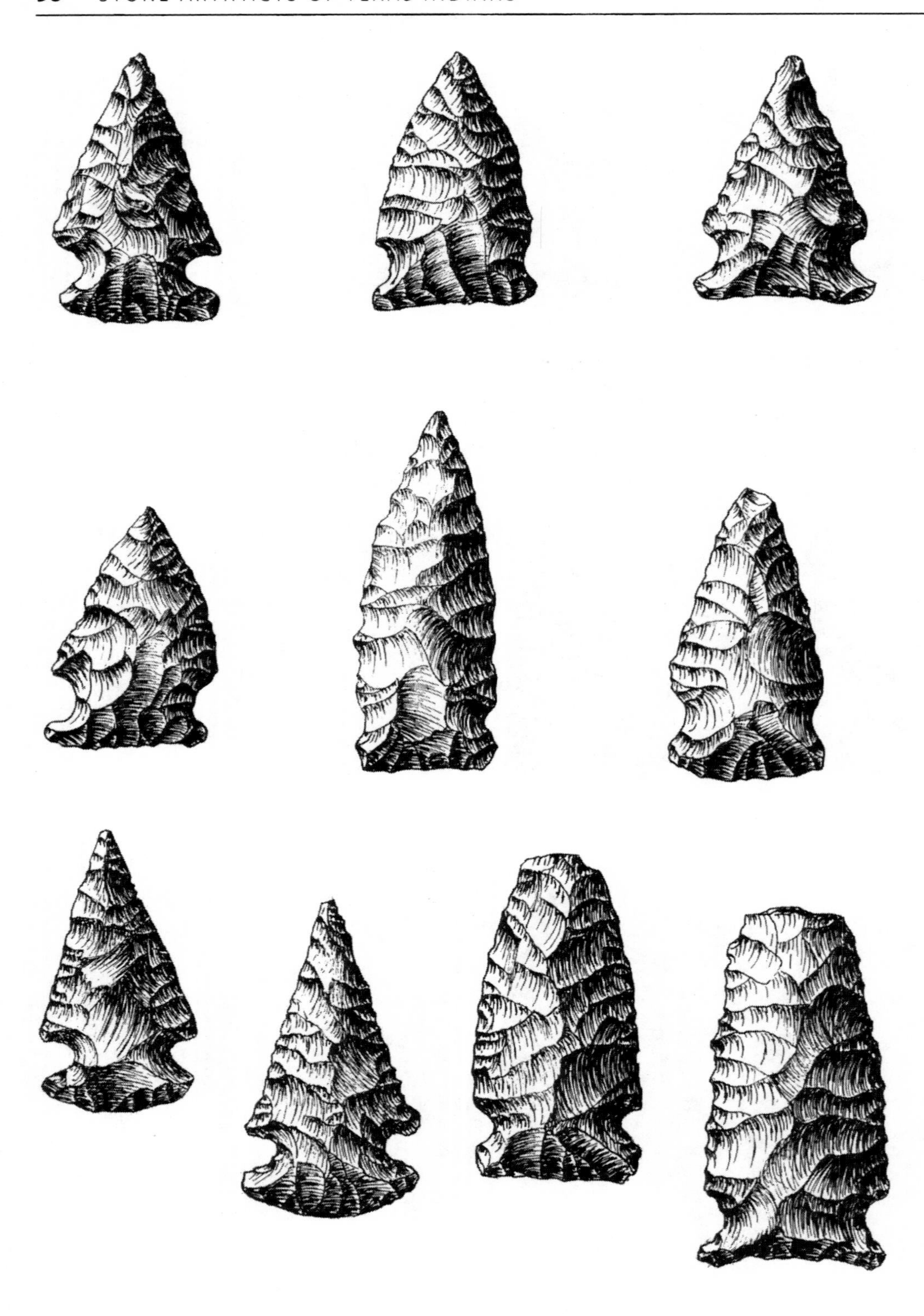

References: Black and McGraw 1985; Hall, Black, and Graves 1982; Hester 1971, 1989b, 2005; Hudler et al. 2003; Lovata 1997; Prewitt 1981a; Story and Bryant 1966.

EVANS

This thick, medium- to large-sized point has mildly convex lateral edges; well-defined shoulders; and a straight to expanded to bulbous stem. The base is sometimes lightly smoothed. Its distinguishing trait is a set of notches cut into the lateral edges a short distance above the shoulders, usually by the bifacial removal of single, deep flakes, leaving sharp edges. Some have finely serrated lateral edges above and below the notches.

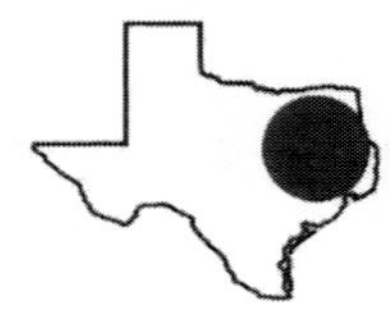

Distribution: Louisiana, Arkansas, and occasionally east Texas. **Period:** Middle Archaic, ca. 2600 BC–1000 BC. **Sites:** (Texas) Gregg County (Sabine River); Newton County; Lake Livingston; (Louisiana) Poverty Point; Jaketown; Caddo Lake; Cowpen Slough; Vernon Parish, Fort Polk (La.).

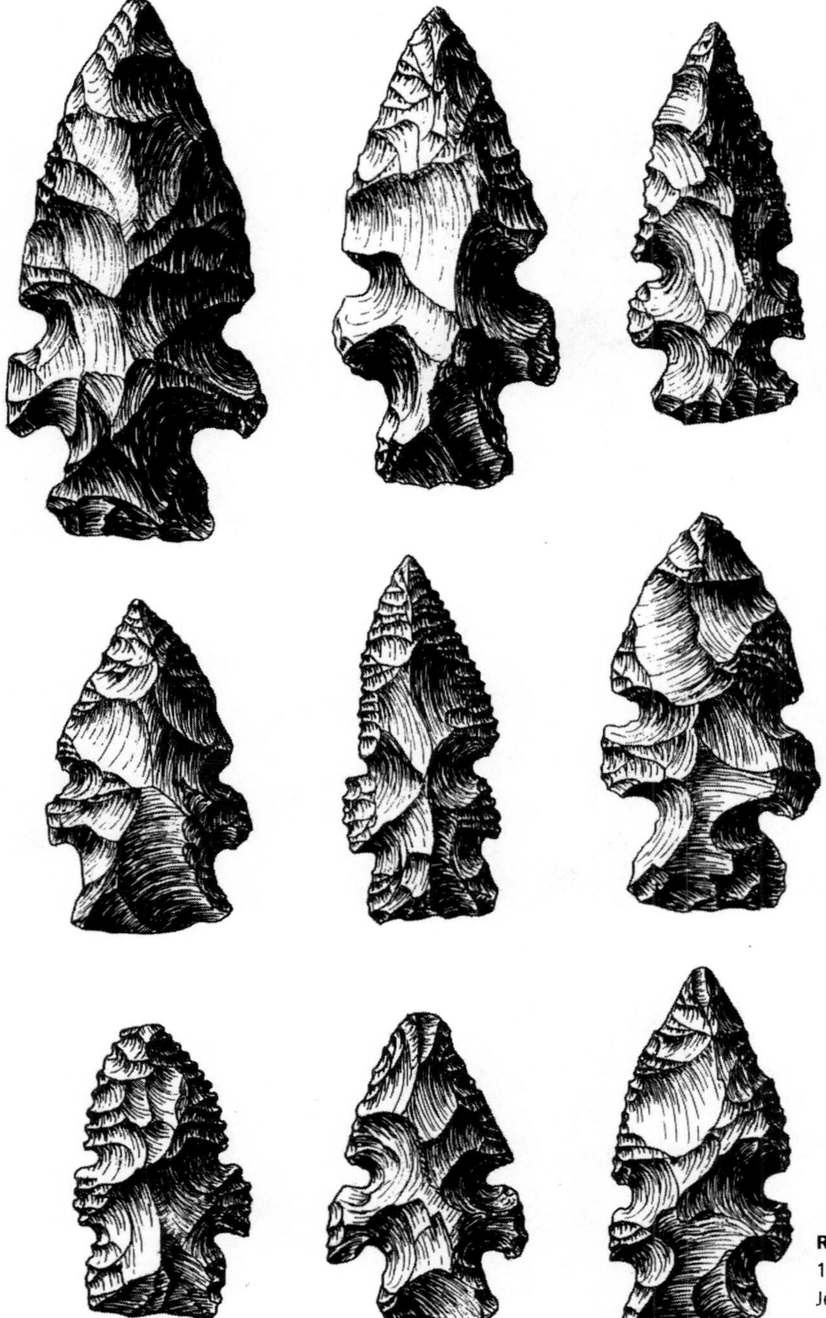

References: Anderson and Smith 2003; Baker and Webb 1978; Bell 1958; Ford et al. 1955; Ford and Webb 1956; Jeter and Williams 1989; Jones 1957; Clarence H. Webb, personal communication.

EVANT

This point has long, narrow, parallel-sided stems. The bases are straight, slightly convex, or slightly concave. Shoulders can be moderate to slight and slant downward toward the base. The bodies are usually slender with straight or fairly convex edges. Because of their simple form, they can be confused with Kent. They are best defined chronologically where they are coeval with Nolan and predate Pedernales, and geographically where they tend to be restricted to the Lampasas Cut Plain (Harry Shafer, personal communication). Schuetz (1957, fig. 37) called these "San Gabriel" points, but the type was never formally defined.

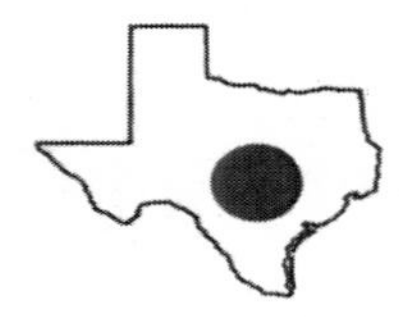

Distribution: Lampasas Cut Plain, Central Texas, cluster in Williamson, Western Bell, Coryell and Hamilton counties along the Lampasas and upper San Gabriel River, Nolan, Cowhouse Creek and middle Leon River drainages. **Period:** Early Archaic.

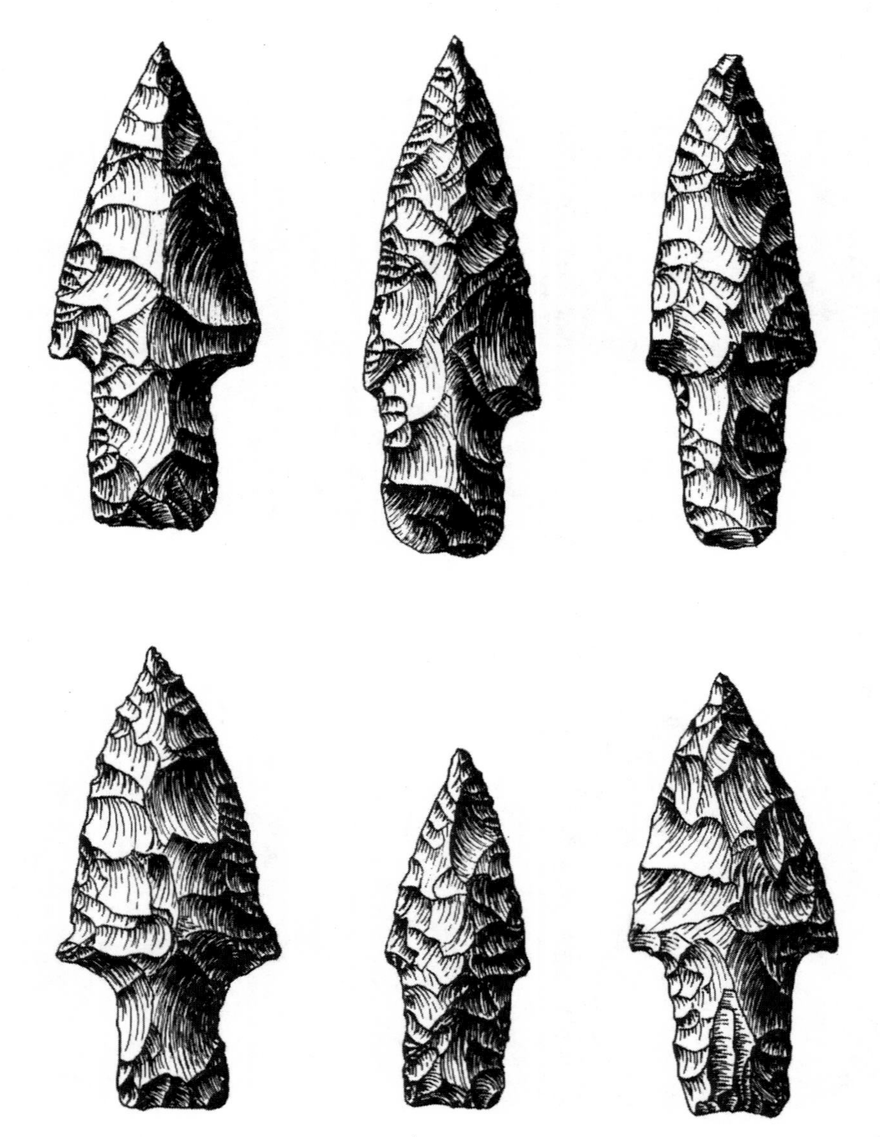

References: Abbott and Trierweiler 1995 (classified as Bulverde); Schuetz 1957; Shafer 1963; Sorrow 1969; Sorrow et al. 1967; Trierweiler 1996 (classified as Kent).

FAIRLAND

This large, broad, triangular point has an expanding stem formed by broad corner notches that produce a strongly flaring base, usually as wide, or wider, than the shoulders. The base has a wide, deep concavity sometimes with fine chipping along the edges. Specimens can be confused with Edgewood and Ellis points. Additionally, at some sites, Ensor, Frio, and Fairland forms overlap, making separation into "types" very difficult (Karbula 2000).

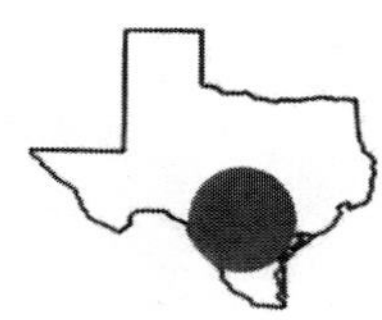

Distribution: Principally central Texas but examples known from south Texas and the lower Pecos. **Period:** Transitional Archaic. **Sites:** Greenhaw; Loeve-Fox; Choke Canyon; Perry Calk; Panther Springs Creek; Eckols; Millican Bench.

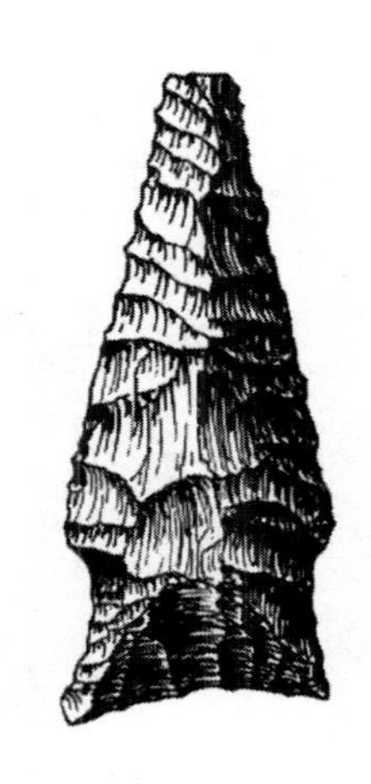

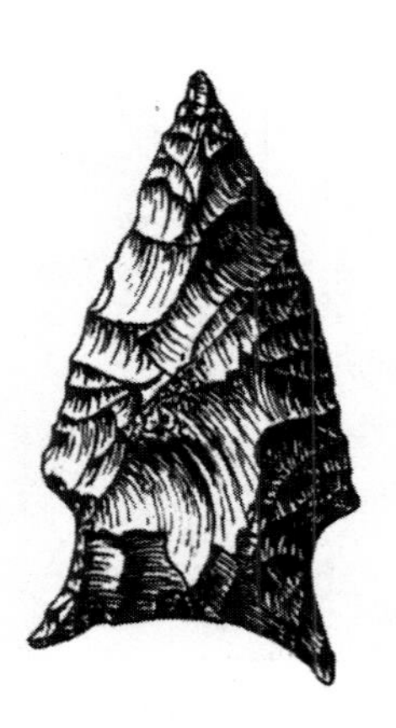

References: Collins 1969; Hall, Black, and Graves 1982; Karbula 2000; Mauldin et al. 2004; Prewitt 1974a; Suhm and Jelks 1962; Weir 1979.

FIRSTVIEW

Examples of the Firstview type are parallel-flaked, broad to relatively narrow, lanceolate points with convex lateral edges that tend to expand gently from the base to midpoint. Points are biconvex in cross section, and the lower lateral edges are heavily ground, with a predominantly straight base that is usually wedge shaped. Some are heavily reworked. Collins and colleagues (1997) consider Firstview to be part of the Cody Complex.

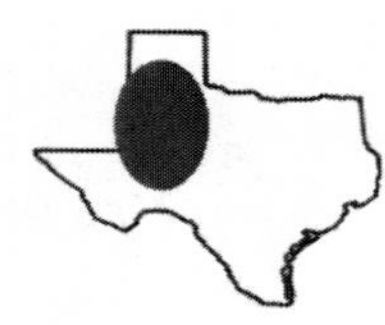

Distribution: Llano Estacado, southern Plains. **Period:** Paleo-Indian, ca. 6700 BC–6050 BC. **Sites:** Seminole-Rose (41GA11); Gaines County; Shifting Sands, Winkler County; Wyche Ranch, Winkler County.

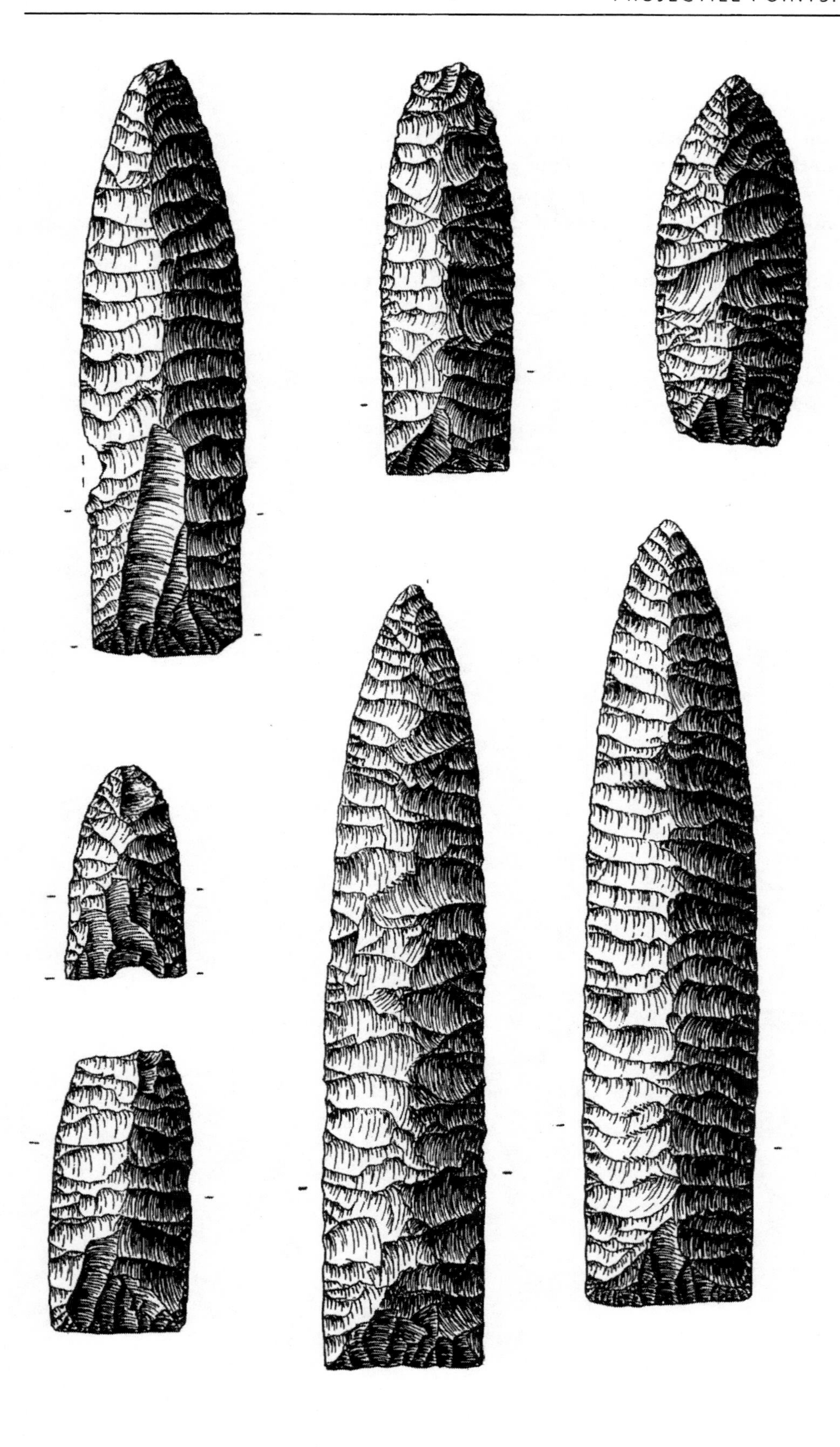

References: Collins et al. 1997; Holliday 1997; Holliday et al. 1983; Kibler 1991; Sellards 1952; Wheat 1972.

FOLSOM

This lanceolate point is easily recognized by its excellent chipping, thinness, and distinctive flutes that have usually been removed from both sides and extend almost to the tip. A nipple, sometimes found in the middle of the base (but often trimmed away), represents the platform for flute removal. An excellent overview of the type and its technological traits is found in works by Ahler and Geib (2000) and Clark and Collins (2002).

At some Folsom sites, large, "ultrathin" bifaces have been found to be part of the Folsom assemblage (Root et al. 1999). Some may have functioned as knives.

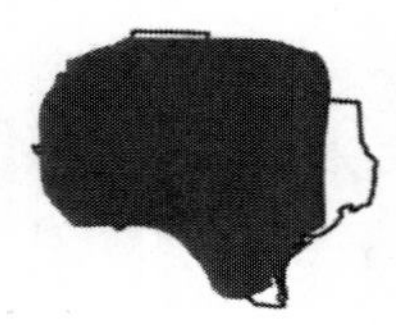

Distribution: Found from the Southwest, including the Trans-Pecos, the Great Plains of south central Canada to central and south Texas, and extending almost to the Gulf Coast. **Period:** Paleo-Indian, ca. 9050 BC–8150 BC. **Sites:** Folsom (N.Mex.); Chispa Creek, Lubbock Lake; Lipscomb; Pavo Real (41BX52); Shifting Sands, Winkler County, 41WK21; Sand Hills, Midland County; Golden Sands, Lee County, Texas; Fort Bliss.

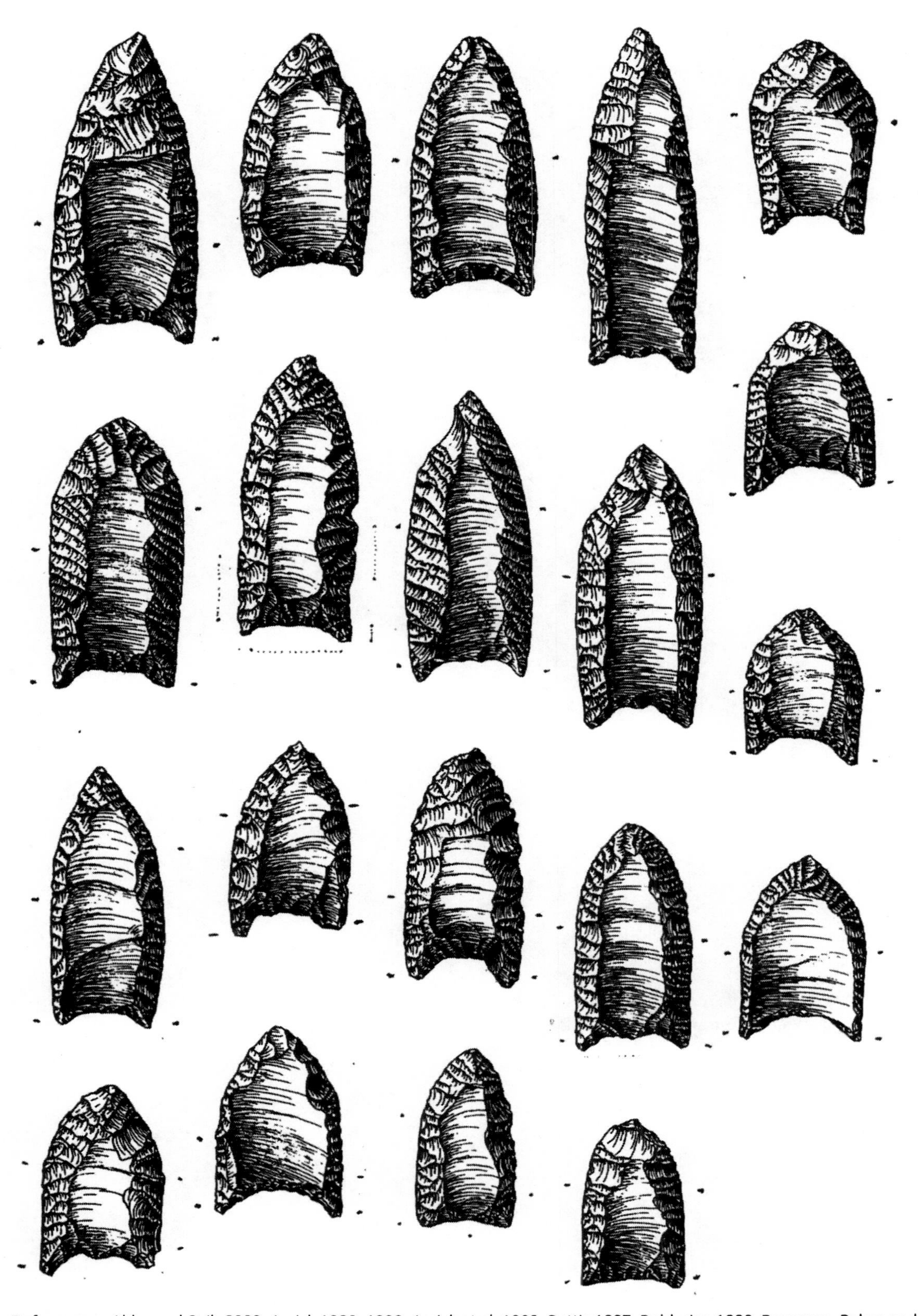

References: Ahler and Geib 2000; Amick 1990, 1999; Amick et al. 1989; Bettis 1997; Boldurian 1990; Bousman, Baker, and Kerr 2004; Brown 2007; Clark and Collins 2002; Collins et al. 2003; Dibble and Lorrain 1968; Figgins 1927; Harrison and Killen 1978; Henderson 1980; Hofman et al. 1990; Holliday et al. 1983; Kelly 1983a; Knudson 2007; Largent 1995; Largent and Waters 1990; Martinez 1990; Miller and Kenmotsu 2004; Rose 2011; Seebach 2004; Sollberger 1989; Suhm and Jelks 1962; Tunnell 1975; Tunnell and Johnson 2000.

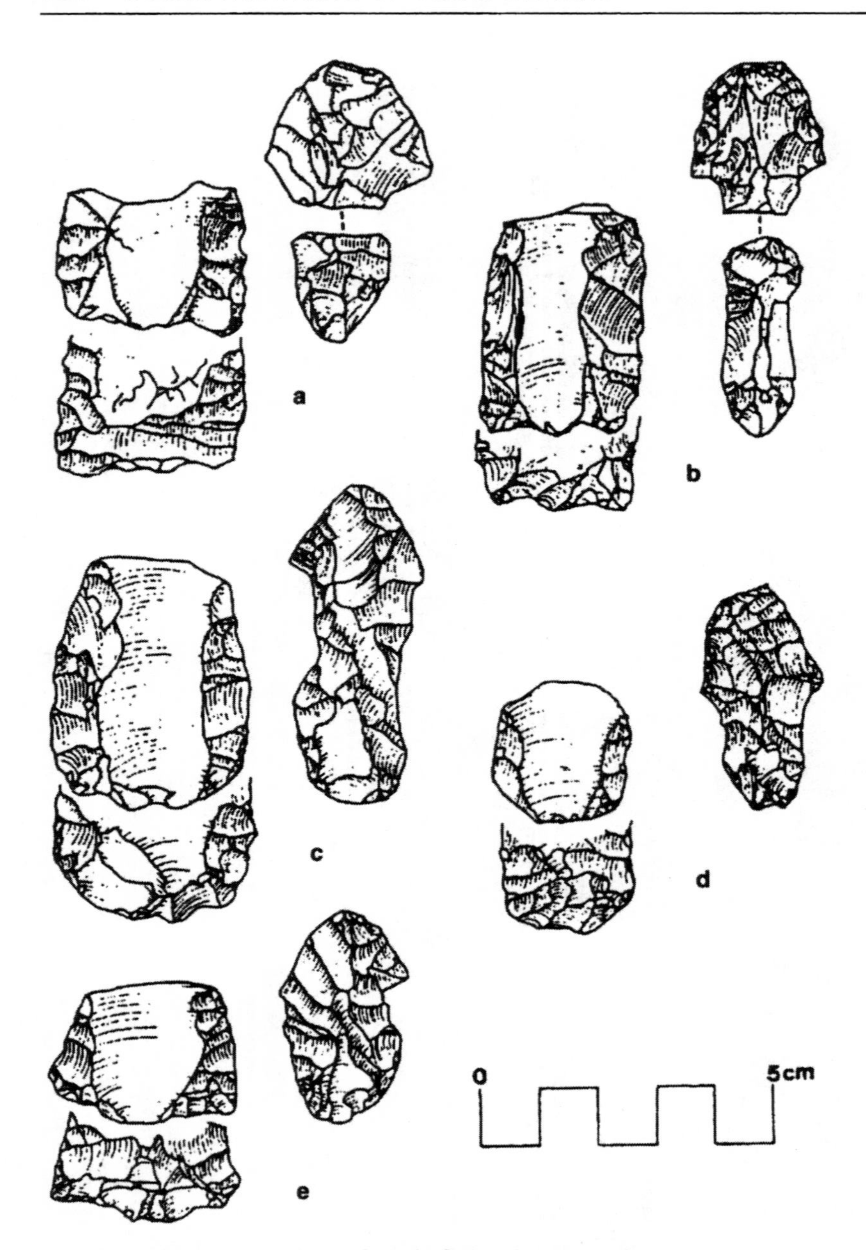

Typical manufacture-related breaks from the fluting of Folsom preforms. Reverse hinge fractures (a–e). From Boldurian (1990, fig. 48). By permission of *Plains Anthropologist*.

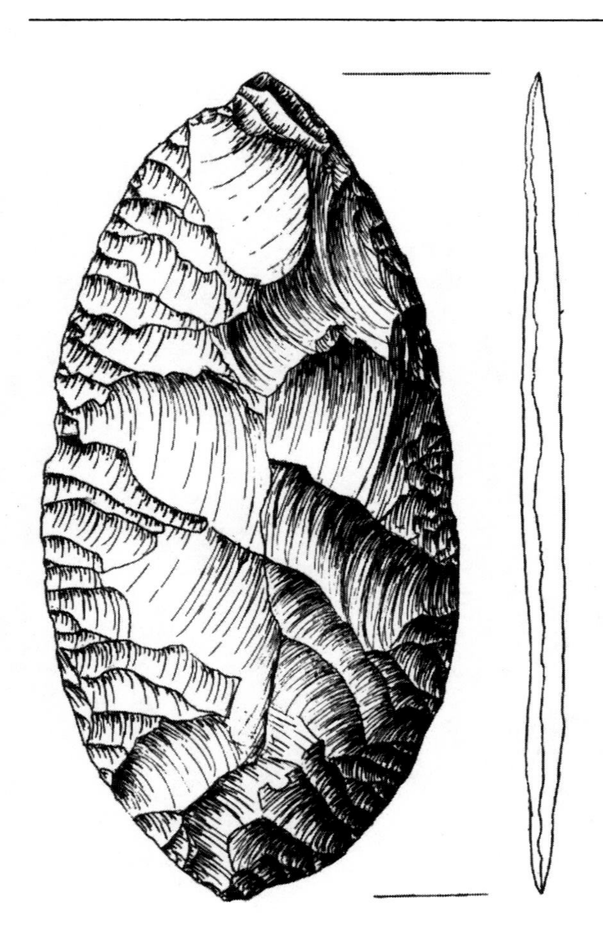

Folsom biface. Thin, carefully flaked bifaces, perhaps knives, are found in Folsom assemblages.

Folsom fluting attempt. Preform and channel flake refits found from January 4, 2001, through April 18, 2006, at Shifting Sands site, 41WK21. Courtesy of Richard Rose (his catalog numbers 2996, 2305, 2414, and 233).

FRIO

This point has a triangular body, often short and broad, with wide side or corner notches and a concave basal indentation that ranges from shallow to a deep U-shaped notch.

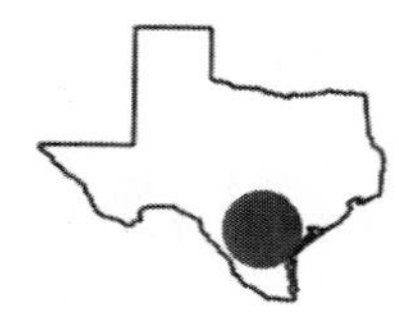

Distribution: Widespread in south and central Texas, extending to the lower Pecos and Trans-Pecos. **Period:** Transitional Archaic, ca. 200 BC–AD 600 (or later). **Sites:** La Jita; Anthon, Roark Cave; Oblate; Devil's Mouth; Blue Hole; Gatlin; Woodrow Heard; Eckols.

References: Decker et al. 2000; Goode 2002; Hester 1971; Houk et al. 2008; Johnson 1964; Karbula 2000; Kelly 1963; Mueggenborg 1994; Story and Bryant 1966; Suhm and Jelks 1962; Tunnell 1962.

GARY

Usually, this is a relatively crude and thick point, but it has a wide range of variation. Diagnostic traits include a triangular body, indistinct to squared shoulders, and a contracting stem. The distal portion of Gary is often heavily reworked. The variability within this type includes points that have been typed as Dawson, Dallas, and some of the so-called Woden type (Harry Shafer, personal communication), among others. We have deleted those types, but they can be found in our second edition.

Some authors have suggested that the type undergoes gradual diminution in size through time (Ford and Webb 1956, 52–54; Young 1981, 73).

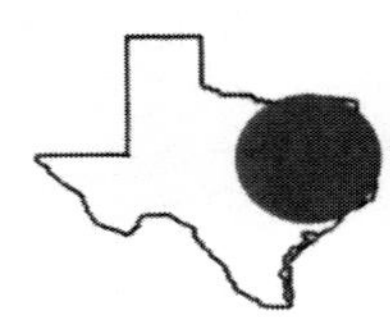

Distribution: Very common in the Trinity River drainage, east Texas, and Louisiana. **Period:** Late Archaic. **Sites:** Cowpen Slough (La.); Tankersley Creek; Harris County; Jasper County; Fayetteville (La.); Harold Williams site, Camp County; Denton County; 41DL30; 41TR21; Stallings Ranch (41LR297).

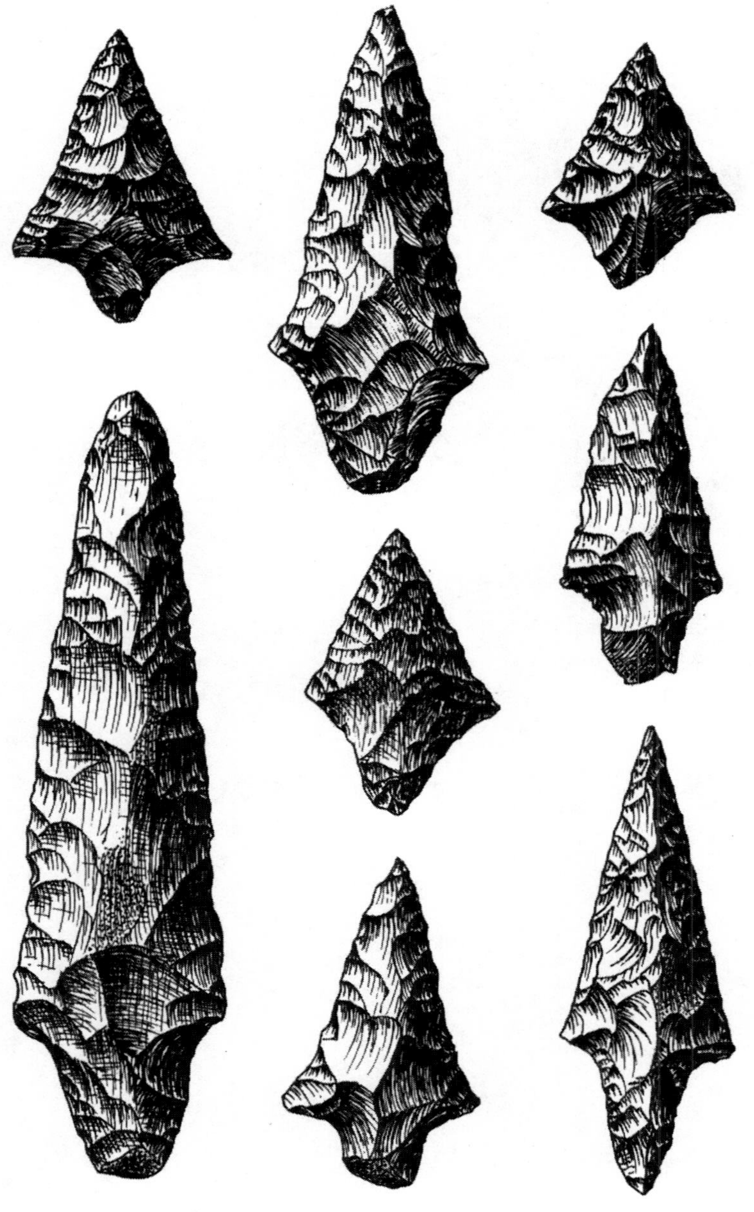

References: Baker and Webb 1978; Bruseth et al. 2009; Duffield 1963b; Ford and Webb 1956; Jensen 1968; Prikryl 1990; Suhm and Jelks 1962; Turner and Smith 2002; C. Webb, personal communication; Young 1981.

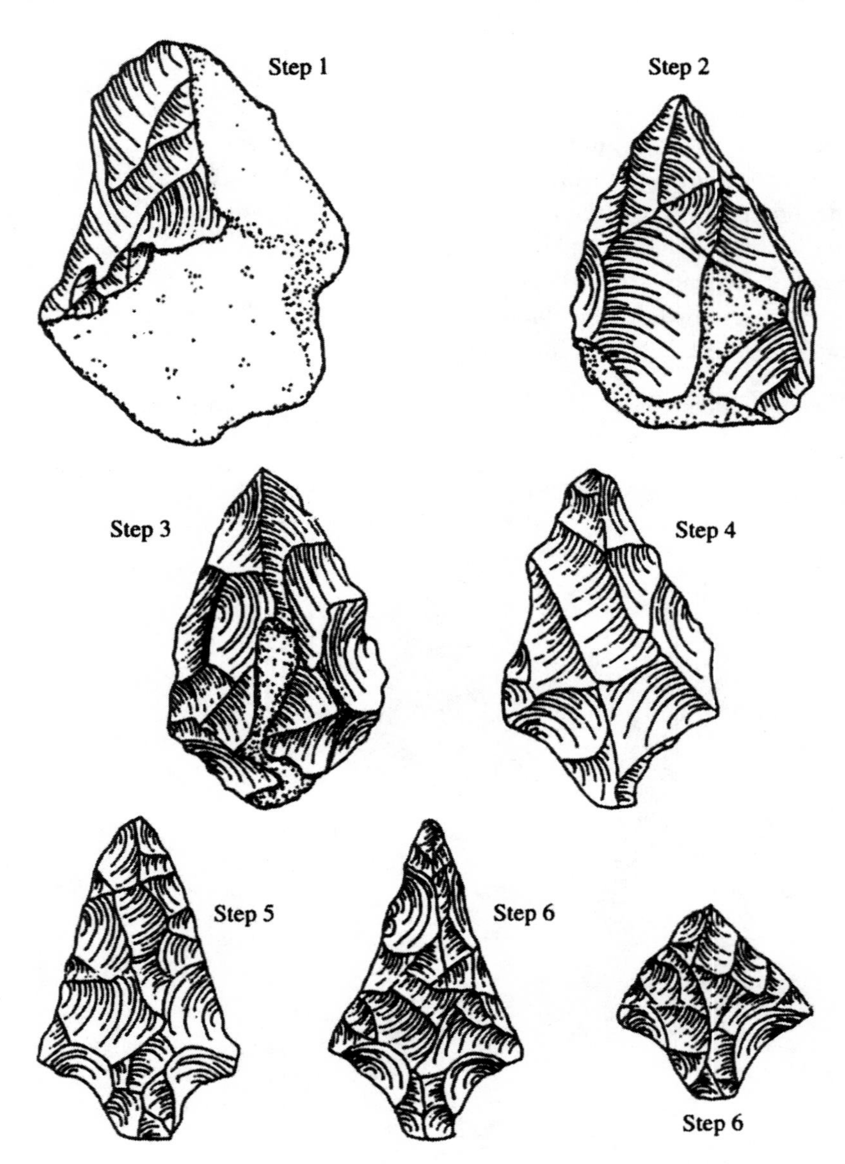

Gary Production Model. From Ensor and Carlson 1991: fig. 85. By permission of Archeological Research Laboratory, Texas A&M University.

GODLEY

This small- to medium-sized triangular point has prominent shoulders but no barbs. The type's most characteristic attribute is a narrow, widely expanding stem with a markedly convex base. Serrations occasionally occur on the lateral edges.

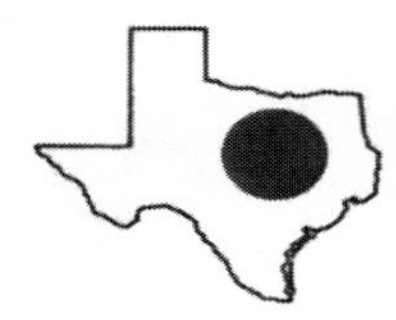

Distribution: Brazos River drainage, but also reported east Texas and into Louisiana. **Period:** Late to Transitional Archaic, but some found in Late Prehistoric. **Sites:** Kyle; Hopewell School; Pecan Springs; Ham Creek; Ernest Witte (41AU36), Fort Hood; Britton; McMillen (41ML262), Fort Polk (La.).

References: Anderson and Smith 2003; Anthony and Brown 1994; Forrester 1964, 1985; Gallagher and Bearden 1976; Jelks 1962; Mehalchick and Kibler 2008; Mueller-Wille and Carlson 1990a, 1990b; Prikryl 1990; Sorrow 1966.

GOLONDRINA

This lanceolate point has a deep basal concavity (more than 4 mm) that varies from a flattened inverted V to recurved. Lateral edges are often beveled. The basal corners or "ears" are somewhat flared, and both the basal edge and concavity are heavily ground. Flaking varies considerably, from well-made parallel-flaked examples to less patterned, more casually flaked specimens. The lower lateral edges are heavily dulled.

While Dial and colleagues (1998) designated a "Golondrina-Barber" type, we see no evidence of any linkage between the two types and continue to recommend the Golondrina label be used.

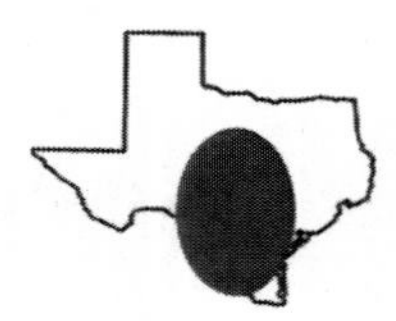

Distribution: South and central Texas, the coastal plain, and the lower Pecos.
Period: Paleo-Indian, at Baker Cave, radiocarbon dated ca. 7080 BC–6830 BC.
Sites: Baker Cave; Devil's Mouth; Strohacker; Johnston-Heller; 41VT141; J2 Ranch; Wilson-Leonard.

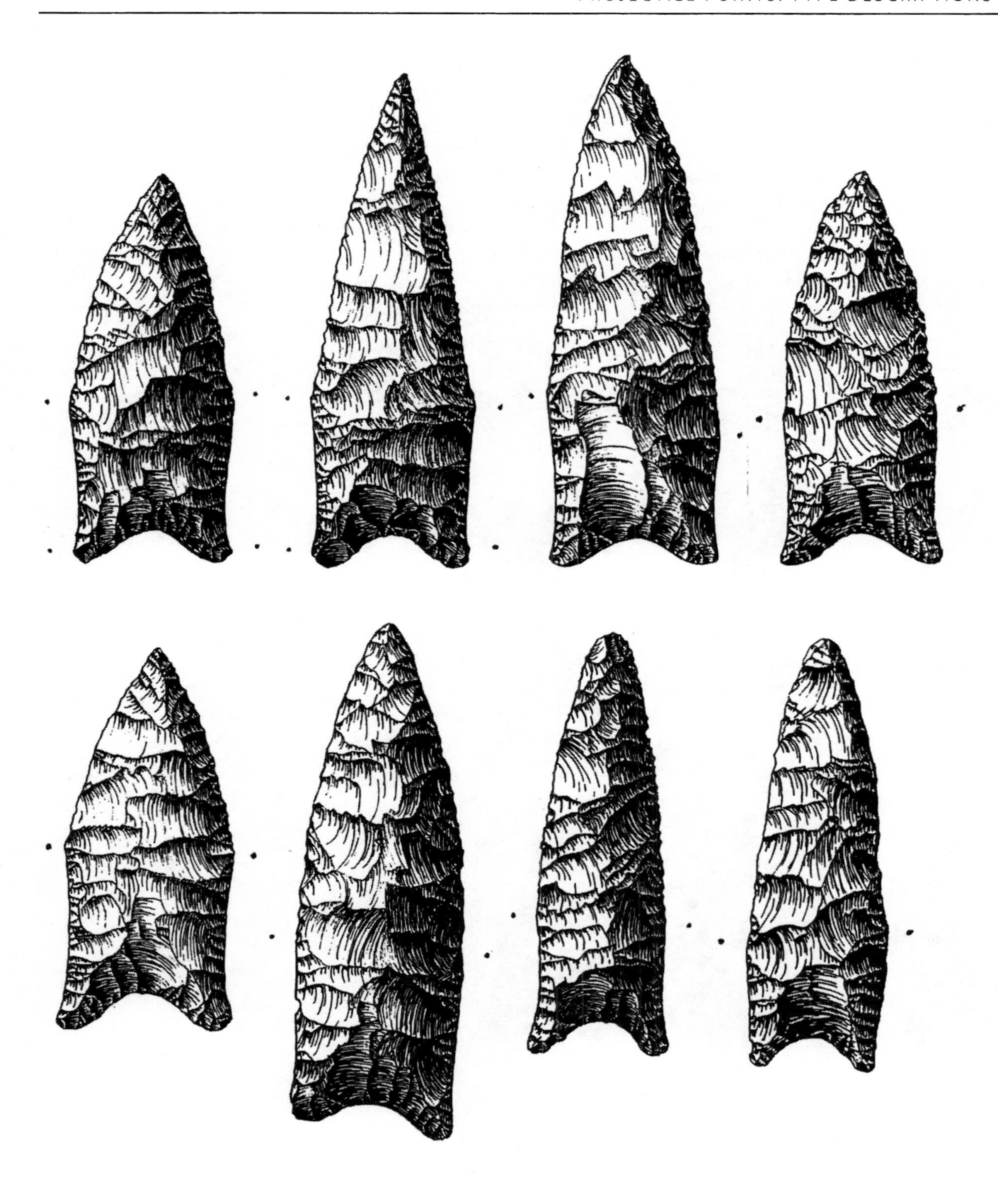

References: Birmingham and Hester 1976; Bousman, Baker, and Kerr 2004; Braun et al. 2008; Collins et al. 1998; Dial et al. 1998; Hester 1983a; Kelly 1982, 1983b; Schroeder 2002; Sollberger and Hester 1972; Sorrow 1968a; Word and Douglas 1970.

GOWER

This point has a short, parallel-edged to expanding stem and a generally short body, usually resulting from extensive reworking during the life of the specimen. Stem and basal edges are heavily dulled. The stem base is markedly concave, the edge often formed by arc-shaped flaking. There has been controversy as to the variations within this type and its dating. At the Varga site (41ED28), points described as Gower points and Merrell points have considerable overlap in form, and other similar specimens are described as Baker points. The Gower points from the Gatlin site (41KR621) also include what would be grouped both as Gower and as Merrell at the Varga site. More typical examples of Gower are found in the work by Dial and colleagues (1998).

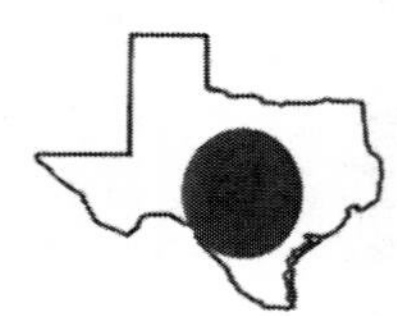

Distribution: Central and south central Texas. **Period:** Early Archaic, 7160–6290 BP (but cf. HY161, 8600–7440 BP). **Sites:** Youngsport; Jetta Court; Landslide; Granite Beach; 41WM570; Sleeper; Varga; Woodrow Heard; Wilson-Leonard; White's Point (41SP156); Gatlin.

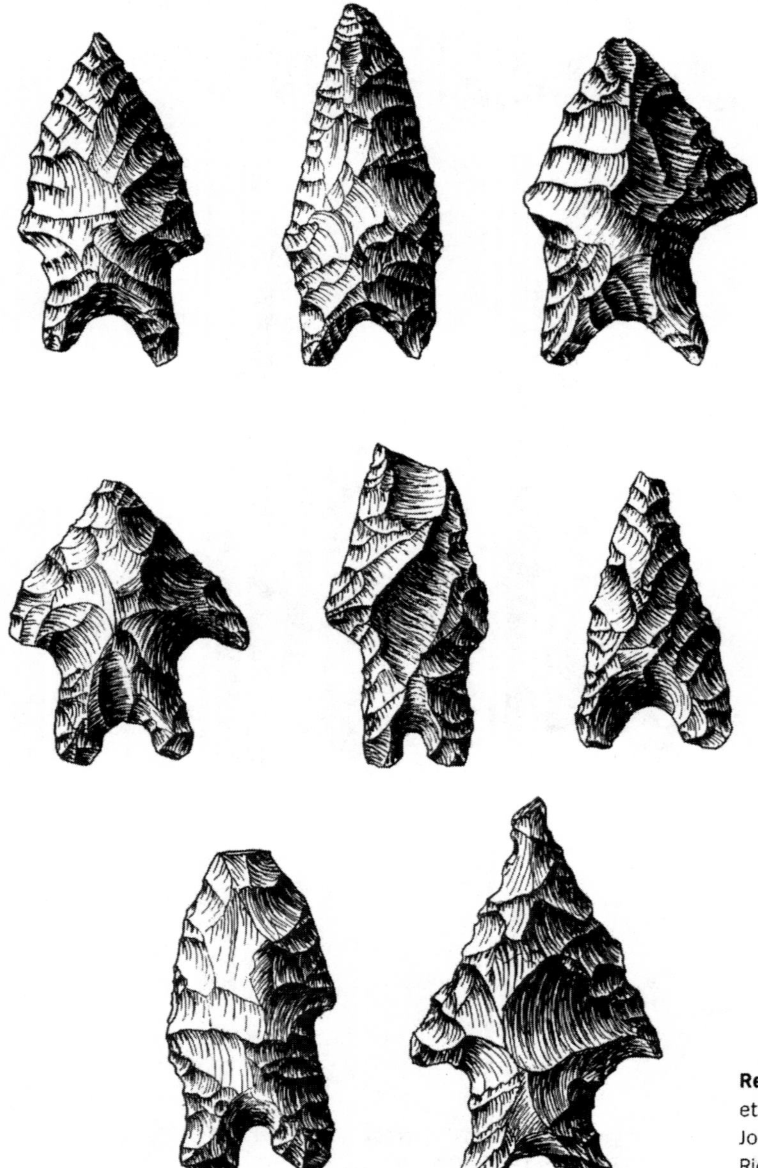

References: Coffman and Prewitt 1985; Crawford 1965; Decker et al. 2000; Dial et al. 1998; Hester 1979b; Houk et al. 2009; Johnson 1991; Kelly 1979; Patterson 1979a; Quigg et al. 2008; Ricklis 1993; Schmiedlin 2000a; Shafer 1963, 1979b; Sorrow et al. 1967; Wesolowsky et al. 1976.

HIDALGO

This is a sturdy point, usually with an expanding stem and more or less bulbous base. It is usually biconvex in cross section and few are less than 10 mm thick. They range from narrow lanceolate to broadly ovate in outline. The shoulders are generally rounded; others, strongly shouldered, verging on barbed. The stem outline is variable, and basal corners are usually rounded. They may be reworked so that one or both lateral edges angle abruptly to a newly placed tip.

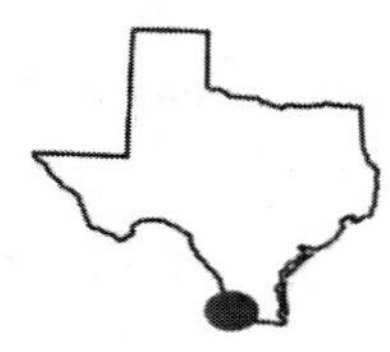

Distribution: Hidalgo, Starr and Zapata counties, northern Tamaulipas and northeastern Nuevo Leon. **Period:** Early Archaic. **Sites:** Los Olmos Creek; Sheldon; 41ZP154; Rio Salado, Tamaulipas.

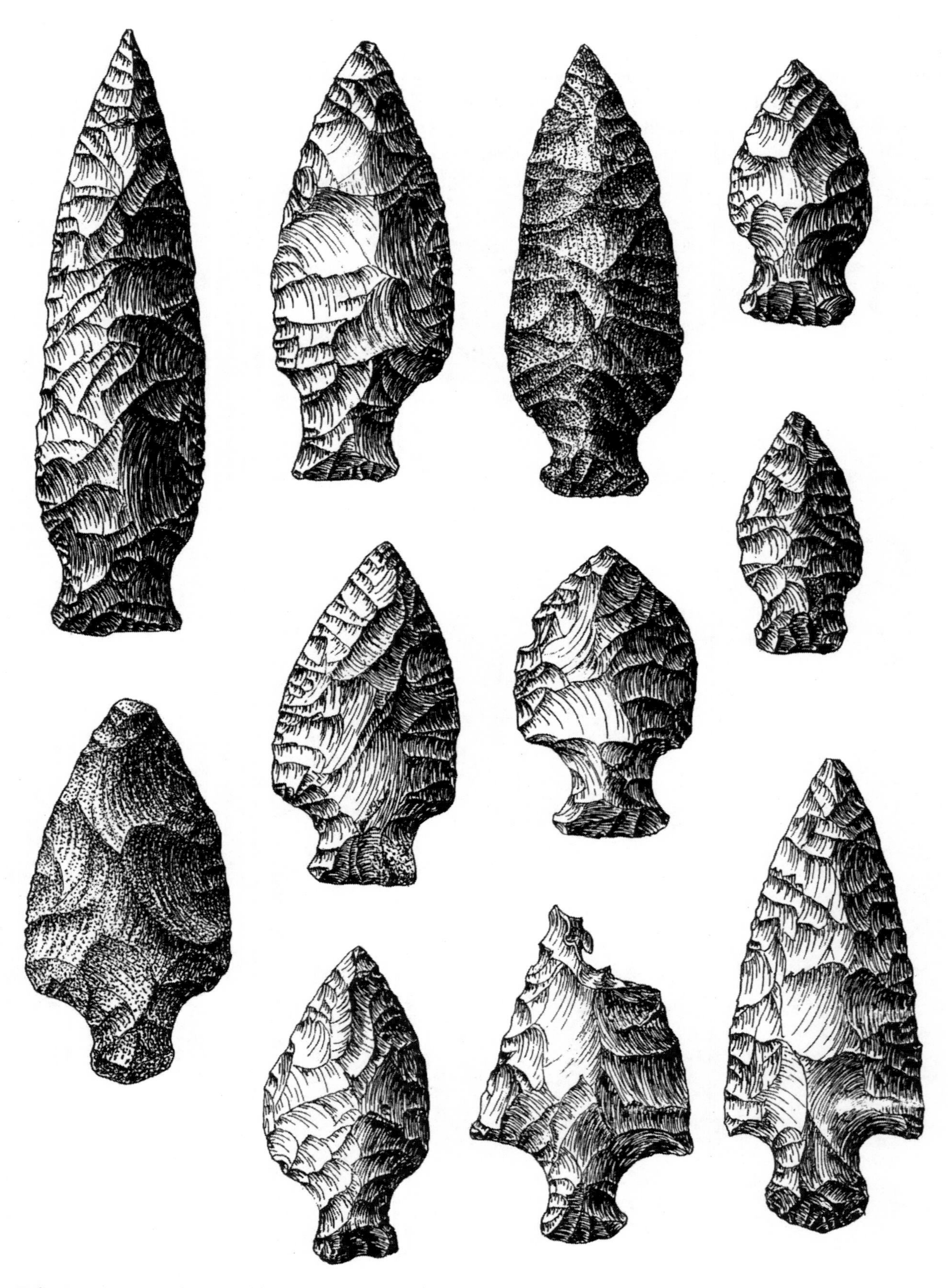

References: Kumpe and McReynolds 2009; Newton 1963; Shiner 1983.

HOXIE

These points are typified by long, heavily ground stems. The body is long, narrow, and often has alternately beveled lateral edges. The basal edge is usually concave and is also ground. An interesting hypothetical resharpening sequence is shown in Dial and colleagues (1998, fig. 13–42).

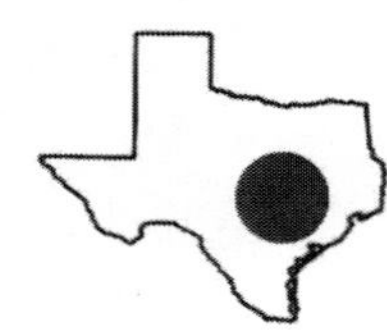

Distribution: Central, north central, and northeastern Texas. **Period:** Early Archaic. **Sites:** Tombstone Bluff; Youngsport; San Geronimo; Granite Beach; Palmetto Bend Reservoir (41JK163); Wilson-Leonard.

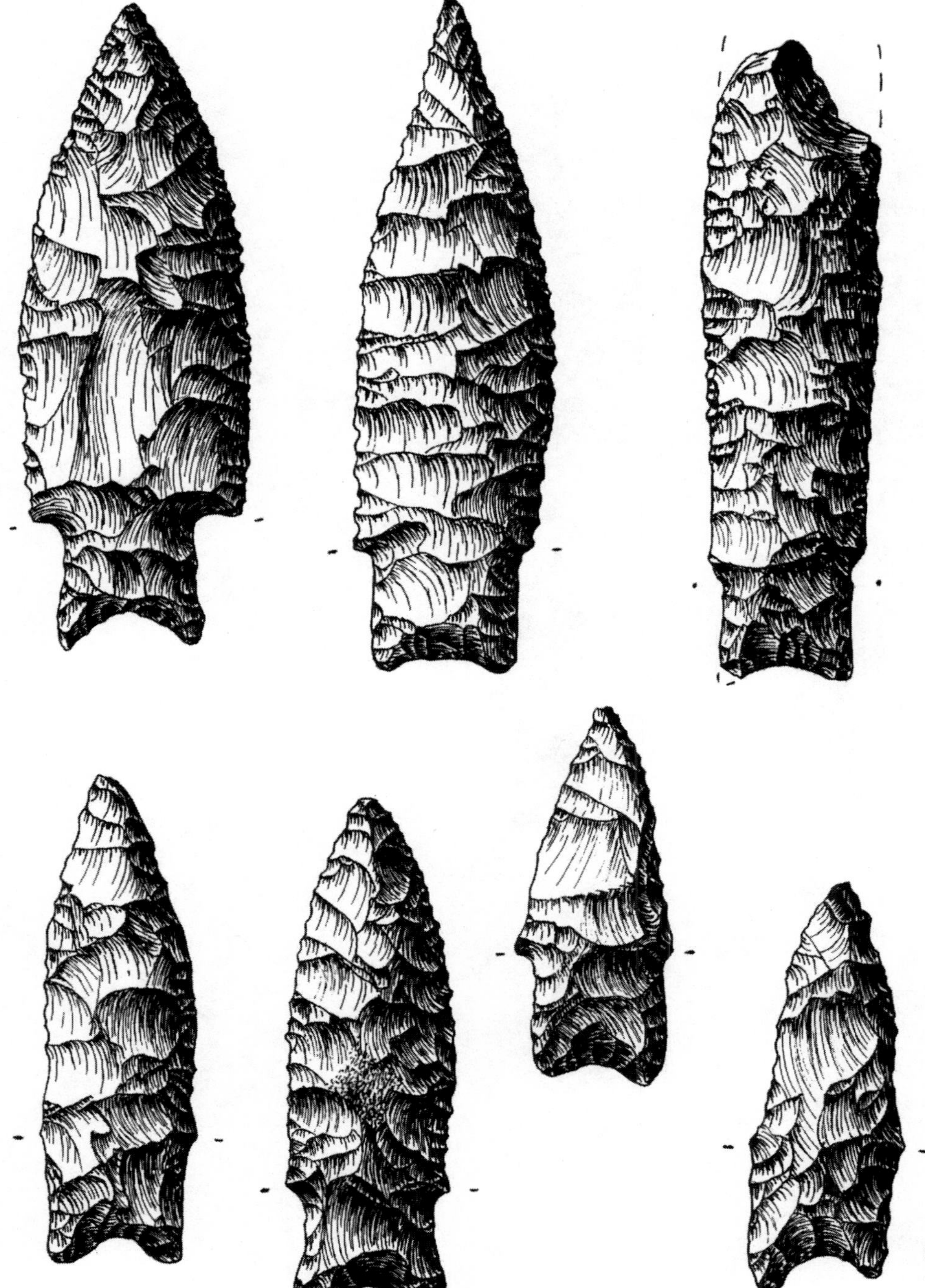

References: Crawford 1965; Dial et al. 1998; Dibble et al. 1981; Peter 1982b; Prewitt 1981a; Shafer 1968; Weir 1976b.

HUECO

This point has similarities with several other types (Carlsbad, San Pedro, Tularosa, and Ellis). For example, Ellis points tend to have straight to only slightly convex stem basal edges, while Hueco points typically have moderate to strongly convex stem basal edges. Ellis points tend to have straight lateral blade edges, while Hueco points typically have convex lateral blade edges. Mallouf (2009) also notes the similarities to San Pedro points in the Southwest.

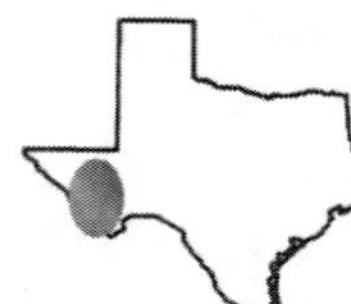

Distribution: Eastern and western Trans-Pecos. **Period:** Late Archaic. **Sites:** Glass Mountains; Bear Creek; Big Bend and eastern Trans-Pecos; Hueco Tanks.

References: Justice 2002; MacNeish 1993; Mallouf 2009c; Howard et al. 2010.

JETTA

This is a very distinctive, carefully flaked point with widely flared barbs, a rectangular stem, and a deep basal notch. The body or distal portion of Jetta points often have parallel to parallel-oblique flaking and are beveled, giving it a slightly twisted form. It is often confused with Pedernales points that occasionally have a deeply concave base.

Distribution: Central Texas. **Period:** Early Archaic. **Sites:** Jetta Court; Granite Beach; Gillespie County (41GL53); Wilson-Leonard.

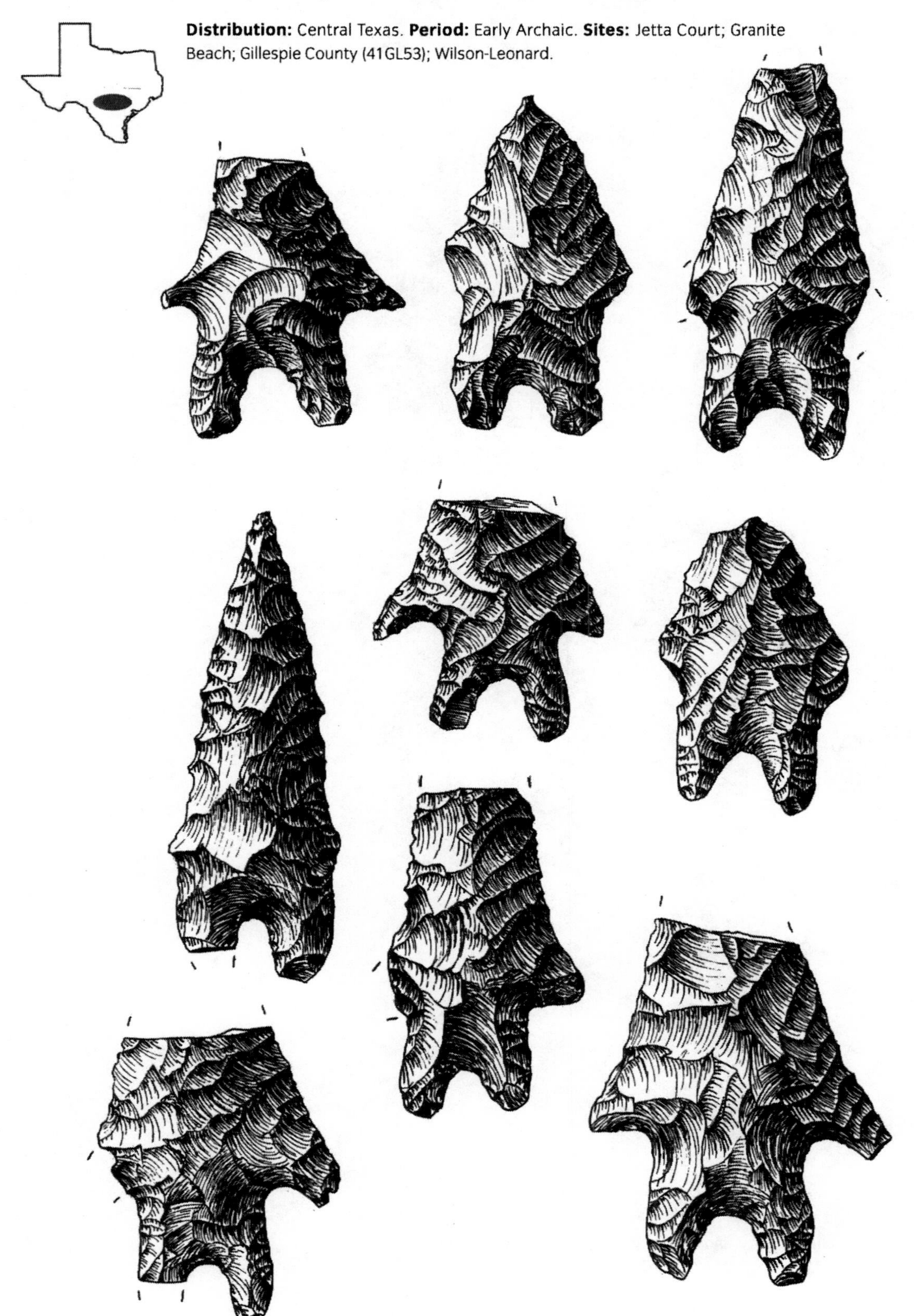

References: Brown 1976; Crawford 1965; Dial et al. 1998; Hester 1979b; Wesolowsky et al. 1976.

JOHNSON

This is a broad point with a wide, expanding to parallel-sided stem. The type has shoulders that vary from sloping to slightly barbed. The essentially straight, broad stems and concave bases are usually smoothed on the edges.

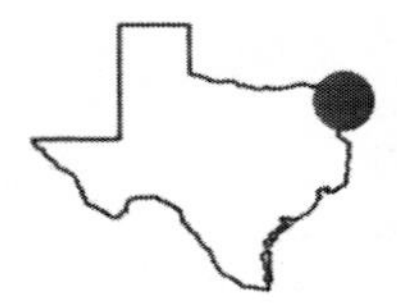

Distribution: Northeast Texas, into southwest Arkansas, east Oklahoma, and northwest Louisiana. **Period:** Early Archaic; Mary Beth Trubitt (personal communication) has a calibrated radiocarbon date of 5980 BC at the Jones Mill site, Arkansas. **Sites:** Tom's Brook shelter (Ark.).

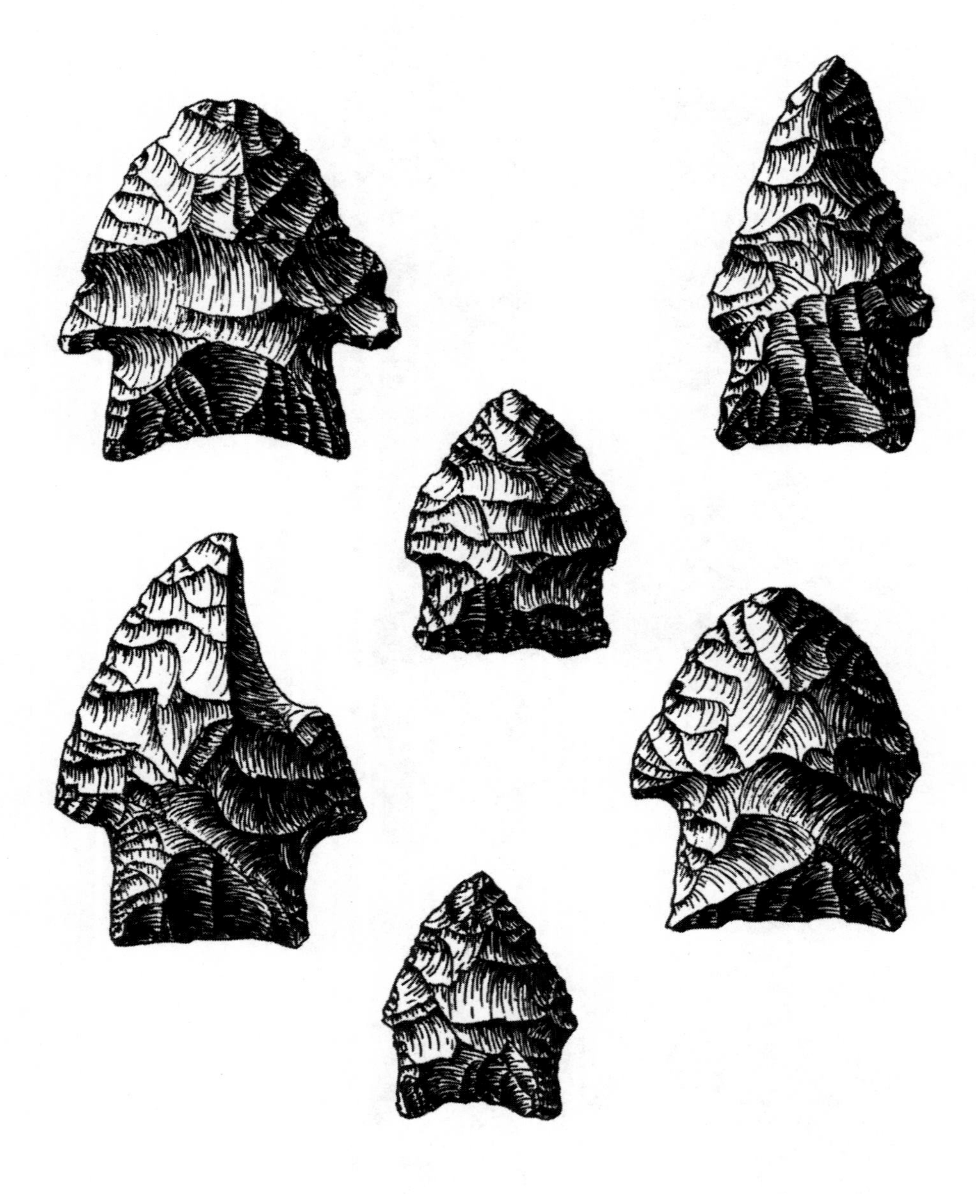

References: Bartlett 1963; Jeter and Williams 1989; Schambach 1970; Scholtz 1967; Story et al. 1990; Trubitt 2009b.

KEITHVILLE

These are small, side-notched dart points with convex sides and wide, expanded stems and concave bases. The lateral edges are sometimes serrated. Basal edges are ground, and it is generally thicker than with the deeply concave base of San Patrice points. A series of Keithville points are illustrated in an article by Webb and colleagues (1971, fig. 6) from the John Pearce site; Webb referred to these as "side notched points, variety B." He subsequently dubbed them Keithville and noted their association with San Patrice points (Webb 1978, 36).

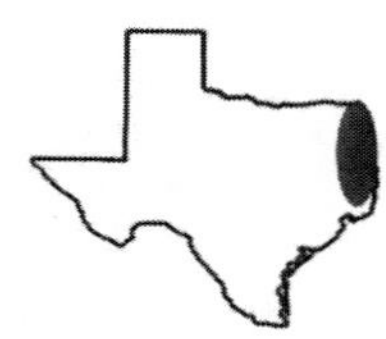

Distribution: Northeast and southeast Texas. **Period:** Late Paleo-Indian; Story et al. (1990, fig. 32) place them prior to 6000 BC. **Sites:** John Pearce; Wolfshead (41SA117); McFaddin Beach (41JF50); Loomis collection (Marion County, Texas Archeological Research Laboratory).

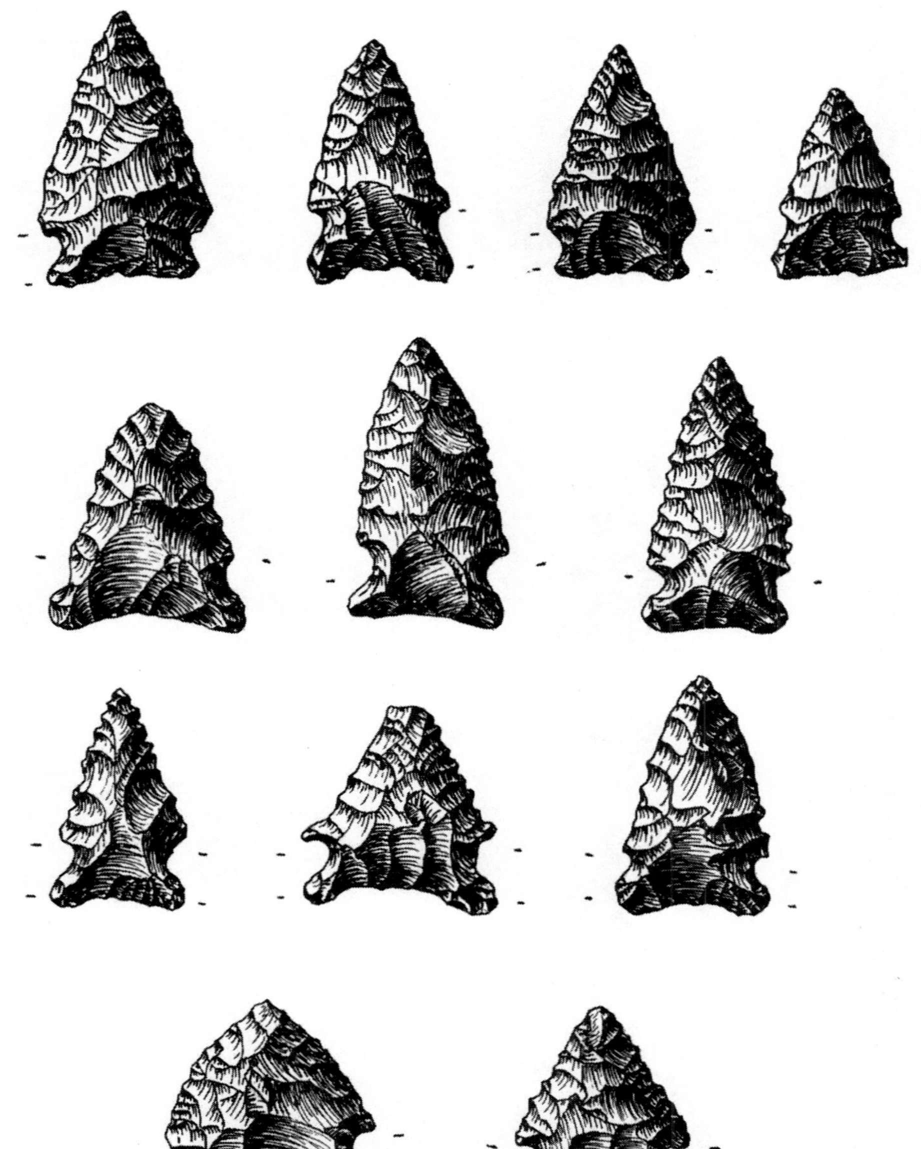

References: Duffield 1963b; Story et al. 1990; Webb 1978; Webb et al. 1971.

KENT

Kent points were first published as a group of dart points found at the Kent-Crane site. Though Campbell (1952) did not name the point form, they were the basis for the Suhm and colleagues (1954) type label. Overall, they are small, with often asymmetrical triangular bodies (perhaps linked to resharpening), and usually with a prominent medial ridge. The shoulders are squared to indistinct, and the stems often have a cortex at the base.

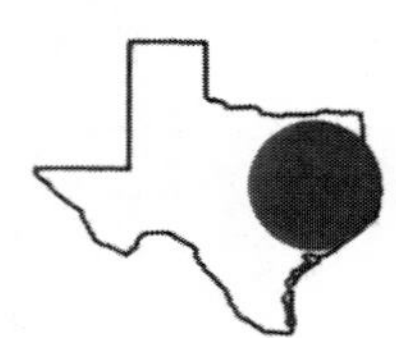

Distribution: Central portion of the coastal area, east and central Texas, and Louisiana. **Period:** Middle Archaic; radiocarbon dated 3156–2873 BP at the Kent-Crane site. **Sites:** Kent-Crane; San Jacinto River Basin; George C. Davis; Poverty Point (La.), Hopkins County; Addicks Reservoir; Titus County; Fresno.

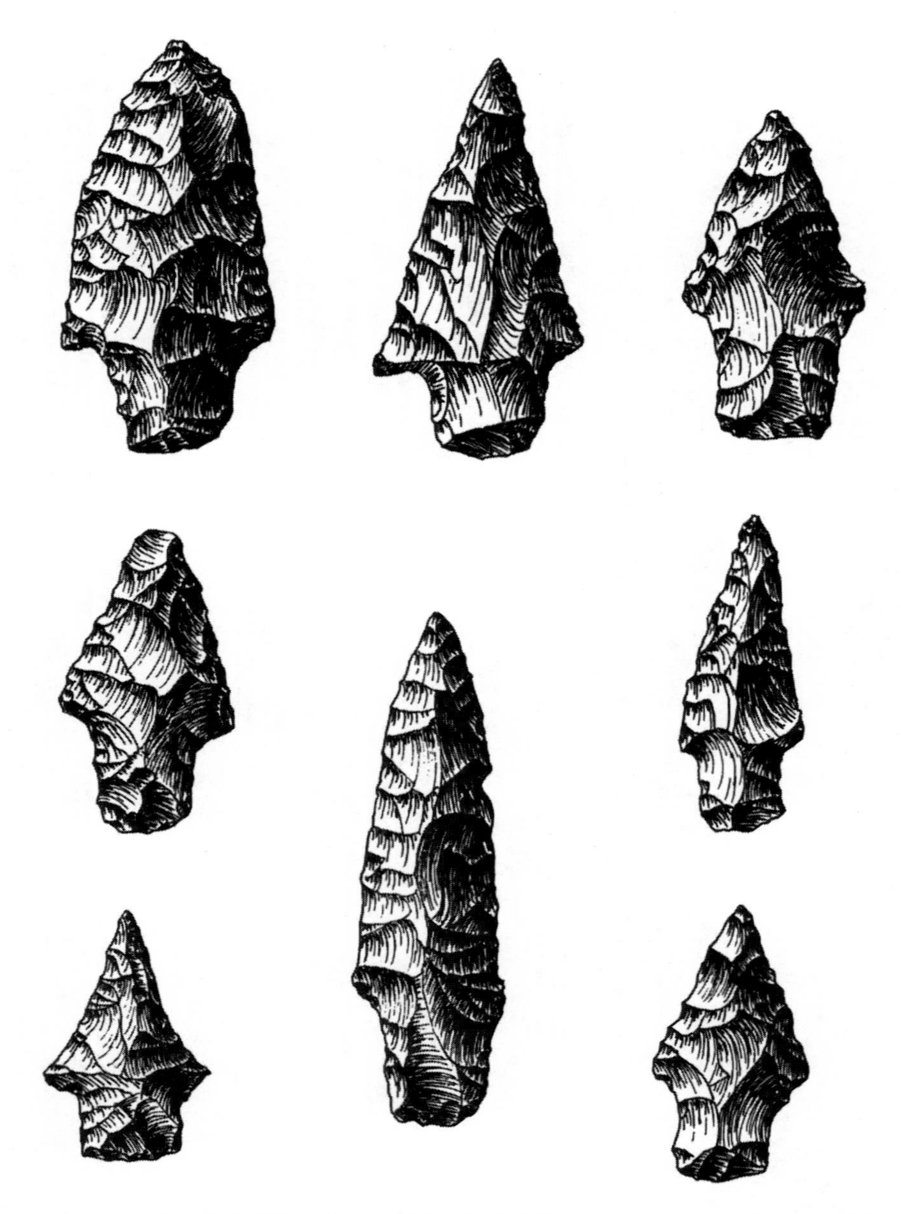

References: Campbell 1952; Patterson 1990b; Ricklis 1995; Shafer 1968, 1973; Story et al. 1990; Suhm et al. 1954; Webb, personal communication; Weir 1956.

KINNEY

This unstemmed triangular to elongate, triangular point has a slightly to more deeply concave base. An extensive study of Kinney has been carried out by Goode (2002), who notes that shape changes through use and resharpening. He further separates the specimens from the Anthon site (41UV60) into four forms, suggesting some were dart points and others were used as knives.

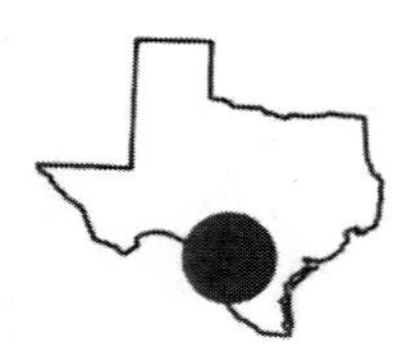

Distribution: Central and south Texas and the lower Pecos. **Period:** Middle Archaic, contemporary with Pedernales. **Sites:** Montell Rockshelter; La Jita; Morhiss; Damp Cave; Anthon; Smith (41UV132).

References: Baker 2003; Campbell 1976; Coleman et al. 2001; Epstein 1963; Goode 2002; Hester 1971; Suhm and Jelks 1962; Weir and Doran 1980.

KIRK

The "Kirk" label has been applied to several point types in the southeast and midwest parts of the United States (see Justice 1987). Story and colleagues (1990, 219) recognize "Kirk" points in northeast Texas and adjacent parts of Oklahoma and Arkansas. The lateral edges are strongly serrated, while the stems are slightly expanded with bases concave or straight. Illustrations shown here are of the Kirk corner-notched variety. The blades are convex, and the shoulders are prominently barbed. The basal edges are straight to slightly concave.

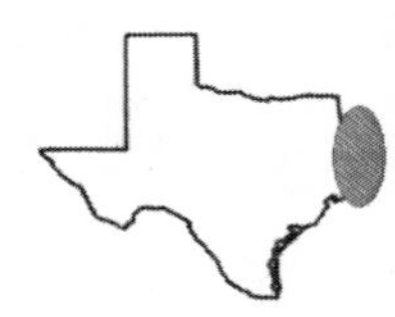

Distribution: Northeast and southeast Texas. **Period:** Story et al. (1990, fig. 32) place them between 4000 and 6000 BC. **Sites:** Dam B, Sandy Creek; Caddel Cove and Julie Creek, Sam Rayburn Lake; McFaddin Beach (41JF50); Sabine River drainage, in Texas and Louisiana.

References: Coe 1964; Justice 1987; Story et al. 1990.

KISATCHIE

This point has a wide body and short stem, and Perino (1985) suggests that the points are possibly part of the San Patrice tradition. Shoulders are slight, and the stems are usually slightly expanded. The basal edge is concave. Stem edges are ground, and basal thinning is common.

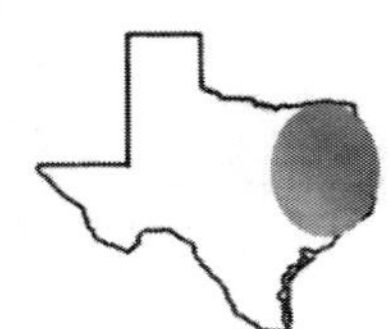

Distribution: East and southeast Texas, Louisiana, Arkansas, and southeastern Arkansas. **Period:** Contemporary with San Patrice; ca. 7500 BC. **Sites:** Harris, Montgomery, Polk, Walker, and Wharton counties.

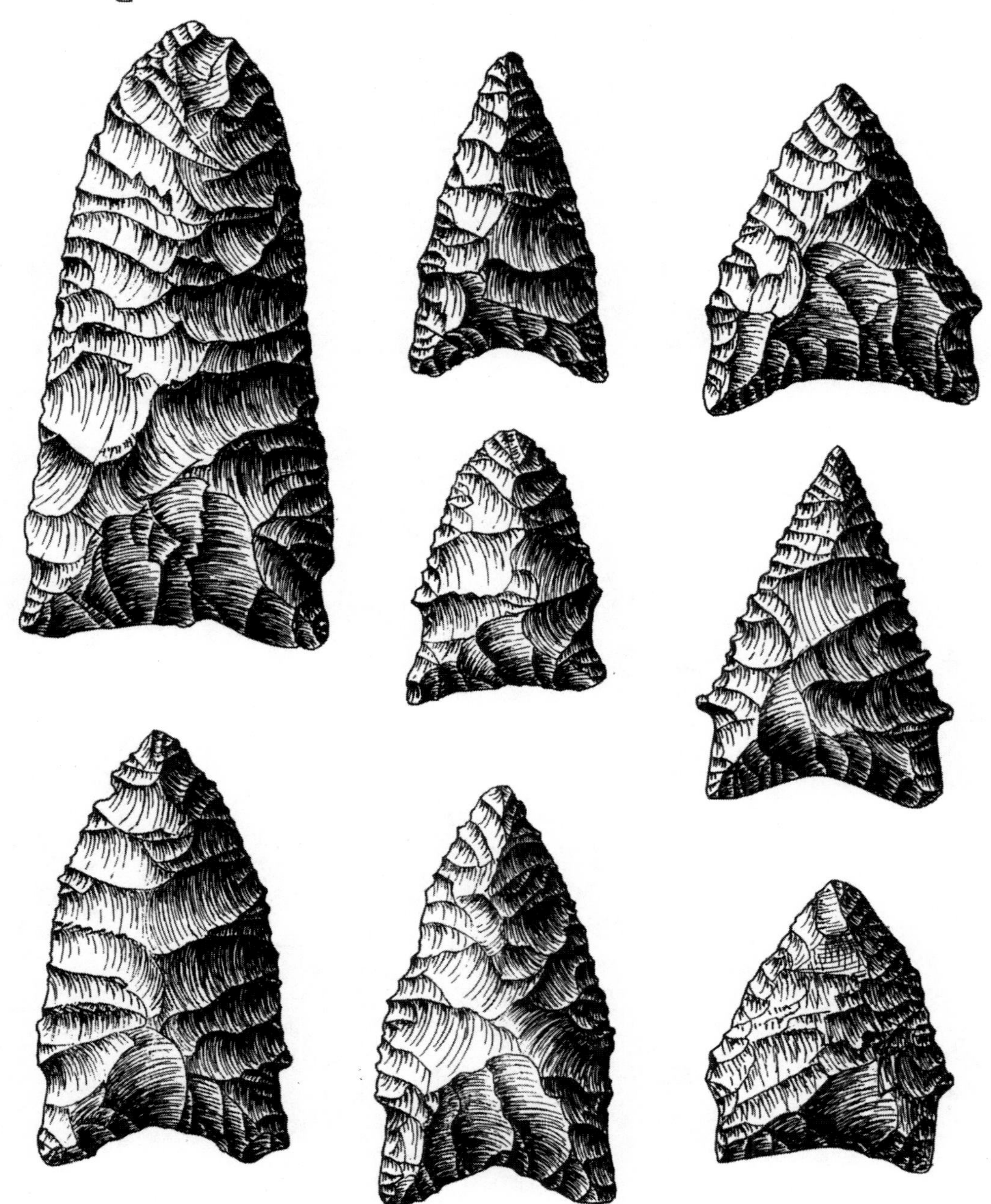

References: Gagliano and Gregory 1965; Perino 1985.

LAGUNA

These points are distinguished by relatively large bodies with concave, recurved edges and V-shaped basal notches that create widely flaring barbs with wide bases. The recurved edges often terminate in a very sharp tip. Laguna points are highly variable in size. Some of the larger specimens are exceptionally well made. Stems have parallel to slightly convex edges and a concave base; some specimens have stems that expand toward the base. In some instances, stem shapes are reminiscent of the much later Pedernales type but are narrower and shorter. Final thinning scars on the body were made, after notching, by removing large pressure flakes. The stem is thicker than the body.

The flaring barbs on these specimens are very distinctive. Laguna points have sometimes been included in the Bell type or linked to the Early Barbed (sometimes Early Barbed Devil's Variant) form in the lower Pecos and southwest Edwards Plateau.

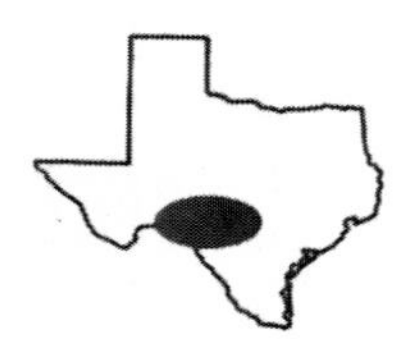

Distribution: Apparently in a swath along the Balcones Escarpment from Val Verde to Bell County. **Period:** Early Archaic. **Sites:** Devil's Rockshelter; Woodrow Heard; Richard Beene; Wilson-Leonard; Gault; Gatlin.

References: Decker et al. 2000; Dial et al. 1998; Houk et al. 2008; Thoms and Mandel 2007; Weber 2009.

LA JITA

The La Jita point is characterized by a short, wide stem, rounded on the edges and generally thinned by the removal of two or three long, broad flakes from both faces. The body is often elongated. The stem is beveled on one edge or sometimes alternately beveled. The largest excavated sample is reported from the Gatlin site (41KR621) in Kerrville. At site 41BN63, La Jita points came from an occupation below the burned rock midden, associated with small pits containing charred acorns.

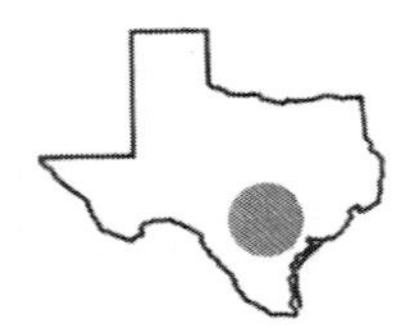

Distribution: Southwestern Edwards Plateau. **Period:** Early Middle Archaic, 4820–3980 BP; BN63, 4260BP. **Sites:** La Jita; Panther Springs Creek; Camp Bullis; Winans Creek; 41UV132; 41BN63; Gatlin; 41BX126; 41ME147.

References: Baker 2003; Black and McGraw 1985; Carroll 1983; Dornheim 2002; Gerstle et al. 1978; Hester 1971, 2010; Houk et al. 2008, 2009; Kelly and Hester 1976; Nickels et al. 2001.

LANGE

This large point has prominent shoulders that are sometimes barbed and an expanding stem. The base is straight to slightly convex, and some are markedly convex. Lange was one of the two most numerous points associated with the burial site at 41LK28 (Taylor and Highley 1995) radiocarbon dated at 850 BC–600 BC.

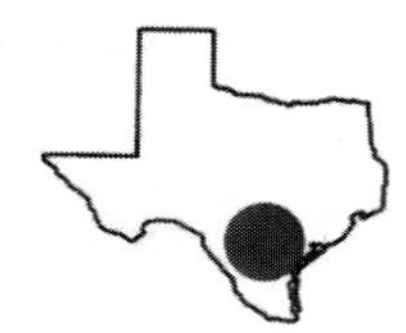

Distribution: Most common in central Texas; also found in the central coastal plain and the lower Pecos. **Period:** Late Archaic. **Sites:** La Jita; Greenhaw; Youngsport; Evoe Terrace; 41LK28; Eckols (41TV528).

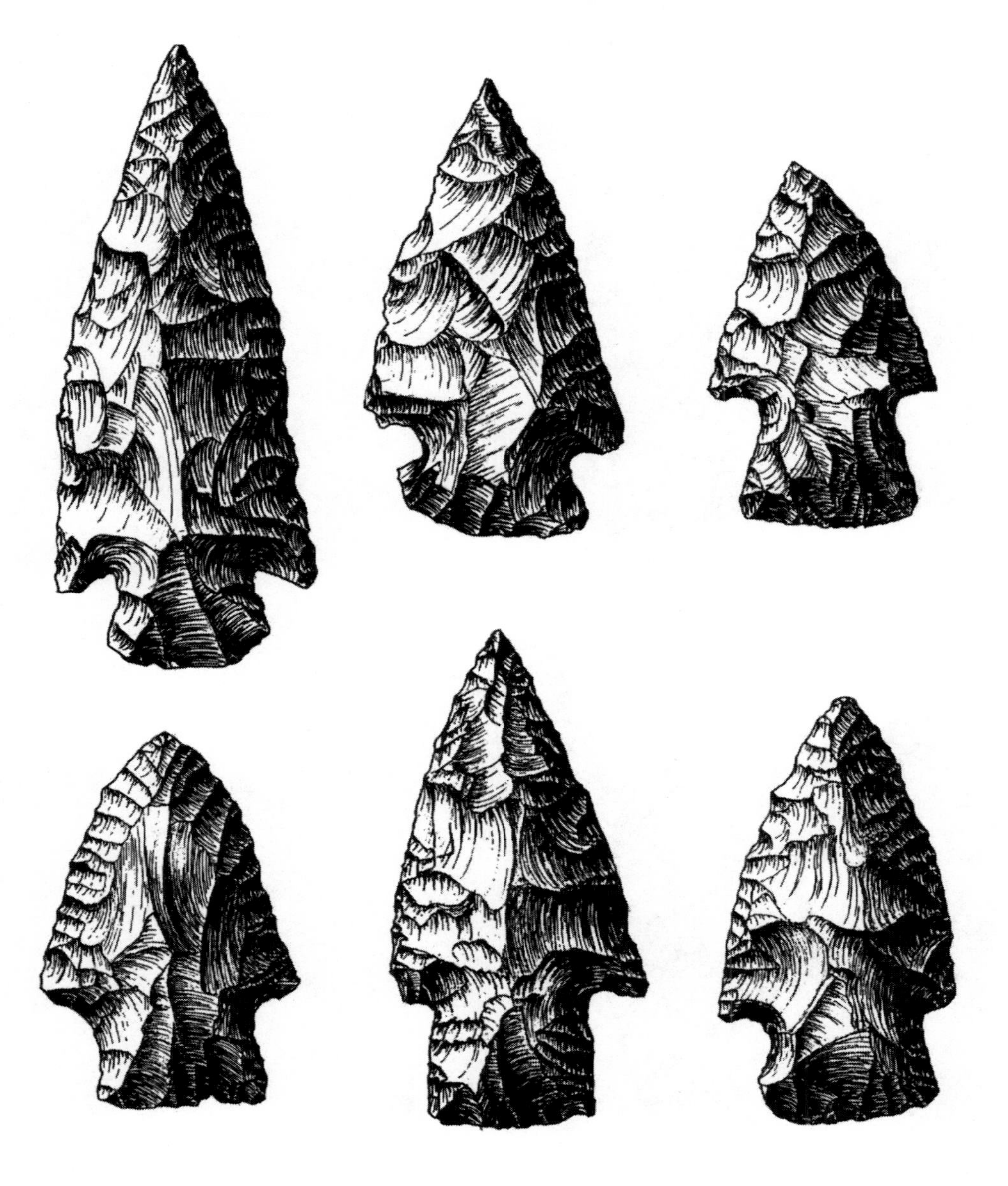

References: Hester 1971; Karbula 2000; Mauldin et al. 2003; Quigg 1997; Sorrow, Shafer, and Ross 1967; Suhm and Jelks 1962; Taylor and Highley 1995; Weir 1979.

LANGTRY

Langtry points are usually thin and well made with straight to slightly concave, lateral edges and strong shoulders. The type is characterized by a tapered stem, sometimes with alternately beveled edges, that terminates in a straight or slightly beveled, concave base. There is much variation within the group in proportions, base shape, and development of shoulders. "Almagre" points, found in our second edition, are clearly preforms for Langtry.

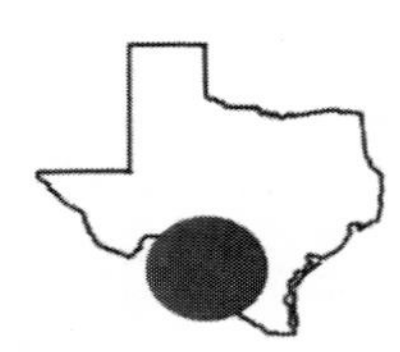

Distribution: Very common in the lower Pecos; occurs in south Texas and the southwestern Edwards Plateau, the Big Bend region, and into Coahuila, Mexico. **Period:** Middle Archaic, ca. 2000 BC. **Sites:** Devil's Mouth; Baker Cave; Roark Cave; Hinds Cave; Fate Bell Rockshelter; Arenosa Shelter; Gatlin; Boiler; 41UV20.

References: Bement 1991a; Bettis 1997; Hester and Whatley 1992a; Houk et al. 2008; Johnson 1964; Kelly 1963; Peck 1991; Quigg et al. 2002; Shafer and Bryant 1977; Story and Bryant 1966; Suhm and Jelks 1962; Word and Douglas 1970; Wulfkuhle 1990.

LERMA

A slender, bipointed outline is characteristic of these points. They have longitudinal symmetry, and thus it sometimes seems difficult to determine which is the proximal and which is the distal end. They have been assumed by some to be Paleo-Indian in age; indeed, some evidence exists to suggest the presence of a small, bipointed form of projectile point in Mexico and south Texas within that time frame. However, points resembling Lerma are generally found in Archaic contexts in south Texas and the coastal plain.

A specimen very similar to those illustrated here was found at Montell Rockshelter (41UV3) with the earliest cultural deposits, likely of Paleo-Indian age (Coleman et al. 2001). Yet, another bipointed biface, closely resembling some of the smaller specimens we have illustrated, was excavated at the base of site 41ZV163, below stratified Archaic and Late Prehistoric occupations (Hester 2000).

Distribution: Lower Pecos, south Texas, and Mexico. **Period:** Paleo-Indian and Archaic. **Sites:** Choke Canyon; La Calsada (Mexico); Devil's Mouth; Hinds Cave; Morhiss; J2 Ranch (41VT6); Montell Rockshelter; 41ZV263.

References: Coleman et al. 2001; Flaigg 1995; Hall, Black, and Graves 1982; Hester 2000; Johnson 1964; Kelly 1989; Nance 1971; Schmiedlin 2000a; Shafer and Bryant 1977; Suhm and Jelks 1962; Weinstein 1992.

MARCOS

Marcos points are distinguished by broad, triangular bodies with straight lateral edges and have expanding stems created by precise corner-notching. It is always barbed. Bases are straight to slightly convex. It is similar in form to Castroville, but the stem of Marcos expands more sharply and the notches cut inward from the corners rather than upward from the base. Points of this type are often exceedingly well made.

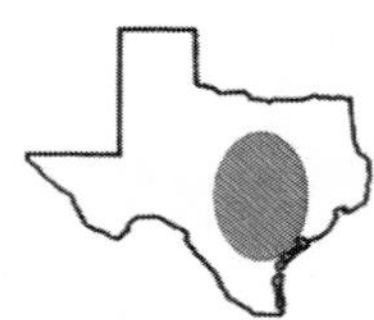

Distribution: Principally central Texas and Edwards Plateau but also found throughout Texas. **Period:** Late to Transitional Archaic, 600 BC–AD 200. **Sites:** Bonfire Shelter; Oblate; Pecan Springs; John Ischy; Haiduk (41KA23); Eckols (41TV526); Harrell; 41UV159; 41UV132.

References: Baker 2003; Dibble and Lorrain 1968; Karbula 2000; Mitchell et al. 1984; Mueggenborg 1994; Sorrow 1966, 1969; Suhm and Jelks 1962; http://www.texasbeyondhistory.net/; Tunnell 1962.

MARSHALL

This is a broad, triangular point with straight to slightly convex lateral edges and strong barbs formed by corner-notching. The stems are relatively short and expanding with concave bases. Most have broad, thinning flakes on the stem. Indeed, typical Marshall preforms feature a finished, thinned stem accomplished before the rest of the biface or thick flake is reduced. An unfinished late-stage Marshall is shown in the upper left of our illustration.

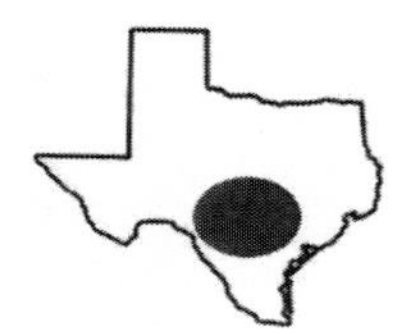

Distribution: Found primarily in central Texas, contemporary with Pedernales. **Period:** Late Middle Archaic. **Sites:** Piedra del Diablo; La Jita; Youngsport; Oblate; Anthon; Jonas Short; 41KE92; No-Name Creek; Gatlin.

References: Denton 1976; Goode 2002; Hester 1971, 1988b; Houk et al. 2008; Johnson 1995; Prewitt 1970; Shafer 1963; Suhm and Jelks 1962; Tunnell 1962.

MARTINDALE

Dart points of the Martindale type have barbs formed by corner-notching. Its most distinguishing feature is the base, which is formed by two convex curves meeting in a depression in the center, giving the base a "fishtail" appearance. Workmanship varies, and many specimens reflect intensive reworking. The Bandy type is apparently the lower Pecos equivalent of Martindale. Or it may simply be a much thinner, often serrated version of Martindale.

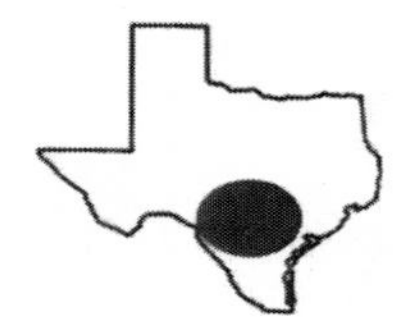

Distribution: Principally central Texas and the lower Pecos but also found in south Texas and much of the rest of the state. **Period:** Early Archaic, with radiocarbon dates 6440–5040 BP and 6410–6280 BP at Smith. **Sites:** Landslide; Tombstone Bluff; Jetta Court; La Jita; 41BN114; 41TR29; Woodrow Heard; Varga; Gatlin; Smith (41UV132).

References: Baker 2003; Decker et al. 2000; Hester 1971; Houk et al. 2008; Prewitt 1981a; Quigg et al. 2008; Sorrow et al. 1967; Suhm and Jelks 1962; Suhm, Krieger, and Jelks 1954; Wesolowsky et al. 1976.

MATAMOROS

This small, often thick, triangular point is similar to Tortugas but markedly smaller. Studies done on Choke Canyon artifacts (Hall et al. 1982) demonstrated that the average length of Tortugas was 4.9 mm to 6.7 mm; Matamoros specimens ranged from 3.2 mm to 4.7 mm in length. Like Catán and Abasolo, Matamoros and the larger Tortugas type may represent a continuum (cf. Mahoney et al. 2002). Matamoros points often have impact fractures at the distal end and are sometimes made of heat-treated chert.

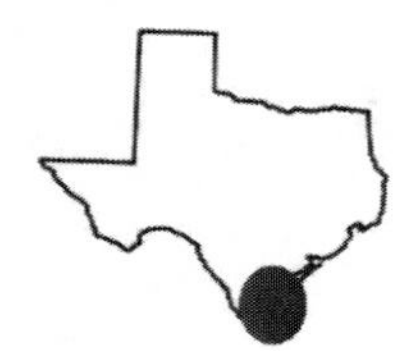

Distribution: Principally south Texas into northeast Mexico. **Period:** Radiocarbon dated about AD 1000 at 41SP120. **Sites:** Becerra Creek (41WB556); Choke Canyon; Ouline; Unland; Cueva de la Zona de Derrumbes Rockshelter, Mexico; 41SP120; Killam Ranch.

References: Bettis 1997; Hall, Black, and Graves 1982; Hester, White, and White 1969; Mahoney et al. 2002; Mallouf and Zavaleta 1979; McClurkan 1966; Ricklis 1995; Suhm and Jelks 1962.

MERRELL

Elton Prewitt has prepared a working draft describing this Early Archaic dart point type and kindly provided us with a copy. He has not completed analysis of the sample of dart points that may represent this type. But he has given us permission to note some of the characteristics he sees for this type. Merrell points often look like Late Archaic–age Frio points, but there is a temporal separation of roughly four thousand years between these two types. Merrell has an asymmetrical stem (one "ear" or "tang" is larger than the other) and a diagonal transverse flaking pattern seen on other Early Archaic types. It is closely associated technologically and temporally with Martindale, and according to Prewitt the two intergrade where there are sufficient numbers of each present within a site.

Merrell points have often been included in the Uvalde type, and at the Varga site, the illustrations suggest considerable similarities in the illustrations of Merrell, Gower, and Bandy. The best examples of Merrell appear to us to be the two or three specimens from the Merrell site and the Landslide site, both north of Austin.

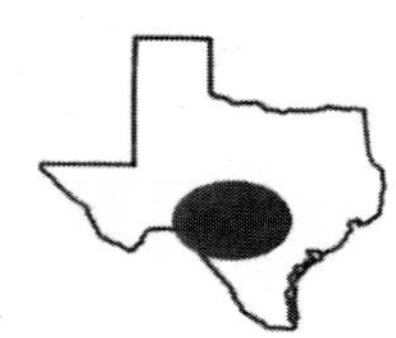

Distribution: Lower Pecos and south and central Texas. **Period:** Early Archaic. **Sites:** Merrell; Landslide; Varga; Wilson-Leonard.

References: Campbell 1948; Collins et al. 1998; Dial et al. 1998; Prewitt 2010; Quigg et al. 2008; Sorrow et al. 1967; Suhm and Jelks 1962.

MIDLAND

This thin lanceolate point has straight to slightly convex lateral edges that have been carefully trimmed. This trimming is usually a diagnostic trait for the type. Both faces have a flat, invasive, regular retouch, which is parallel to subparallel with a marginal retouch on the edges (Martinez 1990). Bases are usually concave, or just slightly so. The point resembles Folsom in shape and size, but it is very thin and unfluted.

Distribution: Southern Llano Estacado area, into central Texas, the coast, and eastern Texas. **Period:** Paleo-Indian. **Sites:** Winkler-1; Wyche Ranch; Rattle Snake Draw; Midland (Scharbauer Ranch); Shifting Sands; Wilson-Leonard; Pavo Real; Golden Sands (Lee County, Tex.); Wilson-Leonard.

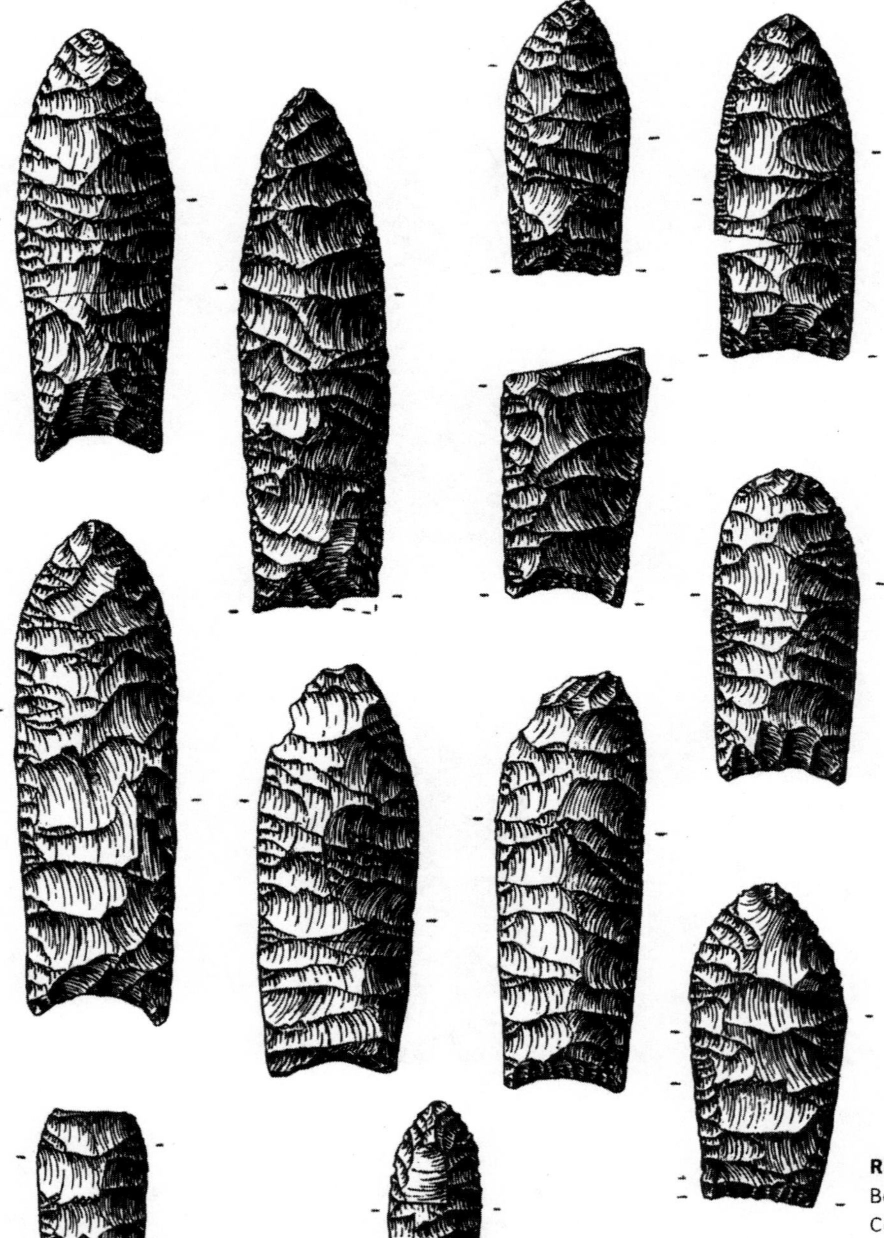

References: Amick et al. 1989; Blaine 1968; Bousman, Baker, and Kerr 2004; Brown 2007; Collins et al. 1998; Collins et al. 2003; E. D. Dorchester, personal communication; Holliday 1997; Martinez 1990; Rose 2011; Wendorf and Krieger 1959; Wendorf et al. 1955; Westfall 2007.

MILNESAND

The Milnesand-type specimens are a relatively broad, parallel-flaked, lanceolate point that has a square, slightly concave to convex, wedge-shaped base. Basal edges are straight to very slightly convex. It tends to be thickest toward the tip. Smoothing of the basal and lateral edges is characteristic. Transverse pressure flaking was used in the manufacture of points from the Milnesand site with flake scars extending from the edge of the point to the center or beyond, but these flake scars do not tend to form a median ridge on the artifact. It is thinner, proportionately broader, and appreciably shorter than Firstview; the majority range between 40 mm and 55 mm in length. An obsidian basal fragment found in Gaines County was sourced using portable X-ray fluorescence (PXRF) to Cerro de Toledo in the Jemez Mountains of northern New Mexico.

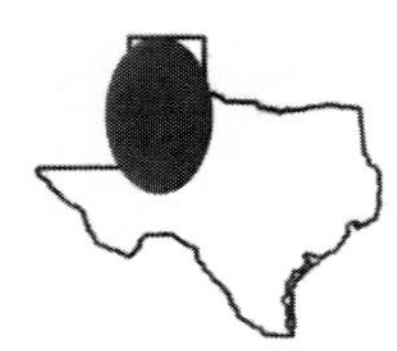

Distribution: Panhandle, Llano Estacado, and to the Texas coastal plain; eastern New Mexico and Colorado. **Period:** Paleo-Indian, ca. 8200 BC–7200 BC. **Sites:** Olsen-Chubbuck (Colo.); Blackwater Draw (N.Mex.); Milnesand (N.Mex.); Wyche Ranch; Scharbauer; 41VT141; 41RF10; Howard County; Lone Wolf Creek; Cedar Lake (Gaines County).

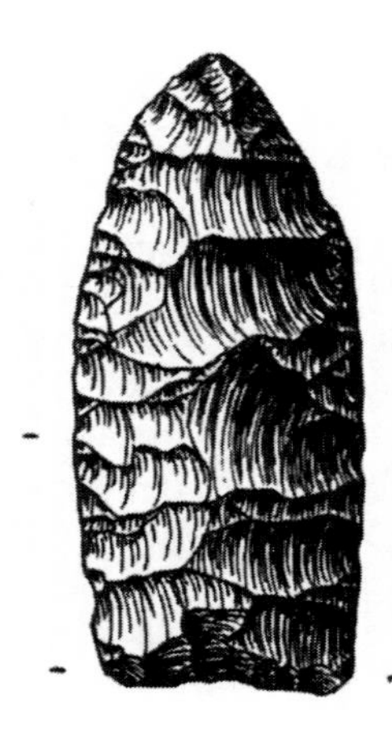

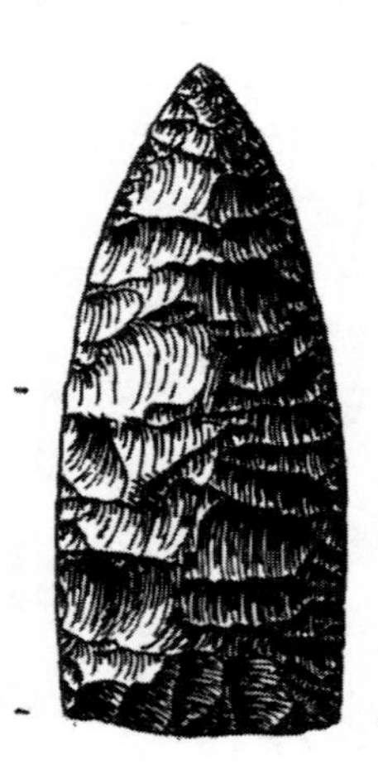

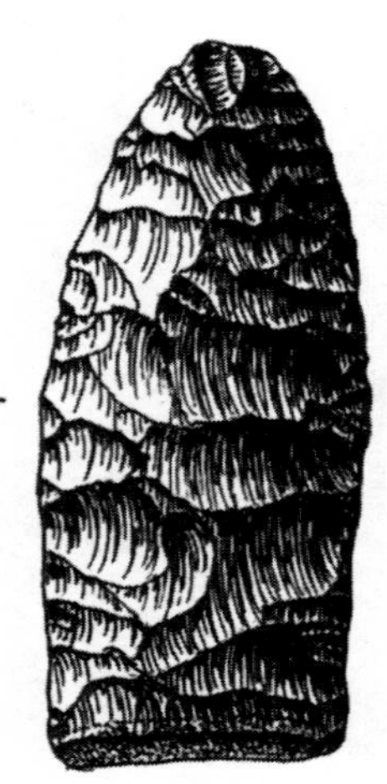

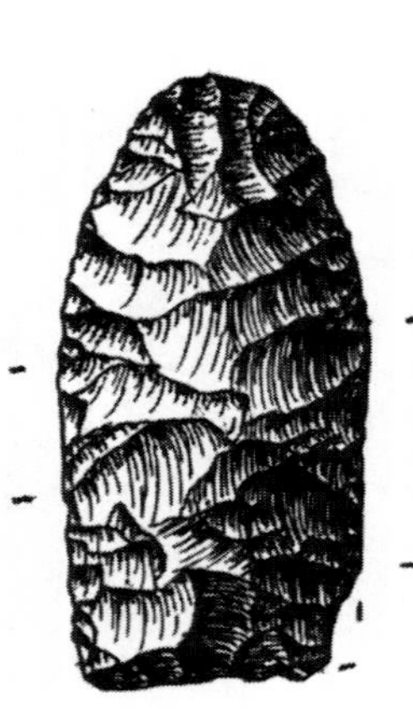

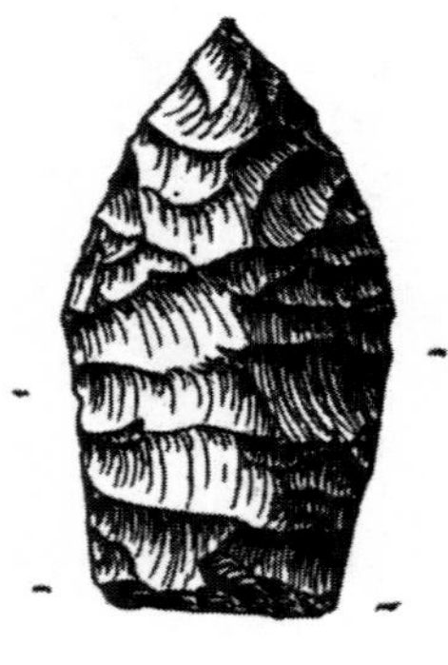

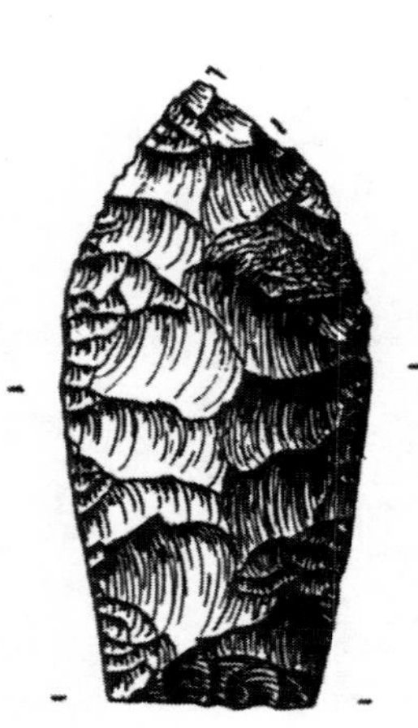

References: Figgins 1927; Hester et al. 2006; Holliday 1997; Justice 2002; Sellards 1955; Warnica and Williamson 1968; Wheat 1972; Wormington 1957.

MONTELL

This triangular point is characterized by a relatively short stem with a V- to U-shaped basal notch. The shoulders are strong and usually barbed. Analysis of a large sample from Jonas Terrace provides details about Montell preforms and the type's overall technology (see also Goode 2002). The points are often heavily reworked causing much variation in size. Preforms and unfinished Montell specimens are fairly common in sites along the Balcones Escarpment. Stems are formed and finished on large flakes or crude biface blanks before the remainder of the point is completed.

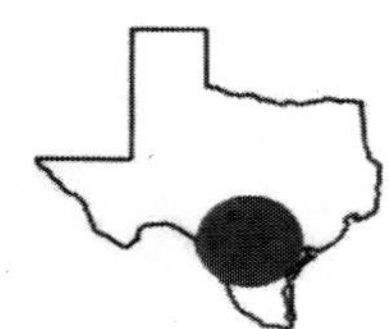

Distribution: Mainly in central Texas and the lower Pecos. **Period:** Late Archaic, ca. 800–400 BC. **Sites:** Piedra del Diablo; La Jita; Youngsport; Wunderlich; Jonas Terrace; Anthon; Gatlin; Varga; Wilson-Leonard; 41UV20.

References: Goode 2002; Hester 1971; Hester and Whatley 1992a; Houk et al. 2008; Johnson 1962a, 1995; Prewitt 1970; Quigg et al. 2008; Shafer 1963; Suhm and Jelks 1962.

MORHISS

This point is usually rather large and heavy, with a long, lanceolate body, a rectangular stem, and generally convex basal edges. There are often traces of asphaltum on the stem, resulting from the use of the gummy natural tar for hafting.

Distribution: Found mainly on the lower reaches of the Guadalupe River in the upper part of the central coastal plain. **Period:** Late Archaic, ca. 800 BC. **Sites:** Morhiss; Berger Bluff; Kent-Crane; Live Oak Point; 41VT141; 41VT98; Smith Creek Bridge (41DW270); Loma Sandia.

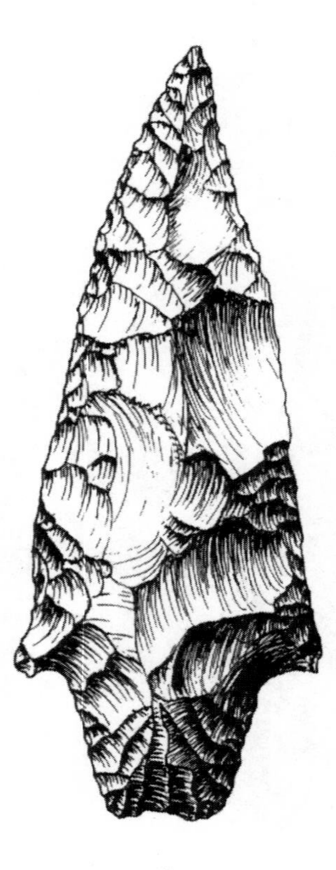

References: Braun et al. 2008; Brown 1983; Campbell 1958, 1976; Fox 1979a; Fox and Hester 1976; Hudler et al. 2002; Jelks 1962; Lintz et al. 1993; Schmiedlin 2000a; Suhm and Weinstein 1992; Taylor and Highley 1995; Weinstein 2002.

MORRILL

This point has a long, slender, triangular body; straight to gently convex lateral edges; weak to squared shoulders; and a long, wide, roughly rectangular stem. Stems are narrower than Carrollton or Bulverde. Stem dulling is sometimes present. In some cases, the type has some similarities to Yarbrough.

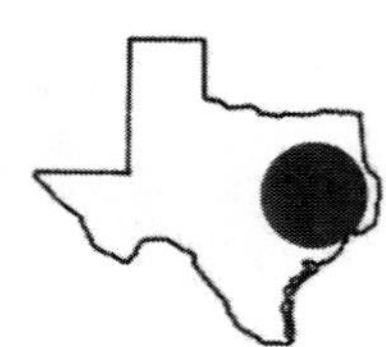

Distribution: Primarily in the central part of east Texas but extending into Louisiana. **Period:** Middle Archaic. **Sites:** Yarbrough and Miller; George C. Davis; Youngsport; Jake Martin; Womack; Allen; Fort Polk (La.).

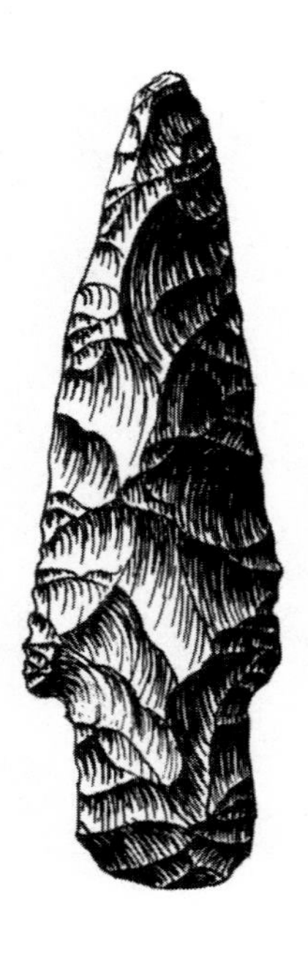
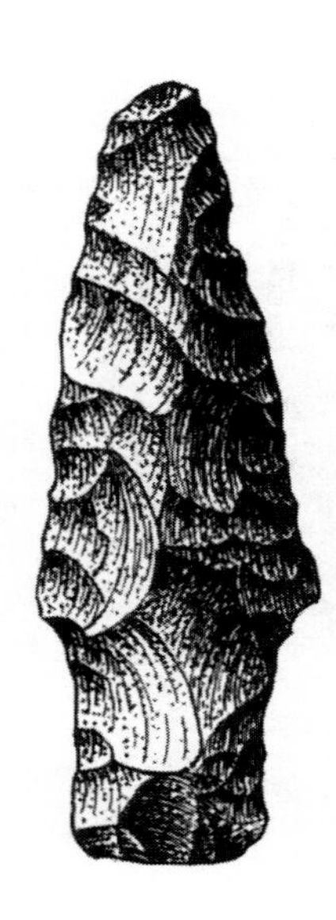
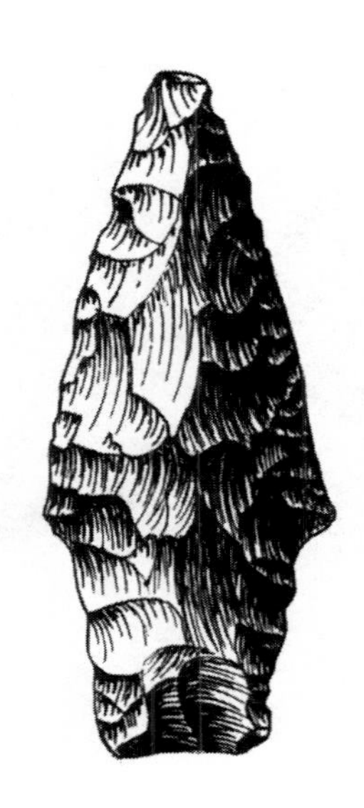

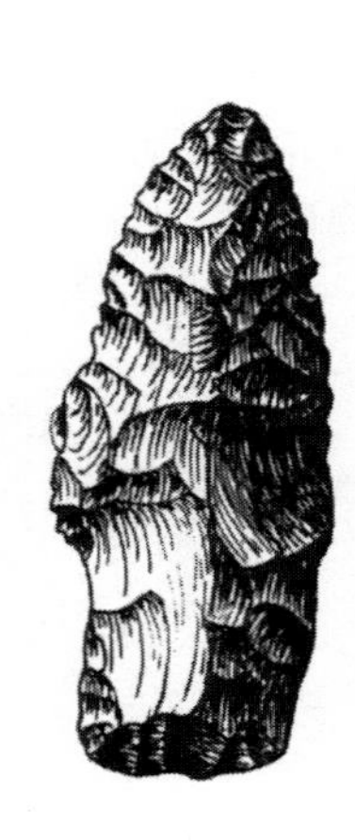

References: Anderson and Smith 2003; Davis and Davis 1960; Johnson 1962b; Newell and Krieger 1949; Shafer 1963; Story et al. 1990; Suhm and Jelks 1962.

MOTLEY

This is a distinctive, well-made point, usually of exotic cherts. It has a triangular, moderately slender body, and deep corner notches produce barbs and an expanding stem with a narrow neck. We have included the so-called Epps type in with the Motley type, as suggested by Justice (1987), who believes they are simply reworked Motley specimens.

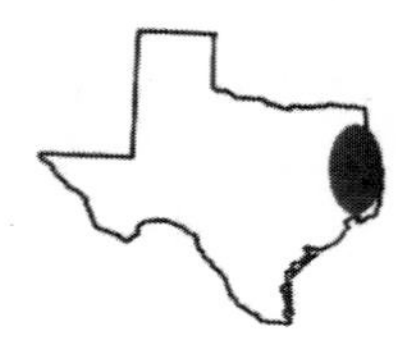

Distribution: Louisiana, and occasionally reported in southeast to northeast Texas. **Period:** Middle to Late Archaic, 1500 BC–500 BC. **Sites:** Poverty Point (La.); Motley Place (La.); Fort Polk (La.); J2 Ranch, Victoria County; McFaddin Beach; Oak Hill (41RK214).

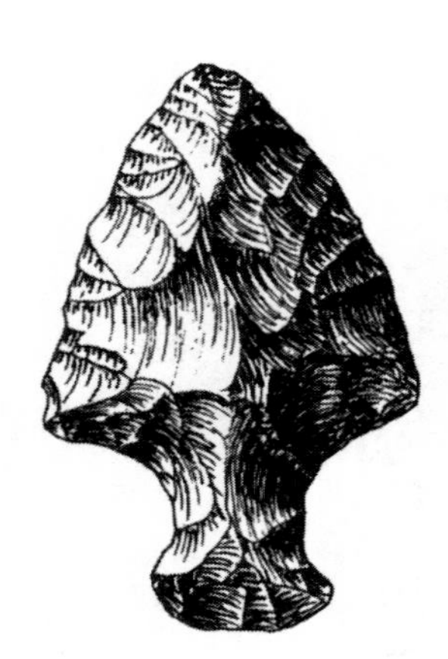

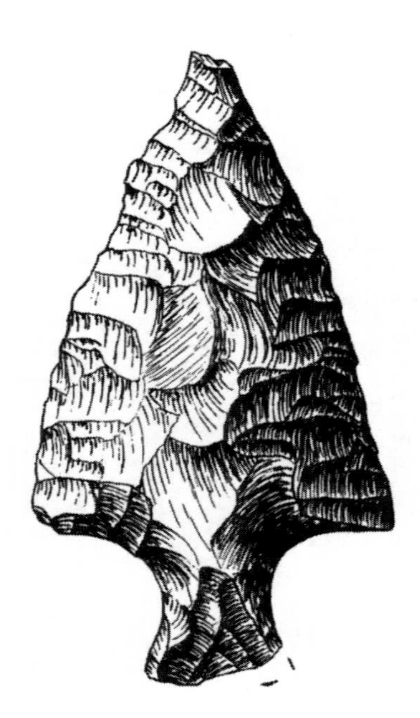

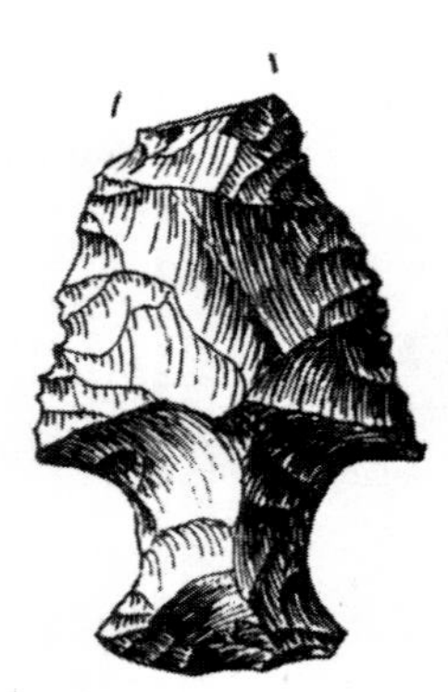

References: Anderson and Smith 2003; Anthony and Brown 1994; Fields et al. 1991; Ford, Phillips, and Haag 1955; Ford and Webb 1956; Rogers et al. 1997; Schmiedlin 2000a; D. A. Story, personal communication; Stright et al. 2000; Webb, personal communication.

NECHES

Known as Neches River in the literature, we have suggested here that the name be shortened to Neches. This triangular point has straight to slightly convex lateral edges that are commonly serrated along the lower two-thirds of their length; the distal one-third is not usually serrated. The tip may be rounded or chipped straight across like a chisel-bit rather than pointed. The stem is strongly expanding or rectangular with straight sides and rounded basal edges. A variant of Neches is typed as Oletha by Prewitt and subsequently used by him as a separate type (Prewitt 2005, 277).

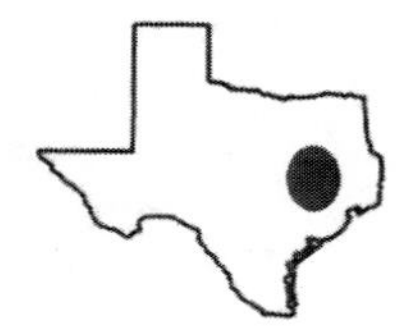

Distribution: East and southeast Texas, into Louisiana. **Period:** Middle Archaic to Woodland. **Sites:** Steinhagen Lake and Sam Rayburn Lake; Toledo Bend; McGee Bend Reservoir; Upper Navasota Reservoir (Carl Sadler and Louis Sadler); Cedar Creek; Strawberry Hill; 41H134; Fort Polk (La.).

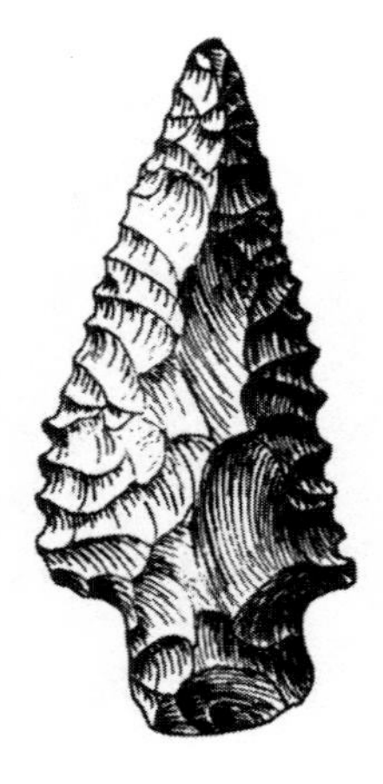

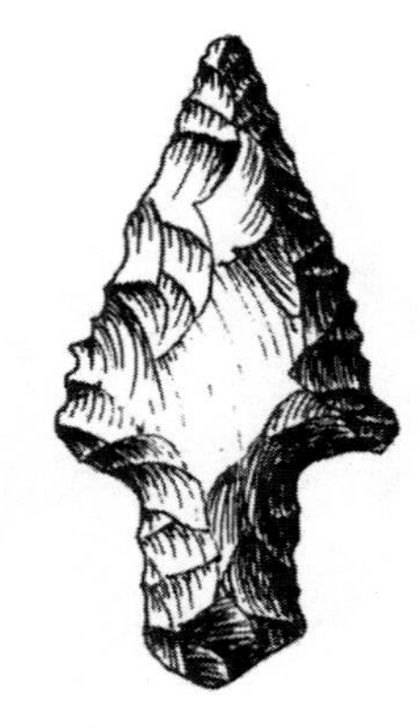

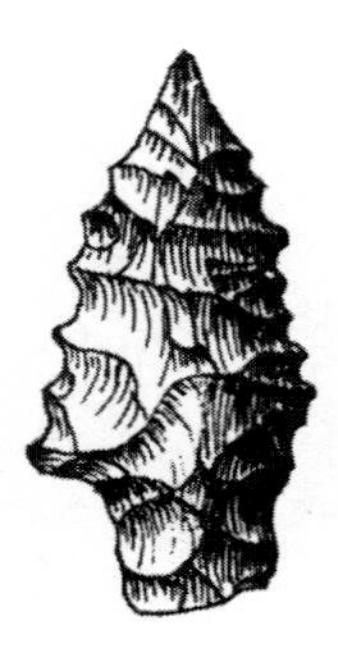

References: Anderson and Smith 2003; Fields 2004; Fields et al. 1990a; Jelks 1965; Keller and Weir 1979; Kent 1961; M. Mallouf 1976; Prewitt 1974b, 1975, 2005; Scurlock and Davis 1962; Story 1965.

NOLAN

This is an elongated point with tapered shoulders; the lateral edges are convex or recurved. The distinctive attribute of this form is steep, alternate beveling on the rectangular stem edges. Specimens can be massive and extremely well made.

Distribution: Primarily central Texas. **Period:** Middle Archaic, ca. 4000 BC–2500 BC. **Sites:** Williams; Greenhaw; Crumley; 41BX1; 41BN115; Eckols (41TV528); Gatlin (41KR621); Millican Bench (41TV163).

References: Houk et al. 2008; Karbula 2000; Kelly 1962; Lukowski 1983; Mauldin et al. 2004; Suhm 1959; Suhm and Jelks 1962; Weir 1979.

PAISANO

These are triangular points, with straight to convex lateral edges that are usually serrated. Some specimens have slight stems formed by shallow side notches, and the base is concave to deeply indented. The specimens can sometimes have a squat lanceolate outline and other variations from reworking that make them a challenge to type. This often leads archaeologists to use the classification for points far from the Paisano range and that have nothing to do with the type.

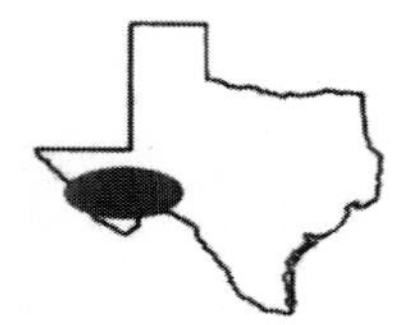

Distribution: Trans-Pecos and Big Bend areas, and into parts of lower Pecos. **Period:** Late to Transitional Archaic, radiocarbon date of AD 560, Fiero site (or later). **Sites:** Bear Creek; Baker Cave; Eagle Cave; Roark Cave; Culberson County; Fiero.

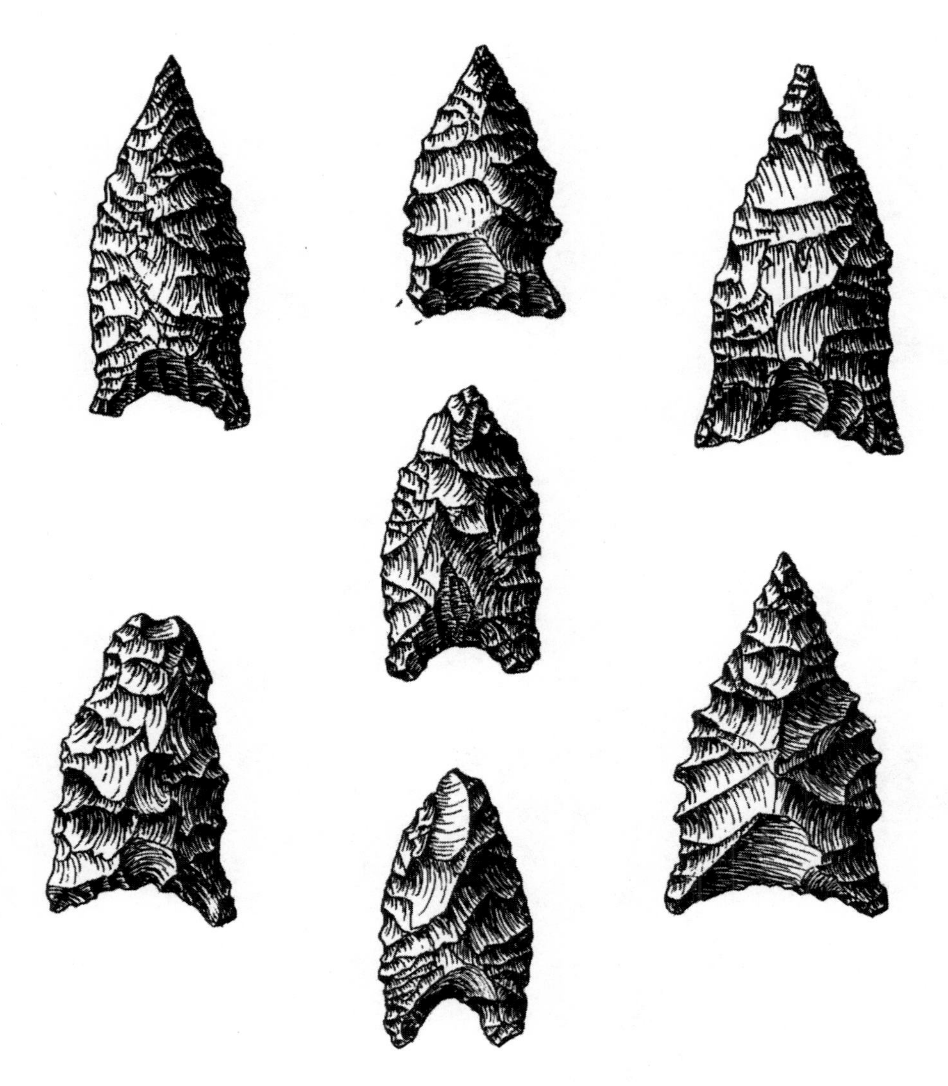

References: Kelly and Smith 1963; Mallouf 1999; Marmaduke 1978; Ross 1965; Story and Bryant 1966; Suhm and Jelks 1962; Word and Douglas 1970; Young 1982.

PALMER

This small, corner-notched point has a straight, thinned, and heavily ground base. The shoulders are barbed and vary from being greater to less than basal width. The lateral edges tend to be straight but may be slightly concave or convex, and most examples are serrated. It is also known as a small variety of Kirk Corner Notched, and Justice (1987) suggests the only observed morphological difference is the heavy basal grinding typical of Palmer.

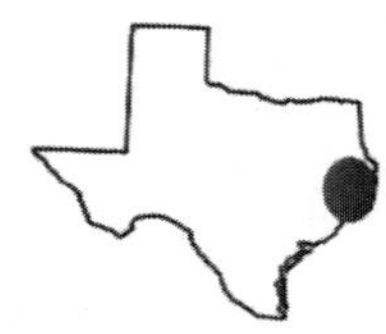

Distribution: Southwestern Arkansas and bordering areas of Oklahoma, Louisiana, and Texas. **Period:** Early Archaic/Paleo-Indian. **Sites:** McFaddin Beach (41JF50); Sam Rayburn Lake; Dam B, Sandy Creek (Neches River drainage); Toledo Bend; Fort Polk (La.).

References: Anderson and Smith 2003; Coe 1964; Justice 1987; Perino 1968; Story et al. 1990.

PALMILLAS

The Palmillas type has a great deal of regional variation. Points vary considerably in size, with a triangular body with mostly convex lateral edges. Points have slight to barbed shoulders formed by shallow side notches. The expanding stem and convex base give the stems a bulbar appearance. It remains a poorly understood type in need of much research.

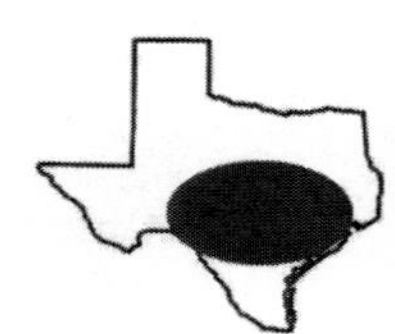

Distribution: Points identified as Palmillas are found from east Texas, the central coastal plain, and south Texas and have been described for the lower Pecos by some authors. **Period:** Middle to Late Archaic. **Sites:** Smith Rockshelter; Livingston Reservoir; San Jacinto River Basin; Panda Cave, Fate Bell Rockshelter; Loma Sandia.

References: Alexander 1970; Anthony and Brown 1994; McClurkan 1968; Peck 1991; Shafer 1968; Suhm 1957; Suhm and Jelks 1962; Taylor and Highley 1995.

PANDALE

Pandale has a long, usually lanceolate point most easily recognized by the distinctive alternate beveling of the body, which creates a peculiar corkscrew twist. Stems are also alternately beveled.

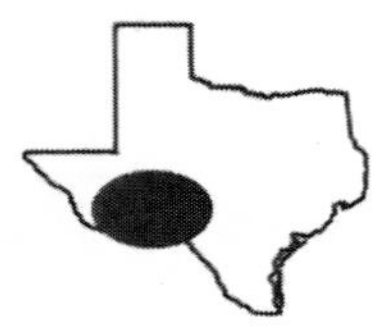

Distribution: Very common in the lower Pecos, the eastern and western Trans-Pecos, and into the southwestern Edwards Plateau. **Period:** Middle Archaic, 4000 BP; at Baker Cave, 4700 BP. **Sites:** Eagle Cave; Damp Cave; Devil's Mouth; Parida Cave; 41VV74; Fate Bell Rockshelter; Gatlin.

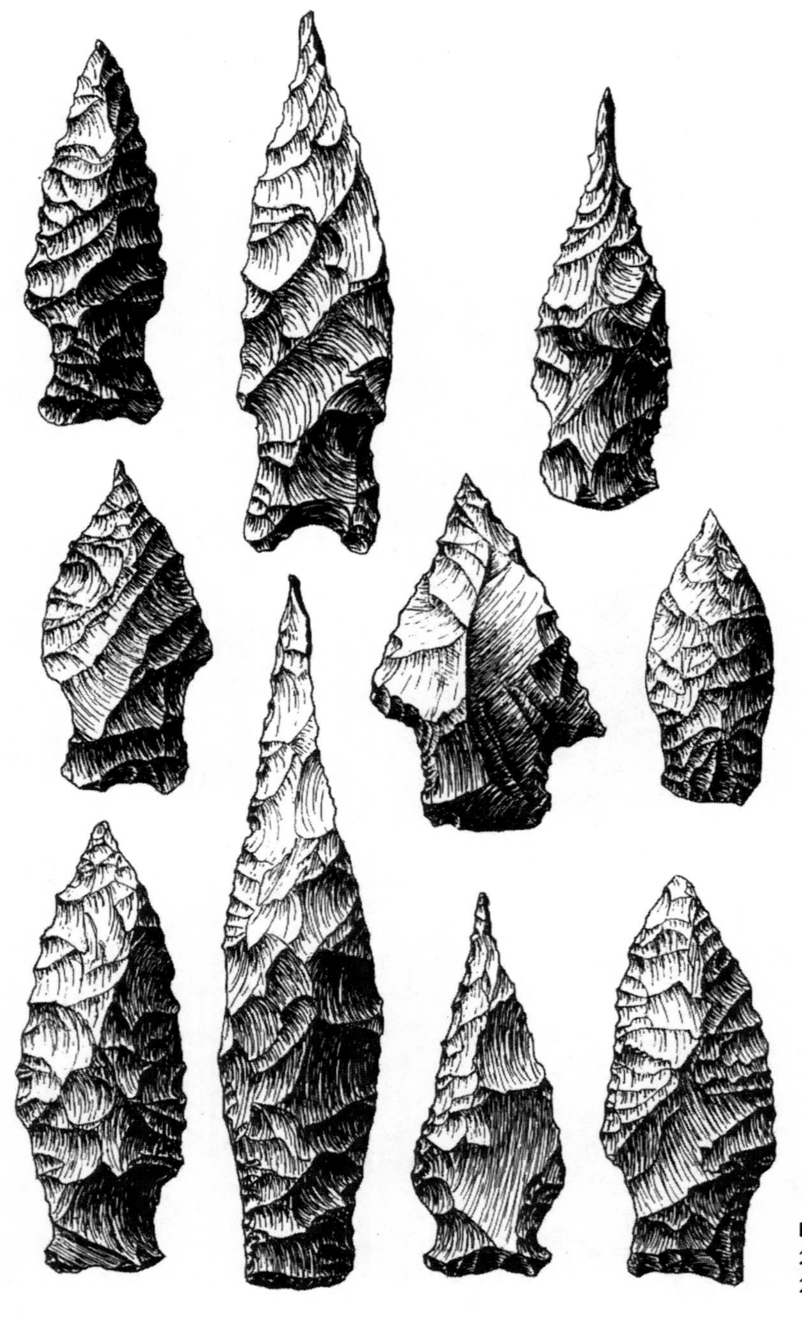

References: Alexander 1970; Epstein 1963; Houk et al. 2008; Johnson 1964; Kelly 1962; Mallouf, Cloud, and Walter 2006; Marmaduke 1978; Peck 1991; Ross 1965.

PANDORA

This elongate, triangular point has a straight to slightly convex base and can be relatively large and crudely chipped. It is a poorly known type, if it is indeed legitimate, and it is quite possible that some are actually preforms or were used for knives.

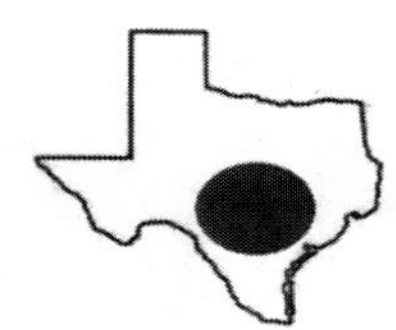

Distribution: Widely distributed from south Texas, across central Texas, and the lower Pecos. **Period:** Middle to Late Archaic. **Sites:** Wheeler; Morhiss; Johnston-Heller; La Perdida.

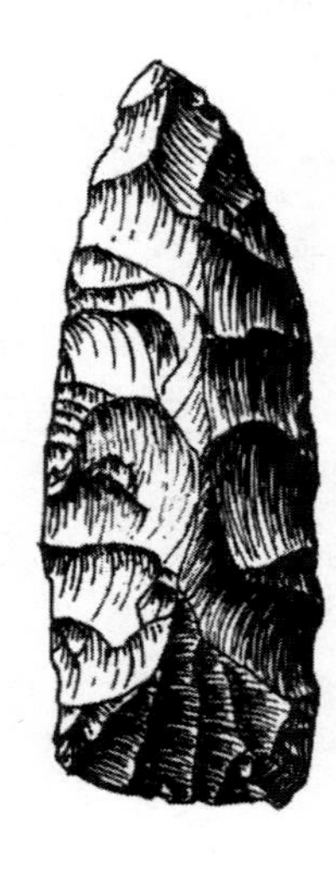

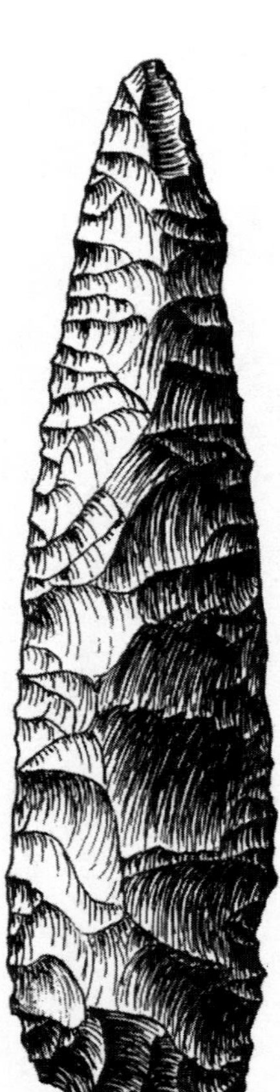
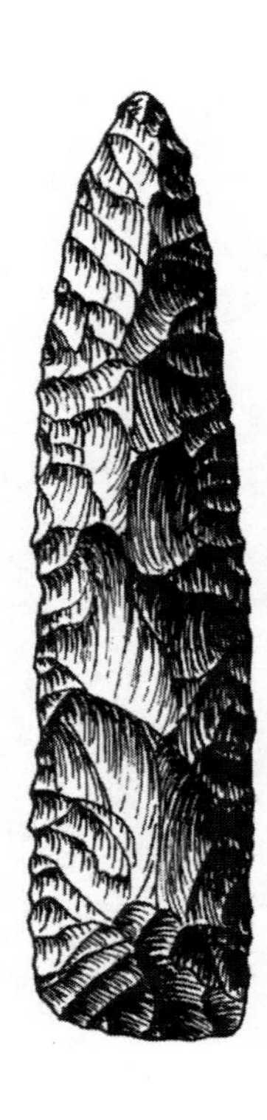
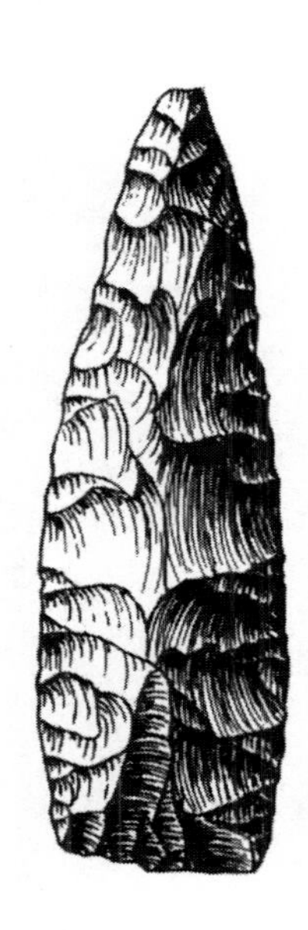

References: Birmingham and Hester 1976; Corbin 1974; Crook and Harris 1954b; Suhm and Jelks 1962; Weir 1956.

PEDERNALES

The most common dart point type in central Texas, Pedernales points vary greatly in overall size, types of barbs, and technology depending on the reworking of a specimen during its life span. The body is triangular with a more or less rectangular, concave-based stem. The stem is often thinned by a broad, flutelike flake on one or both sides. On preforms, stems are usually finished before the body is thinned and the lateral edges straightened. There is so much variation in Pedernales that various scholars have reviewed data on the type (e.g., stem forms) with the goal of defining regional or temporal differences within the type (Mahoney et al. 2003). The large number of points at many central Texas sites have led to some very useful, detailed analyses of the type, including the work of Johnson (1995, 2000); Mahoney and colleagues (2003), and Goode (2002).

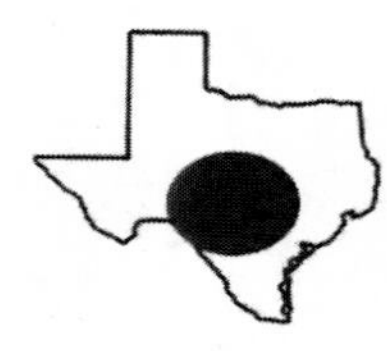

Distribution: Extremely common in central Texas, the northern parts of south Texas and the coastal plain, and into the lower Pecos. **Period:** Middle Archaic, ca. 2500–3500 BP; at the Blue Hole site in Uvalde County, a radiocarbon date of 4,420–4100 BP is attributed to the type; and at the Bessie Kruze site, a date of about 3500 years ago. **Sites:** Centipede Cave; Oblate; Smith Rockshelter; Oulline; Bull Pen; Anthon; Eckols; Jonas Terrace; Blue Hole; Smith; La Jita; Bessie Kruze; Gatlin (41MM340); 41UV20; Woodrow Heard.

References: Decker et al. 2000; Ensor et al. 1988; Epstein 1963; Goode 2002; Hester 1971; Hester and Whatley 1992a; Hester et al. 1969; Houk et al. 2008; Johnson 1995, 2000; Karbula 2000; Mahoney et al. 2003; Mueggenborg 1994; Suhm 1957; Suhm and Jelks 1962; Tunnell 1962.

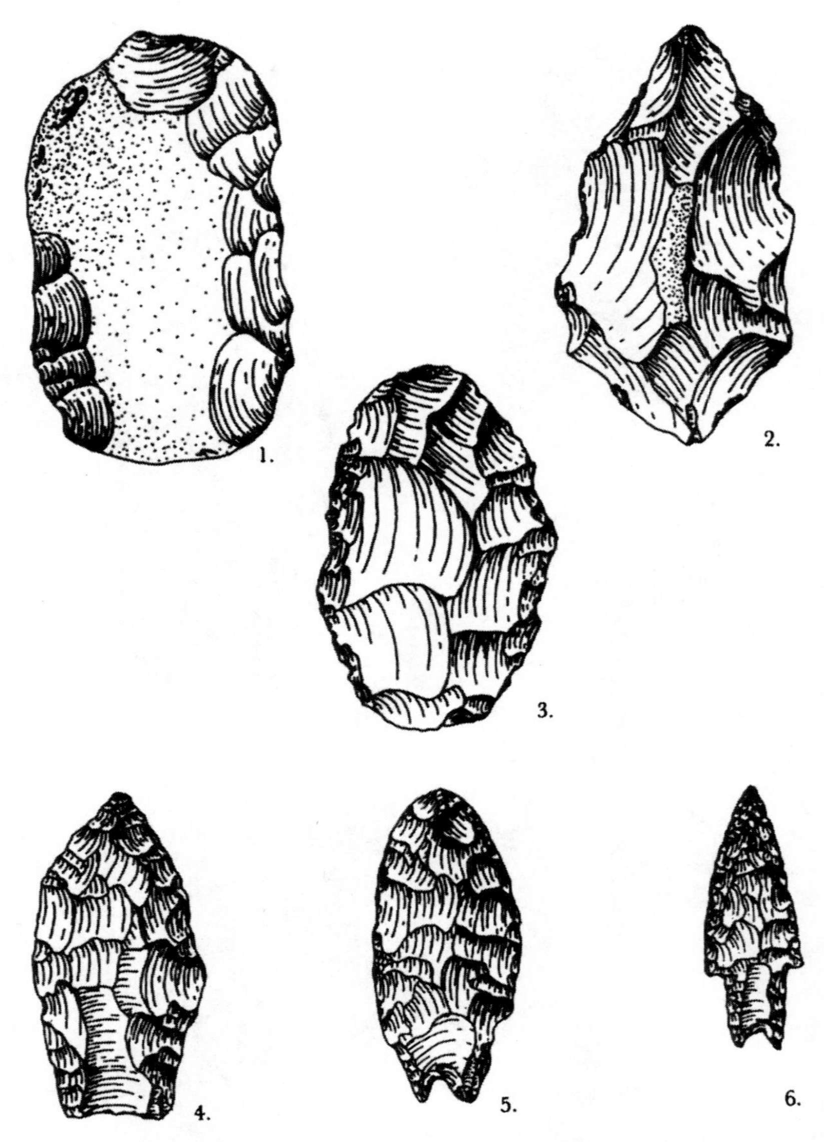

Pedernales reduction model. From Ensor et al. (1988, fig. 61). By permission of Texas State Department of Highways and Public Transportation.

PELICAN

These are short, broad lanceolate points with basal thinning that sometimes takes the form of fluting. The lateral edges are dulled, the extent of which is indicated on the illustrations. The specimens often appear to have been extensively reworked or resharpened.

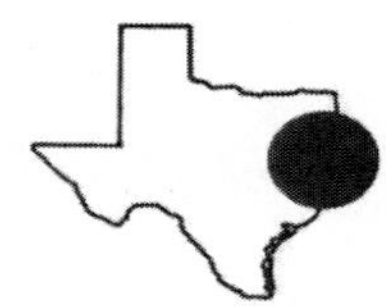

Distribution: In Louisiana; rare in Texas, found mainly in northeast and southeast portions of the state. **Period:** Paleo-Indian, possibly contemporary with San Patrice. **Sites:** McFaddin Beach (41JF50); sites in the Toledo Bend Reservoir area, the lower Trinity River drainage, and the Sabine River drainage (both the Texas and Louisiana sides); Newton, Sabine, and Jasper counties; Fort Polk (La.).

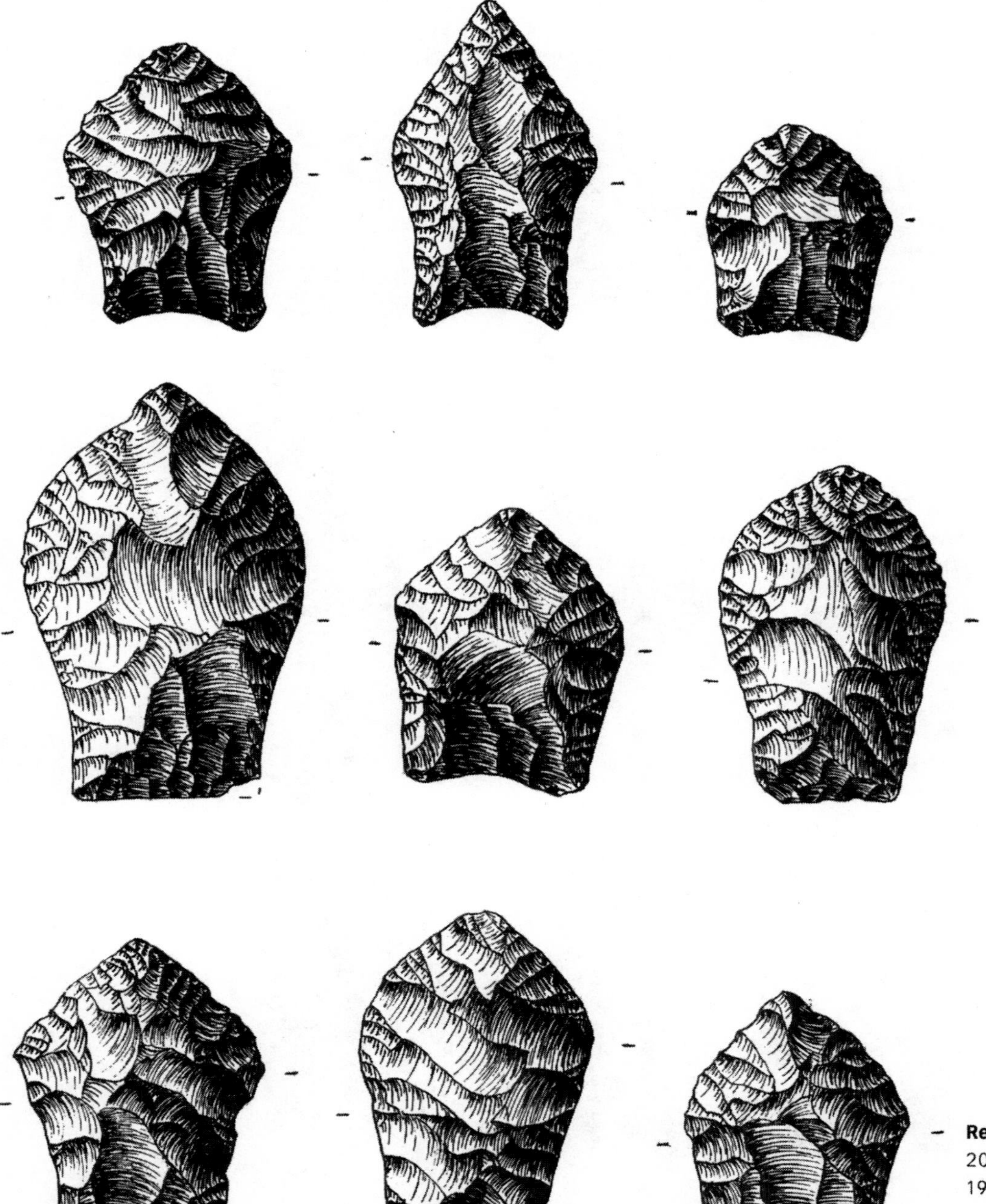

References: Anderson and Smith 2003; Gagliano and Gregory 1965; Perino 1985; Stright, Lear, and Bennett 1999; Waldorf and Waldorf 1987.

PLAINVIEW

The Plainview point is an unfluted, lanceolate point that has parallel or slightly convex lateral edges and a basal concavity ranging from 1 mm to 4 mm in depth (Kelly 1983b). Basal edges are almost always thinned and ground. The body is usually parallel-flaked. This typological label has often been widely applied to similar points across the state. The definition of this type needs extensive reexamination. It has long been a "dumping ground" for unfluted lanceolates in Texas. In using the label, very close comparisons need to be made with specimens from the Plainview type site (41HA1) housed at the Texas Archeological Research Laboratory (TARL; illustrations of these specimens appear in Knudson 1973 and Bousman et al. 2004).

Distribution: Scattered surface finds are reported statewide, but excavated sites are limited to the Texas Panhandle, central Texas, and the lower Pecos. **Period:** Paleo-Indian, ca. 8150 BC–8010 BC. **Sites:** Lubbock Lake; Wilson-Leonard; Bonfire Shelter; 41HA1; Winkler County; Martin County; Rex Rodgers; Ryan's cache; Horace Rivers.

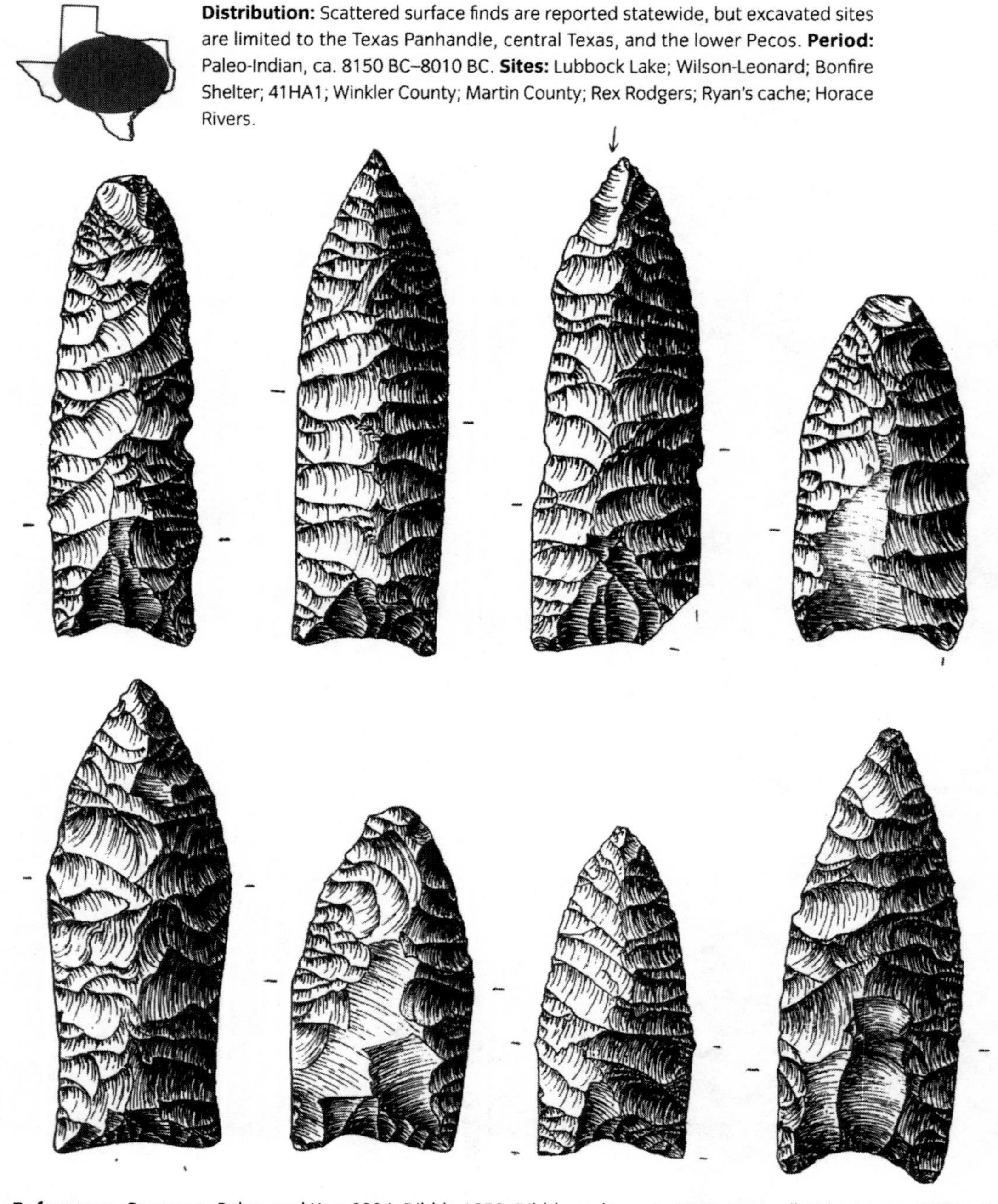

References: Bousman, Baker, and Kerr 2004; Dibble 1970; Dibble and Lorrain 1968; Hartwell 1995; Hester 1979a, 1991; Holliday 1997; Johnson and Holliday 1980, 2004; Kelly 1982, 1983b; Mallouf and Mandel 1996; Sellards et al. 1947; Suhm and Jelks 1962; Weir 1984; Wormington 1957.

PONTCHARTRAIN

This long, slender point has straight to convex lateral edges, with the body shaped by well-executed parallel-flaking. Specimens have squared shoulders, which may be slight, and occasional barbs. The rectangular stem has a straight to slightly convex base that sometimes retains cortex.

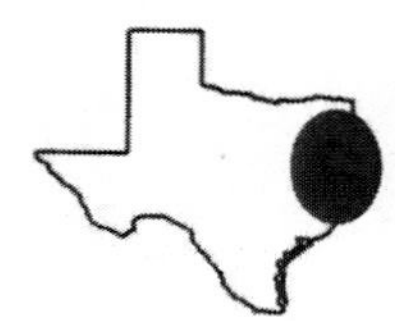

Distribution: Louisiana westward along the Red River and into east Texas. **Period:** Middle to Transitional Archaic, ca. 2000 BC–AD 500. **Sites:** Poverty Point (La.); Jones Hill; Burris 2; Culpepper; San Jacinto County; Austin County; north Sulphur River drainage (Fannin County); Neches River drainage, Polk County; Oak Hill (41RK214).

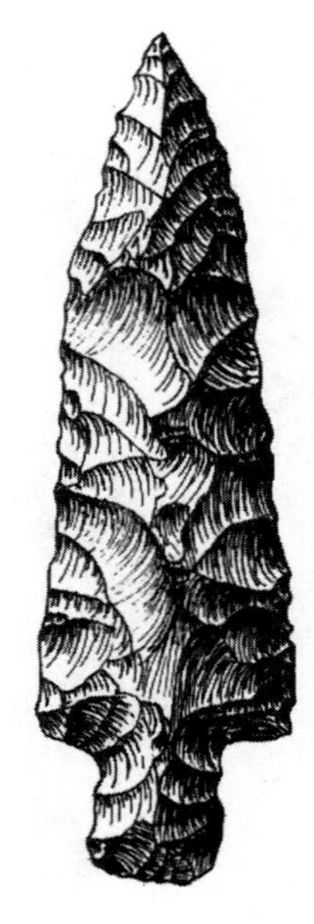

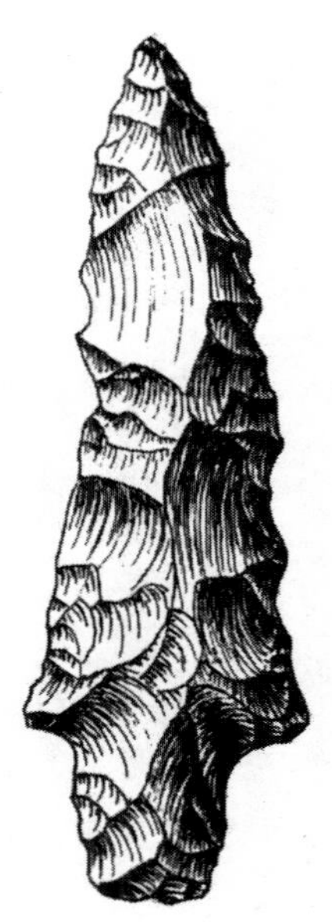

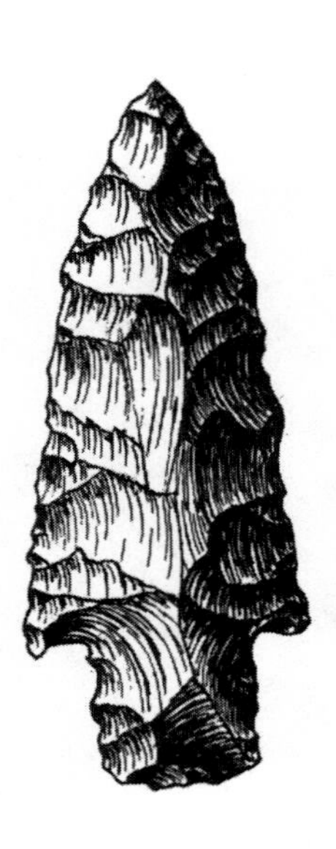

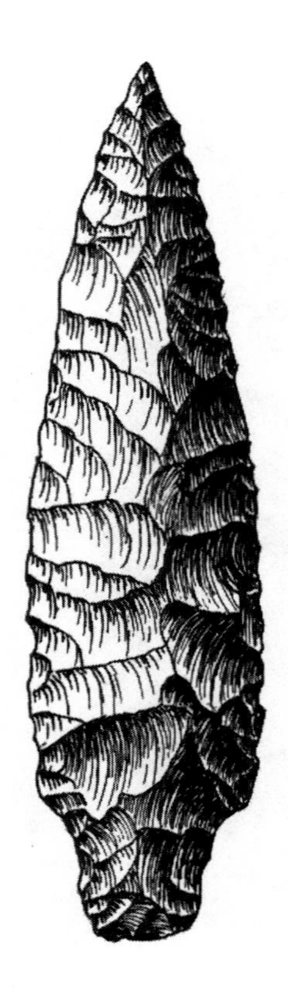

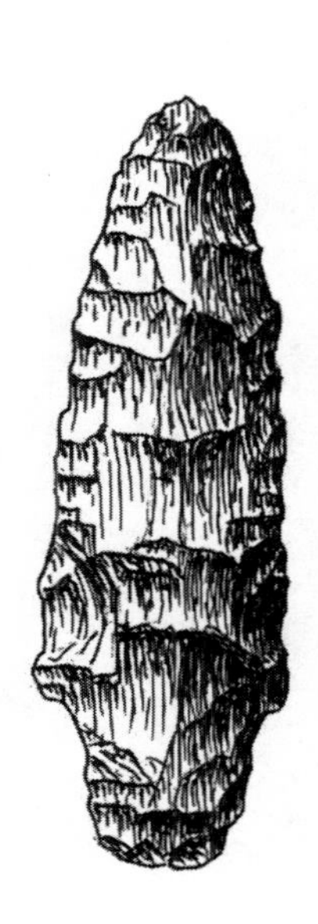

References: Ford and Webb 1956; Hall 1994; McClurkan 1968; Perino 1968; Rogers et al. 1997; Scurlock 1962; Story et al. 1990; Webb 1982; C. Webb, personal communication.

REFUGIO

Refugio specimens are elongate, triangular points with rounded bases and convex lateral edges. Size varies considerably. Some are large and heavy, as at the Morhiss site, while smaller versions are often seen in southern Texas. The base is convex and often thinned. Like Pandora, it is possible that some, or most, are actually preforms or knives.

Distribution: Reported in south Texas, the central coastal plain, and the lower Pecos. **Period:** Late Middle Archaic to Late Archaic, 3400 BP at the Lino site, where the type occurred below Tortugas. **Sites:** Choke Canyon; La Perdida; San Miguel Creek (41AT7); McMullen County; Boiler; Morhiss; Becerra Creek; Lino (41VT141).

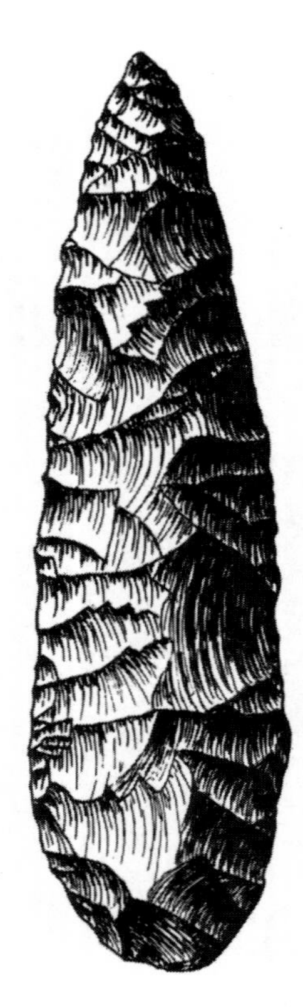

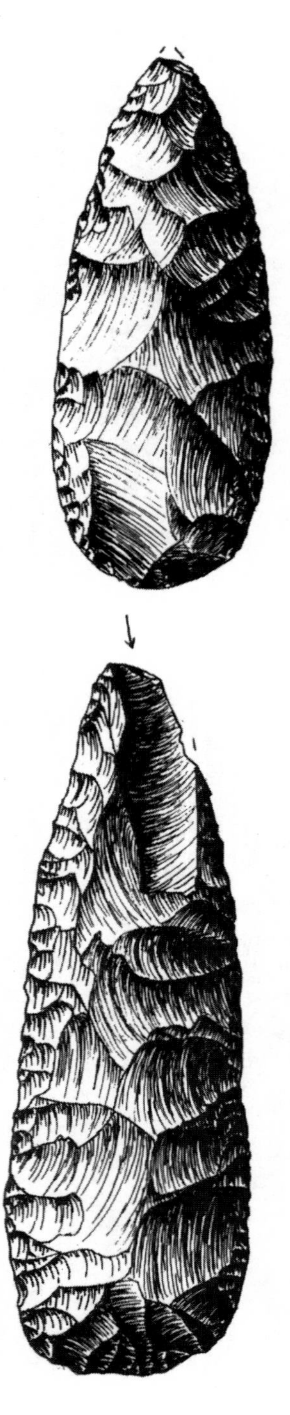

References: Braun et al. 2008; Hall, Black, and Graves 1982; Hester 1968; Mahoney et al. 2002; Quigg et al. 2002; Quigg et al. 2000; Suhm and Jelks 1962; Weir 1956.

ST. CHARLES

A number of points made in the "dovetail" tradition have been found in northeast Texas and eastern Oklahoma. A distinctive specimen was found at the J2 Ranch site in Victoria County. The type is widely distributed from the Midwest into the southeastern United States. They date as early as 7000 BC at Graham Cave in Missouri and are often described as "Early Archaic." Since St. Charles points have such a distinctive shape and technology of manufacture, the specimens are well made, corner to side notched, and are often heavily dulled on the basal edge and along the edges of the notches.

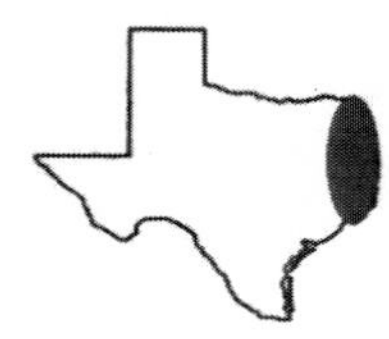

Distribution: Several have been found in northeast Texas sites and onto the coastal plain. **Period:** Early Archaic. **Sites:** Northeast Texas; J2 Ranch, Victoria County; Sabine County and Jasper County; McFaddin Beach (41JF50); Vernon Parish and Calcasieu Parish (La.)

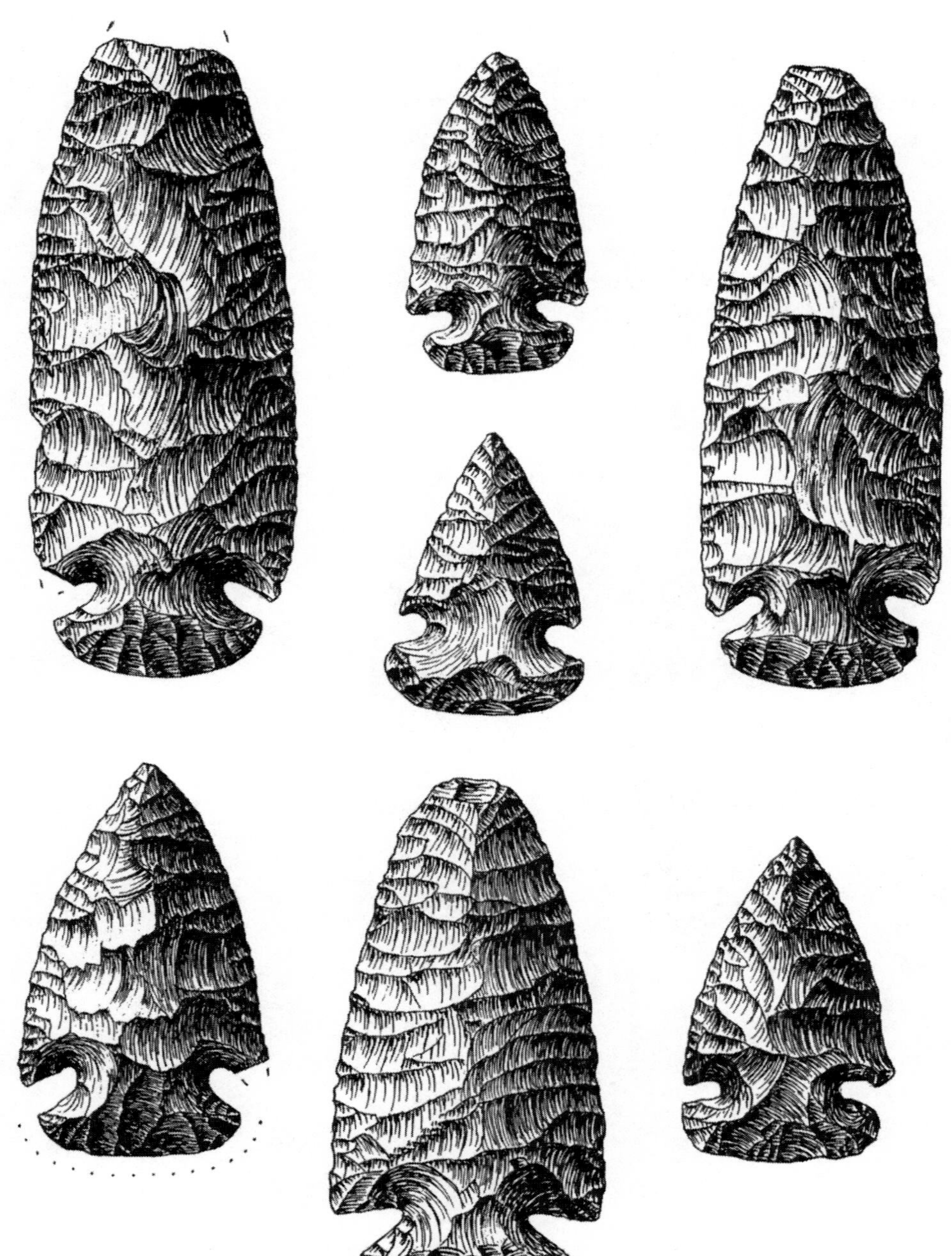

References: Justice 1987; Perino 1985; Schmiedlin 2000b; Scully 1951.

ST. MARY'S HALL

The St. Mary's Hall type was defined by Dial and colleagues (1998), based on excavated materials from the Wilson-Leonard site. Subsequently, Bousman and colleagues (2004) have also provided additional details. Points of this type have often been incorrectly placed in the Plainview category, as Hester (1991) did for the St. Mary's Hall site (41BX229) in San Antonio.

St. Mary's Hall points are narrow, parallel-sided lanceolate points. Parallel-oblique flaking is present on practically all documented specimens. Maximum width is usually in the 18–22 mm range. Bases are concave, mostly 1–3 mm deep, though 6–7 mm on rare occasion. Bases are thinned by two to three adjacent vertical flakes. Lateral edges above the base are dulled, usually for 20–35 mm in length. Points are consistently thin, at 5.5–6.5 mm. Impact and snap fractures are common. Specimens are often reworked into very small pieces, as at St. Mary's Hall.

By far, the largest sample of this type has come from the Wilson County Sand Pit, a sand-mining operation on Cibolo Creek twenty miles southeast of San Antonio. Beginning in the 1980s, points were collected during the sand-sieving and sorting process and passed into the hands of many collectors. Large numbers of other Paleo-Indian types were also found there; unfortunately, there is no contextual information for any of the artifacts.

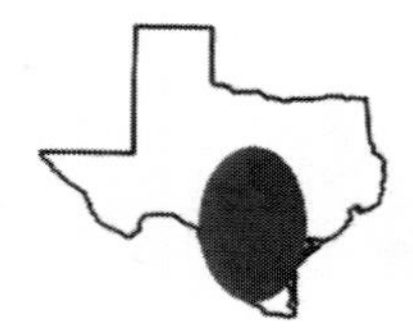

Distribution: Central and south central Texas to the coastal plain, and into southern Texas. **Period:** Paleo-Indian; at Wilson-Leonard, radiocarbon dates of 8700–9990 years ago. **Sites:** St. Mary's Hall; Wilson-Leonard; Lubbock Lake; Levi Rockshelter; J2 Ranch; 41BX411; 41KR243; Chiltipin Creek (San Patricio County); Wilson County Sand Pit.

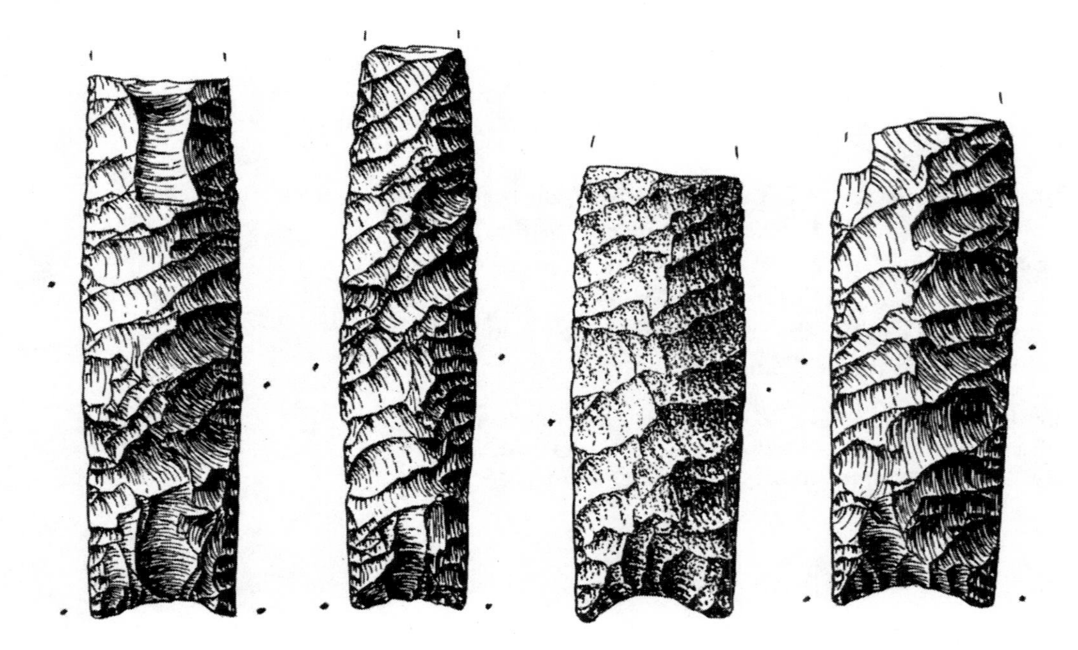

References: Alexander 1963; Bousman, Baker, and Kerr 2004; Chandler 1982; Dial et al. 1998; Flaigg 1995; Hester 1977b, 1991, 2002a; Holliday 1980; Johnson and Brown 1986; Pfeiffer 2001.

SAN PATRICE

This point is characterized by a concave, usually deep, and ground base that has been thinned by the removal of one to three channel flakes to produce a fluting that extends to midpoint or beyond.

Points linked to San Patrice have been found in the Brazos River Valley at Horn Shelter 2 (and termed "Brazos Fishtail"), and in the Texas Panhandle at the Rex Rodgers bison-kill site ("Rodgers Side-Hollowed," illustrated here in two large points on the bottom row). Webb has suggested two variants: "Hope" and "St. Johns" (specimens illustrated here). There is a considerable range in size and commensurate variability in thickness and width even within the two variants (Johnson 1989b).

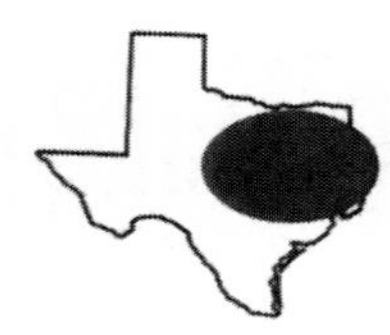

Distribution: East and northeast Texas, Louisiana, and Arkansas. **Period:** Paleo-Indian, perhaps 7500 BC. **Sites:** John Pearce (La.); Fort Polk (La.); Jake Martin; Wolfshead; 41WH19; 41HR233; 41SF20; Lee County; 41JF50; Big Eddy (Mo.).

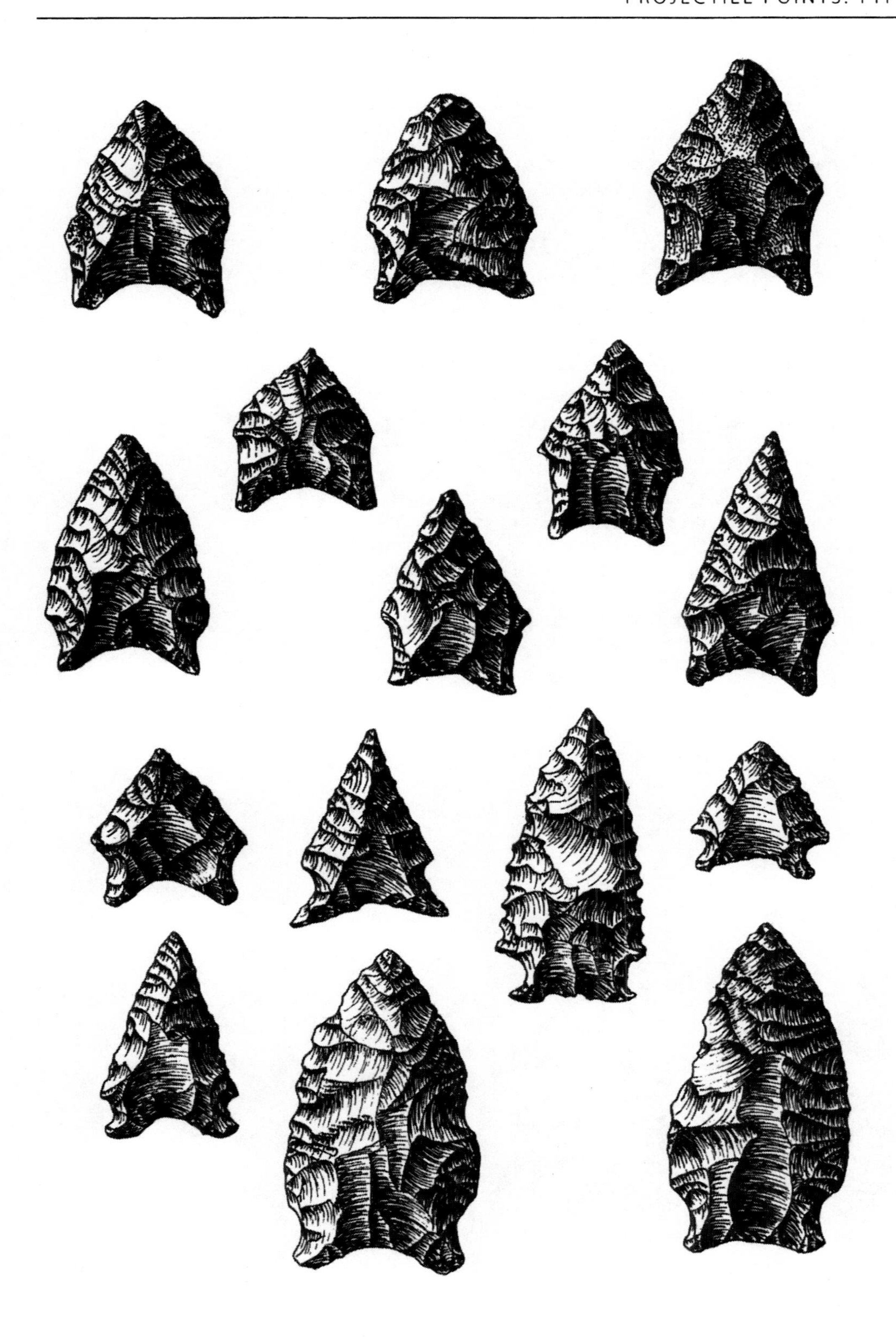

References: Anderson and Smith 2003; Bousman, Baker, and Kerr 2004; Davis and Davis 1960; Duffield 1963b; Hester and Newcomb 1990; Holliday 1996; Hughes and Willey 1978; Jennings 2008; Johnson 1989b; Patterson and Hudgins 1981; Patterson and Marshall 1989; Ray et al. 1998; Stright et al. 1999; Suhm and Jelks 1962; Watt 1978; Webb 1946, 1982; Webb, Shiner, and Roberts 1971.

SCOTTSBLUFF

Initially defined in the Plains, these are fairly large points typified by excellent workmanship, fine parallel-flaking, and a "fat feel" due to their biconvex cross sections. The broad stem edges and base are ground smooth. Texas specimens are usually smaller than their Plains counterparts. Examples from the coastal plain are often heavily resharpened and can also be quite thin.

"Red River Knives" (Johnson 1989b), found in the oak savanna/Cross Timbers area, are refurbished Scottsbluff points, unifacially resharpened and edge-beveled on one lateral edge to a long, concave-cutting, scraping, and sawing edge, which was longer than the opposite edge.

Scottsbluff points have long been known to be very common in eastern Texas. A longtime avocational archaeologist, Bill Young (2008) has estimated that "more Scottsbluff points have been found within a hundred mile radius of Texarkana than any other area of North America."

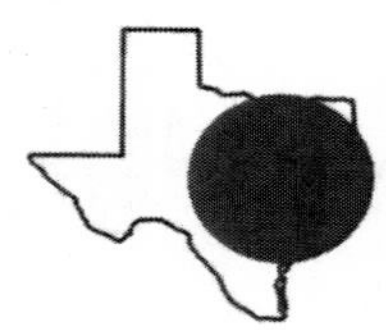

Distribution: Widely scattered over much of Texas with the greatest concentration in east Texas and adjoining portions of Louisiana, and extend onto the Texas coastal plain, extending as far south as Starr County on the lower Rio Grande. **Period:** Late Paleo-Indian, possibly ca. 7120 BC–6650 BC; dated to ca. 7500 BC at Big Eddy (Mo.). **Sites:** Strohacker; La Perdida; 41WH19; Victoria County; 41WD23; 41MR24; 41TT70; Buckner Ranch; Wilson-Leonard, Harris County; Texarkana area; Atascosa, Frio, and McMullen counties.

Red River Knives

References: Bousman et al. 2004; Chandler and Hindes 1993; Collins et al. 1998; Gagliano and Gregory 1965; Hayner 1955; Hester and Birmingham 1976; Hester and Hill 1971; Hudgins and Patterson 1983; Johnson 1989a, 1989b; Kelly 1983a; Ray et al. 2009; Sollberger and Hester 1972; Suhm and Jelks 1962; Weir 1956; Wormington 1957; Young 2008.

SHUMLA

Shumla points are triangular with straight to convex lateral edges that are often slightly serrated. Basal notches form a more or less rectangular stem and short to long barbs. They are usually well made. Specimens linked to this type in south Texas are usually made of heat-treated chert, with the thermal alteration giving the points a pinkish color, a vitreous sheen, and a greasy feeling.

Distribution: Lower Pecos; most common Archaic points to be found in the Big Bend and are found throughout both the eastern and western Trans-Pecos regions. Also found in south Texas. **Period:** Late Archaic, 1000 BC–200 BC. **Sites:** Nopal Terrace; Holdsworth and Stewart; 4lDM59; Middle Rio Grande; Centipede Cave and Damp Cave; Amistad Reservoir (41VV7, 41VV161); Fate Bell Rockshelter; Rosillos Mountains; San Felipe Springs (41MV120).

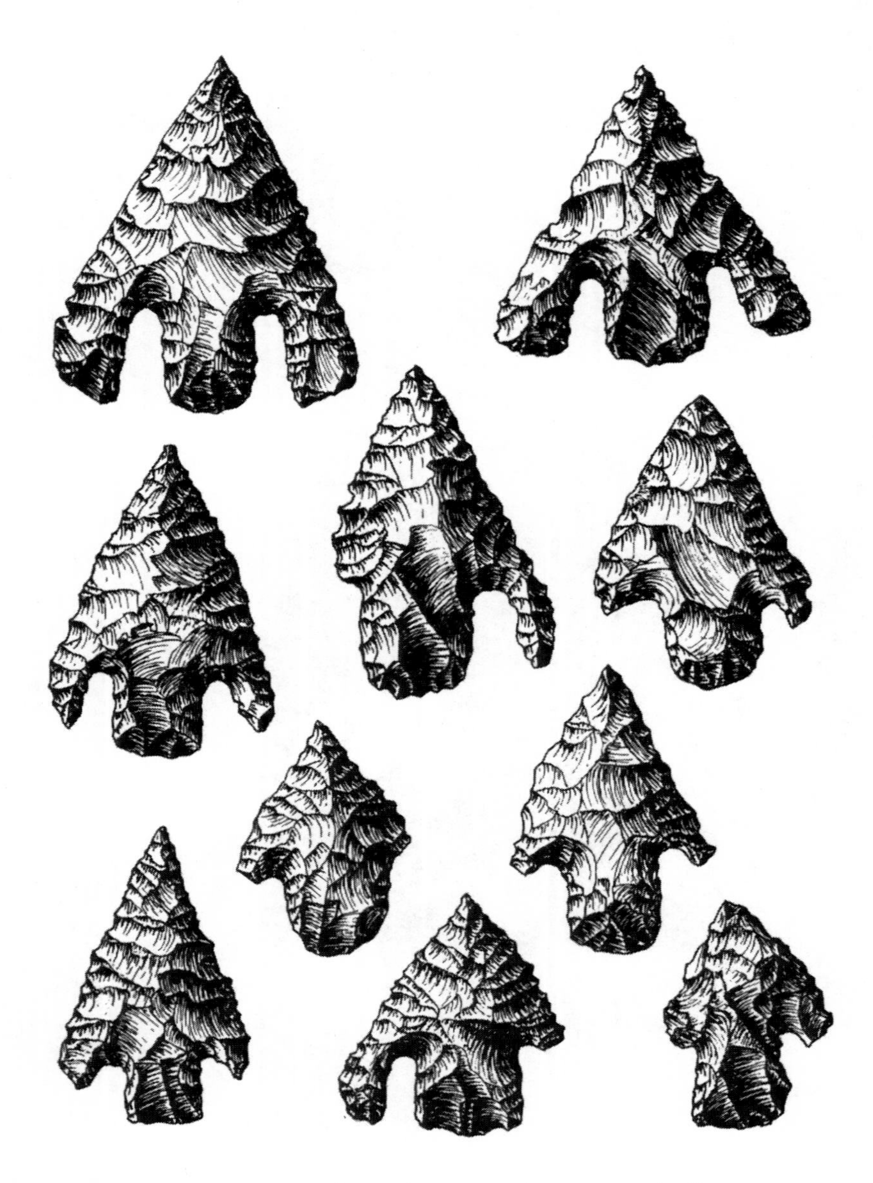

References: Campbell 1970; Collins 1969; Epstein 1963; Hester and Collins 1974; Hester and Hill 1973; Hester and Whatley 1992b, 1997; Ing et al. 1996; Mallouf and Wulfkuhle 1989; Mehalchick et al. 1999; Peck 1991; Vierra 1998.

SINNER

These projectile points have multiple notches or deep serrations along the lateral edges. Stems are squared to slightly expanded. The type was named by Webb and colleagues (1969, 52–53), reporting that it was "related to the Evans type." Evans is distinguished by a single deep notch in each lateral edge, while Sinner points have two to five notches or deep serrations.

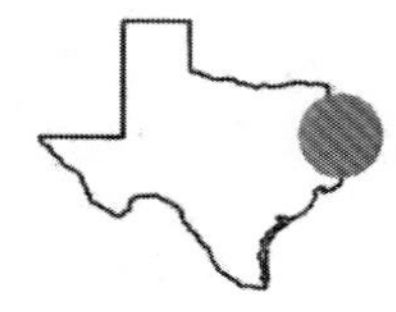

Distribution: Northeast Texas and northwest Louisiana. **Period:** Late Archaic. **Sites:** Resch (41HS16); Catahoula Lake (La.); Sasser Farm (La.); Aired Cottage (La.); Fort Polk (La.); Sam Rayburn Lake.

References: Anderson and Smith 2003; Russell Long, personal communication; Webb et al. 1969.

TORTUGAS

This large, triangular point has a straight to concave base and alternately beveled edges. It is often thick and crudely flaked in the midsection and well thinned basally. There are typological problems (see Matamoros and Early Triangular), and the erroneous inclusion in the nontype "Anthon"), but there is growing evidence that points of this form are characteristic of the late Middle Archaic and Late Archaic in south Texas.

A total of 122 Tortugas points was found at the Loma Sandia cemetery; it was the most numerous point type associated with the burials, which were radiocarbon dated at 850 BC–600 BC (2800–2550 BP; Taylor and Highley 1995). Detailed analysis of Tortugas specimens found in Webb County, Texas, is found in the work of Miller and colleagues (2000). Also in Webb County, studies at the Lino site provide detailed information on the type and reviewed the difficulty in establishing its time range (Quigg et al. 2000).

While impact fractures are common on Tortugas points, microwear studies of some samples indicate that they could, at times, also serve as cutting tools.

Distribution: Characteristic of south Texas and the lower Rio Grande but occasionally found in central Texas and the lower Pecos. **Period:** Middle to Late Archaic; the dates from Loma Sandia, overlapping in part with those from the Lino site, radiocarbon dated 3200–2000 BP. **Sites:** Oulline; Choke Canyon; La Perdida; San Miguel Creek; 41LK28; Camino Colombia; Lino, Webb County.

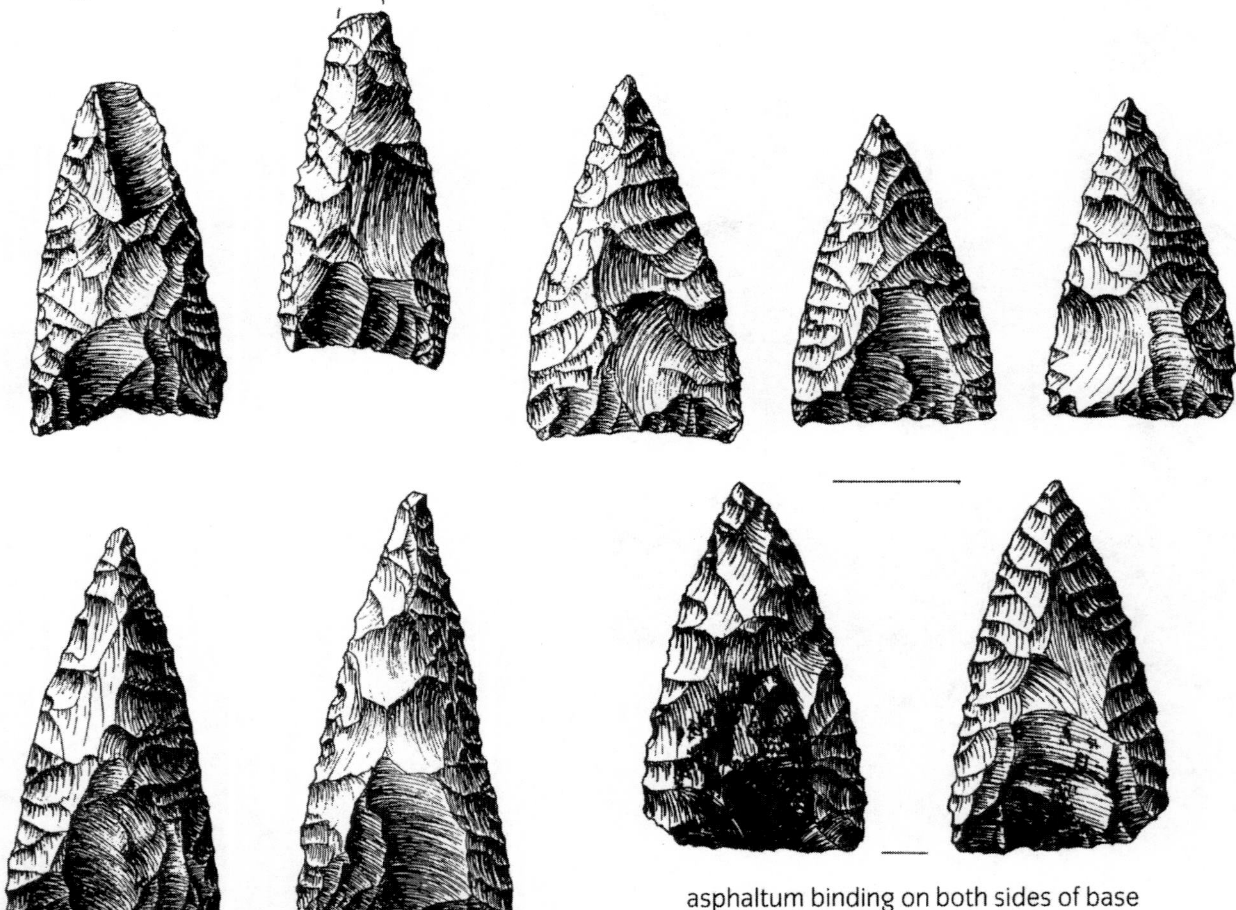

References: Bettis 1997; Hall, Black, and Graves 1982; Hester 1968; Hester et al. 1969; Miller et al. 2000; Quigg et al. 2000; Suhm and Jelks 1962; Taylor and Highley 1995; Weir 1956.

TRAVIS

The Travis type includes specimens that have narrow, triangular bodies with convex lateral edges. Shoulders are rounded, varying from slight to fairly prominent. The stem is usually rectangular with parallel edges; stem edges are not beveled, as seen on Nolan. Similar points were found at the Greenhaw site and called "Buda"; these are now thought to be a local variation of Travis (Frank Weir, personal communication).

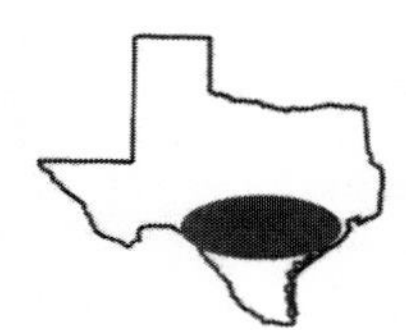

Distribution: Mainly central Texas but, to a lesser degree, in surrounding areas, including the lower Pecos. **Period:** Middle Archaic, ca. 2650 BC–2050 BC. **Sites:** 41BX1; Greenhaw; Kyle; McCann; McKee (41GU117); Burnet County, Hamilton County; Eckols (41TV528).

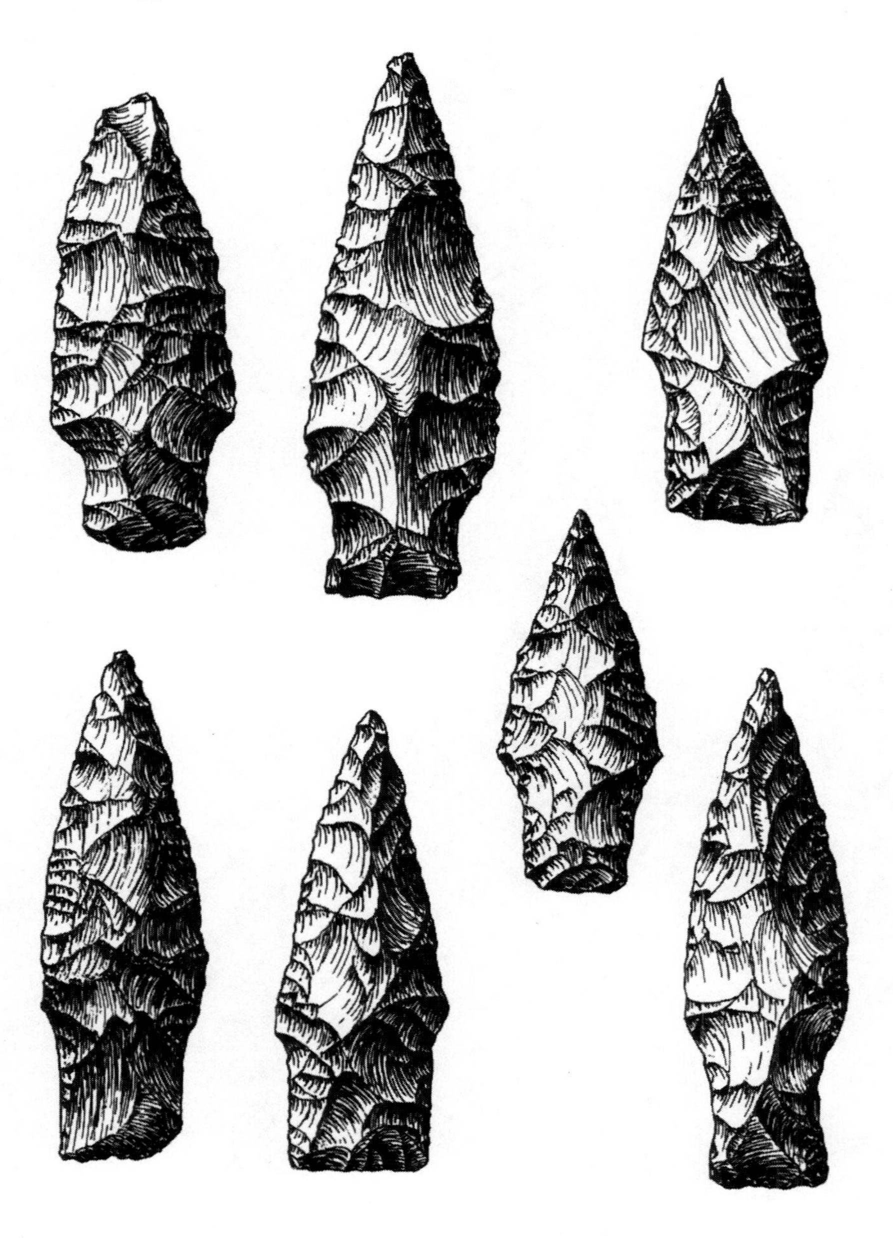

References: Jelks 1962; Karbula 2000; Lukowski 1983; Preston and Shiner 1969; Prewitt 1981b; Suhm and Jelks 1962; Weir 1979.

TRINITY

This is a small- to medium-sized, roughly triangular form, with convex lateral edges and a broad, expanding stem formed by broad side notches. Specimens are sometimes well made and, in some cases, are similar to Yarbrough.

Distribution: Most common in the Dallas area, extending into northeast Texas and southward toward the Brazos area. **Period:** Late Archaic. **Sites:** Yarbrough; Limerick; Big Pine Lake; Jake Martin; 41DL30; 41DN6.

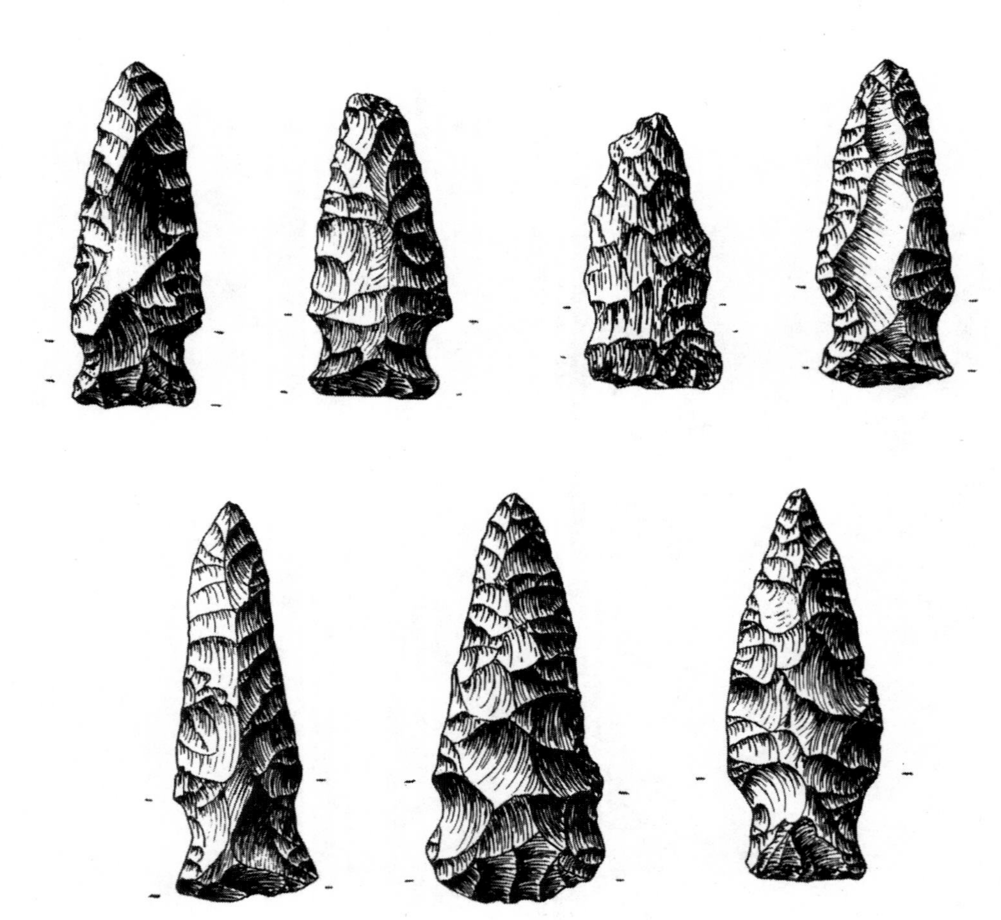

References: Crook and Harris 1954b; Davis and Davis 1960; Duffield 1961; Johnson 1962b; Mallouf 1976; Prikryl 1990; Suhm and Jelks 1962.

UVALDE

This is a broadly defined type that varies considerably. Generally, it has a triangular to elongate body with rounded shoulders or barbs, an expanding stem (edges of which are not ground), and a concave base. It was originally defined as a Middle to Late Archaic type; however, continuing research has shown these points to be Early Archaic in date. Some of the specimens of this general shape have been called "Early Corner-Notched" or lumped into Gower or Merrell groups. Baker, in the lower Pecos, is probably a regional equivalent.

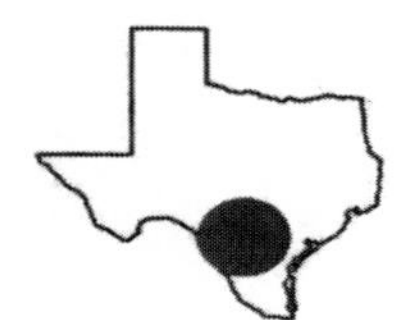

Distribution: Primarily central Texas, along the Balcones Escarpment and south central Texas. **Period:** Early Archaic. **Sites:** Evoe Terrace; Tombstone Bluff; La Jita; Greenhaw; Smith; 41BN114; Baker; Woodrow Heard; Wilson-Leonard.

References: Baker 2003; Decker et al. 2000; Dial et al. 1998; Hester 1971; Prewitt 1981a; Sorrow et al. 1967; Suhm and Jelks 1962; Weir 1979.

VAL VERDE

Val Verde points are thin, triangular, stemmed points similar to the Langtry type. The primary distinction in Val Verde is its expanding stem formed by wide concavities that extend from the shoulder to the base. All of the following variations are found: the stem and base alternately beveled; stem edges beveled to one surface and the base to another; and both stem and base beveled to the same surface.

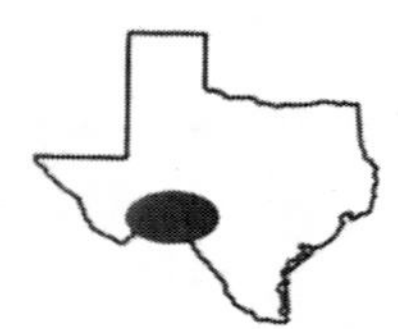

Distribution: Lower Pecos, lower Rio Grande, and Coahuila, Mexico. **Period:** Middle Archaic; contemporary with Langtry. **Sites:** Amistad Reservoir (41VV161, 41VV186, 41VV422); Panda Cave; Nopal Terrace; Coontail Spin; Arenosa Shelter; Fate Bell Rockshelter.

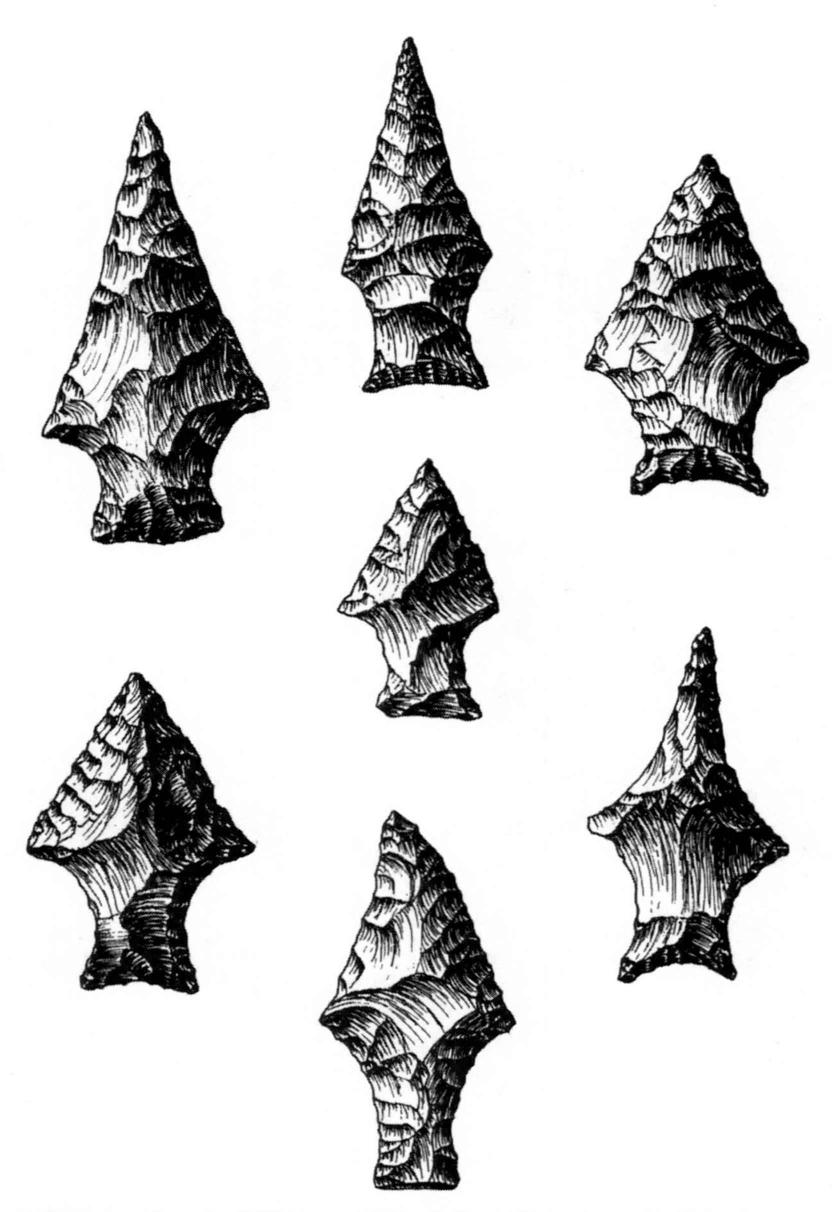

References: Alexander 1970; Bement 1991a; Collins 1969; Nunley and Duffield 1964; Parsons 1965; Peck 1991; Schuetz 1956; Sorrow 1968b; Young 1982.

VAN HORN

Patterned blade-notching is what makes this point unique. The notches often occur above midpoint, and the number of notches on each side varies up to four. None show smoothing, grinding, or abrading of the stem or base. The base may be straight, convex, or rounded. Similar points were included in the Guadalupe type by Justice (2002), but we have adopted Hedrick's (1989) designation of Van Horn to at least lessen the confusion with other "Guadalupe" points and tools in the regional literature. Hedrick had a sample of more than two thousand points from southern Culberson County when he published his detailed type description. It is possible that these specimens could be confused with the Duran type of northeastern Mexico, though Hedrick stated that the technology of the stems are distinctly different.

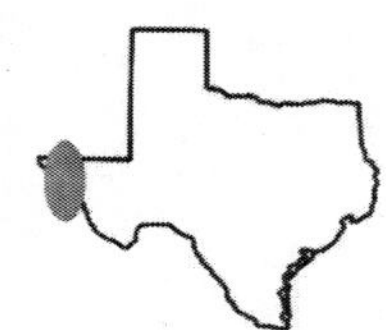

Distribution: Van Horn and Culberson County area of the Trans-Pecos and in northern Chihuahua, Mexico. **Period:** Late Archaic. **Sites:** Plateau Station/Plateau Complex; Wild Horse Draw; 41CU428; 41CU385.

References: Hedrick 1989; Justice 2002; Leslie 1978; Mallouf 1985.

WELLS

Wells points are long, narrow points, with distinct to weak shoulders, and a long, contracting stem. The lateral edges are often serrated, and the stem edges are usually ground smooth.

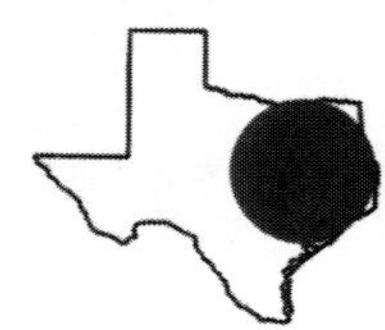

Distribution: East Texas and east central Texas, extending westward into central Texas, and north to Louisiana, Oklahoma, and Arkansas. **Period:** Middle Archaic, possibly 4000–2500 BC. **Sites:** Youngsport; Jake Martin; Culpepper; George C. Davis; Loeve-Fox; Cervenka (41WM267); 41DL30; Trinity River drainage.

References: Davis and Davis 1960; Newell and Krieger 1949; Peter 1982b; Prewitt 1974a; Prikryl 1990; Scurlock 1962; Shafer 1963; Suhm and Jelks 1962.

WILLIAMS

With a broad body and convex lateral edges, Williams points have short barbs and an expanding (or bulbous) stem and a convex, rounded base. An unfinished Williams is shown in the upper left in our illustration. There is significant overlap in form with the Lange type.

Distribution: Common in central Texas and north to the Llano Estacado. Extends into northwest Louisiana, Oklahoma, and western Arkansas. **Period:** Middle to Late Archaic. **Sites:** Crumley; Youngsport; John Ischy; McCann; Cowpen Slough (La.); Whatley (La.).

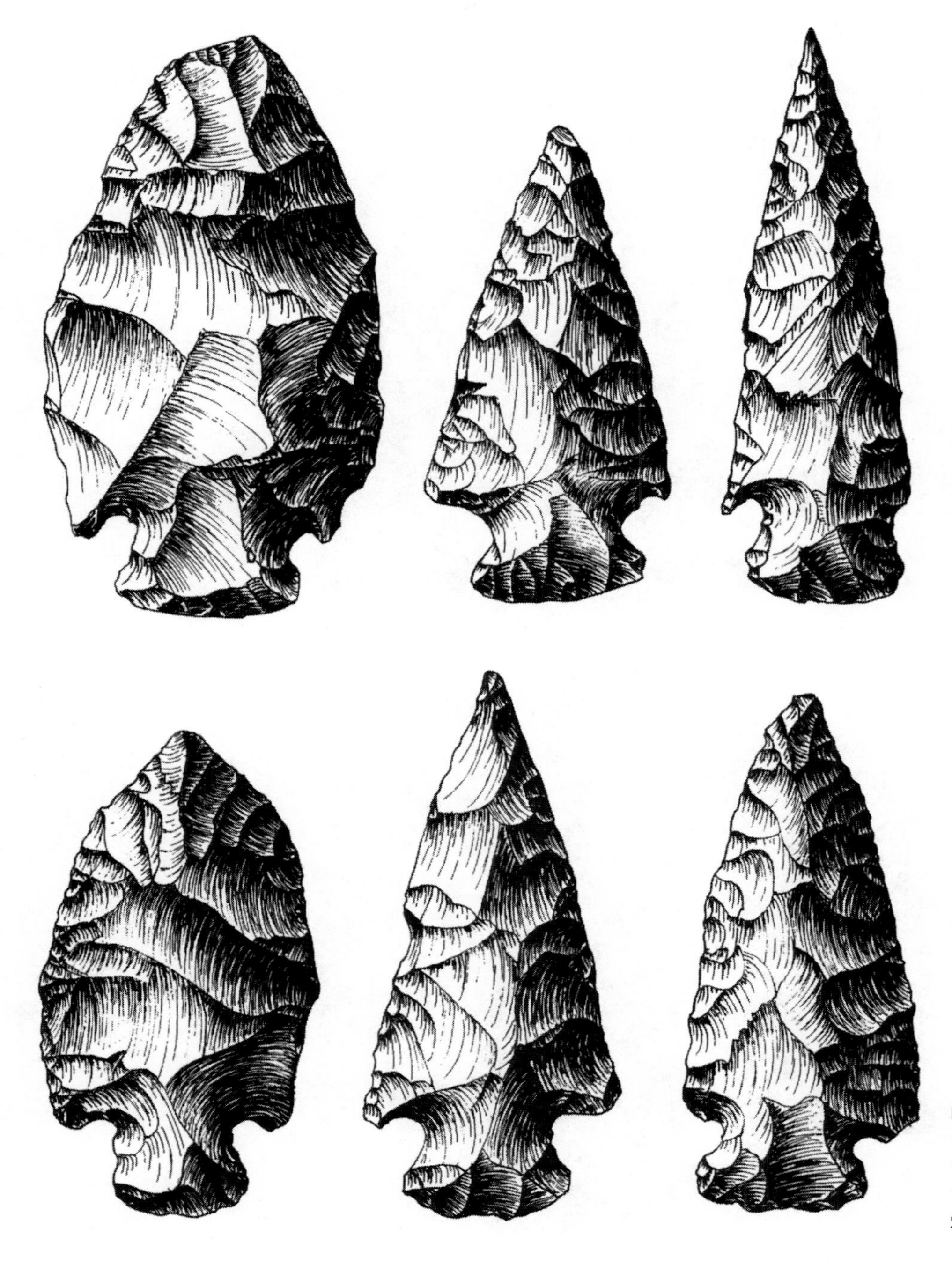

References: Dial et al. 1998; Howard 1996; Jeter and Williams 1989; Kelly 1962; Preston and Shiner 1969; Quigg 1997; Shafer 1963; Sorrow 1969; Suhm and Jelks 1962.

WILSON

These points were originally referred to as Early Stemmed (Turner and Hester 1985). They are characterized by thick, sometimes biconvex, bodies and wide, expanding stems with straight to slightly concave bases. The stems have grinding on all edges, and stems are thinned by two or more vertical flakes. The shoulders are prominent to slightly barbed. There is some regional variation in thickness and stem length between the lower Pecos and central Texas specimens.

First recognized in the early 1960s during excavations at the Devil's Mouth site, it was not until the Wilson-Leonard project that numerous well-dated specimens were recovered. Points of this type are not uncommon in large collections from central Texas down to the middle Rio Grande. There is some difficulty in typing such specimens when dealing with thick, expanded stem points from east central and southeast Texas, most of which do not appear to be linked to Wilson.

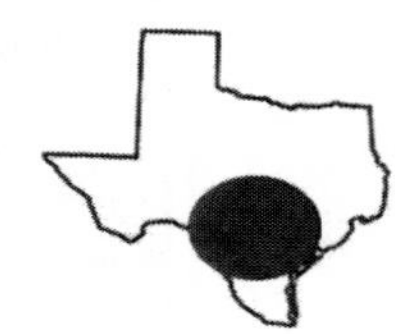

Distribution: Lower Pecos; central, south, and southeastern Texas. **Period:** Late Paleo-Indian, perhaps as early as 8000 BC. **Sites:** Wilson-Leonard; Devil's Mouth; Jack Dies Ranch; 41VV1654; 41ME132; Briscoe Ranch (Dimmit County); 41ME132.

References: Bousman, Baker, and Kerr 2004; Collins et al. 1998; Dial et al. 1998.

YARBROUGH

This slender, elongate point is well made and has straight to convex lateral edges, which are sometimes beveled; small to prominent unbarbed shoulders; and stem edges that are slightly expanded. The stem edges and bases may be lightly smoothed and ground.

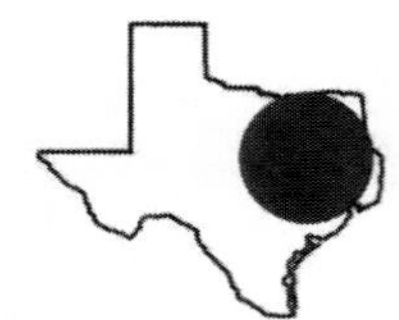

Distribution: Common in north central and east Texas; decreasing. **Period:** Late Archaic. **Sites:** Yarbrough; Tankersley Creek; Jake Martin; Womack; Mackin; Kyle; 41DL30.

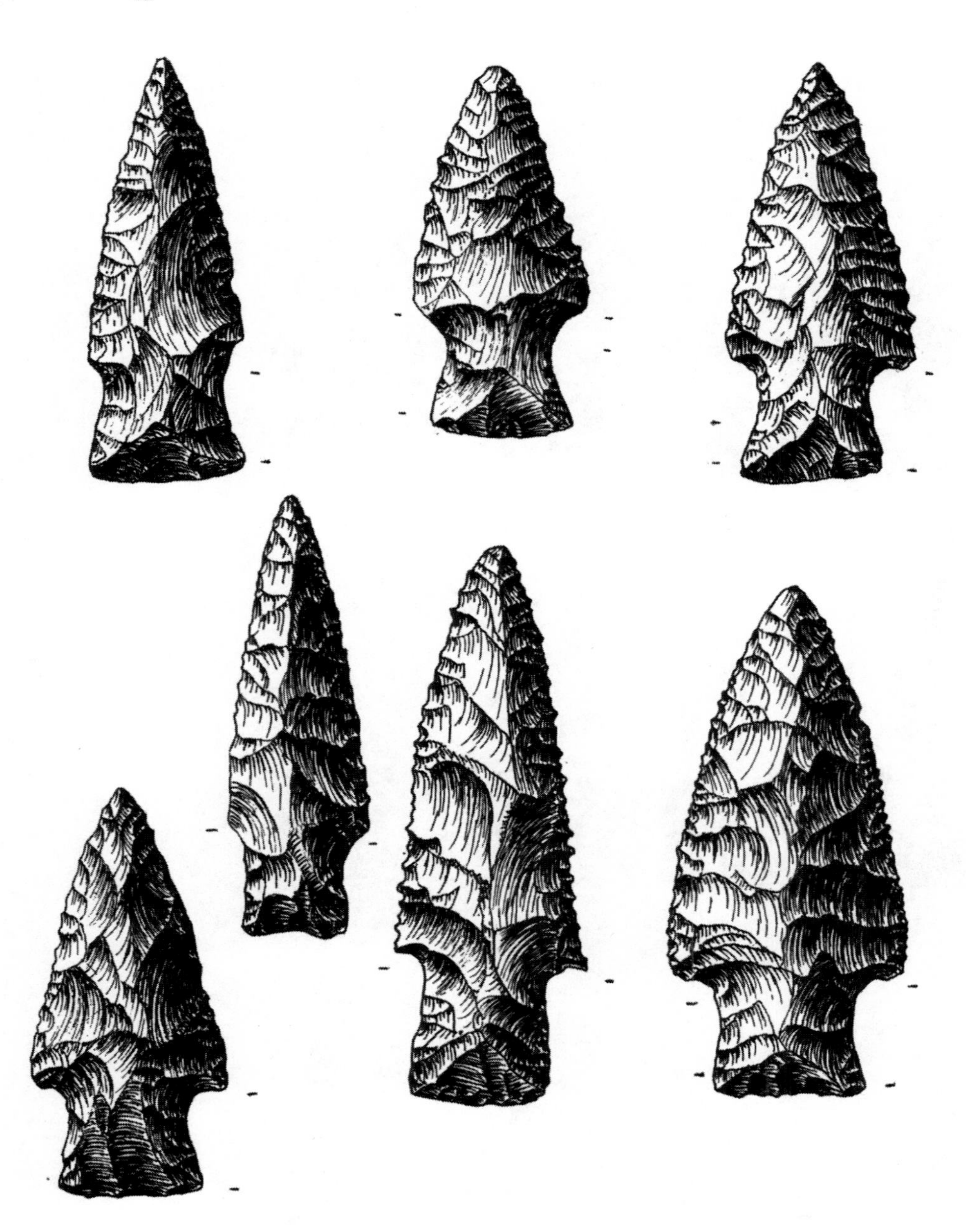

References: Anthony and Brown 1994; Davis and Davis 1960; Jelks 1962; Johnson 1962b; Mallouf 1976; Prikryl 1990; Suhm and Jelks 1962; Young 1981.

ZEPHYR

This point is small to medium sized and lanceolate to triangular, with serrated lateral edges. Stems expand gently toward the base and are parallel-sided or expanded. The basal edge is concave with rounded basal corners, and the stem edges exhibit edge-grinding. The type was originally included in the Darl type (Prewitt 1981b), and Krieger reported Zephyr points in the Harrell site excavations under Kelley's name Sabana Stemmed (Krieger 1946).

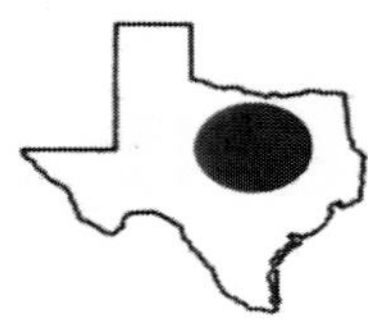

Distribution: Surface finds along the upper Brazos and its tributaries as well as the upper reaches of the Leon and Colorado rivers. **Period:** AD 200–700. **Sites:** Comanche County; Stephens County; Horn Shelter 2; Rogers Springs; 41SE17, where 32 percent of all dart points recovered from the site were Zephyr.

References: Forrester 1987; Krieger 1946; Prewitt 1981b, 1995.

ZORRA

This subtriangular point has convex lateral edges, rounded shoulders, and unifacial beveling on one or both stem edges (a diagnostic attribute). The form is somewhat similar to Pandale, but it is not obliquely flaked and lacks the twisted appearance.

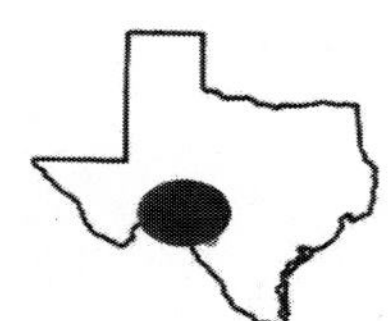

Distribution: Lower Pecos and into south Texas. **Period:** Early Archaic. **Sites:** Baker Cave; Fate Bell Rockshelter; Devil's Mouth; Greenhaw; Choke Canyon.

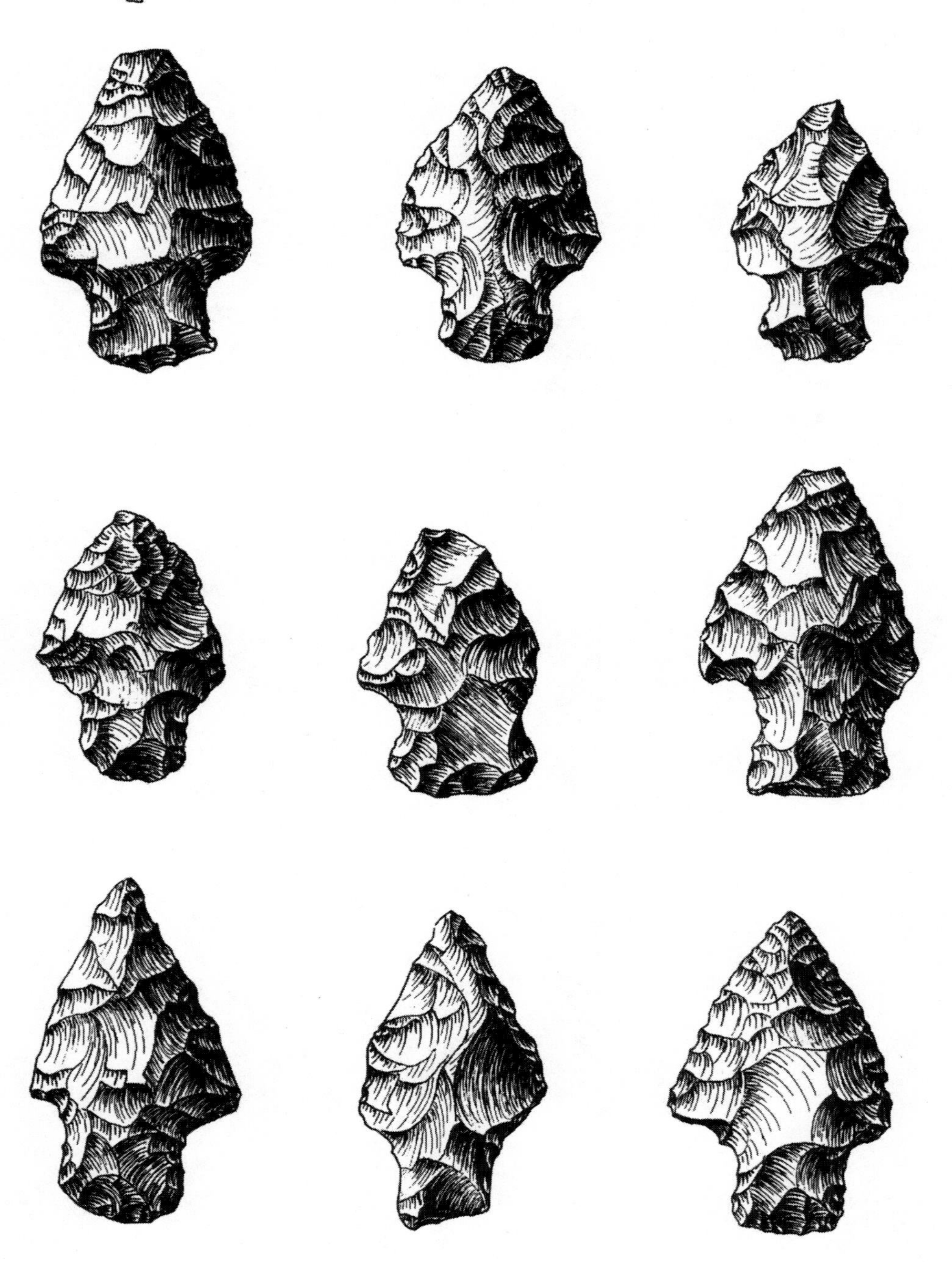

References: Brown et al. 1982; Johnson 1954; Weir 1979; Word and Douglas 1970.

ARROW POINTS

ALAZAN

Newly defined by Mallouf (2009), these points have triangular bodies with variable lateral edge configurations, usually straight, but also concave, convex, or recurved. Lateral edges are frequently serrated, sometimes strongly so. Distal tips are sometimes beveled, giving them a needlelike appearance. The points are often resharpened, making some short and wide relative to the overall length of the artifact. Moderate- to large-sized barbs may project at right angles or slope downward. Narrow or wide stems are typically short and small relative to overall specimen size, and they may be parallel-sided to moderately expanding, usually with a small indentation in the stem basal edge.

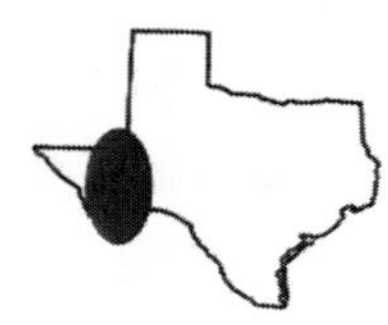

Distribution: Big Bend proper, with increasing frequency to the north. **Period:** Late Prehistoric, AD 1150–1350, including association with Toyah points. **Sites:** Salt Flat; Rosillos Mountains; Plateau Complex.

References: Cloud and Piehl 2008; Hedrick 1975, 1986; Katz and Lukowski 1981; Mallouf 2009a; Mallouf and Wulfkuhle 1989.

ALBA

The body of the Alba point has concave or recurved lateral edges that may be serrated. It also has wide, usually barbed shoulders. The stem is parallel or slightly expanding, sometimes squared, and sometimes with somewhat of a bulbous appearance. Shafer (2006) has proposed a Bonham-Alba classification that encompasses specimens dating around AD 1100, from central Texas into east Texas.

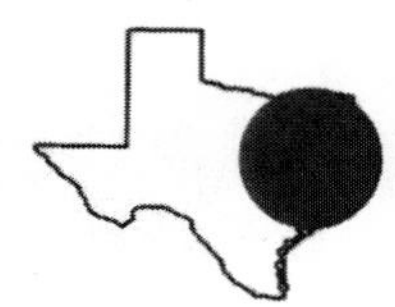

Distribution: Central and east Texas, the coastal plain, and Louisiana. **Period:** Late Prehistoric, ca. AD 800–1200. **Sites:** Mostly northeast Texas, including George C. Davis; Pecan Springs; Mackin; J. B. White (41MM341); Belcher Mound (La.).

References: Gadus et al. 2006; Krieger 1946; Mallouf 1976; Shafer 1973, 2006; Sorrow 1966; Suhm and Jelks 1962; Webb, personal communication.

ANAQUA

This slender, triangular, corner-notched point usually has straight lateral, sometimes slightly convex edges, with well-barbed shoulders. Lateral edges are well flaked with serrations or small notches. The base is deeply concave (U-shaped), and barbs are curved upward to form a fine point, rarely exceeding the barbed shoulders. The cross section is lenticular in shape. Often, traces of asphaltum are found along the basal edges, extending to and including the flake scars and hinges. The point is found in association with pottery, Scallorn points, and Perdiz points, often extending into a later period.

Distribution: Common to lower Guadalupe River drainage system within the central coastal plain. **Period:** Late Prehistoric, possibly contemporaneous with Scallorn. **Sites:** Victoria County (41VT3, 9, 12, 34, 69, 81, and 98); Refugio County (41RF10, 11).

References: Birmingham, Bluhm, Branch, and Vogt collections, curated at the Museum of the Coastal Bend, Victoria College, Victoria, Tex.; Will collection; Ricklis 2009; Weinstein 1992.

BASSETT

This short, wide, triangular point has straight to convex lateral edges, prominent barbs, and a short, pointed contracting stem. When the barbs are long, the stem appears as a tiny protrusion in the middle of a deeply concave base.

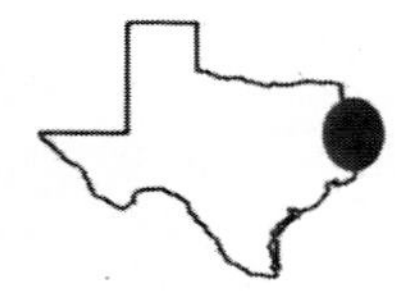

Distribution: Northeast Texas, Louisiana, and Arkansas. **Period:** Late Prehistoric, ca. AD 1400–1700. **Sites:** Carpenter (41CP5); Mackin; Womack; Jones Hill; Burris 2; Belcher Mound (La.).

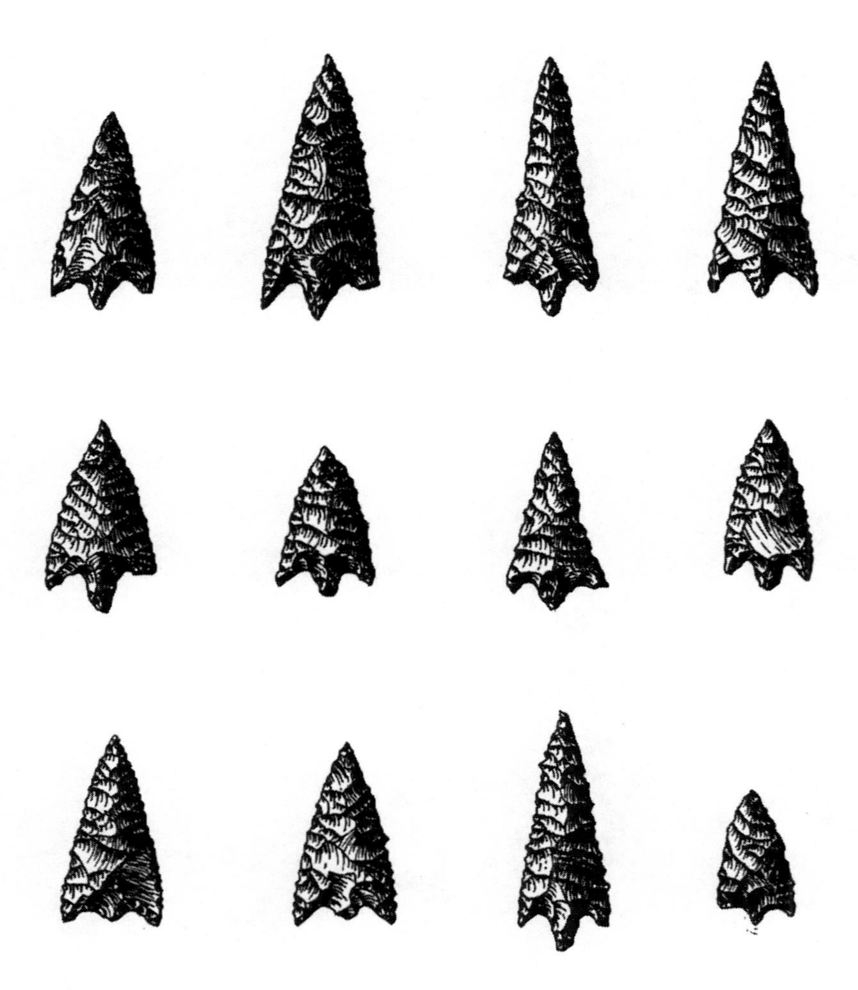

References: Bell 1958; Duncan et al. 2007; Harris et al. 1965; Mallouf 1976; McClurkan 1968; Perttula 1992; Suhm and Jelks 1962; Webb, personal communication.

BONHAM

The Bonham type is a narrow, triangular point with straight to slightly recurved lateral edges, barbs, and a narrow, parallel-sided stem with a flat or rounded basal edge. Most specimens are fully bifacial and have lenticular cross sections. Shafer (2006) proposes a Bonham-Alba grouping for specimens found from central Texas into east Texas, suggesting they are linked to the Caddo of the George C. Davis site.

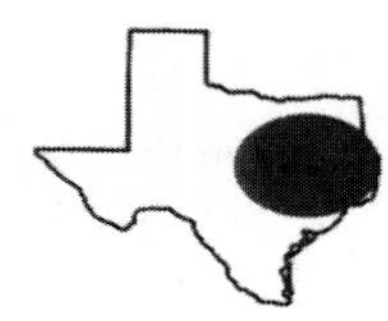

Distribution: North central and northeast Texas. **Period:** Late Prehistoric. **Sites:** Mackin; Sanders; Kyle; Limerick; Baylor; Hoxie Bridge; Loeve-Fox; George C. Davis.

References: Duffield 1961; Duncan et al. 2007; Jelks 1962; Krieger 1946; Mallouf 1976; Ricklis 2010; Shafer 2006; Suhm and Jelks 1962.

BULBAR STEMMED

These points are sometimes similar to Perdiz and may represent a regional variant in the Corpus Christi region and north Padre Island. Although typical examples (as illustrated) are "bulbar stemmed," stem shape is reported to vary in length and width (J. Hudgins, personal communication; E. Mokry, personal communication).

Distribution: South and central Texas Gulf Coast. **Period:** Late Prehistoric into Historic. **Sites:** McGloin Bluff; Oso Creek; north Padre Island; Shanklin (41WH8); Mitchell Ridge (41GV66).

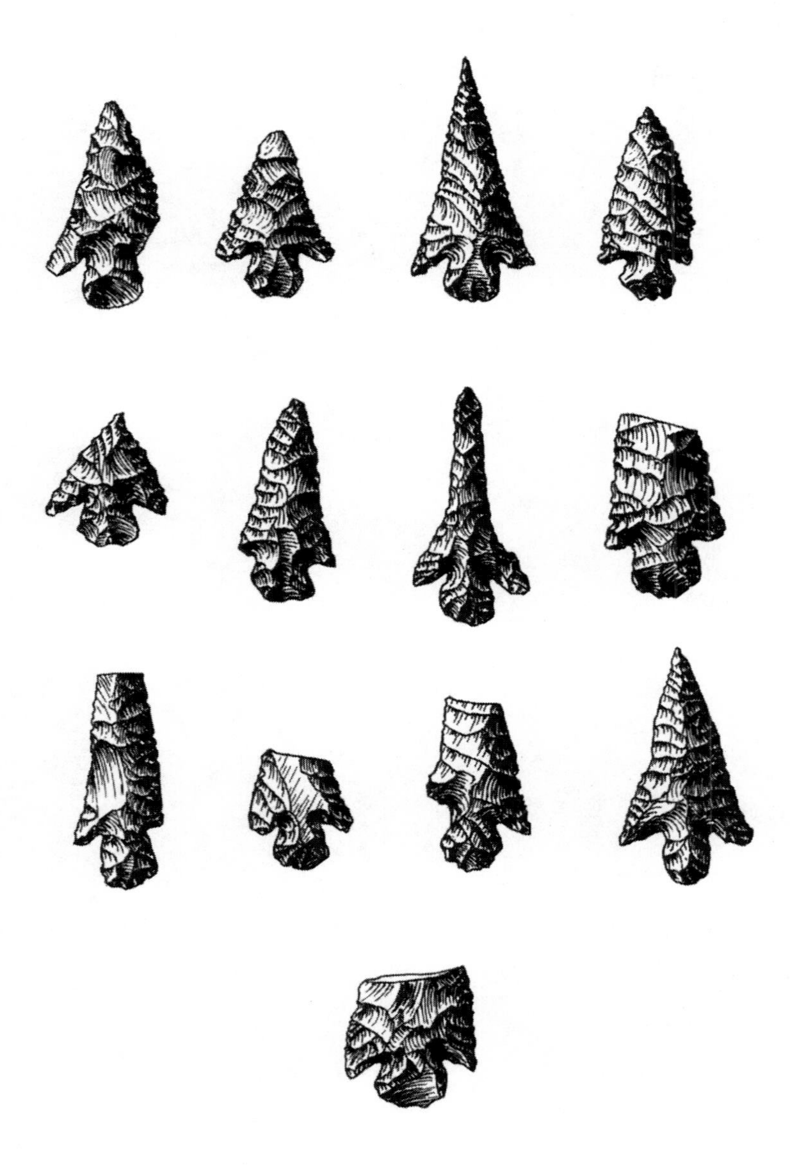

References: Corbin 1963, 1974; Gunter 1985; Hudgins 1982; Ricklis 1994, 1995, 2010.

CAMERON

A tiny, usually equilateral, triangular point with straight to slightly convex edges. A few are unifacially chipped, and some are made of glass. It is similar to the Fresno type but smaller (less than 20 mm in length) and generally much thicker.

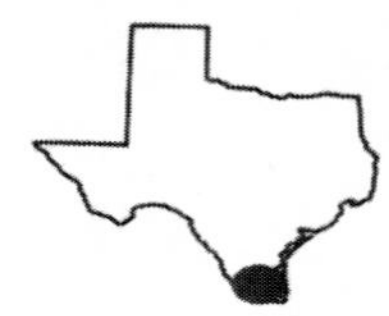

Distribution: Rio Grande Delta, Baffin Bay, and Corpus Christi area. **Period:** Late Prehistoric into Historic. **Sites:** Unland; Kleberg County (41KLI3, 41KL36); McGill Ranch; Hidalgo, Cameron, and Willacy counties; Falcon Lake; Tamaulipas, Mexico.

References: Hester 1969a; MacNeish 1958; Mallouf, Baskin, and Killen 1977; Mallouf and Zavaleta 1979; Saunders 1985.

CARACARA

This side-notched, small, very thin point has been defined by R. K. Saunders. The convex to nearly straight lateral edges of the point are often finely serrated. Flaking is random but usually well executed. The rounded or squared ends of the basal "ears" usually extend slightly beyond the width of the shoulders. Bases are normally straight but may be slightly concave or slightly convex.

Several burials in the Falcon Lake area have been accompanied by Caracara points, some of them embedded in human bones, as evidence of violence or warfare (Boyd and Perttula 2000).

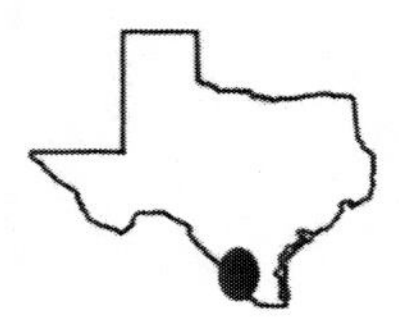

Distribution: Texas and northeast Mexico, centered in the Falcon Lake region. **Period:** AD 1025–1292, perhaps as late as AD 1437, based on radiocarbon dates from Falcon Reservoir. **Sites:** Falcon Reservoir; Starr, Webb, Zapata, Hidalgo, and Duval counties in Texas. Parts of Tamaulipas and Nuevo Leon in Mexico.

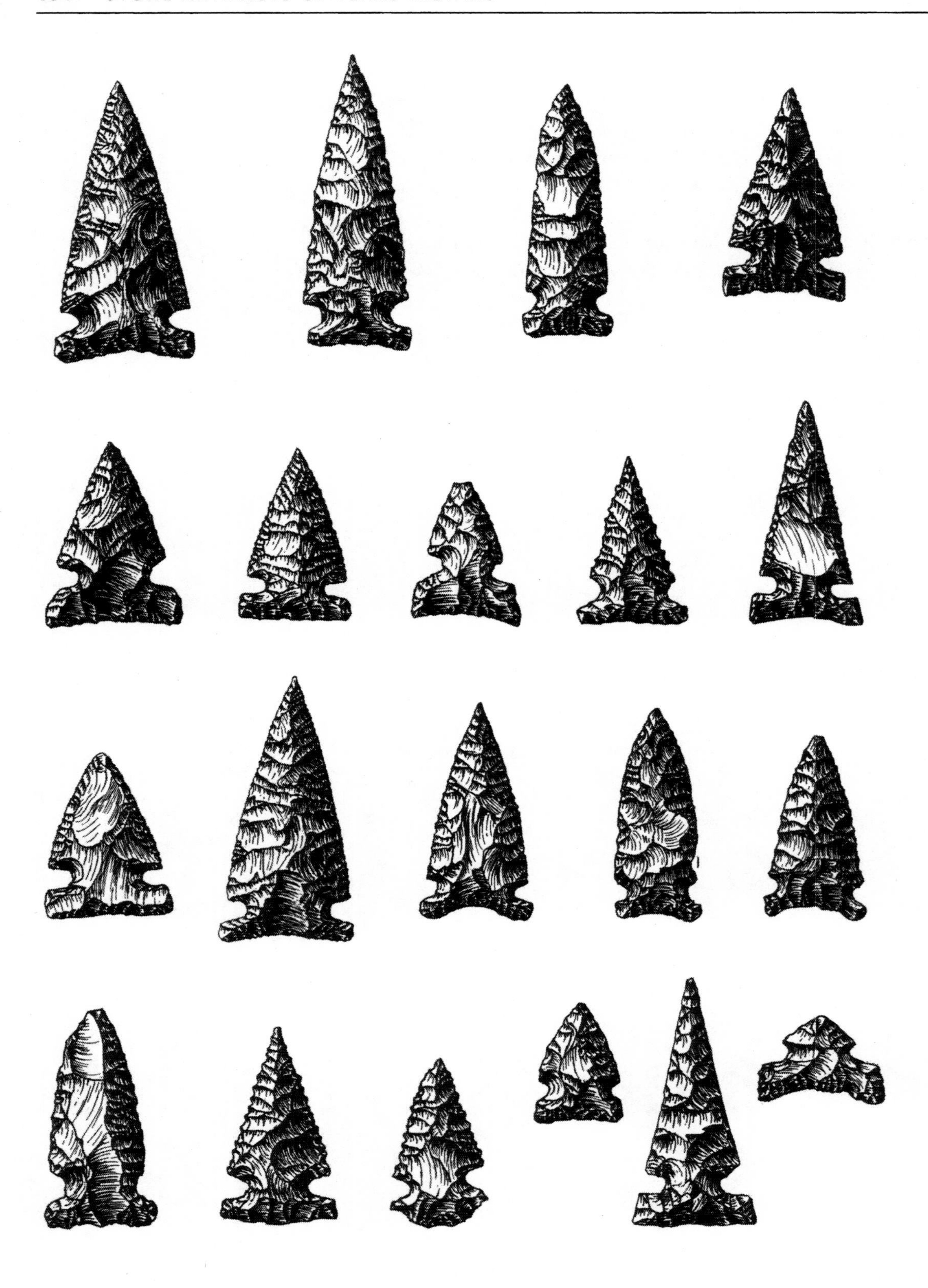

References: Beasley 1978a; Boyd and Perttula 2000; R. K. Saunders, personal communication.

CATAHOULA

The lateral edges of this point are straight to concave or recurved, and they frequently flare at the shoulders to form distinctive, large, rounded, or squared barbs, producing a relatively broad shoulder area. The expanding stem is short, squared, or somewhat expanded, and the base is slightly convex.

"Class A-1" and "Class A-2" (Aten 1967, 1983) in southeast Texas are somewhat similar forms with straight-sided or small, contracting stems that are commonly found on the upper Gulf Coast and have usually been misclassified as Catahoula.

Patterson (1987) describes a drill-like variant of the Catahoula arrow point from site 41HR182, which he calls the Catahoula perforator. The bases have straight stems, and the shoulder barbs are squared like the Catahoula arrow point, inferring that the tool was hafted for use as a drill/perforator. Examination under magnification showed tip smoothing and polish, indicating possible use as a rotary tool.

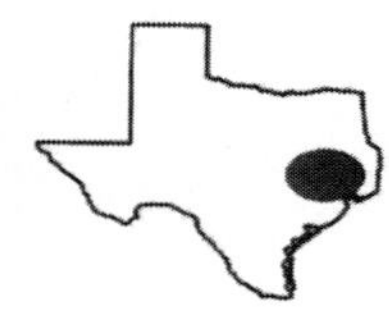

Distribution: Northeast and southeast Texas and Louisiana, as well as southeast Oklahoma and southwest Arkansas. **Period:** Late Prehistoric, ca. AD 700–1100. **Sites:** Grace Creek; Jones Hill; Burris 2; San Jacinto River Basin; Upper Rockwall; Glen Hill; Resch; Harris County.

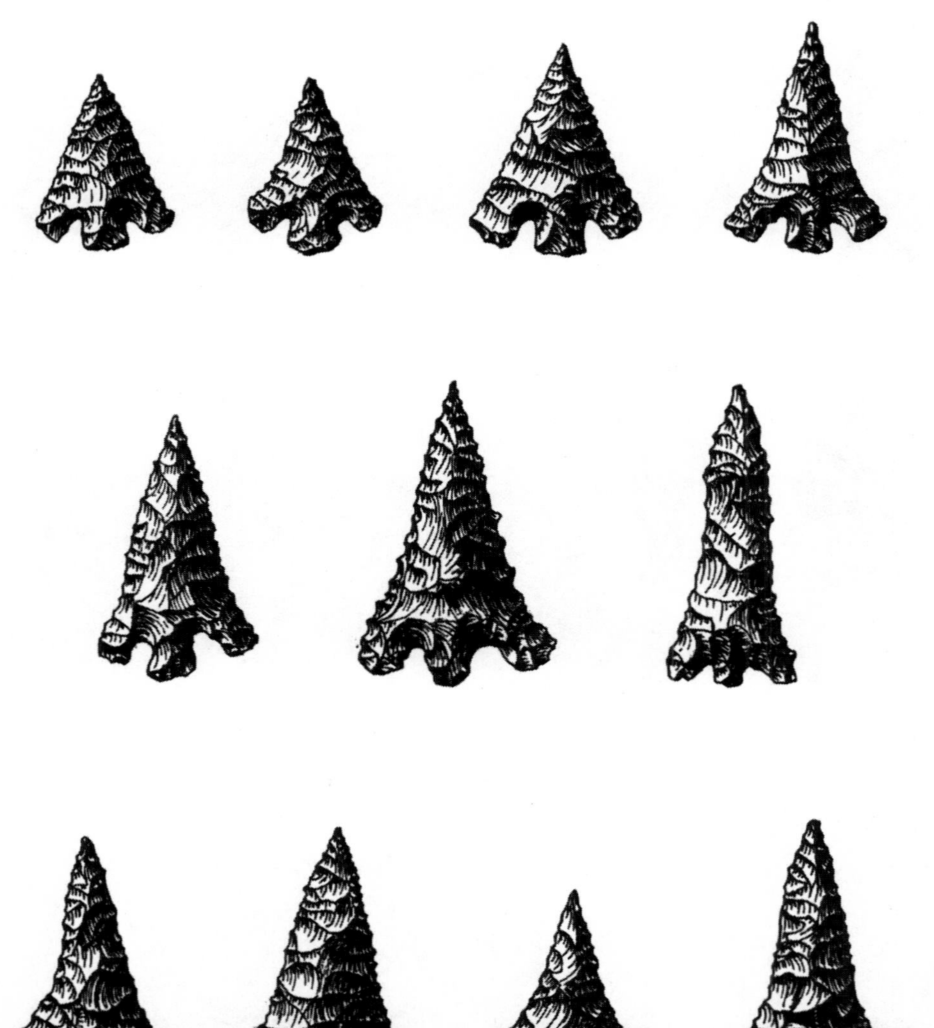

References: Aten 1967, 1983; Baker and Webb 1976; Jones 1957; McClurkan 1968; Patterson 1976, 1987; Ross 1966; Shafer 1968; Webb et al. 1969; C. Webb, personal communication.

CHADBOURNE

This elongate, triangular point has been defined by Darrell Creel (personal communication). It has straight to convex lateral edges, small shoulders, and a wide and slightly expanding stem with a generally concave base. Chadbourne is often found with Scallorn and Moran points.

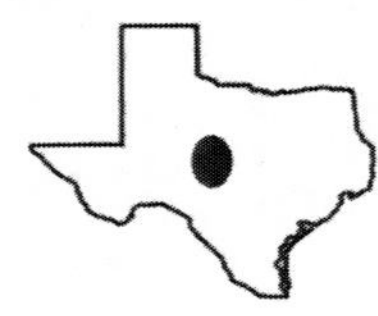

Distribution: Found in west central Texas in the drainages of the Colorado, Concho, and Clear Fork of the Brazos rivers. **Period:** Late Prehistoric, ca. AD 900–1300. **Sites:** 41CK87; 41TA58, 41TA66; Myatt; Airoso; Blowout Mountain Shelter; Sayles collection (Texas Archeological Research Laboratory).

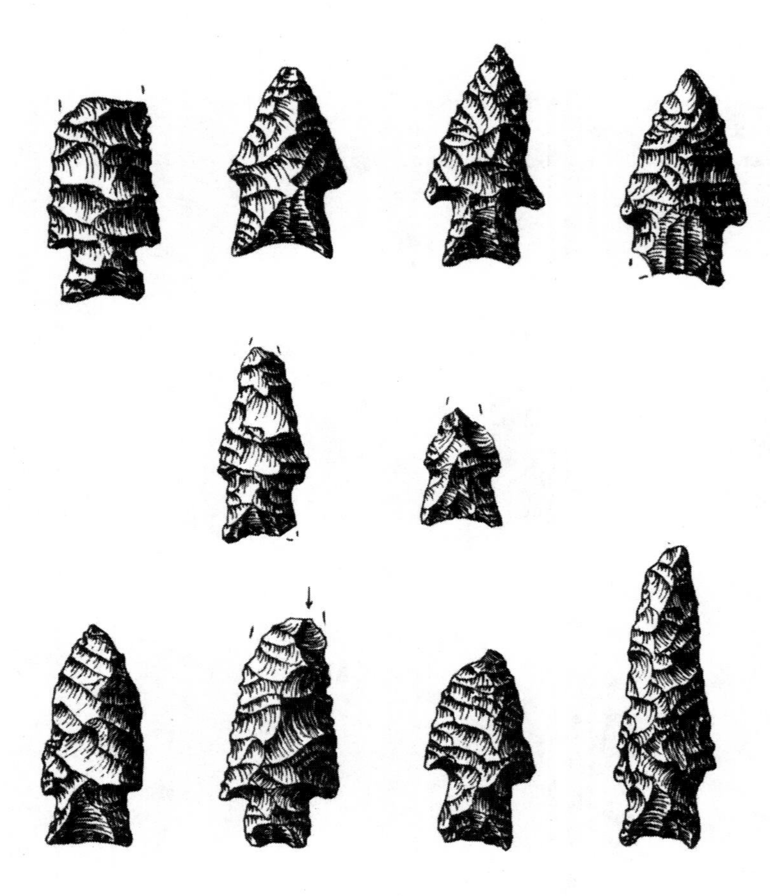

References: Creel 1990; Sayles n.d.; Shafer 1969; Wheat 1947.

CUNEY

This long, narrow point has straight or recurved lateral edges and long barbs that extend downward or flare outward. The base is notched, and the stem is parallel-edged or slightly expanding. Basal edges are concave.

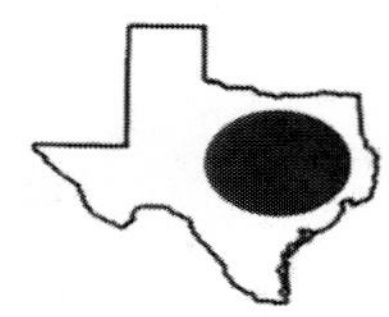

Distribution: Central part of east Texas and occasionally into central and south Texas. **Period:** Late Prehistoric into Historic (Allen phase, Caddo area). **Sites:** Pecan Springs; Scorpion Cave; Smith Rockshelter; 41DM31; Shanklin (41WH8); 41ZV155.

References: Duncan et al. 2007; Highley et al. 1978; Hudgins 1982; Inman et al. 1998; Ricklis 2010; Sorrow 1966; Suhm 1957; Suhm and Jelks 1962.

DEADMAN'S

This short, wide, triangular point has convex lateral edges that are sometimes serrated. The long, slender stem is straight to expanding with a rounded basal edge. Deep basal notches are nearly one-third the length of the point.

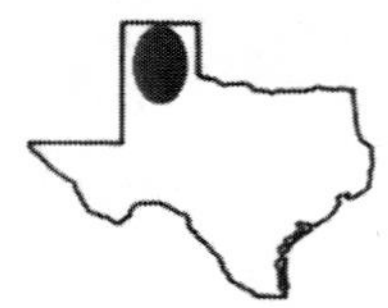

Distribution: Texas Panhandle. **Period:** Late Prehistoric. **Sites:** Deadman's Shelter (41SW23); 41GR256; McKenzie Reservoir; Palo Duro Canyon; Kent Creek; Lake Alan Henry.

References: Boyd 1995, 1997; Boyd et al. 1989; Duncan et al. 2007; Hughes and Willey 1978.

DIABLO

Diablo points, as defined by Mallouf (2009b), are typified by narrow, triangular bodies, having straight to slightly convex lateral edges. In some examples, blade edges are recurved. Moderate to strong serration of lateral edges that extend all the way to the distal tip is common, and occasional notching of the lateral edges just above the barbs serves to exaggerate the lateral edge/barb juncture. Barbs are typically strong to exaggerated, often with an arching, hooklike curve. The deeply corner-notched stems are variable. In both expanding and bulbous stem examples, stem elements usually constitute only 20–30 percent of overall specimen length.

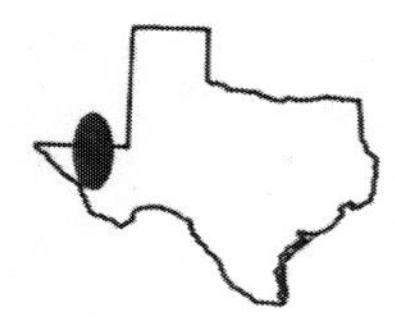

Distribution: Across portions of the central and northern sectors of the eastern Trans-Pecos region of Texas and in areas of southeastern New Mexico. Extremely rare south of the Davis Mountains in the Big Bend region. **Period:** Late Prehistoric, AD 800–1350. **Sites:** John Z. and Exa Means cache; Y6 Hills, Jeff Davis County.

References: Applegarth 1976; Boisvert 1985; Mallouf 2009b.

EDWARDS

These specimens are among the largest of the arrow points and appear to be the earliest form in south and central Texas. They have straight to convex lateral edges that are frequently serrated and occasionally recurved. The prominent shoulders or barbs are pointed, and the expanding stem is deeply divided and recurved, producing projections that may curve upward or downward.

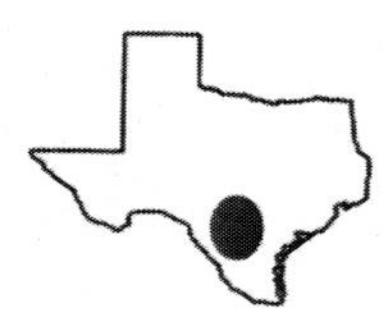

Distribution: Common in south central Texas and onto the south coastal plain. **Period:** Late Prehistoric, 10th and 11th centuries AD, based on radiocarbon dates from Rainey Sinkhole. **Sites:** Goat's Bluff; Kerr County; Panther Springs Creek; Camp Bullis; La Jita; 41BN113; Crystal Rivers; Mingo; Rainey Sinkhole.

References: Black and McGraw 1985; Duncan et al. 2007; Gerstle, Kelly, and Assad 1978; Henderson 2001; Hester 1970a; Houk and Lohse 1993; Sollberger 1978.

FRESNO

This unstemmed, triangular point has straight to slightly convex or concave lateral edges and a convex or slightly concave base. It is similar to Cameron but is over 20 mm in length. Some of these specimens may be preforms and not a distinct type. However, on the Texas coast, carefully chipped specimens appear to represent a typological group.

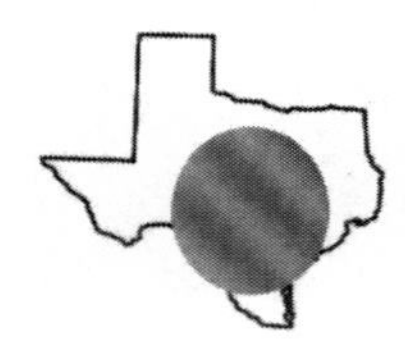

Distribution: Widely reported throughout Texas, though most frequently in central, eastern, and southern parts. **Period:** Late Prehistoric. **Sites:** Kenedy and Kleberg counties (41KL13); Hidalgo and Willacy counties (41HG4, 41HG5, 41HG9); Unland; Landslide; Lubbock Lake; Dillard; Oso (41NU2).

References: Duncan et al. 2007; Hester 1969a; Holliday and Johnson 1990; Jackson et al. 2004; Mallouf, Baskin, and Killen 1977; Mallouf and Zavaleta 1979; Martin 1994; E. Mokry, personal communication; Schmiedlin 2000a; Sorrow, Shafer, and Ross 1967; Suhm and Jelks 1962.

FRILEY

The Friley type is very distinctive. It has an expanding-stem point with prominent shoulders or short barbs that either project laterally or recurve toward the distal end of the point. They are often made of petrified wood of near-opalized quality (C. Webb, personal communication).

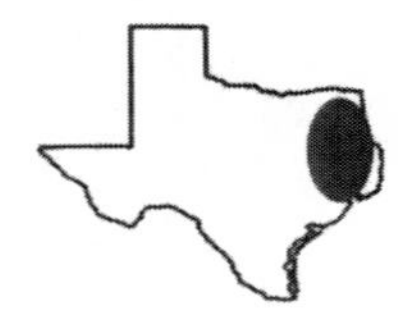

Distribution: East Texas and Louisiana. **Period:** Late Prehistoric, ca. AD 700–1100.
Sites: Jones Hill; 41PK21; Wolfshead; Cedar Creek; Smithport Landing (La.).

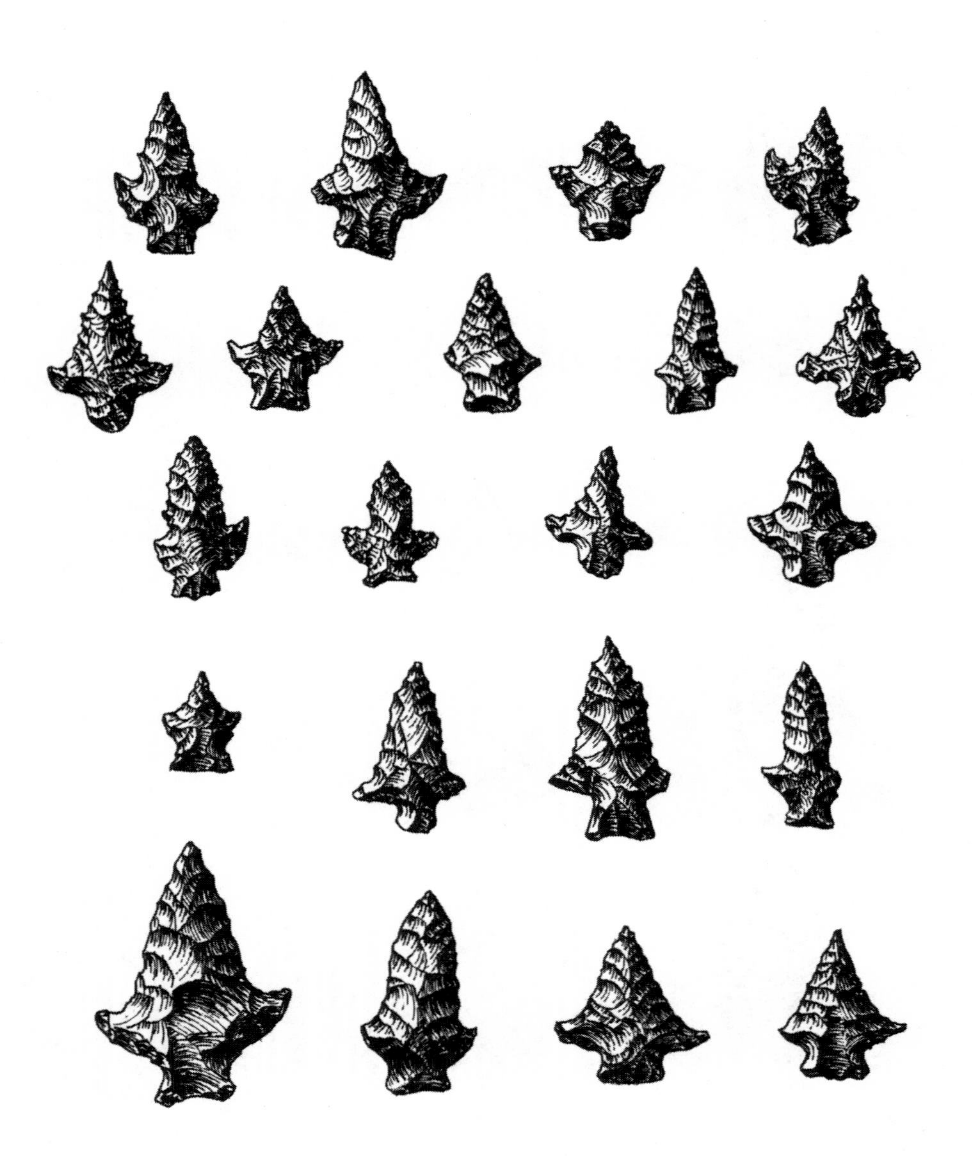

References: Duffield 1963b; Duncan et al. 2007; Fields et al. 1997; McClurkan 1968; Story 1965; Webb 1963.

GARZA

This is a triangular point, often with serrated lateral edges, that has a centrally notched base. The majority of these points are finely made, even though they are only unifacially worked. Points originally described as Garza (Bell 1960, 88) for the El Paso area are now believed to be a regional variant of Toyah, and not an El Paso extension of the range of Garza (F. A. Runkles and E. D. Dorchester, personal communication). However, very similar arrow points are found into northeast Mexico, especially Coahuila (bottom 3), but their context and associations are unknown.

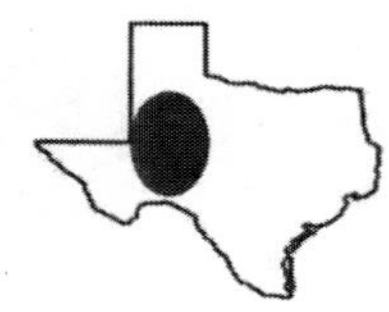

Distribution: Llano Estacado. **Period:** Late Prehistoric, ca. AD 1540–1665. **Sites:** Garza; Johnson; Lubbock Lake; Blue Mountain Rockshelter; Pete Creek; 41GR56; Cielo Bravo.

References: Holden 1938, 1962; Holliday and Johnson 1990; Johnson et al. 1977; Mallouf 1999; Parsons 1967; Runkles 1964; Runkles and Dorchester 1986; Wheat 1955.

GUERRERO

A triangular to lanceolate point made during the Spanish Colonial era (1700s) of Coahuila and Texas, often referred to as "mission" points. They sometimes have very careful parallel-flaking. They are primarily found in mission Indian middens, but they also occur at ranchos and at historic Indian occupation sites. Some specimens are knapped from shards of glass. Most examples are triangular in outline, and distal tips are often reworked. At Mission Espiritu Santo on the Guadalupe River (41VT11), there are both the typical Guerrero points and those that are longer and lanceolate. These are also known from the later, final location of the mission in Goliad (Ricklis 2000). It is tempting to link the lanceolate variant to the Aranama, since they had these points at 41VT11 and then moved with the padres to Goliad in 1749. But, the situation is much more complex, as is our understanding of point types over thousands of years.

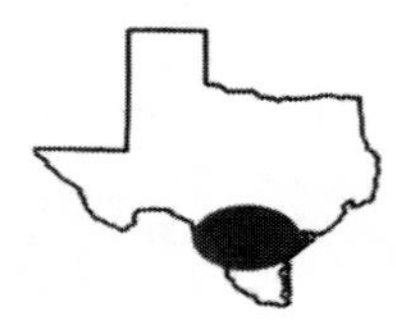

Distribution: South and southeast Texas and into Coahuila, Mexico. **Period:** Historic (18th century). **Sites:** San Jose Mission; San Juan Capistrano Mission; Concepcion Mission; Shanklin (41WH8); Alamo; 4VT11; Middle Rio Grande; Oso (41NU2); Mission Espiritu Santo (41VT11, 41GD1); Mission Rosario (41GD2).

References: Duncan et al. 2007; Fox 1979b; Hester 1977a, 1989c; Hester and Whatley 1997; Hudgins 1982; Inman 1999; Lohse 1999; Ricklis 2000; Schuetz 1968, 1969; Scurlock and Fox 1977; Tomka 1999; Walter 2007.

HARRELL

This triangular point has either side notches or side-and-basal notching, sometimes with finely serrated edges. Bell (1958) suggests that Harrell be applied to specimens having a basal notch, and Washita be applied to those without a basal notch.

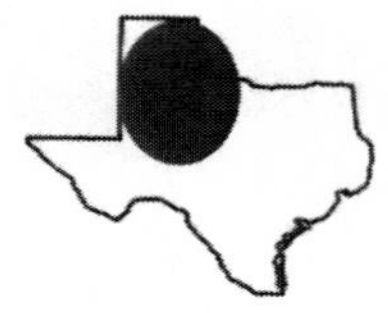

Distribution: Primarily in the Panhandle and Trans-Pecos; similar forms are widely dispersed across North America. **Period:** Late Prehistoric, AD 1200–1500. **Sites:** Possum Kingdom Reservoir; Garza; Texarkana Reservoir (41CS101); Roark Cave; Lubbock Lake; Blue Creek; Harrell.

References: Bell 1958; Briggs and Malone 1970; Couzzourt and Schmidt-Couzzourt 1997; Holliday and Johnson 1990; Kelly 1963; Krieger 1946; Runkles 1964; Schneider 1966; Suhm and Jelks 1962; http://www.texasbeyondhistory.net/.

HAYES

This small, carefully chipped point has a distinctive diamond-shaped stem. The lateral edges are sometimes finely serrated, and the tip might be sharply incut. The flaring shoulders might be barbed or straight.

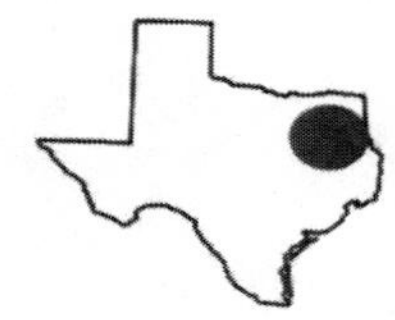

Distribution: Red River bend area and in adjacent corners of Texas, Arkansas, Louisiana, and possibly Oklahoma. **Period:** Late Prehistoric. **Sites:** George C. Davis; Mackin; Crenshaw Mounds (Ark.); Pike County (Ark.).

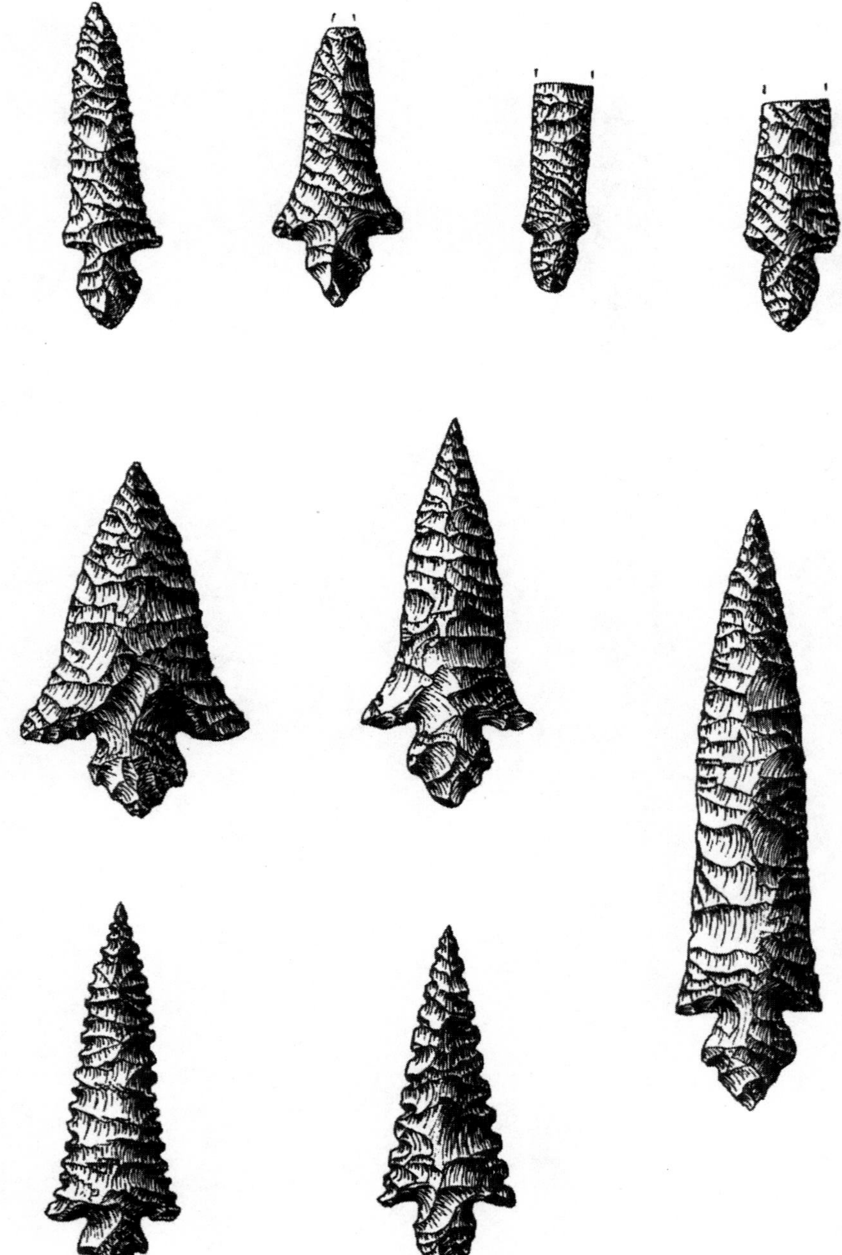

References: Duncan et al. 2007; Lemley 1936; Mallouf 1976; Newell and Krieger 1949; Shafer 1973; Suhm and Jelks 1962.

LIVERMORE

This long, slender point has deeply concave lateral edges and shoulders that project laterally at right angles. The stem is slender and the base, convex. "Livermore" has served as a catchall category for archaeologists for decades. Mallouf (personal communication) reports that the literature dealing with the Guadalupe Mountains is full of a mishmash of point types, all assigned to the Livermore type.

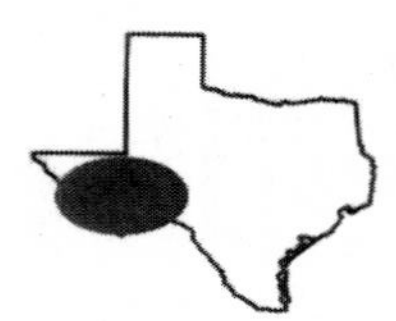

Distribution: Eastern Trans-Pecos and for a short distance south of the Rio Grande. **Period:** Prehistoric, ca. AD 800–1350, making it one of the earliest arrow point types yet documented in the eastern Trans-Pecos. **Sites:** Tall Rockshelter; Wolf Den Cave.

References: Mallouf 1999; Marmaduke 1978; Wulfkuhle 1990.

LOTT

A distinctive triangular point that has an expanding stem and a central basal notch. The lateral edges are trimmed from the base to about one-third the length of the point, forming a shoulder. "Ears" or tangs left by the basal indentation vary from pointed to square.

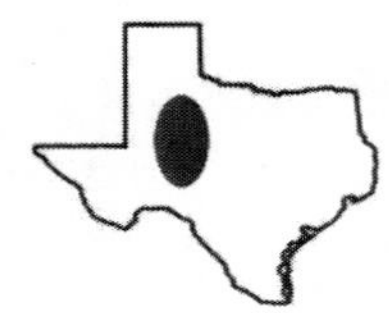

Distribution: Llano Estacado and the rolling plains of north central Texas. **Period:** Late Prehistoric, ca. AD 1390–1500. **Sites:** Lott; Blue Mountain Rockshelter; Lubbock Lake; Floydada Country Club; Crosby and Dickens counties.

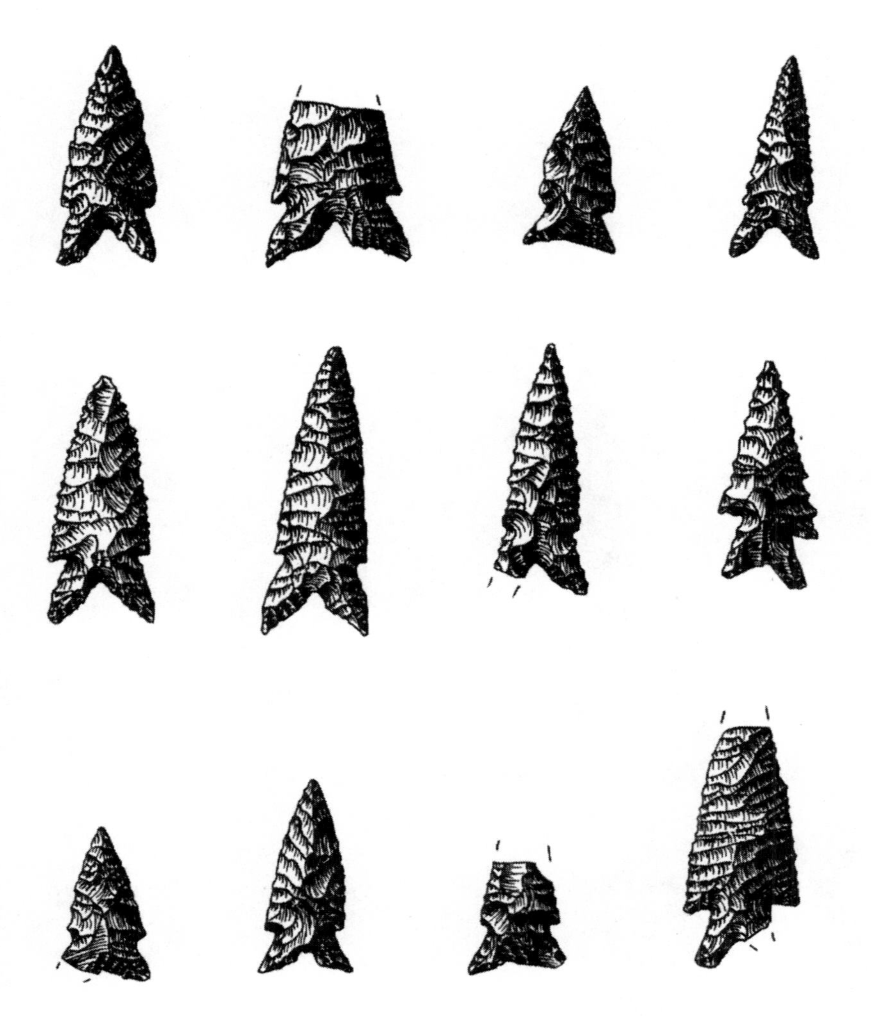

References: Holden 1938; Johnson et al. 1977; Parsons 1967; Runkles and Dorchester 1986; F. A. Runkles and E. D. Dorchester, personal communication; Word 1963; J. Word, personal communication.

LOZENGE

This descriptive name is applied to a point type characterized by an elongated, oval- to diamond-shaped outline. One-half of the point is bifacially worked, resulting in a lenticular cross section; the opposite end is alternately beveled, usually on the right. It is not always clear which end is the distal, and which, the proximal, or if the beveling is the result of resharpening.

Distribution: Texas Gulf Coast from Baffin Bay to Corpus Christi Bay. **Period:** Late Prehistoric. **Sites:** Johnson; Kent-Crane; McGloin Bluff (41SP11); Victoria County; Mitchell Ridge (41GV66).

References: Campbell 1947, 1952; Corbin 1963, 1974; Corbin, personal communication; E. Mokry, personal communication; Ricklis 1994; Weinstein 1992.

MAUD

This slender, stemless, triangular point has a concave to deeply V-shaped base. The lateral edges are straight to slightly convex or recurved. Blade edges are often finely serrated.

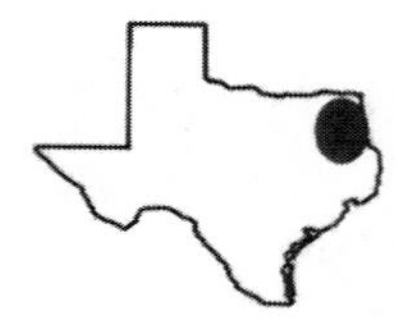

Distribution: Northeast corner of Texas and adjacent areas of Louisiana and Arkansas. **Period:** Late Prehistoric. **Sites:** Jones Hill; Texarkana Reservoir (41CS87, 41CS91); Tuck Carpenter; Alex Justiss; Dan Holdeman.

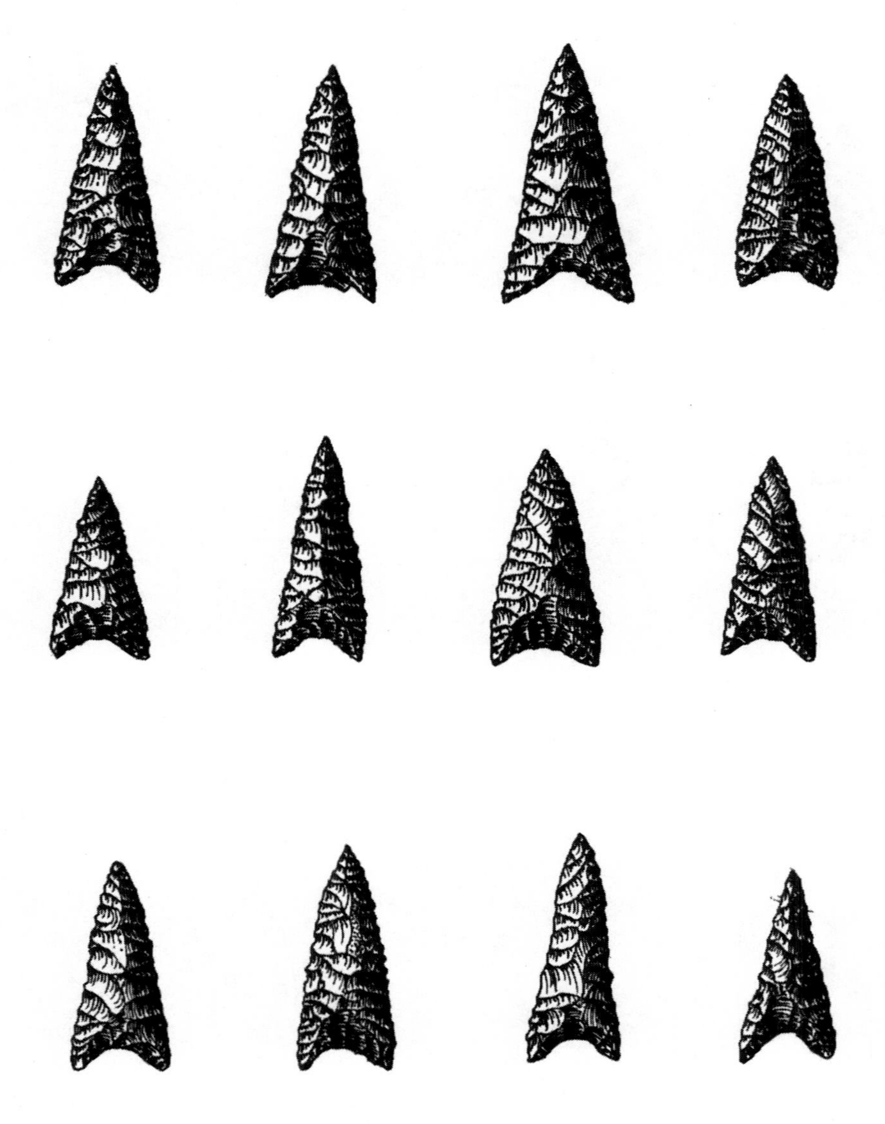

References: Bell 1981; Briggs and Malone 1970; Duncan et al. 2007; McClurkan 1968; Perttula 1995; Turner 1978.

MCGLOIN

This is a triangular point that almost always has a distinctly concave, V-shaped base. McGloin exhibits the characteristics of, and coexists on some sites with, both Fresno and Starr points (E. Mokry, personal communication).

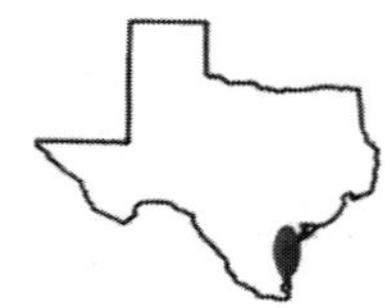

Distribution: Corpus Christi Bay area. **Period:** Late Prehistoric. **Sites:** McGloin Bluff (41SP11); Johnson; Kent-Crane; North Padre Island.

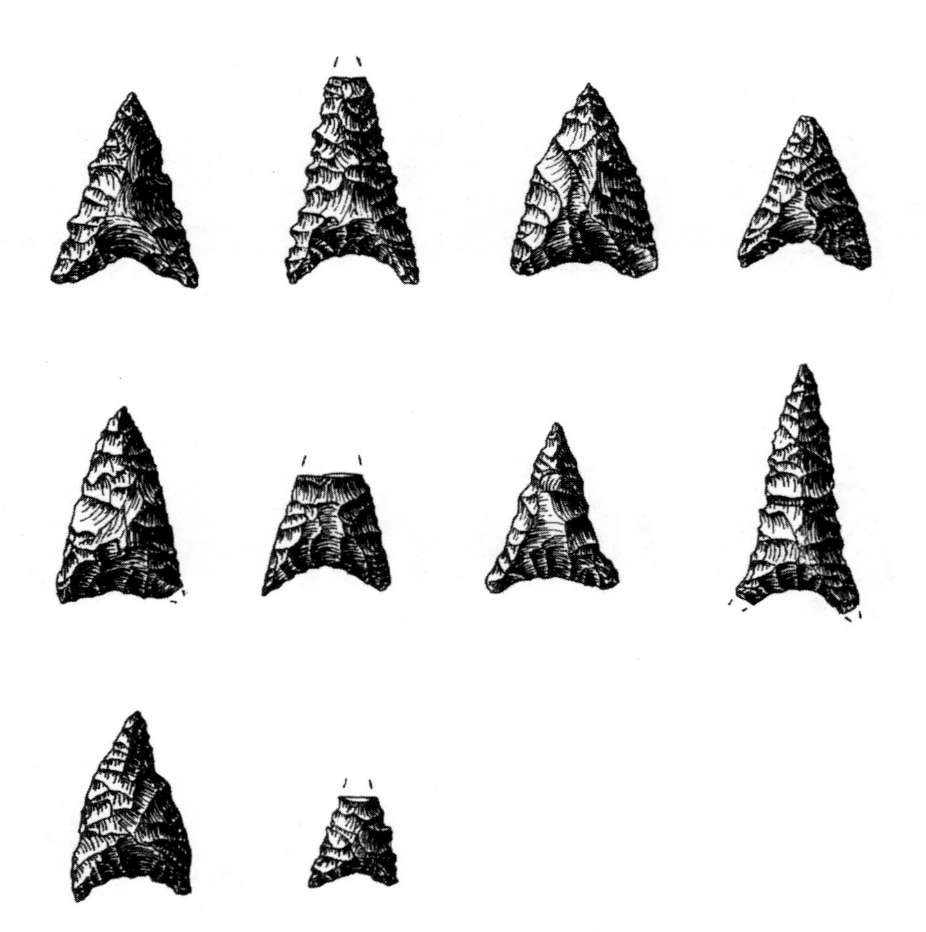

References: Campbell 1947, 1952; Corbin 1963, 1974; Gunter 1985.

MEANS

Robert Mallouf has named and described this new point from the eastern Trans-Pecos region of Texas. These points have long, narrow blades with moderately to strongly serrated lateral blade edges, which are typically straight but may also be recurved. The lateral edges are in some instances strongly beveled to obtain the desired narrow configuration. Distal blade tip beveling is common, sometimes resulting in a tiny, perforator-like tip but with no evidence of wear. Base width of the blade at its juncture with the barbs roughly equates to neck width below the barbs but may be slightly wider or slightly narrower. Well-defined barbs project laterally at roughly right angles to the long axis of the point. In rare instances, strong shoulders may supplant true barbs. Stems are short and fairly wide relative to the overall length of the point, with neck width roughly equivalent to the basal blade width. Stems expand quickly and strongly from the stem neck, and basal edges of stems are commonly straight but may be slightly convex or slightly concave. Width of the basal stem edge often approximates specimen width at the barbs.

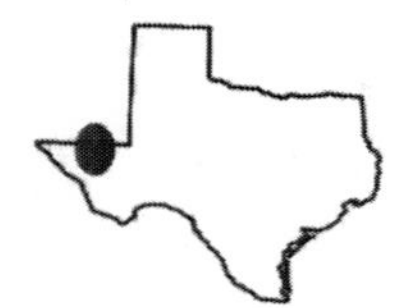

Distribution: Central and northern sections of the eastern Trans-Pecos of far west Texas, probably extending into southeastern New Mexico. Known to occur in the Davis and Guadalupe mountains, in Lobo Valley and the Salt Basin. **Period:** Late Prehistoric, roughly AD 700–1350, based on radiocarbon dates for Toyah points in the region cluster. **Sites:** John A. and Exa Means cache; Y6 Hills, Jeff Davis County.

References: Mallouf 2009c.

MORAN

Moran arrow points are slender, exceptionally well made, and often have straight, serrated lateral edges. The shoulders are sometimes squared but occasionally have small barbs. The stem is narrow (5 to 7 mm in width), parallel-edged, and 4 to 9 mm long. The bases are straight.

Distribution: Presently known only from a limited area bounded by the Colorado River from Colorado City to Ballinger and northeastward to Albany and Moran in Shackelford County. **Period:** Late Prehistoric AD 700–1200 based only on presence of Scallornlike points in two burials at the Salt Prong site with Moran points. **Sites:** Salt Prong; Robert Lee Reservoir basin; 41SF18.

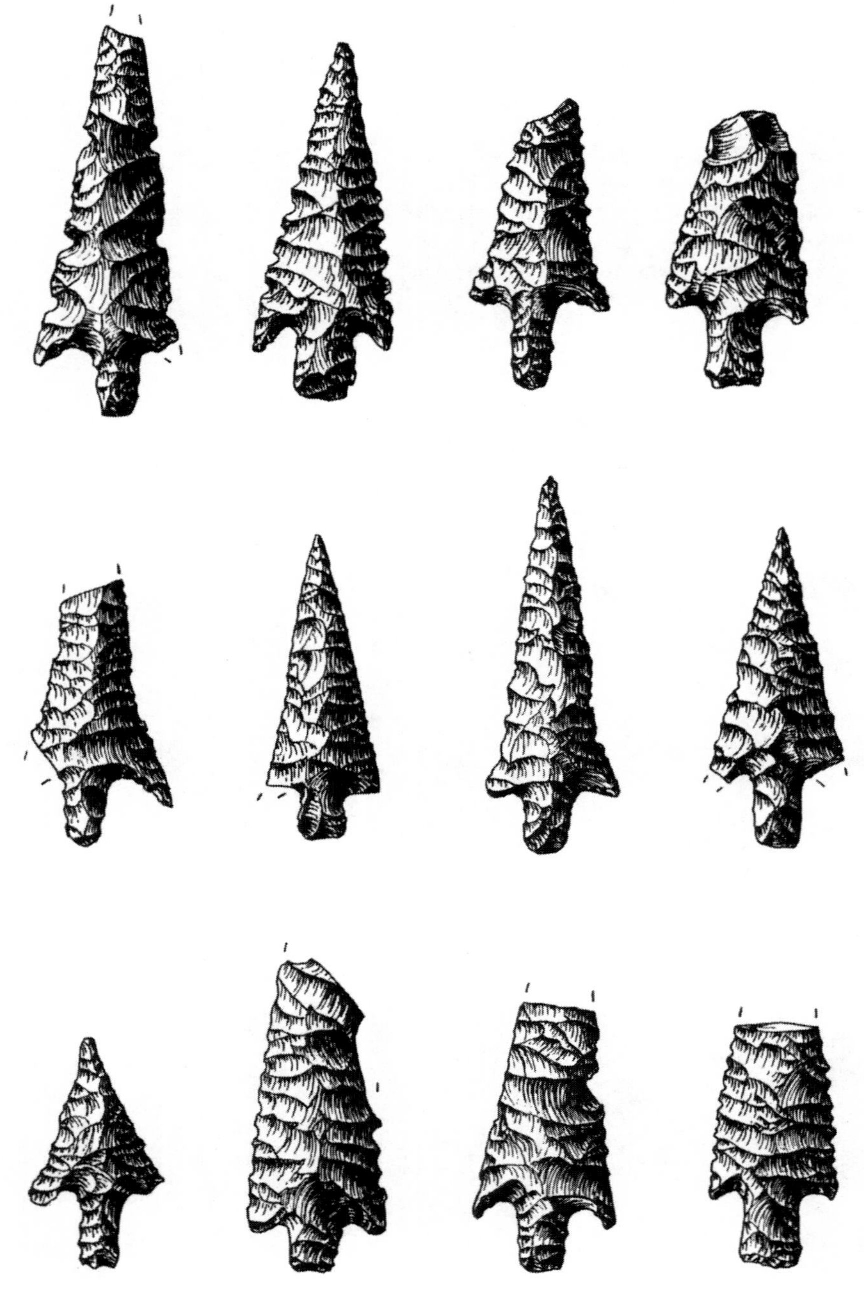

References: Flaigg 1991; Forrester 1951, 1987; Ray 1929; Shafer 1969.

PADRE

A small, triangular, unstemmed point that has convex lateral edges and a rounded base. It exhibits characteristics of both Cameron and Fresno points (E. Mokry, personal communication).

Distribution: Padre Island, and central part of the Texas coast. **Period:** Late Prehistoric. **Sites:** Johnson; Kent-Crane; McGloin Bluff; Oso (41NU2).

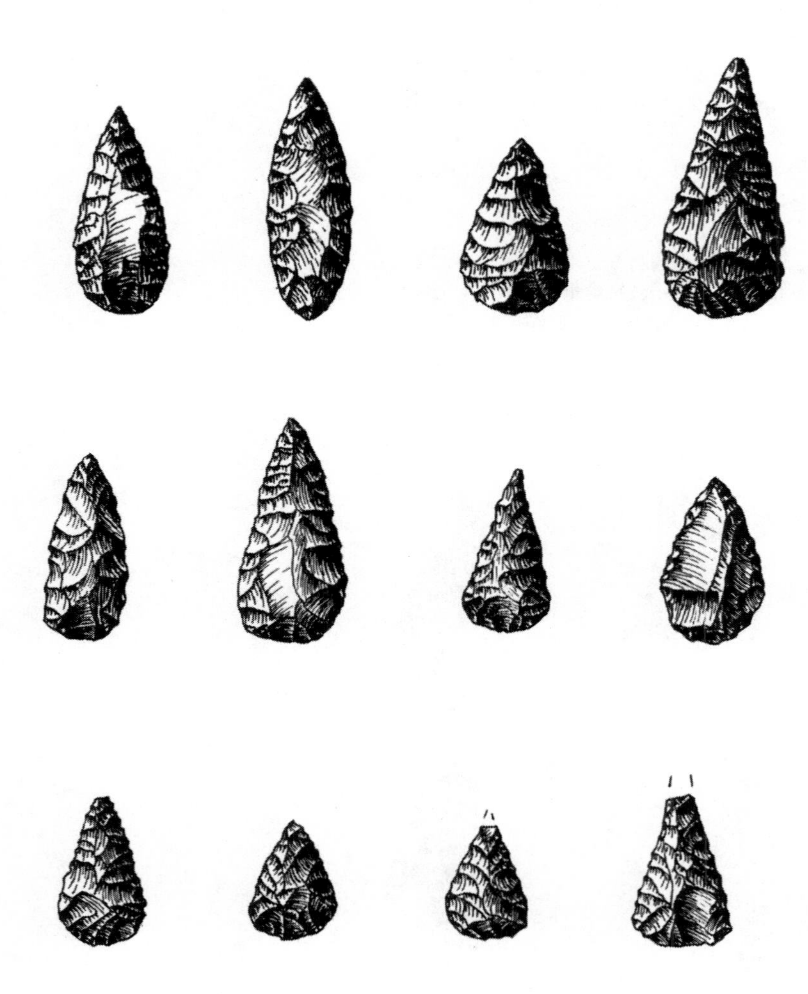

References: Corbin 1974; Corbin, personal communication; Jackson et al. 2004.

PERDIZ

Perdiz points are distinctive, contracting stem arrow points, usually with pointed barbs. There is much variation in size and proportions. Occasionally, specimens may be worked on one side only and are typically made on flakes or blades, but workmanship is generally good, sometimes exceedingly fine with minutely serrated blade edges. Preforms or poorly made Perdiz points have sometimes been called "Cliffton." A detailed study of Perdiz points from the Buckhollow site points to technological data that invalidate Cliffton as a type. Blades for making Perdiz points and other tools (such as end scrapers) were detached from blade cores, sometimes conical and polyhedral in shape. A small workshop containing sixteen Perdiz and Cliffton points was found at the Cardinal site on the Rio Salado, Tamaulipas; data from the site indicated that Cliffton points were preforms (Boyd 1997).

The reasons behind the spread of Perdiz points are unclear. They are a key element of the Toyah phase tool kit, along with beveled knives, end scrapers, bone-tempered ceramics, and bison hunting. In other areas, Perdiz is present but not in a "Toyah context." For example, at Las Haciendas in northern Chihuahua, Mallouf (1987) reports a burial cairn that contained 180 Perdiz points.

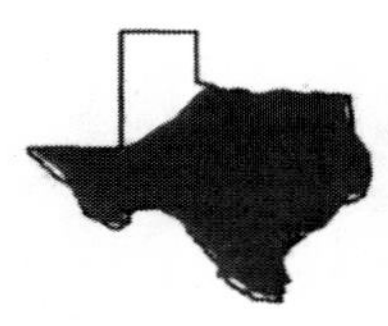

Distribution: Found throughout most of Texas and Louisiana; also found into the border area of the lower Rio Grande and into northern Chihuahua. **Period:** Late Prehistoric, ca. AD 1200–1700. **Sites:** Devil's Mouth; Oblate; Kyle; Wheatley; Finis Frost; Rush; Varga (Cliffton); Hemby (41KA101); Buckhollow; Rainey Sinkhole; Hinojosa; LK201; San Felipe Springs; Mitchell Ridge.

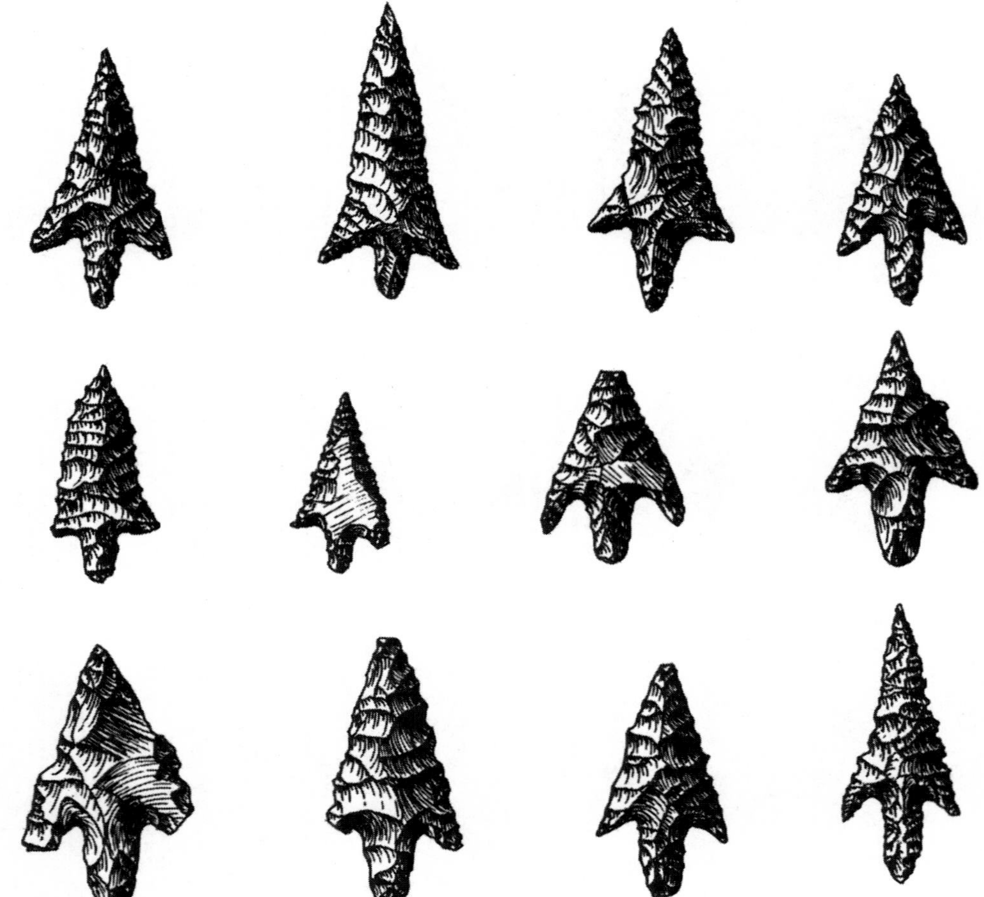

References: Black 1986; Boyd 1997; Duncan et al. 2007; Green and Hester 1973; Greer 1976; Henderson 2001; Highley 1986; Jelks 1962; Johnson 1964, 1994; Karbula 2003; Mallouf 1987; Mehalchick et al. 1999; Quigg and Peck 1995; Ricklis 1994, 1995, 2010; Schmiedlin 1993; Suhm and Jelks 1962; Tunnell 1962.

REVILLA

These are very thin, finely made arrow points of excellent quality chert. They are generally triangular in outline with distinctly deep (at least 4 mm) concave bases. Bases have a rounded apex and convex lateral edges. Prominent serrations begin at the basal corners, usually three to seven per side.

Distribution: Along the old channel of the Rio Grande between Chapote Creek and the Arroyo Clareno in Zapata County and Tamaulipas, Mexico. **Period:** Late Prehistoric. **Sites:** 41ZP83; 41ZP154; 41ZP8; Zapata County.

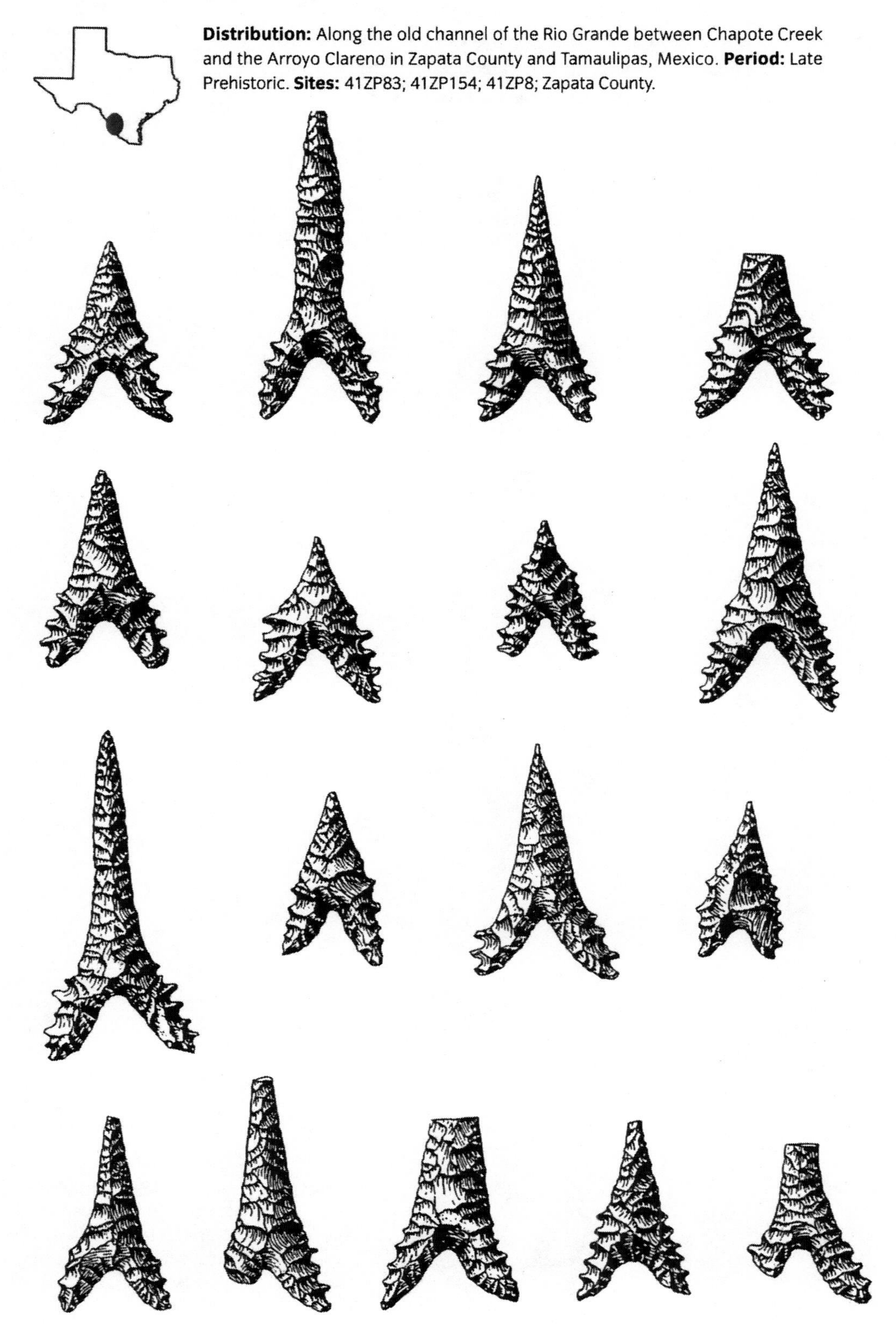

References: Galindo 1998; Kumpe 1993, 1998; Kumpe et al. 2000.

SABINAL

A long, narrow, triangular point that has deeply concave to recurved lateral edges and heavy barbs that flare outward and curve upward. The stem is produced by deep, narrow basal notches and expands moderately. Preforms are common at campsites, typically with flared corners that are later seen as the barb configuration on finished Sabinal points. Sabinal points are tightly defined both in time and space. A number of Texas archaeological reports have wrongly used the "Sabinal" label in areas great distances from its area. Excavations at the Rainey Sinkhole in Bandera County (Henderson 2001, 279) place Sabinal as a "short-lived type," occurring in time between Edwards and Scallorn.

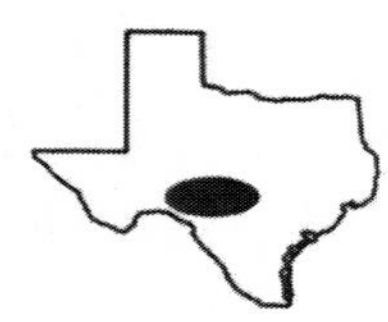

Distribution: Defined initially for a small area in the southwestern Edwards Plateau; similar specimens are sometimes reported from the lower Pecos and south Texas. **Period:** Late Prehistoric, ca. AD 1120–1250. **Sites:** La Jita; Anthon; Choke Canyon; Mason Creek; Leona; Rainey Sinkhole; Montell Rockshelter; 41ZV226; 41UV20.

References: Beasley 1978b; Coleman et al. 2001; Hall, Black, and Graves 1982; Henderson 2001; Hester 1971; Hester and Whatley 1992a; Lukowski 1987; Mauldin et al. 2004; Mitchell 1982; Weir and Doran 1980.

SCALLORN

This triangular, corner-notched point has straight to convex lateral edges and well-barbed shoulders. The expanding stem varies from a broad wedge shape to extremities as wide as the shoulders; the base may be straight, convex, or concave. Schmiedlin (personal communication) noted that sixteen Scallorn specimens at Blue Bayou (41VT94) had asphaltum on the stems.

During the Austin Phase, of which Scallorn points are chronological hallmarks, they are often found with burials (grave goods) and in burials (as cause of death). Indeed, the best evidence for warfare among ancient groups in central, south, and coastal Texas comes from Scallorn-related woundings and deaths.

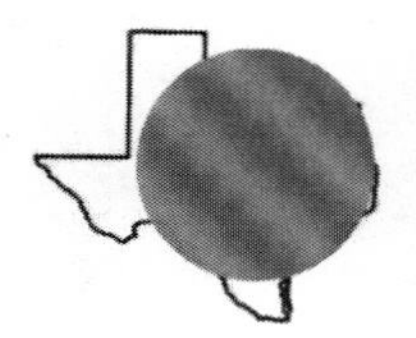

Distribution: Found over much of Texas but diagnostic of the Austin Phase. **Period:** Late Prehistoric, 830±50 BP, at 41FB255; 800–1250 BP, at Buckhollow; radiocarbon dates from the stratified Rainey Sinkhole overlap with Scallorn but occur later in time. **Sites:** Smith Rockshelter; Evoe Terrace; Loeve-Fox; Pat Parker; Frisch Auf!; Blue Bayou; 41FB255; Chytka; Buckhollow; Rainey Sinkhole; Frio County.

References: W. Birmingham, personal communication; Duncan et al. 2007; Greer and Benfer 1975; Henderson 2001; Hester et al. 1993; Hester and Collins 1969; Huebner 1988; Johnson 1994; Peeples 2003; Prewitt 1982; Rogers 2000; Sorrow, Shafer, and Ross 1967; Suhm 1957; Suhm and Jelks 1962.

STARR

A triangular point that is distinguished by slightly concave lateral edges and a pronounced basal concavity. These points are highly restricted in their geographic distribution and should not be used as a "niche" for similar points found at great distances from this distribution.

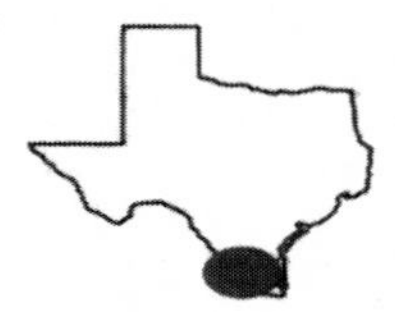

Distribution: Found in the lower Rio Grande Valley, on both sides of the Rio Grande, and extending up the coast to near Oso Creek and into Nuevo Leon at least 125 miles (McClurkan 1966). **Period:** Late Prehistoric. **Sites:** Hidalgo County (41HG4, 5, 6); Kleberg County (41KL13); McGloin Bluff; North Padre Island; Cueva de la Zona de Derrumbes Rockshelter, Mexico (Nuevo Leon).

References: Corbin 1963; Duncan et al. 2007; Gunter 1985; Hester 1969a, 1995; Lintz et al. 1993; Mallouf et al. 1977; McClurkan 1966; Ricklis 1995; Suhm and Jelks 1962.

STEINER

A small, serrated, triangular point that has short projecting spurs at various intervals along the recurved lateral edges. The small, barbed shoulders flare outward, and the stem varies from mildly expanding to rectangular.

Sollberger (1970) defined a type called Rockwall for the Upper Trinity area that is very similar to the Steiner type. Since the Steiner type was defined earlier in the literature (Newell and Krieger 1949), use of this name instead of Rockwall is preferred.

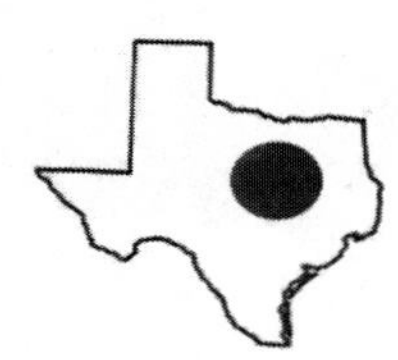

Distribution: East Texas. **Period:** Late Prehistoric. **Sites:** Cedar Creek; Upper Navasota Reservoir; George C. Davis; 41DL240; Cooper Lake.

References: Fields et al. 1997; M. Mallouf 1976; Newell and Krieger 1949; Prikryl 1990; Sollberger 1970.

TALCO

This finely made, Late Caddoan triangular point is characterized by straight to recurved lateral edges and a slightly concave base. The lateral edges are commonly minutely serrated. They seem to occur in graves and are not abundant in residential contexts. According to Perttula (personal communication), they are linked to the Titus Phase and are often found in graves containing Late Ripley Engraved ceramics.

Distribution: Northern part of east Texas. **Period:** Late Prehistoric into Historic, AD 1450–1700. **Sites:** Culpepper; Miller; Tuck Carpenter; Alex Justiss.

References: Bell 1981; Davis et al. 2010; Duncan et al. 2007; Johnson 1962b; Scurlock 1962; Suhm and Jelks 1962; Turner 1978.

TOYAH

A small, triangular point, which has two side notches anywhere from near the base to about the middle of the point and usually a large third notch in the center of the base. The blade edges are often strongly serrated, incut, and narrowed above the notches. Specimens are sometimes carefully flaked; others show up as heavily reworked (Cloud et al. 1994).

Distribution: South Texas, west Texas, and the lower Pecos; less frequently in central Texas. **Period:** Late Prehistoric into Historic. **Sites:** Devil's Mouth; Panda Cave; Perry Calk; Roark Cave; Buckhollow (41KM16); Polvo.

References: Alexander 1970; Cloud et al. 1994; Collins 1969; Duncan et al. 2007; Johnson 1964, 1994; Kelly 1963; Suhm and Jelks 1962; Wulfkuhle 1990.

TURNEY

This slender, thin, triangular point has a broad, V-shaped base. The lateral edges are usually serrated, and the point is finely chipped.

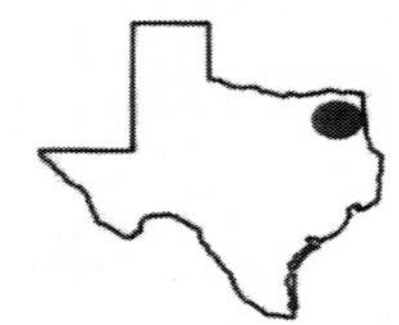

Distribution: Central part of the Neches River Valley, east Texas. **Period:** Historic. **Sites:** Patton; Jim Allen (41CE12); Deshazo (41NA27).

References: Duncan et al. 2007; Fields 1995; Story 1995; Story and Creel 1995; Suhm and Jelks 1962; Suhm, Krieger, and Jelks 1954.

WASHITA

This is a small, side-notched, triangular point with notches on the lateral edges that are often deep and produce an unusually large basal or stem area. The base is the widest part of the point. The stem edges taper gently to merge with the edges of the blade.

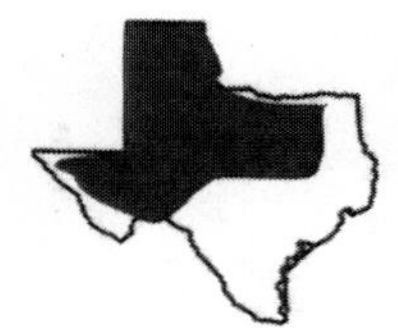

Distribution: Characteristic point in the Washita Focus, Oklahoma. Found in the Panhandle and north central and northeast Texas. **Period:** Late Prehistoric. **Sites:** Denton County; Sam Kaufman; Mackin; 41YN1; Blue Creek; Curtis Lake (Okla.); Sallee G. (Okla.).

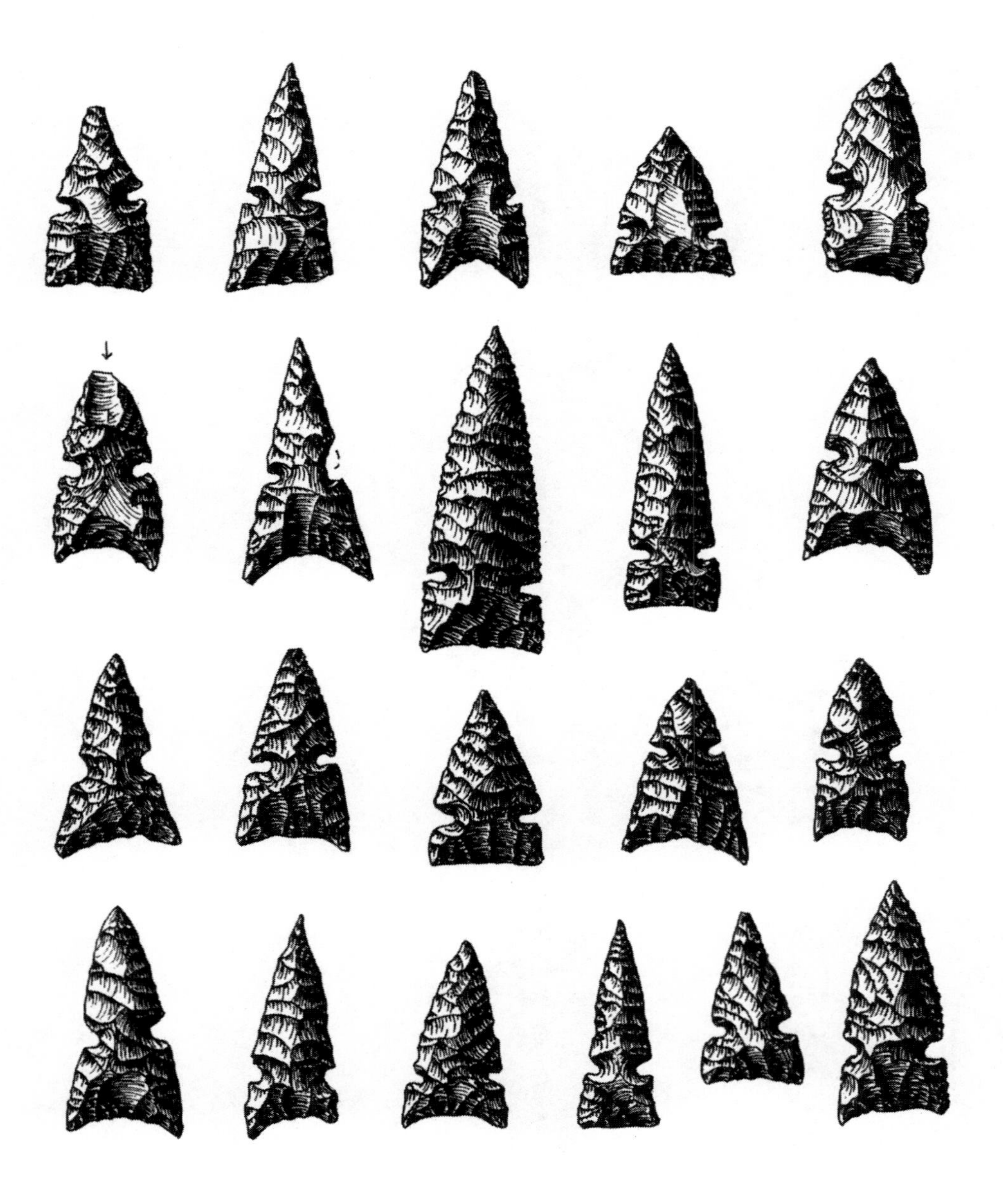

References: Bobalik 1978; Brooks et al. 1985; Couzzourt and Schmidt-Couzzourt 1997; Galm 1978; Mallouf 1976; Prikryl 1990; Skinner, Harris, and Anderson 1969.

YOUNG

This is a subtriangular point made from a thin flake that has been crudely knapped around the edges, the faces showing little or no sign of work. The bases and lateral edges are convex. In practically all (if not all) cases, these specimens are preforms.

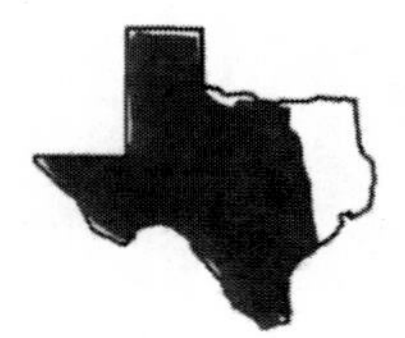

Distribution: North central Texas and southern Oklahoma, and the central Gulf Coast. **Period:** Late Prehistoric. **Sites:** Kyle; Smith Rockshelter; Webb Island; Live Oak Point.

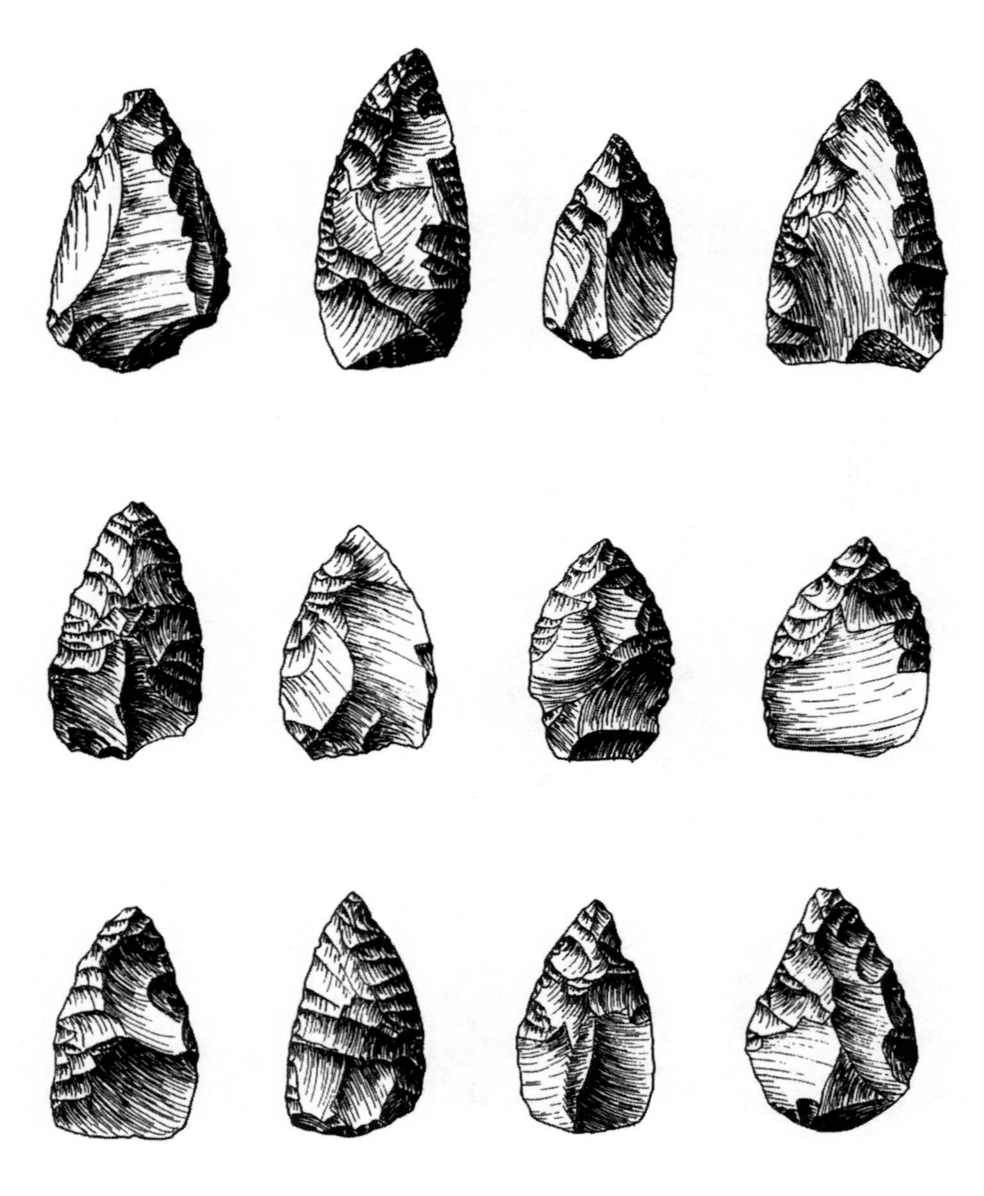

References: Campbell 1956, 1958; Jelks 1962; Suhm 1957; Suhm and Jelks 1962.

ZAPATA

These triangular to lanceolate, unstemmed arrow points were called "Form 1" when first documented at Falcon Reservoir. Specimens have slightly to markedly convex lateral edges near the base, which usually has the widest measurement. The stem and basal areas are slightly to moderately concave and have a "bowlegged" appearance. The points are usually made on flakes and may retain much of the original flake surface. Some specimens appear to have been sharpened while hafted, thus altering the original flake form above the hafted area.

Distribution: Northern portion of the Falcon Reservoir. **Period:** Late Prehistoric. **Sites:** 41ZP83; 41ZP154.

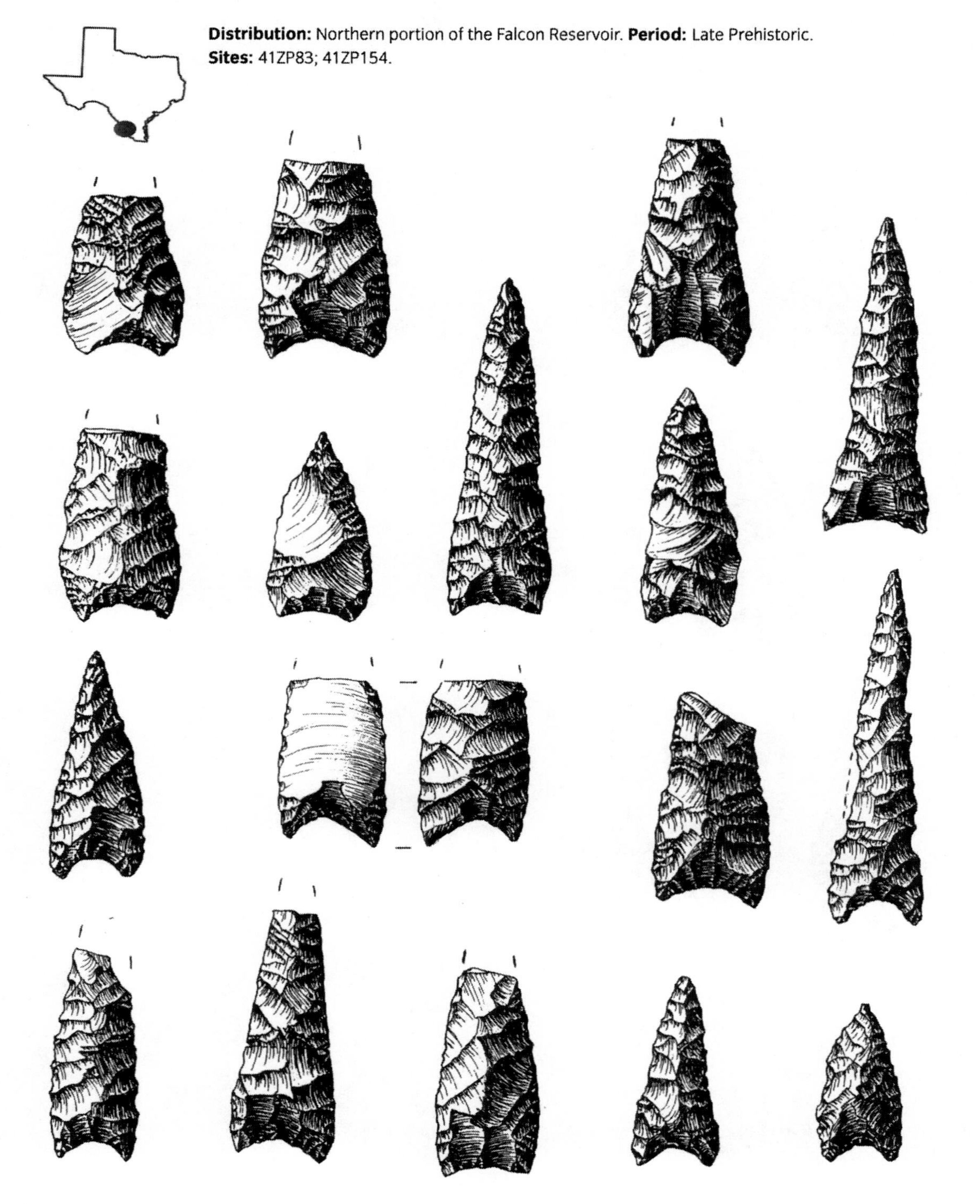

References: Kumpe 1993; Kumpe et al. 2000.

ZAVALA

This is a small, stubby, and thick point that was apparently used as an arrow point in south Texas. Specimens are always associated with contexts containing arrow points. It is similar to the Figueroa type that Johnson (1964) found in a comparable slot in the lower Pecos area. Sometimes, the Figueroa label is carelessly applied to Zavala points, even in the specific area in which the type was defined (Mauldin et al. 2004).

Distribution: South Texas, principally in the Nueces–Rio Grande corridor; possibly into lower Pecos and occasionally central Texas. **Period:** Transitional Archaic, ca. 200 BC–AD 600 (or later). **Sites:** Devil's Mouth; Wunderlich; Coontail Spin; Bear Creek (41BS66, 41BS402); Dos Republicas.

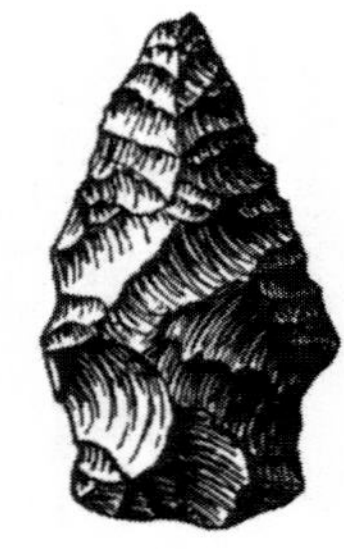

References: Hester 1978a, 2004b; Hester and Hill 1975; Johnson 1962a, 1964; Marmaduke 1978; Mauldin et al. 2004; Montgomery 1978; Nunley and Duffield 1964; Uecker 1994.

Chipped Stone Tools

THE WIDE array of stone tools often found in association with projectile points are usually more difficult to categorize, but they constitute an equally important component of the material culture of a group of people related in time and space. Utilitarian household implements such as knives, scrapers, and drills can be used by the archaeologist to study the behavioral patterns of populations.

Generally, the largest class of tools in an assemblage is the bifaces—artifacts with flaking on both sides or on two opposite faces (see chapter 2). In addition to the projectile points, these include artifacts often called "knives" and "gouges." The other large class of tools is the unifaces—flakes altered on one side or on one face only. Unifaces are usually plano-convex in cross section; the ventral surface is the flat side (plano), and the dorsal surface is the raised (convex) side. These include artifacts that are often labeled scrapers, gravers, flake tools, and unifacial "gouge" forms.

Characteristics of chipped stone tools that have functional importance come in a variety of forms, shapes, and disguises, and the average tool may have been utilized in a number of different ways; thus, it is sometimes very difficult to distinguish a knife from a projectile point or a scraper from a knife. Since form is often simply the by-product of expedience, resharpening, or other modification in a tool's life, the most direct sort of evidence appears to be wear left on the tool while it was being used (chapter 2). Hence, classification and names must be used with caution and only in a general fashion; when used, they should ideally be based on an analysis of manufacturing techniques, shapes, wear patterns, and context.

Some of the best-known and most intensively studied specimens have been named in the past, according to their function suggested as a result of experiments, studies, or hypotheses (or all of these). These are described, together with general morphological classifications (scrapers, perforators, gravers, etc.), and arranged alphabetically. Readers are once again cautioned that we have assembled these from the existing literature; some of these categories are tentative or represent groupings or functions that have not been fully tested through archaeological research. Furthermore, many are very restricted in time and space, and could be used for comparative purposes based on the data provided here and through consultation of the references listed for each.

In this third edition, we have omitted the following groups: Bronson bifaces; Erath bifaces; Friday bifaces; Hare bifaces; Harvey/Mineola bifaces; San Gabriel bifaces; and

Gosset unifaces. Some of these categories have faded from the scene; others have lost their basic definition. The Friday biface is a good example. This artifact was originally described by Jelks (1962) as a relatively thin, bifacially chipped, triangular "knife." At the Kyle site, where Jelks found these, they are all less than 9 cm long and are associated with Scallorn points. But in recent years, the name has been appropriated for much larger, thin, triangular bifaces dating to the Late Archaic in central Texas. Researchers working in Milam County at site 41MM340 have identified "teardrop shaped bifacially flaked celts" labeled as Erath Celts (Mahoney et al. 2003). Similarly, Johnson (2000) illustrates an Erath Adze Blade from site 41WM13 in Williamson County.

We hope that researchers might clarify these categories in the future. Those wishing more information on some of these forms can consult our earlier editions (1985, 1993).

ALBANY TOOLS

These artifacts appear to be hafted spokeshaves or beveled scrapers. Two characteristic features are side-notching, producing an expanded haft with a typically concave or straight base, and a single, concave, beveled lateral edge. They may be flat, waterworn pebbles altered only by chipping of the beveled edge and side notches with some thinning of the base, or they may be chipped over the entire surface. Most of the latter specimens appear to be reworked from projectile points and are typically found in sites with San Patrice points in northwest Louisiana and southeast Texas, perhaps reworked from points of that type.

The diagonal placement and convexity of the bevel plus the generally rough and dull edge suggest a scraping, rather than a cutting, tool.

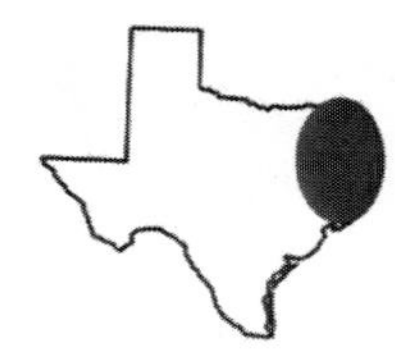

Distribution: East Texas and northwest Louisiana. **Period:** Paleo-Indian. **Sites:** Albany Landing (La.); Wolfshead; 41WH19; 41HR525; 41HR233; 41HR624; 41HR182; 41HR641.

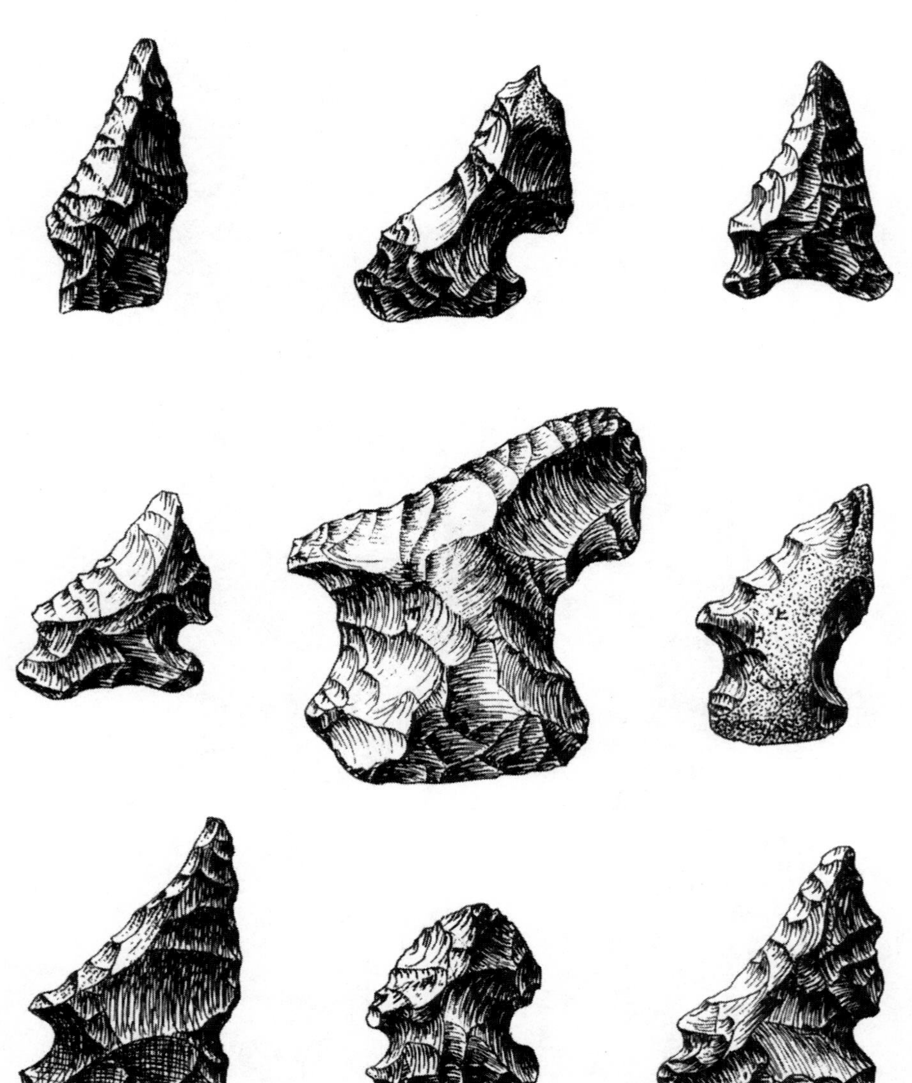

References: Duffield 1963b; Krieger 1943; Patterson 1990a, 1990c, 1991a; Patterson and Hudgins 1981; Patterson and Marshall 1989; Patterson, Murk, and Murk 1984; Patterson et al. 1990; Webb 1946.

BEVELED BIFACES: FOUR-BEVELED AND TWO-BEVELED

Diamond-shaped bifaces with four beveled edges are sometimes called "Harahey Knives." They occur widely in Late Prehistoric sites in the southern Plains and Blackland Prairie and occasionally in the central and eastern parts of the state. They are often made of Alibates-agatized dolomite in the Plains. They are usually characterized by steep bevels on all four alternating edges.

Restricted largely to south Texas is a different, two-beveled form with a shorter, convex-edged proximal segment. The tool form is a regional variant of the better-known four-edged form; the distinctive shape is due to patterned resharpening (Brown et al. 1982). Both forms are frequently associated with bison remains and, in central and south Texas, a trait of the Toyah Horizon.

Distribution: Southern Great Plains and widespread locations in Texas. **Period:** Late Prehistoric and possibly into Historic, ca. AD 1300–1750. **Sites:** Harrell; Buzzard Shelter; Pearson; Choke Canyon (41LK67); Hemby (41KA101); Rainey; Keith site burial.

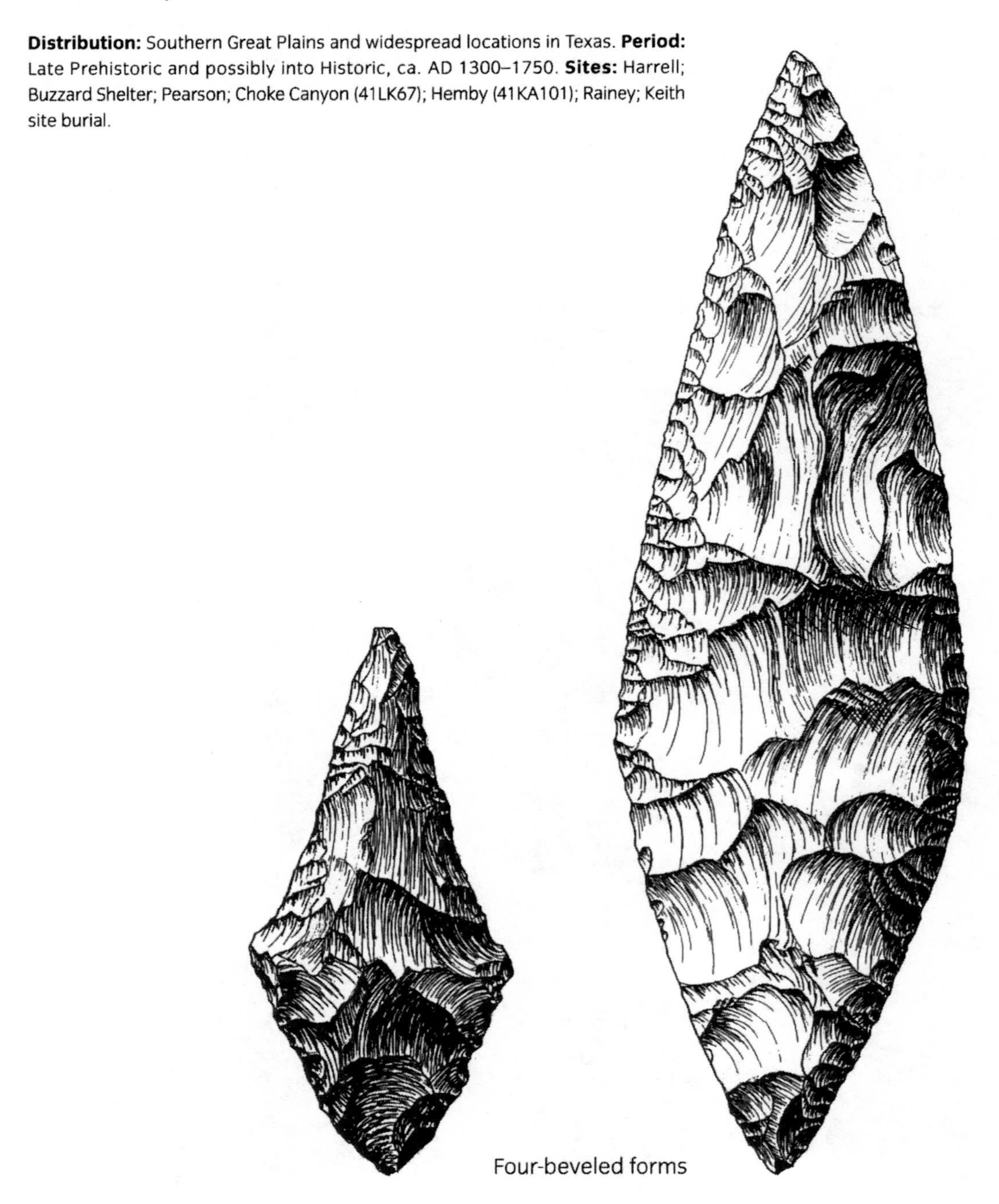

Four-beveled forms

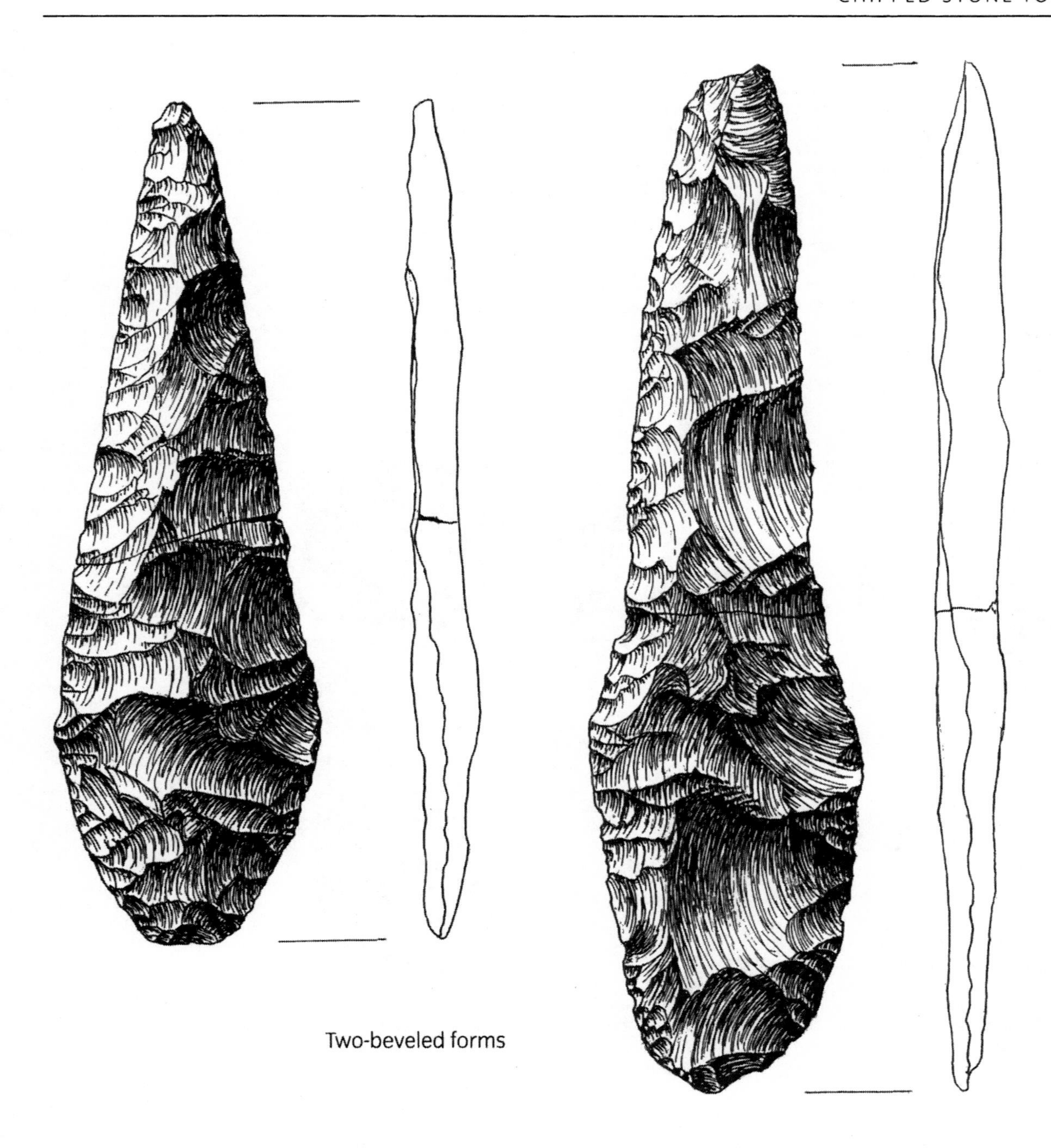

Two-beveled forms

References: Brosowske 2009; Brown et al. 1982; Duffield and Jelks 1961; Henderson 2001; Krieger 1946; Poteet 1938; Schmiedlin 1993; Sollberger 1971; Stephenson 1970.

BRISTOL BIFACES

This relatively small, oval to subtriangular artifact was originally described by Duffield (1963a). The workmanship varies from good to crude; it is usually percussion-flaked, and specimens retain cortex on one or both faces. However, marginal retouching and continuous edging or smoothing are visible on some of the specimens. Its function is unknown.

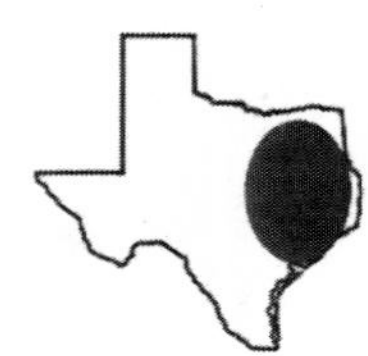

Distribution: East and southeast Texas. **Period:** Late to Transitional Archaic. **Sites:** Strawn Creek; Cedar Creek; Pecan Springs; Burris 1; Richland Creek drainage.

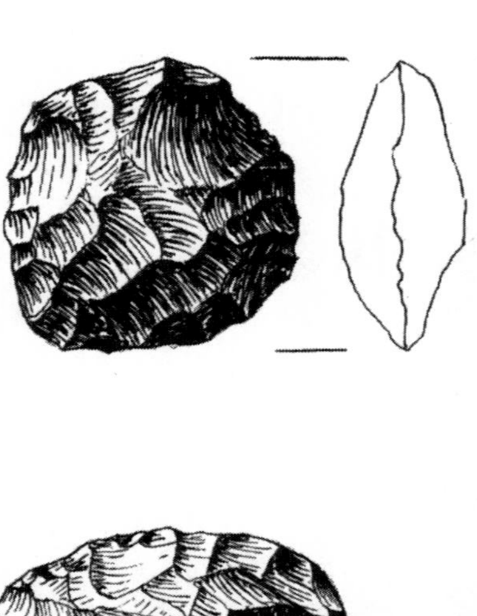

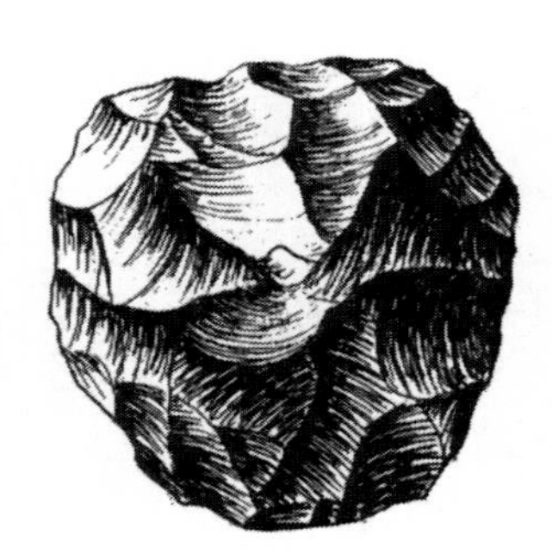

References: Duffield 1963a; McClurkan 1968; McGregor and Bruseth 1987; Sorrow 1966; Story 1965.

CLEAR FORK TOOLS

The Clear Fork tool form was originally defined by Ray (1941). Often called "gouges," these artifacts have triangular to subtriangular outlines, though some vary to lanceolate, rectangular, and ovate. The wide end is considered the working edge or bit. The bit is usually steep and beveled and may be convex, straight, or slightly concave ("scooped out"). In cross section, the tools are plano-convex and at times almost pyramidal; some are biconvex. Edge-wear can sometimes be detected visually or with the aid of a microscope; it is likely that they were utilized in woodworking tasks, as adzes rather than "gouges." The edge angle of the bit end varies from 60 to 75 degrees in most cases.

Large Clear Fork bifaces occur in some Paleo-Indian contexts (e.g., St. Mary's Hall and Baker Cave). Large Clear Fork unifaces often appear in the Early Archaic. The unifacial and bifacial forms of smaller size are very common in south Texas and in the Abilene area, primarily during the Middle Archaic. Boyd and colleagues (1989) illustrate and describe numerous Clear Fork tools in Garza and Kent counties, just off the Llano Estacado.

An intensive study of Clear Fork tool function has been done by Hudler (1997). Through high-power microscopy and replicative experiments, almost all appear to have been used in woodworking tasks, in an adze-like fashion.

Distribution: Found widely in Texas, especially south Texas, north central Texas, and parts of northeast Mexico. **Period:** Some forms begin in the Paleo-Indian and Early Archaic and continue into the Middle Archaic. **Sites:** Baker Cave; St. Mary's Hall; Choke Canyon; Granberg II; Oulline; Granite Beach; Armstrong (41CW54); Justiceburg Reservoir.

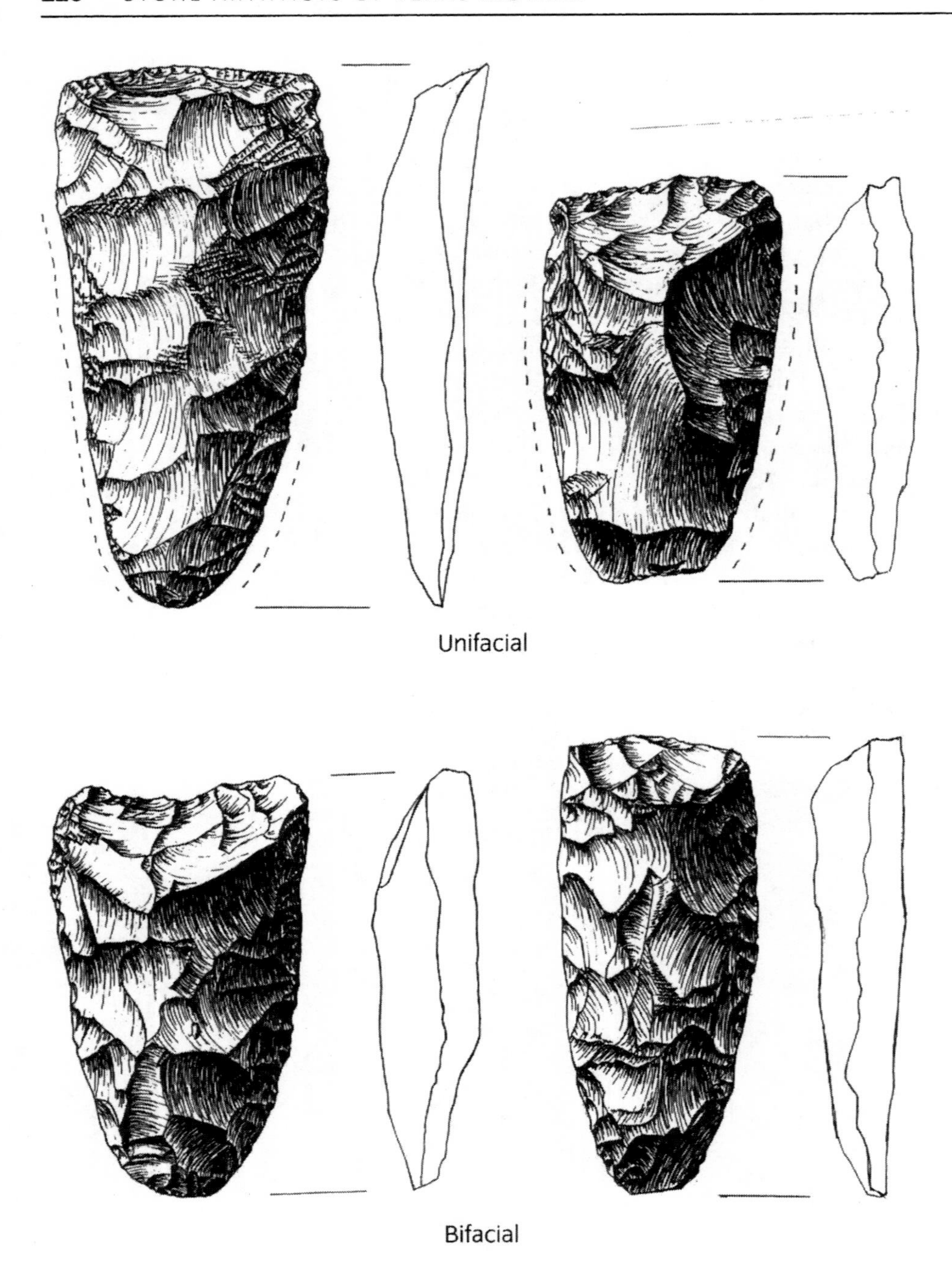

References: Boyd et al. 1989; Chandler 1974; Crawford 1965; Dial 1998; Hall, Black, and Graves 1982; Hester et al. 1973; Hester and Kohnitz 1975; Hester, White, and White 1969; Hofman 1977; Howard 1973; Hudler 1997; Hughes 1980; Ray 1941; Schroeder and Okansen 2002; Shiner 1975.

CORNER-TANG BIFACE

This relatively rare biface has several body and tang variations; the most common form has a tang notched into one corner of the base (Patterson 1936). Most specimens have been found in central and south central Texas and westward in counties along the Balcones Escarpment.

Function is unknown; some have edge-wear indicating hafting for use as a knife (Mitchell and Orchard 1984), others have been reworked as drills, and some were placed with burials. There are corner-tang specimens so outlandish in size and so carefully flaked that a ritual or ceremonial role is presumed when found in Archaic cemeteries like Ernest Witte and Silo.

Distribution: Central Texas and adjoining areas. **Period:** Late Archaic. **Sites:** Ernest Witte; Rudy Haiduk (41KA230); McCann; Morhiss; Silo.

References: Broehm and Lovata 2004; Chandler, Knolle, and Knolle 1983; Hall 1981; Kraft 1993; Lovata 1997; McReynolds and Chandler 1984; Mitchell, Chandler, and Kelly 1984; Mitchell and Orchard 1984; Patterson 1936; Preston and Shiner 1969; http://www.texasbeyondhistory.net/.

DALTON ADZ

This biface has an oval to triangular outline, with a steep bit. The lateral edges are usually heavily dulled, and haft polish is observed on the poll end. Most appear to have been made from flat, long pebbles or small cobbles, and traces of cortex (as illustrated below) are found on many specimens. It is believed that they were used as adzes.

Smaller and thinner bifaces with a beveled bit are referred to as "Quince scrapers" by Johnson (see Story et al. 1990, 197). These are of probable Dalton age and may be related to the Dalton Adz form.

Artifacts matching the form and technology of the Dalton Adz have been reported from south, central, and northeastern Texas.

Distribution: Northeast Arkansas; southwest Missouri; east Texas into central and south Texas. **Period:** Paleo-Indian. **Sites:** Brand; Hawkins cache (Ark.); Horn Shelter 2 (41BQ46); Gault (41BL323); Zavala County; 41DM59.

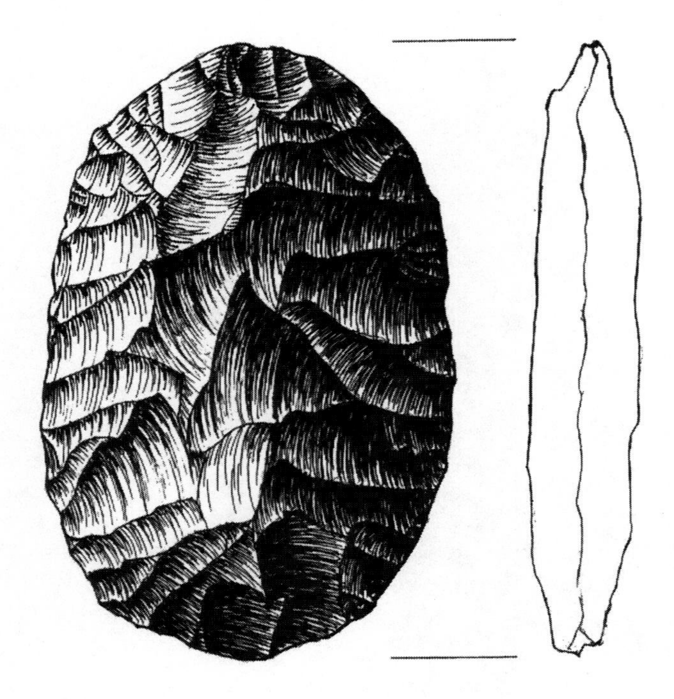

References: Goodyear 1974; Hester and Whatley 1992b; Johnson 1989b; Morse 1973; Morse and Goodyear 1973a.

GAHAGAN BIFACE

The Gahagan biface is a long, parallel-sided to elongated triangular artifact with a base that is generally straight or moderately concave and thinned to about the same degree as the lateral edges. It is often characterized by recurved edges between the base and midpoint of the lateral edges. Edge-wear suggests possible use for cutting vegetal substances or meat (Shafer 1973). Indeed, many of the specimens are heavily resharpened, leading to a reduction in body width and making a specimen much more triangular. Specimens are often from burials, with contexts including elite tombs at the George C. Davis site. The definitive study of the Gahagan biface is found in the work by Shafer (2006).

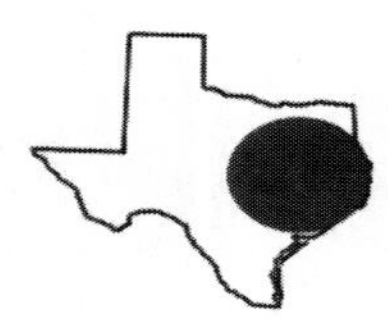

Distribution: Central, east central, and east Texas into south Texas; Louisiana. **Period:** Late Prehistoric. **Sites:** George C. Davis; J. B. White (41MM341); Burris 1; Mackin; Alabonson Road; Grimes Houey (41CV13); Bell, Williamson, Coryell, Limestone, Dallas, Grimes, Milam, Polk, Red River, Robertson, and Washington counties; Gahagan (La.).

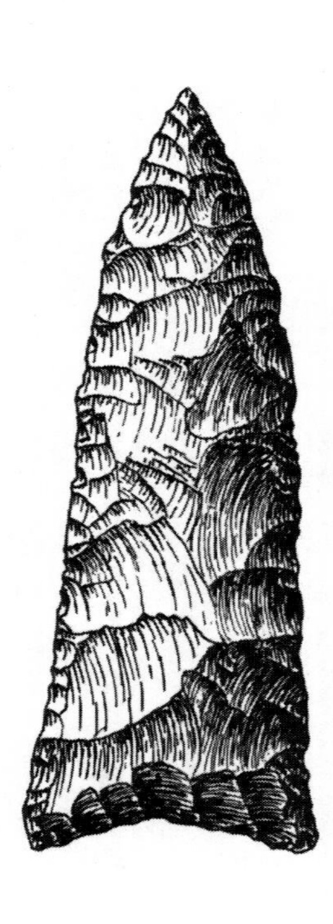

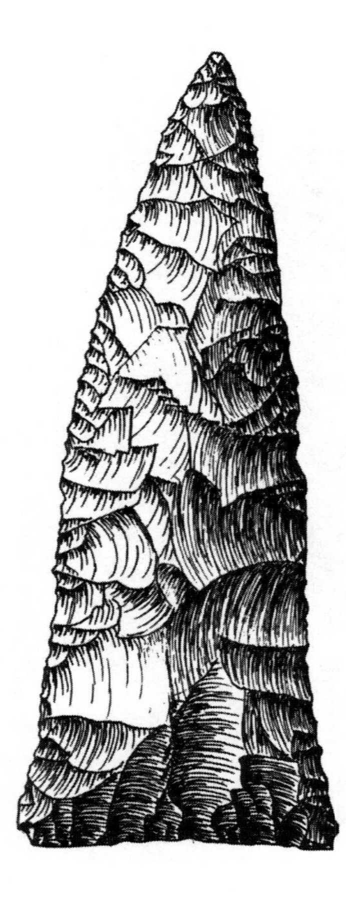

References: Ensor and Carlson 1991; Gadus et al. 2006; Hester 1994b; M. Mallouf 1976; McClurkan 1968; Newell and Krieger 1949; Shafer 1973, 2006; Webb and Dodd 1939.

GRAVERS

Gravers are small, carefully chipped, sharp, beaklike protrusions generally made on flakes or on another tool, for example, combined with a scraper. They were possibly used for cutting and engraving, with various uses in different areas and cultural periods.

Distribution: Throughout Texas. **Period:** Paleo-Indian to Late Prehistoric. **Sites:** Deadman's Shelter; Stillhouse Hollow; Lake Theo; Oblate; Shifting Sands.

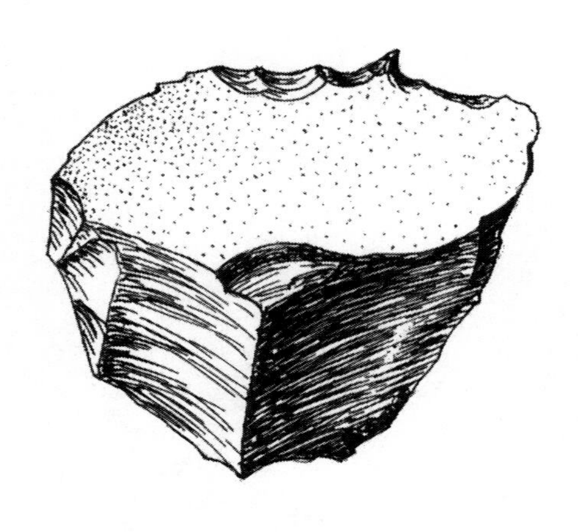

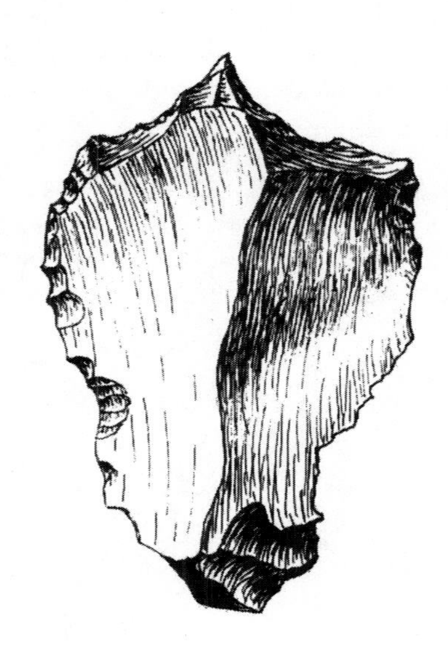

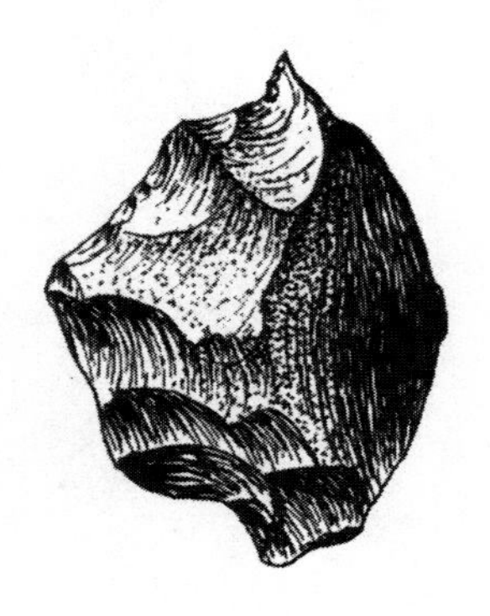

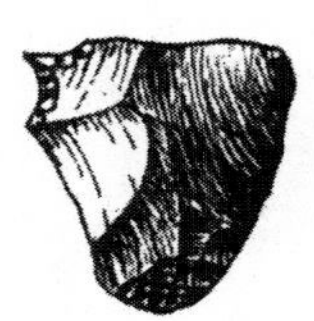

References: Harrison and Killen 1978; Hughes and Willey 1978; Rose 2011; Sorrow, Shafer, and Ross 1967; Tunnell 1962.

GUADALUPE TOOLS

Long known to central Texas archaeologists, and for many years called "Attwater Adzes," these are very unusual artifacts—percussion-flaked, thick, and crude. Most have triangular cross sections, and overall, there is an impression of a "trifacially" flaked artifact. At the distal end, there is an abruptly truncated bit that angles from the dorsal edge toward the proximal end. The bit is usually unifacially worked, often by the removal of narrow, bladelike flakes around the curved distal bit, and the working-edge angles are generally steep, ranging roughly from 55 to 85 degrees. Obvious damage, scarring, and frequent evidence of resharpening are visible on this working edge. Specimens are sometimes extensively reworked, with the artifact being greatly shortened. Black and McGraw (1985) have done an extensive study of the Guadalupe biface and have provided a formal definition of this form.

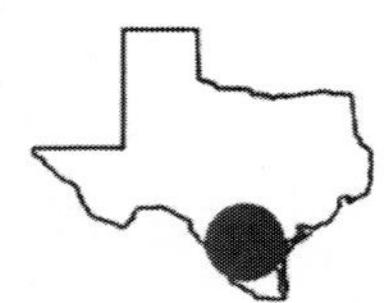

Distribution: Balcones Escarpment to the Rio Grande and across most of the south Texas coastal plain but concentrated in the Guadalupe and San Antonio River basins. **Period:** Early Archaic, ca. 3500 BC or earlier. **Sites:** Morhiss; Panther Springs Creek; Johnston-Heller; Choke Canyon; Granberg II; 41BP19; 41UV132; 41ME34.

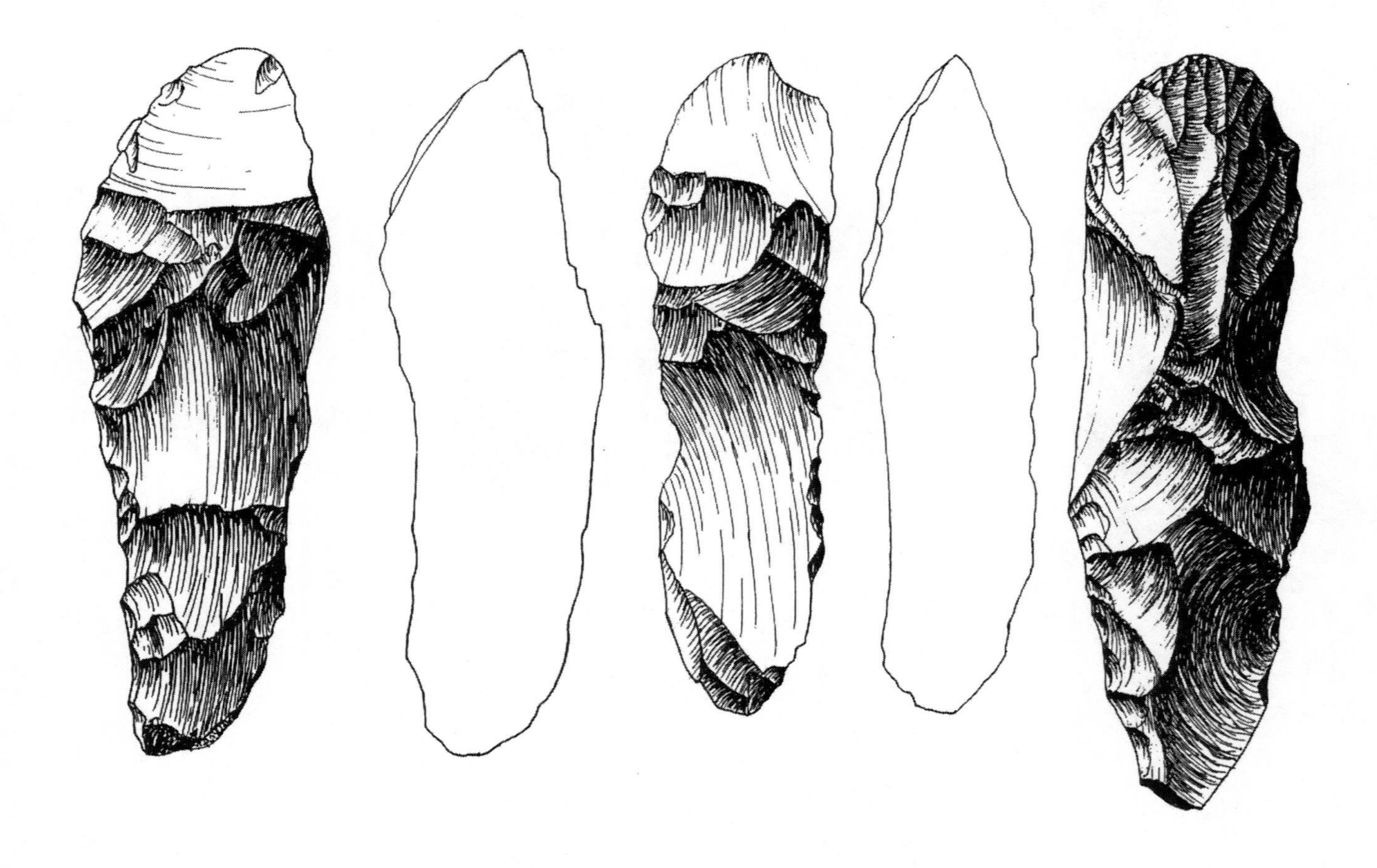

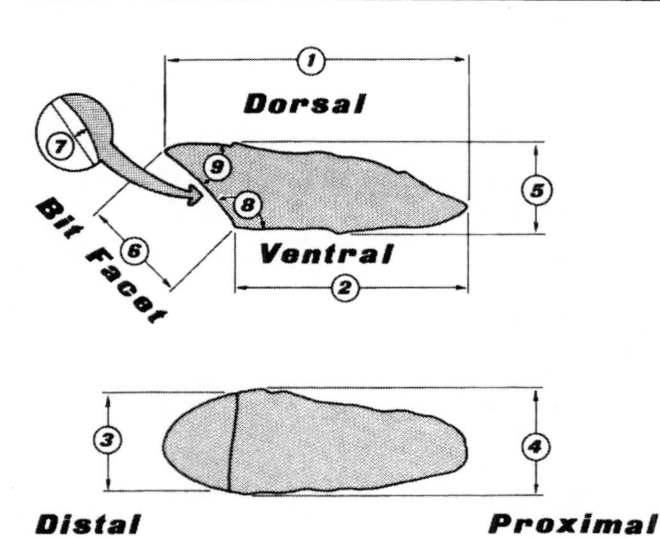

Landmarks and measurements on a Guadalupe biface. Numbered measurements correspond to the following: 1, dorsal length; 2, ventral length; 3, maximum bit width; 4, maximum tool width; 5, maximum tool thickness; 6, bit thickness (e.g., distance from bit apex to intersection with ventral face); 7, maximum depth of bit concavity (the maximum amount of "dishing" of the bit facet, usually just a millimeter or two); 8, bit facet/ventral angle; 9, bit spine-plane angle (working edge angle). From Brown (1985, fig. 3). By permission of the Texas Archeological Society.

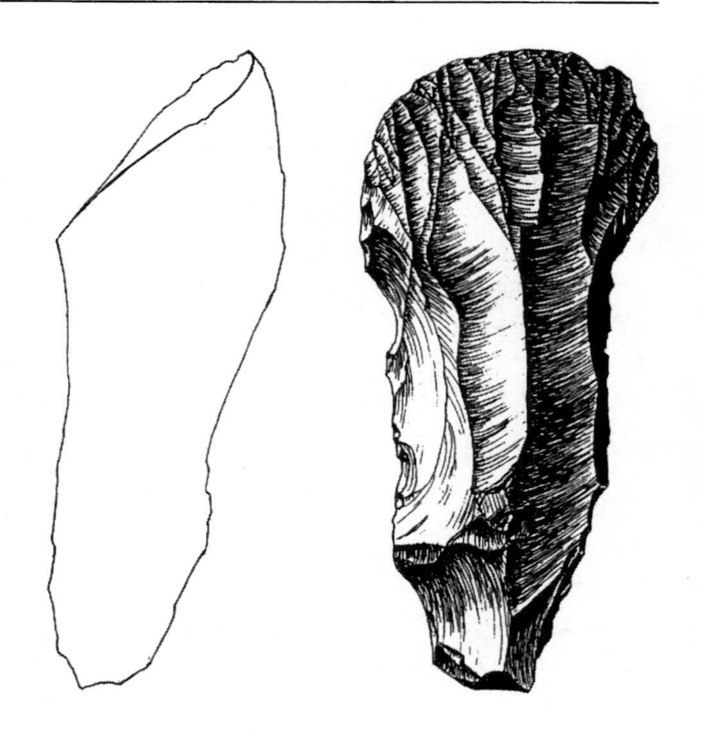

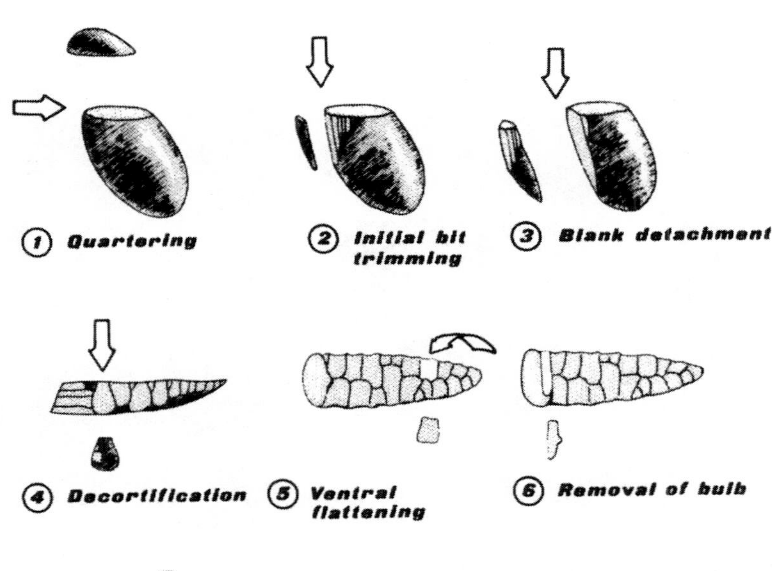

Manufacturing sequence for three caches of Guadalupe bifaces from south Texas. Arrows indicate the direction of percussion blows, which in stages 5 and 6 are directed toward the viewer. From Brown (1985, fig. 2). By permission of the Texas Archeological Society.

References: Baker 2003; Bement et al. 1989; Birmingham and Hester 1976; Black and McGraw 1985; Brown 1985; Hall et al. 1982; Hester and Kohnitz 1975; Highley 1984; Sollberger and Carroll 1985; http://www.texasbeyondhistory.net/.

GUNFLINTS

Gunflints occur commonly in mission collections in Texas and northern Mexico. They are also found in historic Indian sites throughout the state as well as at sites of early settlers. Many are probably of European origin (18th-century English and French) and are of musket, carbine, and pistol sizes. The European flints are very distinctive, the French being honey yellow to blond translucent cherts and the English, nearly black translucent to opaque gray in color range. But aboriginal-made gunflints are quite common, made of local cherts and similar in size and outline to the European specimens. Some are shaped as thin bifaces, and others are trimmed flakes and chips.

Distribution: Texas missions and missions of northern Mexico; Historic Native American occupation sites. **Period:** Spanish Colonial Period. **Sites:** Concepcion Mission; San Jose Mission; San Antonio de Valero Mission; San Juan Capistrano Mission; 41SP68; 41SP69; Gilbert (41RA5); Pearson (41RA13); 41WH8; Mission Espiritu Santo (41VT11, 41GD1).

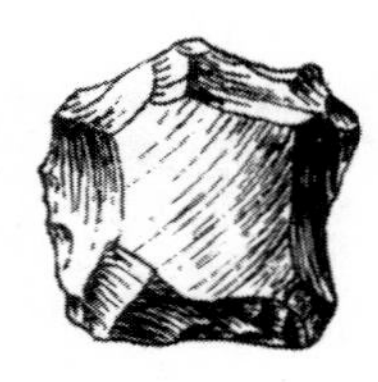

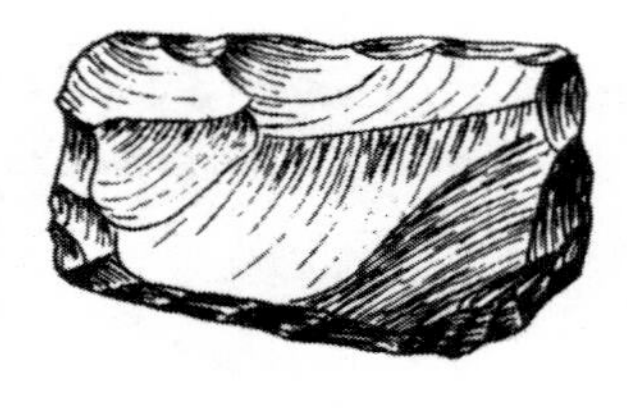

References: Clark 1978; Duffield and Jelks 1961; Fox 1979b; Hester 1989c; Jelks 1967; Kenmotsu 1990; Moore 1991; Ricklis 2000; Walter 2007.

KERRVILLE BIFACES

These generally oblong or pear-shaped artifacts are often called "fist axes" or "carcass cleavers." Specimens have a rounded natural cobble surface on one end (providing the handgrip); the opposite end is rounded to almost pointed, with a worked edge that often exhibits extensive, glossy polish, perhaps from cutting meat or soft plants. They seem ideally fitted for butchering tools; the ends are too thin and delicate for heavy chopping. Specimens get shorter as they are continually resharpened. Some of the larger examples develop concave edges during their use-life.

In our 1985 and 1993 editions, we referred to the specimens as "butted bifaces," utilizing Old World lithic terminology. Perino (1985) published the same artifacts under the new type name of "Kerrville." This term has been adopted fairly widely, and we recommend that it be used, in lieu of our inelegant label.

Distribution: Central and south central Texas and the lower Pecos. **Period:** Late Archaic, ca. 650–300 BC. **Sites:** La Jita; Devil's Mouth; Nopal Terrace; Amistad Reservoir.

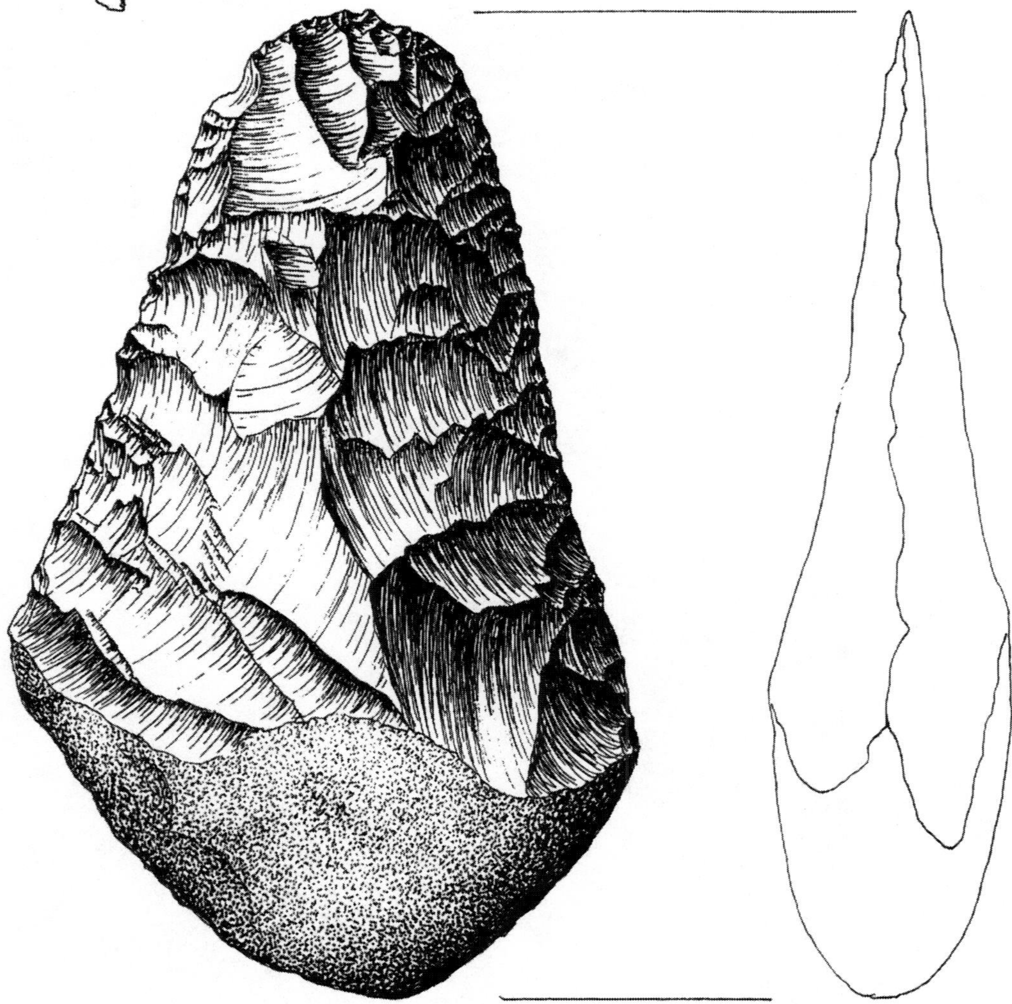

References: Chandler and Marchbanks 1995; Hester 1971, 1985; Johnson 1964; Nunley, Duffield, and Jelks 1965; Priour 1987; Sollberger 1968; Sorrow 1968b.

MULTINOTCHED EARLY ARCHAIC LITHICS

This lithic form is a trait largely of the Calf Creek Horizon, most related to Andice points. Little is known about their function, but it has been suggested that multi-notched specimens might have resulted from the need to "practice" deep-notching skills (Don Wyckoff, personal communication).

This kind of artifact is best known from the Early Archaic. However, there is an occasional later style of dart point with strange or multiple notching.

Distribution: Central and south Texas and neighboring central coastal plain. **Period:** Early Archaic, ca. 5500–3500 BC. **Sites:** 41UV132; 41UV21; 41BP191; 41WN73; 41BX502.

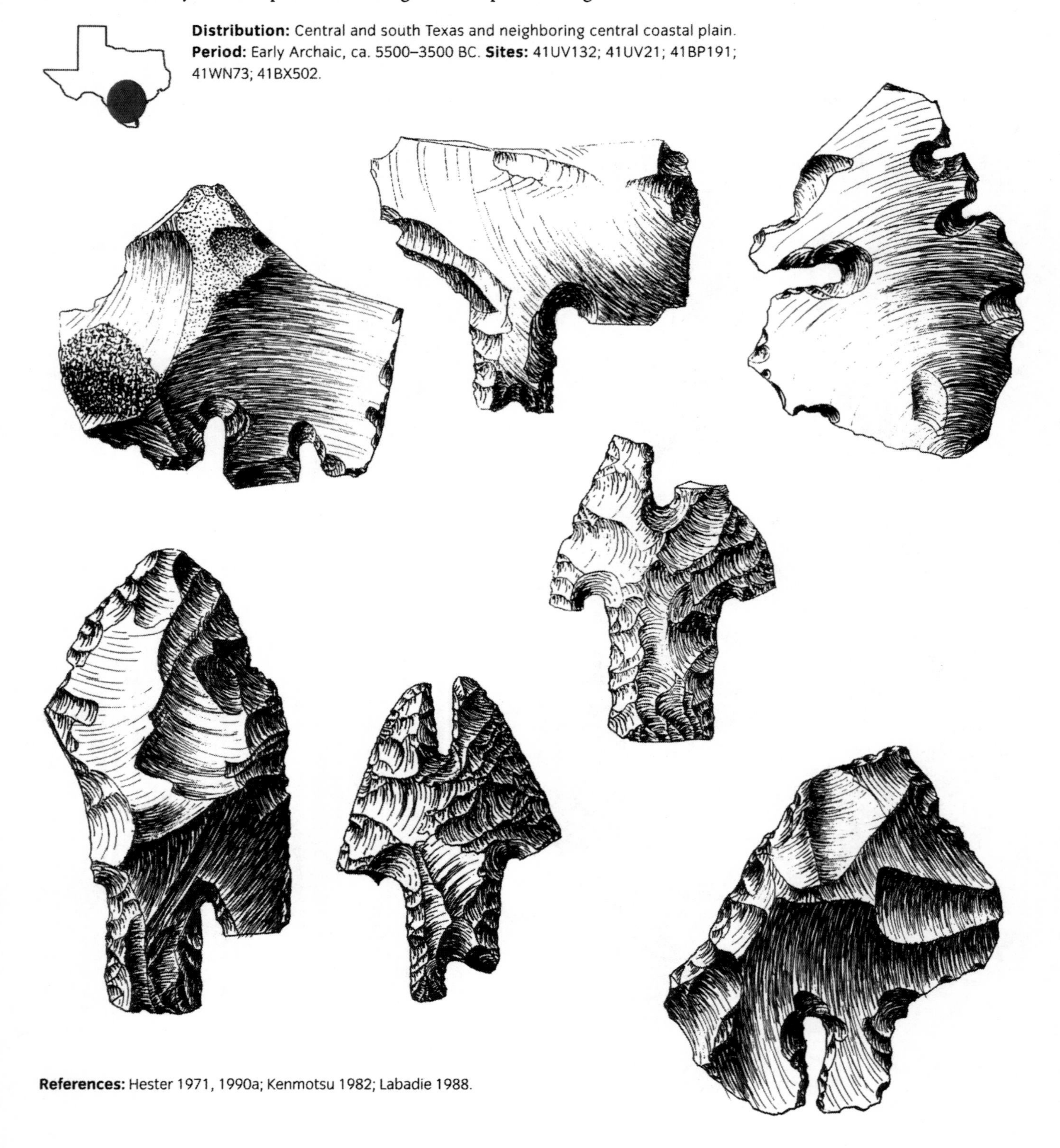

References: Hester 1971, 1990a; Kenmotsu 1982; Labadie 1988.

NUECES TOOLS

These distally beveled bifaces (or occasionally unifaces) were originally described by Hester and colleagues (1969, 148–49) and Wakefield (1968, 26). They are trapezoidal to roughly lunate (or crescentic) in outline with piano-convex cross sections. The widest "bit" edge is steeply beveled, and use-marks along this edge indicate that it may have been employed in scraping or cutting activities.

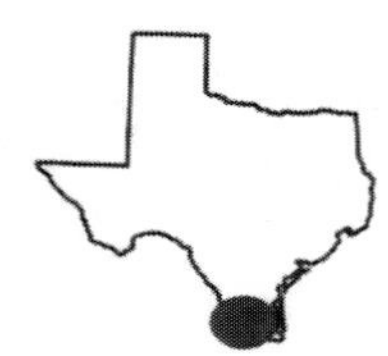

Distribution: Widespread in the interior of south Texas. **Period:** Middle to Late Archaic. **Sites:** Oulline; Choke Canyon; Duval County; Middle Frio River drainage; Killam Ranch.

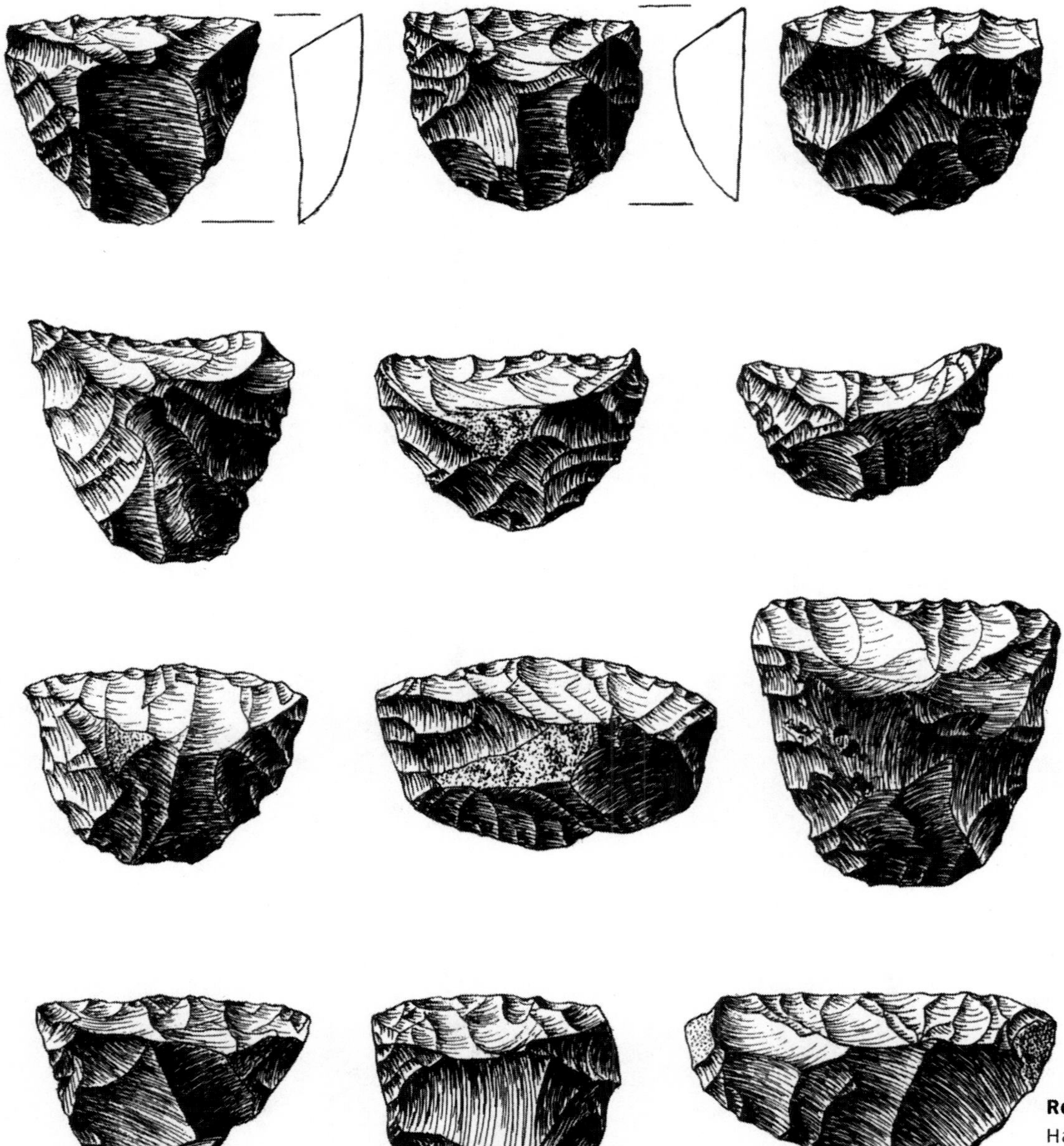

References: Bettis 1997; Hall, Black, and Graves 1982; Hester 1972b, 1969b; Hester, White, and White 1969; Wakefield 1968.

OLMOS BIFACE

These small, distinctive artifacts were first defined by Hester (1969a) and analyzed by Shafer and Hester (1971). They are triangular in outline and bifacially worked and have a beveled-edge bit at the broad end (usually at an angle of 60 degrees or more). The thickest part of the specimen occurs along this edge, which often shows wear in the form of heavy dulling, battering, and striations. Typically, the bit is much resharpened by flakes removed from the ventral edge, and there are often burin spalls struck (as resharpening technology) from the corners of the bit.

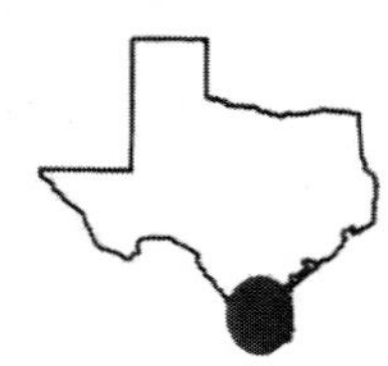

Distribution: From Kleberg County west to the Rio Grande and north into McMullen County. **Period:** Probably Transitional Archaic. **Sites:** Kleberg County (41KL35); Duval County; Choke Canyon.

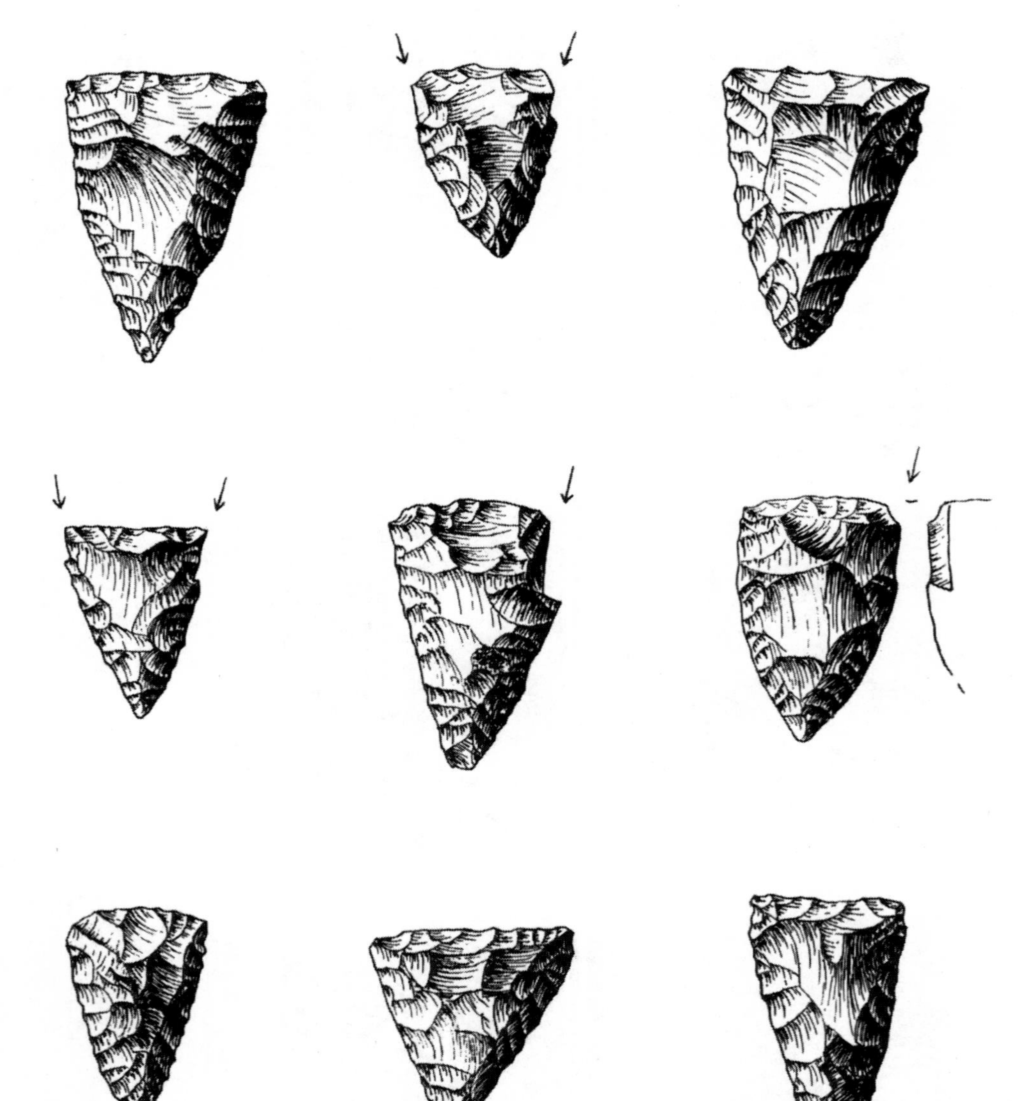

References: Gibson 1981; Hall, Black, and Graves 1982; Hester 1969a, 1972b; Shafer and Hester 1971.

PERFORATORS

Chipped stone artifacts used in perforating tasks are characterized by long, often cylindrical, tapered bits that are diamond-shaped in cross section. Some of these items perhaps functioned as punches—to punch holes through leather or hide—or were perhaps even employed in stitching or weaving tasks. The term "drill," on the other hand, is sometimes used in classifying this type of artifact. They are presumed to be used in a rotary fashion, to create holes in shell, stone, and wood. The tips of drills are usually dulled and worn or have some microfractures around the tip. The bases of Archaic perforators are frequently the same as those of projectile points, suggesting that they probably began as points and were later reworked into drills. It is also likely that some of the "drills" on Archaic points are simply reworking of a broken distal on a hafted point, done to create a new tip.

Late Prehistoric perforators are generally smaller than the large Archaic forms, and most common are long bits on rounded flake bases. These are often associated with Perdiz points and are a key trait of the Toyah Horizon.

"Pin drills" are another distinct form, found in the lower Rio Grande Valley and adjacent Tamaulipas. Similar specimens are also reported from Mitchell Ridge (41GV66). These are bipointed and have careful, minute flaking; some are roughly triangular in cross section. The late C. K. Chandler did microscopic analysis of a number of pin drills, observing circular wear and polish on many examples. Pin drills are Late Prehistoric in age.

Distribution: Widespread in Texas. **Period:** Archaic and Late Prehistoric. **Sites:** Oblate; Baker Cave; Levi Rockshelter; George C. Davis; 41BN111; Rainey; Wilson-Leonard; Mitchell Ridge (pin drills); North Padre Island (pin drills).

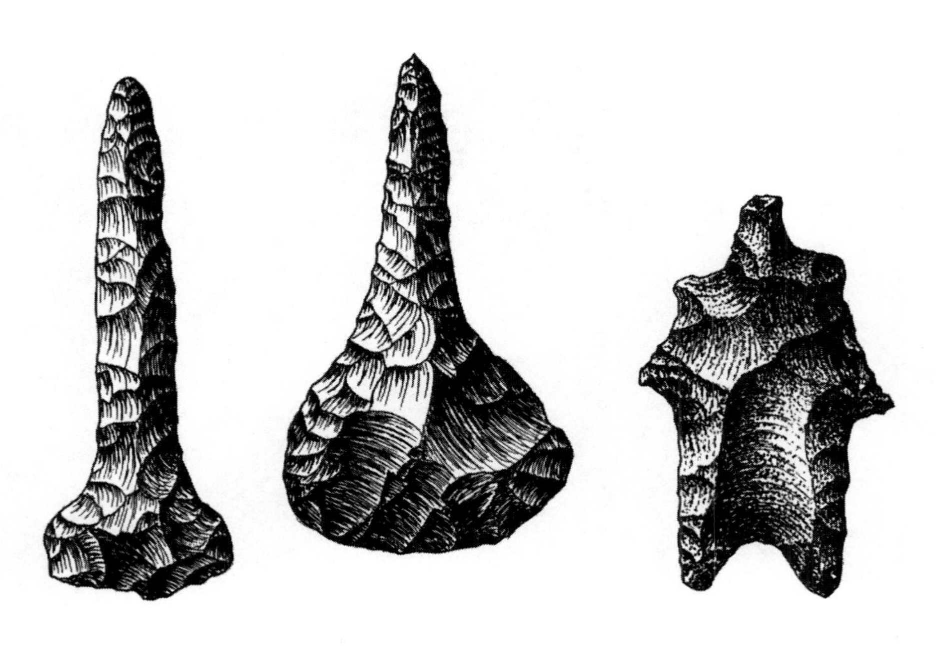

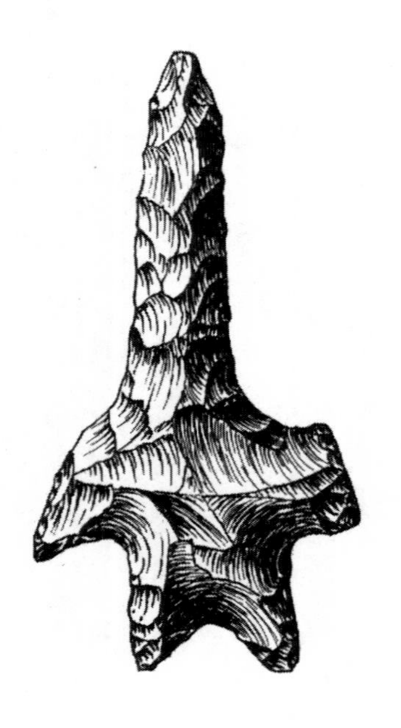

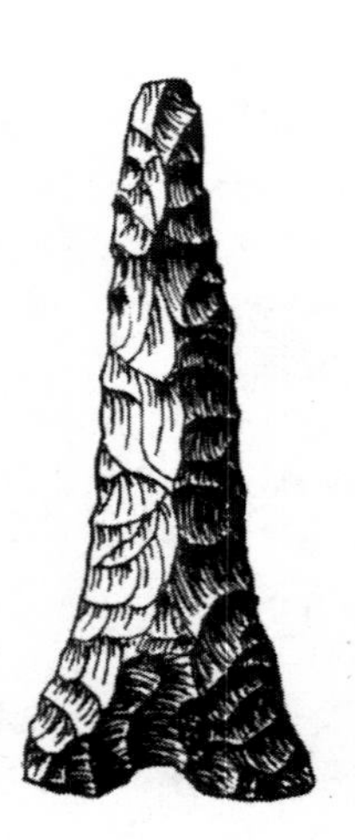

Toyah Phase drill

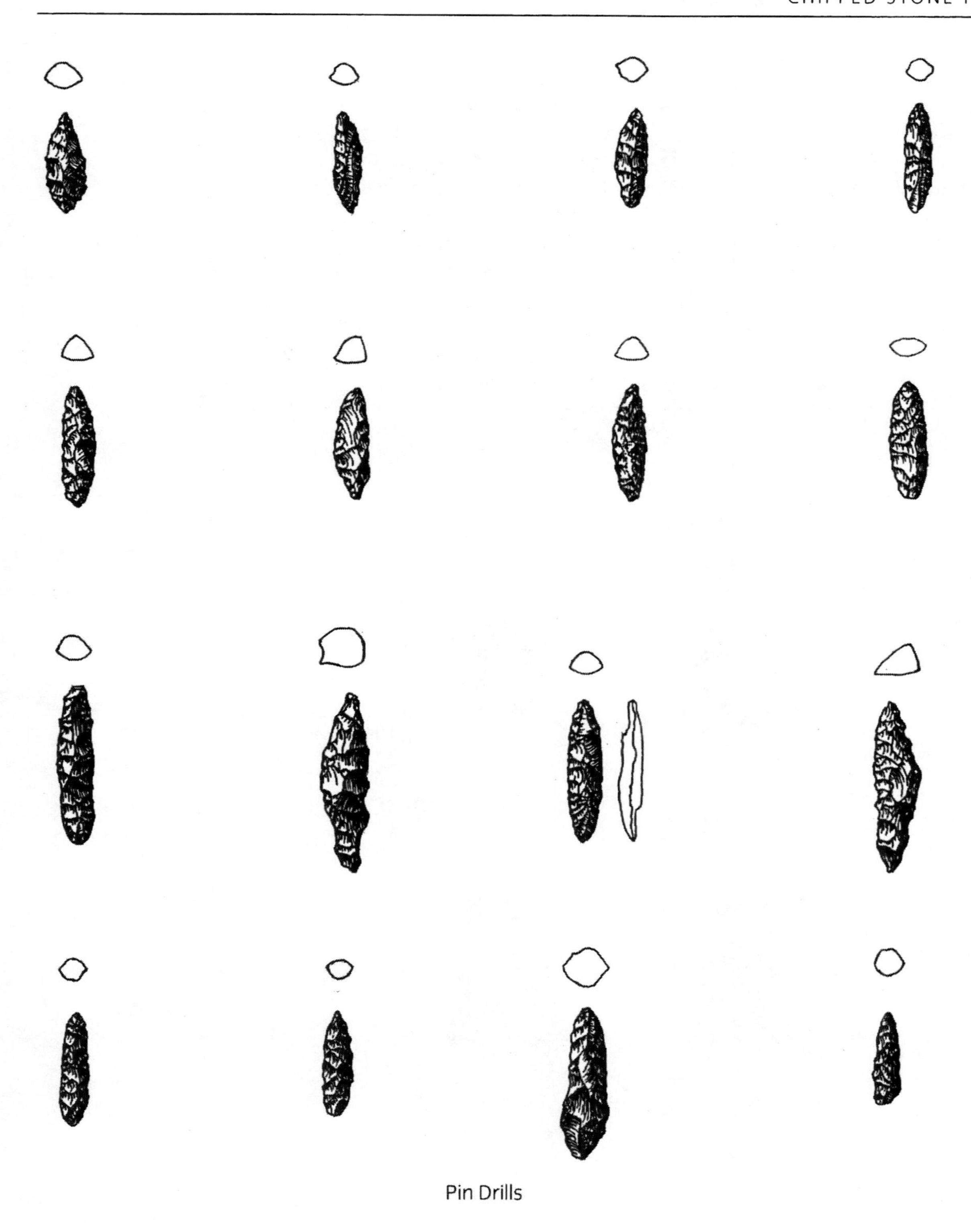

Pin Drills

References: Alexander 1963; Dial and Collins 1998; Gunter 1985; Henderson 2001; Krieger 1946; Ricklis 1994; Shafer 1973; Tunnell 1962; Word and Douglas 1970.

PIPE CREEK BIFACES

These arrow point–sized bifaces have a single, deep corner notch, and workmanship ranges from crudely made to exceptionally fine. The longest lateral edge is straight or slightly convex and often has some serration. The biface is found in association with Edwards points in Late Prehistoric context. The specific use of the tool is not known. Much further research as to function is needed. For example, some specimens may well be final stage preforms for Edwards (some Edwards preforms have a protruding or exaggerated corner) but were not or could not be finished with a second corner notch and shaping of the stem.

Distribution: South central Texas. **Period:** AD 960–1040. **Sites:** 41ME53; 41BN111; 41BN113; 41BNI15; Kyle; Comal County (Ollie Schrank, personal communication); 41UV29 (T. C. Hill, personal communication).

References: Jelks 1962; Turner 1991.

SAN SABA BIFACES

In 1973, Green and Hester published a brief study of microwear found in a sample of five large bifaces, with very small, short stems formed by basal notching. Four of the five had beveled left lateral edges that exhibited microscopic use-wear. The specimens were found at sites near Richland Springs, in San Saba County. Green and Hester did not propose a type or type name for this sample. However, Perino (1985) assembled a group of somewhat similar specimens and labeled them "San Saba Knives."

The problem is that two separate forms are included by Perino and other authors into the San Saba category. Despite similarities at first glance, the Perino specimens have large triangular bodies, with lateral edges generally straight or nearly so. In contrast, the specimens published by Green and Hester, and from which Perino drew his type name, have large bodies and much less triangular—indeed, usually convex—lateral edges. Additionally, the stems from the San Saba County specimens are slightly "askew," while the Perino specimens have broad short stems, slightly expanded. Perhaps most importantly is the occurrence of use-wear on the beveled lateral edge (or edges) on the Green and Hester specimens. These are clearly not restricted to San Saba County, and we have seen excellent examples from other central Texas sites.

According to David Crain (personal communication), the San Saba County form occurs with Marcos and Castroville points, and the Perino San Saba bifaces are associated with Ensor points. Indeed, within the collector community, San Saba has been applied to this latter form. Much more contextual data, from controlled excavations, will be needed to assess the temporal and spatial parameters for these two forms.

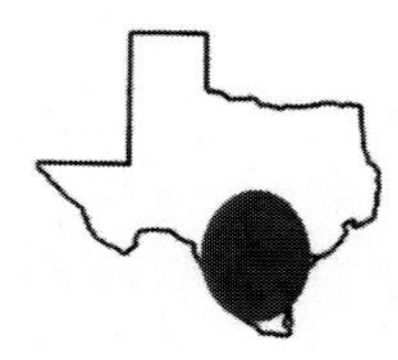

Distribution: Central and west central Texas, into south Texas and the coastal plain. **Period:** Late to Transitional Archaic. **Sites:** San Saba County; Burnet County; Bell County; Cobb; Bexar County; 41VT141; 41UV20; 41RE120; Buckeye Knoll; in a cache at Falcon Reservoir.

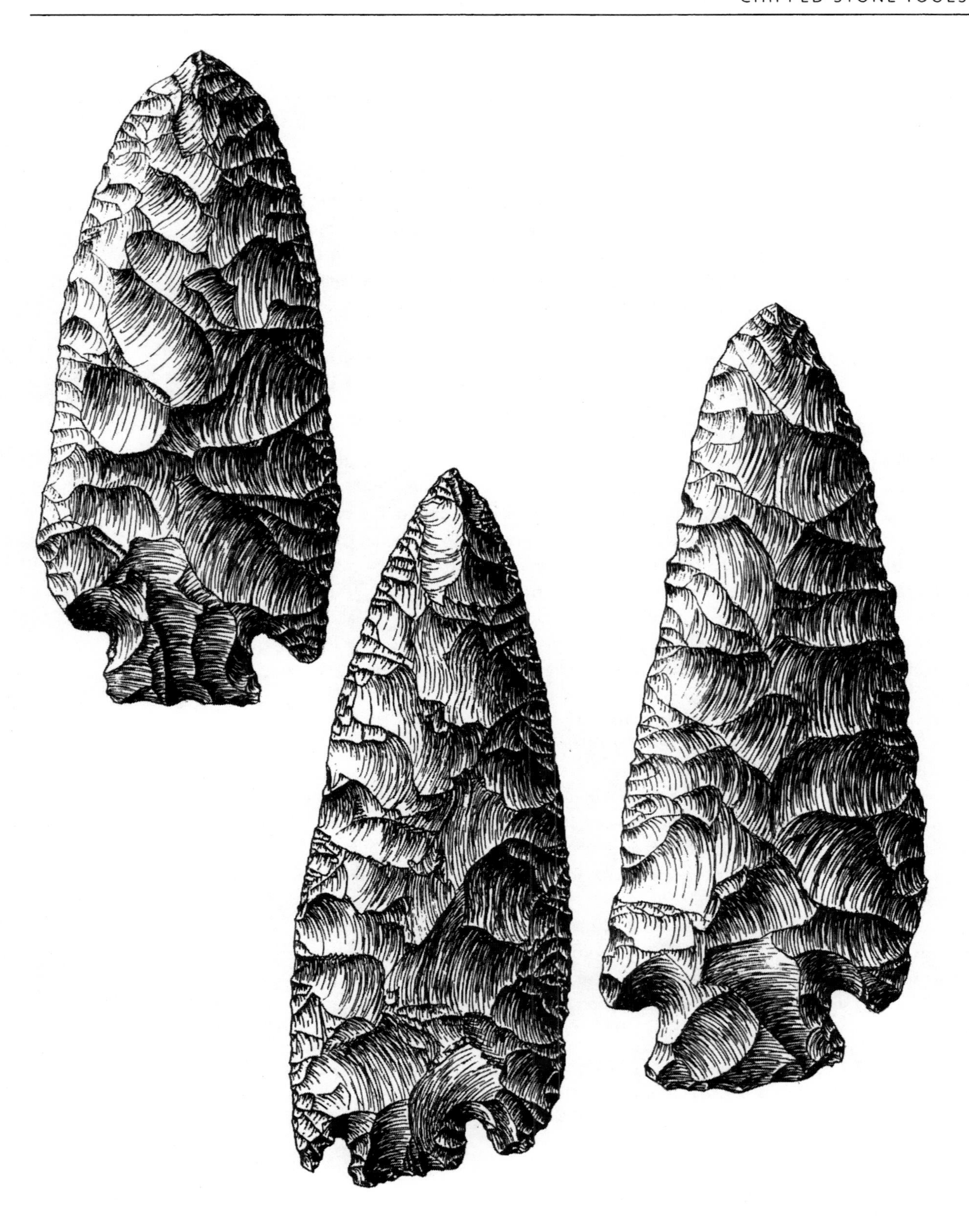

References: Braun et al. 2008; Green and Hester 1973; Hester 1970c, 2004b; Hester and Whatley 1992; Perino 1985; Pfeiffer 2002; Robert Ricklis, personal communication.

SCRAPERS

There is much variation as to form and quality of workmanship in this category of unifacially flaked artifacts that are traditionally referred to, and presumably functioned, as scrapers. They are found in a wide range of shapes and forms; most are made on large flakes or blades and are characterized by a steeply flaked working edge. They are often categorized by archaeologists according to the position of the edge, its location, and the nature of the retouch: *end scrapers* are trimmed to a steep and convex bit at the end of the longest axis (opposite the bulbar or proximal end); *side scrapers* are trimmed on one or two edges and have side and end trimming in combination on one specimen; *convergent scrapers* have edges that meet in a pointed fashion; *concave scrapers* have one edge trimmed in a concave shape; and *transverse scrapers* have a trimmed edge transverse, or obliquely oriented, to the proximal end. Functional studies of specimens (independent of morphological categories) are necessary to determine the usage of a particular artifact; microscopic analysis of edge-wear has shown that some unifacially flaked artifacts were used for cutting, so all unifaces cannot automatically be called scrapers.

We have illustrated a series of end scrapers in this edition. Unlike the other scraper forms, end scrapers are formal tools found in Paleo-Indian times, associated with the Folsom culture, and in the Toyah Horizon of Late Prehistoric age. Used into the Historic era on the Great Plains, similar end scrapers were often hafted on L-shaped handles used by women for bison-hide processing. End scrapers hafted in more ornate ivory handles come from late 19th- and early 20th-century Eskimo culture. Again, they were almost wholly used by women to process skins. Size range can be highly variable; within the Toyah Horizon they can range from "thumbnail" size to elongated specimens made on blades. Folsom scrapers (top row, p. 248) have sharp corners, sometimes with a spur on the corner. While the spur could have been a tool itself, it is also likely that these projections formed during the resharpening of the scrapers and reseating them in their hafts. Eskimo end scrapers exhibit this phenomenon, and the "spur" simply results from the use-life of the end scraper.

End scrapers were sometimes traded or distributed over long distance; caches of specimens or the flakes and blades on which they are made are common in the Texas Panhandle and Llano Estacado. The specimen at the bottom of page 247 comes from Dimmit County in southern Texas; it is made of Alibates chert, the source of which is roughly five hundred miles to the north.

A distinctly regional scraper form is found in the lower Rio Grande Valley and adjacent Tamaulipas. Locally, they are called "button scrapers" (reflecting their outline) and are unifacial. Wear is seen in the trimming of the edges and polish extending onto the flat, ventral surface. Much research is needed. The form is linked to the Late Prehistoric.

Distribution: Various forms throughout Texas. **Period:** Paleo-Indian; Late Prehistoric, especially Toyah Horizon and other cultures very late in this era. **Sites:** Choke Canyon; Devil's Mouth; Levi Rockshelter; Oblate; Oulline; Gilbert; San Felipe Springs; Shifting Sands.

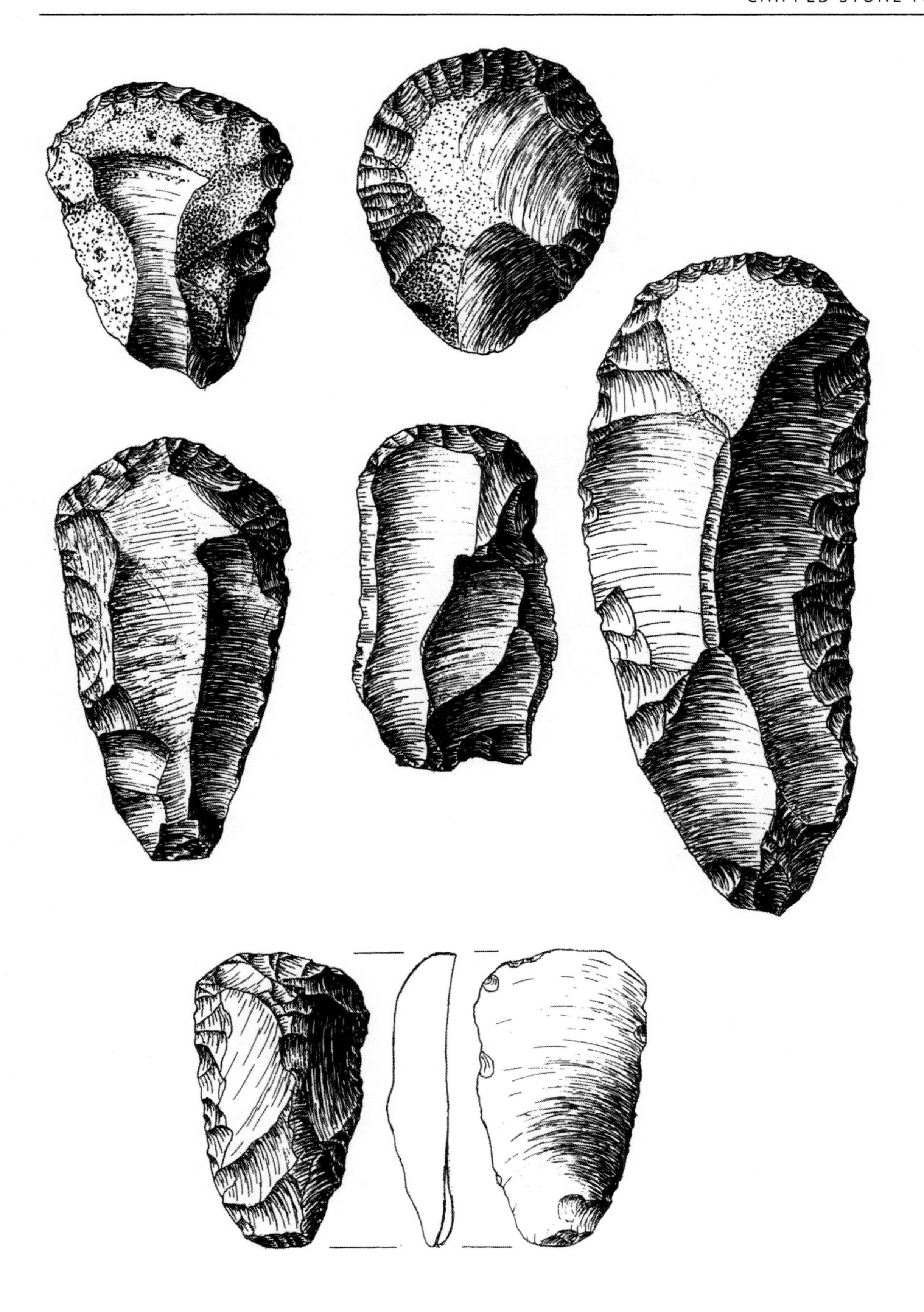

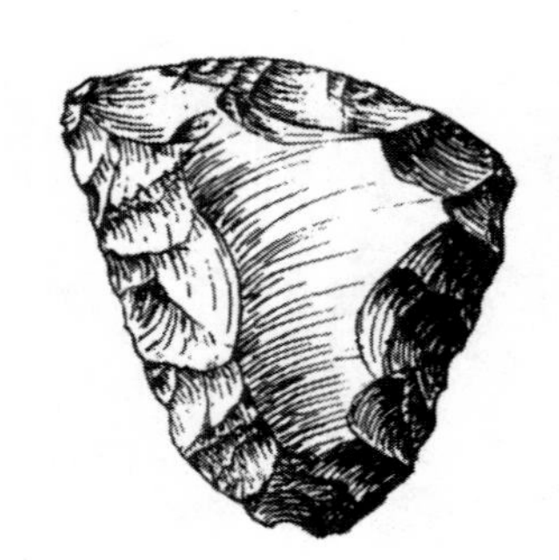

Button scrapers

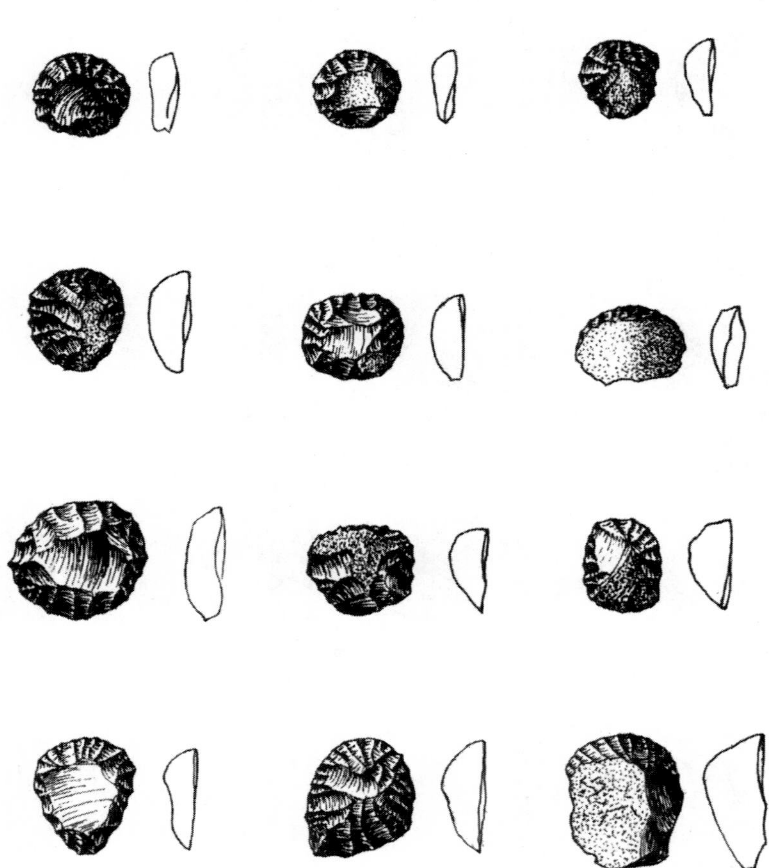

References: Alexander 1963; Coleman et al. 2001; Hall, Black, and Graves 1982; Hester, White, and White 1969; Irwin and Wormington 1970; Jelks 1967; Johnson 1964; Krieger 1946; Mehalchick et al. 1999; Nissen and Dittemore 1974; Rose 2011; Shiner 1971; Tunnell 1962.

SEQUENT FLAKE UNIFACES

These are highly distinctive artifacts, made on oval flakes detached sequentially from elongated chert nodules. Epstein (1963) first described them as "oval cortex scrapers," and Shafer (1986) attributes them to the Baker Interval in the lower Pecos between 8,500 and 5,000 years ago. They are generally oval in outline, with a cortex around a portion of the edge. The edge opposite the cortex has been chipped unifacially for use as a scraper or knife. They have an unusual cross section, with a positive bulb of percussion on one face and a negative bulb (from an earlier flake removal) on the other (see the profile drawn below). A good discussion of the function of these artifacts can be found on the Hinds Cave page of Texas Beyond History (http://www.texasbeyondhistory.net/hinds/index.html).

Distribution: Lower Pecos and into Terrell County and the Big Bend (H. J. Shafer, personal communication). **Period:** Early Archaic, though some examples occur in the Late Archaic. **Sites:** Centipede and Damp caves; Hinds Cave; Devil's Mouth (all in Val Verde County); Sanderson Canyon, Terrell County; Bexar County; Holt (41HY341); Woodrow Heard; Montell Rockshelter.

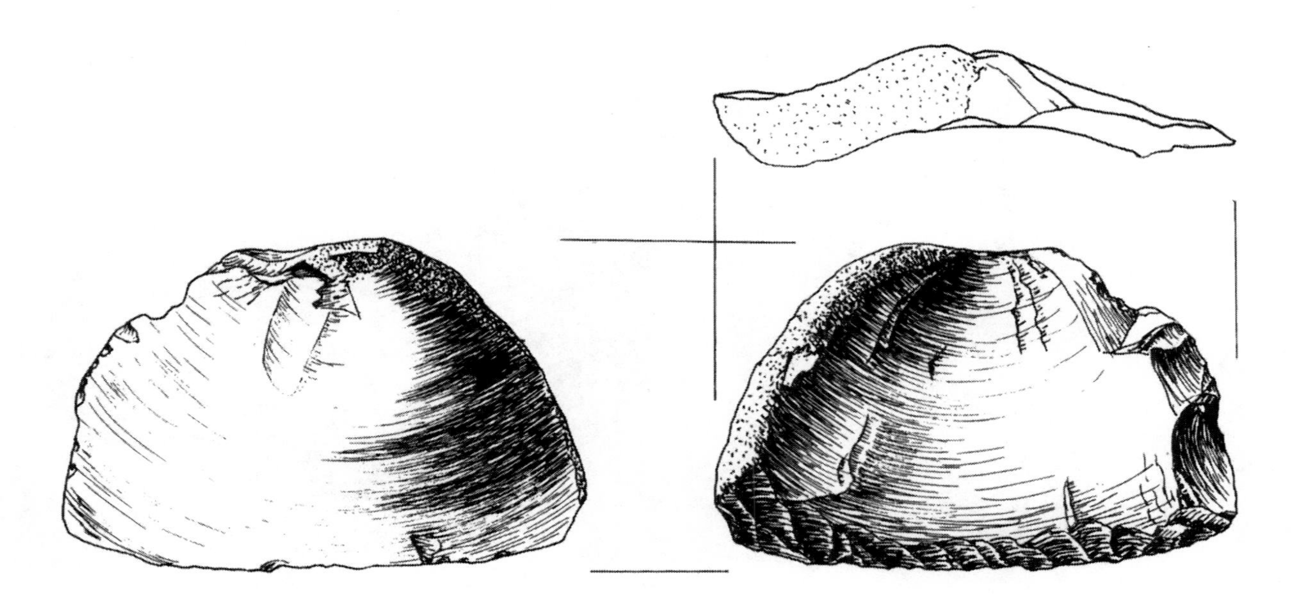

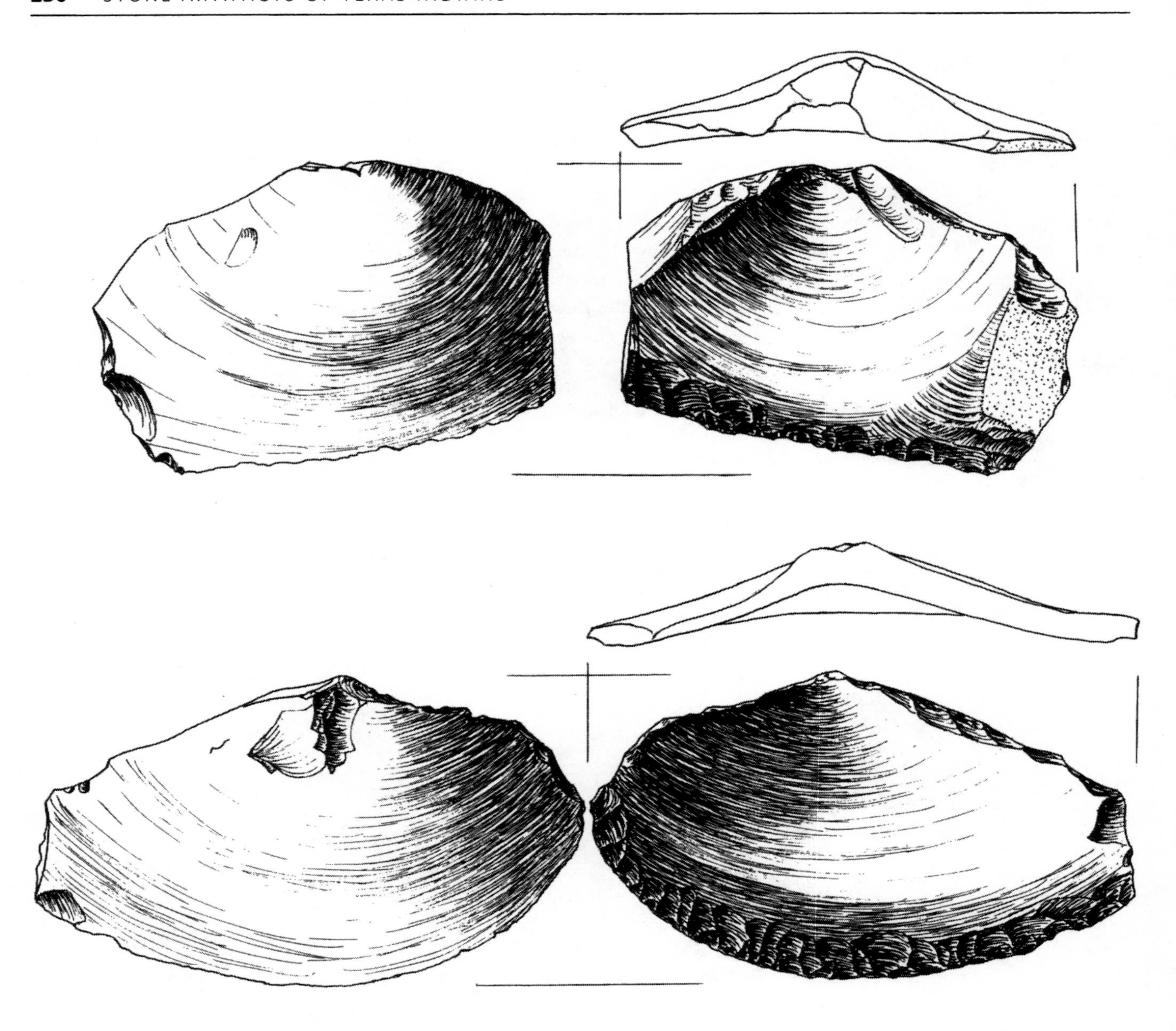

References: Brownlow 2004; Decker et al. 2000; Epstein 1963; Johnson 1964; Shafer 1986.

Ground, Pecked, and Polished Stone Artifacts

THIS CATEGORY includes ground, pecked, and polished stone tools that were shaped and altered intentionally or through use. Implements that have one or more surfaces modified by pecking and grinding and were shaped in the course of food preparation are metates, manos, pestles, and pitted stones. Utilitarian tools used in the process of sharpening, grinding, or honing different tools are described as well as the stones used for straightening arrow shafts. Other stones evidence use in sawing, reaming, polishing, or hammering.

Polished stone artifacts include celts, plummets, boatstones, Waco "sinkers," gorgets, and pipes. Some are relatively crude, but others are beautifully ground, polished, and occasionally decorated. A variety of functions is seen among these categories, from utilitarian to ornamental.

ABRADING STONES

Irregular fragments, usually of sandstone, exhibit grooves formed by use, often V-shaped, longitudinal grooves at various angles. Such artifacts may have been utilized to shape, sharpen, smooth, and polish a number of different implements, such as bone awls and needles. It is also likely that some result from the use of the abrasive stone for smoothing the edges of bifaces during the toolmaking process. The length of the largest is 17.5 cm.

Distribution: Widely found in Texas. **Period:** Archaic to Late Prehistoric. **Sites:** George C. Davis; Oblate; Choke Canyon; Big Pine Lake; Chopek; Harrell; Wheeler; Ellis County; 41VT15; 41VT30; 41VT141; Lino (41WB437); lower Rio Grande and adjacent Tamaulipas.

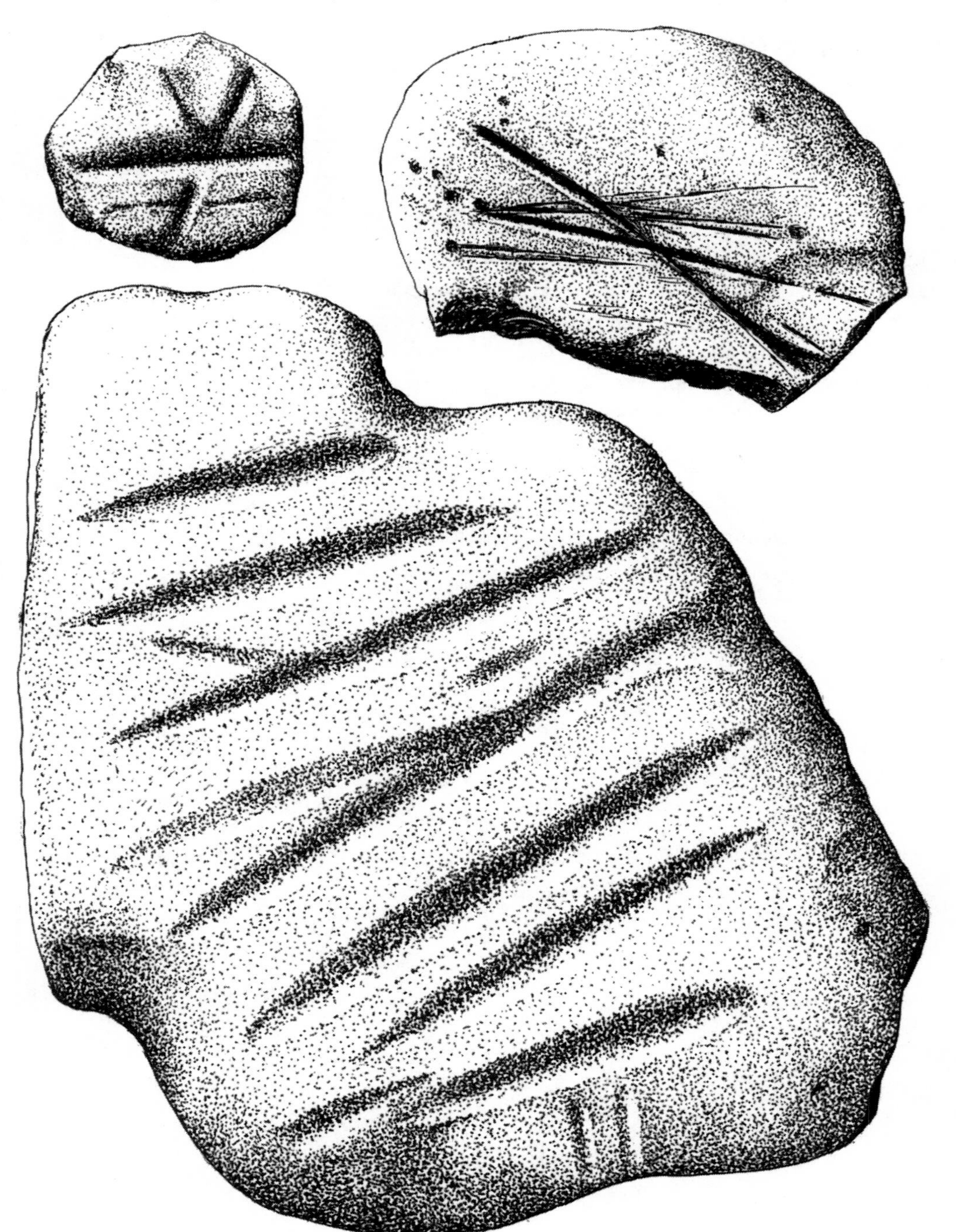

References: Boyd 1997; Brosowske 2009; Chadderdon 1976; Hall, Black, and Graves 1982; Mallouf 1976; Perino and Bennett 1972; Quigg et al. 2000; Shafer 1973; http://www.texasbeyondhistory.net/; Tunnell 1962; Young 1985.

ALTERED QUARTZITE COBBLES

Quartzite cobbles with facets and grooves created by wear are found in central and south Texas, as well as in other areas of the state. In various parts of the country, such altered quartzite cobbles have been called "edge-preparation tools" (Perino and Bennett 1972), thought to have been used to grind and dull the edges of preforms in the bifacing process. Their specific purpose is not known, but their natural waterworn shapes were probably being utilized and modified in various pecking, striking, polishing, abrading, food grinding, and flint-preparation activities (Chadderdon 1976).

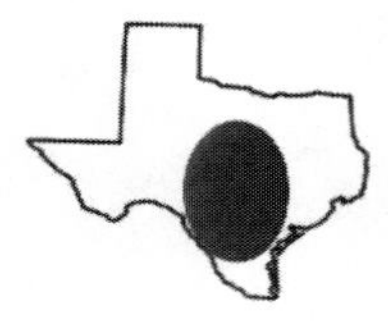

Distribution: Mainly on the south Texas coastal prairie but similar specimens extending into central and perhaps north central Texas. **Period:** Specimens from the south Texas coastal plain appear to date to the Archaic but could well extend into Late Prehistoric times. **Sites:** Victoria and Goliad counties, including sites 41VT16, 41VT15, 41VT20, 4lVT3, and others; Coleto Creek; Stillhouse Hollow; Bexar and Uvalde counties.

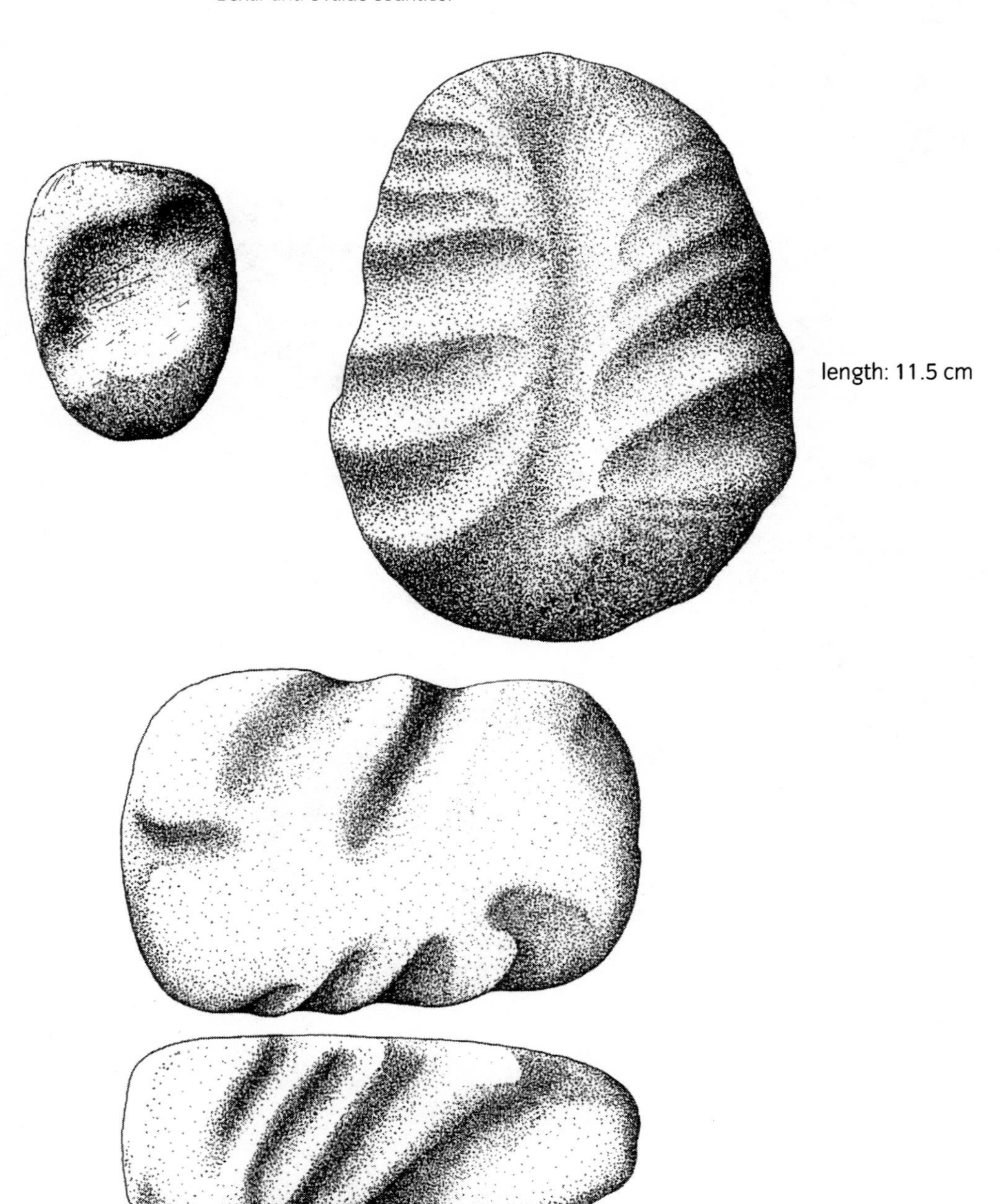

length: 11.5 cm

This broad category of "altered quartzite cobbles" is also used to note elongated grooved quartzite cobbles from the coastal bend, many from Victoria County. These date to the Early Archaic based on work by Ricklis at 41VT98. They are very carefully shaped, finely smoothed, and have a long broad groove on both sides, and the ends are slightly flared. They are obviously not tools of daily use, and given the cemetery context at 41VT98, they may have a ritual function.

Elongate quartzite fully grooved

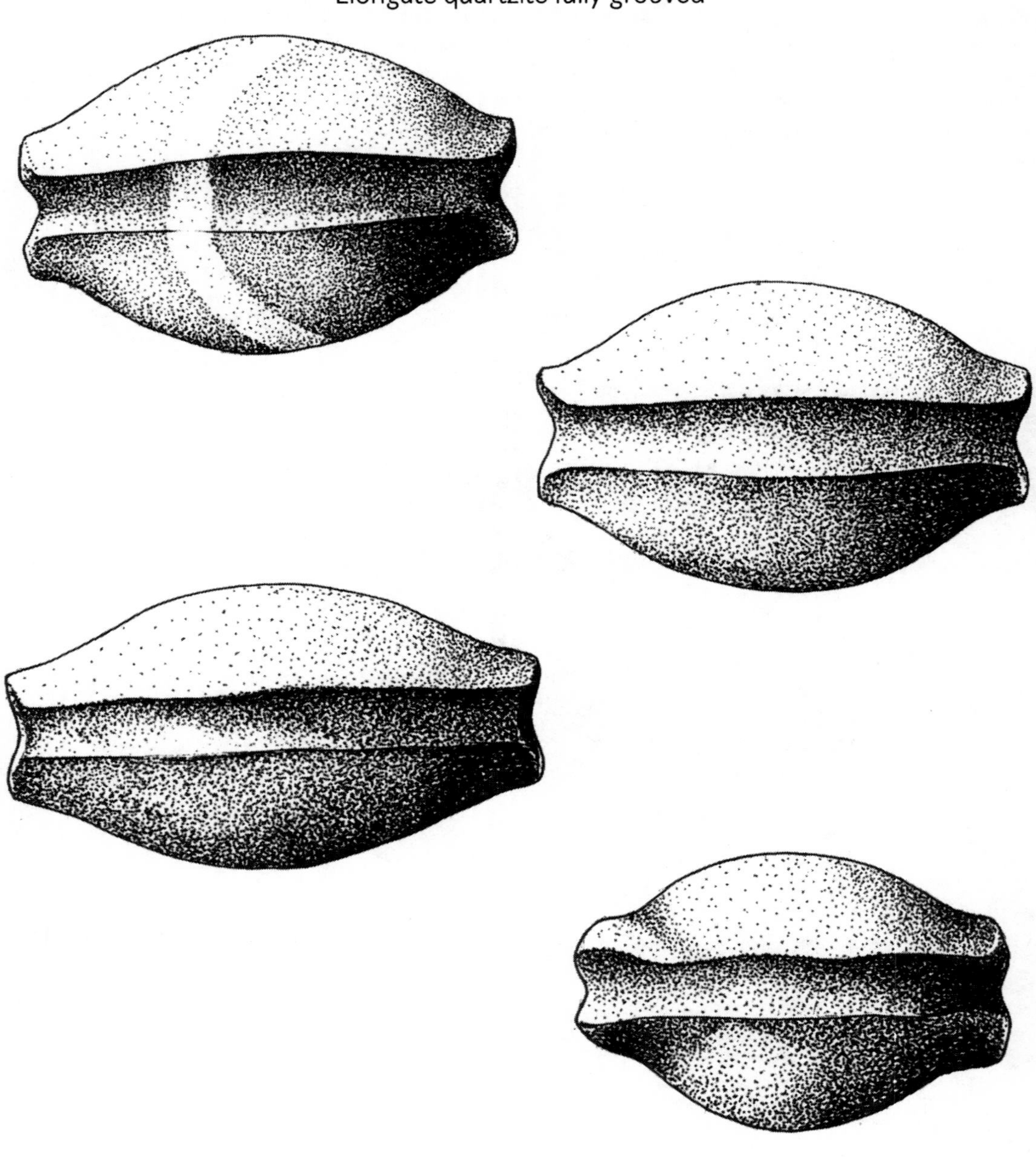

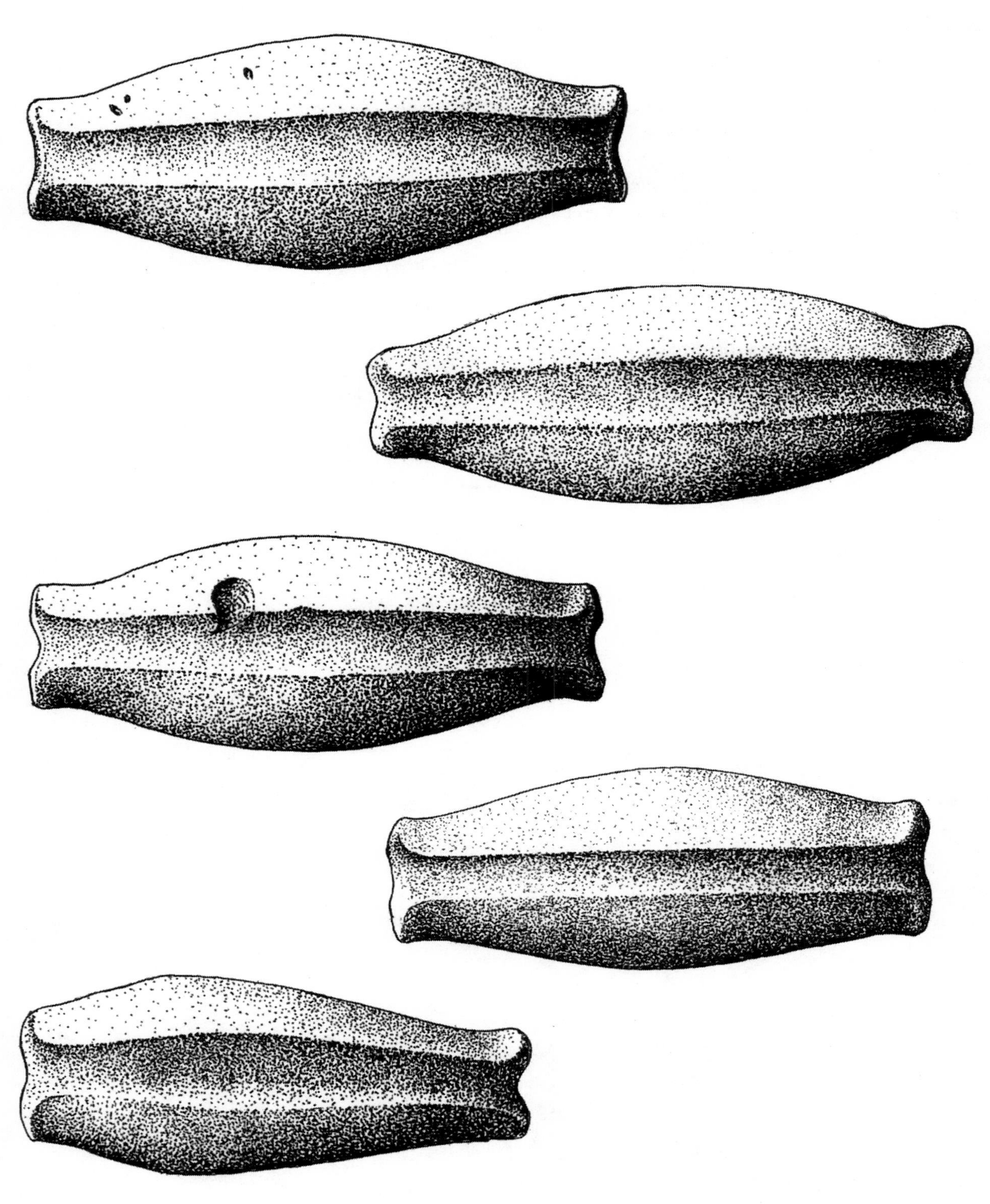

Elongate quartzite fully grooved

References: Chadderdon 1976; Chandler 1997b; Perino and Bennett 1972; Shafer 1979a; Sorrow, Shafer, and Ross 1967.

BANNERSTONES

Bannerstones are found infrequently in Texas. Their function is debatable, but the winged, center-drilled, and "hourglass" varieties were probably used as atlatl weights. They would have been an improvement on the art of spear throwing because they could be moved on spear-thrower shafts with relative ease compared to boatstones that had to be secured (Duke 1989, 14). Adjustment of weight has been demonstrated by modern atlatl experts to be very important in obtaining greater range and accuracy (Annual World's Atlatl Contest, Saratoga, Wyoming; Duke 1985).

Materials vary widely and range from sandstone to jasper and basalt. The holes drilled are relatively uniform, 1.1 cm to 1.4 cm (which could indicate that the size of the atlatl bodies were fairly standard to fit holes in the bannerstones). An unfinished bannerstone, made on fine-grained light-reddish sandstone is known from a Coryell County site. The wings had been shaped and initial efforts had been made to drill the central perforation. The specimen was associated with Bulverde points of the Middle Archaic, ca. 2000 BC.

In the excavations of the Early Archaic cemetery at Buckeye Knoll (41VT98), two winged bannerstones are reported by Ricklis (2009). He places the age of the specimens at 4500 BC.

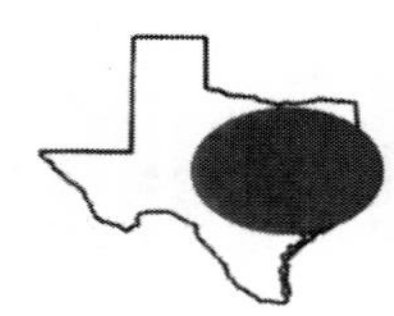

Distribution: East Texas and into the coastal plain. **Period:** Archaic; 4500 BC at 41VT98. **Sites:** 41AU4; 4IAU1; Waller County; Doering; Hays County; Burnet County, Buckeye Knoll; Morhiss; Wilson County Sand Pit; Tamaulipas.

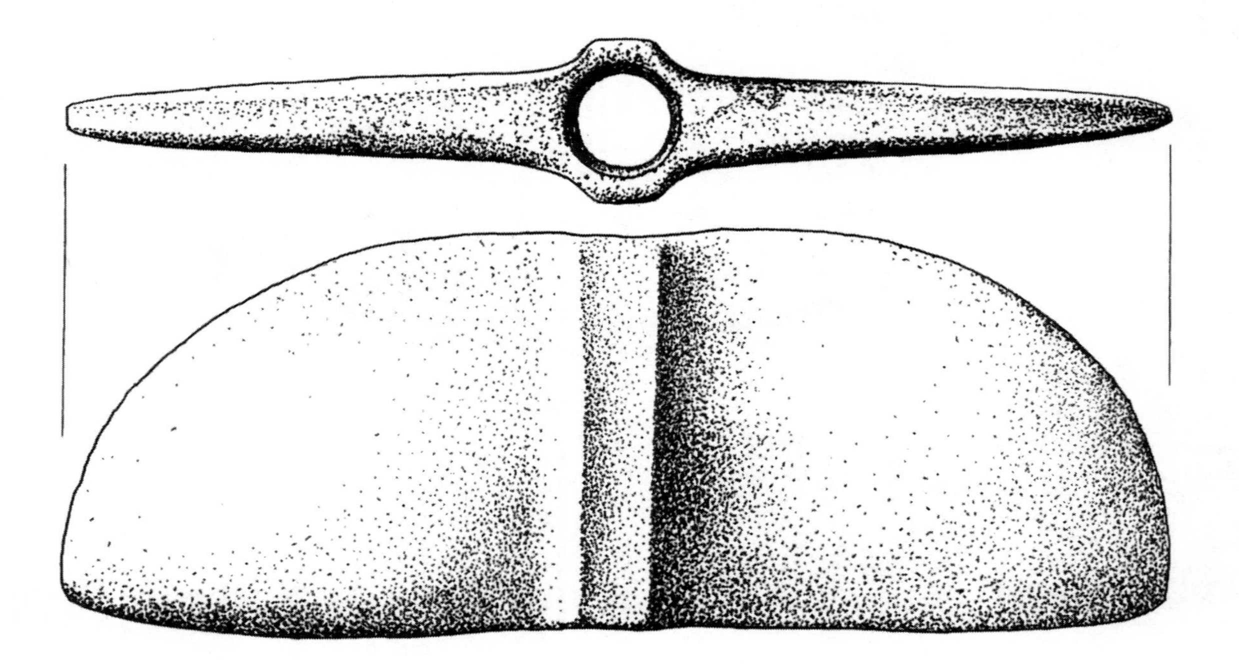

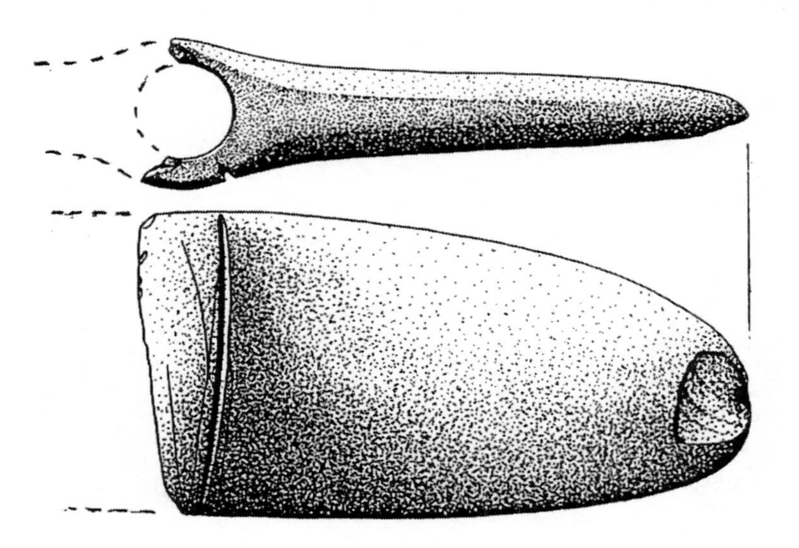

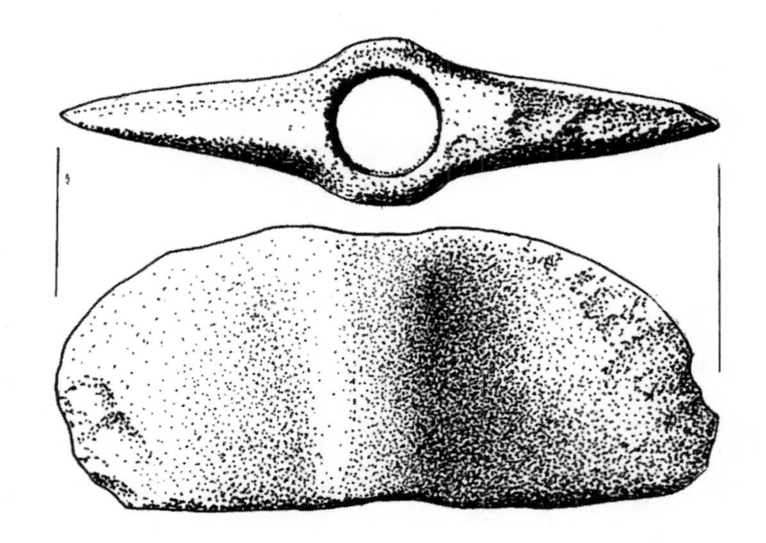

References: Duke 1985; Duke 1989, 1991; Duke and Duke 1988; Ensor et al. 1991; Hester 2002b; Hester et al. 1978; Mitchell et al. 1980; Ricklis 2009; http://www.texasbeyondhistory.net/; Wheat 1953.

BOATSTONES

The basic form of a "boat-shaped" stone is primarily elliptical in plan and plano-convex in longitudinal cross section with rounded ends. The base (flat side) is frequently pecked and ground to form a flat surface or one that is concave. More complex specimens may have a "keel" of varying width extending along the convex surface from one end to the other. This keel may be hollowed out to produce a V-shaped concavity. Specimens are sometimes notched at the ends. The majority of these artifacts are made of local materials, such as hard sandstone or limestone, but obvious cases of importation are commonly found of cryptocrystalline rocks, igneous rocks, and slate. An unfinished boatstone is known from a site in McMullen County.

Boatstones are thought by some to be a weight attached to an atlatl to make it more controllable and hence more accurate. Other authors have suggested use as a charm stone, a fetish, or a ceremonial object. They are sometimes found as grave goods. Indeed, the specimens with pronounced "keels" have sometimes been found containing small, rounded gravels. Three such specimens were found with burials at the Bowser site (41FB3). The significance, here again, is unknown. After finding examples at Jonas Short mound in 1965, Edward B. Jelks jokingly referred to them as weights used on "rattle atlatls."

Figure 1-2 shows an eight-thousand-year-old atlatl from the Great Basin that still has a boatstone attached. An atlatl from Culberson County in the eastern Trans-Pecos had an attached stone weight but not of boatstone form.

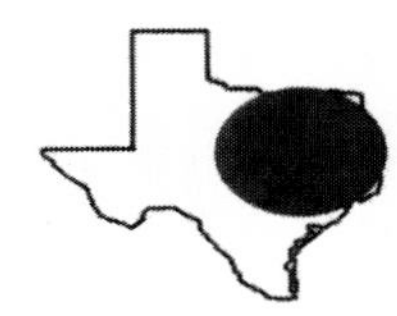

Distribution: Primarily northeast Texas, Arkansas, and Louisiana, southeast Texas, central Texas; scattered in other areas. **Period:** Archaic. **Sites:** Ernest Witte; Fall Creek; Jonas Short; George C. Davis; Smith Rockshelter; 41EL19; Albert George.

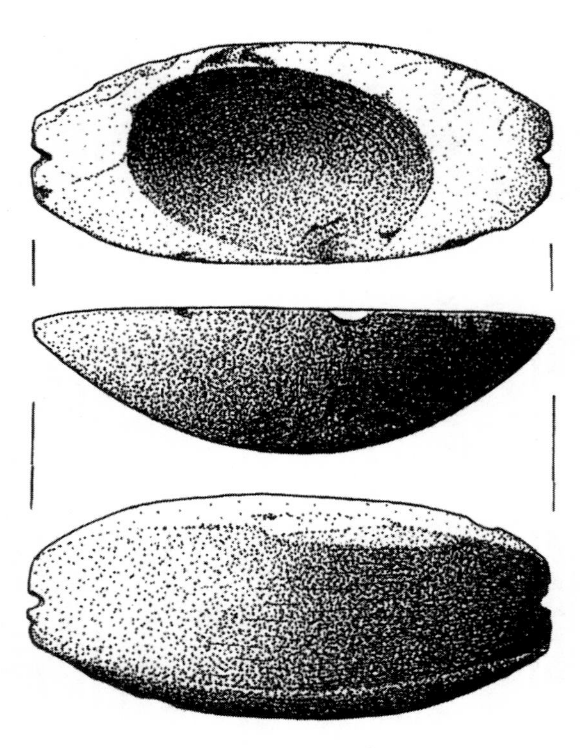

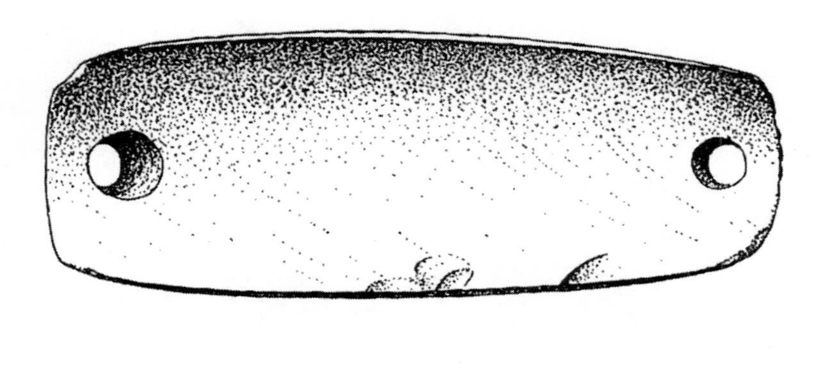

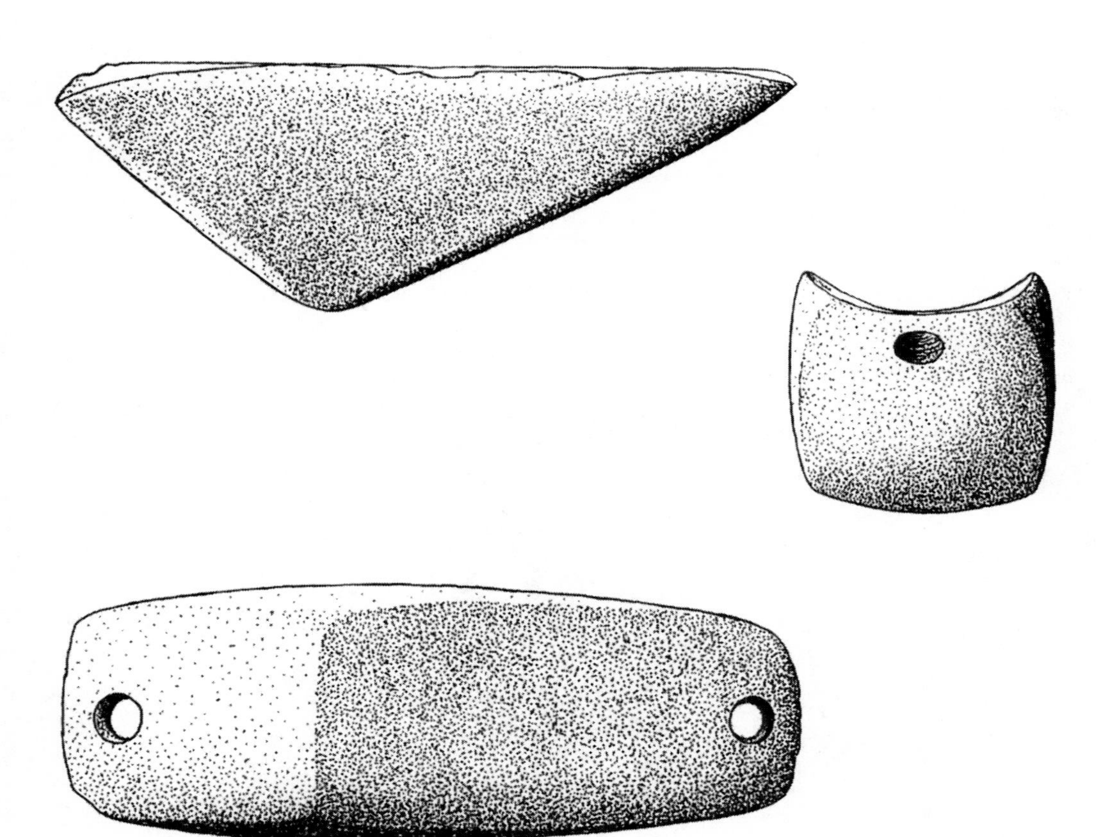

References: Chandler 1996b; Hall 1981; Hester 1974; Hoover and Hester 1972; Jackson and Woolsey 1938; Jelks 1965; Palter 1977; Patterson 1937; Patterson 2000; Shafer 1973; Story et al. 1990; Suhm 1957.

CELTS

Celts are ungrooved, axelike stone implements that have been shaped by pecking and extensive grinding and polishing on the cutting end. They are usually round or oval in cross section at the middle, and one end narrows into a slightly convex bit. The distinction between an adze and a celt is sometimes based on bit morphology; celts have bifacially beveled bits, while adzes are unifacially beveled (Shafer 1973).

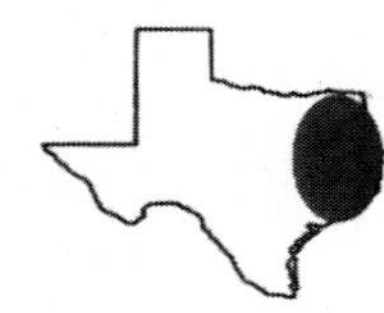

Distribution: Northeast Texas; southeast Texas. **Period:** Late Prehistoric. **Sites:** George C. Davis; Sanders; Austin County; Spiro (Okla.); Harlan (Okla.).

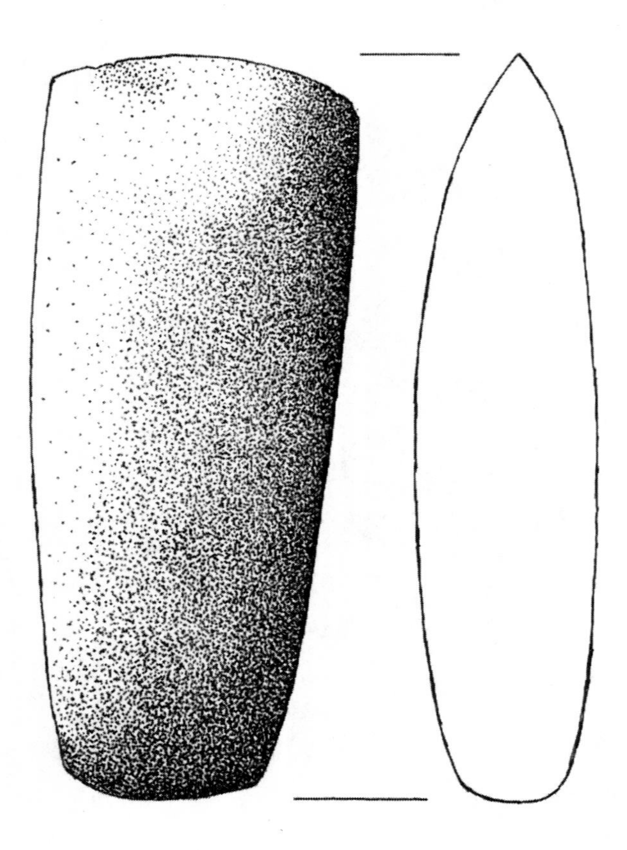

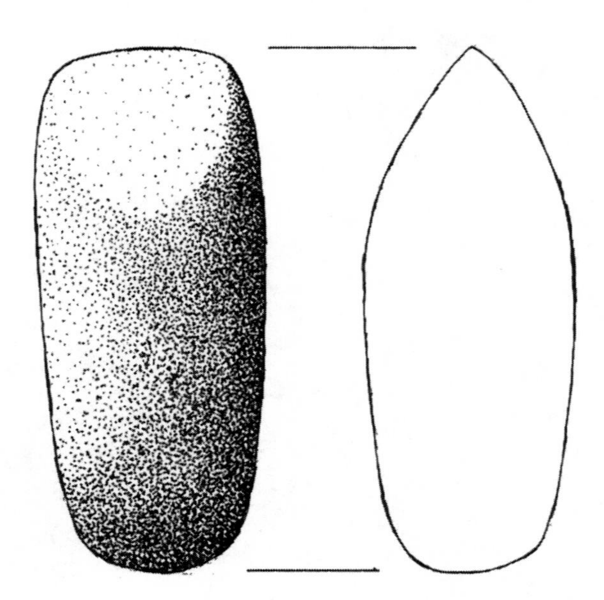

References: Bell 1972; Davis et al. 2010; Hall 1994; Hamilton 1952; Krieger 1946; Shafer 1973.

GORGETS

This term is applied to both shell and stone artifacts that usually have two perforations and are assumed to have been worn around the neck or suspended on the breast area. This interpretation is based on the use of metal gorgets as throat protectors in medieval warfare, and into the 18th century, as signs of status or rank in some militaries. Elaborate engraved metal and silver gorgets were given to Native American chiefs and later became trade items.

Stone gorgets in Texas are usually flat, rectangular, or oval in outline, made of limestone, hard sandstone, slate, and other materials, and with two biconical perforations side by side toward the middle part of the gorget. Often, there are scratches on one or both surfaces (likely from manufacture), but some have incised motifs, and others have shallow notches around the edges. There are occasionally other perforations seen on a gorget, usually related to attempts to repair a broken gorget or for unknown functions.

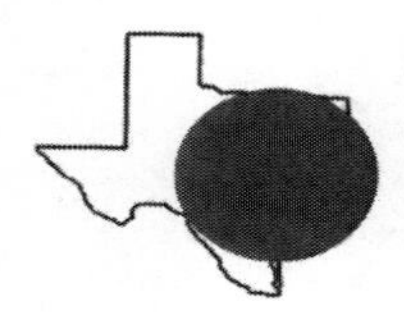

Distribution: Central and south Texas, into lower Rio Grande Valley; central Texas; lower Pecos; east Texas. **Period:** Archaic contexts in most parts of Texas. **Sites:** La Jita; Fall Creek; McGee Bend Reservoir; 41FB250; Ernest Witte (41AU36); 41DM27; Bowman Ranch (Dimmit County).

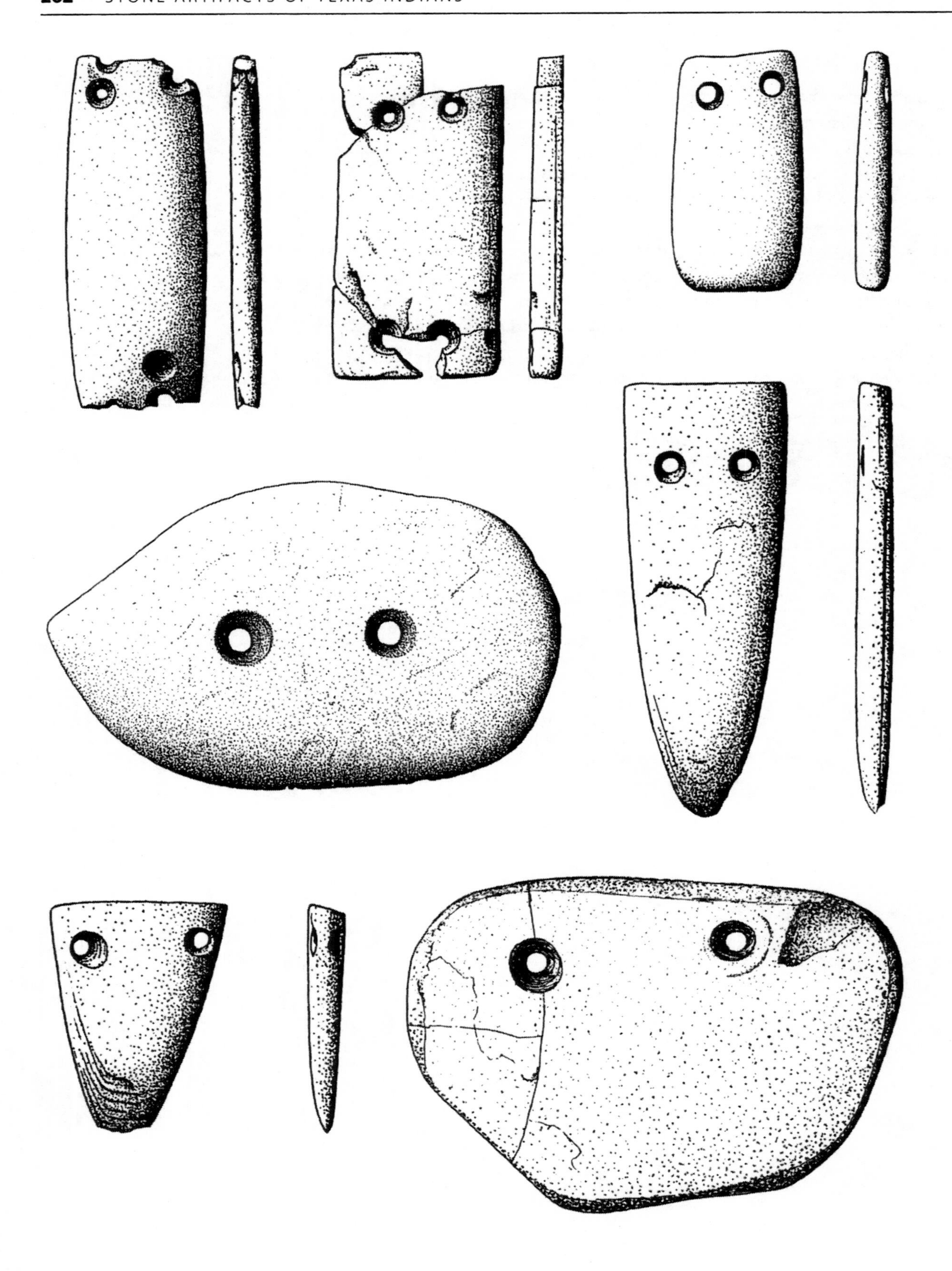

References: Hall 1981; Hester 1971, 1998; Jackson and Woolsey 1938; Patterson 2000; Story et al. 1990.

HAMMERSTONES

Hammerstones are usually modified by use and not intentionally shaped, pecked, or ground before being used to work chert or to process various materials. A wide range of chert, quartzite, granite, and limestone is selected, often from gravel exposures. In south Texas (see fig. 2-6), small egg-sized quartzite cobbles were selected for use as hammerstones. Usually brown to purple in color, there is impact wear on one or both ends, and sometimes, one end will be splintered from use and the hammerstone discarded. Depending on the task involved, hammerstones can vary considerably in size. While stone-working may be a principal task of most hammerstones, they were also used in bone-processing, breaking nuts on a pitted stone, and other food-related activities.

Distribution: All parts of Texas. **Period:** Throughout prehistory. **Sites:** Woodrow Heard; La Jita; Stillhouse Hollow; Jewett Mine; Victoria Co.

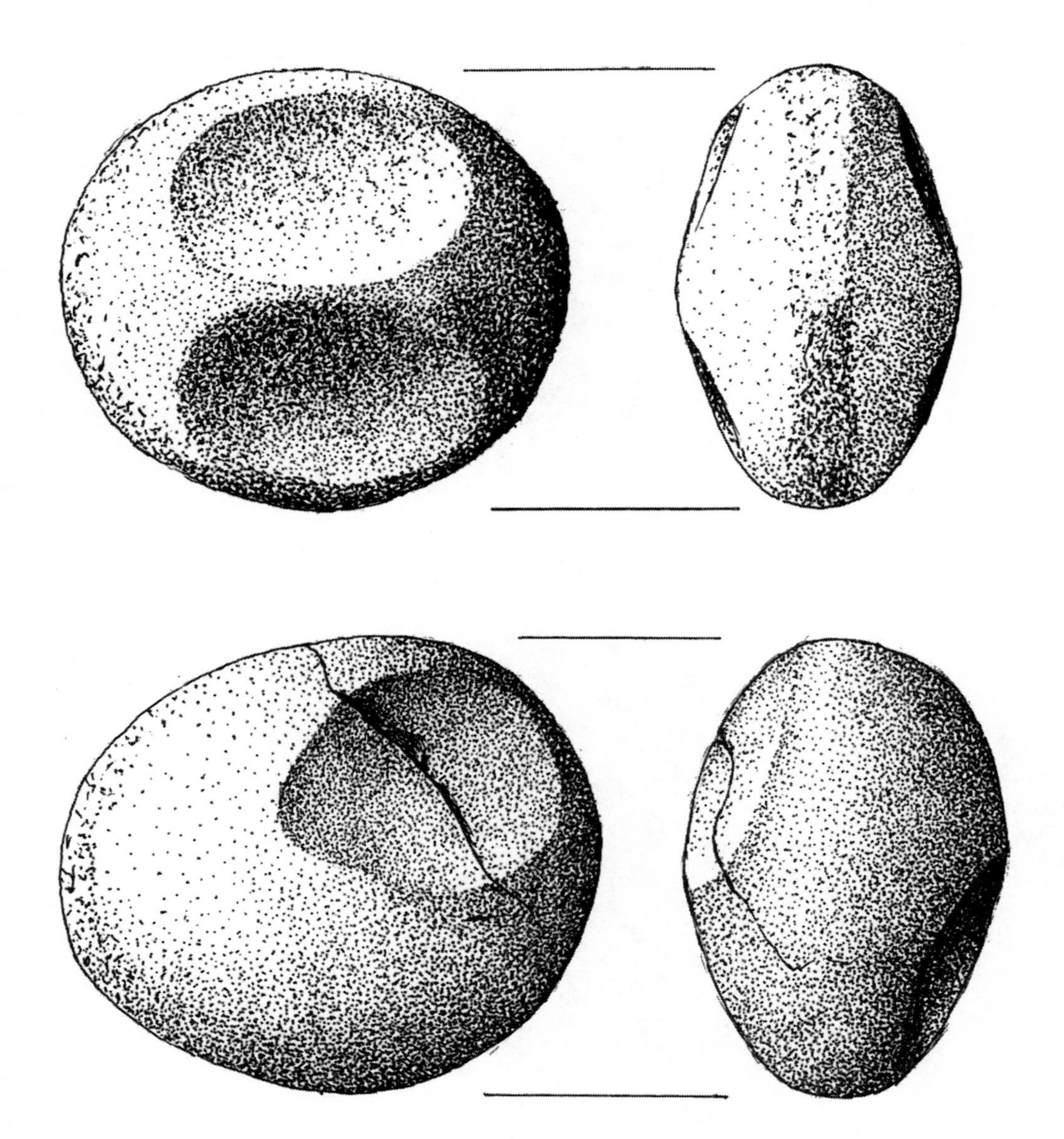

References: Decker et al. 2000; Fields et al. 1990a; Hester 1971; Sorrow et al. 1967.

HEMATITE AXES

Large pieces of siderite (commonly called "hematite") that occur geologically in eastern Texas have been shaped, pecked, and ground into grooved axes. The exterior polish gives them a deep reddish brown color. The axes range considerably in size. Celts shaped of "hematite" are found in north central Texas.

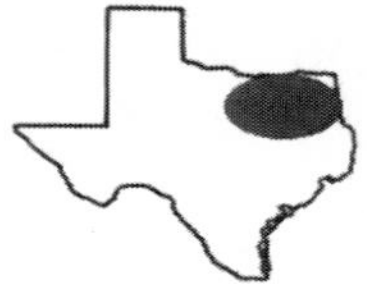

Distribution: Northeast Texas. **Period:** Axes: Archaic into Early Ceramic of northeast Texas; hematite celts: Henrietta Focus; Late Prehistoric. **Sites:** Axes: Williams; Grace Creek; 41UR142; hematite celts: Stallings Ranch; north central Texas, including Brazos River and Trinity River drainage; 41SE17; 41MU53.

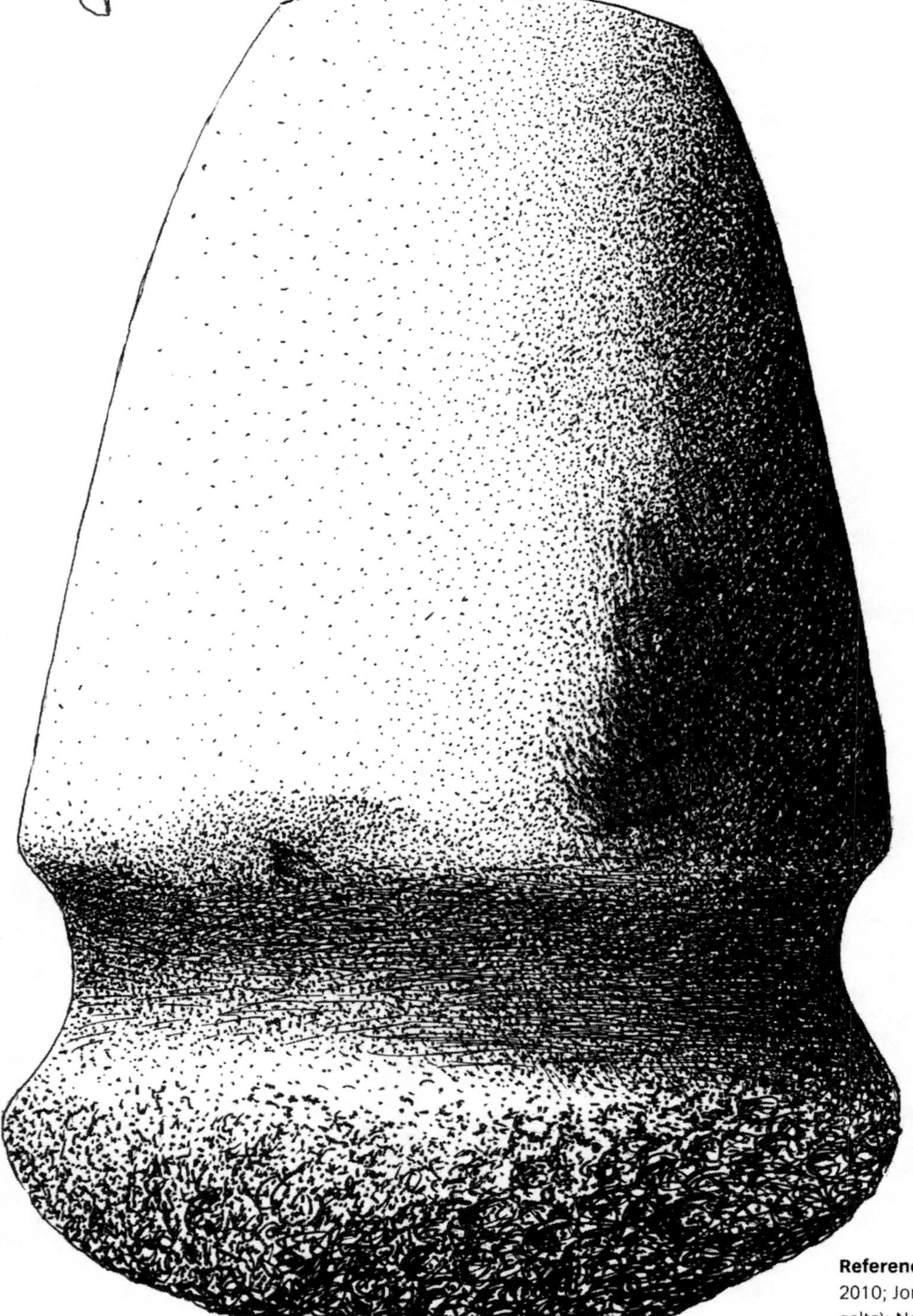

References: Bruseth et al. 2009; Davis et al. 2010; Jones 1957; Moseley 1996 (hematite celts); Nelson et al. 1994; Story et al. 1990; Turner and Smith 2002.

INCISED AND ENGRAVED STONES

Incised and engraved stone artifacts are found in several contexts in Texas. Specimens are made of sandstone, limestone, or soapstone. Designs usually consist of fine lines of deliberate patterns—bands of parallel lines, diamond cross-hatching, zigzag and triangular designs, and largely curvilinear motifs. Two pendants or beads with intricate designs are illustrated here.

Most specimens are Archaic in age, some even Late Prehistoric. The most complex designs, engraved on hard limestone cobbles, are found in the Clovis deposits at the Gault site. A few other incised/engraved stones are known from later Paleo-Indian contexts.

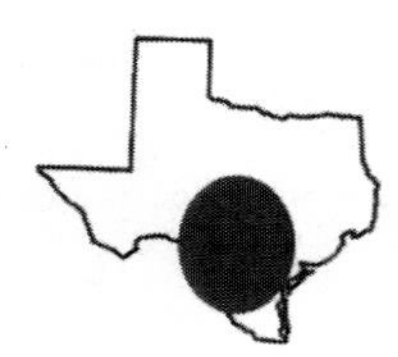

Distribution: South and central Texas, lower Pecos. **Period:** Paleo-Indian (Gault site) to Late Prehistoric. **Sites:** Atascosa; Burnet, Bexar, and Val Verde counties; Gault (41BL323); Bosque County.

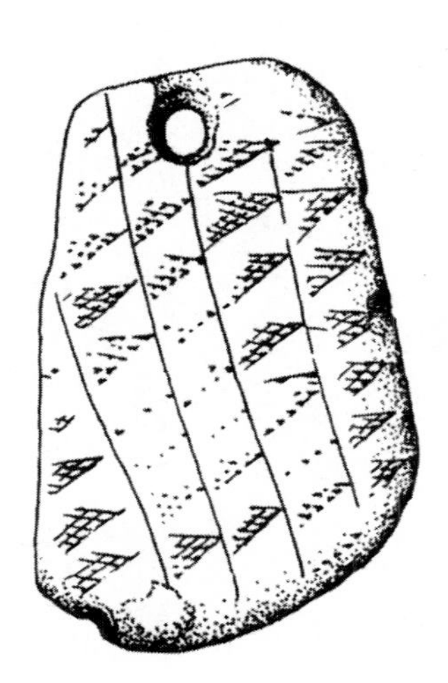

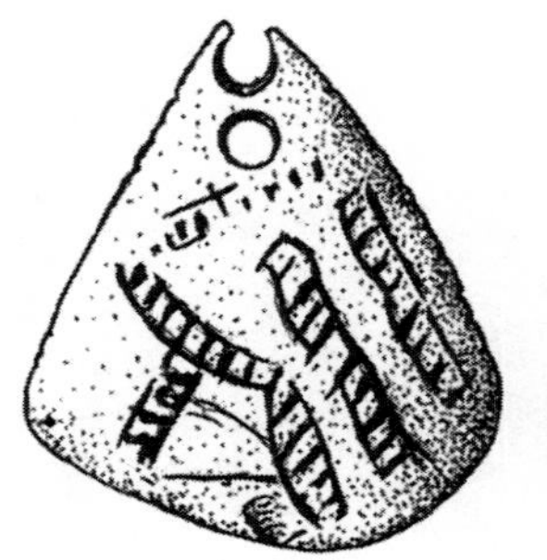

Val Verde Co.

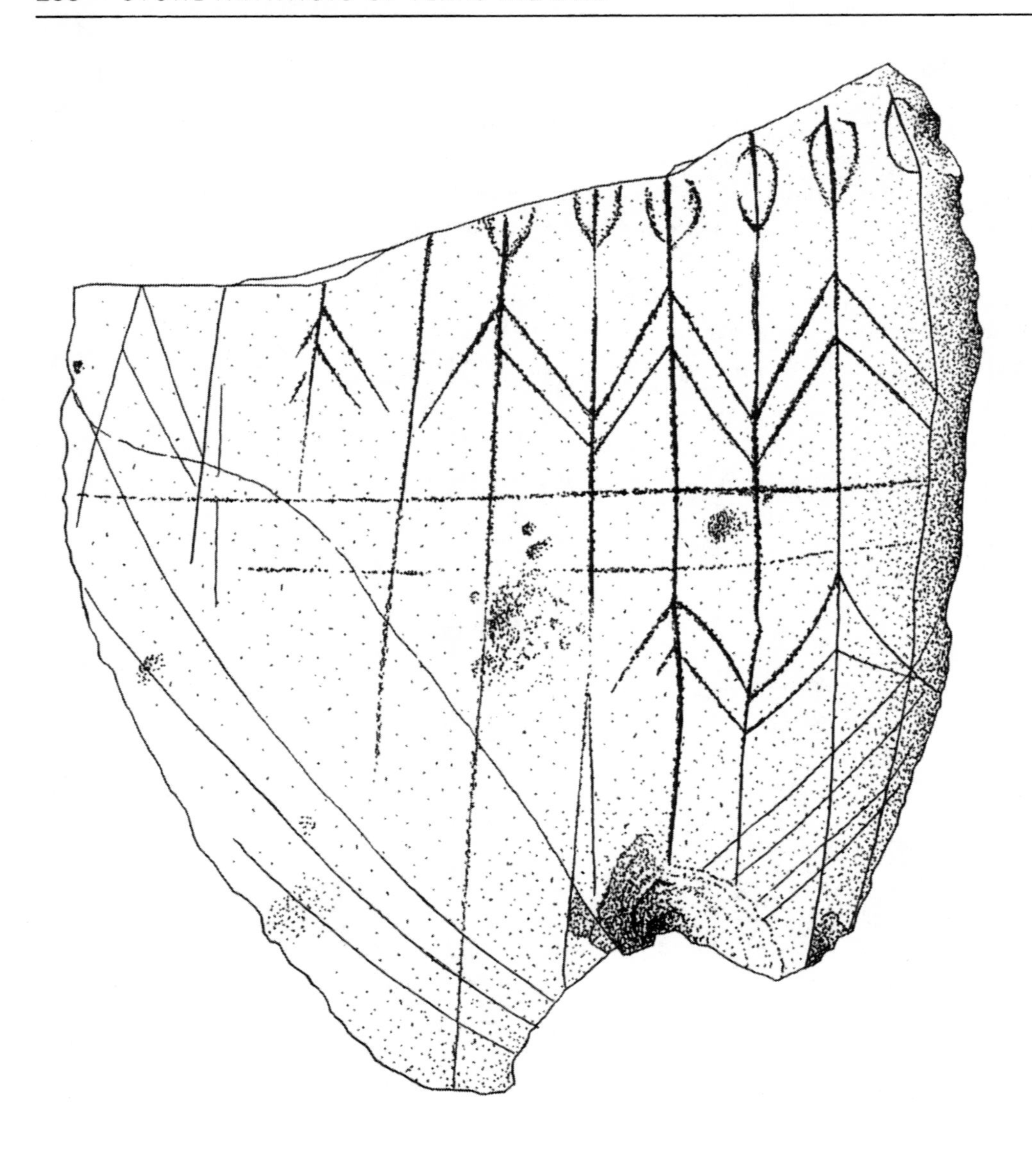

Gault site, 11.8 cm

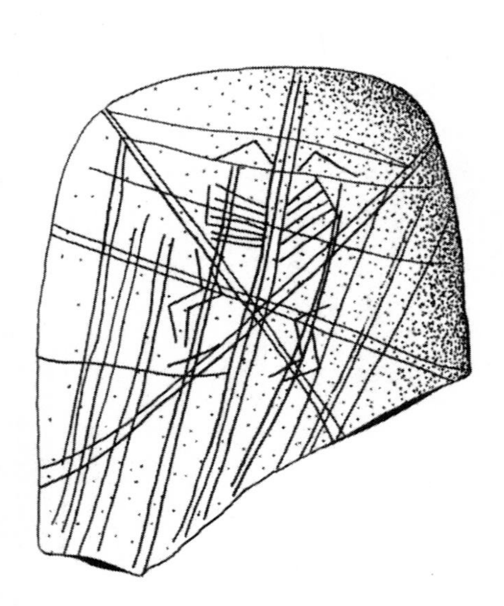

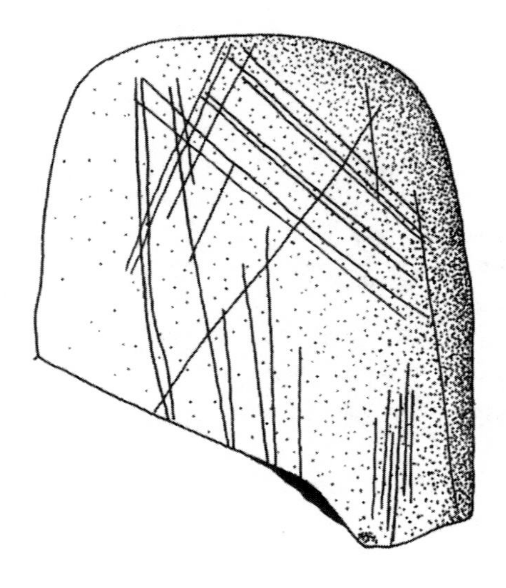

Bexar Co.

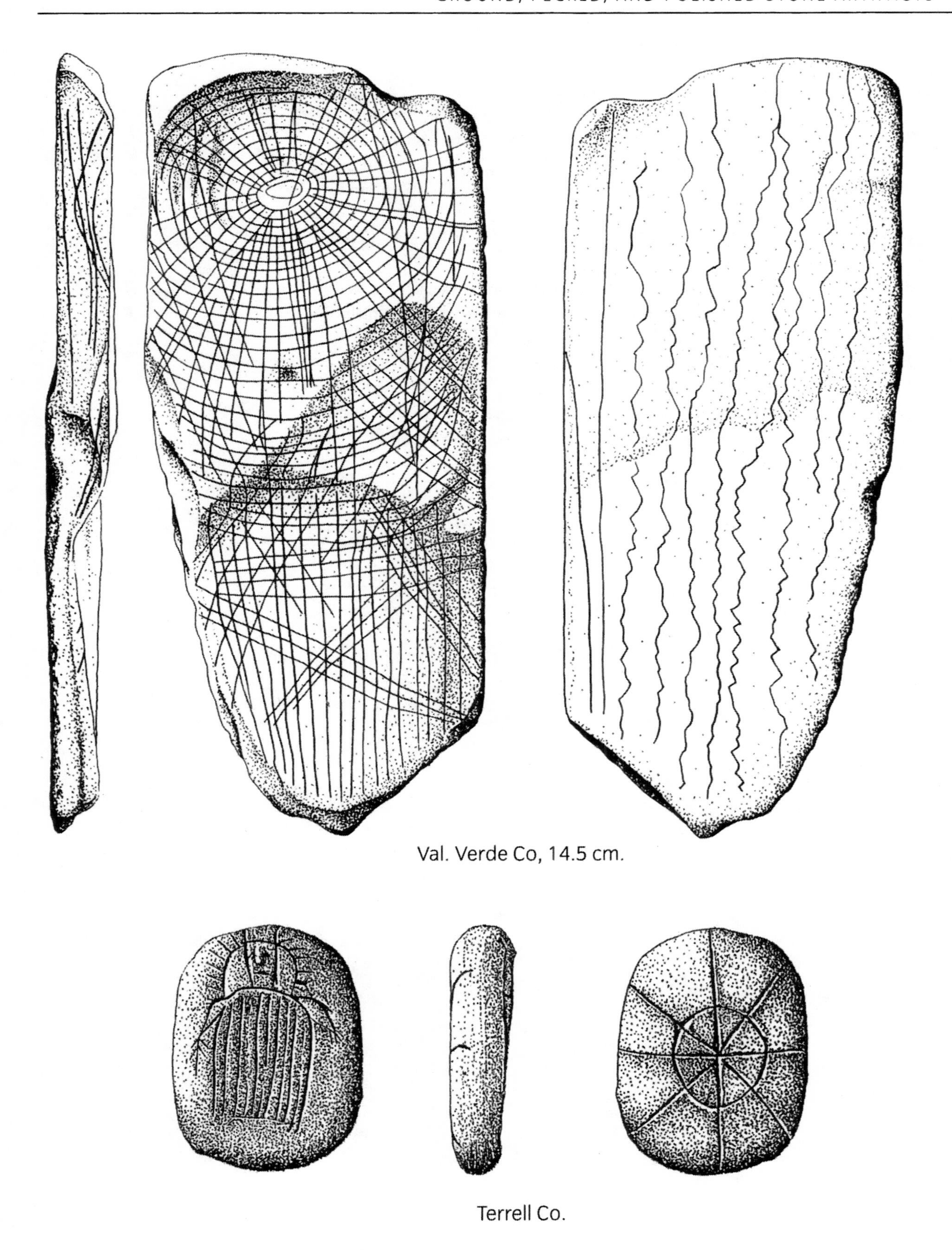

Val. Verde Co, 14.5 cm.

Terrell Co.

References: Chandler 1987, 1991a, 1991b; Collins et al. 1991; Greer and Treat 1975; Parsons 1965; Smith 1994.

MANOS, METATES, MORTARS, AND PESTLES

Metates, or grinding slabs, are usually made of sandstone, indurated sandstone, limestone, or basalt. They may have one or more grinding facets on one or both sides of the slab. They were used to process and grind wild plant foods or, in later cultures in parts of Texas (east Texas, especially), for grinding agricultural plants (maize). Krieger (Newell and Krieger 1949) believes that a distinction should be made between "milling stones," which are grinding slabs upon which a mano was moved in a rotary motion, and "metates," upon which a back-and-forth motion was used, in the Pueblo and Middle American manner.

Manos are small, oval handstones of sandstone, quartzite, limestone, or other stone shaped to match the style of the milling stone on which they were to be used. The basin shape of the milling-stone surface required a rotary-grinding motion or one in which sweeping arcs were made around the perimeter of the basin.

Pestles are long, cylindrical pounding tools, rounded at one or both ends, that were used in association with a stone or wooden mortar for plant processing. Mortars are often bowl-like with cup-shaped to more cylindrical interiors, pecked out, and smoothed. Portable stone mortars in the Trans-Pecos are often made of vesicular basalt or tuff.

Distribution: Throughout Texas. **Period:** Archaic to Late Prehistoric. **Sites:** George C. Davis; Choke Canyon (metates and manos); Fall Creek (manos); Kyle; Oblate; La Jita (metates and manos); Panther Springs Creek (metates and manos); Trans-Pecos; Millington (mortar); Stillhouse Hollow (mortar and manos); Polvo (mortar); John Ischy (metates and manos); Gatlin (metates and manos); Jewett Mine (metates); Evoe Terrace; Dimmit and Zapata counties (manos, metates, and pestles); lower Rio Grande Valley (metates and mortars); Woodrow Heard (metates and manos).

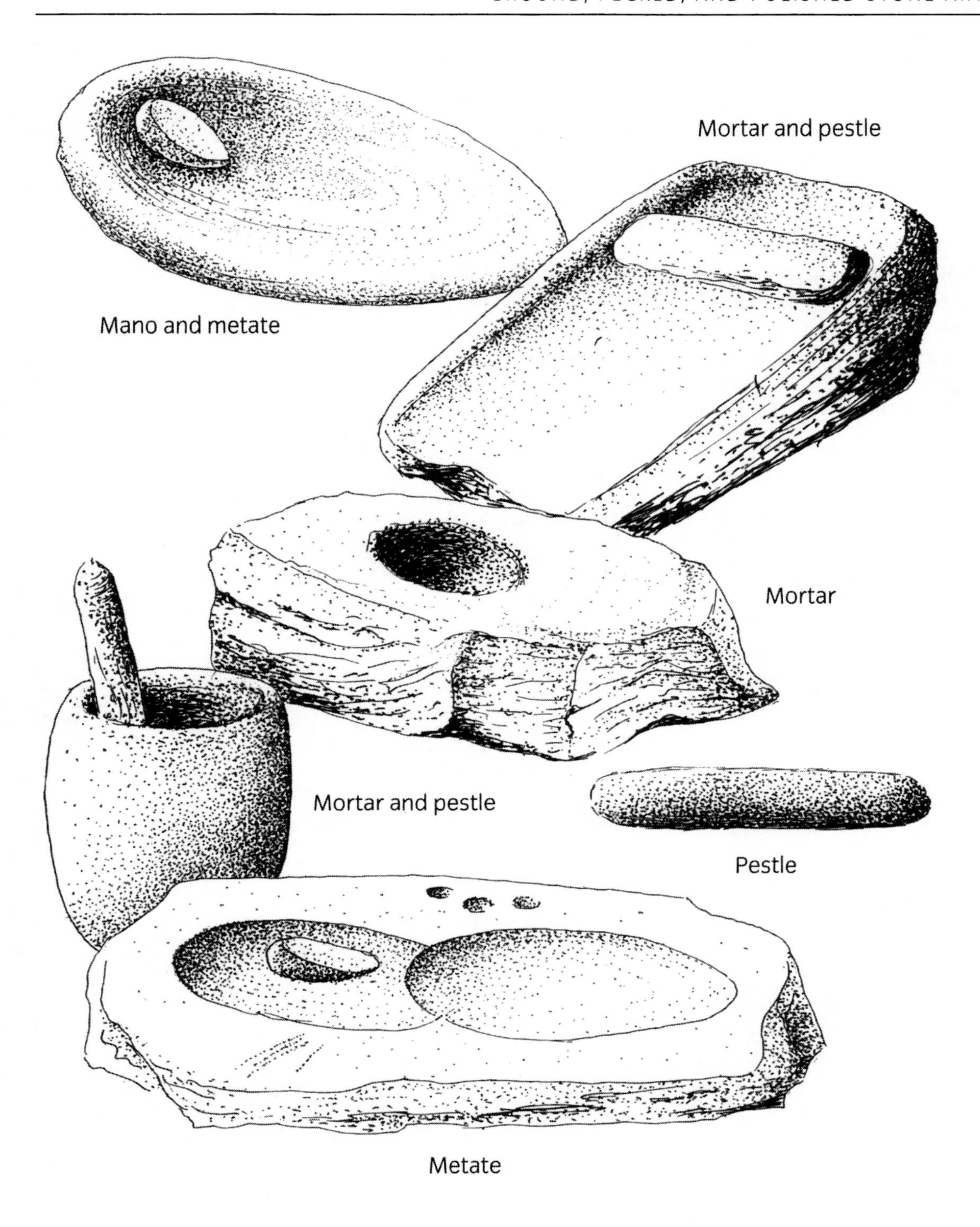

References: Cloud and Piehl 2008; Cloud et al. 1994; Decker et al. 2000; Hall et al. 1982; Hester 1971, 1979c; Houk et al. 2008; Jackson and Woolsey 1938; Jelks 1962; Krieger 1946; Newell and Krieger 1949; Sorrow 1969; Sorrow et al. 1967; Tunnell 1962.

PAINTED PEBBLES

These stone artifacts were modified by the application of painted lines and symbols, usually on the smooth faces (one or both sides) of streamworn cobbles. The meanings of the decorations are unknown, and the subject is of ongoing debate.

Painted pebbles are most common in the rockshelters of the lower Pecos, with black lines dominating (red also is sometimes seen) in terms of color, and with several elements that appear to be repeated. Referred to in the literature as "portable art," we may never know whether the uses of these painted pebbles had great meaning or symbolism, or were something more mundane.

In 1977, the first painted pebble from the south Texas plains was documented on the Nueces River in Zavala County. Its red lines had been preserved only because the river cobble, which had been facedown for a very long time, had been kicked over in a cow trail on a terrace ledge. Later, additional pebbles painted in red were found on ranches in southern Uvalde and northern Zavala counties. A couple of others have come from a rockshelter and a burned rock midden in northern Uvalde County.

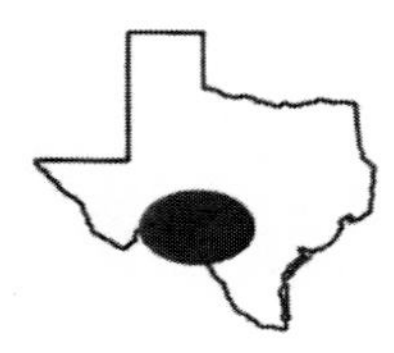

Distribution: Principally lower Pecos but also into northern south Texas and southwestern Edwards Plateau. **Period:** Archaic. **Sites:** Arenosa; Fate Bell Rockshelter; Eagle Cave and numerous Val Verde County rockshelters and caves; 41VV183; Cain Ranch, Uvalde County; Kincaid Rockshelter; Kyle.

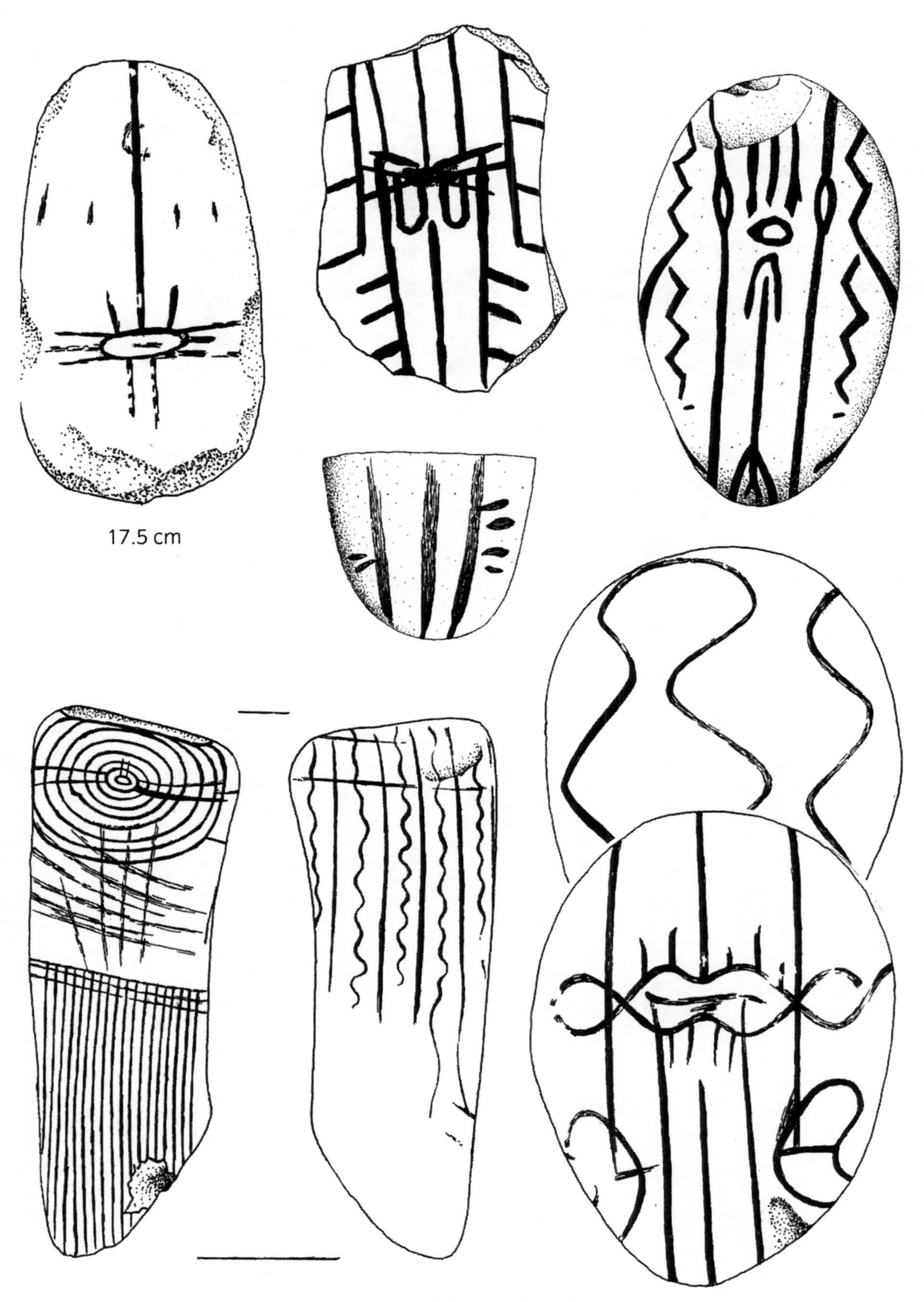

All from Val Verde Co.

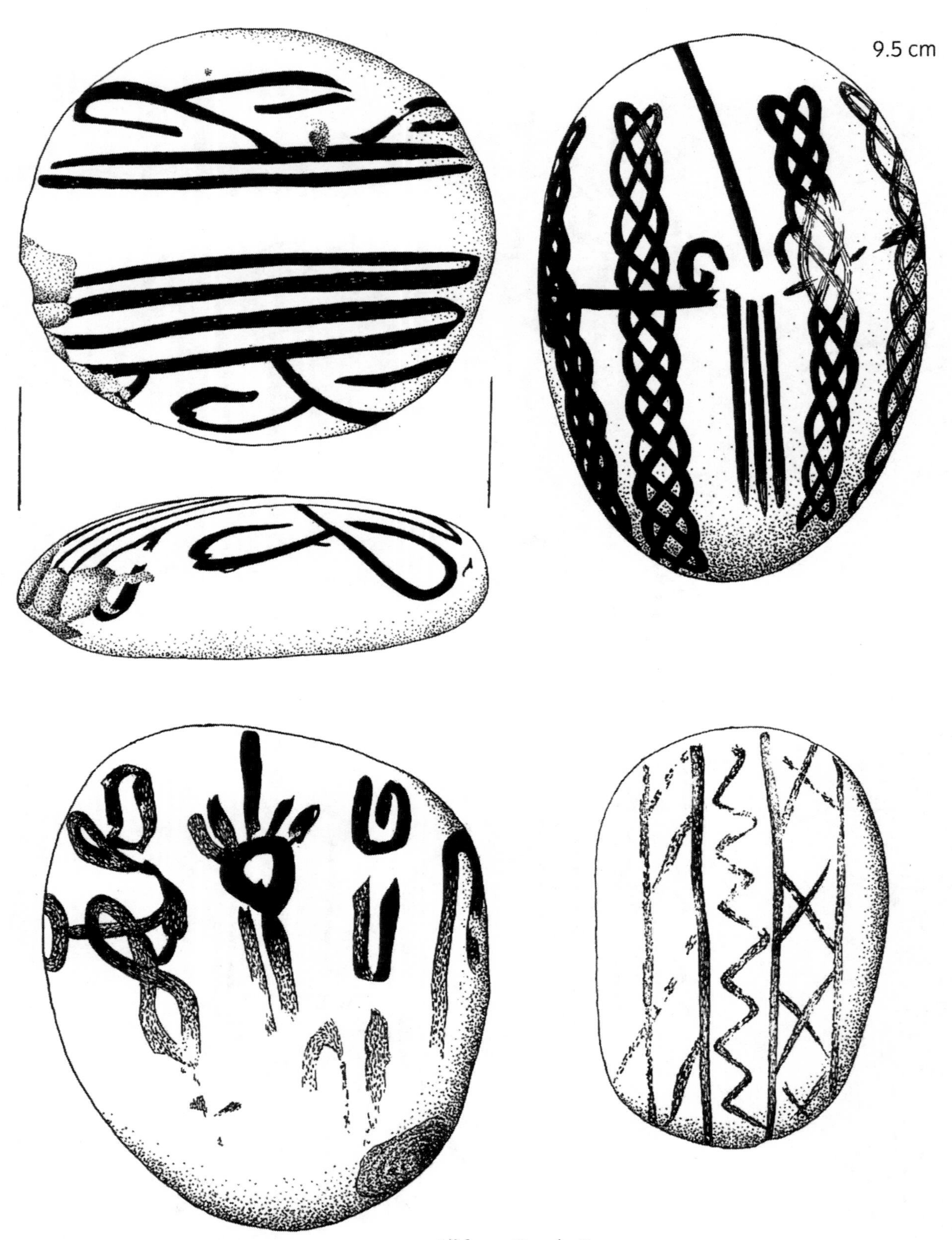

All from Zavala Co.

References: Hester 1977b, 2004b; Mock 1987; Newcomb 1967.

PALETTES

This artifact category is applied to specialized ground stone artifacts in the American Southwest, primarily in the Hohokam culture of Arizona but also in the Mimbres of New Mexico. The specimen we have illustrated here embodies the traits of these palettes. They are rectangular, flat, or tabular artifacts, with a flat to slightly concave depression (smoothed from wear) and a raised border around the edges. It is 15.5 cm long.

The illustrated specimen was found in Terrell County, near the confluence of San Francisco Canyon with the Rio Grande. Made of reddish brown ferruginous sandstone, the interior depression is heavily stained with red hematite; indeed, it seems almost a part of the stone due to such heavy use. It differs from its Southwest counterparts with a hole drilled in one end. It is possible that such palettes are not "Texas" artifacts (although the Terrell County specimen is made from local sandstones) but rather trade items from the Southwest. Regardless, we think its appearance in the third edition might result in more examples being reported.

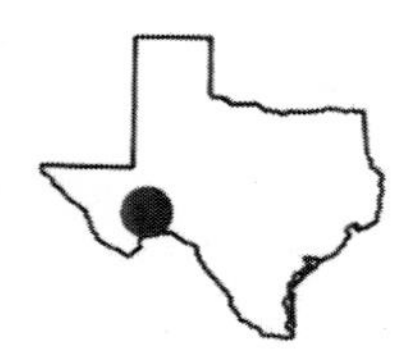

Distribution: Trans-Pecos of Texas; southern New Mexico; Arizona. **Period:** Based on Hohokam and Mimbres chronology, ca. AD 900–1110. **Sites:** Terrell County, Tex.; NAN Ranch (N.Mex.); Snaketown and Casas Grandes (Ariz.).

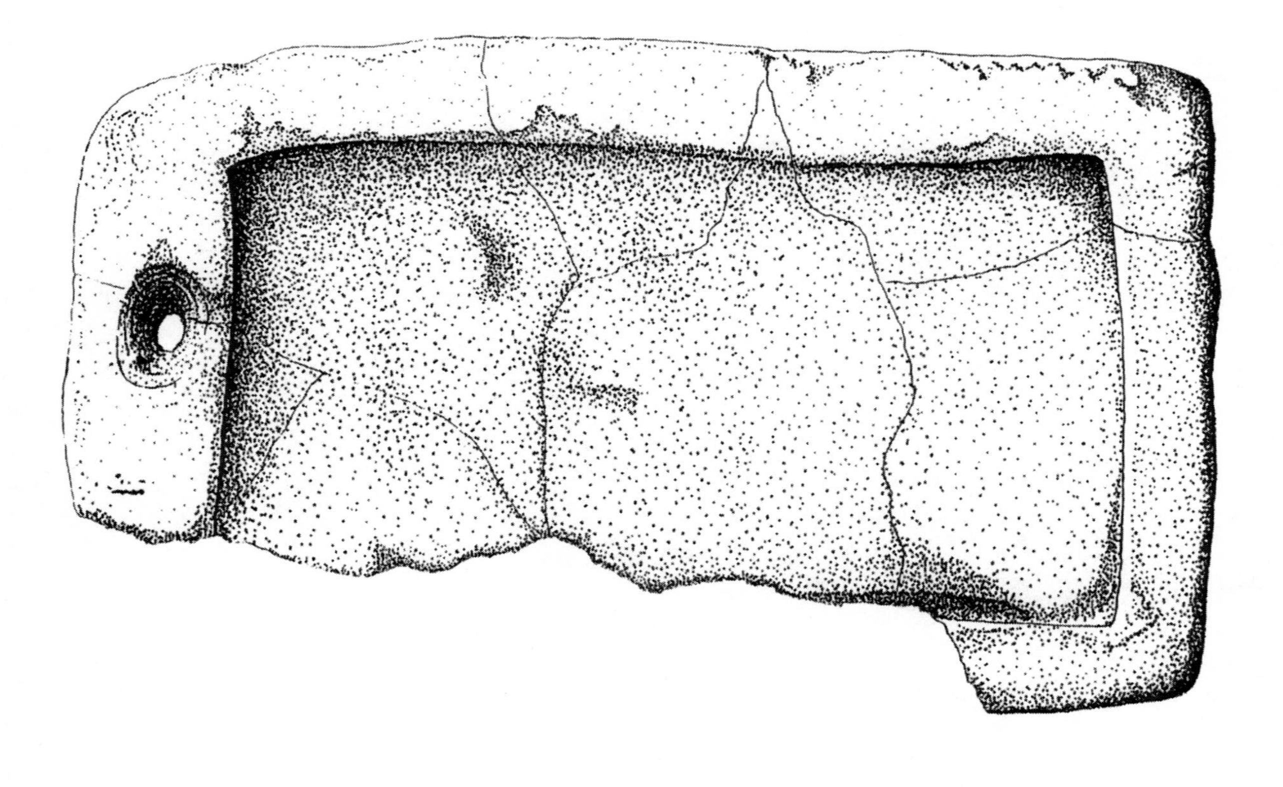

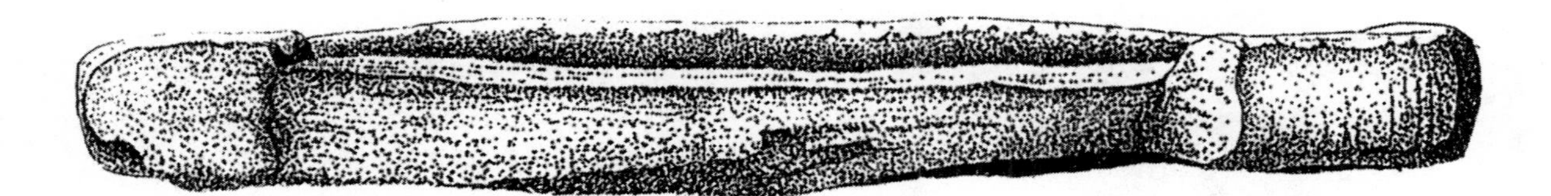

References: Chandler 1994b; Hawley 1947; Shafer 2003.

PITTED STONES

These are tabular pieces of sandstone or hematite having one or more pecked-out circular pits chipped into the grinding face, the worked underside, or both, and generally of a size that could easily be carried in the hand. They are often called "nutting stones" and at times are made on manos; probably they were used interchangeably for milling and for nut-cracking platforms. In central Texas, the pits are often found on limestone manos—in the middle on one or both faces—or they are in the center of mano-sized limestone cobbles. Decker and colleagues (2000) suggest that one use was cracking small native pecans.

Honea (1965) and Johnson (1962b) suggest they were possibly used as anvils in the bipolar-flaking technique—the soft anvil giving the flintknapper better control.

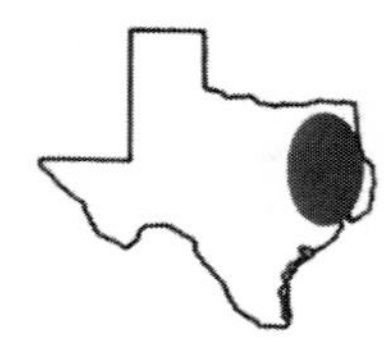

Distribution: East and northeast Texas. **Period:** Archaic into Late Prehistoric. **Sites:** George C. Davis; Yarbrough and Miller; Stillhouse Hollow; San Jacinto River Basin; Burris 1; Texarkana Reservoir; Woodrow Heard; Oak Hill (41RK214); 41ME29.

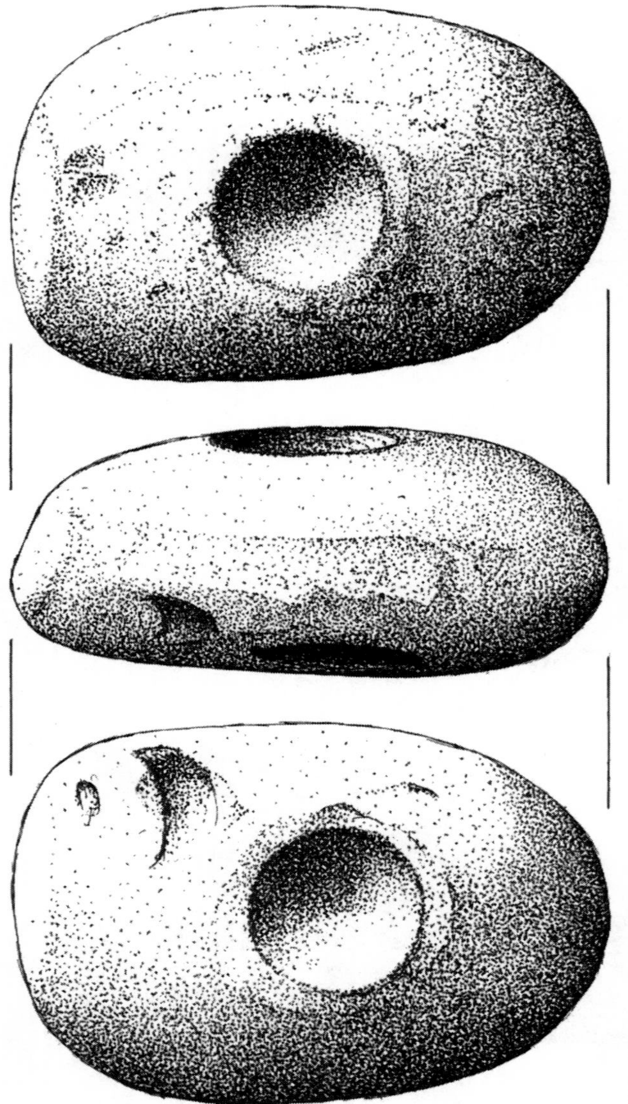

2/3 actual size

References: Briggs and Malone 1970; Decker et al. 2000; Honea 1965; Johnson 1962b, 1995; McClurkan 1968; Newell and Krieger 1949; Rogers et al. 1997; Shafer 1968; 1973; Shott 1989; Sorrow et al. 1967.

PLUMMETS

Possible uses for plummets are as net weights, ornaments, or weights for bolas for capturing small animals or waterfowl (Ford and Webb 1956). Plummets are most commonly known from the eastern United States and the central and lower Mississippi River Valley. Most often, plummets are perforated, but some have a groove around the circumference at the smaller end.

In Texas, scattered examples are found in Late Archaic sites in east and southeast Texas, and at the Buckeye Knoll site (41VT98), where they occur with a formal cemetery of the Early Archaic (Ricklis 2009). The cemetery dates to around 4500 BC.

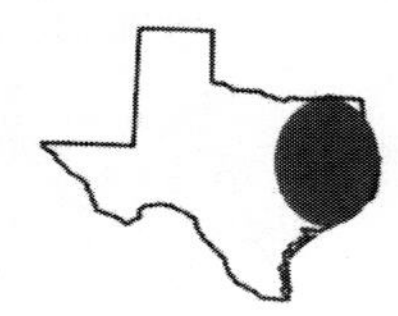

Distribution: East Texas to the southeast Texas coastal plain. **Period:** Early Archaic to Late Prehistoric. **Sites:** George C. Davis; Sam Kaufman; 41JF50; Poverty Point (La.).

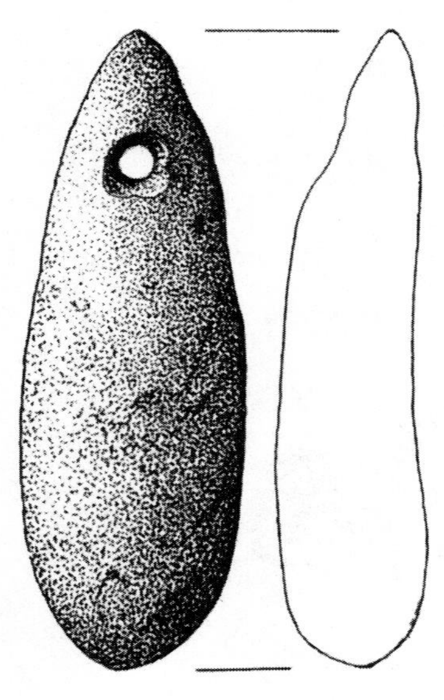

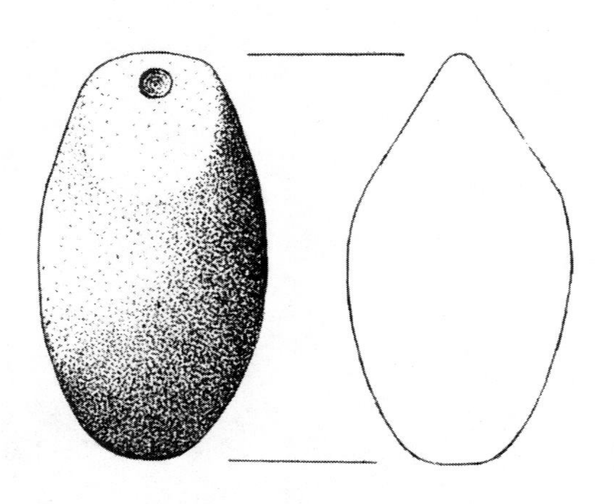

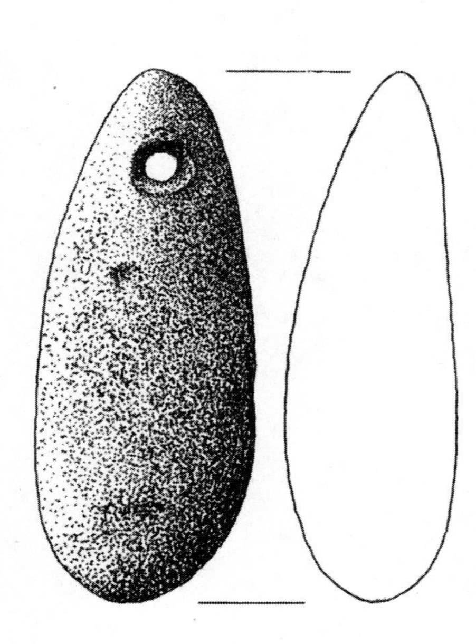

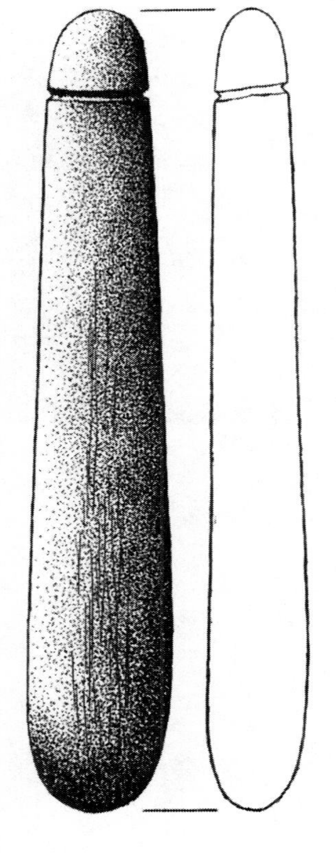

References: Ford and Webb 1956; Ricklis 2009; Shafer 1973; Skinner et al. 1969; Story et al. 1990; Webb 1982.

SHAFT STRAIGHTENERS

These loaf-shaped artifacts are distinguished by the following characteristics: made on oblong, piano-convex cobbles, usually of limestone (sometimes vesicular basalt in western Texas); and a deep transverse groove, which may or may not have perpendicular incised lines adjacent to the groove (quite often, only the incised lines are present). There is a pinkish to red discoloration of the limestone due to heating (most specimens appear to have been fractured through heating).

Similar artifacts are found in the Southwest and in California. The examples from Southern California are much like those from Texas, and their function in arrow shaft straightening has been described by Kroeber (1925, 530, pl. 49): "The joints (of cane arrows) were warmed in the groove and bent by hand or on the ridge after the stone had been heated." Since most grooved stones found in Texas have uncertain contexts, it is not clear whether they have been used for dart shafts or arrow shafts.

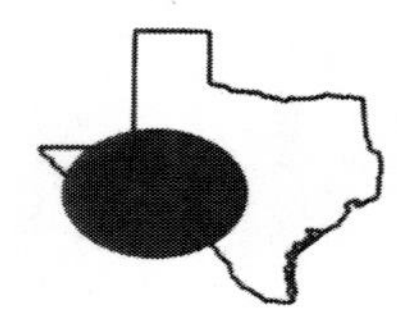

Distribution: South and central Texas, into the eastern Trans-Pecos. **Period:** Late Prehistoric, perhaps Late Archaic. **Sites:** 41BX228; Choke Canyon; Panther Springs Creek; Fall Creek; Edwards Plateau; Uvalde, Terrell, Dimmit, and Zavala counties; 41ME147; 41ED108.

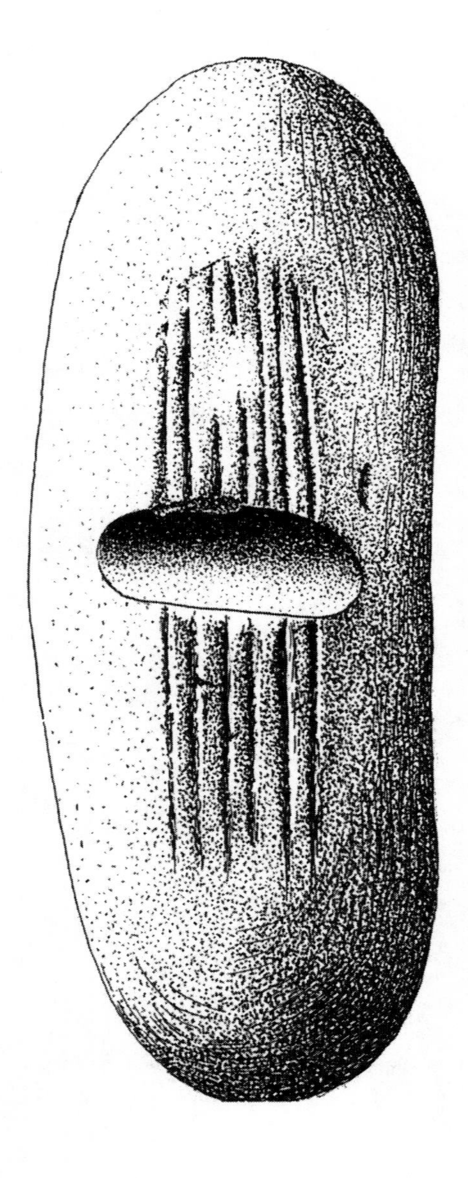

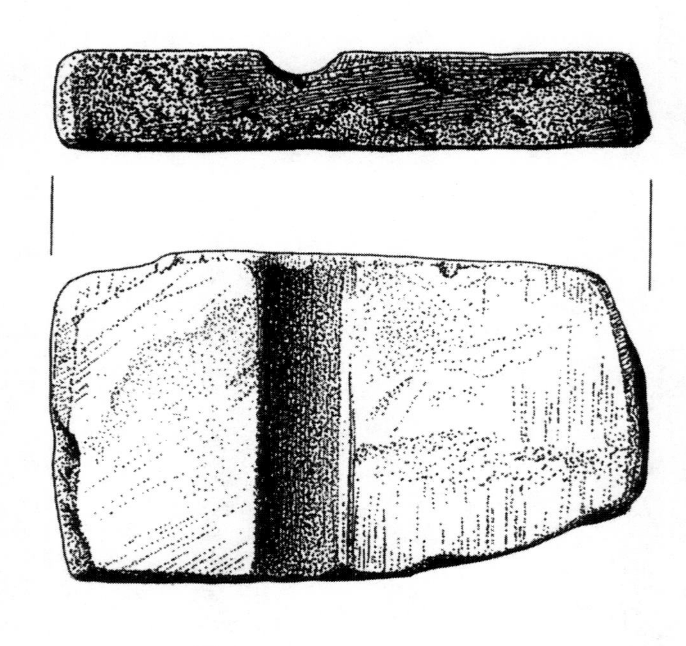

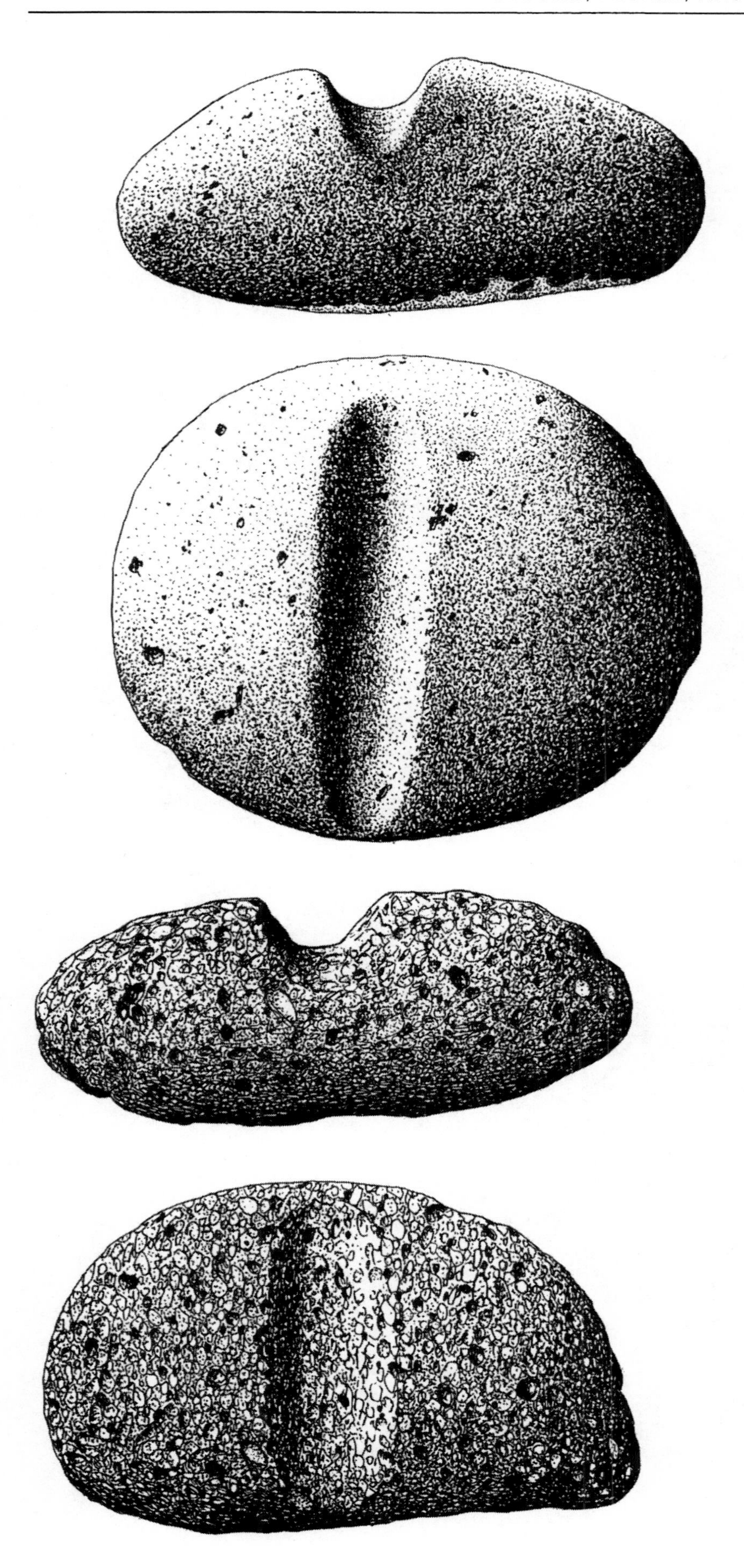

2/3 size

Shaft straighteners in parts of Texas are made of limestone and marked by parallel deep grooves. They are fragments of all size, broken by heat used in the straightening process. Some may have had broad grooves (see page 276, left).

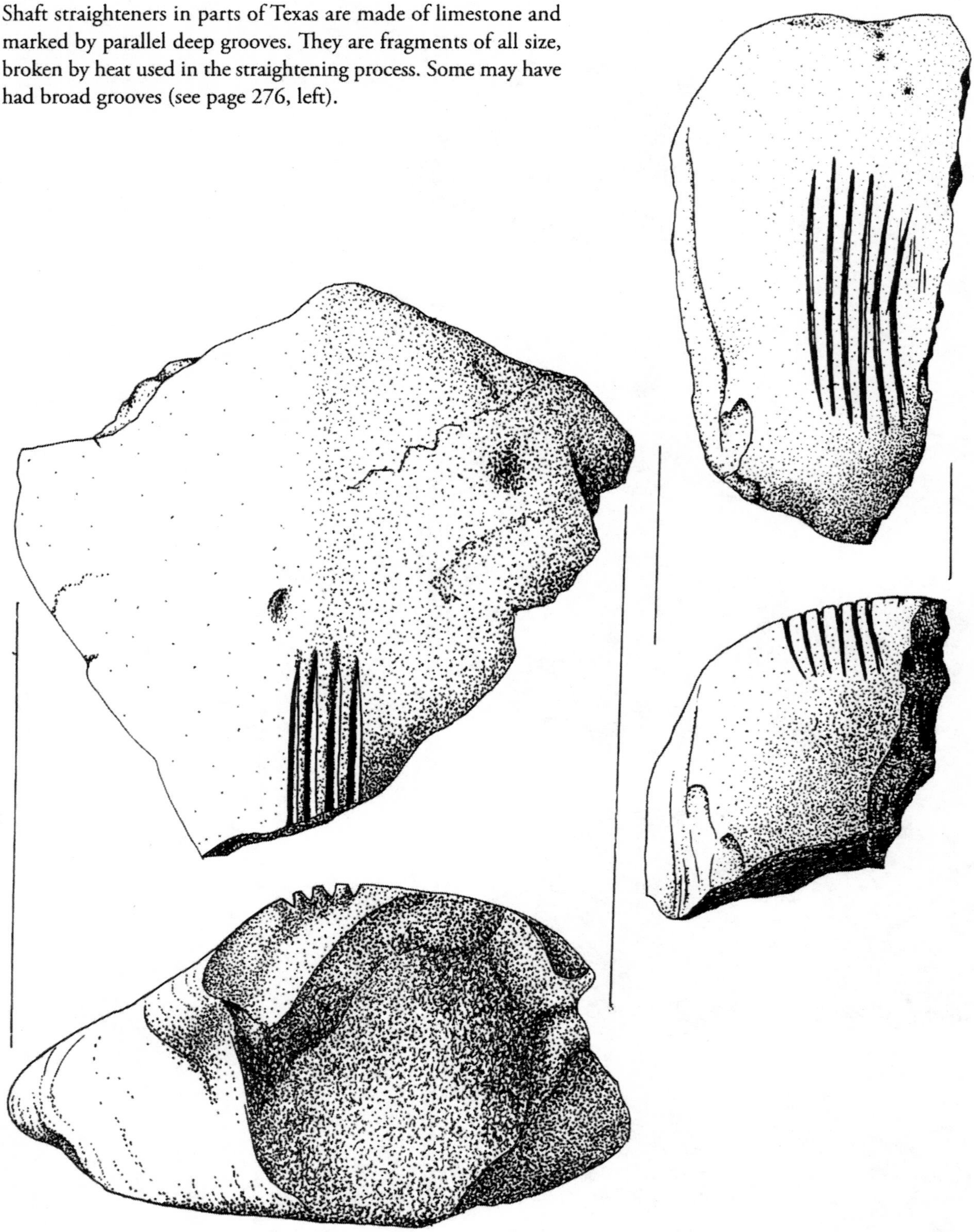

References: Beasley 1980; Black and McGraw 1985; Brown and LeNeave 1987; Hester 1988a; Hester, Stross, and Brown 1988; Hill, House, and Hester 1972; Jackson and Woolsey 1938; Kelley 1948; Kroeber 1925.

STONE MAULS

Ungrooved (handheld) and grooved stone mauls are found in several parts of North America. They are typified by a circular cross section and flattening (from pounding and other use) on both ends. The groove indicates they were hafted and could have been used as needed for hammers, woodworking, hideworking, or other processing tasks that needed a heavy blunt tool.

The specimen illustrated here was found near Dangerfield in Morris County. Another similar specimen is known from Burnet County. Otherwise, few specimens have been documented in Texas.

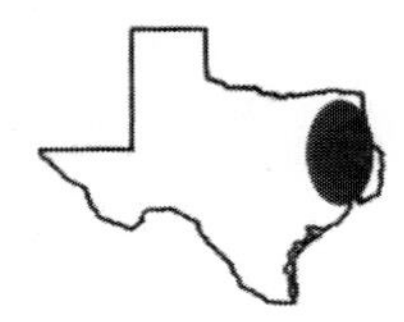

Distribution: Central Texas into northeast Texas; also reported from Antelope Creek sites. **Period:** Archaic and Late Prehistoric. **Sites:** Morris County; Burnet County; Antelope Creek; Canadian River (Studer's Room 55).

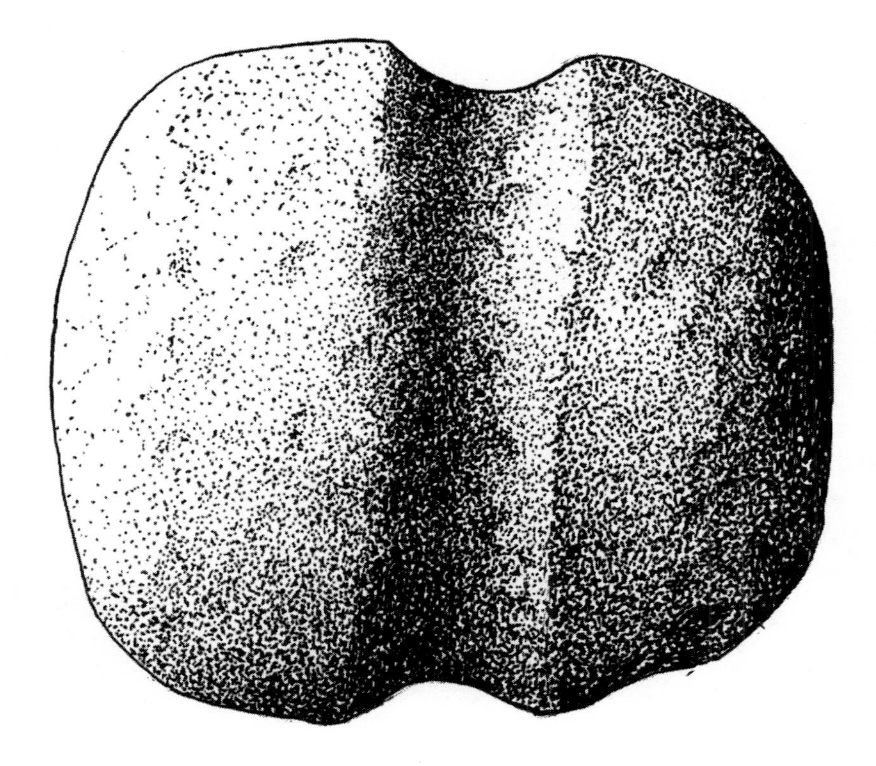

Reference: Krieger 1946.

STONE PIPES

Tubular pipes are hollowed-out, barrel-shaped tubes of stone, usually sandstone, that have been found at both occupation and burial sites; some are quite large. In some cases, as at Loma Sandia, 41LK28 (Hester 1980), the stem of the pipe has been found to be a hollow bone inserted in one end. Some of the pipes will be decorated by engraved exteriors and notches around the mouth.

Other raw materials used for making tubular stone pipes include limestone, vesicular basalt, and travertine. A tubular stone pipe made of travertine found at the Collins site (41TV40) is over 24 cm long and has numerous engraved lines on the exterior.

Effigy pipes were sculptured by pecking and abrading. The pipe bowl and stem were apparently made by pecking and reaming, not drilling (Shafer 1973). An example from the George C. Davis site is illustrated on page 313 of our first and second editions.

Distribution: Tubular pipes are found across the state; effigy pipes are found mainly in east Texas. **Period:** Archaic and Late Prehistoric. **Sites:** Kleberg County; Amistad Reservoir (41VV186); George C. Davis; Harlan (Okla.); Devil's River; 41LK28; Oso (41NU2).

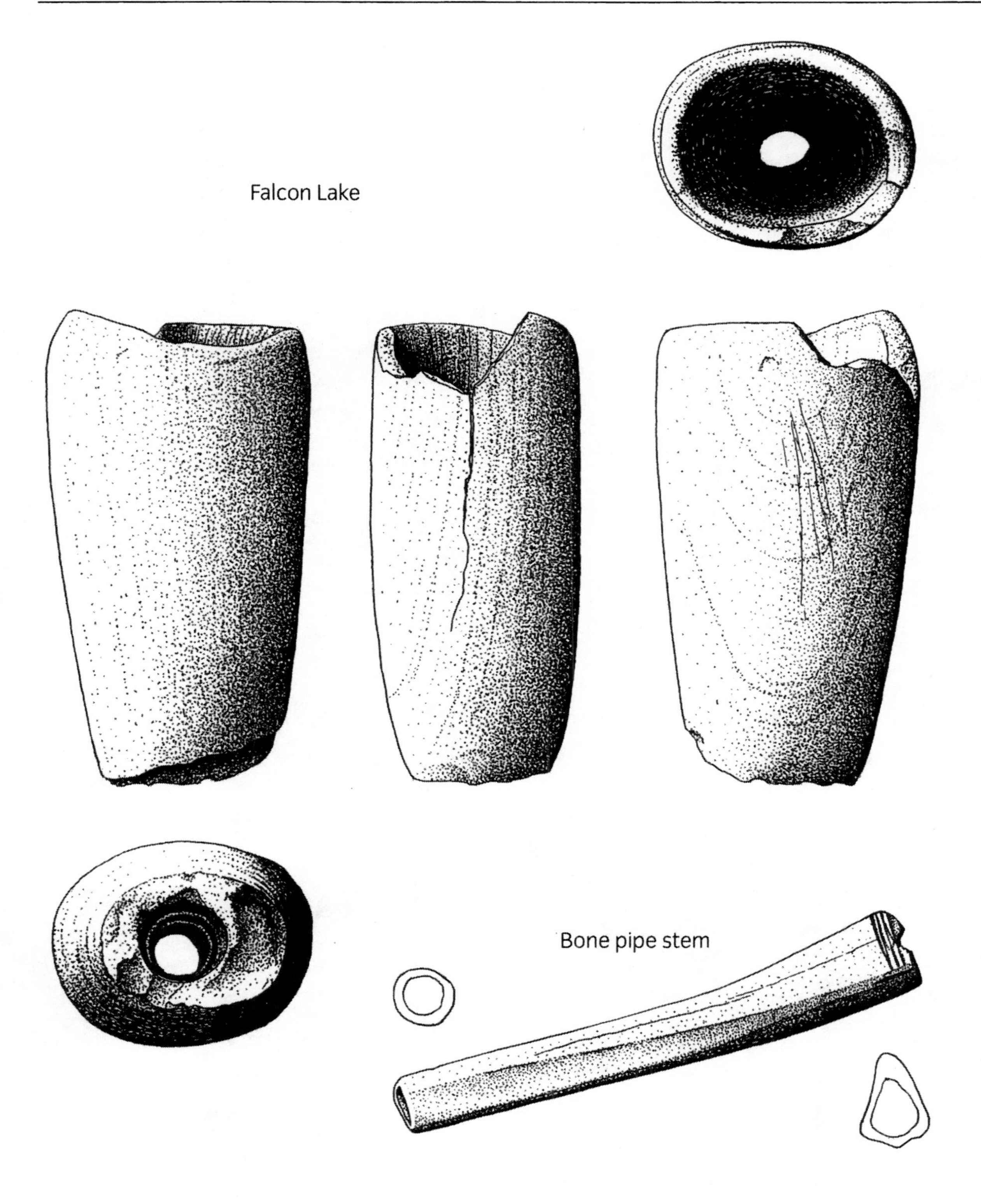
Falcon Lake
Bone pipe stem

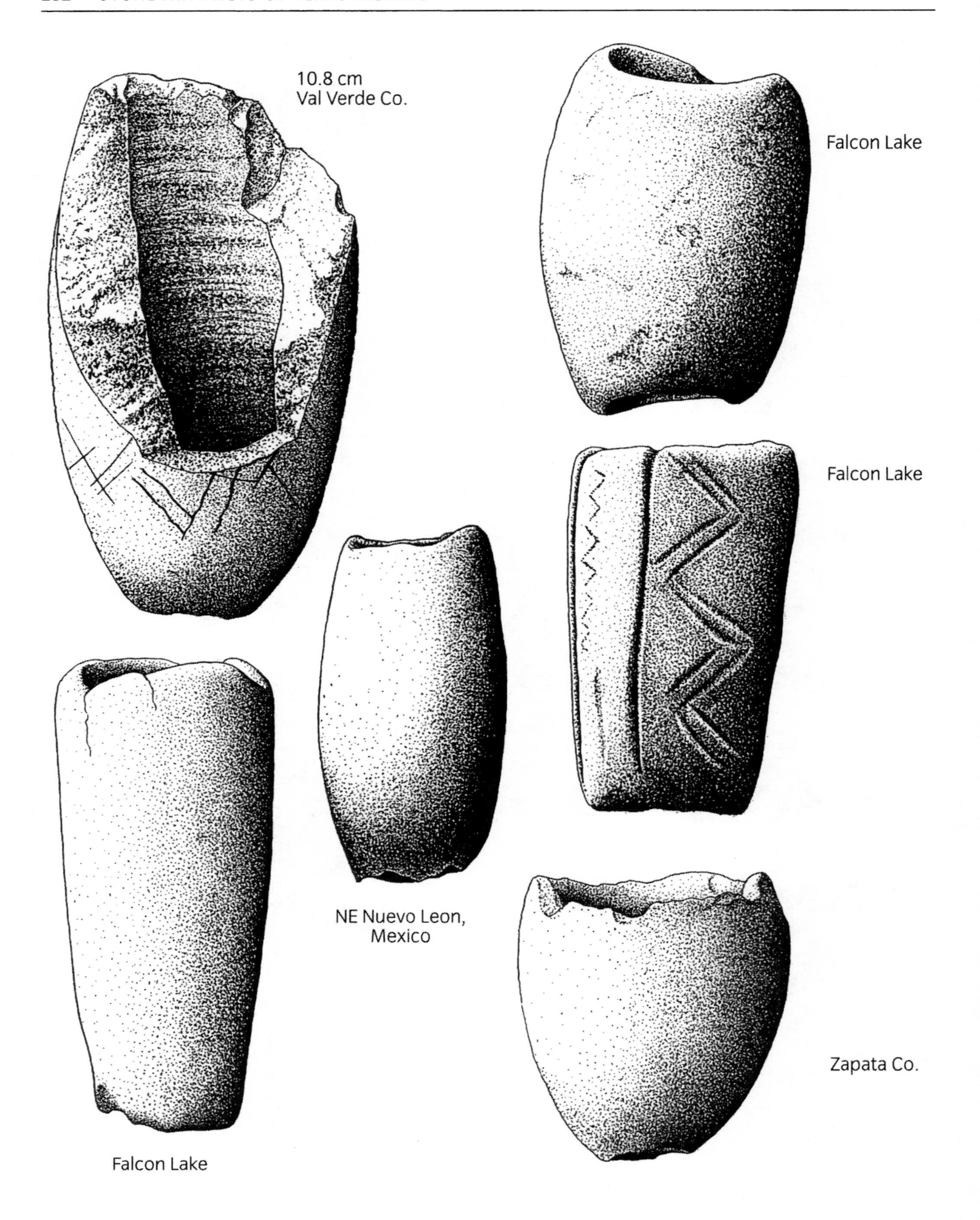
10.8 cm
Val Verde Co.
Falcon Lake
Falcon Lake
NE Nuevo Leon,
Mexico
Zapata Co.
Falcon Lake

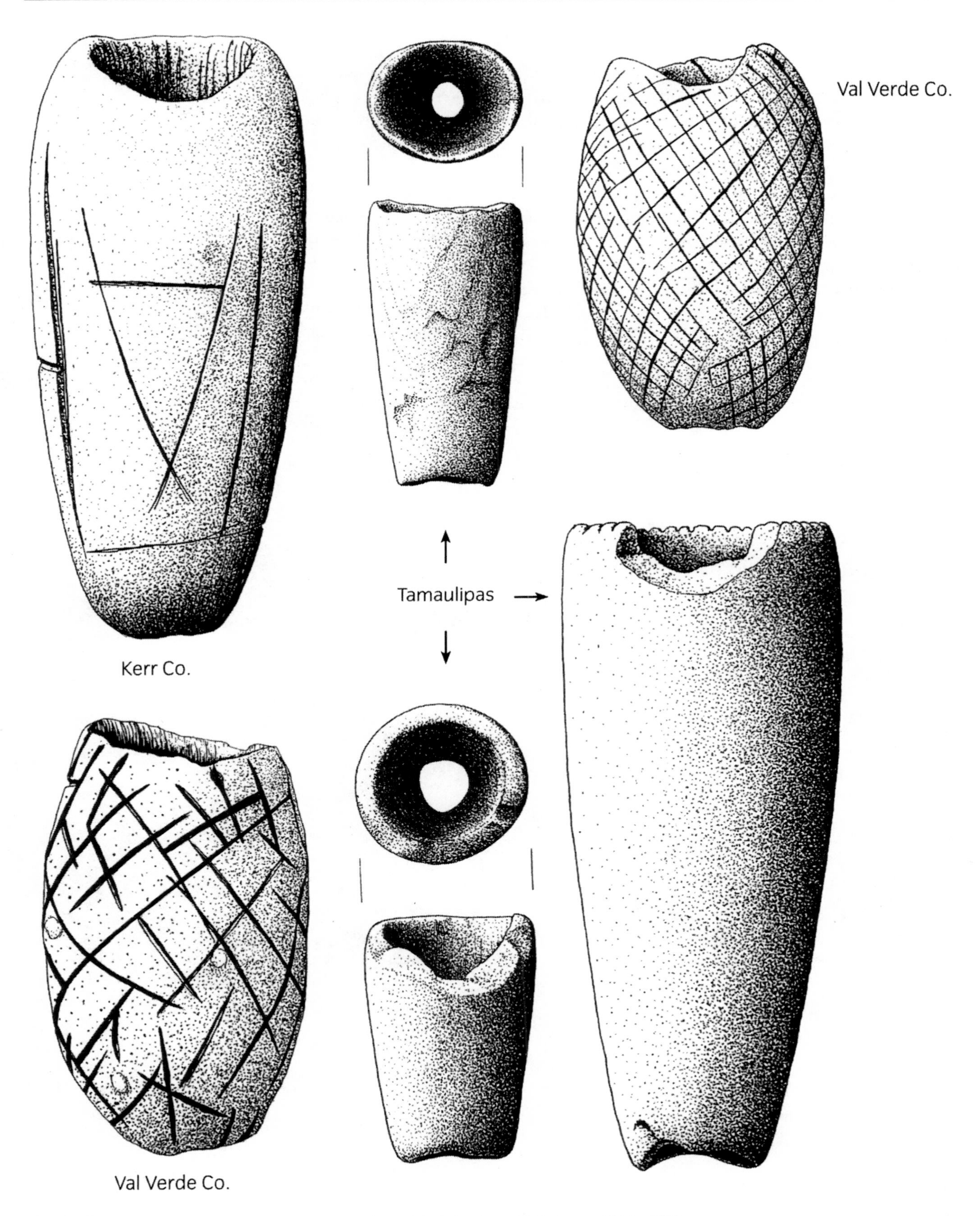

References: Bell 1972; Brown and Leneave 1987; Collins 1969, 2004; Greer 1968; Hester 1969a, 1980, 1994b; Newell and Krieger 1949; Ricklis 1994; Shafer 1973; Taylor and Highley 1995.

WACO ARTIFACTS AND OTHER GROOVED STONES

Waco artifacts (or "sinkers") are Early Archaic in age. Most are medium-sized stone artifacts, generally fashioned from some form of quartz, or quartzite, waterworn pebble. Specimens range from thin, small, and comparatively flat natural pebbles with worked notches in the ends, though crudely chipped and ground, to skillfully shaped objects of highly specialized forms that likely warrant a separate classification.

Their use is undetermined; some have hypothesized that they were intended to function as "sinker weights" or as "bolas" stones. In some areas, small, flat pebbles are notched at both ends and may have been "net sinkers." They do reflect the intensive effort seen on the Waco specimens.

Other grooved stone forms include the elongate, flared end, fully grooved quartzite forms found about 4500 BC at Buckeye Knoll. These had first been published by Hester and colleagues (1978), and they are also known from the Morhiss site and other sites in Victoria and Goliad counties.

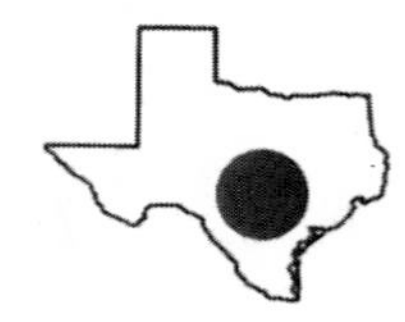

Distribution: Central Texas but also found in adjacent areas. **Period:** Early Archaic. **Sites:** Yarbrough and Miller; Scorpion Cave; Wheeler and Lake Dallas; Fort Hood; Polvo.

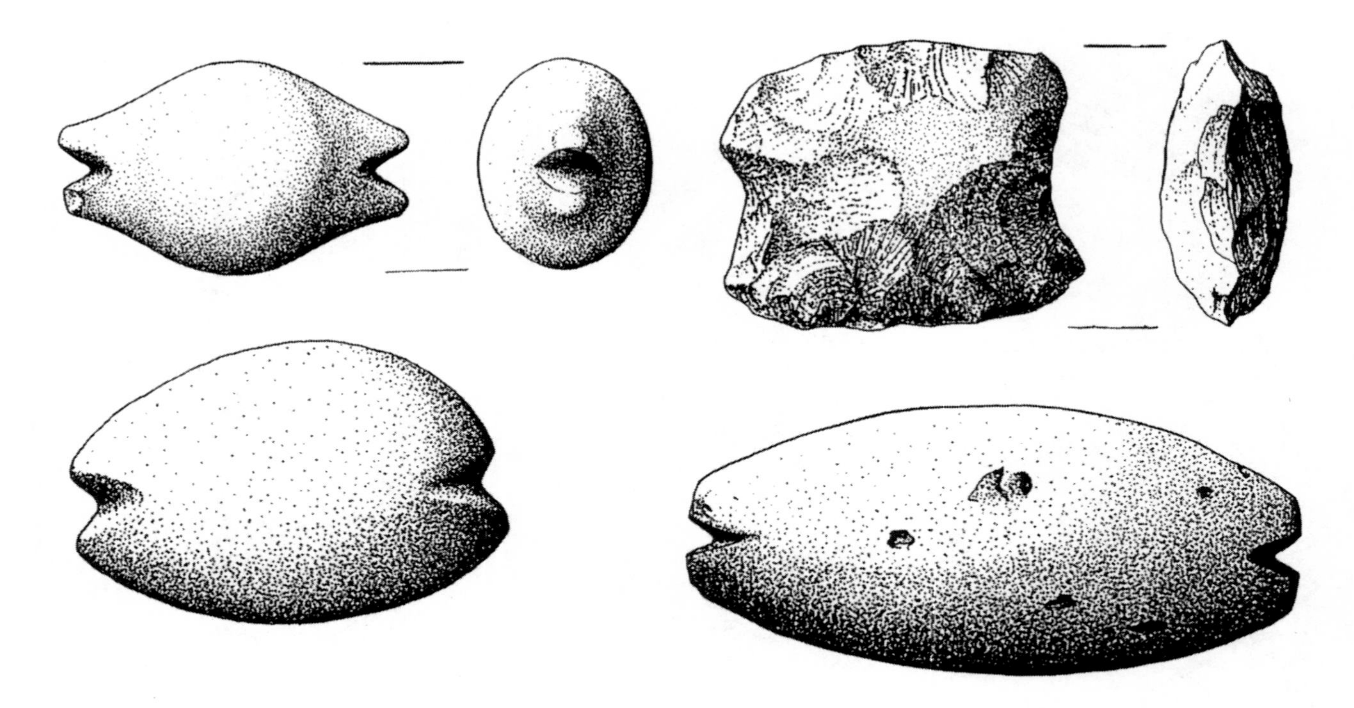

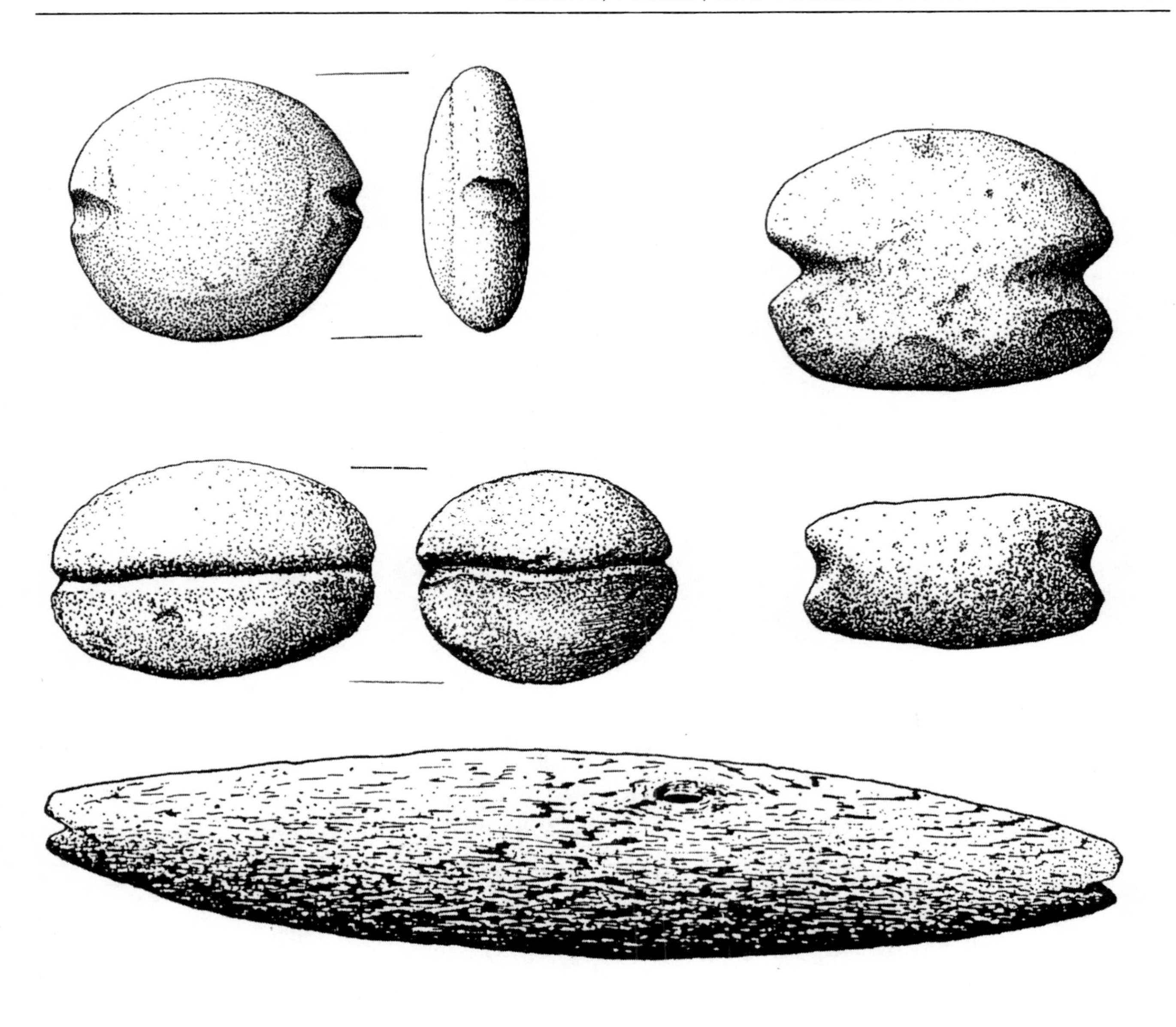

References: Boyd and Shafer 1997; Cloud et al. 1994; Collins 2004; Crook and Harris 1952; Fields et al. 1990a; Highley et al. 1978; Johnson 1962b; Ricklis 2009; Story et al. 1990; Thomas 1978; Watt 1938.

Appendix 1

Archaeological Societies in Texas

Big Bend Archaeological Society
P.O. Box 1
Big Bend National Park, TX 79834
cbbs@sulross.edu
http://www.bigbendarch.org/

Brazosport Archaeological Society
Brazosport Museum of Natural Science
400 College Drive
Clute, TX 77531
Contact: Johnney Pollan, jpollan@brazosport.cc.tx.us

Central Texas Archaeological Society
345 Rainbow Drive
Woodway, TX 76712
254-776-2900
central@texasarchaeology.org
http://texasarchaeology.org/

Coastal Bend Archeological Society
12912 McBurnett
Corpus Christi, TX 78410
361-241-9447
ibman172@aol.com

Collin County Archeological Society
c/o Heard Natural Science Museum
One Nature Place
McKinney, TX 75069

Concho Valley Archeological Society
Fort Concho, Texas
4222 North Rd. 3
Miles, TX 76861
Contact: Larry Riemenschneider, larremjo@wcc.net
915-653-8216

Deep East Texas Archeological Society
c/o Phyllis Summers
RR2, Box 50
Burkeville, TX 75932
409-565-2022
psummers@sabinenet.com

East Texas Archeological Society
P.O. Box 632398
Nacogdoches, TX 75961
TMdlbrk@aol.com

El Paso Archaeological Society
P.O. Box 4345
El Paso, TX 79914-4345
http://www.epas.com/

Fort Bend Archeological Society
Fort Bend Museum
500 Houston St.
Richmond, TX 77469
http://www.facebook.com/pages/
Fort-Bend-Archeological-Society/55005563362

Hill Country Archeological Association
P.O. Box 290393
Kerrville, TX 78029-0393
sanerjr@ktc.com
sodbustr@ktc.com

Houston Archeological Society
P.O. Box 13061
Houston, TX 77219-0631
713-983-8105
http://www.houstonarcheology.org/

Iraan Archeological Society
P.O. Box 183
Iraan, TX 79744

Llano Uplift Archeological Society
P.O. Box 302
Kingsland, TX 78639-0302
http://www.texasluas.org/

Midland Archaeological Society
P.O. Box 4224
Midland, TX 79704-4224
432-570-1253
http://midarcsoc.org/

Panhandle Archeological Society
P.O. Box 814
Amarillo, TX 79105
jdcrogers@sbcglobal.ne

Parker County Archeological Society
Doss Heritage and Culture Center
1400 Texas Drive
Weatherford, TX 76086
Contact: Laurie Moseley, moseley@airmail.net

Rio Grande Delta Archeological Society
8801 Boca Chica #54
Brownsville, TX 78521
riograndeltarch@aol.com

Southern Texas Archaeological Association
P.O. Box 791032
San Antonio, TX 78279-1032
http://www.staa.org/

Tarrant County Archaeological Society
P.O. Box 24679
Fort Worth, TX 76124-1679
817-295-0266
http://www.tarrantarch.org/

Texas Archeological Society
Center for Archaeological Research at UTSA
One UTSA Circle
San Antonio, TX 78249-0658
210-458-4393
tasoffice@txarch.org
http://www.txarch.org/

Texas Beyond History
(Txarch.org)
6900 N. Loop 1604 W
CAR at UTSA
San Antonio, TX 78249-0658
210-458-4393
http://www.texasbeyondhistory.net/

Travis County Archeological Society
P.O. Box 9250
Austin, TX 78766
travisco.arch@gmail.com
http://travis.txarch.org/

Valley of the Caddo Archeological Society
Paris, Texas
Contact: Dr. Richard Proctor, 903-785-0229

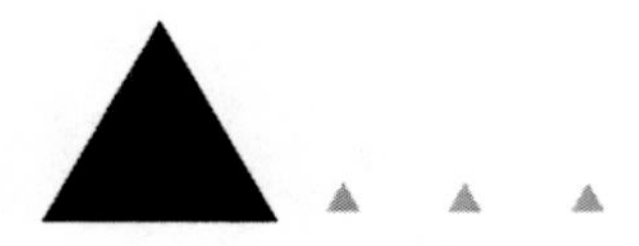

Appendix 2
Sources of Illustrations

CHAPTER 2

Cache biface: John Haberer collection; five of nine-piece cache found in Williamson County.
Cores: Wedge-shaped cores from Kerr County; Toyah core from Webb County; Clovis core from Museum of the Coastal Bend, Victoria; large core from Hollywood Park, Bexar County; small core from Killam Ranch, Webb County; Rusty Vereen collection; Dan Davis collection: Encino Park.
Fakes: TARL (Texas Archeological Research Laboratory, University of Texas at Austin).
Flake saws: Hale collection, Burnet County; Bill Birmingham collection: 41VT141; Museum of the Coastal Bend, Victoria.
Geofacts: Larry Oefinger collection: Oefinger Ranch; Wilson McKinney collection.
Hafted projectile points: Witte Museum, Shumla Cave.
Hafted scraper: Joe Guillory collection: hafted with fiber cord, northern Mexico.
Hafted Shumla: Joe Guillory collection: Shumla hafted with fiber cord and then coated with resin, shelter in Val Verde County.
Hammerstones: Richard and Ben McReynolds collections: Atascosa, Val Verde, and McMullen counties.
Overshot flake: 41BL323, AM305-55, Gault site, Bell County.
Partial overshot flake: 41BL323, AM392-F2, Gault site, Bell County.
Preforms of Sabinal points: Uvalde County.
Primary and secondary cortex flakes: 41BL323, AM292-A, Gault site, Bell County.
Starch fractures: Hollywood Park, Bexar County; Colha, Belize; 41TV1364.
Trade blank: Medina County.

CHAPTER 4

Dart Points

Abasolo: All from McMullen County, Texas.
Andice: Mrs. John West collection: Medina County; Don Kumpe collection: Starr and Zapata counties; David Calame collection: 41UV351, Uvalde County; Barry

Holleron collection: Sutherland Springs Sand Pit, Wilson County; Marc Land collection: Gillespie County; C. K. Chandler collection: Tehuacana Creek Limestone Co.

Angostura: Richard McReynolds collection: McMullen County; J. Neil Hernandez collection: 41BX502; J2 Ranch, 41VT6; Museum of the Coastal Bend, Victoria, 41VT141.

Arenosa: Rockshelters in Val Verde County.

Axtell: Calvin F. Mansell collection: Falls and McLennan counties.

Baker: Ben McReynolds collection: Val Verde County Rockshelter; Witte Museum, Shumla #5, 1933, Val Verde County; TARL: 41VV213, Baker site; 41VV74, Fate Bell Rockshelter.

Bandy: Witte Museum, Jacal Cañon, Val Verde County; Ben McReynolds collection: Atascosa and Val Verde counties; 5H, 41WM235; E. R. Long collection: Val Verde County; 55M, 41WM235; Rusty Vereen collection: Bexar County; Richard McReynolds collection: Val Verde County; Michael McReynolds collection: Val Verde County.

Barber: TARL: Barber site, Gillespie county, 41GL53, 41GL54, 41GL94; Mike Redwine collection: Bexar County, Harris Sand Pit; Tom Gudergan collection: Scorpion Cave.

Bell: Tom Atkinson collection: Corpus Christi Bay Dredge Spoil (island), Nueces County; Wedemeist site, 41VT78, Museum of the Coastal Bend, Victoria; Bill Birmingham and S. Schmiedlin collections: J2 Ranch, 41VT6; E. Sue Turner collection; Mike Krzywonski collection: #69, 41ZP8, Zapata County, #297 Falcon Lake; Tamaulipas, Mexico, #569, Zapata County.

Big Sandy: Mary Beth Trubitt collection: 3CL34, 3HS35, 3CA9, and 3P157, Arkansas, Henderson State University; Joseph Louvier collection: McFaddin Beach; V. V. Turner collection: Milam County, 41MM376; Lewis B. Smith collection: Baker's Creek, near Fannin-Delta County line; 41RF10, 11, Hopper's Landing, Refugio County.

Bulverde: Hale collection, Burnet County; Witte Museum, Friedrich collection; Richard McReynolds collection: Six Mile Creek, Bexar County, Val Verde County.

Carlsbad: All from Roy and Cindy Smyers collection: Culberson County.

Carrizo: TARL: Kothmann Ranch, Frio County.

Carrollton: TARL: Wood Pit site, 41DL; M. O. Laun site, 41KF; Obshner site, 41DL; Wheeler site, 41DL; TARL cast: Dallas and Kaufman counties; V. V. Turner collection: 41MM376, Milam County.

Castroville: Richard McReynolds collection: Bexar and Bandera counties; J. Neil Hernandez collection: Bexar County; Witte Museum, Bexar County, Friedrich collection; Hale collection.

Catán: La Salle, McMullen, and Webb counties.

Charcos: TARL: Riley family type collection from Coahuila, Mexico.

Clovis: Hondo Creek; 41ME75L, Medina County; Mike Redwine collection: Tom Green County, Tres Casal, Atascosa County; Dwain Rogers collection; Vince Ayers collection: Montgomery County, south side of Falcon Lake, Tamaulipas, Mexico; Richard Flores collection: Sutherland Springs Sand Pit, Wilson County; Nell Taylor collection: McFaddin Beach, 41JF50, courtesy of Joel Zachary Taylor.

Conejo: Ben McReynolds collection: Val Verde County Rockshelter; Earl Bly collection: Devil's River, Val Verde County; TARL cast: Castle Canyon, 41VV7 (J. Greer); Witte Museum, Shumla Cave, Val Verde County.

Dalton: Paul Tanner collection: McFaddin Beach, 41JF50; Bo Nelson collection: 41CP42, Camp County, "Dalton/Meserve," 41CP276; Mark Walters collection: surface, 41SM204, Smith County; Arkansas Archaeological Survey, Winthrop Rockefeller Institute, Chowning collection: Conway, Faulkner, and Perry counties, Arkansas, courtesy of Leslie C. "Skip" Stewart-Abernathy.

Darl: Hale collection; Burnet County; Richard McReynolds collection: Bell County; Harry Shafer collection: Stempede Creek Mounds #6 and #3, Bell County; Witte Museum, Bell County.

Delhi: Phillip Lee Green collection: Hopkins County; Don Black collection: Polk and San Jacinto counties, Trinity River drainage; David Crain collection: Matagorda County.

Desmuke: La Salle and McMullen counties.

Duran: TARL type collection: Coahuila, Mexico.

Early Stemmed Lanceolate: 41VT15 casts from Johnson-Heller site; Roy Ekstrum collection: Runge and Karnes counties; Geffert-Barrett collection: DeWitt County; Victor Mireles collection: Manahuilla Creek and San Antonio River, Goliad County.

Early Triangular: Ben McReynolds collection: Atascosa County, Goliad County, Bexar County.

Edgewood: Phillip Lee Green collection: 41HP237 Hopkins County; J. Neil Hernandez collection: Bexar County; Richard McReynolds collection: Val Verde County Rockshelter.

Elam: Phillip Lee Green collection: Tuinier Farm site, Hopkins County; Bo Nelson collection: 41CP25, 41CP42, Camp County, 41TT726, Titus County; TARL: D. Lehard collection: Hightower, Kirkpatrick, and W. Slaughter collections: HITT15.

Ellis: Richard McReynolds collection: Val Verde County; Robert Mallouf collection: Big Bend counties.

Ensor: Harry Shafer collection: Stempede Creek Mounds, Bell County; Richard McReynolds collection: La Salle, Atascosa, Val Verde, and Duval counties; Witte Museum, Eagle Cave, Val Verde County.

Evans: David Crain collection; David Benson collection: Vernon Parish, La.; Randy Holden Brand collection: Delhi, La., Lake Livingston; Paul Tanner and E. Sue Turner collections: Newton County.

Evant: David Crain collection: Coryell County; Oakalla, Burnet County; B. Arnold collection: Mound on Mathis Farm, Leon River, Coryell County; Oakalla, Burnet County.

Fairland: Floyd and Jody McKee collection: 41GU117; Witte Museum, 37-110, Bexar County, Friedrich collection; J. Neil Hernandez collection: Bexar County; TARL type collection cast; Ben McReynolds collection.

Firstview: Richard Rose collection: 41GA11, R2, Gaines County; 41GA11, R1, Gaines County; 41WK, W2-91, near Shifting Sands, Winkler County; 41AD, 1A2, Wyche Ranch, Winkler County; David Burrows collection; Larry Roach collection: Winkler County, 1979; David Crain collection: Gaines County.

Folsom: Michael Redwine collection: Bexar County, Harris Sand Pit; Bastrop, Culberson, and Crane counties. Tom Valley collection: Llano County, Sand Hills; Midland, Culberson, and Limestone counties. James Kasper collection: Aransas County; Hue Fadal collection: Kendall County; Carl Dillard collection: Atascosa County; James Richmond collection: Denton and Tarrant counties; Jon Gerber collection: Atascosa County; Buck Maspero collection: Goose Creek, Atascosa

County; Kirk Loftin collection: Live Oak County; John Boland collection: Hidalgo County; Al Lopez collection: 41DV133, Duval County; T. Wooten collection: Maverick County; Richard Rose collection: Winkler County, Folsom preforms 2296, 2305, 2414, 2433; pieces plus channel flake refits found from 1-04-01 through 4-18-06 at Shifting Sands site, 41WK21; Richard Dobie collection.

Folsom knife: Richard Rose collection: Shifting Sands site, 41WK21.

Frio: Richard and Ben McReynolds collections: Val Verde County Rockshelter; Shepherd Road, Bexar County; Camp Wood, Uvalde County; Witte Museum, Friedrich collection: Dimmit County; Keith Horton collection: Atascosa County, Charlotte; Boerne Stage Road, Bexar County.

Gary: David Crain collection: Harris County; Colorado River, Fayetteville; Curtis Hodge and Sammy Ray collections: Jasper County; Randy Heldenbrand collection: Marksville, La.; two of petrified wood.

Godley: TARL: 41HI1 Kyle site 41TV39; Baird site, Brian Miles collection: Bell County; Waco Lake Testing TASP 1964 (Kimbal and Klondike varieties).

Golondrina: Joe Guillory collection: Harris Sand Pit, south Bexar County; 41VT141, Museum of the Coastal Bend, Victoria; Richard and Ben McReynolds collections: San Miguel Creek, Atascosa County.

Gower: J. Neil Hernandez collection: Bexar County; Richard McReynolds collection: Burnet County; Travis Lake, Bexar County; 41VT3, Victoria County, Museum of the Coastal Bend, Victoria.

Hidalgo: Don Kumpe collection: Hidalgo, Starr, and Zapata counties; Terry Kumpe collection: Starr County; Bill Yoder collection: Tamaulipas, Mexico, Zapata County; Mike Krzywonski collection: Tamaulipas, Mexico, Zapata County.

Hoxie: V. V. Turner collection: found by Lane Greyson, Huntsville, Walker County; Museum of the Coastal Bend, Victoria; Calhoun and Victoria counties.

Hueco: Glass Mountains and Bear Creek areas of the Big Bend; Homer Mills collection (Alpine), courtesy of Robert Mallouf.

Jetta: TARL: 41TV151, Wilson-Leonard (41WM235); John Garrett collection: 41RE120.

Johnson: From Arkansas sites: Mary Beth Trubitt collection: 3CI34, 3HS28, 3GA9, 3P13, Henderson State University; Bo Nelson collection; Margaret I. Bunce McReynolds collection: Franklin County, AR.

Keithville: Bo Nelson collection: Sulphur River, Delta County, 41CP42, 41CP241, 41CP303. David Crain collection: Toledo Bend, Angelina County; Lake Livingston, Lee County; Earl Bly collection: Sabine County.

Kent: Phillip Lee Green collection: Stout's Creek, Hopkins County; TARL type collection: 41TT15, Addicks Reservoir.

Kinney: J. Neil Hernandez collection: Bexar County; Richard McReynolds collection: Uvalde County; McMullen County; La Salle County; J2 Ranch, Victoria County.

Kirk: Curtis Hodge collection: counties and parishes from both sides of the Sabine River, lower Sabine River drainage.

Kisatchie: Curtis Hodge collection: Newton County, Jasper County, X-John Fish, Angelina County, Vernon Parish, and Calcasieu Parish, La.; David Crain collection: east Texas.

Laguna: Ted Nemec Jr. collection: Williamson County; Jay Roach collection: Bexar County; James Wright collection: Travis County; Todd Chism collection: Bexar and Kerr counties; Billy Woods collection: Bell and Lynn counties.

La Jita: T. C. Hill collection: 41UV29; TARL from casts, 41BN63; Barney Sam collection: Bexar County near Helotes.

Lange: Jody and Floyd McKee collection: 41GU117; 41VT141, Victoria County; J2 Ranch, Victoria County; Coleto Creek, 41VT6, Victoria County, Museum of the Coastal Bend.

Langtry: Ben McReynolds collection: Val Verde and McMullen counties.

Lerma: Ray Myers collection: Falcon Lake, Zapata County; Dorothy Lee Hindes collection; Bill Birmingham collection: 41VT6, J2 Ranch, Victoria County.

Marcos: Barber site, Gillespie County, redrawn from *La Tierra* 14 (1) (1987); Randy Haiduk site, 41KA23, Karnes County, *La Tierra* 2 (1984); Hale collection: Burnet County; Ben McReynolds collection: Val Verde County Rockshelter.

Marshall: Hale collection: Burnet County; Witte Museum, Friedrich collection, Kendall County; J. Neil Hernandez collection: west Bexar County.

Martindale: Ben McReynolds collection: Val Verde County; Richard McReynolds collection: Val Verde County; Parker Ranch, Kimble County; Hale collection, Burnet County; Dan Davis collection: Walker Ranch, Bexar County; Terry Kelly collection: Val Verde County.

Matamoros: Richard McReynolds collection: McMullen County; Webb County; La Salle County.

Merrell: TARL: Merrell site and Landslide.

Midland: Richard Rose collection: Shifting Sands site, 41WK21, Winkler County, Andrews County; Floyd and Jody McKee collection: 41GU117; Paul Tanner collection: McFaddin Beach, 41JF50; David Burrows collection.

Milnesand: Shannon Jones collection: Copano Bay, San Patricio County; Jimmy Bluhm collection: Hopper's Landing, 41RF10, Museum of the Coastal Bend, Victoria; McNeil Gonzales Ranch, 41VT14/sand pit; Richard Rose collection: Sand Hills, Andrews County; Wyche Ranch, Scharbauer Ranch, Midland County; plowed hill north of Big Spring, Howard County.

Montell: J. Neil Hernandez collection: Bexar County; Ben McReynolds collection: Gillespie County; Hale collection; Richard McReynolds collection: Bexar County.

Morhiss: Museum of the Coastal Bend, Victoria, 41VT15, 41VT141.

Morrill: TARL type collection: H. E. Womack collection, Allen site.

Motley: Lewis B. Smith collection: Navasota River, Limestone County, Hopper's Landing, Refugio County (41RF10, 11), Museum of the Coastal Bend, Victoria; Bill Young collection: 41RK200, Mission San Jose de la Nazoni.

Neches: Bill Young collection: 41HI242; 41NV201, 41NV202, Navarro County sites, Chambers Creek; Lewis B. Smith collection: Limestone County.

Nolan: Hale collection, Burnet County; Ben and Richard McReynolds collection: Val Verde County.

Paisano: Roy and Cindy Smyers collection: Culberson County; Richard McReynolds collection: Val Verde County.

Palmer: Curtis Hodge collection: counties and parishes from both sides of the Sabine River, lower Sabine River drainage.

Palmillas: Robert Mallouf collection; TARL type collection: 41TT15, Addicks Reservoir; Floyd and Jody Mckee collection: 41GU117; Ben McReynolds collection: Val Verde County.

Pandale: Ben and Richard McReynolds collection: Val Verde County rockshelter; Homer Mills collection (Alpine), courtesy of Robert Mallouf.

Pandora: TARL type collection.

Pedernales: Ben McReynolds collection: Shepherd Road, Bexar County; STAA Eagles Bluff, 41ME147, Medina County; Steve Schwarz, Tony Hardson, and Ben

McReynolds collections: Kerr County; Cliff Scott collection: Buda, Tex.; J2 Ranch, 41VT6; Tommy Long collection: Poteet, Atascosa County.

Pelican: Don Black collection; Earl Bly collection: Sabine County; Joe Louvier collection: McFaddin Beach; Curtis Hodge collection: Newton, Sabine, and Jasper counties, Vernon Parish and Sabine Parish, La.

Plainview: Richard Rose collection: W2-95, Winkler County; Rex Rodgers site, Panhandle-Plains Historical Museum; TARL casts: San Augustine Plains, N.Mex.; Plainview site, Texas Memorial Museum, Hale County; Brian Miles collection: Gault site.

Pontchartrain: Don Black collection: San Jacinto County; Lewis B. Smith collection: North Sulphur drainage in Fannin County; V. V. Turner collection: petrified wood, Polk County, off the Neches River; TARL: 41HS16.

Red River knives: Joe Guillory collection.

Refugio: TARL type collection; Leyendecker collection; Riley family collection; Richard Brady collection: Nuevo Leon, Mexico; Bill Yoder collection: Falcon Reservoir, Tamaulipas, Mexico.

San Patrice: David Crain collection: Lee and Angelina counties, Sabine Pass and Leesville, La.; Earl Bly collection: Sabine County; Clayton Vandergriff collection: tributaries of the San Jacinto, Harris County; Panhandle-Plains Historical Museum, Rex Rodgers site, McKenzie Reservoir.

Scottsbluff: Joe Guillory collection: south Bexar County sand pit; David Crain collection: edge-fractured specimen from Keith Brown, Bluff Creek, Lee County; J. Neil Hernandez collection: Bexar County; Dorothy Lee Hindes collection: McMullen County; Clayton Vandergriff collection: Harris County.

Shumla: Ben McReynolds collection: Val Verde County Rockshelter.

Sinner: David Beason collection: Vernon Parish, La.

St. Charles: Curtis Hodge collection: Sabine and Jasper County, McFaddin Beach (41JF50); Vernon Parish and Calcasieu Parish, La.

St. Mary's Hall: David Crain collection: Travis County, Horse Creek, Coryell County; Jay Roach collection: Cibolo Creek Sand Pit, Wilson County; Terry Kumpe collection: Cedar Gap, Taylor County.

Tortugas: La Salle, McMullen, and Victoria counties; Brian Miles collection: point with asphaltum on both sides from Baird site, Bell County.

Travis: Floyd and Jody McKee collection: 41GU117; David Crain collection: Oakalla, Burnet County; Leon River, Hamilton County; TARL: 41TT15 cast from type collection.

Trinity: TARL casts: 6-154: 130-h-1629, 146-1-1589, 126-L-667.

Uvalde: Richard McReynolds collection: Bandera County; J. Neil Hernandez collection: Bexar County; Robert Mallouf collection: Center for Big Bend Studies, Big Bend area.

Val Verde: Richard McReynolds collection: all from rockshelters on the Pecos River.

Van Horn: Roy and Cindy Smyers collection: Culberson County.

Wells: Bob Bonneau collection: Bell County; Leon River, Coryell County; Mathis Farm, Leon River, Coryell County; Oakalla, Burnet County; Lampasas County; Pat Gilstrap collection: central Texas; Leon River, Gatesville, 41CVH, Coryell County; David Crain collection: Travis County.

Williams: TARL: H. E. Womack collection.

Wilson: David Crain collection: Bluff Creek, Lee County, Austin County; Wilson Co. Elison; Bastrop County; High Island, McFaddin Beach; Wilson Co. Richard Mentzer; Coryell County.

Yarbrough: Phillip Lee Green collection: Tuinier Farm site, Hopkins County; TARL: H. E. Womack collection.

Young: TARL type collection.
Zephyr: Hugh O'Brien collection: Comanche County; R. E. Forrester collection: 41SE17, Stephens County.
Zorra: TARL: 41VV74, Fate Bell Rockshelter.

Arrow Points

Alazan: Bear Creek, Big Bend, 41BS466, 41BS522; Robert Mallouf collection: John Z. and Exa Means cache, Center for Big Bend Studies; Robert Haynes collection (Alpine); Homer Mills collection (Alpine).
Alba: Bo Nelson collection: 41CP241; TARL collection: 41CE19; TARL cast; Earl Bly collection: Sabine County.
Anaqua: Hopper's Landing, Refugio County; different sites in Victoria County, Museum of the Coastal Bend, Victoria.
Bassett: R. L. Turner collection: Camp County, Carpenter site, 41CP5; Bo Nelson collection: 41CP25.
Bonham: TARL type collection; Harry Shafer collection: Smith and Waller counties; Don Black collection: Polk and San Jacinto counties.
Bulbar Stemmed: Museum of the Coastal Bend, Victoria, 41VT12, 41VT81 (Linn Lake), 41CL2, Calhoun County.
Cameron: Mike Krzywonski collection: Cameron County; John Boland collection: Cameron and Hidalgo counties; Don Kumpe collection: Hidalgo County; Armando Vela collection: Hidalgo County, Tamaulipas, Mexico.
Caracara: Don Kumpe, John Boland, Doug Bryan, and Richard Brady collections: Zapata, Starr, and Hidalgo counties; Tamaulipas, Mexico.
Catahoula: Clayton Vandergriff collection: Harris County.
Chadbourne: TARL: 41CK87, GP Abilene; Taylor County, 41TA58, 41TA66; Coke County 41CK9, 41CK24, 41CK14, 41CK87.
Cuney: TARL type collection; T. C. Hill collection: 41DM31; Earl Bly collection: Sabine County; Museum of the Coastal Bend, Victoria.
Deadman's: Panhandle-Plains Historical Museum, McKenzie Reservoir, Palo Duro Canyon, Pop Technology and Rockshelter, Swisher County.
Diablo: Robert Mallouf collection: John Z. and Exa Means cache, Y6 Hills, western Jeff Davis County, Center for Big Bend Studies.
Edwards: Witte Museum, Friedrich collection, Atascosa County; Richard McReynolds collection: Bexar County; Tom Atkinson collection: McMullen County.
Fresno: Don Kumpe collection: Hidalgo County; Jimmy Bluhm collection: Harper's Landing, 41RF41; John Boland collection: Hidalgo County; Mike Krzywonski collection: Cameron County, Tamaulipas, Mexico.
Friley: Mark Walters collection: 41SM195A, Smith and Gregg counties; Bo Nelson collection: 41TT266, 41TT730; Earl Bly collection: Sabine County; Phillip Lee Green collection: 41HP237, Hopkins County, Tuinier Farm.
Garza: Richard Rose collection: 41AD2, Ector, Tom Green, Andrews, Midland, and Pecos counties; TARL: Sayles Coll.; Coahuila, Mexico; Barth Robbins collection: Loving and Ector counties.
Guerrero: CAR, UTSA: Alamo, 41BX6; Mission Rosario, Goliad County; Mission Espiritu Santo, 41GO35; 41VT3; Padre Island, Nueces County; Museum of the Coastal Bend, Victoria; specimen G is light green bottle glass.
Harrell: Panhandle-Plains Historical Museum, Greenbelt site, 41DY17.

Hayes: TARL casts; Michael Walker collection: Pike County, Ark.

Livermore: Homer Mills and Robert Haynes collections (Alpine), courtesy of Robert Mallouf, Center for Big Bend Studies.

Lott: Richard Rose collection: 41AD2, Ector, Tom Green, Andrews, Midland, and Pecos counties; Barth Robbins collection: Midland, Pecos, and Ector counties, Sand Hills blowout; TARL: 41TA66.

Lozenge: Ed Mokry collection: 41NU33, Nueces County; Museum of the Coastal Bend, Victoria, 41VT10, 41VT12, 41VT34, 41VT81, 41CL2.

Maud: Burial points from Carpenter site, 41CP5, Camp County, Tommy Johns collection: BTAS 49; Bo Nelson collection: 41TT730.

McGloin: Tom Atkinson collection: 41SP238, San Patricio County; Ed Mokry collection: 41NU164, Oso Creek, Pequeine and Pradera sites, Nueces County.

Means: John A. and Exa Means cache, Y6 Hills of Jeff Davis County, courtesy of Robert Mallouf, Center for Big Bend Studies; Robert Haynes collection (Alpine); Homer Mills collection (Alpine).

Moran: TARL: 41CK87, 41HL10, 41TA58, Coke, Nolan, and Taylor counties.

Padre: John Boland collection: Hidalgo County; Ed Mokry collection: Nueces County; Mike Krzywonski collection: Zapata County, Cameron County; coastal Tamaulipas, Mexico.

Perdiz: Tom Atkinson collection: San Patricio County, 41SP238; Richard McReynolds collection: Val Verde, Bexar, and McMullen counties; Witte Museum, Friedrich collection, Atascosa County.

Revilla: Don Kumpe, James Boyd, Douglas Bryan, Erick Kruger, and Mike Krzywonski collections: northern portion of Falcon Reservoir, 41ZP83, 41ZP154.

Sabinal: Allen Mitchell collection: Uvalde County; Richard McReynolds collection: Val Verde County.

Scallorn: Clayton Vandergriff collection: Lee and Harris counties; Museum of the Coastal Bend, Victoria; Richard McReynolds collection: La Salle County; Witte Museum, Friedrich collection, Atascosa County; Richard McReynolds collection: Bexar, La Salle, and McMullen counties; Tom Atkinson collection: Heinz Bay, Calhoun County; Bill Hindes collection: San Miguel and Atascosa counties.

Starr: Don Kumpe collection: Hidalgo and Starr counties; Eugene Pilarczyk collection: Zapata County.

Steiner: Mark Walters collection: 41SM195A; Earl Bly collection: Sabine County; Museum of the Coastal Bend, Victoria; Coryell County.

Talco: R. L. Turner collection: burial from Carpenter site, Camp County, 41CP5.

Tortugas point with asphaltum: Baird site, Bell County; Brian Miles collection: Lake Jackson.

Toyah: Bill Yoder collection: Falcon Reservoir; Don Kumpe collection: Hidalgo County; T. C. Hill collection: Zavala County; Ben McReynolds collection: Val Verde County.

Turney: TARL: Miklas site, Trinidad site, D. O. Harper collection: Kirkpatrick, Conant Farm, 41DL, Haymarket site, Lake Dallas, Walnut site, TARL cast; Michal Walters collection: Case County, Ark.

Washita: Panhandle-Plains Historical Museum, courtesy of Jeff Indeck.

Zapata: Don Kumpe collection: northern portion of Falcon Reservoir, 41ZP83, 41ZP154.

Zavala: Dimmit County 41DM14.

CHAPTER 5

Bifaces and Unifaces

Albany bifaces: David Black collection; Jerry Collins collection: Goliad County; David Crain collection: Sabine Parish, La., Matagorda County, Sabine County, Tex., Lake Livingston.

Bristol bifaces: CAR, UTSA: C. K. Chandler collection.

Button scrapers: Mike Krzywonski collection: Cameron County; Tamaulipas, Mexico; John Boland collection: Hidalgo County; Don Kumpe collection.

Clear Fork uniface and biface: 41VT41, Victoria County.

Corner-tang: Joe Guillory and Jay Roach collections: Knibbe Ranch, Spring Branch, Comal County.

Dalton adz: TARL: T. C. Hill coll., Zavala Co.

End scrapers: Richard Rose collection: Shifting Sands site, Winkler County; Tom Hester collection: 41ME88, 41ME91; Witte Museum; Pickens collection: Gillespie County.

Gahagan: Harry Shafer collection: 41HM2D, Horsehead Creek Midden.

Gravers: CAR: Varga site, 41ED28; Richard Rose collection: Folsom gravers from Shifting Sands site.

Guadalupe biface: M. F. Palmer collection: Frio County; David Calame collection: Medina County; Floyd and Jody McKee collection: 41GU117, Guadalupe County.

Gunflints: Excavations at the Alamo, 41BX6; UTSA; French, English, and native made, Bexar County.

Kerrville bifaces: Wright Friday collection: Friday Ranch, Uvalde County.

Multinotched Early Archaic lithics: Carey Weber collection: 41BL323; Bill Birmingham collection: Kerr County; John Haberer collection: Comal County; La Jita site, 41UV21.

Nueces biface and uniface: Richard McReynolds collection: La Salle and McMullen counties.

Olmos biface: TARL: Riley family collection.

Perforators/drills: John Boland collection: Uvalde County; Hale collection: Burnet county; Ben McReynolds collection: Val Verde County; Richard McReynolds collection: Shepherd Road (red quartzite), Bexar County.

Pin drills: Terry Kumpe, Lily Kumpe, and Don Kumpe collections: northeast Tamaulipas, Mexico; Mike Krzywonski collection: Cameron County.

Pipe Creek biface: J. Neil Hernandez collection: 41BX502; Randy Snider collection: Bexar County; David Calame collection; Richard McReynolds collection: Bexar County.

Potlidded biface: Larry Oefinger collection: Oefinger Ranch, Medina County.

San Saba knives: TARL: 41VT141; Joe Guillory collection; David Crain collection: McLennan and Limestone county line.

Sequent flake: Cibolo Creek, Bexar County.

Four-beveled biface: Joe Guillory collection: Coryell County.

Two-beveled biface: Two of a six-piece cache in San Saba County. Bill Breckenridge collection; O'Connor Ranch, Bundick Lake, Goliad County; Kai Buckert collection.

CHAPTER 6

Abrading stones: Richard McReynolds collection: McMullen County; 41VT141, Victoria County; Museum of the Coastal Bend, Victoria; Jimmy Bluhm collection: Coleto Creek, Goliad County.

Altered quartzite cobbles: Museum of the Coastal Bend, Victoria; INVISTA casts, 41VT98.

Axe, red hematite: TARL, Bradfield collection: Earl Vaughn Farm, Morris County (6 1/2 lbs.).

Bannerstones: 1/2 banded slate, Frank Dudley collection: south of Mier, Tamaulipas, Mexico, Rancho Penitas, owned by Robert Gonzales, east of Rio Alamo; INVISTA casts, 41VT98.

Boatstones: Steve Schwarz and Tony Hardin collections: burned rock midden, Kerr County; Joe Guillory collection: Sutherland Springs Sand Pit, Wilson County.

Bowl with mortar and pestle: Starr County.

Celt: Joe Guillory collection: Sam Rayburn Reservoir.

Geofacts: Wilson McKinney collection.

Gorgets: Don Kumpe collection: Starr County, Falcon Lake, and Tamaulipas, Mexico; Dick Clardy collection: Nuevo Leon, Mexico; Scott Reilly collection: Cibolo Creek; Bucky Densford collection: Pipe Creek, Tex.

Grooved and polished quartzite stones: Vic Urban site, 41VT12; Victoria Barge Canal, 41VT98.

Incised and engraved stones: Steve Portillo collection: Val Verde County Rockshelter; Walt and Ruth Carruthers collection: San Francisco Canyon, Terrell County; Mike Redwine collection: 41BL323, Gault site; Robert Flores collection: Bexar County.

Maul: Richard McReynolds collection: Northeast Texas.

Milling stones, metate, mano, pestle: Val Verde, Brewster, and El Paso counties.

Modified quartzite pebbles: C. K. Chandler collection: 41EL18, Ellis County; Claude Haby collection: Uvalde County; Calvin F. Mansell collection: Bexar County.

Painted pebbles in black: Ben McReynolds collection: 41VV156; Michael McReynolds collection: Val Verde County; Terry Kelly collection: Coahuila, Mexico, opposite Pecos River; Keith Grunswald collection.

Painted pebbles in red: Cain Ranch, Zavala County.

Palette: Ruth and Walt Carruthers collection: San Francisco Canyon, Terrell County.

Pendants: Ben McReynolds collection: Val Verde County; Don Kumpe collection: Starr County; Howard and Marilyn Hunt collection: Val Verde County; Jack St. John collection: Medina County; Scott Riley collection: Cibolo Creek, Comal County.

Pipes: Mike Krzywonski collection: Mosquito Cave (41VV215), Tamaulipas, Mexico; Jim Schroeder collection: Tamaulipas, Mexico; Mike Ryan collection: hematite, Nuevo Leon, Mexico; Troy Bauer collection: Falcon Lake, Tamaulipas, Mexico; five views of stone pipe with bone insert: Steve Schwarz collection: midden in Kerr County; Mike Krzywonski collection: Tamaulipas, Mexico; Thomas Wooten collection: Val Verde County Rockshelter; George S. Meyer collection: Still Canyon, Val Verde County; Connie and Keith Mohan collection: Falcon Lake, Tamaulipas, Mexico; James Boyd collection: stone pipe and bone stem from juvenile burial, Falcon Lake, Tamaulipas, Mexico.

Pitted stones: Leonard Phillips collection: Red River County.

Plummets: Joe Guillory collection: Wilson County Sand Pit; INVISTA cast: 41VT98; Hale collection, Burnet County.

Shaft straighteners: C. K. Chandler, BRM, Terrell County; Harry Shafer collection: vesicular basalt, Rattle Snake Canyon, Val Verde; TARL: Uvalde County; Tom Miller collection: 41KR38, Kerr County; Jimmy Moos collection: 41BX708.

Waco "sinker": Calvin F. Mansell collection: Falls and McLennan counties; John Boland collection: Starr County; Ben McReynolds collection: Atascosa and Goliad counties; Frank Dudley collection: hematite, Tamaulipas, Mexico; Larry Wilhoit collection: Ellis County; Erwin Kramer collection: petrified palmwood, DeWitt County; 41VT141.

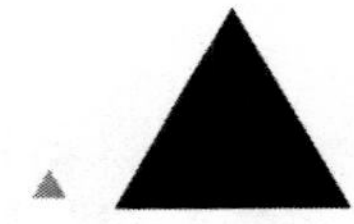

Appendix 3

County Symbols for Archaeological Site Designation: Texas (41)

County	Symbol
Anderson	AN
Andrews	AD
Angelina	AG
Aransas	AS
Archer	AR
Armstrong	AM
Atascosa	AT
Austin	AU
Bailey	BA
Bandera	BN
Bastrop	BP
Baylor	BY
Bee	BE
Bell	BL
Bexar	BX
Blanco	BC
Borden	BD
Bosque	BQ
Bowie	BW
Brazoria	BO
Brazos	BZ
Brewster	BS
Briscoe	BI
Brooks	BK
Brown	BR
Burleson	BU
Burnet	BT
Caldwell	CW
Calhoun	CL
Callahan	CA
Cameron	CF
Camp	CP
Carson	CZ
Cass	CS
Castro	CAS
Chambers	CH
Cherokee	CE
Childress	CI
Clay	CY
Cochran	CQ
Coke	CK
Coleman	CN
Collin	COL
Collingsworth	CG
Colorado	CD
Comal	CM
Comanche	CJ
Concho	CC
Cooke	CO
Coryell	CV
Cottle	CT
Crane	CR
Crockett	CX
Crosby	CB
Culberson	CU
Dallam	DA
Dallas	DL
Dawson	DS
Deaf Smith	DF
Delta	DT
Denton	DN
DeWitt	DW
Dickens	DK
Dimmit	DM
Donley	DY
Duval	DV
Eastland	EA
Ector	EC
Edwards	ED
Ellis	EL
El Paso	EP
Erath	ER
Falls	FA
Fannin	FN
Fayette	FY
Fisher	FS
Floyd	FD
Foard	FD
Fort Bend	FB
Franklin	FK
Freestone	FT
Frio	FR

County	Code
Gaines	GA
Galveston	GV
Garza	GR
Gillespie	GL
Glasscock	GC
Goliad	GD
Gonzales	GZ
Gray	GV
Grayson	GS
Gregg	GG
Grimes	GM
Guadalupe	GU
Hale	HA
Hall	HL
Hamilton	HM
Hansford	HF
Hardeman	HX
Hardin	HN
Harris	HR
Harrison	HS
Hartley	HT
Haskell	HK
Hays	HY
Hemphill	HH
Henderson	HE
Hidalgo	HG
Hill	HI
Hockley	HQ
Hood	HD
Hopkins	HP
Houston	HO
Howard	HW
Hudspeth	HZ
Hunt	HU
Hutchinson	HC
Irion	IR
Jack	JA
Jackson	JK
Jasper	JP
Jeff Davis	JD
Jefferson	JF
Jim Hogg	JH
Jim Wells	JW
Johnson	JN
Jones	JS
Karnes	KA
Kaufman	KF
Kendall	KE
Kenedy	KN
Kern	KT
Kerr	KR
Kimble	KM
King	KG
Kinney	KY
Kleberg	KL
Knox	KX
Lamar	LR
Lamb	LA
Lampasas	LM
La Salle	LS
Lavaca	LC
Lee	LE
Leon	LN
Liberty	LB
Limestone	LT
Lipscomb	LP
Live Oak	LK
Llano	LL
Loving	LV
Lubbock	LU
Lynn	LY
Madison	MA
Marion	MR
Martin	MT
Mason	MS
Matagorda	MG
Maverick	MV
McCulloch	MK
McLennan	ML
McMullen	MC
Medina	ME
Menard	MN
Midland	MD
Milam	MM
Mills	MI
Mitchell	MH
Montague	MU
Montgomery	MQ
Moore	MO
Morris	MX
Motley	MY
Nacogdoches	NA
Navarro	NV
Newton	NW
Nolan	NL
Nueces	NU
Ochiltree	OO
Oldham	OL
Orange	OR
Palo Pinto	PP
Panola	PN
Parker	PR
Parmer	PM
Pecos	PC
Polk	PK
Potter	PT
Presidio	PS
Rains	RA
Randall	RD
Reagan	RG
Real	RE
Red River	RR
Reeves	RV
Refugio	RF
Roberts	RB
Robertson	RT
Rockwall	RW
Runnels	RN
Rusk	RK
Sabine	SB
San Augustine	SA
San Jacinto	SJ
San Patricio	SP
San Saba	SS
Schleicher	SL
Scurry	SC
Shackelford	SF
Shelby	SY
Sherman	SH
Smith	SM
Somervell	SV
Starr	SR
Stephens	SE
Sterling	ST
Stonewall	SN
Sutton	SU
Swisher	SW

Tarrant	TR
Taylor	TA
Terrell	TE
Terry	TY
Throckmorton	TH
Titus	TT
Tom Green	TG
Travis	TV
Trinity	TN
Tyler	TL
Upshur	UR
Upton	UT
Uvalde	UV
Val Verde	VV
Van Zandt	VN
Victoria	VT
Walker	WA
Waller	WL
Ward	WR
Washington	WT
Webb	WB
Wharton	WH
Wheeler	WE
Wichita	WC
Wilbarger	WG
Willacy	WY
Williamson	WM
Wilson	WN
Winkler	WK
Wise	WS
Wood	WD
Yoakum	YK
Young	YN
Zapata	ZP
Zavala	ZV

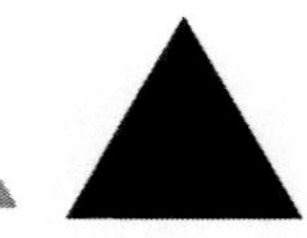

Appendix 4

Texas Archeology Awareness Month

TEXAS HISTORICAL COMMISSION
real places telling real stories

Office of the State Archeologist, Texas Historical Commission.

THE ANNUAL Texas Archeology Awareness Month was first celebrated in 1989. Governor Clements made the official proclamation, and concurrent resolutions were read in the Texas House of Representatives and Senate. Archeology Month, which takes place in October each year, is a program of events oriented toward informing the public about archaeology in the state and involving them in archeological activities. The program focuses on how individuals can get involved in a positive way, what makes archaeology interesting, and what the past has to offer. The program reflects a continuing tradition of commitment to public awareness and involvement and has developed into a major public relations effort that involves museums, historical societies, libraries, schools, and other federal, state, municipal, and private organizations. The Archeology Awareness Committee has an official logo (above), a motto, and information on sources of video, filmstrips, and speakers. They also have promotional materials and suggestions for activities.

Dedicated members of the Texas Historical Commission, the Texas Archeological Society, and the Texas Archeological Stewardship Network organize Archeology Month events. Local archeological and historical societies, museums, state and federal agencies, private companies, and individuals also sponsor events through the state. For more information:

Archeology Division
Texas Historical Commission
P.O. Box 12276
Austin, TX 78711-2276
Phone: 512-463-6096
Email: archeology@thc.state.tx.us
Website: www.thc.state.tx.us

Appendix 5

Groups to Contact Around the State

THE FOLLOWING are agencies and institutions that may be able to provide either information or assistance in matters concerning the study and preservation of archeological sites in Texas.

Amistad National Recreation Area
4121 Veterans Blvd.
Del Rio, TX 78840
830-775-7491
Fax: 830-778-9248
http://www.nps.gov/amis

Baylor University, Mayborn Museum Complex
(formerly Stecker Museum)
One Bear Place # 97154
Waco, TX 76798-7154
254-710-1110
Fax: 254-710-1173
http://www.baylor.edu/mayborn

Catholic Archives of Texas
P.O. Box 13124, Capitol Station
Austin, TX 78711
512-476-6296
cat@onr.com

Center for American History
Dolph Briscoe Center for American History
University of Texas at Austin
Sid Richardson Hall 2.101
1 University Station D1100
Austin, TX 78712-0335
Reference desk: 512-495-4532
Information desk: 512-495-4518
http://www.cah.utexas.edu

Center for Environmental Archaeology
University of North Texas
Department of Geography
P.O. Box 305279
1704 W Mulberry, EESAT 210
Denton, TX 76203
940-565-2091
Fax: 940-369-7550
geog@unt.edu
http://www.geog.unt.edu/research.html

Council of Texas Archeologists
Cultural Resource Program
P.O. Box 5218
Austin, TX 78763-5218
http://www.counciloftexasarcheologists.org/

Fort Concho National Historic Landmark
630 South Oakes Street
San Angelo, TX 76903
325-481-2646
http://www.fortconcho.com/

Gault School of Archaeological Research
Texas State University, San Maneos
P.O. Box 2620
San Marcos, TX 78667-2620
512-245-8734
http://www.gaultschool.org/

Institute of Texan Cultures
UTSA HemisFair Park Campus
801 South Bowie Street
San Antonio, TX 78205-3296 (mail)
851 Durango Blvd.
San Antonio, TX 78205-3296 (physical)
210-458-2300
archeology@thc.state.TX.us

Museum of the Coastal Bend
The Victoria College
2200 East Red River
Victoria, TX 77901
Phone: 361-582-2511

Panhandle-Plains Historical Museum
2503 4th Avenue
Canyon, TX 79015
806-651-2244
Fax: 806-651-2250
http://www.panhandleplains.org/

Rice University
Department of Anthropology MS-20
Rice University
P.O. Box 1892
Houston, TX 77251-1892
Fax: 713-348-5455
anth@rice.edu
http://anthropology.rice.edu/

Rock Art Foundation
18160 US Highway 281 North, Suite 108
PMB 257
San Antonio, TX 78232
888-ROCKART (888-762-5278)
Or 210-525-9907
http://www.rockart.org/

SHUMLA School
P.O. Box 627
Comstock, TX 78837
432-292-4848
info@shumla.org
http://www.shumla.org/

Southern Methodist University
Department of Anthropology
3225 Daniel Avenue
Heroy Bldg. 408
Dallas, TX 75275
214-768-2684
Fax: 214-768-2906
phogan@smu.edu
http://smu.edu/anthro/smu_anthro

Stephen F. Austin State University
Center for Regional Heritage Research
SFA Station
Nacogdoches, TX 75962
gavery@sfasu.edu
http://www.sfasu.edu/heritagecenter

Sul Ross State University
Center for Big Bend Studies
Ferguson Hall, Suite 114
P.O. Box C-71
Alpine, TX 79832
432-837-8179
Fax: 432-837-8381
cbbs@sulross.edu
http://www.sulross.edu/cbbs

Texas A&M University
Department of Anthropology
4352 TAMU
College Station, TX 77844
979-845-5242
Fax: 979-845-4070
http://anthropology.tamu.edu/

Texas Archeological Society
Center for Archaeological Research at UTSA
One UTSA Circle
San Antonio, TX 78249-0658
210-458-4393
Fax: 210-458-4870
tasoffice@txarch.org
http://www.txarch.org/

Texas Beyond History
(Txarch.org)
6900 N. Loop 1604 W
CAR at UTSA
San Antonio, TX 78249-0658
210-458-4393
http://www.texasbeyondhistory.net/www.texasbeyondhistory.net

Texas Department of Transportation Environmental Affairs Division
125 11th Street
Austin, TX 78701-2483
512-374-5424
http://www.dot.state.TX.us/

Texas Historical Commission
Archeology Division
P.O. Box 12276
Austin, TX 78711-2276
512-463-6090
http://www.thc.state.TX.us/

Texas Memorial Museum
Texas Natural Science Center
2400 Trinity Street
University of Texas
Austin, TX 78705
http://www.utexas.edu/tmm

Texas Parks and Wildlife Department
4200 Smith School Road
Austin, TX 78744
Toll free: 800-792-1112
Austin: 512-389-4800
http://www.tpwd.state.TX.us/

Texas State University
Department of Anthropology
601 University Drive
San Marcos, TX 78666
512-245-8272
http://www.txstate.edu/anthropology

Texas Tech University
Southwest Collection
15th and Detroit
P.O. Box 41041
Lubbock, TX 79409-1041
806-742-3749
Fax: 806-742-0496
http://www.swco.ttu.edu/

University of Texas at Austin
Department of Anthropology
1 University Station C3200
Austin, TX 78712
512-471-4206
Fax: 512-471-6535
http://www.utexas.edu/cola/depts/anthropology

University of Texas at Austin
Texas Archeological Research Laboratory (TARL)
1 University Station, R7500
Austin, TX 78712-0714
512-471-5960
Fax: 512-471-5973
http://www.utexas.edu/research/tarl

University of Texas at El Paso
Department of Sociology and Anthropology
Old Main Bldg., Room 108
El Paso, TX 79968
915-747-5740
Fax: 915-747-5505
soci@utep.edu
http://academics.utep.edu/

University of Texas at San Antonio
Center for Archaeological Research
One UTSA Circle
San Antonio, TX 78249
210-458-4378
http://car.utsa.edu/

References

Abbott, James T., and W. Nicolas Trierweiler, eds. 1995. *NRHP Significance Testing of 57 Prehistoric Archeological Sites on Fort Hood, Texas.* Vol. 2. Archeological Resource Management Series, Research Report. Fort Hood, Tex.: U.S. Army Fort Hood.

Agogino, George A. 1961. A New Point Type from Hell Gap Valley, Eastern Wyoming. *American Antiquity* 26:558–60.

Ahler, Stanley A., and Phil Geib. 2000. Why Flute? Folsom Point Design and Adaptation. *Journal of Archaeological Science* 27:799–820.

Alexander, Herbert L., Jr. 1963. The Levi Site: A Paleo-Indian Campsite in Central Texas. *American Antiquity* 28 (4): 510–27.

Alexander, R. K. 1970. *Archaeological Investigations at Panda Cave, Val Verde County, Texas.* Papers of the Texas Archeological Salvage Project 19. Austin: Texas Archeological Salvage Project.

Amick, Daniel S. 1990. Dimensioning Folsom Variability: Lessons from the Shifting Sands Site. In *Transactions of the 25th Regional Archaeological Symposium for Southeastern New Mexico and Western Texas,* edited by P. Brothers, 1–24. Midland, Tex.: Midland Archeological Society.

———, ed. 1999. *Folsom Lithic Technology: Explorations in Structure and Variation.* Archaeological Series 12. Ann Arbor, Mich.: International Monographs in Prehistory.

Amick, Daniel S., Jack L. Hofman, and Richard O. Rose. 1989. The Shifting Sands Folsom-Midland Site in Texas. *Current Research in the Pleistocene* 6:1–2.

Anderson, David G., and Steven D. Smith. 2003. *Archaeology, History and Productive Modeling: Research at Fort Polk, 1972–2002.* Tuscaloosa: University of Alabama Press.

Anthony, Dana, and David O. Brown, eds. 1994. *Archeological Investigations in the Denton Creek Floodplain: Data Recovery Excavations at 41DL270, Denton and Dallas Counties, Texas.* Archeological Series 37. Austin: Hicks and Company.

Applegarth, Susan Marjorie. 1976. Prehistoric Utilization of the Environment of the Eastern Slopes of the Guadalupe Mountains, Southeastern, New Mexico. PhD diss., Department of Anthropology, University of Wisconsin at Madison.

Assad, Cristi. 1978. *An Evaluation of Archaeological Sites in the Vicinity of Floodwater Retarding Structure No. 2, Dry Comal Creek, Comal County, Texas.* Archaeological Survey Report 50. San Antonio: Center for Archaeological Research, University of Texas.

Aten, Lawrence E. 1967. *Excavations at the Jamison Site (41LB2), Liberty County, Texas.* Report 1. Houston: Houston Archeological Society.

———. 1983. *Indians of the Upper Texas Coast.* New York: Academic Press.

Aveleyra Arroyo de Anda, L., M. Maldonado-Koerdell, and P. Martinez del Río. 1956. *Cueva de la Candelaria.* Vol. 1. Memorias del Instituto Nacional de Antropología e Historia 5. Mexico: Instituto Nacional de Antropología e Historia.

Bailey, Gail L., and Douglas K. Boyd. 1980. *Archeological Investigations at 41 TL38, Tyler County, Texas.* Technical Reports 10. Austin, Tex.: Prewitt and Associates.

Baker, Ed. 2003. The University of Texas and 1990: Texas Archeological Society Excavations at 41UV132, the Smith Site, Uvalde County, Texas. *Bulletin of the Texas Archeological Society* 74:1–30.

Baker, William S., and Clarence H. Webb. 1976. Catahoula Type Projectile Points. *Louisiana Archaeology* 3:225–52.

———. 1978. Burials at the Cowpen Slough Site (16CT147). *Louisiana Archaeology Society* 5 (2): 16–18.

Ballenger, Jesse A. M. 2001. *Dalton Settlement in the Arkoma Basin of Eastern Oklahoma.* R. E. Bell Monographs in Anthropology 2. Norman: University of Oklahoma.

Banks, Larry D. 1990. *From Mountain Peaks to Alligator Stomachs: A Review of Lithic Sources in the Trans-Mississippi South, the Southern Plains, and Adjacent Southwest.* Oklahoma Anthropological Society, Memoir 4. Norman: University of Oklahoma.

Barker, Philip. 1982. *Techniques of Archaeological Excavation.* New York: Universe Books.

Barnes, Alfred S. 1939. The Difference between Natural and Human Flaking in Prehistoric Flint Implements. *American Anthropologist* 41:99–112.

Bartlett, C. S., Jr. 1963. The Tom's Brook Site—3J0L: A Preliminary Report. In *Arkansas Archaeology,* edited by C. R. McGimsey III, 15–65. Fayetteville: University of Arkansas.

Bartlett, R. 1994. The Calf Creek Component at the Stillman Pit Site (34MR71) and Its Relation to Calf Creek Caching Strategy. *Bulletin of the Oklahoma Anthropological Society* 40:69–90.

Beasley, Tom S. 1978a. A Late Prehistoric Site in Webb County. *La Tierra* 5 (2): 4–9.

———. 1978b. A Site with *Edwards* Points in Bandera County, Texas. *La Tierra* 5 (4): 23–31.

———. 1980. Incised Stones from Kinney and Webb Counties. *La Tierra* 7 (2): 19–21.

Bell, Milton. 1981. *The Alex Justiss Site: A Caddoan Cemetery in Titus County, Texas.* Publication in Archaeology Report 21. Austin: Texas State Department of Highways and Public Transportation.

Bell, Robert E. 1958. *Guide to the Identification of Certain American Indian Projectile Points.* Special Bulletin 1. Norman: Oklahoma Anthropological Society.

———. 1960. *Guide to the Identification of Certain American Indian Projectile Points.* Special Bulletin 2. Norman: Oklahoma Anthropological Society.

———. 1972. *The Harlan Site, CK-6: A Prehistoric Mound Center in Cherokee County, Eastern Oklahoma.* Memoir 2. Norman: Oklahoma Anthropological Society.

Bement, Leland C. 1991a. The Statistical Analysis of Langtry Variants from Arenosa Shelter, Val Verde County, Texas. In *Papers on Lower Pecos Prehistory,* edited by Solveig A. Turpin, 51–64. Studies in Archeology 8. Austin: Texas Archeological Research Laboratory, University of Texas.

———. 1991b. The Thunder Valley Burial Cache: Group Investment in a Central Texas Sinkhole Cemetery. *Plains Anthropologist* 36 (135): 97–109.

———. 1994. *Hunter-Gatherer Mortuary Practices during the Central Texas Archaic.* Austin: University of Texas Press.

Bement, Leland C., Wayne Bartholomew, Glen T. Goode, Stephen A. Hall, and David G. Robinson. 1989. *Excavations at 41BP19 the Kennedy Bluffs Site Bastrop County, Texas.* Report 5. Austin: Texas State Department of Highways and Public Transportation, Highway Design Division.

Bement L. C., and K. J. Buehler. 1994. Preliminary Results from the Certain Site: A Late Archaic Bison Kill in Western Oklahoma. *Plains Anthropologist* 39 (148): 173–83.

Bement, L. E., E. Lundelius Jr., and R. Ketchum. 2004. Driving Home a Point: A Data Package from the Arkansas River. *Oklahoma Archaeological Society Newsletter* 23 (4): 1–3.

Bettinger, Robert L., James F. O'Connell, and David Hurst Thomas. 1991. Projectile Points as Time Markers in the Great Basin. *American Anthropologist* 93:166–73.

Bettinger, Robert L., and Jelmer Eerkens. 1999. Point Typologies, Cultural Transmission, and the Spread of Bow-and-Arrow Technology in the Prehistoric Great Basin. *American Antiquity* 64 (2): 231–42.

Bettis, Allen C. 1997. Chipped Stone Artifacts from the Killam Ranch, Webb County, Texas. *TARL Research Notes* 5 (2): 3–23.

Bever, Michael R., and David J. Meltzer. 2007. Exploring Variation in Paleoindian Lifeways: The Third Revised Edition of the Texas Clovis Fluted Point Survey. *Bulletin of the Texas Archeological Society* 78:65–99.

Birmingham, W. W., and James E. Bluhm. 2003. A Clovis Polyhedral Core from Northwest Victoria County, Texas. *La Tierra* 30 (3 and 4): 55–58.

Birmingham, W. W., and T. R. Hester. 1976. *Late Pleistocene Archaeological Remains from the Johnston-Heller Site, Texas Coastal Plain*. Special Report 3. San Antonio: Center for Archaeological Research, University of Texas.

Black, Stephen L. 1986. *Archaeological Investigations at the Clemente and Herminia Hinojosa Site (41JW8), Jim Wells County, Southern Texas*. Archaeological Survey Report 100. San Antonio: Center for Archaeological Research, University of Texas.

Black, S. L., and A. J. McGraw. 1985. *The Panther Springs Creek Site: Culture Change and Continuity within the Upper Salado Creek Drainage, South Central Texas*. Archaeological Survey Report 100. San Antonio: Center for Archaeological Research, University of Texas.

Blackmar, Jeannette M., Richard O. Rose, and Jack L. Hofman. 2000. 1A2: A West Texas Cody Campsite. *Current Research in the Pleistocene* 17:9–11.

Blaine, Jay C. 1968. A Preliminary Report of an Early Man Site in West Texas. *Transactions of the Third Archeological Symposium for Southwestern New Mexico and Western Texas*. South Plains Archeological Society, Lubbock, Tex.

Bobalik, Sheila J. 1978. *Archeological Investigations at the Sallee G. Site (34-Pu-99), Pushmataha County, Oklahoma*. Studies in Oklahoma's Past 3. Norman: Oklahoma Archeological Survey, University of Oklahoma.

Boisvert, Richard. 1985. A Technological Analysis of Lithic Assemblages from Guadalupe Mountains National Park, Texas. *Bulletin of the Texas Archeological Society* 54:1–104.

Boldurian, Anthony T. 1990. Lithic Technology at the Mitchell Locality of Blackwater Draw: A Stratified Folsom Site in Eastern New Mexico. *Plains Anthropologist*, Memoir 24 (35–130): 90.

Bond, Clell L. 1978. *Three Archeological Sites at Hoxie Bridge, Williamson County, Texas*. Anthropological Laboratory Report 43. College Station: Texas A&M University.

Bousman, C. Britt, Barry W. Baker, and Anne Kerr. 2004. Paleoindian Archeology in Texas. In *The Prehistory of Texas*, edited by Timothy K. Perttula, 15–100. College Station: Texas A&M University Press.

Bowers, Rodger Lee. 1975. Petrography and Petrogenesis of the Alibates Dolomite and Chert (Permian) Northern Panhandle of Texas. Master's thesis, University of Texas at Arlington.

Boyd, Charles L., and Harry J. Shafer. 1997. Another Look at the Distribution, Age and Function of "Waco Sinkers." *Bulletin of the Texas Archeological Society* 68:263–72.

Boyd, Douglas K. 1995. The Palo Duro Complex: Redefining the Early Ceramic Period in the Caprock Canyonlands. *Bulletin of the Texas Archeological Society* 66:461–518.

———. 1997. *Caprock Canyonlands Archeology: A Synthesis of the Late Prehistory and History of Lake Alan Henry and the Texas Panhandle-Plains*. Vol. 2. Reports of Investigations 110. Austin, Tex.: Prewitt and Associates.

Boyd, Douglas K., Martha Doty Freeman, Michael D. Blum, Elton R. Prewitt, and J. Michael Quigg. 1989. *Phase 1 Cultural Resources Investigations at Justiceburg Reservoir on the Double Mountain Fork of the Brazos River, Garza and Kent Counties, Texas.* Reports of Investigations 66. Austin, Tex.: Prewitt and Associates.

Boyd, James B. 1997. A Cliffton/Perdiz Atelier on the Rio Salado, Tamaulipas, Mexico. *La Tierra* 24 (4): 5–10.

Boyd, James B., and Timothy K. Perttula. 2000. On the Association of Caracara Arrow Points with Late Prehistoric Burials in the Falcon Reservoir Area. *La Tierra* 27 (4): 5–14.

Bradley, Bruce A., Michael B. Collins, and Andrew Hemmings, with contributions by Marilyn Shoberg and Jon C. Lohse. 2010. *Clovis Technology.* Ann Arbor, Mich.: International Monographs in Prehistory.

Braun, Pat, Jimmy Bluhm, and William W. Birmingham. 2008. An Initial Review of Archaeological Research at 41VT141, McNeill Ranch, Victoria County, Texas. *La Tierra* 35 (1–2): 17–40.

Brewington, Robbie L., John C. Dockall, and Harry J. Shafer. 1995. *Archaeology of 41MX5: A Late Prehistoric Caddoan Hamlet in Morris County, Texas.* Reports of Investigations 1. Austin: Center for Environmental Archaeology, Texas A&M University.

Briggs, A. K., and J. Malone. 1970. *An Archeological Survey of the Texarkana Reservoir Enlargement Area: Report on the First Season.* Archeological Survey Report 7. Austin: Texas Historical Survey Committee, and Texas Water Development Board.

Broehm, Cory J., and Troy R. Lovata. 2004. Five Corner Tang Bifaces from the Silo Site, 41KA102: A Late Archaic Mortuary Site in South Texas. *Plains Anthropologist* 49 (189): 59–77.

Brooks, Robert L., Richard R. Drass, and Fern E. Swenson. 1985. *Prehistoric Farmers of the Washita River Valley: Settlement and Subsistence Patterns during the Plains Village Period.* Archeological Resource Survey Report 23. Norman: Oklahoma Archeological Survey, University of Oklahoma.

Brosowske, Scott. 2009. *Guide to the Identification of Prehistoric Artifact Classes of the Southern High Plains.* Perryton, Tex.: Courson Archaeological Research.

Brown, David O. 1983. *The Berger Bluff Site (41 GD30A): Excavations in the Upper Deposits, 1979.* Archaeological Survey Report 115. San Antonio: Center for Archaeological Research, University of Texas.

Brown, Keith. 2007. The Gold Sand Site, Lee County, Texas. *Prehistoric American: The Journal for the Documentation of Prehistoric America* 41 (4): 23.

Brown, Kenneth M. 1976. Fused Volcanic Glass from the Manning Formation. *Bulletin of the Texas Archeological Society* 47:189–208.

———. 1985. Three Caches of Guadalupe Tools from South Texas. *Bulletin of the Texas Archeological Society* 56:75–126.

———. 1986. *Archaeological Testing at Sunrise Canyon Subdivision (41BX441), Universal City, Texas.* Archaeological Survey Report 133. San Antonio: Center for Archaeological Research, University of Texas.

———. 2008. A Surface-Collected Assemblage from Berger Bluff, Goliad County. *La Tierra* 35 (1–2): 1–16.

Brown, Kenneth M., and Rochelle J. Leneave. 1987. An Incised and Grooved Limestone Cobble from Edwards County. *La Tierra* 14 (3): 24–27.

Brown, Kenneth M., D. R. Potter, G. D. Hall, and S. L. Black. 1982. *Excavations at 41 LK67: A Prehistoric Site in the Choke Canyon Reservoir, South Texas.* Choke Canyon Series 7. San Antonio: Center for Archaeological Research, University of Texas.

Brownlow, Russ. 2004. *Data Recovery at the Holt Site, San Marcos, Hays County, Texas.* Austin, Tex.: Horizon Environmental Services.

Bruseth, Jim, Jeff Durst, Richard Proctor, Larry Banks, Gary Sykes, and Bill Pierson. 2009. Investigations at the Gene and Ruth Ann Stallings Ranch Site (41LR297). *Bulletin of the Texas Archeological Society* 80:195–205.

Bryan, Frank. 1930. Archeological Remains in the Black and Grand Prairies of Texas. *Bulletin of the Texas Archeological and Paleontological Society* 2:76–84.

———. 1936. Preliminary Report on the Archeology of Western Limestone County. *Bulletin of the Central Texas Archeological Society* 2:81–95.

Calame, David, Carey Weber, Larry Banks, and Richard McReynolds. 2002. Projectile Points of the Calf Creek Horizon from Frio, Medina and Uvalde Counties, Southern Texas. *La Tierra* 29 (4): 29–30.

Cambron, J. W., and D.C. Hulse. 1975. *Handbook of Alabama Archaeology.* Part 1, *Point Types.* Tuscaloosa: Alabama Archaeological Society.

Campbell, T. N. 1947. The Johnson Site: Type Site of the Aransas Focus of the Texas Coast. *Bulletin of the Texas Archeological and Paleontological Society* 18:40–75.

———. 1948. The Merrell Site: Archaeological Remains Association with Alluvial Terrace Deposits in Central Texas. *Bulletin of the Texas Archeological and Paleontological Society* 19:7–35.

———. 1952. The Kent-Crane Site: A Shell Midden on the Texas Coast. *Bulletin of the Texas Archeological Society* 23:39–77.

———. 1956. Archeological Materials from Five Islands in the Laguna Madre, Texas Coast. *Bulletin of the Texas Archeological Society* 27:7–46.

———. 1958. Archeological Remains from the Live Oak Point Site, Aransas County, Texas. *Texas Journal of Science* 10 (4): 423–42.

———. 1967. Archeological Survey of the Big Bend National Park, Texas: Part 1. Mimeographed report submitted to the National Park Service.

———. 1970. *Archeological Survey of the Big Bend National Park, 1966–1967.* Austin: University of Texas.

———. 1976. Archaeological Investigations at the Morhiss Site, Victoria County, Texas, 1932–1940. In *An Archaeological Survey of Coleto Creek, Victoria and Goliad Counties, Texas,* edited by A. A. Fox and T. R. Hester, 81–85. Archaeological Survey Report 18. San Antonio: Center for Archaeological Research, University of Texas.

Carmichael, David L., Robert H. Lafferty, III, and Brian L. Moyneaux. 2003. *Excavation.* Archaeologist's Toolkit 5. Walnut Creek, Calif.: AltaMira.

Carroll, W. B. 1983. The Medina Point: A New Dart Point Type. *La Tierra* 10 (1): 29–31.

Chadderdon, Mary Frances. 1976. An Analysis of Altered Quartzite Cobbles from Victoria County, Texas. *La Tierra* 3 (1): 7–14.

———. 1984. *Baker Cave, Val Verde County, Texas: The 1976 Excavations.* Special Report 13. San Antonio: Center for Archaeological Research, University of Texas.

Chandler, C. K. 1974. Use Wear Analysis of "Clear Fork" Tools from the Falcon Reservoir Area, Southern Texas. *La Tierra* 1 (4): 15–21.

———. 1982. Paleo-Indian Projectile Points from San Patricio County, Texas, Texas Coastal Bend. *La Tierra* 9 (2): 26–33.

———. 1987. An Incised Stone from Bexar County. *La Tierra* 14 (2): 31–33.

———. 1990. An Arrow Shaft Straightener from the Texas Trans-Pecos. *La Tierra* 17 (3): 11–23.

———. 1991a. An Incised Pebble from Val Verde County. *La Tierra* 18 (2): 32–37.

———. 1991b. An Incised Stone Pendant from Val Verde County. *La Tierra* 18 (1): 29–32.

———. 1994a. Paleo-Indian Projectile Points from the Olmos Basin in San Antonio, Texas. *La Tierra* 21 (1): 11–19.

———. 1994b. Sandstone Artifacts from Terrell County, Texas. *La Tierra* 21 (4): 27–29.

———. 1996a. A Basalt Shaft Straightener from Rattlesnake Canyon in Val Verde County. *La Tierra* 23 (1): 8–9.

———. 1996b. A Boatstone and Other Artifacts from Site 41EL19, Ellis County, North-Central Texas. *The Cache* 3:27–34.

———. 1996c. Tubular Stone Pipes and Pipe Fragments from the Lower Rio Grande of Texas. *La Tierra* 23 (2): 11–24.

———. 1997a. An Arrowshaft Straightener from Terrell County, Texas. *La Tierra* 24 (2): 41–43.

———. 1997b. Quartzite Cobbles Altered from Use. *La Tierra* 24 (2): 13–17.

Chandler, C. K., and Kay Hindes. 1993. Scottsbluff Points from Atascosa, Frio, and McMullen Counties, South Central Texas. *La Tierra* 20 (1): 31–36.

Chandler, C. K., Florence Knolle, and Mary Margaret Knolle. 1983. Paleo-Indian Projectile Points from Jim Wells and Nueces Counties, Texas. *La Tierra* 10 (2): 23–27.

Chandler, C. K., and Don Kumpe. 1993. Pin Drills from Tamaulipas, Mexico. *La Tierra* 20 (4): 5–7.

———. 1994. Tubular Stone Pipes from the Lower Rio Grande Valley. *La Tierra* 21 (3): 14–21.

———. 1996. Stone Pestles from the Lower Rio Grande, Texas. *La Tierra* 23 (2): 24–34.

Chandler, C. K., and Michael Marchbanks. 1995. Butted Bifaces and Their Use. *La Tierra* 23 (2): 24–35.

Clark, John E., and Michael Collins. 2002. *Folsom Technology and Lifeways*. Special Publication 4: *Lithic Technology*. Tulsa, Okla.: Department of Anthropology, University of Tulsa.

Clark, John W., Jr. 1978. *Mission San José y San Miguel de Aguayo: Archeological Investigations, December 1974*. Report 20. Austin: Office of the State Archeologist, Texas Historical Commission.

Cloud, William A., Robert J. Mallouf, Pat Mercado-Alinger, Cathryn A. Hoyt, Nancy A. Kenmotus, J. M. Sanchez, and Enrique R. Madrid. 1994. *Archeological Testing at the Polvo Site, Presidio County, Texas*. Report 39. Austin: Office of the State Archeologist, Texas Historical Commission.

Cloud, William A., and Jennifer C. Piehl. 2008. *The Millington Site: Archaeological and Human Osteological Investigations, Presidio County, Texas*. Papers of the Trans-Pecos Archaeological Program 4. Alpine, Tex.: Center for Big Bend Studies, Sul Ross State University.

Coe, Joffre Lanning. 1964. The Formative Cultures of the Carolina Piedmont. *Transactions of the American Philosophical Society*, New Series, 54 (5).

Coffman, Robert, and Elton R. Prewitt. 1985. *Phase 2 Cultural Resources Investigations in Portions of the Buttercup Creek Subdivision, Williamson County, Texas*. Reports of Investigations 36. Austin, Tex.: Prewitt and Associates.

Coleman, Shawn, Glen L. Evans, and Thomas R. Hester. 2000. An Overview of the Archeology at Montell Rockshelter, Uvalde County, Texas. *TARL Research Notes* 7:121–31.

Collins, M. B., G. L. Evans, T. N. Campbell, M. C. Winans, and C. E. Mear. 1989. Clovis Occupation at Kincaid Rockshelter, Texas. *Current Research in the Pleistocene* 6:3–5.

Collins, M. B., T. R. Hester, D. Olmstead, and P. J. Headrick. 1991. Engraved Cobbles from Early Archaeological Contexts in Texas. *Current Research in the Pleistocene* 8:13–15.

Collins, Michael B. 1968. A Note on Broad Corner-Notched Projectile Points Used in Bison Hunting in Western Texas. *The Bull-Roarer, The University of Texas Anthropological Society* 3 (2): 13–14.

———. 1969. *Test Excavations at Amistad International Reservoir, Fall 1967*. Papers of the Texas Archeological Salvage Project 16. Austin: University of Texas.

———. 1971. A Review of Llano Estacado Archaeology and Ethnohistory. *Plains Anthropologist* 16 (52): 85–104.

———. 1990. Observations on Clovis Lithic Technology. *Current Research in the Pleistocene* 7:73–74.

———, ed. 1998. *Wilson-Leonard: An 11,000-year Archeological Record of Hunter-Gatherers in Central Texas*. Vol. 1, *Introduction, Background and Synthesis*, edited by Michael B.

Collins et al. Studies in Archeology 31. Austin: Texas Archeological Research Laboratory, University of Texas; Austin Archeology Studies Program Report 10, Environmental Affairs Division, Texas Department of Transportation.

———. 1999. *Clovis Blade Technology*. Austin: University of Texas Press.

———. 2004. Archeology in Central Texas. In *Prehistory of Texas*, edited by T. K. Pertulla, 101–26. College Station: Texas A&M University Press.

Collins, Michael B., Michael D. Blum, Robert A. Ricklis, and Salvatore Valastro Jr. 1990. Quaternary Geology and Prehistory of the Vera Daniels Site, Travis County, Texas. *Current Research in the Pleistocene* 7:8–10.

Collins, Michael B., and C. Andrew Hemmings. 2005. Lesser-known Clovis Diagnostic Artifacts I: The Bifaces. *La Tierra* 32 (2): 9–20.

Collins, Michael B., Dale B. Hudler, and Stephen L. Black, et al. 2003. *Pavo Real (41BX52): A Paleoindian and Archaic Camp and Workshop on the Balcones Escarpment, South-Central Texas*. Studies in Archeology 41. Austin: Texas Archeological Research Laboratory, University of Texas.

Collins, Michael B., et al. 1997. Cody Down South: The Seminole-Rose Site in West Texas. *Current Research in the Pleistocene* 14: 15–18.

Cook, Harold J. 1927. New Geological and Palaeontological Evidence Bearing on the Antiquity of Mankind in America. *Natural History* 27:240–47.

Corbin, J. E. 1963. Archeological Materials from the Northern Shore of Corpus Christi Bay, Texas. *Bulletin of the Texas Archeological Society* 34:5–30.

———. 1974. A Model for Cultural Succession for the Coastal Bend Area of Texas. *Bulletin of the Texas Archeological Society* 45:29–54.

Couzzourt, Jim, and Beverly A. Schmidt-Couzzourt. 1997. The 1969 Texas Archeological Field School at Blue Creek, Moore County, in the Texas Panhandle. *Bulletin of the Texas Archeological Society* 67:1–114.

Crawford, Daymond D. 1965. The Granite Beach Site, Llano County, Texas. *Bulletin of the Texas Archeological Society* 36:71–97.

Creel, Darrell. 1990. *Excavations at 41TG91, Tom Green County, Texas, 1978*. Publications in Archaeology Report 38. Austin: Texas Department of Highways and Public Transportation.

Crook, Wilson W., Jr., and R. K. Harris. 1952. Trinity Aspect of the Archaic Horizon: The Carrollton and Elam Foci. *Bulletin of the Texas Archeological and Paleontological Society* 23:7–38.

———. 1954a. Another Distinctive Artifact: The Carrollton Ax. *The Record* 13 (2): 10–14.

———. 1954b. Traits of the Trinity Aspect Archaic: Carrollton and Elam Foci. *The Record* 12 (1): 2–16.

Dancey, William S. 1981. *Archaeological Field Methods: An Introduction*. Minneapolis: Burgess Publishing.

Das, Sudhir Ranjan. 1968. *Stone Tools: History and Origins*. Calcutta, India: Pilgrim Publishers.

Davis, Dan R., Jr. 1991. *Prehistoric Artifacts of the Texas Indians*. Special ed. San Antonio, Tex.: Pecos Publishing.

Davis, William A., and E. Mott Davis. 1960. *The Jake Martin Site: An Archaic Site in the Ferrell's Bridge Reservoir Area, Northeastern Texas*. Archaeology Series 3. Austin: Department of Anthropology, University of Texas.

Davis, E. Mott, W. A. Davis, Jules R. Gipson, and Bernard Golden. 2010. Archeological Investigations at the Lake O' the Pines, Marion and Upshur Counties, Texas, 1957–1959. Archival Series 4. Austin: Texas Archeological Research Laboratory, University of Texas.

Day, D. William. 1984. *Archeological Mitigation at the Doyle Martin Site, 41LN178 and the P.I. Ridge Site, 41FT52, Leon and Freestone Counties, Texas*. Austin, Tex.: Espy, Huston and Associates.

Decker, Susan, Stephen L. Black, and Thomas Gustavson. 2000. *The Woodrow Heard Site, 41UV88, A Holocene Terrace Site in the Western Balcones Canyonlands of Southwestern Texas.* Studies in Archeology 33. Austin: Texas Archeological Research Laboratory, University of Texas; Archeology Studies Program Report 14, Environmental Affairs Division, Texas Department of Transportation.

Denton, Joe T. 1976. *No-Name Creek: A Terrace Site of the Middle and Late Archaic Period in Gillespie County, Texas.* Report 7. Austin, Tex.: Publications in Archaeology, State Department of Highways and Public Transportation.

Dial, Susan W. 1998. Clear Fork Tools. In *Wilson-Leonard: An 11,000-Year Record of Hunter-Gatherers in Central Texas.* Vol. 2, *Chipped Stone Artifacts,* edited by Michael B. Collins et al., 507–25. Studies in Archeology 31. Austin: Texas Archeological Research Laboratory, University of Texas; Austin Archeology Studies Program Report 10, Environmental Affairs Division, Texas Department of Transportation.

Dial, Susan, and Michael Collins. 1998. Bifaces, Bifacial Tools, Perforator, Burins and Spalls. In *Wilson-Leonard: An 11,000-Year Record of Hunter-Gatherers in Central Texas.* Vol. 2, *Chipped Stone Artifacts,* edited by Michael B. Collins et al., 537–96. Studies in Archeology 31. Austin: Texas Archeological Research Laboratory, University of Texas; Austin Archeology Studies Program Report 10, Environmental Affairs Division, Texas Department of Transportation.

Dial, Susan W., Anne C. Kerr, and Michael Collins. 1998. Projectile Points. In *Wilson-Leonard: An 11,000-year Archeological Record of Hunter-Gatherers in Central Texas.* Vol. 2, *Chipped Stone Artifacts,* edited by Michael B. Collins et al., 313–445. Studies in Archeology 31. Austin: Texas Archeological Research Laboratory, University of Texas; Austin Archeology Studies Program Report 10, Environmental Affairs Division, Texas Department of Transportation.

Dibble, D. S., and D. Lorrain. 1968. *Bonfire Shelter: A Stratified Bison Kill Site, Val Verde County, Texas.* Miscellaneous Papers 1. Austin: Texas Memorial Museum, University of Texas.

Dibble, David S. 1967. Excavations at Arenosa Shelter, 1965–66. Report submitted to the National Park Service by the Texas Archeological Salvage Project, University of Texas, Austin.

———. 1970. On the Significance of Additional Radiocarbon Dates from Bonfire Shelter, Texas. *Plains Anthropologist* 15 (50): I:251–54.

Dibble, David S., Alf Sjoberg, Raymond W. Neck, and Melissa Winans. 1981. *Phase III: Prehistoric Research within Palmetto Bend Reservoir, Jackson County, Texas.* Research Report 82. Palmetto Bend Reservoir Series 6. Austin: Texas Archeological Survey, University of Texas.

Dickens, William A., and James E. Wiederhold. 2003. Some Notes on Bison, the Texas Post Oak Savanna, and the Late Prehistoric Period of Texas. *Bulletin of the Texas Archeological Society* 74:31–54.

Dickson, D. Bruce. 1985. The Atlatl Assessed: A Review of Recent Anthropological Approaches to Prehistoric North American Weaponry. *Bulletin of the Texas Archeological Society* 56:1–37.

Dillehay, Tom D., and David M. Meltzer. 1991. *The First Americans: Search and Research.* Boca Raton, Fla.: CRC Press.

Dockall, John E., and Stephen L. Black. 2006. Morhiss Mound. Texas Beyond History. September 18. http://www.texasbeyondhistory.net/morhiss.

Dornheim, Sharon Kay Lubka. 2002. The Archaeology of Site 41BN63. Master's thesis, University of Texas at Austin.

Duffield, Lathel F. 1959. Archeological Reconnaissance at Cooper Reservoir, Delta and Hopkins Counties, Texas, February 1959. Mimeographed report submitted to the National Park Service by the Texas Archeological Laboratory, University of Texas at Austin.

———. 1961. The Limerick Site at Iron Bridge Reservoir, Rains County, Texas. *Bulletin of the Texas Archeological Society* 30:51–116.

———. 1963a. The Strawn Creek Site: A Mixed Archaic and Neo-American Site at Navarro Mills Reservoir, Navarro County, Texas. Mimeographed report submitted to the National Park Service by the Texas Archeological Salvage Project, University of Texas at Austin.

———. 1963b. The Wolfshead Site: An Archaic-Neo-American Site in San Augustine County, Texas. *Bulletin of the Texas Archeological Society* 34:83–141.

Duffield, Lathel F., and Edwards B. Jelks. 1961. *The Pearson Site: A Historic Indian Site in Iron Bridge Reservoir, Rains County, Texas.* Archaeology Series 4. Austin: Department of Anthropology, University of Texas.

Duke, Alan R. 1989. Additional Bannerstones from Texas. *Houston Archeological Society Journal* 95:12–15.

———. 1991. Another Bannerstone from Harris County, Texas. *Houston Archeological Society Journal* 100:6–7.

Duke, Alan R., and Bruce R. Duke. 1988. A Bannerstone from Austin County, Texas. *Houston Archeological Society Journal* 90:11–13.

Duke, B. R. 1985. Surface Surveys at Site 41AU4, Austin Co., Texas. *Houston Archeological Society Journal* 82:12–15.

Duncan, Marjorie, Larry Neal, Don Shockey, Don Wyckoff, Michael Sullivan, and L. M. Sullivan. 2007. *Southern Plains Lithics: The Small Points.* Special Bulletin 26. Norman: Oklahoma Anthropological Society.

Durham, James M., and Michael K. Davis. 1975. Report on Burials Found at Crenshaw Mound "C," Miller County, Arkansas. *Oklahoma Anthropological Society Bulletin* 13:1–90.

Ensor, H. Blaine. 1987. San Patrice and Dalton Affinities on the Central and Western Gulf Coastal Plain. *Bulletin of the Texas Archeological Society* 57:69–82.

———. 1990. Comments on Prehistoric Chronology Building in Southeast Texas. *Journal of the Houston Archeological Society* 98:1–11.

Ensor, H. Blaine, and David L. Carlson. 1991. *Alabonson Road: Early Ceramic Period Adaptation to the Inland Coastal Prairie Zone, Harris County, Southeast Texas.* Reports of Investigations 8. College Station: Archeological Research Laboratory, Texas A&M University.

Ensor, H. Blaine, John E. Dockall, and Frank Winchell. 1991. *National Register Eligibility Testing and Assessment at the Al Soloman I and Al Soloman II Sites, Cypress Creek, Harris County, Texas.* Reports of Investigations 12. College Station: Archeological Research Laboratory, Texas A&M University.

Ensor, H. Blaine, and Catherine S. Mueller-Wille, et al. 1988. *Excavations at the Bull Pen Site 41BP280 Colorado River Drainage, Bastrop County, Texas.* Contract Reports in Archaeology 3. Austin: Texas State Department of Highways and Public Transportation.

Epstein, Jeremiah F. 1963. Centipede and Damp Caves: Excavations in Val Verde County, Texas, 1958. *Bulletin of the Texas Archeological Society* 33:2–129.

Fagan, Brian M. 1981. *In the Beginning.* 4th ed. Boston: Little, Brown.

Ferring, C. Reid. 1990. The 1989 Investigations at the Aubrey Clovis Site, Texas. *Current Research in the Pleistocene* 7:10–12.

Fields, R. C., M. E. Blake, and K. W. Kibler. 1997. *Synthesis of the Prehistoric and Historic Archeology of Cooper Lake, Delta and Hopkins Counties, Texas.* Reports of Investigations 104. Austin, Tex.: Prewitt and Associates.

Fields, Ross C. 1988. *Cultural Resources Investigations along White Oak Bayou, Harris County, Texas.* Reports of Investigations 62. Texas Antiquities Committee Permit 540. Austin, Tex.: Prewitt and Associates.

———. 1995. The Archeology of the Post Oak Savannah of East Central Texas. *Bulletin of the Texas Archeological Society* 66:301–30.

———. 2004. The Archeology of the Post Oak Savannah of East-Central Texas. In *The Prehistory of Texas*, edited by T. K. Perttula, 347–69. College Station: Texas A&M University Press.

Fields, Ross C., L. Wayne Klement, C. Britt Bousman, David H. Jurney, and Melissa M. Green. 1990a. *National Register Assessments of Eight Prehistoric and Four Historic Sites at the Jewitt Mine, Freestone and Leon Counties, Texas.* Reports of Investigations 73. Austin, Tex.: Prewitt and Associates.

Fields, Ross C., L. Wayne Klement, C. Britt Bousman, Steve A. Tomka, Eloise F. Gadus, and Margaret A. Howard. 1991. *Excavations at the Bottoms, Rena Branch, and Moccasin Springs Site, Jewett Mine Project, Freestone and Leon Counties, Texas.* Reports of Investigations 82. Austin, Tex.: Prewitt and Associates.

Fields, Ross C., Steve Tomka, C. Britt Bousman, L. Wayne Klement, Gail L. Bailey, William A. Bryan, Eloise A. Howard, and J. Michael Quigg. 1990b. *Excavations at the Charles Cox, Lambs Creek Knoll, and Buffalo Branch Sites, Jewett Mine Project, Leon and Freestone Counties, Texas.* Vol. 1. Reports of Investigations 70. Austin, Tex.: Prewitt and Associates.

Figgins, J. D. 1927. The Antiquity of Man in America. *Natural History* 27:229–39.

Fladmark, Knut R. 1978. *A Guide to Basic Archaeological Field Procedures.* Publication 4. Burnaby, Canada: Department of Archaeology, Simon Fraser University.

Flaigg, Norman G. 1991. A Surface Collection of Prehistoric Artifacts from Coke County, Texas. Manuscript on file at Texas Archeological Research Laboratory, University of Texas at Austin.

———. 1995. A Study of Some Early Projectile Points from the J2 Ranch Site (41VT6), Victoria County, Texas. *La Tierra* 22 (4): 16–55.

Flenniken, J. Jeffrey, and Anan W. Raymond. 1986. Morphological Projectile Point Typology: Replication Experiments and Technological Analysis. *American Antiquity* 51 (3): 603–14.

Flenniken, J. Jeffrey and Philip J. Wilke. 1989. Typology, Technology and Chronology of Great Basin Dart Points. *American Anthropologist* 91:149–58.

Flinn, R., and J. Flinn. 1968. The High Bluff Site on the Clear Fork of the Brazos River. *Bulletin of the Texas Archeological Society* 38:93–125.

Ford, James A., Philip Phillips, and William G. Haag. 1955. *The Jaketown Site in West Central Mississippi.* Anthropological Papers of the American Museum of Natural History 45, part 1. New York: American Museum of Natural History.

Ford, James A., and Clarence H. Webb. 1956. *Poverty Point: A Late Archaic Site in Louisiana.* Anthropological Papers of the American Museum of Natural History 46, part 1. New York: American Museum of Natural History.

Forrester, Robert E. 1951. A Series of Eighteen Indian Skeletons Excavated in Shackelford County, Texas. *Bulletin of the Texas Archeological and Paleontological Society* 22:132–43.

———. 1964. *The Ham Creek Site; An Edwards Plateau Aspect Site in Johnson County, Texas.* Fort Worth, Tex.: Tarrant County Archeological Society.

———. 1985. Horn Shelter Number 2: The North End, A Preliminary Report. *Central Texas Archaeologist* 10:21–35.

———. 1987. The Moran Point from North-Central Texas. *Bulletin of the Oklahoma Anthropological Society* 36:131–36.

———. 1991. Pestles for Boat-Shaped Mortars in Texas. *Bulletin of the Texas Archeological Society* 60 (for 1989): 191–207.

Fox, Anne A., and Thomas R. Hester. 1976. *An Archaeological Survey of Coleto Creek, Victoria and Goliad Counties, Texas.* Archaeological Survey Report 18. San Antonio: Center for Archaeological Research, University of Texas.

Fox, D. E. 1979a. *Archaeological Investigations of Two Prehistoric Sites on the Coleto Creek Drainage, Goliad County, Texas.* Archaeological Survey Report 69. San Antonio: Center for Archaeological Research, University of Texas.

———. 1979b. *The Lithic Artifacts of Indians at the Spanish Colonial Missions, San Antonio, Texas.* Special Report 8. San Antonio: Center for Archaeological Research, University of Texas.

———. 1983. *Traces of Texas History: Archeological Evidence of the Past 450 Years.* San Antonio, Tex.: Corona Publishing.

Fox, Daniel E., Robert J. Mallouf, Nancy O'Malley, and William M. Sorrow. 1974. *Archeological Resources of the Proposed Cuero I Reservoir, Dewitt and Gonzales Counties, Texas.* Archeological Survey Report 12. Austin: Texas Historical Commission and Texas Water Development Board.

Frison, G. C. 1968. A Functional Analysis of Chipped Stone Tools. *American Antiquity* 33 (2): 149–55.

———. 1974. Archeology of the Casper Site. In *The Casper Site: A Hell Gap Bison Kill on the High Plains,* edited by G. C. Frison, 1–111. New York: Academic Press.

———. 1982. Hell Gap Components. In *The Agate Basin Site: A Record of Paleoindian Occupation of the Northwestern High Plains,* by G. C. Frison and D. J. Stanford, 135–42. New York: Academic Press.

Gadus, E. Frances, Ross C. Fields, and Karl W. Kibler. 2006. *Data Recovery Excavations at the J. B. White Site (41MM341), Milam County, Texas.* Archeological Studies Program Report 87. Report of Investigations 145, Environmental Affairs Division, Texas Department of Transportation. Austin, Tex.: Prewitt and Associates.

Gagliano, S. M., and H. F. Gregory Jr. 1965. A Preliminary Study of Paleo-Indian Points in Louisiana. *Louisiana Studies* 4 (1): 62–67.

Galindo, Mary Jo. 1998. Analysis of the Riley Projectile Point Collection from Mier, Tamaulipas, Mexico. Draft Manuscript on file at Texas Archeological Research Laboratory, Austin.

Gallagher, Joseph G., and Susan E. Bearden. 1976. *The Hopewell School Site: A Late Archaic Campsite in the Central Brazos River Valley.* Contributions in Anthropology 19. Dallas: Southern Methodist University.

Galm, Jerry R. 1978. *The Archaeology of the Curtis Lake Site (34Lf-5A), LeFlore County, Oklahoma.* Research Series 2. Norman: Archaeological Research and Management Center, University of Oklahoma.

Gerstle, Andrea, Thomas C. Kelly, and Cristi Assad. 1978. *The Fort Sam Houston Project: An Archaeological and Historical Assessment.* Archaeological Survey Report 40. San Antonio: Center for Archaeological Research, University of Texas.

Gibson, Eric C. 1981. *The San Antonio Project: An Archaeological Reconnaissance for Urex, Inc. Southeastern Webb County, Texas.* Archaeological Survey Report 102. San Antonio: Center for Archaeological Research, University of Texas.

Goode, Glenn T. 2002. *The Anthon Site: A Prehistoric Encampment in Southern Uvalde County, Texas.* Report 38. Austin: Environmental Affairs Division, Texas Department of Transportation.

Goodyear, Albert C. 1974. *The Brand Site. A Techno-Functional Study of a Dalton Site in Northeast Arkansas.* Research Series 7. Fayetteville: Arkansas Archeological Survey.

———. 1982. The Chronological Position of the Dalton Horizon in the Southeastern United States. *American Antiquity* 47 (2): 382–95.

———. 2000. The Topper Site 2000: Results of the Allendale Paleoindian Expedition. *Legacy* 5 (2): 18–25. Newsletter of the South Carolina Institute of Archaeology and Anthropology, University of South Carolina, Columbia.

Graham, John A., and William A. Davis. 1958. *Appraisal of the Archeological Resources of Diablo Reservoir, Val Verde County, Texas.* Austin, Tex.: Archeological Salvage Program Field Office, U.S. National Park Service.

Green, F. E. 1963. The Clovis Blades: An Important Addition to the Llano Complex. *American Antiquity* 29:145–65.

Green, L. M. 1970. An Introduction to the Archaeology of the Richland Springs Creek Area, Western San Saba County, Texas. *Lower Plains Archaeological Society* 1:38.

Green, L. M., and Thomas R. Hester. 1973. The Finis Frost Site: A Toyah Phase Occupation in San Saba County, Texas. *Bulletin of the Texas Archeological Society* 44:69–88.

Greene, L. H. 1971. Archeological Investigations in the Desierto de Charcos de Risa, Coahuila, México. Master's thesis, University of Texas at Austin.

Greer, John W. 1966. Results of Archaeological Excavations at the Castle Canyon Site, Val Verde County, Texas. *Southwestern Lore* 32 (1): 10–18.

———. 1968. Some Unusual Artifacts from Val Verde County, Texas. *Texas Journal of Science* 20 (2): 184–91.

———. 1976. Neo-American Occupation at the Wheatley Site, Pedernales Falls State Park, Blanco, Texas. *Bulletin of the Texas Archeological Society* 47:89–169.

Greer, John W., and Robert A. Benfer. 1975. Austin Phase Burials at the Pat Parker Site, Travis County, Texas. *Bulletin of the Texas Archeological Society* 46:189–216.

Greer, John W., and Patricia A. Treat. 1975. Incised and Painted Pebbles From the Levi Site. *Plains Anthropologist* 20 (69): 231–37.

Guderjan, Thomas H., Bob Baker, Britt Bousman, Maureen Brown, Charles K. Chandler, Anne Fox, and Barbara Meissner. 1992. Prehistoric Settlement in the Medina Valley and the 1991 STAA/ITC Field School. *La Tierra* 19 (2): 14–28.

Gunter, Rita R. 1985. The Ben Bickham Collection from North Padre Island, Texas. *La Tierra* 12 (1): 6–17.

Hall, Grant D. 1981. *Allens Creek: A Study in the Cultural Prehistory of the Lower Brazos River Valley, Texas.* Research Report 61. Austin: Texas Archeological Survey, University of Texas.

———. 1994. The Cunningham-Gray Collection from Austin County, Texas. *Bulletin of the Texas Archeological Society* 62 (for 1991): 87–104.

Hall, Grant D., Stephen L. Black, and Carol Graves. 1982. *Archaeological Investigations at Choke Canyon Reservoir, South Texas: The Phase I Findings.* Choke Canyon Series 5. San Antonio: Center for Archaeological Research, University of Texas.

Hall, Grant D., Thomas R. Hester, and Stephen L. Black. 1986. *The Prehistoric Sites at Choke Canyon Reservoir, Southern Texas: Results of Phase II Archaeological Investigations.* Choke Canyon Series 10. San Antonio: Center for Archaeological Research, University of Texas.

Hamilton, Henry W. 1952. *The Spiro Mound.* Missouri Archaeologist 14. Columbia: Missouri Archaeologist.

Harris, R. K. 1953. The Sam Kaufman Site, Red River County, Texas. *Bulletin of the Texas Archeological Society* 24:43–68.

Harris, R. K., I. N. Harris, J. C. Blaine, and Jerry Lee Blaine. 1965. A Preliminary Archeological and Documentary Study of the Womack Site, Lamar County, Texas. *Bulletin of the Texas Archeological Society* 36:287–364.

Harrison, Bill R., and Kay L. Killen. 1978. *Lake Theo: A Stratified, Early Man Bison Butchering and Camp Site, Briscoe County, Texas.* Special Archeological Report 1. Canyon, Tex.: Panhandle-Plains Historical Museum.

Hartwell, William T. 1995. The Ryan's Site Cache: Comparisons to Plainview. *Plains Anthropologist* 40 (152): 165–84.

Hawley, Fred G. 1947. The Use of Lead Minerals by the Hohokam in Cremation Ceremonials. *Southwestern Journal of Anthropology* 3 (1): 69–71.

Hayner, E. W. 1955. Research in East Texas Projectile Points. *Bulletin of the Texas Archeological Society* 26:235–43.

Haynes, C. V., Jr. 1955. Evidence of Early Man in Torrance County, New Mexico. *Bulletin of the Texas Archeological and Paleontological Society* 26:144–64.

———. 1966. Elephant Hunting in North American. *Scientific American* 214:104–12.

Haynes, C. Vance, Jr., and George Agogino. 1966. Prehistoric Springs and Geochronology of the Clovis Site, New Mexico. *American Antiquity* 31:812–21.

Heartfield, Lorraine. 1975. Archeological Investigations of Four Sites in Southwestern Coahuila, México. *Bulletin of the Texas Archeological Society* 46:127–78.

Hedrick, John A. 1968. Plateau Station Area Survey (EPAS-68; CM-31:104:14:1). *The Artifact* (El Paso Archeological Society) 6 (1): 1–16.

———. 1975. Archaeological Survey of the Plateau Complex. *The Artifact* 13 (4): 45–82.

———. 1986. Five Arrow Point Types from the Plateau Complex, Van Horn, Texas. In *Transactions of the 22nd Regional Archaeological Symposium for Southwestern New Mexico and Western Texas*, 15–27.

———. 1989. A Preliminary Report on Archeological Resources in Southern Culberson County, Texas, in the Vicinity of Van Horn, Texas. *Bulletin of the Texas Archeological Society* 59:129–56.

———. 1993. Patterned Blade-Notched Projectile Points from Southern Culbertson County, Texas. In *Why Museums Collect: Papers in Honor of Joe Ben Wheat*, edited by Meliha S. Duran and David T. Kirkpatrick, 89–101. Papers of the Archaeological Society of New Mexico 19. Albuquerque: Archaeological Society of New Mexico.

Heizer, Robert F. 1970. A Mescal Knife from Near Overton, Moapa Valley, Southern Nevada. *Contributions, University of California Archaeological Research Facility* 7:28–37.

Heizer, Robert F., and Thomas R. Hester. 1978. *Great Basin Projectile Points: Forms and Chronology*. Socorro, N.Mex.: Ballena Press.

Hemion, Roger H. 1983. *Field and Laboratory Handbook*. Special Publication 2. San Antonio: Southern Texas Archaeological Association

Henderson, Jerry. 1980. Update on the Texas Highway Department's Excavations at 41BX52 on Leon Creek. Paper presented at the meeting of the Southern Texas Archaeological Association, San Antonio.

———. 2001. *Excavations at the Rainey Site (41BN33), A Late Prehistoric Sinkhole Site in Bandera County, Texas*. Report 5. Austin: Archeological Studies Program, Texas Department of Transportation.

Hester, Thomas R. 1968. Paleo-Indian Artifacts from Sites along San Miguel Creek: Frio, Atascosa and McMullen Counties, Texas. *Bulletin of the Texas Archeological Society* 39:147–62.

———. 1969a. *Archeological Investigations in Kenedy and Kleberg Counties, Texas, August, 1967*. Archeological Program Report 15. Austin, Tex.: State Building Commission.

———. 1969b. Notes on South Texas Archeology: Sites along the Middle Frio River Drainage. *The Record, Journal of the Dallas Archeological Society* 25 (4): 25–31.

———. 1970a. Notes on the Edwards Arrow Point Type. *The Record, Journal of the Dallas Archeological Society* 26 (2): 17–18.

———. 1970b. A Study of Wear Patterns on Hafted and Unhafted Bifaces from Two Nevada Caves. *Contributions of the University of California Archaeological Research Facility* 7:44–54.

———. 1970c. Burned Rock Middens on the Southwestern Edge of the Edwards Plateau. *Plains Anthropologist* 15 (50): I:237–50.

———. 1971. Archeological Investigations at the La Jita Site, Uvalde County, Texas. *Bulletin of the Texas Archeological Society* 42:51–148.

———. 1972a. Ethnographic Evidence for the Thermal Alteration of Siliceous Stone. *Tebiwa* 15:63–65.

———. 1972b. The Surface Archeology of Three Sites in Duval County, Southern Texas. *Lower Plains Archeological Society Bulletin* 2:45–71.

———. 1974. Archaeological Materials from Site NV-WA-197, Western Nevada: Atlatl and Animal Skin Pouches. *Contributions of the University of California Archaeological Research Facility* 21:1–43.

———. 1975. Chipped Stone Industries on the Rio Grande Plain, Texas: Some Preliminary Observations. *Texas Journal of Science* 26 (1–2): 213–22.

———, ed. 1976. *The Texas Archaic: A Symposium.* Special Report 2. San Antonio: Center for Archaeological Research, University of Texas.

———. 1977a. The Lithic Technology of Mission Indians in Texas and Northeastern Mexico. *Lithic Technology* 6 (1–2): 9–13.

———. 1977b. A Painted Pebble from a Site on the Nueces River, Nueces County, Texas. *Bulletin of the Texas Archeological Society* 48:139–44.

———. 1978a. *Background to the Archaeology of Chaparrosa Ranch, Southern Texas.* Special Report 6. San Antonio: Center for Archaeological Research, University of Texas.

———. 1978b. *Early Human Occupations in South Central and Southwestern Texas: Preliminary Papers on the Baker Cave and St. Mary's Hall Sites.* San Antonio: Center for Archaeological Research, University of Texas.

———. 1979a. Early Populations in Texas. *Archaeology* 32 (6): 26–33.

———. 1979b. Notes on *Gower, Jetta* and Other Projectile Points of the Pre-Archaic Period. *La Tierra* 6 (3): 5–8.

———. 1979c. A Stone Pestle from Dimmit County, Southern Texas. *La Tierra* 6 (3): 24.

———. 1980. *Digging into South Texas Prehistory.* San Antonio, Tex.: Corona Publishing.

———. 1983a. Late Paleo-Indian Occupations at Baker Cave, Southwestern Texas. *Bulletin of the Texas Archeological Society* 53:101–19.

———. 1983b. Problems in Typology: The Case of the "Medina" Points. *La Tierra* 10 (3): 41–43.

———. 1985. Form and Function: Hand Axes, Fist Axes and Butted Knives. *La Tierra* 12 (3): 3–5.

———. 1986. On the Misuse of Projectile Point Typology in Mesoamerica. *American Antiquity* 51 (2): 412–14.

———. 1988a. Arrow Shaft Straighteners in Southern Texas and Some California Ethnographic Comparisons. *La Tierra* 15 (3): 3.

———. 1988b. On Preforms and Projectile Points. *La Tierra* 15 (1): 2–4.

———. 1989a. Chronological Framework for Lower Pecos Prehistory. *Bulletin of the Texas Archeological Society* 59:53–64.

———. 1989b. A Late Archaic Burial from the Lower Nueces Drainage, Live Oak County, Texas. *La Tierra* 16 (2): 2–3.

———. 1989c. Perspectives on the Material Culture of the Mission Indians on the Texas-Northeastern Mexico Borderlands. In *Columbian Consequences*, edited by D. H. Thomas, 213–30. Vol. 1. Washington, D.C.: Smithsonian Institution Press.

———. 1990a. Early Archaic "Eccentric" Lithic Artifacts in Southern and Central Texas. *La Tierra* 17 (3): 1–5.

———. 1990b. Radiocarbon Dates from Archaeological Excavations in Medina County. *La Tierra* 17 (4): 1–2.

———. 1991. The Plainview Points from the St. Mary's Hall Site, South Central Texas. *La Tierra* 18 (2): 1–4.

———. 1992a. Archaeological Materials from Site 41UV20, Uvalde County, South-Central Texas. *La Tierra* 19 (1): 3–8.

———. 1992b. Chipped Stone Artifacts from Site 41DM59, Dimmit County, Southern Texas. *La Tierra* 19 (3): 1–7.

———. 1994a. Large Triangular Bifaces as Grave Goods in Southern Texas: An Example from 41LC4, Lavaca County. *La Tierra* 21 (4): 1–5.

———. 1994b. On TARL's Doorstep. *Newsletter of the Friends of the Texas Archeological Research Laboratory* 12 (2): 25, 28.

———. 1995. The Prehistory of South Texas. *Bulletin of the Texas Archeological Society* 66:427–60.

———. 1997. Archaeological Materials from the Middle Rio Grande, Southern Texas and Coahuila. *La Tierra* 24 (2): 3–12.

———. 1998. Closing a Chapter in the History of South Texas Archaeology: J. W. House, 1905–1998. *La Tierra* 25 (3): 2–7.

———. 2000. An Artifact Sequence from 41ZV263, Zavala County, Texas: The Lost Manuscript from the Lost Peacock Site. *La Tierra* 27 (2): 2–8.

———. 2002a. Problems in Typology in South Texas and Northeastern Mexico. *La Tierra* 29 (4): 5–11.

———. 2002b. An Unfinished Bannerstone from a Site in Coryell County, Texas. *La Tierra* 29 (1): 1–3.

———. 2004a. The Lithics of 41HY431. In *Data Recovery at the Holt Site, San Marcos, Hays County, Texas*, edited by Russ Brownlow, 78–94. Austin, Tex.: Horizon Environmental Services.

———. 2004b. The Prehistory of South Texas. In *The Prehistory of Texas*, edited by T. K. Perttula, 127–54. College Station: Texas A&M University Press.

———. 2005. An Overview of the Late Archaic in Southern Texas. *The Late Archaic across the Borderlands, from Foraging to Farming*, edited by Bradley J. Vierra, 259–78. Austin: University of Texas Press.

———. 2010. A Radiocarbon Date from 41BN63. *An Introduction to the Archaeology of the Southwestern Edwards Plateau*, edited by Thomas R. Hester. Utopia, Tex.: Seco Creek Publications.

Hester, Thomas R., Frank Asaro, Fred Stross, Anne C. Kerr, and Robert D. Giauque. 1991a. Trace Element Analyses and Geologic Source Studies of Obsidian Artifacts from Arenosa Shelter, Val Verde County, Texas. In *Papers on Lower Pecos Prehistory*, edited by S. A. Turpin, 191–98. Studies in Archeology 8. Austin: Texas Archeological Research Laboratory, University of Texas.

Hester, Thomas R., Frank Asaro, Fred Stross, Helen Michel, Anne C. Kerr, and Pamela Headrick. 1991b. An Overview of the Results of the Texas Obsidian Project. *La Tierra* 18 (1): 4–7.

Hester, Thomas R., and Byron D. Barber. 1990. A Large Biface from Atascosa County, with Comments on the Function of Such Artifacts in Prehistoric South Texas. *La Tierra* 17 (2): 2–4.

Hester, Thomas R., and W. W. Birmingham. 1976. *Papers on Paleo-Indian Archaeology in Texas I.* Special Report 3. San Antonio: Center for Archaeological Research, University of Texas.

Hester, Thomas R., Stephen Black, D. Gentry Steele, Ben W. Olive, Anne A. Fox, Karl J. Reinhard, and Leland C. Bement. 1989. *From the Gulf to the Rio Grande: Human Adaptation in Central, South and Lower Pecos Texas.* Research Series 33. Fayetteville: Arkansas Archeological Survey.

Hester, Thomas R., and Michael B. Collins. 1969. Burials from the Frisch Auf! Site: 41FY42. *Texas Journal of Science* 20 (3): 261–72.

———. 1974. Evidence for Heat Treating of Southern Texas Projectile Points. *Bulletin of the Texas Archeological Society* 45:219–24.

Hester, Thomas R., David Burrows, Frank Asaro, Fred H. Stross, and Robert Giauque. 2006. Trace Element Analysis of an Obsidian Milnesand Point, Gaines County, Texas. *Current Research in the Pleistocene* 23:106–7.

Hester, Thomas R., Glen L. Evans, Frank Asoro, Fred Stross, T. N. Campbell, and Leland Helen Michel. 1985. Trace Element Analysis of an Obsidian PaleoIndian Projectile Point from Kincaid Rockshelter, Texas. *Bulletin of the Texas Archeological Society* 56:143–54.

Hester, Thomas R., Robert F. Heizer, and John A. Graham. 1975. *Field Methods in Archaeology.* 6th ed. Palo Alto, Calif.: Mayfield Publishing.

Hester, Thomas R., and T. C. Hill Jr. 1971. Notes on *Scottsbluff* Points from the Texas Coastal Plain. *Southwestern Lore* 37 (1): 27–33.

———. 1973. Prehistoric Occupation at the Holdsworth and Stewart Sites on the Rio Grande. *Bulletin of the Texas Archeological Society* 43:33–75.

———. 1975. *Some Aspects of Late Prehistoric and Protohistoric Archaeology in Southern Texas.* Special Report 1. San Antonio: Center for Archaeological Research, University of Texas.

Hester, Thomas R., Delbert Gilbow, and Alan D. Albee. 1973. A Functional Analysis of "Clear Fork Artifacts" from the Rio Grande Plain, Texas. *American Antiquity* 38 (1): 90–96.

Hester, Thomas R., and Harvey Kohnitz. 1975. Chronology and Placement of "Guadalupe" Tools. *La Tierra* 2 (2): 22–25.

Hester, Thomas R., Michael Mildner, and Lee Spencer. 1974. *Great Basin Atlatl Studies.* Socorro, N.Mex.: Ballena Press.

Hester, Thomas R., and Sam W. Newcomb. 1990. Projectile Points of the San Patrice Horizon on the Southern Plains of Texas. *Current Research in the Pleistocene* 7:17–19.

Hester, Thomas R., E. H. Schmiedlin, and W. W. Birmingham. 1978. A Record of Several Ground Stone Artifacts from the Texas Coastal Plain. *La Tierra* 5 (3): 22–25.

Hester, Thomas R., and Harry J. Shafer. 1975. An Initial Study of Blade Technology on the Central and Southern Texas Coast. *Plains Anthropologist* 20 (69): 175–85.

Hester, Thomas R., Harry J. Shafer, and Kenneth L. Feder. 1997. *Field Methods in Archaeology.* 7th ed. Mountain View, Calif.: Mayfield Publishing.

Hester, Thomas R., Fred H. Stross, and Dorothy M. Brown. 1988. Arrow Shaft Straighteners in South Texas and Some California Ethnographic Comparisons. *La Tierra* 15 (3): 130–65.

Hester, Thomas R., and Charles M. Whatley. 1992. Chipped Stone Artifacts from Site 41DM59, Southern Texas. *La Tierra* 19 (3): 1–7.

———. 1997. Archaeological Materials from the Middle Rio Grande, Southern Texas and Coahuila. *La Tierra* 24 (2): 3–12.

Hester, Thomas R., L. D. White, and J. White. 1969. Archeological Materials from the Oulline Site and Other Sites in LaSalle County, Texas. *Texas Journal of Science* 21 (2): 130–65.

Hester, Thomas R., Diane Wilson, and Pamela Headrick. 1993. An Austin Phase Burial from Frio County, Southern Texas: Archaeology and Physical Anthropology. *La Tierra* 20 (1): 5–8.

Hibben, Frank C. 1941. Evidences of Early Occupation in Sandia Cave, New Mexico, and Other Sites in the Sandia-Manzano Region. *Smithsonian Miscellaneous Collections* 99 (23): 1–64.

———. 1946. The First Thirty-Eight *Sandia* Points. *American Antiquity* 11 (4): 257–58.

———. 1986. *Archaeological Investigations at 41 LK 201, Choke Canyon Reservoir, Southern Texas.* Choke Canyon Series 11: San Antonio: Center for Archaeological Research, University of Texas.

Highley, L., C. Graves, C. Land, and G. Judson. 1978. Archeological Investigations at Scorpion Cave (41ME7), Medina County, Texas. *Bulletin of the Texas Archeological Society* 49:139–98.

Highley, Lynn. 1984. Guadalupe Tools from Zavala County. *La Tierra* 11 (1): 28–35.

Hill, R. T. 1891. Notes on Geology of the Southwest. *American Geologist* 7:254–55, 336–70.

Hill, T. C., Jr., and T. R. Hester. 1971. Isolated Late Prehistoric and Archaic Components at the Honeymoon Site (41ZV34), Southern Texas. *Plains Anthropologist* 15 (51): 52–59.

Hill, T. C., Jr., J. W. House, and T. R. Hester. 1972. Notes on Incised and Grooved Stones from Southern and Western Texas. *Lower Plains Archeological Society Bulletin* 3:1–10.

Hofman, J. L., Robert L. Brooks, Joe S. Hays, Douglas W. Owsley, Richard L. Jantz, Murray K. Marks, and Mary H. Manheim. 1989. *From Clovis to Comanchero: Archeological Overview of the Southern Great Plains*. Research Series 35. Fayetteville: Arkansas Archeological Survey.

Hofman, Jack L. 1977. A Technological Analysis of Clear Fork Gouge Production. *Bulletin of the Oklahoma Anthropological Society* 26:105–21.

Hofman, Jack L., Daniel S. Amick, and Richard O. Rose. 1990. Shifting Sands: A Folsom-Midland Assemblage from a Campsite in Western Texas. *Plains Anthropologist* 35 (129): 221–54.

Holden, William Curry. 1938. Blue Mountain Rock Shelter. *Bulletin of the Texas Archeological and Paleontological Society* 10:208–21.

———. 1962. The Land. In *A History of Lubbock*, edited by L. L. Graves, 17–44. Lubbock: West Texas Museum Association.

Holliday, Vance T. 1996. *Paleoindian Geoarchaeology of the Southern High Plains*. Austin: University of Texas Press.

———. 1997. *Paleoindian Geoarchaeology of the Southern High Plains*. Austin: University of Texas Press.

Holliday, Vance T., and Eileen Johnson. 1981. An Update on the Plainview Occupation at the Lubbock Lake Site. *Plains Anthropologist* 26 (93): 251–53.

———. 1990. *Fifty Years of Discovery: The Lubbock Lake Landmark*. Lubbock Lake Landmark Quarternary Research Series 2. Lubbock: Museum of Texas Tech University.

Holliday, Vance T., Eileen Johnson, Herbert Haas, and Robert Stuckenrath. 1983. Radiocarbon Ages from the Lubbock Lake Site, 1950–1980: Framework for Cultural and Ecological Change on the Southern High Plains. *Plains Anthropologist* 28 (101): 165–82.

Holliday, Vance T., and Curtis M. Welty. 1981. Lithic Tool Resources of the Eastern Llano Estacado. *Bulletin of the Texas Archeological Society* 52:201–14.

Honea, K. M. 1965. The Bipolar Flaking Technique in Texas and New Mexico. *Bulletin of the Texas Archeological Society* 36:259–67.

Hoover, A. J., and Thomas R. Hester. 1974. Technological Notes on an Unfinished Boatstone Artifact from Southern Texas. *Lower Plains Archeological Society Bulletin* 4:21–24.

Houk, Brett A., and Jon C. Lohse. 1993. Archeological Investigations at the Mingo Site, Bandera County, Texas. *Bulletin of the Texas Archeological Society* 61:193–247.

Houk, Brett A., Kevin A. Miller, and Eric R. Oksanen, et al. 2008. *The Gatlin Site (41KR621): Investigating Archaic Lifeways on the Southern Edwards Plateau of Central Texas*. SWCA Project 9862-053-AUS, SWCA Cultural Resources Report 2008-149. Austin: Texas Department of Transportation.

———. 2009. The Gatlin Site and the Early-to-Middle Archaic Chronology of the Southern Edwards Plateau, Texas. *Bulletin of the Texas Archeological Society* 80:51–75.

Houk, Brett A., Steve Tomka, Britt Bousman, C. K. Chandler, Bruce Moses, Marcie Renner, and Mike Lyons. 1997. The Greenbelt Core: A Polyhedral Blade Core from San Antonio, Texas. *Current Research in the Pleistocene* 14:104–6.

House, J. W., and T. R. Hester. 1963. *The Carrizo Point*. Special Publication of the Carrizo (Texas) High School Archeological Society.

———. 1967. New Point Type Description: The *Carrizo* Point. *Texas Archeology* 11 (3): 7–9.

Howard, C. D. 1973. A Study of the Clear Fork Gouge. *Bulletin of the Texas Archeological Society* 44:51–60.

———. 1990. The Clovis Point: Characteristics and Type Description. *Plains Anthropologist* 35 (129): 255–62.

Howard, Edgar B. 1935a. *Evidence of Early Man in North America.* University of Pennsylvania *Museum Journal* 24 (2–3): 53–171.

———. 1935b. Occurrence of Flints and Extinct Animals in Pluvial Deposits near Clovis, New Mexico, Part 1. *Introduction, Proceedings, Philadelphia Academy of Natural Sciences* 86:229–303.

Howard, Margaret. 1996. Cowhead Mesa. In *The New Handbook of Texas,* edited by Ron Tyler, 380–81. Vol. 2. Austin: Texas State Historical Association.

Howard, Margaret, Logan McNutt, Terri Myers, Tim Roberts, and Amy Ringstaff. 2010. *10,000 years at Hueco Tanks State Park and Historic Site, El Paso County, Texas.* Austin: Cultural Resources Program, Texas Parks and Wildlife Department.

Hudgins, Joe D. 1982. Historic Indian Sites in Wharton County, Texas. *Journal of the Houston Archeological Society* 74:2–7.

Hudgins, Joe D., and L. W. Patterson. 1983. *Scottsbluff* Point Site 41WH19. *Journal of the Houston Archeological Society* 75:1.

Hudler, Dale, Keith Prillman, and Thomas Gustavson. 2002. *The Smith Creek Bridge Site (41DW270): A Terrace Site in DeWitt County, Texas.* Studies in Archeology 35. Austin: Texas Archeological Research Laboratory, University of Texas; Archeology Studies Program Report 17, Texas Department of Transportation.

Hudler, Dale B. 1997. *Determining Clear Fork Tool Function through Use-Wear Analysis: A Discussion of Use-Wear Methods and Clear Fork Tools.* Studies in Archeology 25. Austin: Texas Archeological Research Laboratory.

———. 2003. Wear Analysis of Selected Pavo Real Artifacts. Appendix in *Pavo Real (41BX52): A Paleoindian and Archaic Camp and Workshop on the Balcones Escarpment, South-Central Texas,* by Michael B. Collins, Dale B. Hudler, and Stephen L. Black. Studies in Archeology 42. Austin: Texas Archeological Research Laboratory, University of Texas; Archeological Studies Program Report 50, Environmental Affairs Division, Texas Department of Transportation.

Huebner, Jeffery A. 1988. The Archaeology of Blue Bayou: A Late Prehistoric and Archaic Mortuary Site, Victoria County, Texas. Master's thesis, University of Texas at San Antonio.

Hughes, Jack T. 1976. The Panhandle Archaic. In *The Texas Archaic: A Symposium,* edited by Thomas R. Hester, 28–38. Special Report 2. San Antonio: Center for Archaeological Research, University of Texas.

———. 1980. Some Early and Northerly Occurrences of the Clear Fork Gouge. In *Papers on the Prehistory of Northeast Mexico and Adjacent Texas,* edited by J. F. Epstein, T. R. Hester, and C. Graves, 143–46. Special Report 9. San Antonio: Center for Archaeological Research, University of Texas.

———. 1991. Prehistoric Cultural Developments on the Texas High Plains. *Bulletin of the Texas Archeological Society* 60:1–55.

Hughes, Jack T., and Patrick S. Willey. 1978. *Archeology at Mackenzie Reservoir.* Archeological Survey Report 24. Austin: Texas Historical Commission, Office of the State Archeologist.

Hughes, Richard E., and Thomas R. Hester. 2009. Geochemical Evidence for a Mexican Source of Origin for an Obsidian Artifact from South Central Texas. *Bulletin of the Texas Archeological Society* 80:77–84.

Ing, J. David, Sheron Smith-Savage, William A. Cloud, and Robert J. Mallouf. 1996. *Archeological Reconnaissance on Big Bend Ranch State Park, Presidio and Brewster Counties, Texas, 1988–1994.* Center for Big Bend Studies Occasional Papers 1. Alpine, Tex.: Sul Ross State University.

Inman, Betty. 1999. The Lithic Artifacts of the Native Americans at the Spanish Colonial Missions at Guerrero, Coahuila, Mexico. *Bulletin of the Texas Archeological Society* 70:363–84.

Inman, Betty J., T. C. Hill Jr., and Thomas R. Hester. 1998. Archeological Investigations at the Tortuga Flat Site (41ZV155), Zavala County, Southern Texas. *Bulletin of the Texas Archeological Society* 69:11–33.

Inman, Betty J., and Dale B. Hudler. 1998. Preliminary Results from a Use-Wear Analysis of Clovis Blades from the Gault Site. *TARL Research Notes* 6 (1): 18–20.

Irwin, Henry T., and H. M. Wormington. 1970. Paleo-Indian Tool Types in the Great Plains. *American Antiquity* 5 (1): 24–34.

Irwin-Williams, C., H. Irwin, G. Agogino, and C. V. Haynes Jr. 1973. Hell Gap: Paleo-Indian Occupation on the High Plains. *Plains Anthropologist* 18 (59): 40–53.

Jackson, A. T., and A. M. Woolsey. 1938. *The Fall Creek Sites and Additional Buchanan Lake Sites*. University of Texas Publications 3802. Austin: University of Texas.

Jackson, A. T., Steve Tomka, Richard B. Mahoney, and Barbara A. Meissner. 2004. *The Cayo del Oso Site (41NU2)*. Vol. 1, *A Historical Summary of Exploration of a Prehistoric Cemetery on the Coast of False Oso Bay, Nueces County, Texas*. Archaeological Survey Report 350. San Antonio: Center for Archaeological Research, University of Texas; Archeological Studies Program Report 68, Texas Department of Transportation.

Jelks, Edward B. 1962. *The Kyle Site: A Stratified Central Texas Aspect Site in Hill County, Texas*. Archaeology Series 5. Austin: Department of Anthropology, University of Texas.

———. 1965. The Archaeology of McGee Bend Reservoir, Texas. PhD diss., University of Texas at Austin.

———, ed. 1967. The Gilbert Site, A Norteno Focus Site in Northeastern Texas. *Bulletin of the Texas Archeological Society* 37 (whole volume).

———. 1978. Diablo Range. In *Chronologies in New World Archeology*, edited by R. E. Taylor and Clement W. Meighan, 71–111. New York: Academic Press.

Jelks, Edward B., and Curtis D. Tunnell. 1959. *The Harroun Site: A Fulton Aspect Component of the Caddoan Area, Upshur County, Texas*. Archaeology Series 2. Austin: Department of Anthropology, University of Texas.

Jennings, Thomas A. 2008. *San Patrice Technology and Mobility across the Plains-Woodland Border*. R. E. Bell Monographs in Anthropology 5; Memoir 12. Norman: Oklahoma Anthropological Society.

Jensen, Harold P., Jr. 1968. Coral Snake Mound (X16SA48). *Bulletin of the Texas Archeological Society* 39:9–44.

Jeter, Marvin D., and G. Ishmael Williams Jr. 1989. Lithic Horizons and Early Cultures. In *Archeology and Bioarcheology of the Lower Mississippi Valley and Trans-Mississippi South in Arkansas and Louisiana*, edited by M. Jeter, J. Rose, G. Williams Jr., and A. Harmon, 111–70. Research Series 37. Fayetteville: Arkansas Archeological Survey.

Johnson, Eileen, and Vance T. Holliday. 1980. A Plainview Kill/Butchering Locale on the Llano Estacado: The Lubbock Lake Site. *Plains Anthropologist* 25 (88): I:89–111.

———. 2004. Archeology and Late Quaternary Environments of the Southern High Plains. In *Prehistory of Texas*, edited by T. K. Perttula, 283–95. College Station: Texas A&M University Press.

Johnson, Eileen, Vance T. Holliday, Michael J. Kaczor, and Robert Stuckenrath. 1977. The Garza Occupation at the Lubbock Lake Site. *Bulletin of the Texas Archeological Society* 48:83–109.

Johnson, Leroy, Jr. 1962a. Wunderlich: A Burned-Rock Midden Site. In *Salvage Archeology of Canyon Reservoir: The Wunderlich, Footbridge and Oblate Sites*, edited by Leroy Johnson Jr., Dee Ann Suhm, and Curtis D. Tunnell, 13–48. Bulletin of the Texas Memorial Museum 5. Austin: Texas Memorial Museum, University of Texas.

———. 1962b. The Yarbrough and Miller Sites of Northeastern Texas, with a Preliminary Definition of the La Harpe Aspect. *Bulletin of the Texas Archeological Society* 32:141–284.

———. 1964. *The Devil's Mouth Site: A Stratified Campsite at Amistad Reservoir, Val Verde County, Texas*. Archeology Series 6. Austin: Department of Anthropology, University of Texas.

———. 1989a. Classification of Stone Projectile Points by a Small Texan Folk Community: A Case Study. *Texas Journal of Science* 41 (2): 194–203.

———. 1989b. *Great Plains Interlopers in the Eastern Woodlands during Paleo-Indian Times*. Report 36. Austin: Texas Historical Commission, Office of the State Archeologist.

———. 1991. *Early Archaic Life at the Sleeper Archaeological Site, 41BC65 of the Texas Hill Country, Blanco County, Texas*. Publications in Archaeology Report 39. Austin: Texas State Department of Highways and Public Transportation.

———. 1994. *The Life and Times of Toyah-Culture Folk: The Buckhollow Encampment, Site 41KM16, Kimble County, Texas*. Report 38. Austin: Office of the State Archeologist, Texas Department of Transportation and Texas Historical Commission.

———. 1995. *Past Cultures and Climates at Jonas Terrace 41ME29, Medina County, Texas*. Report 40. Austin: Office of the State Archeologist, Texas Department of Transportation and Texas Historical Commission.

———. 2000. *Life and Death as Seen at the Bessie Kruze Site (41WM13) on the Blackland Prairie of Williamson County, Texas*. Archeology Studies Program Report 22. Austin: Texas Department of Transportation.

Johnson, LeRoy, Jr., with the collaboration of Glenn T. Goode. 1994. A New Try at Dating and Characterizing Holocene Climates, as Well as Archeological Periods, on the Eastern Edwards Plateau. *Bulletin of the Texas Archeological Society* 65:1–54.

Jones, Buddy C. 1957. The Grace Creek Sites, Gregg County, Texas. *Bulletin of the Texas Archeological Society* 28:198–231.

Joukowsky, Martha. 1980. *A Complete Manual of Field Archaeology*. Englewood Cliffs, N.J.: Prentice-Hall.

Justice, Noel D. 1987. *Stone Age Spear and Arrow Points of the Midcontinental and Eastern United States*. Bloomington: Indiana University Press.

———. 2002. *Stone Age Spear and Arrow Points of the Southwestern United States*. Bloomington: Indiana University Press.

Karbula, James William. 2000. Investigations of the Eckols Site (41TV528): A Stratified Prehistoric Terrace Site on Barton Creek in Travis County, Texas. PhD diss., Department of Anthropology, University of Texas at Austin.

———. 2003. The Toyah Bluff Site (41TV441) Changing Notions of Late Prehistoric Subsistence in the Blackland Prairie, Travis County, TX. *Bulletin of the Texas Archeological Society* 74:55–83.

Katz, Paul R. 1987. *Archaeological Mitigation at 41BX300, Salado Creek Watershed, South-Central Texas*. Archaeological Survey Report 130. San Antonio: Center for Archaeological Research, University of Texas.

Katz, Paul R., and Paul D. Lukowski. 1981. Results of Archaeological Survey in the Salt Flat Locality of Northern Hudspeth County, Texas. In *Five Archeological Investigations in the Trans-Pecos Region of Texas*, 1–26. Permit Series 6. Austin: Texas Antiquities Committee.

Keeley, Lawrence H. 1980. *Experimental Determination of Stone Tool Uses: A Microwear Analysis*. Chicago: University of Chicago Press.

Keller, John E., and Frank A. Weir. 1979. *The Strawberry Hill Site*. Report 13. Austin: Highway Design Division, Texas State Department of Highways and Public Transportation Publications in Archaeology.

Kelley, J. Charles. 1947. The Lehmann Rock Shelter: A Stratified Site of the Tovah, Uvalde, and Round Rock Foci. *Bulletin of the Texas Archeological and Paleontological Society* 18:115–28.

———. 1948. Arrow or Dart Shaft Tools and Problematical Incised Tools from Central and Western Texas. *El Palacio* 55 (3): 73–84.

———. 1978. *Seminar: Native Indian Culture in the Texas Big Bend: A Public Discussion.* Alpine, Tex.: Museum of the Big Bend, Sul Ross State University. Published with assistance from the Texas Committee for the Humanities and the National Endowment for the Humanities.

———. 1986. *Jumano and Patarabueye Relations at La Junta de Los Rios.* Anthropological Papers 77. Ann Arbor: Museum of Anthropology, University of Michigan.

Kelly, Thomas C. 1962. The Crumley Site: A Stratified Burnt Rock Midden, Travis County, Texas. *Bulletin of the Texas Archeological Society* 31:239–72.

———. 1963. Archeological Investigations at Roark Cave, Brewster County, Texas. *Bulletin of the Texas Archeological Society* 33:191–227.

———. 1979. Comments on Patterson's, Hester's and Shafer's Comments. *La Tierra* 6 (3): 11.

———. 1982. Criteria for Classification of *Plainview* and *Golondrina* Projectile Points. *La Tierra* 9 (3): 2–25.

———. 1983a. The *Barber* Paleo-Indian Point. *La Tierra* 10 (4): 10–25.

———. 1983b. The Brom Cooper Paleo-Indian Collection from McMullen County, Texas. *La Tierra* 10 (3): 17–40.

———. 1989. Morphological Study of the Lerma/Desmuke Problem. Paper presented to the Texas Archeological Society Meeting, Amarillo, Tex., October 28.

Kelly, Thomas C., Philip Green, Sylvia Bento, and Wayne Cox. 1983. *The Chacon Creek Project: Archaeological Investigations in Maverick and Zavala Counties, Texas.* Archaeological Survey Report 112. San Antonio: Center for Archaeological Research, University of Texas.

Kelly, Thomas C., and Thomas R. Hester. 1975. *Additional Archaeological Survey in the Dry Corral Watershed, Corral County, South Central Texas.* Archaeological Survey Report 10. San Antonio: Center for Archaeological Research, University of Texas.

———. 1976. *Archaeological Investigations at Sites in the Cibolo Creek Watershed, Central Texas.* Archaeological Survey Report 17. San Antonio: Center for Archaeological Research, University of Texas.

Kelly, Thomas C., and H. P. Smith. 1963. An Investigation of Archaeological Sites in Reagan Canyon, Brewster County, Texas. *Bulletin of the Texas Archeological Society* 33:167–90.

"Kelpie." 1908. Arrowhead Making: Letter to the Editor. *Forest and Stream,* September 5.

Kenmotsu, Nancy. 1990. Gunflints: A Study. *Historical Archaeology* 24 (2): 92–124.

Kenmotsu, Ray D., with contributions by Leland C. Bement and David G. Robinson. 1982. *Cultural Resource Investigations at the Powell Bend Prospect, Bastrop, Texas.* Research Report 84. Austin: Texas Archeological Survey, University of Texas.

Kent, D. T., Jr. 1961. Letter to Lathel F. Duffield containing description of *Neches River* dart points in McGee Bend Reservoir files, Texas Archeological Research Laboratory, University of Texas at Austin.

Kibler, Karl W. 1991. Surface Distributions of Sites and Survey Strategies for Draws on the Southern Llano Estacado. Master's thesis, Department of Anthropology, University of Texas at Austin.

Kibler, Karl W., and Ann M. Scott. 2000. *Archaic Hunters and Gatherers of the Balcones Canyonlands: Data Recovery at the Cibolo Crossing Site (41BX377), Camp Bullis Military Reservation.* Report of Investigations 126. Austin, Tex.: Prewitt and Associates.

Knudson, Ruthann. 1973. Organizational Variability in Late Paleo-Indian Assemblages. PhD diss., Department of Anthropology, Washington State University, Pullman.

———. 1998. Plainview Complex. In *Paleoindian,* edited by George C. Frison, in *Archaeology of Prehistoric Native America: An Encyclopedia,* edited by Guy E. Gibbon, 653–55. New York: Garland.

———. 2005. On Plainview. *Prehistoric American* 39 (2): 3–8.

Knudson, Ruthann, and Susanne J. Miller. 2007. The Wasden Owl Cave Folsom Material from Eastern Idaho. *Inside Prehistoric American: The Journal for the Documentation of Prehistoric America* 41 (4): 62–64.

Kotter, Steven M., Thomas M. Byrd, and Michael W. Davis. 1985. *Cherry Tree Shelter: Excavations of a Stratified Late Archaic and Neoarchaic Rockshelter, Travis County, Texas.* Research Report 92. Austin: Texas Archeological Survey, University of Texas.

Kotter, Steven M., Patience E. Patterson, Dan K. Utley, and Henry B. Moncure. 1991. *Final Report of Cultural Resource Investigations at the Cummins Creek Mine, Fayette County, Texas.* Studies in Archeology 11. Austin: Texas Archeological Research Laboratory, University of Texas.

Kraft, Kenneth C. 1993. *Corner-Tang Artifacts of the Plains.* Master's thesis, Texas Tech University, Lubbock.

Krieger, Alex. 1943. Archaeological Horizons in the Caddo Area. In *El Norte de México y el Sur de Estados Unidos.* Mexico: Sociedad Mexicana de Antropologia.

———. 1944. The Typological Concept. *American Antiquity* 9:271–88.

———. 1946. *Culture Complexes and Chronology in Northern Texas.* University of Texas Publications 4640. Austin: University of Texas.

Krieger, Alex, and J. T. Hughes. 1950. *Archaeological Salvage in the Falcon Reservoir Area: Progress Report 1* (mimeographed). Austin: University of Texas.

Kroeber, A. L. 1925. *Handbook of the California Indians.* Bureau of American Ethnology 78. Washington, D.C.: Government Printing Office.

Kumpe, Don. 1993. Site form for 41ZP154. On record at Texas Archeological Research Laboratory, University of Texas at Austin.

———. 1998. Site form for 41ZP83. On record at Texas Archeological Research Laboratory, University of Texas at Austin.

Kumpe, Don, and Richard McReynolds. 2009. Hidalgo: A Dart Point Type of the Lower Rio Grande. *La Tierra* 36 (1–2): 1–8.

Kumpe, Don, Richard McReynolds, and C. K. Chandler. 2000. A Highly Serrated Arrow Point from Falcon Reservoir, Zapata County, Texas. *La Tierra* 27 (1): 33–45.

Labadie, Joseph H. 1988. *Archaeological Investigations at the Shrew Site, 41 WJV73, Wilson County, Southern Texas.* Contract Reports in Archaeology 2. Austin: Highway Design Division, State Department of Highways and Public Transportation.

Largent, Floyd B., Jr. 1995. Some New Additions to the Texas Folsom Point Database. *Plains Anthropologist* 40 (151): 69–72.

Largent, Floyd B., Jr., and Michael R. Waters. 1990. The Distribution of Folsom Points in Texas. *Current Research in the Pleistocene* 7:27–28.

Lemley, H. J. 1936. Discoveries Indicating a Pre-Caddo Culture on the Red River in Arkansas. *Bulletin of the Texas Archeological and Paleontological Society* 8:25–55.

Leslie, Robert H. 1978. Projectile Point Types and Sequences of the Eastern Jornada Mogollon: Extreme Southeastern New Mexico. In *Transactions of the 13th Regional Archaeological Symposium for Southeastern New Mexico and Western Texas,* 81–157.

Lintz, Chris, and Bryant Saner. 2002. The Hoerster Cache from 41MS67, Mason County, Texas. *La Tierra* 29 (1): 12–47.

Lintz, Christopher, et al. 1993. *Cultural Resource Investigations in the O.H. Ivie Reservoir, Concho, Coleman, and Runnels Counties, Texas.* Vol. 1. Technical Report 346-1. Austin, Tex.: Mariah Associates.

Logan, Wilfred D. 1952. Gr*aham Cave, An Archaic Site in Montgomery County, Missouri.* Memoir 2. Springfield: Missouri Archaeological Society.

Lohse, Jon C. 1999. Lithics from the San Antonio de Valero Mission: Analysis from 1979. Excavations at the Alamo. *Bulletin of the Texas Archeological Society* 70:265–80.

Long, Russell J. 1977. *McFaddin Beach.* Patillo Higgins Series of Natural History and Anthropology 1. Beaumont, Tex.: Spindletop Museum, Lamar University.

Lovata, Troy R. 1997. Archeological Investigations at the Silo Site (41KA102): A Prehistoric Cemetery in Karnes County, Texas. Master's thesis, Department of Anthropology, University of Texas at Austin.

Loy, Thomas. 1983. Prehistoric Blood Residues: Detection on Tool Surfaces and Identification of Species of Origin. *Science* 270:1269–71.

Luchterhand, Kubet. 1970. *Early Projectile Points and Hunting Patterns in the Lower Illinois Valley*. Research Papers 3, Springfield: Illinois Valley Archaeological Program.

Luedtke, Barbara E. 1992. *An Archaeologist's Guide to Chert and Flint*. Archaeological Research Tools 7. Los Angeles: Institute of Archaeology, University of California.

Luke, Clive J. 1980. *Continuing Archaeology on State Highway 16: The Shep Site (41KR109) and the Wounded Eye Site (41KR107)*. Publications in Archaeology Report 16. Austin: Texas State Department of Highways and Public Transportation.

———. 1983. *Continuing Archaeology on Interstate Highway 10: The Musk Hog Canyon Project, Crockett County, Texas*. Publications in Archaeology Report 24. Austin: Texas State Department of Highways and Public Transportation.

Lukowski, Paul D. 1983. *Archaeological Investigations at 41BX1, Bexar County, Texas*. Archaeological Survey Report 126. San Antonio: Center for Archaeological Research, University of Texas.

———. 1987. *Archaeological Investigations along the Leona River Watershed, Uvalde County, Texas*. Archaeological Survey Report 132. San Antonio: Center for Archaeological Research, University of Texas.

Lynott, Mark J. 1981. A Model of Prehistoric Adaptation in Northern Texas. *Plains Anthropologist* 26 (92): 97–110.

MacNeish, Richard S. 1958. Preliminary Archaeological Investigations in the Sierra de Tamaulipas, Mexico. *Transactions of the American Philosophical Society* 4 (6): 1–210.

———. 1993. *Preliminary Investigation of the Archaic in the Region of Las Cruces, New Mexico*. Historic and Natural Resources Report 9. Fort Bliss, Tex.: Cultural Resources Managements Program, Directorate of Environment.

Mahoney, Richard B., Raymond Maudlin, and Steve Tomka, et al. 2002. *Archaeological Data Recovery Excavations along Becerra Creek (41WB556), Webb County, Texas*. Archaeological Survey Report 321. San Antonio: Center for Archaeological Research, University of Texas.

Mahoney, Richard B., Harry J. Shafer, Steve A. Tomka, Lee C. Nordt, and Raymond P. Mauldin. 2003. *Royal Coachman (41CM111): An Early Middle Archaic Site along Cordova Creek in Comal County, Texas*. Archaeological Survey Report 332. San Antonio: Center for Archaeological Research, University of Texas; Archaeological Studies Program Report 49, Texas Department of Transportation, Austin.

Mahoney, Richard B., Steve A. Tomka, Raymond P. Mauldin, Harry J. Shafer, Lee C. Nordt, Russell D. Greaves, and Rebecca R. Galdeano, et al. 2003. *Data Recovery Excavations at 41MM340: A Late Archaic Site along Little River in Milam County, Texas*. Archeological Studies Program Report 54. Austin: Texas Department of Transportation; Archaeological Survey Report 340, Center for Archaeological Research, University of Texas at San Antonio.

Mallouf, Robert B. 1976. *Archeological Investigations at Proposed Big Pine Lake, 1974–1975, Lamar and Red River Counties, Texas*. Archeological Survey Report 18. Austin: Texas Historical Commission.

Mallouf, R. J., B. J. Baskin, and K. L. Killen. 1977. *A Predictive Assessment of Cultural Resources in Hidalgo and Willacy Counties, Texas*. Survey Report 25. Austin: Texas Historical Commission, Office of the State Archeologist.

Mallouf, R. J., and R. D. Mandel. 1996. Horace Rivers: A Late-Plainview Component in the Northeastern Texas Panhandle. *Current Research in the Pleistocene* 15:50–52.

Mallouf, R. J., and Anthony N. Zavaleta. 1979. *The Unland Site. A Prehistoric Group Burial from Laguna Atascosa National Wildlife Refuge, Cameron County, Texas*. Special Report 25. Austin: Office of the State Archeologist.

Mallouf, Robert J. 1979. *Archeological Investigations at Lake Limestone*. Research Report 71. Austin: Texas Archeological Survey, University of Texas.

———. 1981a. *A Case Study of Plow Damage to Chert Artifacts: The Brookeen Creek Cache, Hill County, Texas*. Report 33. Austin: Office of the State Archeologist.

———. 1981b. Observations Concerning Environmental and Cultural Interactions during the Terminal Pleistocene and Early Holocene in the Big Bend of Texas and Adjoining Regions. *Bulletin of the Texas Archeological Society* 52:121–46.

———. 1985. A Synthesis of Eastern Trans-Pecos History. Master's thesis. Austin: Department of Anthropology, University of Texas.

———. 1987. *Las Haciendas. A Cairn-Burial Assemblage from Northeastern Chihuahua, Mexico*. Report 35. Austin: Office of the State Archeologist, Texas Historical Commission.

———. 1988. The Yellow Hawk Site: A Clovis Quarry in North-Central Texas. *Current Research in the Pleistocene* 5:17–18.

———. 1990. Hell Gap Points in the Southern Rolling Plains of Texas. *Current Research in the Pleistocene* 7:32–35.

———. 1999. Comments on the Prehistory of Far Northeastern Chihuahua, the La Junta District and the Cielo complex. *Journal of Big Bend Studies* 11:49–92.

———. 2009a. Alazan: An Arrow Point Type from the Eastern Trans-Pecos and Big Bend Region of Texas. Alpine, Tex.: Center for Big Bend Studies, Sul Ross State University.

———. 2009b. Diablo Arrow Point. Alpine, Tex.: Center for Big Bend Studies, Sul Ross State University.

———. 2009c. Hueco Dart Points. Alpine, Tex.: Center for Big Bend Studies, Sul Ross State University.

———. 2009d. The John Z. and Exa Means Cache: New Discovery Yields Insights into Big Bend's Prehistoric Indians. *La Vista de la Frontera* 20:1–3.

———. 2009e. The Means Arrow Point: A New Arrow Point Type from the Eastern Trans-Pecos Region of Texas. Alpine, Tex.: Center for Big Bend Studies, Sul Ross State University.

Mallouf, Robert J., William A. Cloud, and Richard W. Walter. 2006. *The Rosilla Peak Site: A Prehistoric Mountaintop Campsite in Big Bend National Park, Texas*. Papers of the Trans-Pecos Archaeological Program 1. Alpine, Tex.: Center for Big Bend Studies, Sul Ross State University.

Mallouf, Robert J., and Curtis Tunnell. 1979. Field Notes at 41SR137: Geological Notes and Postulations Concerning "Opalite" (opalized tuffaceous bentonitic clay) Found in Starr County. On file at Office of State Archeologist, Austin, Tex.

Mallouf, Robert J. and Virginia A. Wulfkuhle. 1989. An Archeological Reconnaissance in the Rosillos Mountains, Brewster County, Texas. *Journal of Big Bend Studies* 1:1–34.

———. 1991. Notes on the Helton-Harrel Biface Cache from Seward County, Kansas. *Kansas Anthropologist* 12 (1): 1–12.

Manning, Andrew P. 1991. An Examination of Techniques Involved in the Qualitative and Quantitative Analysis of Blood Residues on Stone Tools. Master's thesis, University of Texas at Austin.

Marchbanks, Michael L. 1989. Lipid Analysis in Archaeology: An Initial Study of Ceramics and Subsistence at the George C. Davis Site. Master's thesis, University of Texas at Austin.

Marmaduke, William S. 1978. *Prehistory at Bear Creek*. State Archeologist Survey Report 25. Austin: Texas Historical Commission.

Martin, Ernest A. 1994. The Dillard Site: A Late Prehistoric Plains Village Site in Cooke County, Texas. *Bulletin of the Texas Archeological Society* 62 (for 1991): 105–200.

Martinez, Valentina L. 1990. Folsom-Midland Sites of the Southern High Plains. Paper presented at the 55th Annual Meeting of the Society for American Archaeology, Las Vegas.

Mauldin, Raymond P., Steve A. Tomka, and Harry J. Shafer, et al. 2004. *Millican Bench (41TV163): A Multicomponent Site in Travis County*. Archeological Studies Program Report 66. Austin: Center for Archaeological Research, University of Texas at San Antonio; Archaeological Survey Report 351, Texas Department of Transportation.

Mauldin, Raymond P., et al. 2003. *Archeological Survey and Testing of Selected Prehistoric Sites Along FM 481, Zavala County, Texas*. Archaeological Survey Report 352. San Antonio: Center for Archaeological Research, University of Texas; Archeological Studies Program Report 67, Texas Department of Transportation.

McClurkan, Burney B. 1966. The Archaeology of Cueva de la Zona de Derrumbes, a Rockshelter in Nuevo León, México. Master's thesis, University of Texas at Austin.

———. 1968. *Livingston Reservoir, 1956–1966*. Papers of the Texas Archeological Salvage Project 12. Austin: University of Texas.

McCormick, Olin F. 1976. The Archaic Period in North Central Texas. In *The Texas Archaic: A Symposium*, edited by Thomas R. Hester, 39–45. Special Report 2. San Antonio: Center for Archaeological Research, University of Texas.

McGraw, A. Joachim, and Jerry Thompson. 1998. *Campfires and Coal Dust on the Rio Grande: The Archaeology and History of the Laredo-Columbia Solidarity International Bridge Site, Nuevo Leon, Mexico and Webb County, Texas*. Archeological Studies Program 8. Austin: Texas Department of Transportation.

McGraw, A. Joachim, and Fred Valdez Jr. 1978. *41BX68: A Prehistoric Quarry-Workshop in Northern Bexar County, Texas*. Archaeological Survey Report 56. San Antonio: Center for Archaeological Research, University of Texas.

McGregor, Daniel E., and James E. Bruseth, eds. 1987. *Hunter-Gatherer Adaptations along the Prairie Margin, Site Excavations and Synthesis of Prehistoric Archaeology*. Richland Creek Technical Series 3. Dallas: Archaeology Research Program, Southern Methodist University.

McKinney, Wilson W. 1981. Early Holocene Adaptations in Central and Southern Texas: The Problem of the Paleo-Indian Archaic Transition. *Bulletin of the Texas Archeological Society* 52:91–120.

McReynolds, Richard. 2002. Calf Creek Horizon Points from Wilson County, Texas. *La Tierra* 29 (4): 39–44.

McReynolds, Richard, Ben McReynolds, and Mike McReynolds. 1979. Additional Paleo-Indian Artifacts from San Miguel Creek, Atascosa County, Texas. *La Tierra* 6 (2): 20.

McReynolds, Richard L., and C. K. Chandler. 1984. Two Tanged Knife Forms from Val Verde County, Texas. *La Tierra* 11 (2): 6–11.

———. 1990. An Incised Stone from Atascosa County, South Central Texas. *La Tierra* 17 (4): 3–7.

Medlar, Carole A. 1991. A Functional Morphological Microwear Study of Central Texas Early Triangular Bifaces. Manuscript on file at Texas Archeological Research Laboratory, University of Texas at Austin.

Mehalchick, Gemma, and Karl W. Kibler. 2008. *Hunters and Gatherers of the North Bosque River Valley: Excavations at the Baylor, Britton, McMillan, and Higginbotham Sites, Waco Lake, McLennan County, Texas*. Reports of Investigations 156. Austin, Tex.: Prewitt and Associates.

Mehalchick, Gemma, Terri Myers, Karl W. Kibler, and Douglas K. Boyd. 1999. *"Val Verde on the Sunny Rio Grande": Geoarchaeological and Historical Investigations at San Felipe Springs, Val Verde County*. Texas Reports of Investigations 122. Austin, Tex.: Prewitt and Associates.

Meltzer, David J. 1987. The Clovis Paleoindian Occupation of Texas: Results of the Texas Fluted Point Survey. *Bulletin of the Texas Archeology Society* 57:27–68.

Metcalf, George. 1970. Some Wooden Scraper Handles from the Great Plains and the Southwest. *Plains Anthropologist* 15 (47): 46–53.

Miller, Kevin. 1991. Two Large Biface Caches from Texas: The Fairview Cache (41TV9) and the Baird Cache. Manuscript on file at Texas Archeological Research Laboratory, University of Texas at Austin.

———. 2007. A Study of Prehistoric Biface Caches from Texas. *La Tierra* 34 (1–2): 1–88.

Miller, Kevin A., Steve Carpenter, Lee C. Nordt, and Christopher W. Ringstaff. 2000. *Archaeological Investigations along the Camino Colombia Toll Road, Webb County, Texas.* Cultural Resource Report 97–120. Austin: SWCA.

Miller, Myles R., and Nancy A. Kenmotsu. 2004. Prehistory of the Jornada Mogollon and Eastern Trans-Pecos Regions of West Texas. In *The Prehistory of Texas,* edited by T. K. Perttula, 205–65. College Station: Texas A&M University Press.

Mitchell, J. L., C. K. Chandler, and T. C. Kelly. 1984. The Rudy Haiduk Site (41KA23): A Late Archaic Burial in Karnes County, Texas. *La Tierra* 11 (2): 12–39.

Mitchell, J. L., T. R. Hester, and Wayne Parker. 1980. A Bannerstone from Padre Island on the Texas Coast. *La Tierra* 7 (2): 23–25.

Mitchell, J. L., and C. D. Orchard. 1984. Three Corner Tang Artifacts from the Olmos Dam Area, Bexar County, Texas. *La Tierra* 11 (2): 2–5.

Mitchell, Jimmy L. 1975. Ground Stone Ornaments in Southern Texas. *La Tierra* 2:18–14.

———. 1982. The *Sabinal* Point. *La Tierra* 9 (4): 1–6.

Mock, Shirley. 1987. The Painted Pebbles of the Lower Pecos: A Study of Medium, Form, and Content. Master's thesis, Department of Anthropology, University of Texas at San Antonio.

Montgomery, John L. 1978. *The Mariposa Site: A Late Prehistoric Site on the Rio Grande Plain of Texas.* Special Report 6. San Antonio: Center for Archaeological Research, University of Texas.

Moore, William E. 1989. An Andice Point from the Fietsam Site (41FY52) Fayette County, Texas. *La Tierra* 16 (4): 8–9.

———. 1991. A Probable Aboriginal Gunflint from Site 41LK293 in Live Oak County, Texas. *La Tierra* 18 (2): 38–39.

Morrow, Juliet E. 1995. Clovis Projectile Point Manufacture: A Perspective from the Ready/Lincon Hills Site, 11JY45, Jersey County, Illinois. *Midcontinental Journal of Archaeology* 20 (2): 167–91.

Morse, D. F., and A. C. Goodyear. 1973a. The Hawkins Cache: A Significant Dalton Find in Northeast Arkansas. *Arkansas Archeologist* 12 (1): 9–20.

———. 1973b. The Significance of the Dalton Adz in Northeast Arkansas. *Plains Anthropologist* 19 (63): 316–22.

Morse, Dan F. 1973. Dalton Culture in Northeast Arkansas. *Florida Anthropologist* 26 (1): 23–38.

———. 1997. *Sloan: A Paleoindian Dalton Cemetery in Arkansas.* Washington, D.C.: Smithsonian Institution Press.

Moseley, Laurie. 1996. Hematite Celts from North-Central Texas Sites. *The Cache* 3:35–44.

Mueggenborg, Henry. 1994. Excavations at the Blue Hole Site, Uvalde County, Texas. *Bulletin of the Texas Archeological Society* 62 (for 1991): 1–74.

Mueller-Wille, C. S., and David L. Carlson. 1990a. *Archaeological Survey at Fort Hood, Texas Fiscal Year 1986: Other Training Areas.* Archeological Resource Management Series Research Report 21. Fort Hood, Tex.: U.S. Army.

———. 1990b. *Archaeological Survey at Fort Hood, Texas Fiscal Year 1986: The Shoal Creek Watershed.* Archeological Resource Management Series Research Report 20. Fort Hood, Tex.: U.S. Army.

Myers, Thomas P., and Ray Lambert. 1983. Meserve Points: Evidence of a Plains-Ward Extension of the Dalton Horizon. *Plains Anthropologist* 28 (100): 109–14.

Nance, C. R. 1971. The Archaeology of La Calsada: A Stratified Rock Shelter Site, Sierra Madre Oriental, Nuevo León, México. PhD diss., University of Texas at Austin.

Nelson, Bo, Tim Perttula, and Mike Turner. 1994. Caddoan Archaeology in the Little Cypress Creek Valley: Recent Investigations at the Griffin Mound Site (41UR142), Upshur County, Texas. *Caddoan Archeology Newsletter* 5 (3): 6–17. [See also Nelson and Turner in *The Cache* 3:49–66.]

Newcomb, W. W., Jr. 1967. *The Rock Art of Texas Indians*. Paintings by Forrest Kirkland. Austin: University of Texas Press.

Newell, H. Perry, and Alex D. Krieger. 1949. *The George C. Davis Site, Cherokee County, Texas*. Memoirs of the Society for American Archaeology 5. Menasha, Wis.: Society for American Archaeology and University of Texas.

Newton, Milton B. 1963. Summary of Reconnaissance on Arroyo Los Olmos, Starr County, Texas. Paper distributed at the Southern Archeological Association annual meeting, Boulder, Colo.

Nickels, David L., C. Britt Bousman, Jeff D. Leach, and Diane A. Cargill, et al. 2001. *Test Excavations at the Culebra Creek Site, 41BX126, Bexar County, Texas*. Archaeological Survey Report 265. San Antonio: Center for Archaeological Research, University of Texas.

Nightengale, B. A., J. M. Jackson, and H. B. Moncure. 1985. *Additional Intensive Survey of Cultural Resources in the Cummins Creek Prospect, Fayette County, Texas*. Texas Archeological Survey Research Report 89. Austin: University of Texas.

Nissen, Karen M., and Margaret E. Dittemore. 1974. Ethnographic Data and Wear Pattern Analysis: A Study of Socketed Eskimo Scrapers. *Tebiwa* 17 (1): 67–88.

Nunley, J. Parker, and Lathel F. Duffield. 1964. Salvage Excavations at the Coontail Spin Rockshelter, Amistad Reservoir, Texas. Manuscript on file at the Texas Archeological Salvage Project, University of Texas at Austin.

Nunley, J. Parker, and Thomas R. Hester. 1966. Preliminary Investigations in Dimmit County, Texas. *Texas Journal of Science* 18 (3): 233–53.

———. 1975. *An Assessment of Archaeological Resources in Portions of Starr County, Texas*. Archaeological Survey Report 7. San Antonio: Center for Archaeological Research, University of Texas.

Nunley, John Parker, Lathel F. Duffield, and E. B. Jelks. 1965. *Excavations at Amistad Reservoir: 1962 Season*. Miscellaneous Papers 3. Austin: Texas Archeological Salvage Project.

Oksanen, Eric R. 2008. Archaeological Investigations at the Icehouse Site 41HY161: A Revaluation of Early Archaic Technology, Subsistence and Settlement along the Balcones Escarpment and Central Texas. Master's thesis, Texas State University at San Marcos.

Palter, John L. 1977. A New Approach to the Significance of the "Weighted" Spear Thrower. *American Antiquity* 41 (4): 500–10.

Parsons, Mark L. 1965. *1963 Test Excavations at Fate Bell Shelter, Amistad Reservoir, Val Verde County, Texas*. Miscellaneous Papers 4. Austin: Texas Archeological Salvage Project.

———. 1967. *Archeological Investigations in Crosby and Dickens Counties, Texas, during the Winter 1966–1967*. Archeological Program Report 7. Austin: Texas State Building Commission.

Patterson, J. T. 1936. *The Corner-Tang Flint Artifacts of Texas*. Bulletin 3618. Anthropological Papers 1 (4). Austin: University of Texas.

———. 1937. *Boat-Shaped Artifacts of the Gulf Southwest States*. Bulletin 3732. Anthropological Papers 1 (2). Austin: University of Texas.

Patterson, L. W., and Joe Hudgins. 1981. Site 41WH19: A Long Occupation Period in Wharton County, Texas. *Houston Archeological Society Journal* 70:4–13.

———. 1985. Paleo-Indian Occupations in Wharton County, Texas. *Bulletin of the Texas Archeological Society* 56:155–70.

———. 1998. Comments on Boatstones. *Ohio Archaeologist* 49 (2): 18–19.

Patterson, L. W., K. Marriott, and L. Marriott. 1990. Site 41HR624: Another Long Sequence in Harris Co., Texas. *Houston Archeological Society Journal* 96:21–26.

Patterson, L. W., Ron Murk, and Suzanne Murk. 1984. Site 41HR525: Another Long Occupation Sequence in Harris County, Texas. *Houston Archeological Society Journal* 78:11–15.

Patterson, Leland W. 1975. The Catahoula Projectile Point: A Distributional Study. *Louisiana Archaeology* 3:217–24.

———. 1976. Technological Changes in Harris County, Texas. *Bulletin of the Texas Archeology Society* 47:171–88.

———. 1979a. An Alternate Explanation of Edge Damage on Gower Points. *La Tierra* 6 (3): 3–4.

———. 1979b. A Review of the Prehistory of the Upper Texas Coast. *Bulletin of the Texas Archeological Society* 50:103–234.

———. 1987. The Catahoula Perforator: A Possible New Artifact Type. *Houston Archeological Society Journal* 88:19–21.

———. 1990a. Additional Data from Site 41HR624, Harris Co., Texas. *Houston Archeological Society Journal* 96:15–20.

———. 1990b. Relationships of Certain Dart Point Types in Southeast Texas. *Houston Archeological Society Journal* 96:1–3.

———. 1990c. The Seaberg Collections (41HR641, 642), Harris Co., Texas. *Houston Archeological Society Journal* 98:12–20.

———. 1991a. The Albany-Edgefield Hafted Scraper. *Chesopiean* 29 (2): 7–13.

———. 1991b. Arrow Point Chronology in Southeast Texas. *Houston Archeological Society Journal* 101:6–11.

———. 1991c. Dart Point Chronologies of Southeast Texas. *Houston Archeological Society Journal* 101:1–5.

———. 2000. Late Archaic Mortuary Tradition of Southeast Texas. *La Tierra* 27 (2): 28–44.

Patterson, Leland W., and M. A. Marshall. 1989. Some Archeological Sites on Upper Jacinto Bay. *Houston Archeological Society Journal* 94:1–8.

Patterson, Leland W., and J. B. Sollberger. 1990. The Significance of Beveled Edges on Projectile Points. *La Tierra* 17 (2): 37–38.

Patterson, Patience E. 1977. A Lithic Reduction Sequence: A Test Case in the North Fork Reservoir Area, Williamson County, Texas. *Bulletin of the Texas Archeological Society* 48:53–82.

Peck, Jay. 1991. An Analysis of the Projectile Points from the 1932: Excavation of Fate Bell Rockshelter. In *Papers on Lower Pecos Prehistory*, edited by Solveig A. Turpin, 65–86. Studies in Archeology 8. Austin: Texas Archeological Research Laboratory, University of Texas.

Peckham, Stewart. 1965. *Prehistoric Weapons in the Southwest*. Popular Series Pamphlet 3. Santa Fe: Museum of New Mexico Press.

Peeples, Matthew. 2003. An Analysis of the Projectile Points from the Chytka Site (41JK66), Jackson County, Texas. *La Tierra* 30 (1–2): 37–63.

Perino, G., and W. J. Bennett Jr. 1972. More Edge-Trimming Tools. *Central States Archaeological Journal* (October): 147–51.

Perino, Gregory. 1968. *Guide to the Identification of Certain American Projectile Points*. Special Bulletin 3. Oklahoma City: Oklahoma Anthropological Society.

———. 1971. *Guide to the Identification of Certain Indian Projectile Points*. Special Bulletin 4. Oklahoma City: Oklahoma Anthropological Society.

———. 1985. *Selected Preforms, Points, and Knives of the North American Indians*. Vol. 1. Idabel, Okla.: Points & Barbs Press.

Perttula, Timothy K. 1992. *The Caddo Nation: Archaeological and Ethnographic Perspectives.* Texas Archaeology and Ethnohistory Series. Austin: University of Texas Press.

———. 1995. A Reconsideration of the Chronological and Cultural Placement of Mortuary Remains and Grave Goods from the Dan Holdeman Site. *Journal of Northeast Texas Archaeology* 6:57–87.

———, ed. 2004. *The Prehistory of Texas.* College Station: Texas A&M University Press.

———. 2009. Typological Labeling of Early Holocene Projectile Points. *Proceedings of the National Academy of Sciences* 106 (27): E74.

Perttula, Timothy K., et al. 2002. Archeological Investigations on the Red River and Tributaries: Summary Findings of the Findings of the 1991 and 1992 Texas Archeological Society Field School in Red River and Lamar Counties. *Bulletin of the Texas Archeological Society* 72:165–250.

Peter, Duane E. 1982a. An Experiment in the Assessment of Projectile Point Variability. In *Archaeological Investigations at San Gabriel Reservoir Districts, Central Texas,* edited by T. R. Hays, 14-35–14-69. Denton: Institute of Applied Sciences, North Texas State University.

———. 1982b. Projectile Point Classification. In *Archaeological Investigations at San Gabriel Reservoir Districts, Central Texas,* edited by T. R. Hays, 14-3–14-35. Denton: Institute of Applied Sciences, North Texas State University.

Pfeiffer, Leslie. 2001. The Cibolo Creek Site. *Central States Archaeological Society Journal* 48 (1): 56–57.

———. 2002. San Saba Knives. *Central States Archaeological Society Journal* 49 (2): 56–57.

Pillaert, E. Elizabeth. 1963. The McLemore Site of the Washita River Focus. *Bulletin of the Oklahoma Anthropological Society* 11 (March): 1–114.

Pitzer, Jean M. 1977. *A Guide to the Identification of Burins in Prehistoric Chipped Stone Assemblages.* Guidebooks in Archaeology 1. San Antonio: Center for Archaeological Research, University of Texas.

Poteet, S. 1938. The Occurrence and Distribution of Beveled Knives. *Bulletin of the Texas Archeological and Paleontological Society* 10:245–62.

Preston, Nolan E., and Joel L. Shiner. 1969. The McCann Site. *Bulletin of the Texas Archaeological Society* 40:167–92.

Prewitt, E. R., and D. A. Lawson. 1972. *An Assessment of the Archeological and Paleontological Resources of Lake Texoma, Texas-Oklahoma.* Survey Reports 10. Austin: Texas Archeological Salvage Project, University of Texas.

Prewitt, Elton R. 1970. The Piedra del Diablo Site, Val Verde County, Texas. *Texas Historical Survey Committee Archeological Report* 18 (1): 1–31.

———. 1974a. *Archeological Investigations at the Loeve-Fox Site, Williamson County.* Research Report 49. Austin: Texas Archeological Survey, University of Texas.

———. 1974b. *Upper Navasota Reservoir: An Archeological Assessment.* Research Report 47. Austin: Texas Archeological Survey, University of Texas.

———. 1975. *Upper Navasota Reservoir: Archeological Test Excavations at the Barkley and Louie Sadler Sites.* Research Report 53. Austin: Texas Archeological Survey, University of Texas.

———. 1981a. *Archeological Investigations at the Loeve-Fox, Loeve and Tombstone Bluff Sites in the Granger Lake District of Central Texas.* Archaeological Investigations at the San Gabriel Reservoir Districts 4. Denton: Institute of Applied Sciences, North Texas State University.

———. 1981b. Cultural Chronology in Central Texas. *Bulletin of the Texas Archeological Society* 52:65–89.

———. 1983. *Andice*: An Early Archaic Dart Point Type. *La Tierra* 10 (3): 1–6.

———. 1985. From Circleville to Toyah: Comments on Central Texas Chronology. *Bulletin of the Texas Archeological Society* 54:201–38.

———. 1995. Distributions of Typed Projectile Points in Texas. *Bulletin of the Texas Archeological Society* 66:83–173.

———. 2005. Review of *The Prehistory of Texas*, edited by Timothy K. Perttula (College Station: Texas A&M University Press, 2004). *Bulletin of the Texas Archeological Society* 76:266–77.

———. 2010. Merrell: An Early Archaic Dart Point Type. Working draft manuscript.

Prewitt, Elton R., and C. K. Chandler. 1992. Axtell: A Middle Archaic Dart Point Type. *La Tierra* 19 (1): 15–20.

Prikryl, Daniel J. 1990. *Lower Elm Fork Prehistory*. Report 37. Austin: Texas Historical Commission, Office of the State Archeologist.

Prilliman, Keith L. 1998. Gault Site Andice Bifaces. *TARL Research Notes* 6 (1): 13–17.

Priour, Donald J. 1987. A Preliminary Report on the "Butted Knife" Biface Survey. *La Tierra* 14 (2): 5–18.

Quigg, J. M., and J. Peck. 1995. *The Rush Site (41TG346): A Stratified Late Prehistoric Locale in Tom Green County, Texas*. Technical Report 816C. Austin, Tex.: Mariah Associates.

Quigg, J. Michael. 1997. *The Sanders Site (41HF128): A Single Event Late Archaic Camp/Bison Processing Site, Hansford County, Texas*. Technical Report 19751. Austin, Tex.: Mariah Associates.

———. 1998. A Late Archaic Bison Processing Event in the Texas Panhandle. *Plains Anthropologist* 43 (166): 367–84.

Quigg, J. Michael, Chris Lintz, Grant Smith, and Scott Wilcox. 2000. *The Lino Site: A Stratified Late Archaic Campsite in a Terrace of the San Idelfonzo Creek, Webb County, Southern Texas*. Archeological Studies Program Report 20. Austin: Texas Department of Transportation.

Quigg, J. Michael, Jeffrey D. Owens, Paul M. Matchen, Grant D. Smith, Robert Ricklis, Mercedes C. Cody, and Charles D. Frederich. 2008. *Varga Site: A Multicomponent, Stratified Campsite in the Canyonlands of Edwards County, Texas*. Vol. 1. Archeological Studies Program Report 110. Austin: Environmental Affairs Division, Texas Department of Transportation.

Quigg, J. Michael, Shane Pritchard, and Grant Smith. 2002. *The Boiler Site (41WB557): Utilization of an Upland Setting over the Last 4200 Years, Webb County, Texas*. Archeological Studies Program Report 45. Austin: Environmental Affairs Division, Texas Department of Transportation.

Quimby, George I., Jr. 1957. *The Bayou Goula Site, Iberville Parish, Louisiana*. Fieldiana Anthropology 47 (2). Chicago: Chicago Natural History Museum.

Ray, Cyrus E. 1929. A Differentiation of the Prehistoric Cultures of the Abilene Section. *Bulletin of the Texas Archeological and Paleontological Society* 5:14–24.

———. 1940. The Deeply Buried Gibson Site. *Bulletin of the Texas Archeological and Paleontological Society* 12:223–37.

———. 1941. The Various Types of the Clear Fork Gouge. *Bulletin of the Texas Archeological and Paleontological Society* 13:152–62.

Ray, J. H., N. H. Lopinot, E. R. Hajic, and R. D. Mandel. 1998. The Big Eddy Site: A Multicomponent Paleoindian Site on the Ozark Border, Southwest Missouri. *Plains Anthropologist* 43 (163): 73–81.

Ray, Jack H., Neal Lopinot, and Edwin R. Hajic. 2009. Archaic Prehistory of the Western Ozarks of Southwest Missouri. In *Archaic Societies: Diversity and Complexity across the Midcontinent*, edited by T. F. Emerson, D. L. McElrath, and A. C. Fortier, 155–98. Albany: State University of New York Press.

Richner, Jeffrey J., and Joe Bagot. 1978. *A Reconnaissance Survey of the Trinity River Basin*. Research Report 113. Dallas: Archaeology Research Program, Southern Methodist University.

Ricklis, Robert A. 1993. *A Model of Holocene Environmental and Human Adaptive Change on the Central Texas Coast: Geoarchaeological Investigation at White's Point, Nueces Bay, and Surrounding Area*. Corpus Christi, Tex.: Coastal Archaeological Research.

———. 1994. *Aboriginal Life and Culture on the Upper Texas Coast: Archaeology at the Mitchell Ridge Site, 41GV66, Galveston Island.* Corpus Christi, Tex.: Coastal Archaeological Research.

———. 1995. Prehistoric Occupations of the Central and Lower Coast: A Regional Overview. *Bulletin of the Texas Archeological Society* 66:265–300.

———. 2000. *Archaeological Testing at the Spanish Colonial Mission Sites of Espiritu Santo (41GD1) and Nuestra Senora del Rosario, Goliad County, Texas*. Corpus Christi, Tex.: Coastal Archaeological Research.

———. 2009. *The Buckeye Knoll Archaeological Site, Victoria County, Texas*. Corpus Christi, Tex.: Coastal Archaeological Research.

———. 2010. Data Recovery at the McGloin Bluff Site (41SP11): A Late Prehistoric Rockport Phase Fishing Camp on Corpus Christi Bay. *Current Archeology in Texas* 12 (2): 8–15.

Ricklis, Robert A., and Michael B. Collins. 1994. *Archaic and Late Prehistoric Human Ecology in the Middle Onion Creek Valley, Hays County, Texas*. Studies in Archeology 19. Austin: Texas Archeological Research Laboratory, University of Texas.

Ricklis, Robert A., and Kim A. Cox. 1991. Toward a Chronology of Adaptive Change during the Archaic of the Texas Coastal Bend Area. *La Tierra* 18 (2): 13–31.

Rogers, Robert. 2000. Excavations at Site 41FB255. *Current Archeology in Texas* 2 (1): 16–17.

Rogers, Robert, Brett Cruse, Maria Cruse, Kathyrn Reese-Taylor, J. Matthew Tanner, Tom Gosdin, and Wayne P. Chandler. 1997. Archaeological Investigations at the Oak Hill Village Site (41RK214), Rusk County, Texas. Paper presented at the 14th Annual Meeting of the American Society for Surface Mining and Reclamation, Austin, Tex., May 10–16.

Roney, John. 1995. Prehistory of the Guadalupe Mountains. *Artifact* 33 (1): 53.

Roosa, William B. 1956a. The Lucy Site in Central New Mexico. *American Antiquity* 21 (3): 310.

———. 1956b. Preliminary Report on the Lucy Site. *El Palacio* 63 (2): 36–49.

Root, Matthew, Darle D. Ferguson, and Douglas Harro. 2008. Use Wear Analysis. Appendix D in *The Gatlin Site (41KR621): Investigating Archaic Lifeways on the Southern Edwards Plateau of Central Texas*, by Brett Houk, Kevin Miller, and Eric Oksansen. SWCA Cultural Resources Report 149. Austin: SWCA Environmental Consultants; Archeological Studies Program Report 108, Texas Department of Transportation.

Root, Matthew J., Jerry D. William, Marvin Kay, and Lisa K. Shifrin. 1999. Folsom Ultrathin Biface and Radial Break Tools in the Knife River Flint Quarry Area. In *Folsom Lithic Technology: Explorations in Structure and Variation*, edited by Daniel S. Amick, 144–48. Archaeological Series 12. Ann Arbor, Mich.: International Monographs in Prehistory.

Rose, Richard O. 2011. The Shifting Sands Site: A Southern Plains Folsom-Midland Assemblage. *Bulletin of the Texas Archeological Society* 82: 299–324.

Roskams, Steve. 2001. *Excavation*. Cambridge: Cambridge University Press.

Ross, R. E. 1965. *The Archaeology of Eagle Cave*. Papers of the Texas Archeological Salvage Project 7. Austin: University of Texas.

———. 1966. *The Upper Rockwall and Glen Hill Sites, Forney Reservoir, Texas*. Papers of the Texas Archeological Salvage Project 9. Austin: University of Texas.

Runkles, Frank A. 1964. The Garza Site: A Neo-American Campsite Near Post, Texas. *Bulletin of the Texas Archeological Society* 35:101–25.

Runkles, Frank A., and E. D. Dorchester. 1986. The Lott Site (41GR56): A Late Prehistoric Site in Garza County, Texas. *Bulletin of the Texas Archeology Society* 57:83–115.

Saunders, R. K. 1985. Recovery of Drowned Rio Grande River Artifacts, Zapata and Starr Counties, South Texas. *La Tierra* 12 (2): 6–20.

———. 1988. A Possible Late Paleoindian Site on Chiltipin Creek, San Patricio County, Texas. *La Tierra* 15 (2): 27–35.

Sayles, E. B. n.d. Unpublished notes on file at the Texas Archeological Research Laboratory, University of Texas at Austin.

Schambach, Frank F. 1970. Pre-Caddoan Cultures in the Trans-Mississippi South: A Beginning Sequence. PhD diss., Department of Anthropology, Harvard University, Cambridge, Mass.

Schmiedlin, E. H. 1993. Investigation of a Toyah Horizon Site in Karnes County, Texas. *The Cache* 1:33–45.

———. 2000a. Archaic and Late Prehistoric Projectile Points from the J-2 Ranch Site (41VT6). *La Tierra* 27 (4): 20–39.

———. 2000b. St. Charles Point: J-2 Ranch, Victoria County. *La Tierra* 27 (4): 20–39.

Schneider, Fred. 1966. The Harrell Point: A Discussion. *Papers in Anthropology* 7 (1): 33–45. Norman: University of Oklahoma Anthropology Club.

Scholtz, J. A. 1967. An Archaeological Survey of the Beaver Reservoir Area in Northwest Arkansas. Master's thesis, University of Arkansas, Fayetteville.

Schroeder, Eric. 2002. *Data Recovery at the Armstrong Site (41CW54), Caldwell County, Texas.* Vol. 2, *Cultural Interpretations.* PPA Cultural Resources Report 0330. Austin, Tex.: Paul Price Associates.

Schroeder, Eric A., and Erick A. Okansen. 2002. *Data Recovery at the Armstrong Site (41CW54), Caldwell County, Texas.* Vol. 1, *Background, Methods, and Site Context.* PPA Cultural Resources Report 0284. Austin, Tex.: Paul Price Associates.

Schuetz, M. K. 1956. An Analysis of Val Verde County Cave Material. *Bulletin of the Texas Archeological Society* 27:129–60.

———. 1957. A Report on Williamson County Mound Material. *Bulletin of the Texas Archeological Society* 28:135–68.

———. 1968. *The History and Archeology of Mission San Juan Capistrano, San Antonio, Texas.* Vol. 1, *Historical Documentation and Description of the Structures.* Archeological Program Report 10. Austin: Texas State Building Commission.

———. 1969. *The History and Archeology of Mission San Juan Capistrano, San Antonio, Texas.* Vol. 2, *Description of the Artifacts and Ethnohistory of the Coahuiltecan Indians.* Archeological Program Report 11. Austin: Texas State Building Commission.

Scully, Edward G. 1951. Some Central Mississippi Valley Projectile Point Types. Mimeographed paper, Museum of Anthropology, University of Michigan, Ann Arbor.

Scurlock, J. D., and W. A. Davis. 1962. *Appraisal of the Archeological Resources of Toledo Bend Reservoir, Panola, Newton, Sabine and Shelby Counties, Texas: Sabine and De Soto Parishes, Louisiana.* Report submitted to the National Park Service by the Texas Archeological Salvage Project, University of Texas.

Scurlock, J. D., and D. E. Fox. 1977. *An Archeological Investigation at Mission Concepcion, San Antonio, Texas.* Report 28. Austin: Texas Historical Commission, Office of the State Archeologist.

Scurlock, J. Dan. 1962. The Culpepper Site: A Late Fulton Aspect Site in Northeastern Texas. *Bulletin of the Texas Archeological Society* 32:285–316.

Seebach, Jo. 2004. Past and Present at the Chispa Creek Folsom Site, Culberson County, Texas. *Journal of Big Bend Studies* 16:1–30.

Sellards, E. H. 1940. Pleistocene Artifacts and Associated Fossils from Bee County, Texas. *Bulletin of the Geological Society of America* 51:1627–57.

———. 1952. *Early Man in North America.* Austin: University of Texas Press.

———. 1955. Fossil Bison and Associated Artifacts from Milnesand, New Mexico. *American Antiquity* 20 (4): 336–44.

Sellards, E. H., G. L. Evans, and G. E. Meade, with Description of Artifacts by A. D. Krieger. 1947. Fossil Bison and Associated Artifacts from Plainview, Texas. *Bulletin of the Geological Society of America* 58:927–54.

Semenov, S. A. 1964. *Prehistoric Technology*. Translated by M. W. Thompson. London: Cory, Adams and Mackay.

Shafer, Harry J. 1963. Test Excavations at the Youngsport Site: A Stratified Terrace Site in Bell County, Texas. *Bulletin of the Texas Archeological Society* 24:57–82.

———. 1968. *Archeological Investigations in the San Jacinto River Basin, Montgomery County, Texas*. Papers of the Texas Archeological Salvage Project 13. Austin: University of Texas.

———. 1969. *Archeological Investigations in the Robert Lee Reservoir Basin, West Central Texas*. Papers of the Texas Archeological Salvage Project 17. Austin: University of Texas.

———. 1973. Lithic Technology at the George C. Davis Site, Cherokee County, Texas. PhD diss., Department of Anthropology, University of Texas at Austin.

———. 1979a. Additional Comments on Altered Cobbles and Pebbles from Central and Southern Texas. *La Tierra* 6 (1): 28–29.

———. 1979b. Comments on Kelly's "*Gower* Projectile Point?" *La Tierra* 6 (3): 9–10.

———. 1981. The Adaptive Technology of the Prehistoric Inhabitants of Southwest Texas. *Plains Anthropologist* 26 (92): 129–38.

———. 1984. Early Holocene Occupations at Hinds Cave, Texas. Paper presented at the Paleo-Indian Archaeology in Texas Symposium, Texas Academy of Science, San Antonio, March.

———. 1986. *Ancient Texans, Rock Art and Lifeways along the Lower Pecos*. Photographs by Jim Zintgraff. Austin: Texas Monthly Press.

———. 2003. *Mimbres Archaeology at the NAN Ranch Ruin*. Albuquerque: University of New Mexico Press.

———. 2006. *People of the Prairie: A Possible Connection to the Davis Site Caddo*. Module prepared for the Archeological Studies Program. Austin: Texas Department of Transportation and Prewitt and Associates.

Shafer, Harry J., and Vaughn M. Bryant Jr. 1977. *Archeological and Botanical Studies at Hinds Cave, Val Verde County, Texas*. Special Series 1. College Station: Anthropology Research Laboratory, Texas A&M University.

Shafer, Harry J., and Thomas R. Hester. 1971. *A Study of the Function and Technology of Certain Bifacial Tools from Southern Texas*. Archeological Report 20. Austin: Texas Historical Survey Committee.

Shafer, Harry J., and Richard G. Holloway. 1979. Organic Residue Analysis in Determining Stone Tool Function. In *Lithic Use-Wear Analysis*, edited by Brian Hayden, 385–400. New York: Academic Press.

Shafer, Harry J., Dee Ann Suhm, and J. Dan Scurlock. 1964. *Investigation and Appraisal of the Archeological Resources of Belton Reservoir, Bell and Coryell Counties, Texas: 1962*. Miscellaneous Papers 1. Austin: Texas Archeological Salvage Project.

Shaller, Rolla, Christopher Linz, and Douglas W. Owsley. 1998. Description and Analysis of the Keith Site Burial, 41RD52, Randall County, Texas. *Steward* 4:14–29.

Shiner, J. L. 1971. *Scrapers and Things like That*. Handbook Series 2. El Paso: El Paso Archaeological Society.

———. 1975. The Clear Fork Gouge Revisited. *Bulletin of the Texas Archeological Society* 46:179–88.

———. 1983. Archeology of the Sheldon Site, Hidalgo County, Texas. *Bulletin of the Texas Archeological Society* 54:309–18.

Shoberg, Marilyn. 2010. Functional Analysis of Stone Tools. In *Clovis Technology*, edited by Bruce A. Bradley, Michael B. Collins, and Andrew Hemmings, 138–56. Archaeological Series 17. Ann Arbor, Mich.: International Monographs in Prehistory.

Shott, Michael L. 1989. Bipolar Industries: Ethnographic Evidence and Archaeological Implications. *North American Archaeologist* 10 (1): 1–24.

Sieveking, Gale de Giberne, and Christopher J. Clayton. 1986. Frost Shatter and the Structure of Frozen Flint. In *The Scientific Study of Flint and Chert*, edited by G. de G. Sieveking and M. B. Hart, 283–90. Cambridge: Cambridge University Press.

Silva, John P., and Thomas R. Hester. 1973. Archaeological Materials from a Nonceramic Site in Eastern Durango, Mexico. In *Studies in Ancient Mesoamerica*, edited by J. A. Graham, 40–166. Contributions of the University of California Archaeological Research Facility 18. Berkeley: University of California.

Simmons, Alan H., Ann Lucy Wiener Stodder, Douglas D. Dykeman, and Patricia A. Hicks. 1989. *Human Adaptations and Cultural Change in the Greater Southwest*. Research Series 32. Fayetteville: Arkansas Archeological Survey.

Skinner, S. Alan, R. King Harris, and Keith M. Anderson, eds. 1969. *Archaeological Investigations at the Sam Kaufman Site, Red River County, Texas*. Contributions in Anthropology 5. Dallas: Southern Methodist University.

Smith, James E., II. 1994. Geometrically Etched Pebbles from Bosque County, Texas. *The Cache* 2:17–22.

Smyers, Cindy, and David Calame. 2004. A Study of Corner-Tang Bifaces from 41RV49, Reeves Co., Texas. *La Tierra* 31 (2): 77–83.

Sollberger, J. B. 1968. A Partial Report on Research Work Concerning Lithic Typology and Technology. *Bulletin of the Texas Archeological Society* 39:95–109.

———. 1970. The Rockwall Point. *Newsletter of the Oklahoma Anthropological Society* 18 (2).

———. 1971. A Technological Study of Beveled Knives. *Plains Anthropologist* 16 (53): 209–18.

———. 1978. A New Type of Arrow Point with Speculations as to Its Origin. *La Tierra* 5 (4): 13–20. Reprinted from *The Record* 23 (3): 16–22, 1967, with permission of the Dallas Archeological Society.

———. 1989. On Replicating Fluted Projectile Points. *Bulletin of the Texas Archeology* 59:1–18.

Sollberger, J. B., and William B. Carroll. 1985. Guadalupe Tools: Were They Used for Defleshing Hides? *La Tierra* 12 (1): 18–22.

Sollberger, J. B., and Thomas R. Hester. 1972. The Strohacker Site: A Review of Pre-Archaic Manifestations in Texas. *Plains Anthropologist* 17 (58): 327–44.

Sorrow, William M. 1966. *The Pecan Springs Site, Bardwell Reservoir, Texas*. Papers of the Texas Archeological Salvage Project 10. Austin: Texas Archeological Salvage Project.

———. 1968a. *The Devil's Mouth Site: The Third Season, 1967*. Papers of the Texas Archeological Salvage Project 14. Austin: Texas Archeological Salvage Project.

———. 1968b. *Test Excavations at the Nopal Terrace Site, Val Verde County, Texas, Spring 1967*. Papers of the Texas Archeological Salvage Project 15. Austin: Texas Archeological Salvage Project.

———. 1969. *Archeological Investigations at the John Ischy Site: A Burnt Rock Midden in Williamson County, Texas*. Papers of the Texas Archeological Salvage Project 18. Austin: Texas Archeological Salvage Project.

Sorrow, William M., Harry J. Shafer, and Richard E. Ross. 1967. *Excavations at Stillhouse Hollow Reservoir*. Papers of the Texas Archeological Salvage Project 11. Austin: Texas Archeological Salvage Project.

Stephenson, R. L. 1970. Archaeological Investigations in the Whitney Reservoir Area, Central Texas. *Bulletin of the Texas Archeological Society* 41:37–277.

Stevens, D. E., and G. A. Agogino. 1975. *Sandia Cave: A Study in Controversy*. Contributions to Anthropology 7 (1). Portales: Paleo-Indian Institute, Eastern New Mexico University.

Story, D. A., and V. M. Bryant Jr. 1966. A Preliminary Study of the Paleoecology of the Amistad Reservoir Area. Final report submitted to the National Science Foundation by University of Texas at Austin.

Story, Dee Ann. 1965. The Archeology of Cedar Creek Reservoir, Henderson and Kaufman Counties, Texas. *Bulletin of the Texas Archeological Society* 36:163–257.

———. 1976. The Archaic of East Texas. In *The Texas Archaic: A Symposium*, edited by Thomas R. Hester, 46–59. Special Report 2. San Antonio: Center for Archaeological Research, University of Texas.

———. 1981. An Overview of the Archaeology of East Texas. *Plains Anthropologist* 26 (92): 139–56.

———. 1995. The Cultural Setting. In *The Deshazo Site, Nacogdoches County, Texas*, edited by Dee Ann Story. Vol. 1. Permit Series Report 7. Austin: Texas Antiquities Committee.

Story, Dee Ann. 1995. *The DeShazo Site, Nacogdoches County, Texas. Volume 2. Artifacts of Native Manufacture.* Studies in Archeology 21. Texas Archeological Research Laboratory, The University of Texas at Austin.

Story, Dee Ann, Janice A. Guy, Barbara A. Burnett, Martha Doty Freeman, Jerome C. Rose, D. Gentry Steele, Ben W. Olive, and Karl J. Reinhard. 1990. *The Archeology and Bioarcheology of the Gulf Coastal Plain.* 2 vols. Research Series 38. Fayetteville: Arkansas Archeological Survey.

Story, Dee Ann, and Harry J. Shafer. 1965. *1964 Excavations at Waco Reservoir, McLennan County, Texas: The Baylor and Britton Sites.* Miscellaneous Papers 6. Austin: Texas Archeological Salvage Project, University of Texas.

Stright, Melanie, Jr., Eileen M. Lear, and James F. Bennett. 1999. *Spatial Data Analysis of Artifacts Redeposited by Coastal Erosion: A Case Study of McFaddin Beach, Texas.* Washington, D.C.: Minerals Management Services, U.S. Department of the Interior.

Suhm, D. A., and E. B. Jelks. 1962. *Handbook of Texas Archeology: Type Descriptions.* Special Publications 1. Austin: Texas Archeological Society; Bulletin 4, Texas Memorial Museum.

Suhm, Dee Ann. 1955. Excavations at the Collins Site, Travis County, Texas. *Bulletin of the Texas Archeological Society* 26:7–54.

———. 1957. Excavations at the Smith Rockshelter, Travis County, Texas. *Texas Journal of Science* 9 (1): 26–58.

———. 1959. The Williams Site and Central Texas Archaeology. *Texas Journal of Science* 11 (2): 218–50.

Suhm, Dee Ann, Alex D. Krieger, and Edward B. Jelks. 1954. *An Introductory Handbook of Texas Archeology.* Bulletin of the Texas Archeological Society 25. Austin: Texas Archeological Society.

Tamers, M. A., F. J. Pearson, and E. M. Davis. 1964. University of Texas Radiocarbon Dates II. *Radiocarbon* 6:138–59.

Taylor, Anna J., and Cheryl L. Highley. 1995. *Archaeological Investigations at the Loma Sandia Site (41LK28): A Prehistoric Cemetery and Campsite in Live Oak County, Texas.* Studies in Archeology 20. Austin, Texas Archeological Research Laboratory, The University of Texas.

Taylor, Walter W. 1966. Archaic Cultures Adjacent to the Northeastern Frontiers of Mesoamerica. In *The Handbook of Middle American Indians*, edited by Gordon F. Ekholm and Gordon R. Willey, 59–94. Vol. 4. Austin: University of Texas Press.

Thomas, David Hurst. 1979. *Archaeology.* New York: Holt, Rinehart and Winston.

———. 1981. How to Classify the Projectile Points from Monitor Valley, Nevada. *Journal of California and Great Basin Anthropology* 3 (1): 7–43.

Thomas, George B. 1978. A Survey and Assessment of the Archeological Resources of Fort Hood, Texas. *Bulletin of the Texas Archeological Society* 49:195–240.

Thoms, Alston V. 1992. Late Pleistocene and Early Holocene Regional Land Use Patterns: A Perspective from the Preliminary Results of Archaeological Studies at the Richard

Beene Site, 41BX831, Lower Medina River, South Texas. In *Late Cenozoic Alluvial Stratigraphy and Prehistory of the Inner Gulf Coastal Plain, South-Central Texas*, edited by Rolfe D. Mandel and S. Christopher Caran, 2–37. Guidebook for the 10th annual meeting of the South-Central Friends of the Pleistocene field trip. Lubbock Lake Landmark Quaternary Research Center Series 4. San Antonio, Tex.: South-Central Friends of the Pleistocene.

———. 1993. Knocking Sense from Old Rocks: Typologies and Narrow Perspective of the Angostura Type. *Lithic Technology* 18 (1–2): 16–27.

Thoms, Alston V., and Rolfe D. Mandel, eds. 2007. *Archaeological and Paleoecological Investigations at the Richard Beene Site, South-Central Texas.* Reports of Investigations 8. College Station: Center for Ecological Archaeology, Texas A&M University.

Thurmond, John P. 1981. Archeology of the Cypress Creek Drainage Basin, Northeastern Texas and Northwestern Louisiana. Vols. 1 and 2. Master's thesis, University of Texas at Austin.

Tomka, Steve A. 1999. Historic Period Lithic Technology at Mission San Jose y San Miguel de Aguayo. *Bulletin of the Texas Archeological Society* 70:241–64.

Toulouse, J. H., Jr. 1939. Arrow Shaft Tools (with Notes on General Distribution). In *Preliminary Report on the 1937 Excavations, Bc50–51, Chaco Canyon, New Mexico*, edited by Clyde Kluckhohn and Paul Reiter, 80–89. University of New Mexico Bulletin, Anthropology Series 3 (2). Albuquerque: University of New Mexico Press.

Townsend, Richard E., Jr. 1990. Possible Almagre Points from the Panther Springs Creek Site, Bexar County, Texas. *La Tierra* 17 (3): 32–37.

Trierweiler, W. Nicolas, ed. 1996. Archeological Testing at Fort Hood: 1994–1995. Vol. 2. Archeological Resource Management Series, Research Report 35. Fort Hood, Tex.: U.S. Army Fort Hood.

Trubitt, Mary Beth. 2009a. Investigating the Middle Archaic at the Jones Mill Site. *Arkansas Archeologist* 48:71–84.

———. 2009b. Putting an Age on the Archaic at Jones Mill. *Newsletter of the Arkansas Archeological Society* 349:3–7.

Tunnell, Curtis, and Leroy Johnson. 2000. *Comparing Dimensions for Folsom Points and Their By-products from the Adair-Steadman and Lindenmeier Sites and Other Localities.* Archeological Reports 1. Austin: Texas Historical Commission.

Tunnell, Curtis D. 1962. Oblate: A Rockshelter Site. In *Salvage Archeology of Canyon Reservoir: The Wunderlich, Footbridge, and Oblate Sites*, edited by L. Johnson Jr., D. A. Suhm and C. D. Tunnell, 77–116. Austin: Texas Memorial Museum, University of Texas.

———. 1975. Fluted Projectile Point Production as Revealed by Lithic Specimens from the Adair-Steadman Site in Northwest Texas. Paper presented at a Symposium on Paleo-Indian Lifeways held at The Museum, Texas Tech University, Lubbock, Tex., October 16–18.

———. 1978. *The Gibson Lithic Cache from West Texas.* Report 30. Austin: Texas Historical Commission, Office of the State Archeologist.

Tunnell, Curtis D., and Jack T. Hughes. 1955. An Archaic Bison Kill. *Panhandle-Plains Historical Review* 28:63–70.

Turner, Ellen Sue. 1991. A Corner-Notched Biface from South Central Texas. *La Tierra* 18 (3): 21–22.

Turner, Ellen Sue, and Thomas R. Hester. 1985. *A Field Guide to Stone Artifacts of Texas Indians.* Austin: Texas Monthly Press.

———. 1993. *A Field Guide to Stone Artifacts of Texas Indians.* Houston: Gulf Publishing Company.

Turner, Ellen Sue, and Paul Tanner. 1994. The McFaddin Beach Site on the Upper Texas Coast. *Bulletin of the Texas Archeological Society* 65:319–36.

Turner, Robert L. 1978. The Tuck Carpenter Site and Its Relation to Other Sites within the Titus Focus. *Bulletin of the Texas Archeological Society* 49:1–110.

Turner, Robert L., Jr., and James E. Smith II, with contributions by T. K. Perttula, B. Nelson, M. Walters, and B. Gonzales. 2002. The Harold Williams Site (41CP10) and the

Texas Archeological Society Field School of 1967. *Bulletin of the Texas Archeological Society* 73:1–68.

Turpin, Solveig A. 1982. *Seminole Canyon: The Art and the Archeology, Val Verde County, Texas.* Research Report 83. Austin: Texas Archeological Survey, University of Texas.

———. 1991. Time Out of Mind: The Radiocarbon Chronology of the Lower Pecos River Region. In *Papers on Lower Pecos Prehistory*, edited by S. A. Turpin, 1–50. Studies in Archaeology 8. Austin: Texas Archeological Research Laboratory, University of Texas.

Uecker, Herbert G. 1994. *The Dos Republicas Project: Phase II Archaeological Investigations at a Proposed Coal Strip Mine, Maverick County, Texas.* Archaeological Survey Report 215. San Antonio: Center for Archaeological Research, University of Texas.

Utberg, Neil S. 1969. *The Indian Artifacts of Mexico and Southern Texas.* Edinburg, Tex.: privately printed.

Versar, Inc., and Parsons. 2008. *Phase 1 Archaeological Survey of Dixie Target and the Operations Center, McMullen Range Complex, McMullen County, Texas.* Report prepared for Naval Facilities Engineering Command, Southern Division. Springfield, Va.: Versar; Norfolk, Va.: Parsons.

Vierra, Bradley J. 1998. *41MV120: A Stratified Late Archaic Site in Maverick County, Texas.* Archaeological Survey Report 251. San Antonio: Center for Archaeological Research, University of Texas; Archaeological Studies Program Report 7, Texas Department of Transportation.

Wakefield, Walter H. 1968. *Archaeological Surveys of Palmetto Bend and Choke Canyon Reservoirs, Texas.* Survey Reports 5. Austin: Texas Archeological Salvage Project.

Waldorf, D. C., and Val Waldorf. 1987. *Story in Stone, Flint Types of the Central and Southern U.S.* Branson, Mo.: Mound Builder Books.

Walter, Tamra L. 2007. *Espiritu Santo de Zuniga: A Frontier Mission in Texas.* Austin: University of Texas Press.

Warnica, James M. 1961. The Elida Site, Evidence of a Folsom Occupation in Roosevelt County, Eastern New Mexico. *Bulletin of the Texas Archeological Society* 30:205–15.

Warnica, James M., and Ted Williamson. 1968. The Milnesand Site: Revisited. *American Antiquity* 33 (1): 16–24.

Watt, Frank H. 1938. The Waco Sinker. *Central Texas Archeologist* 4:21–70.

———. 1978. Radiocarbon Chronology of Sites in the Central Brazos Valley. *Bulletin of the Texas Archeological Society* 49:111–38.

Webb, C. H., J. A. Ford, S. M. Gagliano, and R. T. Saucier. n.d. Poverty Point Culture and the American Formative. Unpublished manuscript provided by Webb to Dee Ann Story; copy on file at the Texas Archeological Research Laboratory, Austin.

Webb, Clarence H. 1946. Two Unusual Types of Chipped Stone Artifacts from Northwest Louisiana. *Bulletin of the Texas Archeological and Paleontological Society* 17:9–17.

———. 1959. *The Belcher Mound: A Stratified Site in Caddo Parish, Louisiana.* Memoir 16. Salt Lake City, Utah: Society for American Archaeology.

———. 1963. The Smithport Landing Site: An Alto Focus Component in De Soto Parish, Louisiana. *Bulletin of the Texas Archeological Society* 34:143–87.

———. 1978. Changing Archeological Methods and Theory in the Trans-Mississippi South. In *Texas Archeology*, edited by K. D. House, 27–45. Dallas: Southern Methodist University Press.

———. 1982. *Geoscience and Man: The Poverty Point Culture.* Vol. 17. 2nd rev. ed. Baton Rouge: School of Geoscience, Louisiana State University.

Webb, Clarence H., and Monroe Dodd Jr. 1939. Further Excavations at the Gahagan Mound: Connections with a Florida Culture. *Bulletin of the Texas Archeological and Paleontological Society* 11:92–128.

Webb, Clarence H., Forrest E. Murphy, Wesley G. Ellis, and H. Roland Green. 1969. The Resch Site, R1HS16, Harrison County, Texas. *Bulletin of the Texas Archeological Society* 40:3–106.

Webb, Clarence H., Joel L. Shiner, and E. Wayne Roberts. 1971. The John Pearce Site (16CD56): A *San Patrice* Site in Caddo Parish, Louisiana. *Bulletin of the Texas Archeological Society* 42:1–49.

Weber, C. D., and L. W. Patterson. 1985. A Quantitative Analysis of Andice and Bell Points. *La Tierra* 12 (2): 21–27.

———. 1986. An Analysis of Discriminant Function Values of Andice and Bell Points. *La Tierra* 13 (3): 32–38.

Weber, Carey D. 2000. Andice/Bell Resharpening Attributes. *La Tierra* 27 (4): 45–61.

———. 2009. The Laguna Point: Projectile Point Variation in the Early Archaic Prehistoric Period of Texas. *La Tierra* 36 (1–2): 99–117.

Weber, Carey D., and Michael B. Collins. 1994. A Replication Technique for Andice/Bell Points. In *Archaic and Late Prehistoric Human Ecology in the Middle Onion Creek Valley, Hays County, Texas*, edited by Robert Ricklis and Michael B. Collins, 629–51. Studies in Archeology 19. Austin: Texas Archeological Research Laboratory, University of Texas.

Wedel, Waldo R. 1970. Antler Tine Scraper Handles in the Central Plains. *Plains Anthropologist* 15 (47): 36–45.

Weinstein, Richard A. 1992. *Archaeology and Paleogeography of the Lower Guadalupe River/San Antonio Bay Region: Cultural Resources Investigations along the Channel to Victoria, Calhoun and Victoria Counties, Texas.* Baton Rouge: La.: Coastal Environments.

———, ed. 2002. *Archaeological Investigations at the Guadalupe Bay Site (41CL2): Late Archaic through Historic Occupation along the Channel to Victoria, Calhoun County, Texas.* 2 vols. Baton Rouge, La.: Coastal Environments.

Weir, Frank A. 1956. Surface Artifacts from La Perdida, Starr County, Texas. *Bulletin of the Texas Archeological Society* 27:59–78.

———. 1976a. The Central Texas Archaic. PhD diss., Washington State University, Pullman.

———. 1976b. The Central Texas Archaic Reconsidered. In *The Texas Archaic: A Symposium*, edited by Thomas R. Hester, 60–66. Special Report 2. San Antonio: Center for Archaeological Research, University of Texas.

———. 1979. Greenhaw: An Archaic Site in Central Texas. *Bulletin of the Texas Archeological Society* 50:5–67.

———. 1984. The Wilson-Leonard Site: A Late Paleo-Indian Village in Central Texas. Paper presented at the Paleo-Indian Archaeology Symposium, Texas Academy of Sciences, San Antonio, Tex., March.

———. 1985. An Early Holocene Burial at the Wilson-Leonard Site in Central Texas. *Mammoth Trumpet* 2 (1): 1–3.

Weir, Frank A., and Glen H. Doran. 1980. Anthon Site (41UV60). *La Tierra* 7 (3): 17–23.

Wendorf, Fred, and Alex D. Krieger. 1959. New Light on the Midland Discovery. *American Antiquity* 25 (1): 68–78.

Wendorf, Fred, Alex D. Krieger, Claude C. Albritton, and T. D. Stewart. 1955. *The Midland Discovery.* Austin: University of Texas Press.

Wesolowsky, Al B., Thomas R. Hester, and Douglas R. Brown. 1976. Archeological Investigations at the Jetta Court Site (41TV151), Travis County, Texas. *Bulletin of the Texas Archeological Society* 47:25–88.

Westfall, Tom. 2007. The Shifting Sands Folsom/Midland Site (41WK21). *Prehistoric American: The Journal for the Documentation of Prehistoric America* 41 (4): 72–74.

Whalen, Michael E. 1980. *Special Studies in the Archeology of the Hueco Bolson.* Publications in Anthropology 9. El Paso: El Paso Centennial Museum, University of Texas.

Wheat, Joe Ben. 1947. Notes on the W. A. Myatt Site. *Bulletin of the Texas Archeological and Paleontological Society* 18:87–93.

———. 1953. *An Archeological Survey of the Addicks Dam Basin, Southeast Texas.* River Basin Survey Papers 4. Bureau of American Ethnology 154. Washington, D.C.: Government Printing Office.

———. 1955. Two Archeological Sites near Lubbock, Texas. *Panhandle-Plains Review* 28:71–77.

———. 1972. *The Olsen-Chubbuck Site: A Paleo-Indian Bison Kill.* Memoirs 26. Washington, D.C.: Society for American Archaeology.

———. 1979. *The Jurgens Site.* Memoir 15. Lincoln, Neb.: Plains Anthropologist.

Wishoff, Ira R. 2010. An Analysis of Quarrying Behavior at Alibates Flint Quarries National Monument, Fritch, Texas. Master's thesis, Texas State University at San Marcos.

Wood, W. R. 1962. Breckenridge Shelter-3CR2: An Archeological Chronicle in the Beaver Reservoir Area. In *Arkansas Archeology*, edited by C. R. McGimsey, III, 67–96. Fayetteville: Arkansas Archeological Survey.

———. 1963. Two New Projectile Points: *Homan* and *Agee* Points. *Arkansas Archaeologist* 4 (2): 1–6.

Wood, W. Raymond, and R. Bruce McMillan. 1967. Recent Investigations at Rodgers Shelter, Missouri. *Archaeology* 20 (1): 52–55.

Word, James H. 1963. Floydada Country Club Site, 41FL-1. *Bulletin of the South Plains Archeological Society* 1:53.

Word, James H., and C. L. Douglas. 1970. *Excavations at Baker Cave, Val Verde County, Texas.* Bulletin 16. Austin: Texas Memorial Museum.

Wormington, H. M. 1957. *Ancient Man in North America.* Popular Series 4. Denver, Colo.: Denver Museum of Natural History.

Wulfkuhle, Virginia A. 1990. The 1933 Excavation of Meriwether Rockshelter C (41BS809) in Brewster County, Texas. In *Papers from the Third Symposium on Resources of the Chihuahuan Desert Region, United States and Mexico, 10–12 November, 1988*, edited by A. Michael Powell et al., 117–32. Alpine, Tex.: Chihuahuan Desert Research Institute.

Wyckoff, D. G. 1964. *The Archaeological Survey of the Kaw Reservoir, Kay and Osage Counties, Oklahoma.* Oklahoma River Basin Survey Report 6. Norman: University of Oklahoma.

———. 1994. Introduction to the 1991 Bulletin. *Bulletin of Oklahoma Anthropological Society* 40 (for 1991): 1–8.

Young, Bill. 2008. The Overall Distribution of Scottsbluff and San Patrice Points. *Corsicana Daily Sun*, September 13.

Young, Bill, and Michael B. Collins. 1989. A Cache of Blades With Clovis Affinities from Northeastern Texas. *Current Research in the Pleistocene* 6:26–28.

Young, Wayne C. 1981. *Test Excavations at the Tankersley Creek Site: A Multicomponent Campsite in Titus County, Texas.* Publications in Archaeology Report 22. Austin: Texas State Department of Highways and Public Transportation.

———. 1982. *Excavations at the Ram's Head Site, 41PC35, Pecos County, Texas.* Publications in Archaeology Report 23. Austin: Texas State Department of Highways and Public Transportation.

———. 1985. *Archaeological Excavations at Site 41 BT6, Burnet County, Texas.* Publications in Archaeology Report 28. Austin: Texas State Department of Highways and Public Transportation, Highway Design Division.

About the Authors

Ellen Sue Turner has served as a research associate at the Center for Archeological Research, University of Texas at San Antonio, as editor and author of a number of anthropological publications, and as regional director, Region 12, of the Texas Archeological Society. She was elected 1993–1994 president of the Texas Archeological Society and is a fellow of the Texas Archeological Society.

Thomas R. Hester is professor of anthropology, emeritus, and former director of the Texas Archeological Research Laboratory at the University of Texas at Austin. He was the first director of the Center for Archaeological Research at the University of Texas at San Antonio, where he also served as professor of anthropology. He is a fellow, and was elected president in 1992–1993, of the Texas Archeological Society. Hester continues to work on a number of archaeological reports from work in Texas, Belize, and Mexico.

Richard L. McReynolds has illustrated extensively in Texas archaeological reports, articles, journals, newsletters, and dissertations. His artistic renderings of Texas artifacts are sought after and respected throughout the state. He is retired from civil service in the U.S. Air Force.

Made in United States
Cleveland, OH
27 October 2024

10324628R00215